Communications in Computer and Information Science   **1297**

More information about this series at http://www.springer.com/series/7899

Ana Fred · Ana Salgado ·
David Aveiro · Jan Dietz ·
Jorge Bernardino · Joaquim Filipe (Eds.)

Knowledge Discovery, Knowledge Engineering and Knowledge Management

11th International Joint Conference, IC3K 2019
Vienna, Austria, September 17–19, 2019
Revised Selected Papers

Springer

Editors
Ana Fred
Instituto de Telecomunicações
Lisbon, Portugal

University of Lisbon
Lisbon, Portugal

David Aveiro (iD)
University of Madeira
Funchal, Portugal

Jorge Bernardino
Polytechnic Institute of Coimbra
Coimbra, Portugal

Ana Salgado
Federal University of Pernambuco
Recife, Brazil

Jan Dietz
Delft University of Technology
Delft, The Netherlands

Joaquim Filipe
Polytechnic Institute of Setúbal
Setúbal, Portugal

ISSN 1865-0929   ISSN 1865-0937   (electronic)
Communications in Computer and Information Science
ISBN 978-3-030-66195-3   ISBN 978-3-030-66196-0   (eBook)
https://doi.org/10.1007/978-3-030-66196-0

This Springer imprint is published by the registered company Springer Nature Switzerland AG
The registered company address is: Gewerbestrasse 11, 6330 Cham, Switzerland

Preface

The present book includes extended and revised versions of a set of selected papers from the 11th International Joint Conference on Knowledge Discovery, Knowledge Engineering and Knowledge Management (IC3K 2019), held in Vienna, Austria, during September 17–19, 2019.

IC3K 2019 received 220 paper submissions from 57 countries, of which 11% were included in this book. The papers were selected by the event chairs and their selection is based on a number of criteria that include the classifications and comments provided by the Program Committee members, the session chairs' assessment, and also the program chairs' global view of all papers included in the technical program. The authors of selected papers were then invited to submit a revised and extended version of their papers, having at least 30% innovative material.

The purpose of the IC3K is to bring together researchers, engineers, and practitioners in the areas of Knowledge Discovery, Knowledge Engineering, and Knowledge Management. IC3K is composed of three co-located conferences (KDIR, KEOD, and KMIS), each specialized in at least one of the aforementioned main knowledge areas.

The papers selected to be included in this book contribute to the understanding of relevant trends of current research on Knowledge Discovery, Knowledge Engineering, and Knowledge Management.

KDIR collected a set of 8 papers that represent the best presentations delivered at the conference and their authors produced revised, extended versions that incorporated the comments of reviewers and subsequent reflections and research work. The resulting papers are focused on themes such as Datamining, Business Intelligence, Machine Intelligence, including applications such as Recommender Systems, OLAP Mining, Machine Translation, or Credit Scoring.

We had a very interesting set of papers presented at KEOD, from which we selected 12 to be part of this book. A good number of them were dedicated to applications on practical scenarios/contexts such as: social networks, energy, health, and food. Some focused on important theoretical aspects like knowledge life cycle, knowledge loss, modularization, and versioning. The extended versions of these papers bring more examples and new interesting insights from research that advanced in the meantime.

In KMIS conference, we had very good papers, from which we selected only 5 papers to be published in this book. This collection of papers from KMIS focused mainly on the study and application of all perspectives of Knowledge Management and Information Systems. All these extended versions of KMIS papers bring more research insights into these themes.

We would like to thank all the authors for their contributions and also to the reviewers who helped ensure the quality of this publication.

September 2019

Ana Fred
Ana Salgado
David Aveiro
Jan Dietz
Jorge Bernardino
Joaquim Filipe

Organization

Conference Chair

Joaquim Filipe   Polytechnic Institute of Setúbal, INSTICC, Portugal

Program Co-chairs

KDIR

Ana Fred   Instituto de Telecomunicações, University of Lisbon, Portugal

KEOD

Jan Dietz   Delft University of Technology, The Netherlands
David Aveiro   University of Madeira, Madeira-ITI, Portugal

KMIS

Jorge Bernardino   Polytechnic Institute of Coimbra, ISEC, Portugal
Ana Salgado   Federal University of Pernambuco, Brazil

KDIR Program Committee

Amir Ahmad   United Arab Emirates University, UAE
Mayer Aladjem   Ben-Gurion University of the Negev, Israel
Maria Aramburu Cabo   University Jaume I, Spain
Sabeur Aridhi   LORIA France, France
Eva Armengol   IIIA CSIC, Spain
Zeyar Aung   Masdar Institute of Science and Technology, UAE
Vladan Babovic   National University of Singapore, Singapore
Kerstin Bach   Norwegian University of Science and Technology (NTNU), Norway
Vladimir Bartik   Brno University of Technology, Czech Republic
Gloria Bordogna   CNR, Italy
Amel Borgi   Université de Tunis El Manar, Institut Supérieur d'Informatique, LIPAH, Tunisia
Pavel Brazdil   University of Porto, Portugal
Ivana Burgetová   Faculty of Information Technology, Czech Republic
Yi Cai   South China University of Technology, China
Jesús Carrasco-Ochoa   INAOE, Mexico
Arnaud Castelltort   LIRMM, France
Chien-Chung Chan   The University of Akron, USA
Keith Chan   The Hong Kong Polytechnic University, Hong Kong

Chien Chen	National Taiwan University College of Management, Taiwan, China
Zhiyuan Chen	University of Maryland, USA
Patrick Ciarelli	Universidade Federal do Espírito Santo, Brazil
Paulo Cortez	University of Minho, Portugal
Luis M. de Campos	University of Granada, Spain
Emanuele Di Buccio	University of Padua, Italy
Thanh-Nghi Do	College of Information Technology, Can Tho University, Vietnam
Antoine Doucet	University of La Rochelle, France
Markus Endres	University of Augsburg, Germany
Iaakov Exman	Azrieli College of Engineering Jerusalem, Israel
Alvis Fong	Auckland University of Technology, New Zealand
Philippe Fournier-Viger	University of Moncton, Canada
Ana Fred	Instituto de Telecomunicações, University of Lisbon, Portugal
Panorea Gaitanou	Universidad de Alcala, Spain
Susan Gauch	University of Arkansas, USA
Angelo Genovese	Università degli Studi di Milano, Italy
Rosario Girardi	Federal University of the State of Rio de Janeiro, Brazil
Nuno Gonçalves	Superior School of Technology, Polytechnic Institute of Setúbal, Portugal
Alfonso Gonzalez Briones	University of Salamanca, Spain
Francesco Gullo	UniCredit R&D, Italy
Yaakov Hacohen-Kerner	Jerusalem College of Technology, Israel
Jennifer Harding	Loughborough University, UK
Lynette Hirschman	The MITRE Corporation, USA
Yo-Ping Huang	National Taipei University of Technology, Taiwan, China
Beatriz de la Iglesia	University of East Anglia, UK
Roberto Interdonato	DIMES, Unversità della Calabria, Italy
Ahmedul Kabir	University of Dhaka, Bangladesh
Mouna Kamel	IRIT, France
Mehmed Kantardzic	University of Louisville, USA
Ron Kenett	Samuel Neaman Institute, Israel
Margita Kon-Popovska	Ss. Cyril and Methodius University, North Macedonia
Donald Kraft	Colorado Technical University, USA
Nuno Lau	Universidade de Aveiro, Portugal
Anne Laurent	Lirmm, Montpellier University, France
Carson Leung	University of Manitoba, Canada
Jerry Chun-Wei Lin	Western Norway University of Applied Sciences, Norway
Michel Liquiere	University of Montpellier II, France
Jun Liu	University of Ulster, UK
Juan Manuel Corchado	University of Salamanca, Spain
Ricardo Marcacini	University of São Paulo, Brazil

KDIR Additional Reviewers

Jerry Bonnell	University of Miami, USA
Kevin Labille	University of Arkansas, USA
Cristiano Russo	LISSI Laboratory, UPEC, France
Bishnu Sarker	Inria, France
Akrem Sellami	LIS, France

KEOD Program Committee

Alia Abdelmoty	Cardiff University, UK
Mamoun Abu Helou	Al-Istiqlal University, Palestine
Francisco Antunes	Institute of Computer and Systems Engineering of Coimbra, Beira Interior University, Portugal
David Aveiro	University of Madeira, Madeira-ITI, Portugal
Petra Bago	University of Zagreb, Croatia
Claudio Baptista	Universidade Federal de Campina Grande, Brazil
Jean-Paul Barthes	Université de Technologie de Compiègne, France
Ines Ben Messaoud	Laboratory Mir@cl, Tunisia
Vladimír Bureš	University of Hradec Kralove, Czech Republic
Radek Burget	Brno University of Technology, Czech Republic
Ismael Caballero	Universidad de Castilla-La Mancha (UCLM), Spain
Gabriella Casalino	Università degli Studi di Bari, Italy
Davide Ciucci	Università degli Studi di Milano-Bicocca, Italy
João Costa	Institute of Computer and Systems Engineering of Coimbra, Portugal
Christophe Cruz	Laboratoire LIB, EA 7534, France
Pierpaolo D'Urso	Sapienza Università di Roma, Italy
Christof Ebert	Vector Consulting Services, Germany
John Edwards	Aston University, UK
Dieter Fensel	University of Innsbruck, Austria
Arnulfo Garza	Instituto Tecnologico de Tijuana, Mexico
James Geller	New Jersey Institute of Technology, USA
Manolis Gergatsoulis	Ionian University, Greece
Yoan Gutiérrez	University of Alicante, Spain
Josiane Hauagge	UNICENTRO, Brazil
Martina Husáková	University of Hradec Králové, Czech Republic
Sarantos Kapidakis	University of West Attica, Greece
Nikos Karacapilidis	University of Patras, Greece
Pinar Karagoz	METU, Turkey
Jakub Klímek	Charles University, Czech Technical University in Prague, Czech Republic
Kouji Kozaki	Osaka Electro-Communication University, Japan
Deniss Kumlander	Tallinn University of Technology, Estonia
Yuan-Fang Li	Monash University, Australia
Antoni Ligeza	AGH University of Science and Technology, Poland

Elena Lloret	University of Alicante, Spain
Paulo Maio	Polytechnic of Porto, Portugal
Riccardo Martoglia	University of Modena and Reggio Emilia, Italy
Luca Mazzola	Lucerne University of Applied Sciences and Arts, Switzerland
Andre Menolli	Universidade Estadual do Norte do Parana, Brazil
Nives Mikelic Preradovic	University of Zagreb, Croatia
Andres Montoyo	University of Alicante, Spain
Óscar Mortágua Pereira	University of Aveiro, Portugal
Erich Neuhold	University of Vienna, Austria
Jørgen Nilsson	Technical University of Denmark, Denmark
Alex Norta	Tallinn University of Technology, Estonia
Femke Ongenae	Ghent University, imec, Belgium
Carlos Periñán-Pascual	Universidad Politécnica de Valencia, Spain
Laura Po	University of Modena and Reggio Emilia, Italy
Daniele Porello	Free University of Bozen-Bolzano, Italy
Violaine Prince	LIRMM-CNRS, France
Frank Puppe	University of Würzburg, Germany
Amar Ramdane-Cherif	Versailles Saint-Quentin-en-Yvelines University, France
Stephan Reiff-Marganiec	University of Leicester, UK
Thomas Risse	University Library Johann Christian Senckenberg, Germany
Eduardo Rodriguez	University of Wisconsin, USA
Mariano Rodríguez Muro	Google LLC, USA
Oscar Rodríguez Rocha	Teach on Mars, France
Colette Rolland	Université Paris 1 Panthèon Sorbonne, France
Loris Roveda	Dalle Mole Institute for Artificial Intelligence (IDSIA), Switzerland
Fabio Sartori	University of Milano-Bicocca, Italy
Nuno Silva	Polytechnic of Porto, Portugal
Antonio Soares	FEUP, INESC TEC, Portugal
Deborah Stacey	University of Guelph, Canada
Gerson Sunye	University of Nantes, France
Orazio Tomarchio	University of Catania, Italy
Petr Tucnik	University of Hradec Kralove, Czech Republic
Manolis Tzagarakis	University of Patras, Greece
Hironori Washizaki	Waseda University, Japan
Dianxiang Xu	Boise State University, USA
Yue Xu	Queensland University of Technology, Australia
Veruska Zamborlinini	Institute for Logic, Language and Computation (ILLC), University of Amsterdam, The Netherlands
Gian Zarri	Sorbonne University, France
Ying Zhao	Naval Postgraduate School, USA
Nianjun Zhou	IBM, USA
Qiang Zhu	University of Michigan - Dearborn, USA

KEOD Additional Reviewers

Kevin Angele	University of Innsbruck, Austria
Duarte Gouveia	Universidade da Madeira, Portugal
Elwin Huaman	University of Innsbruck, Austria
Elias Kärle	Semantic Technologie Institute, Austria
Oleksandra Panasiuk	Semantic Technology Institute, Austria
Diogo Regateiro	University of Aveiro, Portugal
Umutcan Simsek	University of Innsbruck, Austria

KMIS Program Committee

Marie-Helene Abel	HEUDIASYC, CNRS, University of Compiègne, France
Samia Aitouche	Université Batna 2, Laboratoire D'automatique Et Productique, Algeria
Miriam Alves	Institute of Aeronautics and Space, Brazil
Michael Arias	Universidad de Costa Rica, Costa Rica
Ana Azevedo	CEOS.PP, ISCAP, P.PORTO, Portugal
Giuseppe Berio	University of Southern Brittany, France
Dickson Chiu	The University of Hong Kong, Hong Kong
Ritesh Chugh	Central Queensland University, Australia
Michael Fellmann	Universität Rostock, Germany
Joan-Francesc Fondevila-Gascón	University of Gerona, Open University of Catalonia, Spain
Annamaria Goy	University of Turin, Italy
Gabriel Guerrero-Contreras	University of Cádiz, Spain
Mounira Harzallah	LS2N, Polytech Nantes, University of Nantes, France
Anca Ionita	University Politehnica of Bucharest, Romania
Paul Johannesson	Royal Institute of Technology, Sweden
Nikos Karacapilidis	University of Patras, Greece
Radoslaw Katarzyniak	Wroclaw University of Science and Technology, Poland
Tri Kurniawan	Universitas Brawijaya, Indonesia
Dominique Laurent	ETIS Laboratory, CNRS, Cergy-Pontoise University, ENSEA, France
Michael Leyer	University of Rostock, Germany
Kecheng Liu	University of Reading, UK
Carlos Malcher Bastos	Universidade Federal Fluminense, Brazil
Federica Mandreoli	University of Modena and Reggio Emilia, Italy
Nada Matta	University of Technology of Troyes, France
Rodney McAdam	University of Ulster, UK
Brahami Menaouer	National Polytechnic School of Oran, Algeria
Michele Missikoff	ISTC-CNR, Italy
Owen Molloy	National University of Ireland Galway, Ireland
Jean-Henry Morin	University of Geneva, Switzerland

Wilma Penzo   University of Bologna, Italy
José Pérez-Alcázar   University of São Paulo, Brazil
Erwin Pesch   University of Siegen, Germany
Filipe Portela   Centro ALGORITMI, University of Minho, Portugal
Arkalgud Ramaprasad   University of Illinois at Chicago, USA
Marina Ribaudo   Università di Genova, Italy
Colette Rolland   Université Paris 1 Panthèon-Sorbonne, France
Ana Salgado   Federal University of Pernambuco, Brazil
Christian Seel   University of Applied Sciences Landshut, Germany
Mukhammad Setiawan   Universitas Islam Indonesia, Indonesia
Malgorzata Sterna   Poznan University of Technology, Poland
Deborah Swain   North Carolina Central University, USA
Tan Tse Guan   Universiti Malaysia Kelantan, Malaysia
Shu-Mei Tseng   I-Shou University, Taiwan, China
Uffe Wiil   University of Southern Denmark, Denmark
Qiang Zhu   University of Michigan - Dearborn, USA

KMIS Additional Reviewers

Sara Balderas-Díaz   University of Cadiz, Spain
Daniel Hilpoltsteiner   University of Applied Sciences Landshut, Germany
Fabienne Lambusch   University of Rostock, Germany
Michael Poppe   Germany

Invited Speakers

Robert Pergl   Czech Technical University in Prague, Czech Republic
Eduard Babkin   National Research University Higher School
                             of Economics, Russia
Heimo Müller   Medical University of Graz, Austria
Kayyali Mohamed   International Federation of Global & Green
                             Information Communication Technology, USA

Contents

Knowledge Discovery and Information Retrieval

Predicting the Quality of Translations Without an Oracle

Yi Zhou(✉) and Danushka Bollegala

Department of Computer Science, University of Liverpool, Liverpool, UK
{y.zhou71,danushka}@liverpool.ac.uk

Abstract. Even though machine translation (MT) systems have shown promise for automatic translations, the quality of translations produced by MT systems is still far behind professional human translations (HTs), because of the complexity of grammar and word usage in natural languages. As a result, HTs are still commonly used in practice. Nevertheless, the quality of HTs is strongly depending on the skills and knowledge of translators. How to measure the quality of translations produced by MT systems and human translators in an automatic manner has faced a lot of challenges. The transitional way to manually checking the accuracy of translation quality by bilingual speakers is expensive and time-consuming. Therefore, we propose an unsupervised method to assess HTs and MTs quality without having access to any labelled data. We compare a range of methods which are able to automatically grade the quality of HTs and MTs, and observe that the Bidirectional Minimum Word Mover's Distance (BiMWMD) obtains the best performance on both HTs and MTs dataset.

Keywords: Bidirectional Minimum Word Mover's Distance · Human translation · Machine translation · Cross-lingual word embeddings · Word Mover's Distance · Translation quality evaluation

1 Introduction

Although MT systems have reach impressive performance in cross-lingual translation tasks, their requirement of large parallel corpora remains a common issue for training the systems. Such parallel corpora might be difficult to obtain for resource poor language pairs, such as Hindi and Sinhalese, etc. On the other hand, the complexity of grammar and word usage in natural languages results in the quality of translations produced by MT systems are still far behind professional HTs. For this reason, HTs are still be extensively used in various areas.

L1 language refers to the native language of a person, while L2 language is the second language spoken by that person. The various levels of experiences and knowledge of L2 speakers results in the HTs created by such human translators can be erroneous. Therefore, HTs provided by L2 speakers must be manually verified by qualified translators. In general, a good translation has six properties:

© Springer Nature Switzerland AG 2020
A. Fred et al. (Eds.): IC3K 2019, CCIS 1297, pp. 3–23, 2020.
https://doi.org/10.1007/978-3-030-66196-0_1

intelligibility, fidelity, fluency, adequacy, comprehension, and informativeness [1]. Nevertheless, manually evaluating the quality of HTs is both time consuming and expensive.

MTs are evaluated by measuring the syntactic and semantic similarity between the source and target languages pairs. The most common used automatic method for MT quality evaluation is the bilingual evaluation understudy (BLEU) method, which is proposed by Papineni et al. [2]. This method compares MTs to golden references, that refers to professional HT, and considers a better MT is the one closer to the professional HTs. On the other hand, traditional HT quality evaluation is often done manually by bilingual speakers due to such golden references are not available in HTs. However, the number of such bilingual speakers are not enough and might not exist for rare languages. Also, manually evaluating the quality of HTs is not re-usable and time consuming. Therefore, MT evaluation methods such as BLEU are not able to be used for the purpose of HT evaluation.

In this paper, we propose a method which can be used for evaluating the quality of either MTs or HTs without any supervision. We indicate translation quality evaluation as an unsupervised graph matching problem. Given a source document and its target translation S and T, we measure the semantic similarity between a set of source words $\{s_1, s_2, \ldots, s_n\}$ in S and a set of target words $\{t_1, t_2, \ldots, t_m\}$ in T by using different distance and similarity metrics. The Word Mover's distance [3] is one of the distance metrics, which considers the distance between documents as the minimum cost of transforming embedded words from one language to another language. Inspired by this, we take the advantage of cross-lingual word embeddings and propose a novel approach to evaluate the quality of translations without having access to any references.

We report and evaluate different unsupervised translation quality evaluation methods, and measure the Spearman rank and Pearson correlation of the similarity scores produced by these methods against professional human judgements. The results in the experiments show that the Bidirectional Minimum Word Mover's distance (BiMWMD) has the greatest agreement with human ratings, which demonstrates that our proposed method has the capability to distinguish high quality and low quality translations without requiring any human supervision.

2   Related Work

Translation quality can be accessed by comparing a source text against its translation using similarity and distance methods by taking advantage of cross-lingual embeddings. Prior work on measuring text similarity measures the similarity between two texts by taking the average over the word similarities of the words that occur in the text [4–6]. Supervised system which combines different similarity measures, such as lexicon-semantic, syntactic and string similarity showed impressive performance at SemEval 2012 [7,8]. Later, an unsupervised system based on word alignment proposed by Sultan et al. [9] drew attentions to the benefits from using unsupervised quality evaluation model. After that, Brychcín and Svoboda [10] and Tian et al. [11] model semantic similarity for multilingual and cross-lingual sentence pairs by first translating source texts into target language using MT, then applying monolingual Semantic Textual Similarity (STS) models. To tackle the limitation of human annotated data for resource poor languages, Brychcín [12] makes use of bilingual dictionary to map monolingual word embeddigns into a shared space via linear transformations for cross-lingual semantic similarity.

Word embeddings are learned based on the distributional hypothesis [13], which states that words appearing in the same context tend to have similar meanings. In light of this hypothesis, Mikolov et al. [14] present distributed Skip-gram and Continuous Bag-of-Words (CBOW) models to learn semantic representations of words from a large quantity of unstructured texts data. Recently, researches on mapping words from two (bilingual word embeddings) [15–17] or more (multilingual word embeddings) [18,19] languages to a common shared vector space regard as cross-lingual word embeddings learning. The distance between words indicates the dissimilarity between such word embeddings.

Most approaches for learning cross-lingual word embeddings require different kinds of alignment as supervision. Taking advantage of word alignment, Luong et al. [20] propose the bilingual Skip-Gram model (BiSkip) to train cross-lingual word embeddings by using a parallel corpus. This model can be seen as an extension of monolingual skip-gram model. Hermann and Blunsom [18] present The Bilingual Compositional Model (BiCVM) to learn cross-lingual word embeddigns on sentence alignment. In terms of document alignment, Vulić and Moens [21] indicate a model to learn cross-lingual word embeddings from non-parallel data by extending the skip-gram model with negative sampling (SGNS) model and generating cross-lingual word embeddings through a comparable corpus.

The Word Mover's Distance proposed by Kusner et al. [3] is used for measuring the semantic distance between the source and the target documents. This method regards the distance between documents as the minimal cost for transforming each word in a source document to the words in a target document. Nevertheless, taking the alignment of each word from source document to all the words in the translated document is expensive. To handle this problem, we study the sentence alignment and propose the Bidirectional Minimum Word Mover's distance (BiMWMD) method. We consider the distance between texts to be the cumulative minimal cost of translating each source word to its corresponding target word. Furthermore, the method we proposed computes the translation flow from both the source to the target and the target to the source directions.

3 Translation Quality Evaluation

Most of the existing translation quality evaluation approaches require gold references, which are the professional HTs manually created by qualified human translators. Hence, we aim to propose an automatic method to accurately and efficiently evaluate the quality of cross-lingual translations without any supervision. In our work, we consider the scenario that there are no golden references available.

Given the source language text S and the target language text T. For instance, when translating Japanese text into English one, S is the Japanese text and T is the English text. Denote that the vocabularies for the source and the target languages are $\mathcal{V}_S$, $\mathcal{V}_T$ respectively. A cross-lingual word embedding $v \in \mathbb{R}^d$ of a word $w \in \mathcal{V}_S \cup \mathcal{V}_T$ can be regarded as an embedding which is shared between both S and T. Many different methods have been presented for learning cross-lingual word embeddings. In this paper, we presume that the set of cross-lingual word embeddigns for both the source and the target languages are available.

We consider an text in source language $S = v_{s_1}, v_{s_2}, \ldots, v_{s_n}$, and its translation in target language $T = v_{t_1}, v_{t_2}, \ldots, v_{t_m}$. Here, $v_{s_i} \in \mathbb{R}^d$ represents the embedding of the i-th word in source sentence, $v_{t_j} \in \mathbb{R}^d$ represents the embedding of the j-th word in the target sentence. n and m here represent the number of words in the source and the target texts respectively. In our work, source and target texts are not restricted to single sentence. Our proposed method do not require any sentence-level processing, which means that this method can be applied to either single sentence or documents with multiple sentences.

3.1   Averaged Vector (AV)

Previous researches on learning sentence embeddings have discovered that one simple way to obtain sentence embeddings is to take the average over word embeddings for the words appearing in a sentence [22]. Inspired by this, we represent the embeddings for both source and target language texts by taking the average of cross-lingual word embeddings for the words occurring in each of the texts. We name this method as the Averaged vector (AV) method. Particularly, given an embedded source language text $S = v_{s_1}, v_{s_2}, \ldots, v_{s_n}$ and its $T = v_{t_1}, v_{t_2}, \ldots, v_{t_m}$, we are able to obtain the embeddings of two texts by $\bar{v}_s, \bar{v}_t \in \mathbb{R}^d$ as given by (1) and (2).

$$\bar{v}_s = \frac{1}{n} \sum_{i=1}^{n} v_{s_i} \tag{1}$$

$$\bar{v}_t = \frac{1}{m} \sum_{j=1}^{m} v_{t_j} \tag{2}$$

$$\mathrm{sim}(S, T) = \cos(\bar{v}_s, \bar{v}_t)$$
$$= \frac{\bar{v}_s^\top \bar{v}_t}{||\bar{v}_s|| \, ||\bar{v}_t||}. \tag{3}$$

Here, we provide a measure of translation quality by regarding the similarity between S and T as a proxy of the semantic agreement between the source text and the target texts. In our preliminary experiments, we implemented term frequency inverse document frequency (tfidf) weighting and smooth inverse frequency (SIF) [22] methods to obtain sentence embeddings. However, we did not observe significant improvement for our tasks by using these weighting methods. Hence, we decided to use the unweighted averaging method as given in (1) and (2).

3.2 Source-Centred Maximum Similarity (SMS)

The AV method described in Sect. 3.1 takes the averaged embedding as sentence embedding, regardless of the alignment between source and target words. This is a symmetric method, which means that the method will return the same similarity score even if we swap the source and the target texts. However, one word in a source text might be related to only a few words in the corresponding target text, rather than all the words appearing in the target text. Hence, we modify the AV method and propose the source-centred maximum similarity (SMS) method, which is able to compare each source word against its most related target word in the translation. We will describe more details about this method below.

We firstly measure the cosine similarity of each embedded word v_{s_i} in the source text against all the embedded words $v_{t_1}, v_{t_2}, \ldots, v_{t_m}$ in the target translated text. We consider the maximal similarity score between v_{s_i} and any of $v_{t_1}, v_{t_2}, \ldots, v_{t_m}$ as the similarity between two words. Finally, the averaged similarity score over all the maximum scores is reported as the similarity between the source text S and the target text T as given by (4).

$$\text{sim}(S, T) = \frac{1}{n} \sum_{i=1}^{n} \max_{j=1,\ldots,m} \cos(v_{s_i}, v_{t_j}) \tag{4}$$

3.3 Target-Centred Maximum Similarity (TMS)

The SMS method measures the similarity from the source text to the target text only. To evaluate the similarity from the opposite direction (from the target text to the source text), we modify the SMS method and present the TMS method. This method computes the cosine similarity of each embedded target word v_{t_j} against all the embedded source words $v_{s_1}, v_{s_2}, \ldots, v_{s_n}$ in the source text. Similar to the SMS method, the maximal similarity score is then calculated as the similarity score of transforming each target word v_{t_j} back to its corresponding word v_{s_i} in the source text. Finally, the averaged score over all the maximum similarity scores is regarded as the similarity between the target and the source texts, as given by (5).

$$\text{sim}(S, T) = \frac{1}{m} \sum_{i=1}^{m} \max_{i=1,\ldots,n} \cos(v_{s_i}, v_{t_j}) \tag{5}$$

3.4   Word Mover's Distance (WMD)

In the light of the Earth Mover's Distance (EMD) [23], Kusner et al. [3] propose the WMD, which has the capability of measuring the dissimilarity between two text documents. Specifically, the WMD computes the minimal cost that has to spend for transferring words from a source text to reach the corresponding words in a target text. This method enables us to assess the similarity between two documents even if there is no common words contained in those two documents.

Assume that the two text documents are represented as normalised bag-of-words vectors. The i-th source embedded word v_{s_i} appears $h(v_{s_i})$ times in the source text S. The normalised frequency $f(v_{s_i})$ of v_{s_i} can be defined as given by (6).

$$f(v_{s_i}) = \frac{h(v_{s_i})}{\sum_{j=1}^{m} h(v_{s_j})} \tag{6}$$

Likewise, the normalised frequency $f(v_{t_j})$ of a word v_{t_j} in the target text T is given by (7).

$$f(v_{t_j}) = \frac{h(v_{t_j})}{\sum_{i=1}^{n} h(v_{t_i})} \tag{7}$$

Next, the transformation problem can be specified as the minimum cumulative amount of cost that is required to transfer words from a source text S to a target text T under the certain constraints defined in the following linear programme (LP).

$$\min \sum_{i=1}^{n} \sum_{j=1}^{m} \mathbf{T}_{ij} c(i,j) \tag{8}$$

$$\text{subject to: } \sum_{j=1}^{m} \mathbf{T}_{ij} = f(v_{s_i}), \forall i \in \{1, \ldots, n\} \tag{9}$$

$$\sum_{i=1}^{n} \mathbf{T}_{ij} = f(v_{t_j}), \forall j \in \{1, \ldots, m\} \tag{10}$$

$$\mathbf{T} \geq 0 \tag{11}$$

Here, $\mathbf{T} \in \mathbb{R}^{n \times m}$ represents a non-negative transformation *flow* matrix learnt by the aforementioned LP. We take the Euclidean distance between the embedded words v_{s_i} and v_{t_j} to be the dissimilarity between them, and define the equation by (12).

$$c(i,j) = \left\| v_{s_i} - v_{t_j} \right\|_2 \tag{12}$$

In order to reduce the objective given by (8), we can assign the (i, j) element T_{ij} of $\mathbf{T}$ to be a small value (possibly zero) when $c(i, j)$ is high for transforming an embedded source word $\boldsymbol{v}_{s_i}$ to its corresponding target word $\boldsymbol{v}_{t_j}$. The equality constraints given in (9) and (10) demonstrate the column and row stochasticity constraints for $\mathbf{T}$ respectively. These equality constraints make sure that the total weights are able to be transferred from each source word to the target text, and contrariwise are preserved. This makes $\mathbf{T}$ a *double stochastic* matrix.

3.5   Bidirectional Minimum WMD (BiMWMD)

As we described in Sect. 3.4 before, WMD is a symmetric. So the same dissimilarity score between two documents will be observed even though we switch the source and the target texts. In contrast, the SMS and TMS methods presented in Sect. 3.2 and 3.3, respectively, are both asymmetric translation quality evaluation methods. Following the SMS and TMS, we modify the WMD and take into account the translation quality from the perspective of the source text, which we call it the *Source-centric Minimum WMD* (SMWMD), and from the perspective of the target text, which we refer it to the *Target-centred Minimum WMD* (TMWMD). We will describe the details about the SMWND, TMWMD and BiMWMD methods below.

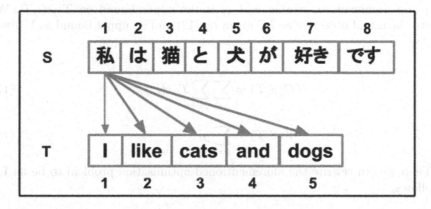

Fig. 1. Translating a word from the Japanese text (S) into the English (T) text. The perfect alignment between S and T is $s_1 \rightarrow I$, $s_2 \rightarrow null$, $s_3 \rightarrow cats$, $s_4 \rightarrow and$, $s_5 \rightarrow dogs$, $s_6 \rightarrow null$, $s_7 \rightarrow like$ and $s_8 \rightarrow null$. The thin arrow in the figure represents the minimum cost of translating the Japanese word to the corresponding word I in English text. The accurate translations tend to have smaller distances (costs) associated with.

SMWMD: The Source-centred Minimum WMD (SMWMD) takes into account the translation flow from a source text to its corresponding target text. Figure 1 indicates an example of how the method measures the semantic distance between a source text S and a target text T. The SMWMD method measures the minimal cost of transforming each embedded source word v_{s_i} to its corresponding target word v_{t_j} in T, and considers the sum of transforming cost to be the objective function for the LP. Similar to the WMD, $\mathbf{T}_{ij} \geq 0$ can be denoted as the flow matrix that is used to translate embedded source word v_{s_i} to the corresponding target word v_{t_j} according to the cost $c(i,j)$ given by (12). From the experiments, we observe that the normalised frequencies $f(v_{s_i})$ and $f(v_{t_j})$ do not have significant effect on the results. Therefore, we set both frequencies to be 1 to simplify the objective function.

Hence, the optimisation problem can be defined as follows:

$$\min \sum_{i=1}^{n} \min_{j=1,\ldots,m} \mathbf{T}_{ij}c(i,j) \tag{13}$$

$$\text{subject to: } \sum_{j=1}^{m} \mathbf{T}_{ij} = 1, \forall i \in \{1,\ldots,n\} \tag{14}$$

$$\sum_{i=1}^{n} \mathbf{T}_{ij} = 1, \forall j \in \{1,\ldots,m\} \tag{15}$$

$$\mathbf{T} \geq 0 \tag{16}$$

In order to further simplify the objective function given in (13), we replace $\mathbf{T}_{ij}c(i,j)$ to y_i, where $\mathbf{T}_{ij}c(i,j)$ represents the actual cost of translating words from one document to another and y_i is the upper bound on $\mathbf{T}_{ij}c(i,j)$. We denote the actual objective as TC given by (17) and its upper bound as Y given by (18).

$$TC(S,T) = \sum_{i=1}^{n}\sum_{j=1}^{m} T_{ij}c(i,j) \tag{17}$$

$$Y(S,T) = \sum_{i=1}^{n} y_i \tag{18}$$

Then we can rewrite the aforementioned optimisation problem to be an LP as follows:

$$\min \sum_{i=1}^{n} y_i \tag{19}$$

$$\text{subject to: } \mathbf{T}_{ij}c(i,j) \leq y_i \tag{20}$$

$$\sum_{j=1}^{m} \mathbf{T}_{ij} = 1, \forall i \in \{1,\ldots,n\} \tag{21}$$

$$\sum_{i=1}^{n} \mathbf{T}_{ij} = 1, \forall j \in \{1\ldots,m\} \tag{22}$$

$$\mathbf{T} \geq 0 \tag{23}$$

We measure the minimal translation cost of transforming a source text S into a target text T by solving the LP above. Here, SMWMD(S, T) can be either $TC(S, T)$ or $Y(S, T)$. In the Sect. 4.4, we will show more details about the difference between the actual objective (TC) and its upper bound for the purpose of evaluating the quality of cross-lingual translations.

TMWMD: As we know that a correct translation must not only accurately translate the information from the source text, but also not add any extra information to the target text. A simple way to verify this is to translate the target text back to the source text, then calculate the semantic distance between them. To quantitatively capture this idea, we modify the WMD objective as we have done for SMWMD, and proposed a reverse method which pivots on the target text rather than the source text. We regard this method as the Target-centred Minimum WMD (TMWMD).

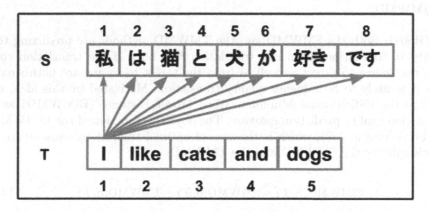

Fig. 2. The transformation of a word in the English target (T) text to the Japanese source (S) text. The perfect alignment between S and T is $s_1 \rightarrow I$, $s_2 \rightarrow null$, $s_3 \rightarrow cats$, $s_4 \rightarrow and$, $s_5 \rightarrow dogs$, $s_6 \rightarrow null$, $s_7 \rightarrow like$ and $s_8 \rightarrow null$. The thin arrow represents the minimal cost alignment.

Similar to SMWMD, TMWMD can also be calculated using either the actual objective $(TC(S, T))$ or the upper bound $(Y(S, T))$. We collectively define these two variants as TMWMD(S, T).

We assign the semantic distance between the source text S and the target text T as the minimum cumulative cost that has to paid for transforming all words from T to S. Figure 2 shows an example of the way that this method calculates distance from T to S. In this figure, the embedded target word I is compared against all the source words, which is indicated by arrows. The closet Japanese translation s_1 is mapped by the thinnest arrow. We define the objective of TMWMD as the following LP:

$$\min \sum_{j=1}^{m} y_j \tag{24}$$

$$\text{subject to: } \mathbf{T}_{ij} c_{(i,j)} \leq y_j \tag{25}$$

$$\sum_{j=1}^{m} \mathbf{T}_{ij} = 1, \forall i \in \{1, \ldots, n\} \tag{26}$$

$$\sum_{i=1}^{n} \mathbf{T}_{ij} = 1, \forall j \in \{1 \ldots, m\} \tag{27}$$

$$\mathbf{T} \geq \mathbf{0} \tag{28}$$

To clarify that the TMWMD is the mirror image of the SMWMD in the sense that by swapping source text S and target text T we will obtain the LP for SMWMD.

BiMWMD: Both the SMWMD and the TMWMD methods are predicting the quality of translations from one translation flow only. If the translation cost from the source to target as well as from the target to source are both small, then it is likely to be a higher quality translation. Motivated by this idea, we propose the Bidirectional Minimum Word Mover Distance (BiMWMD) as a translation quality prediction measure. The objective function of the BiMWMD can be defined as (29), which is the sum of optimal translation costs returned individually by the SMWMD and the TMWMD.

$$\text{BiMWMD}(S,T) = \text{SMWMD}(S,T) + \text{TMWMD}(S,T) \tag{29}$$

Likewise to the WMD, the BiMWMD is a symmetric translation quality prediction measure. Owing to the SMWMD and TMWMD measures solve different LPs, they return different translation quality predictions. The minimal cumulative cost for transforming each word in the source text S to all the words in the target text T that computed by the WMD is returned as the objective. In contrast, the result of BiMWMD comes from two independent LPs. Each of them consider only a single direction: the SMWMD considers the translation flow from source to target, while the TMWMD takes into account the translation flow from target to source. From the results showed in Sect. 4.4, we observed that BiMWMD obtains a higher degree of correlation with professional human judgements for translation quality prediction than WMD.

4   Experiments

In this section, we evaluate the aforementioned translation quality evaluation methods described in Sect. 3. We create a translation dataset, where we use correlation against human ratings as the evaluation criteria. More details about the dataset will be described in Sect. 4.1. The experimental results will be showed in Sect. 4.4.

4.1 Dataset

In order to assess the different translation quality prediction methods described in Sect. 3, we provide a dataset containing 1030 sentences from Japanese user manuals on Digital cameras. Afterwards, we ask a group of 50 human translators, whose L1 language is Japanese and have learned English as a L2 language. These human translators were recruited using a crowd-sourcing platform that is operational in Japan. To clarify that the human translators have various levels of experience in technical documents translation, ranging widely from experienced translator to beginners. We believe this will give us a broad spectrum of translations for quality evaluation purposes. Specifically, each of the Japanese sentences was translated by one of the human translators in the pool, that is, the translator was asked to write a single English translation for a Japanese sentence.

Afterwards, we randomly chose 130 such Japanese to English translation pairs and hired four human judges, who are familiar with both Japanese and English and are professionally qualified translator with more than 10 years of experience in translating technical documents. We asked them to rate the quality of each of the chosen translation pairs. In order to distinguish these four professional human translators from the pool of human translators who have written the English translations, we call them as *judges*. Particularly, we asked each of the four judges to rate a translation pair by the following grades:

Grade 1 Quality Translations: A perfect translation. There are no further modifications required. The translation pair is scored in a range of $0.76 - 1.00$.

Grade 2 Quality Translations: A good translation. There are some incorrectly translations of words. But the overall meaning can be understood. The translation pair is scored in a range of $0.51 - 0.75$.

Grade 3 Quality Translations: A bad translation. There are more incorrectly translated words than correctly translated words in the translation. The translation pair is scored in a range of $0.26 - 0.50$.

Grade 4 Quality Translations: A translation which requires re-translation. The translation cannot be comprehend or conveys a significantly different meaning to the source sentence. The translation pair is scored in a range of $0.00 - 0.25$.

We consider the average of the grades assigned by the four judges to a translation pair as its final grade.

4.2 Cross-Lingual Word Embeddings

All the aforementioned translation quality measures in Sect. 3 require cross-lingual word embeddings. In order to study the effects of different types of embeddigns (context-independent embeddings and contextualised embeddings at word-level) on translation quality prediction, we obtain cross-lingual word embeddings using different methods.

Context-Independent Word Embeddings. The word embeddings learnt based on the distributional hypothesis are often referred to context-independent word embeddings. To obtain the context-independent word embeddings between Japanese and English languages, we make the usage of publicly available monolingual word embeddings. These monolingual embeddigns are trained on Wikipedia and Common Crawl using fastText [24]. Owing to the dataset contains words in both Japanese and English, we train two sets of monolingual word embeddings for Japanese and English separately. Afterwards, the unsupervised adversarial training methods proposed by Conneau et al. [25] and implemented in MUSE[1] is used to map Japanese and English word embeddings into a common vector spaces, without having access to any bilingual dictionary or parallel corpora. By using bilingual lexical resources, we could possibly further improve the performance of cross-lingual alignment. But in our case, even if such resources are not available, we are still able to elastically estimate the performance of methods that we described in Sect. 3.

Contextualised Word Embeddings. Even though context-independent word embeddings are able to represent words in a vector space, they create a single representation for each word, which results in all senses of a polysemous word need to share a single vector. To tackle the limitation of context-independent word embeddings, the study on learning contextualised embeddings starts to draw more and more attentions. Contextualised word embeddings are learnt based on the context that a word occurs in. These word embeddings are able to capture different senses of a word. In this manner, they are able to distinguish polysemous words using the contexts.

In order to study whether contextualised information has the capability to improve the performance of our proposed method, we use the Language-Agnostic SEntence Representations (LASER)[2] [26], which is a model to create multilingual sentence embeddings. This model is trained on 93 input language corpora selected from Europarl, United Nations, Open-Subtitles-2018, Global Voices, Tanzil and Tatoeba (available on the OPUS website [3] [27]). The architecture of LASER is showed in Fig. 3.

As shown in Fig. 3, words in the training corpora are fed in to the model after tokenising using byte-pair encoding (BPE) [28]. Then sentence embeddings are obtained as the output of BiLSTM encoder by applying a max-pooling operation on top of it. Afterwards, the learned sentence embeddings are used to initialise the decoder with the concatenation of its input embeddings. In our work, we

---

[1] https://github.com/facebookresearch/MUSE.
[2] https://github.com/facebookresearch/LASER.
[3] http://opus.nlpl.eu.

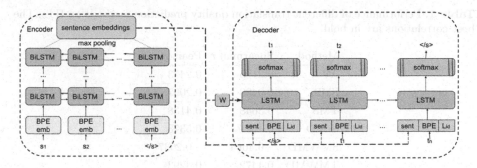

Fig. 3. The architecture of LASER. The system is able to learn multilingual contextualised embeddings. Adapted from "Massively multilingual sentence embeddings for zero-shot cross-lingual transfer and beyond" by Artetxe, Mikel and Schwenk, Holger, 2019, Transactions of the Association for Computational Linguistics, 7, pp. 597–610 [26].

obtain the cross-lingual contextualised embeddings at word-level from LASER. Specially, we apply LASER on the aforementioned HTs dataset to obtain cross-lingual contextualised embeddings.

4.3   Evaluation Measures

Recall that our aim of this work is to predict translation quality without having access to any supervision. To evaluate the performance of different methods, we would like the check whether the translation qualities predicted by the afore-mentioned methods, which we described in Sect. 3, are having a high agreement with the grades provided by the professional human judges to each of the translation pairs in the dateset that we generated in Sect. 4.1. Specially, to assess the level of agreement of predicted scores generated by different methods against the human ratings, we calculate the Spearman rank and Pearson correlation coefficients between them. Unlike the Spearman rank which takes into account only the relative ordering, the Pearson correlation coefficient considers the linear relationship among variables.

4.4   Results

Table 1 summarises the result of comparing different translation quality evaluation methods, which we described in Sect. 3. In this experiment, we apply LASER to obtain cross-lingual contextualised embeddings on the HTs dataset. Note that some of the methods, such as AV, SMS and TMS, return similarity scores, while others (WMD, SMWMD, TMWMD and BiMWMD) generate the semantic distances between translation pairs. In order to make sure both similarity scores and semantic distance are equally comparable, we convert distances to similarity scores for WMD, SMWMD, TMWMD and BiMWMD by

$$1 - \frac{distance}{maximum\ distance}.$$

Table 1. Performance of different translation quality prediction methods on HTs. The best correlations are in bold.

Method	Spearman r	Pearson ρ
AV	0.2185	0.2473
SMS	0.0488	0.2097
TMS	0.3648	0.4138
WMD	0.4507	0.5378
SMWMD	−0.4064	−0.2637
TMWMD	0.4472	0.4293
BiMWMD	**0.5912**	**0.5412**

Table 2. Different configurations for the BiMWMD method with contextualised word embeddings on HTs. Normalisation of word embeddings: ℓ_1, ℓ_2 and unnormalised (**No**), **Row** and **Column** denote using only row or column stochasticity constraints in the LP. In addition, we consider the actual objective (**TC**) or its upper bound (**Y**) as the value of BiMWMD.

Method	Spearman r	Pearson ρ
ℓ_2+Y+Row	−0.0568	0.1061
ℓ_2+Y+Column	**0.5912**	**0.5412**
ℓ_2+TC+Row	−0.2510	−0.0733
ℓ_2+TC+Column	−0.2510	−0.0663
ℓ_1+Y+Row	0.1619	−0.0385
ℓ_1+Y+Column	0.5870	0.5239
ℓ_1+TC+Row	−0.2510	−0.0707
ℓ_1+TC+Column	−0.2510	−0.0638
No+Y+Row	0.0771	0.2748
No+Y+Column	0.5258	0.4952
No+TC+Row	−0.2107	−0.0465
No+TC+Column	−0.2053	−0.0366

We use interior-point method to solve the aforementioned LPs in all cases and consider the degree of correlation with the ratings provided by the professional human judges for the translation pairs to be a predictor of the translation quality of a method. From Table 1, we see that the AV method returns a low-level of correlation with human ratings. This is because that taking the average over word embeddings for the words appearing in a sentence to create text/sentence embeddings only provides a naive alignment between the two languages, which results in the cosine similarity between a source and target text to be unreliable. Comparing the SMS and TMS methods, we observe that estimating the translation by centering on the target obtains a high correlation against

Table 3. Different configurations for the BiMWMD method with context-independent word embeddings on HTs. Normalisation of word embeddings: ℓ_1, ℓ_2 and unnormalised (**No**), **Row** and **Column** denote using only row or column stochasticity constraints in the LP. In addition, we consider the actual objective (**TC**) or its upper bound (**Y**) as the value of BiMWMD.

Method	Spearman r	Pearson ρ
ℓ_2+Y+Row	−0.0510	0.1396
ℓ_2+Y+Column	0.5743	**0.5457**
ℓ_2+TC+Row	−0.2599	−0.0661
ℓ_2+TC+Column	−0.2599	−0.0562
ℓ_1+Y+Row	0.0924	0.0011
ℓ_1+Y+Column	**0.5893**	0.5446
ℓ_1+TC+Row	−0.2599	−0.0667
ℓ_1+TC+Column	−0.2599	−0.0565
No+Y+Row	0.2218	0.2259
No+Y+Column	0.4608	0.4764
No+TC+Row	−0.2815	−0.1026
No+TC+Column	−0.2496	−0.0850

Table 4. Performance of different translation quality prediction methods on MTs. The best correlations are in bold.

Method	Spearman r	Pearson ρ
AV	0.0171	0.0092
SMS	−0.1642	−0.0036
TMS	0.1829	0.0364
WMD	−0.0620	0.0272
SMWMD	0.4027	0.4321
TMWMD	0.5190	0.5095
BiMWMD	**0.5296**	**0.5482**

professional human ratings than centering on the source. A similar trend can be observed when we compare the SMWMD and TMWMD methods. In particular, the SMWMD method returns negative correlations for both Spearman rank and Pearson correlation coefficient, which are the lowest correlation values returned among all methods. This validates our hypothesis that the translation is different when considering different translation directions. On the other hand, we observe that the BiMWMD method obtains the highest correlations against professional judgements among all methods. This result indicates that taking into account both direction of translation flow is essential for obtaining more accurate estimates of the quality of the translations.

Table 5. Different configurations for the BiMWMD method with contextualised word embeddings on MTs. Normalisation of word embeddings: ℓ_1, ℓ_2 and unnormalised (**No**), **Row** and **Column** denote using only row or column stochasticity constraints in the LP. In addition, we consider the actual objective (**TC**) or its upper bound (**Y**) as the value of BiMWMD.

Method	Spearman r	Pearson ρ
ℓ_2+Y+Row	−0.3056	−0.3247
ℓ_2+Y+Column	0.0313	0.0594
ℓ_2+TC+Row	**0.5296**	**0.5482**
ℓ_2+TC+Column	**0.5296**	0.5471
ℓ_1+Y+Row	0.1421	−0.0065
ℓ_1+Y+Column	−0.0297	0.0521
ℓ_1+TC+Row	0.5024	0.5450
ℓ_1+TC+Column	0.5024	0.5437
No+Y+Row	−0.1591	−0.2771
No+Y+Column	0.1560	0.2551
No+TC+Row	0.5053	0.5346
No+TC+Column	0.4967	0.5327

In order to study the impact of the different parameters and settings that is associated with the BiMWMD method, we estimate it under different configurations. In particular, to study the effect of the normalisation for word embeddings, we consider three settings, ℓ_1 normalisation, ℓ_2 normalisation and no normalisation (**No**). In order to analyse differences between the actual objective $TC(S,T)$ of LP (given by (17)) and its upper bound $Y(S,T)$ (given by (18)), we consider each of the two parameters separately as the prediction returned by BiMWMD, then measure the correlation against professional human ratings. On the other hand, the row and column stochasticity constraints add a large amount of equality constraints to the LPs described in Sect. 3. Therefore, taking into account both row and column stochasticity constraints simultaneously makes the LP infeasible. To relax the constraints and to empirically study the significance of the row and the column stochasticity constraints, we analyse BiMWMD with either row stochasticity constraints (denoted by **Row**) or column stochasticity constraints (denoted by **Column**). The result of all possible combinations of the different configurations are shown in Table 2. In this experiment, we take the advantage of contextualised word embeddings obtained by running LASER on the HT dataset.

Table 2 indicates that the best performance is obtained with ℓ_2 normalised cross-lingual word embedding settings. Furthermore, The column stochasticity constraints are more essential than the row stochasticity constraints. In addition, using upper bound of the actual objective of LPs ($Y(S,T)$) as the prediction of BiMWMD returns higher degree of agreement against with human ratings than

Table 6. Different configurations for the BiMWMD method with context-independent word embeddings on MTs. Normalisation of word embeddings: ℓ_1, ℓ_2 and unnormalised (**No**), **Row** and **Column** denote using only row or column stochasticity constraints in the LP. In addition, we consider the actual objective (**TC**) or its upper bound (**Y**) as the value of BiMWMD.

Method	Spearman r	Pearson ρ
ℓ_2+Y+Row	−0.1365	−0.1681
ℓ_2+Y+Column	0.1243	0.1253
ℓ_2+TC+Row	**0.4599**	0.4818
ℓ_2+TC+Column	**0.4599**	0.4819
ℓ_1+Y+Row	−0.0042	−0.1536
ℓ_1+Y+Column	0.1183	0.1413
ℓ_1+TC+Row	**0.4599**	**0.4825**
ℓ_1+TC+Column	**0.4599**	**0.4825**
No+Y+Row	0.25831	0.1818
No+Y+Column	0.2329	0.2356
No+TC+Row	0.4253	0.4491
No+TC+Column	0.4253	0.4498

using the actual objective $(TC(S,T))$. Note that the translation flow matrix **T** has nm number of parameters. The number of parameters grows with the lengths of source and target texts. Hence, to minimise the actual objective of LPs, it is possible to consider most of the nm elements to be zero, which thereby satisfies the inequality $T_{ij}c(i,j) \leq y_j$ in LP. Therefore, the total sum of upper bounds $\sum_j y_j$, that is the objective minimised by the reformed LP, is a better proxy as the BiMWMD method.

Table 3 shows the performance of the BiMWMD method under different configurations with context-independent embeddings on HTs. From this table, we observe that the BiMWMD method obtains the highest correlations for Spearman rank and Pearson correlation coefficient with different settings. The best performance is obtained with ℓ_1 normalisation for Spearman rank, whereas with ℓ_2 normalisation for Pearson correlation coefficient. Comparing with the result showed in Table 2, the BiMWMD method obtains better performance with contextualised word embeddings than with context-independent word embeddings, which indicates that contextualised word embeddings contain more useful contextual information in a text than context-independent embeddings.

4.5   Comparison Against Machine Translations

Machine Translation (MT) systems have also significantly improved in quality over the last few years due to large-scale neural network language models. Recently, Neural Machine Translation (NMT) has emerged as the state-of-the-art approach for MT [30–34].

Japanese	English	Grade	Score
カメラをテレビに接続するための映像と音声用のケーブル。映像と音声信号を送信する。	A cable used to connect the camera to a standard definition television or video device, supplying both audio and video signals	0.76	0.255
写真撮影用レンズの絞りは、微調整できるようにするために複数枚の板（絞り羽根）を重ね合わせて作られている。6枚羽根絞りの場合、6枚の羽根で6角形ができており、このような絞りを虹彩絞りという。	A type of stop mechanism with multiple overlapping blades offering fine control over aperture. The six blades create a hexagonal opening referred to as an iris diaphragm.	0.54	0.212
各部名称。いわゆる「撮影設定変更ボタン」。ボタンを押すと、液晶モニターに撮影に関する情報が表示される。	Camera part; the "shooting information" button, used to display shooting settings in the monitor. The term in parentheses is represented by an icon in the manuals except when it appears in the list of camera parts.	0.43	0.233
カメラを縦に構えて撮影すること	Of images: Taller than it is wide (a.k.a. portrait orientation). "Tall" images are taken with the camera in "tall" or "portrait" orientation.	0.23	0

Fig. 4. Scores that predicted by the BiMWMD method and the ratings graded by human judges to several translation pairs. We have scaled both BiMWMD scores and judges' grades to [0,1] range for the ease of comparison. The figure is adapted from "Unsupervised Evaluation of Human Translation Quality" by Zhou, Yi and Bollegala, Danushka, 2019, KDIR, 1, pp. 55–64 [29].

It is therefore an interesting research question to compare the translations generated by MT systems against HTs for the same input source texts using the automatic evaluation measures that we proposed in this paper. For this purpose, we translate the 130 Japanese source sentences in the HTs dataset used in Sect. 4.1 to English using Google Translate[4]. In the remainder of this paper, we refer to this translated version of the HTs dataset as the MTs dataset.

Similar to the experiments conducted on the HTs dataset, we evaluate the performance of different automatic translation quality prediction measures on this MTs dataset. The results are showed in Table 4. In contrast to the results showed in Table 1, the WMD method obtains a low degree of both Spearman rank and Pearson correlation coefficient compared to the BLEU scores on the MTs dataset. Furthermore, both the SMWMD and TMWMD methods return better performances on the MT dataset than on the HT dataset, which indicates that the quality of the MTs is more stable in both directions of translations. From the table, we observe that the translation quality scores predicted by the BiMWMD method have the highest degree of agreement with the scores generated by BLEU for MTs evaluation.

Table 5 shows the performance of the BiMWMD method under different configurations with contextualised embeddings on MTs dataset. From the table, we see that similar to the prediction on HTs, the best performance is obtained with ℓ_2 normalisation. However, in comparison to the evaluation on HTs, the BiMWMD method returns the highest correlation under a different setting.

---

[4] https://translate.google.com/.

Specifically, the highest correlation is obtained with the actual objective of LPs (TC) and the row stochasticity constraints. Overall, the actual objective of LPs become more important when evaluating MTs than HTs.

Table 6 shows the performance of the BiMWMD method under different configurations with context-independent embeddings on MTs. From this table, we observe that the BiMWMD method obtains the highest correlations for Spearman rank under 4 different configurations. The ℓ_1 normalised cross-lingual word embedding setting and ℓ_2 normalised cross-lingual word embedding setting return similar correlations for both Spearman and Pearson coefficients.

A reliable method for predicting the quality of translations must have the capability to distinguish low quality translations from high quality translations. If we are able to decide whether a certain translation is of lower quality automatically, without requiring a professional translator to read it, then it is perhaps better to prioritise such low quality translation for re-translating or to be justified by a qualified translator in order to quality control. This is essential when we need to efficiently verify the accuracy of a large number of translations and would like to check the ones which are most likely to be incorrect. In order to understand the predicted scores generated by the BiMWMD method to translations with different grades that are provided by human judges, we randomly select several human translation pairs with different grades and show the scores assigned by the BiMWMD, which was the best performing the methods according to Sect. 3. We show the HT examples in Fig. 4. The predictions are generated by the BiMWMD method with ℓ_2 normalisation, upper bound of the actual objective and the column stochasticity. We can observe that translations with high grades as assigned by the human judges are also predicted to be of high quality by the BiMWMD method, while low quality translations are assigned with lower scores by both BiMWMD and professional human judges.

5 Conclusion

In this paper, we proposed different translation quality evaluation prediction measures. These measures are able to automatically evaluate the quality of translations without having accessing to any gold standard references. Particularly, we proposed a broad range of methods covering both symmetric and asymmetric measures.

The experimental results show that the Bidirectional Minimum Word Mover's Distance method obtains the best performance on both HTs and MTs datasets among all the proposed translation quality evaluation prediction measures. Between contextualised vs. context-independent embeddings, we see that the proposed Bidirectional Minimum Word Mover's Distance method obtains better performance with contextualised word embedings.

References

1. Han, L.: Machine translation evaluation resources and methods: A survey. arXiv:1605.04515 (2016)
2. Papineni, K., Roukos, S., Ward, T., Zhu, W.J.: Bleu: a method for automatic evaluation of machine translation. In: Proceedings of ACL. pp. 311–318 (2002)
3. Kusner, M., Sun, Y., Kolkin, N., Weinberger, K.: From word embeddings to document distances. In: Proceedings of ICML. pp. 957–966 (2015)
4. Corley, C., Mihalcea, R.: Measuring the semantic similarity of texts. In: Proceedings of ACL Workshop. pp. 13–18 (2005)
5. Li, Y., McLean, D., Bandar, Z.A., Crockett, K., et al.: Sentence similarity based on semantic nets and corpus statistics. IEEE Trans. Knowl. Data Eng. 18(8), 1138–1150 (2016)
6. Islam, A., Inkpen, D.: Semantic text similarity using corpus-based word similarity and string similarity. ACM Trans. Knowl. Discovery from Data (TKDD) 2(2), 10 (2008)
7. Bär, D., Biemann, C., Gurevych, I., Zesch, T.: Ukp: Computing semantic textual similarity by combining multiple content similarity measures. In: Proceedings of SemEval. pp. 435–440 (2012)
8. Šarić, F., Glavaš, G., Karan, M., Šnajder, J., Bašić, B.D.: Takelab: Systems for measuring semantic text similarity. In: Proceedings of SemEvaluation Association for Computational Linguistics pp. 441–448 (2012)
9. Sultan, M.A., Bethard, S., Sumner, T.: Dls$@$ cu: Sentence similarity from word alignment and semantic vector composition. In: Proceedings of SemEvaluation pp. 148–153 (2015)
10. Brychcín, T., Svoboda, L.: Uwb at semeval-2016 task 1: Semantic textual similarity using lexical, syntactic, and semantic information. In: Proceedings of SemEval. pp. 588–594 (2016)
11. Tian, J., Zhou, Z., Lan, M., Wu, Y.: Ecnu at semeval-2017 task 1: Leverage kernel-based traditional nlp features and neural networks to build a universal model for multilingual and cross-lingual semantic textual similarity. In: Proceedings of SemEval. pp. 191–197 (2017)
12. Brychcín, T.: Linear transformations for cross-lingual semantic textual similarity. arXiv:1807.04172 (2018)
13. Harris, Z.S.: Distributional structure. Word pp. 146–162 (1954)
14. Mikolov, T., Chen, K., Corrado, G., Dean, J.: Efficient estimation of word representations in vector space. In: Proceedings of ICLR (2013)
15. Artetxe, M., Labaka, G., Agirre, E.: Learning bilingual word embeddings with (almost) no bilingual data. In: Proc. of ACL. pp. 451–462 (2017)
16. Chandar, A.P.S., Lauly, S., Larochelle, H., Khapra, M., Ravindran, B., Raykar, V.C., Saha, A.: An autoencoder approach to learning bilingual word representations. In: Proceedings of NIPS. pp. 1853–1861 (2014)
17. Zou, W.Y., Socher, R., Cer, D., Manning, C.D.: Bilingual word embeddings for phrase-based machine translation. In: Proceedings of EMNLP. pp. 1393–1398 (2013)
18. Hermann, K.M., Blunsom, P.: Multilingual models for compositional distributed semantics. In: Proceedings of ACL. pp. 58–68 (2014)
19. Lauly, S., Boulanger, A., Larochelle, H.: Learning multilingual word representations using a bag-of-words autoencoder. arXiv:1401.1803 (2014)

20. Luong, T., Pham, H., Manning, C.D.: Bilingual word representations with monolingual quality in mind. In: Proceedings of VSMNLP Workshop. pp. 151–159 (2015)
21. Vulić, I., Moens, M.F.: Bilingual word embeddings from non-parallel document-aligned data applied to bilingual lexicon induction. In: Proceedings of IJCNLP. pp. 719–725 (2015)
22. Arora, S., Liang, Y., Ma, T.: A simple but tough-to-beat baseline for sentence embeddings. In: Proceedings of ICLR (2017)
23. Rubner, Y., Tomasi, C., Guibas, L.J.: The earth mover's distance as a metric for image retrieval. International J. Comput. Vis. **40**, 99–121 (2000)
24. Grave, E., Bojanowski, P., Gupta, P., Joulin, A., Mikolov, T.: Learning word vectors for 157 languages. In: Proceedings of LREC. pp. 3483–3487 (2018)
25. Conneau, A., Lample, G., Ranzato, M., Denoyer, L., Jégou, H.: Word translation without parallel data. arXiv:1710.04087v3 (2017)
26. Artetxe, M., Schwenk, H.: Massively multilingual sentence embeddings for zero-shot cross-lingual transfer and beyond. Trans. Assoc. Comput. Ling. **7**, 597–610 (2019)
27. Tiedemann, J.: Parallel data, tools and interfaces in opus. In: Proceedings of LREC. pp. 2214–2218 (2012)
28. Sennrich, R., Haddow, B., Birch, A.: Neural machine translation of rare words with subword units. In: Proceedings of the 54th Annual Meeting of the Association for Computational Linguistics. vol. 1, pp. 1715–1725. Association for Computational Linguistics, Berlin, Germany (2016)
29. Zhou., Y., Bollegala., D.: Unsupervised evaluation of human translation quality. In: Proceedings of the 11th International Joint Conference on Knowledge Discovery, Knowledge Engineering and Knowledge Management - Volume 1: KDIR. pp. 55–64. INSTICC, SciTePress (2019)
30. Wu, Y., et al.: Google's neural machine translation system: Bridging the gap between human and machine translation. arXiv:1609.08144 (2016)
31. Johnson, M., et al.: Google's multilingual neural machine translation system: Enabling zero-shot translation. Trans. Assoc. Comput. Ling. **5**, 339–351 (2017)
32. Blackwood, G., Ballesteros, M., Ward, T.: Multilingual neural machine translation with task-specific attention. In: Proceedings of the 27th International Conference on Computational Linguistics. pp. 3112–3122 (2018)
33. Gu, J., Hassan, H., Devlin, J., Li, V.O.: Universal neural machine translation for extremely low resource languages. In: Proceedings of the 2018 Conference of the North American Chapter of the Association for Computational Linguistics: Human Language Technologies, vol. 1, pp. 344–354 (2018)
34. Barrault, L., et al.: Findings of the 2019 Conference on Machine Translation (wmt 2019). In: Proceedings of the Fourth Conference on Machine Translation. Vol. 2, pp. 1–61 (2019)

Active Learning and Deep Learning
for the Cold-Start Problem
in Recommendation System: A Comparative
Study

Rabaa Alabdulrahman[1(✉)], Herna Viktor[1(✉)], and Eric Paquet[1,2(✉)]

[1] School of Electrical Engineering and Computer Science, University of Ottawa,
Ottawa, Canada
{ralab054, hviktor}@uottawa.ca,
eric.paquet@nrc-cnrc.gv.ca
[2] National Research Council of Canada, Ottawa, Canada

Abstract. Recommendation systems, which are employed to mitigate the information overload e-commerce users face, have succeeded in aiding customers during their online shopping experience. However, to be able to make accurate recommendations, these systems require information about the items for sale and about users' individual preferences. Making recommendations to new customers, who have no prior data in the system, is therefore challenging. This scenario, called the "cold-start problem," hinders the accuracy of recommendations made to a new user. In this paper, we introduce the popular users personalized predictions (PUPP-DA) framework to address cold starts. Soft clustering and active learning are used to accurately recommend items to new users in this framework. Additionally, we employ deep learning algorithms to improve the overall predictive accuracy. Experimental evaluation shows that the PUPP-DA framework results in high performance and accurate predictions. Further, focusing on frequent, or so-called popular, users during our active-learning stage clearly benefits the learning process.

Keywords: Recommendation systems · Collaborative filtering · Cold-start · Active learning · Deep learning · CNN

1 Introduction

Increasingly, investors and businesses are turning to online shopping when aiming to maximize their revenues. With the rapid development in technology and the exponential increase in online businesses, however, the amount of information to which clients are submitted is overwhelming. Recommendation systems were introduced to aid customers in dealing with this vast amount of information and guide them when making purchasing decisions [2]. A persistent drawback, though, is that these systems cannot always provide a personalized or human touch [3]. When a business owner does not directly, or verbally, interact with the customer, he or she has to rely intuitively on historic data collected from previous purchases. In general, research has shown that

© Springer Nature Switzerland AG 2020
A. Fred et al. (Eds.): IC3K 2019, CCIS 1297, pp. 24–53, 2020.
https://doi.org/10.1007/978-3-030-66196-0_2

vendors are better at recognizing and segmenting users [3] than existing recommendation systems are. This observation holds especially for new customers.

The primary purpose of recommendation systems is to address the information overload users experience and to aid the users in narrowing down their purchase options. These systems aim to achieve this goal by understanding their customers' preferences not only by recognizing the ratings they give for specific items but also by considering their social and demographic information [4]. Consequently, these systems create a database for both items and users where ratings and reviews of these items are collected [5]. The more information and ratings collected about the users, the more accurate the recommendations the systems make [6].

Generally speaking, recommendation systems are either content-based filtering (CBF) [7], collaborative filtering (CF) [8], or hybrid approaches [9]. These systems rely on two basic inputs: the set of users in the system, U (also known as customers), and the set of items to be rated by the users, I (also known as the products) [10]. All these systems employ matrices based on past purchase patterns. With CBF, the system focuses on item matrices where it is assumed that if a user liked an item in the past, he or she is more inclined to like a similar item in the future [5, 11]. These systems therefore study the attributes of the items [8]. On the other hand, CF systems focus on user-rating matrices, recommending items that have been rated by other users with preferences similar to those of the targeted user [12]. Thus, these systems rely on the historic data of user rating and similarities across the user network [5]. Since the hybrid systems employ both CBF and CF approaches, they concurrently consider items based on users' preferences and on the similarity between the items' content [11]. In recent years, research has trended toward hybrid systems [8]. Another growing trend is the use of data mining and machine learning algorithms [13] to identify patterns in users' interests and behaviors [13].

Deep learning algorithms have had much success in industry and academia recently, especially when addressing complex problems that involve big data, focusing on domains such as image processing and text analysis [13, 14]. Notably, deep learning has been employed in recommender systems that involve movies and music [13–15]. Deep learning methods are used to extract hidden features and relationships and build on earlier work within the field of neural networks [16]. The advantage of deep learning techniques comes from their ability to construct multi-layer, nonlinear, and layer-to-layer network structures [14]. Therefore, in recommendation systems they effectively capture the nonlinear and insignificant user-item relationships [14]. Deep learning technology also has the ability to use diverse data sources to make accurate recommendations and overcome the data sparsity and cold-start problems, notably in the area of social and text recommendation systems [15, 16]. Specifically, deep learning based on convolution neural networks [13, 14, 19] has been employed extensively within the recommender system domain due to their known success in computer vision and text mining domains.

In this paper, we present the popular users personalized predictions (PUPP-DA) framework, designed to address the cold-start problem in recommendation systems. We combine cluster analysis and active learning, or so-called user-in-the-loop, to assign new customers to the most appropriate groups in our framework. The novelty of our approach lies in the fact that we construct user segmentations via cluster analysis.

Subsequently, as new users enter the system, classification methods intelligently assign them to the best segment. Based on this assignment, we apply active learning to describe the groups. That is, cluster analysis is used to group similar user profiles, while active learning is employed to learn the labels associated with these groups. We extend our earlier work as reported in [1] by incorporating deep convolutional neural networks (CNNs) into the learning process.

The remainder of this paper is organized as follows: In Sect. 2, we present related work, then Sect. 3 presents our PUPP-DA framework and components; Sect. 4 discusses our experimental setup and data preparation, and Sect. 5 details the results. Finally, Sect. 6 concludes the paper.

2 Related Work

In active learning, or user in the loop, a machine learning algorithm selects the best data samples to present to a domain expert for labelling. These samples are then used to bootstrap the learning process in that these examples are subsequently used in a supervised learning setting. In recommendation systems, active learning presents a utility-based approach to collect more information about the users [17]. Showing the users a number of questions about their preferences, or asking for more personal information such as age or gender, may benefit the learning process [18].

The literature addressing the cold-start problem [19] is divided into implicit and explicit approaches. On the implicit side, the system uses existing information to create its recommendations by adopting traditional filtering strategies or by employing social network analysis. For instance, Wang et al. rely on an implicit approach based on questionnaires and active learning to engage the users in a conversation aimed at collecting additional preferences. Based on the previously collected data, the users' preferences and predictions, the active learning method is used to determine the best questions to be asked [18]. Similarly, standard explicit approaches may be extended by incorporating active learning methods in the data collection phase [19]. Fernandez-Tobias et al., for example, use an explicit framework to compare three methods based on the users' personal information [20]. First, they include the personal information to improve a collaborative filtering framework performance. Then they use active learning to further improve the performance by adding more personal information from existing domains. Finally, they supplement the lack of preference data in the main domain using users' personal information from supporting domains.

There are many examples in the literature of machine learning techniques being utilized in recommendation systems. Although hybrid filtering was proposed as a solution to the limitations of CBF and CF, hybrid filtering still does not adequately address issues such as data sparsity, where the number of items in the database is much larger than the items a customer typically selects, and grey sheep, which refers to atypical users. Further, a system may still be affected when recommending items to new users (cold starts). To this end, Pereira and Hruschka proposed a simultaneous co-clustering and learning framework to deal with new users and items. According to their data mining methodology, a cluster analysis approach is integrated in the hybrid recommendation system, which results in better recommendations [21].

In addition, performances may be improved by implementing classification according to association rule techniques [22]. Such a system was built to deal with sparsity and scalability in both CF and CBF approaches. In [23], clustering and classifications are used to identify criminal behavior. Also, Davoudi and Chatterjee in [24] use clustering to recognize profile injection attacks. Both methods apply clustering techniques to create user segmentations prior to classification. In our PUPP framework, as reported in [1], we showed that the use of cluster analysis and active learning leads to improvements in terms of recommendation quality during cold starts. We review current advances within the area of deep active learning for recommendation systems in the next section.

2.1 Deep Active Learning in Recommendation Systems

Deep learning methods, and specifically CNNs, have been successfully used to solve complex computational problems within the recommendation systems domain. As noted above, a drawback of recommendation systems is that they often do not perform well when aiming to recommend items to new users. That is, the lack of information about the users, or their preferences, make it difficult to establish relationships with other users in the system. To this end, CNNs have been utilized to learn such missing information to alleviate the cold-start problem and to deal with data sparsity [25, 26]. Specifically, CNNs have been widely used in recommendation systems that employ images.

For example, in [26] a Siamese CNN architecture is used in a clothing recommendation system to capture the latent feature space from clothing images as available in the system. These features are integrated with other available data, such as personal interest and fashion style, and fed to the personalized recommendation model using probabilistic matrix factorization. A similar approach is employed by [27], where a CNN is also used to extract more features to deal with new item cold-start recommendations. In this work, the authors employ the CNN approach to extract textual item descriptions that are fed into two different recommendation models based on item, time, and text correlations. In [16], text and images from the users' browsing history are both utilized to make article recommendations. In this study, a CNN is first used to create a text eigenvector, and a Visual Geometry Group method is used to construct the corresponding image eigenvector. This combined eigenvector is input to a multilayer perceptron that outputs the recommendation.

As discussed above and in our earlier work [1], it follows that employing active learning in recommendation systems produces some promising results when considering the customer cold-start problem. However, the integration of active learning within a deep learning paradigm has not been widely explored in this scenario [31]. As reported in [31, 32], the use of deep active learning in detecting cancer through the selection of informative samples and training a CNN has shown some success. Similarly, in [33], active learning is used to label new images prior to training. To the best of our knowledge, this is the first work that studies the use of deep active learning for alleviating the cold-start and data sparsity problems in recommendation systems. The next section introduces our PUPP-DA framework, which employs both traditional machine learning and deep active learning methods to address the cold-start and data sparsity problems.

3 PUPP-DA Framework

Algorithm 1: Popular User Personalized Prediction (PUPP) [1].

Input
R: a set of r class labelled training inputs;
$anonA_j$: Clustering algorithm;
k: Number of clusters;
R_i: ratings per user;
Y: class label of r;
x: unkown sample;

User Segmentation
   1. A_j discover k objects from D as initial cluster
      center
   2. Repeat:
   - (re)assign each object to cluster according to
      A_j distance measure
   - Update A_j
   - Calculate new value
  Until no change
   3. Output models $(M_1, \dots M_n)$
Initialization for classification and prediction:
   1. Classify (R_i, Y, x);
   2. **Output** classification model
   3. Test model on R_i^{test}
   4. **Output** prediction list
Initialization for active user rating stage:
   1. Select 2 highest prediction rate
   2. Return 2 highest r_n, r_k
   3. Remove r_n, r_k from R_i^{test}
Append r_n, r_k to R_i^{train}

Our PUPP-DA framework extends our earlier work, the PUPP framework, for prediction-based personalized active learning that was designed to address the cold-start and data sparsity problems in recommendation systems [1].

The PUPP-DA framework includes clustering and classification algorithms and active learning. We employ the expectation maximization (EM) soft clustering method, subspace clustering, and k-nearest neighbors (k-NN). Additionally, we use CNNs during training to extend our previous framework, as well as active learning to facilitate labeling. The results from our framework are compared with the traditional CF (using k-NN) framework, which constitutes our baseline.

Learners in any active learning setting query the instances' labels using different scenarios. In the PUPP-DA framework, we use pool-based sampling wherein instances are drawn from a pool of unlabeled data [28]. These instances are selected by focusing on the items with the highest prediction rates and using explicit information extraction [28, 29]. As mentioned above, active learning is an effective way to collect more information about the user. Hence, in this framework, if a new user rates a small number of highly relevant items, that may be sufficient for first analyzing the items features and then calculating the similarity to other items in the system.

3.1 Traditional Machine Learning Component

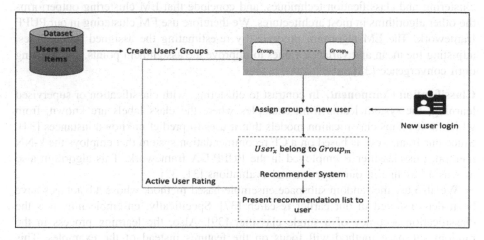

Fig. 1. Workflow of out methodology [1].

Figure 1 shows the steps involved in the machine learning component of our PUPP framework [1]. Initially, we employ cluster analysis to assign customers to groups using the soft clustering approach [30]. This approach results in overlapping clusters where a user may belong to more than one cluster, and it accurately reflects the human behavioral complexity. Once the groups are created, we apply two splitting methods to generate the training and test sets. We use a random split method—a common practice in machine learning. In addition, we designed an approach that focuses on so-called popular users, as detailed in Sect. 4.4. The cold-start problem is addressed as follows. When a new user logs in to the system, the initial model is employed to find user groups with similar preferences. As stated before, we employ the k-NN algorithm to assign a new user to a given group [31, 32]. A machine learning algorithm is used to evaluate and potentially improve the group assignment. To this end, a human expert evaluates the predictive outcome and selects two records (for each user) with the highest prediction rate. These are appended to the training set [29, 33]. Then, a new model is trained against the new, enlarged data set. This process is repeated until a stopping criterion is met. The following two subsections will discuss these steps in detail.

Cluster Analysis Component. Cluster analysis is an unsupervised learning technique used to group data when class labels are unknown [33]. Cluster analysis allows for determining the data distribution while discovering patterns and natural groups [34]. In an e-commerce setting, the goal is to maximize the similarity of individuals within the group while minimizing the similarity of characteristics between groups [35]. Therefore, similarities in opinions, likes, and ratings of the users are evaluated for each group [36].

Numerous options for algorithms are available for cluster analysis. With soft clustering, the groups may overlap; as a result, a data point may belong to more than one group. Intuitively, users' group memberships are often fuzzy in recommendation systems. In work done by [37], the authors compare the performance of different clustering and classification techniques, and conclude that EM clustering outperforms the other algorithms in most architectures. We therefore use EM clustering in our PUPP framework. The EM algorithm proceeds by re-estimating the assigned probabilities, adjusting the mean and variance values to improve the assignment points, and iterating until convergence [38].

Classification Component. In contrast to clustering, with classification or supervised learning, the system learns from examples where the class labels are known, from which it develops classification models that it uses to predict unknown instances [34]. Since our framework is based on a CF recommendation system that employs the k-NN method, this classifier is employed in the PUPP-DA framework. This algorithm also acts as a baseline in our experimental evaluations [31, 32].

We also use the random subspace ensemble-based method, whose advantages have been demonstrated in our earlier research [37]. Specifically, ensemble improves the classification accuracy of a single classifier [39]. Also, the learning process in the random subspace method will focus on the features instead of the examples. This approach, therefore, will evaluate all features in the subspace and select the most informative ones based on the selected features. That is, feature subsets will be created randomly with replacements from the training set. Then each individual classifier will learn from the created subsets while considering all training examples [40]. We further utilize the CNN deep learning algorithm during classification, as will be detailed next.

Deep Learning Component. This section provides an overview of the deep learning component of our system. A CNN is, in essence, a feedforward neural network with convolution and pooling layers [14]. As the name suggests, a convolutional layer performs a so-called convolution, which is a linear operation, in between the previous layer and a kernel (also called a filter or convolution matrix), which is essentially a small window. The convolution is simply the element-to-element product in between the parameters of the previous layer and the parameters of the kernel for every possible position of the kernel with respect to the previous layer. The benefits are twofold: The convolution provides translation invariance, and the training is more efficient since the number of parameters to be estimated for the kernel is much smaller than for its dense layer counterpart. Intuitively, the former entailed a much smaller number of parameters.

Multiple kernels or filters are often associated with the same convolutional layer, each one of them being in charge of capturing a particular aspect about the data. For instance, in image detection, each filter has a specific task, e.g., to detect eyes, nose, or shapes such as circles and squares. Each filter corresponds to a matrix with a predefined number of rows and column [14, 41]. A convolutional layer is often followed by a subsampling layer, better known as a pooling layer, which applies an aggregative function, such as maximum, minimum, or mean. Pooling is applied to the outcome of the convolution operation for each particular position of the kernel with respect to the previous layer, resulting in nonlinear subsampling and dimensionality reduction. In our architectures, the maximum pooling function is used, as illustrated in Fig. 2.

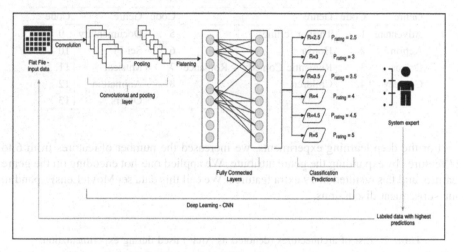

Fig. 2. Deep active learning component.

4   Experimental Setup

The experimental evaluation was conducted on a desktop with an Intel i7 Core 2.7 GHz processor and 16 GB of RAM. Our framework was implemented using the WEKA data-mining environment [42].

4.1   Data Set Description

We used two data sets to evaluate the machine learning component of our PUPP framework. We tested our framework on the Serendipity data set [43], which contains 2,150 movie ratings as well as descriptions of the movies and users' responses to questionnaires about the movies they have rated. The second data set is the famous MovieLens data set [44]. It is well-known in recommendation system research and contains 100,836 ratings on 9,742 movies.

4.2 Data Set Pre-processing

Initially, the movie genres were determined with the help of statista.com and imdb.-com, as shown in Table 1. Additional preprocessing steps involved removing all ratings lower than 2.5 out of 5 to focus the recommendations on popular movies. Also, for the Serendipity data set, attributes S_1 to q provide information about survey answers. These answers relate to users' experience using the recommendation system and of the movie suggestions presented to them. If fewer than 5 questions were answered, the record was removed for lack of information. We eliminated a total of 18 records.

Table 1. Genre feature coding [1].

Genre	Code	Genre	Code	Genre	Code
Adventure	1	Thriller (crime)	5	Documentary	9
Action	2	Horror	6	Sci-Fi	10
Drama	3	Romantic Comedy – Romance	7	Musical	11
Comedy	4	Children	8	Animation	12
				Others	13

For the deep learning experiments, we increased the number of features from 6 to 24 features by expanding the genre attribute. We applied one-hot encoding on the genre feature, and this resulted in 19 extra features. We call this data set MovieLensExpand in our subsequent discussions.

Table 2. List of architectures (denoted as Arch.) used during experimentation.

	Without clustering		With EM clustering
Arch. 1	1 Layer – 100 Filter	Arch. 7	1 Layer – 100 Filter
Arch. 2	2 Layers – 100, 50 filters	Arch. 8	2 Layers – 100, 50 filters
Arch. 3	3 Layers – 100, 50, 25 filters	Arch. 9	3 Layers – 100, 50, 25 filters
Arch. 4	1 Layer with 4 × 4 patch size and 2 × 2 pool size	Arch. 10	1 Layer with 4 × 4 patch size and 2 × 2 pool size
Arch. 5	2 Layers – 100, 50 filter each with 4 × 4 patch 2 × 2 pool	Arch. 11	2 Layers – 100, 50 filter each with 4 × 4 patch 2 × 2 pool
Arch. 6	3 Layers – 100, 50, 25 filters each with 4 × 4 patch and 2 × 2 pool	Arch. 12	3 Layers – 100, 50, 25 filters each with 4 × 4 patch - 2 × 2 pool

List of Architectures and Parameters. Table 2 shows the architectures of the different deep learning algorithms used for our experimental evaluation. For convenience, our experiments are referred to as architectures 1 to 12. For architectures 1 to 3 and 7 to 9, the neural network has three convolutional layers with 100, 50, and 25 filters, respectively, without any pooling layer. The kernel size is 4 × 4. However, for architectures 4 to 6 and 10 to 12, a pooling layer of size 2 × 2 with a maximum aggregation function was inserted after the first hidden layer. The sizes of both the kernels and the pooling layer were determined by inspection to maximize the accuracy of the system. Recall that the maximum pooling function was used. As expected, adding a pooling layer after each hidden layer resulted in longer training time and lower accuracy as demonstrated by our experimental results.

4.3   Experimental Setup

In our experimental evaluation, we employed the EM cluster analysis algorithm to segment users into potentially overlapping clusters. We initially utilized two baseline classifiers: k-NN and the random subspace ensemble method with k-NN as the base learner. The value of k was set to 5, while the number of features to be included in a subspace was fixed at 0.50 (50%); both values were set by inspection.

In active learning, we proceed in a number of iterations, where in each iteration we select for each user the 2 records with the highest prediction rate. After labelling, these two records are appended to the original training set and removed from the test set. The number of iterations in the present work is limited to 5 to process the request in near real time. Our model was evaluated using the 10-fold cross-validation approach.

4.4   Cold-Start Simulation

This section explains the approach for simulating the cold-start problem. We employ two techniques to split our data sets, random split and popularity split. Initially, each technique was evaluated against the traditional k-NN, EM-k-NN, and EM-subspace.

In the random split method, the data set is divided randomly between training (70%) and testing (30%) sets, where the training data set contains the known rating by the system, as already provided by the users. The test set, on the other hand, includes unknown ratings. Note that this approach is commonly taken in the literature [33].

Popularity split evaluates the popularity associated with the users and the items. In this scenario, we consider the users with the highest number of ratings and refer to them as "popular users," i.e., those who use the system frequently. These users are removed from the training set and used as test subjects for cold-start simulations. A removed user must have rated at least 5 popular movies to be considered for removal; the choice of 5 movies was determined by inspection. By removing members in this manner, we increase the chance for the system to find similarities among more users' segmentations in the system. This is, as far as we are aware, the first research to use the notion of popular, or frequent, users for guiding the determination of the recommendations made to cold starts. We do so based on the assumption of trends (such as in clothing recommendation systems) and top rating systems for movies or music (such as in Netflix and iTunes).

For a user to be considered as a test subject in the popularity split, the following criteria must be met:

- The user must have a high number of ratings, as opposed to a random split, where the number of items rated by the user is ignored, as shown in Table 3.

Table 3. Test subject from the MovieLens dataset [1].

Popular users		Random split	
User ID	#Rating	User ID	#Rating
599	1096	1	226
474	1280	225	67
414	1491	282	190
182	805	304	194
477	772	34	56
603	773	374	32
448	698	412	90
288	724	450	48
274	780	510	74
68	677	602	118

- The rated movies must have a rating greater than 2.5 (out of 5).
- The user rated popular movies. The unpopular movies create a grey sheep problem, which refers to users who are atypical. We do not address grey sheep in the present work.

We illustrate our results with 10 users. Table 3 shows some information about the selected users in the MovieLens data set. It is important to stress that we need to ensure that each selected user does not have any remaining records in the training set. This verification ensures a properly simulated cold-start problem.

4.5 Evaluation Criteria

As mentioned, k-NN is widely employed in CF systems. Consequently, it is used as our baseline as well as the base learner in our feature subspace ensemble. The mean absolute error (MAE) measure, which indicates the deviation between predicted and actual ratings, is employed as a predictive measure [45]. In addition, the model accuracy and the F-measure (geometric mean of recall and precision) are employed to determine the usefulness of the recommendation list [45].

5   Results and Discussions

In this section we discuss the performance of the model in terms of accuracy, MAE, and F-measure [45]. Individual users are taken into account in our evaluation.

5.1   System Evaluation

Table 4 and Table 5 show the classification accuracy of the traditional machine learning methods in the PUPP-DA framework system for random and popularity splits. In both cases, active learning improves the performance—by 39.66% for the Serendipity data set and 59.95% for the MovieLens data set. When considering the random split results, we notice increases of 20.56% for the Serendipity data set and 42.8% for the MovieLens data set. These results are obtained using the EM clustering technique.

We also enhanced the performance of the traditional CF framework by introducing the subspace method. Recall that instead of using the k-NN algorithm as a single classifier, we apply an ensemble subspace method using k-NN as a base learner and a subspace of 50% features. Again, we notice improvement over the traditional CF system. Specifically, the random split method improves results by 23.91% for the Serendipity data set and 47.47% for the MovieLens data set, compared to the traditional framework. Also, using the popularity split method, the accuracy increases by 40.96% and 60.31%, respectively. One may conclude from Table 4 and Table 5 that the popularity split method always results in a much higher accuracy (Table 6 and Table 7).

Table 8 and Table 9 depict the results for the F-measure, which again confirm the benefit of focusing on popular users while training. The same observation holds when the MAE metric is employed.

Table 10 contains a summary of the improvement in percentage over the traditional CF framework for both data sets. Notice that these improvements were calculated only for the first iteration since we are interested in the immediate, cold-start problem. The outcome of the last four iterations confirms that the system can make appropriate recommendations to new users while performing adequately for existing users (Fig. 3).

Table 4. Model accuracy for the MovieLens dataset [1].

		Iteration 1	Iteration 2	Iteration 3	Iteration 4	Iteration 5
Popularity split	kNN	38.50	38.43	38.28	38.37	38.44
	EM-kNN	98.45	98.47	98.44	98.50	98.47
	EM-Subspace	**98.81**	**99.18**	**98.83**	**98.86**	**98.68**
Random split	kNN	39.08	38.94	38.91	39.11	39.22
	EM-kNN	81.88	81.76	81.81	81.87	81.83
	EM-Subspace	**86.55**	**88.51**	**87.23**	**87.14**	**86.38**

Table 5. Model accuracy for the Serendipity dataset [1].

		Iteration 1	Iteration 2	Iteration 3	Iteration 4	Iteration 5
Popularity split	kNN	42.18	42.35	43.29	43.07	44.83
	EM-kNN	81.84	81.63	81.87	82.58	**82.58**
	EM-Subspace	**83.14**	**83.18**	**84.04**	**84.17**	81.60
Random split	kNN	43.87	44.18	45.08	45.24	46.51
	EM-kNN	64.43	65.07	65.23	65.33	66.47
	EM-Subspace	**67.78**	**68.40**	**69.27**	**69.21**	**69.77**

Table 6. MAE results for popularity split test method [1].

	kNN		EM-kNN		EM-Subspace	
	Serendipity	MovieLens	Serendipity	MovieLens	Serendipity	MovieLens
Iteration 1	0.214	0.237	0.120	0.039	0.167	0.106
Iteration 2	0.213	0.237	0.119	0.039	0.170	0.108
Iteration 3	0.211	0.237	0.119	0.039	0.167	0.110
Iteration 4	0.211	0.237	0.118	0.039	0.167	0.110
Iteration 5	0.210	0.237	0.118	0.039	0.167	0.095

Table 7. MAE results for random split test method [1].

	kNN		EM-kNN		EM-Subspace	
	Serendipity	MovieLens	Serendipity	MovieLens	Serendipity	MovieLens
Iteration 1	0.210	0.237	0.175	0.116	0.204	0.164
Iteration 2	0.210	0.237	0.173	0.116	0.201	0.161
Iteration 3	0.209	0.237	0.171	0.116	0.199	0.168
Iteration 4	0.206	0.237	0.170	0.116	0.201	0.166
Iteration 5	0.205	0.236	0.168	0.116	0.198	0.163

Table 8. F-measure results for popularity split method [1].

	kNN		EM-kNN		EM-Subspace	
	Serendipity	MovieLens	Serendipity	MovieLens	Serendipity	MovieLens
Iteration 1	0.594	0.352	0.818	0.984	0.830	0.988
Iteration 2	0.595	0.351	0.816	0.985	0.831	0.992
Iteration 3	0.604	0.350	0.819	0.984	0.840	0.988
Iteration 4	0.602	0.351	0.826	0.985	0.841	0.989
Iteration 5	0.619	0.352	0.826	0.985	0.815	0.987

Table 9. F-measure for the random split test method [1].

	kNN		EM-kNN		EM-Subspace	
	Serendipity	MovieLens	Serendipity	MovieLens	Serendipity	MovieLens
Iteration 1	0.610	0.359	0.629	0.817	0.656	0.864
Iteration 2	0.613	0.358	0.636	0.816	0.660	0.884
Iteration 3	0.622	0.357	0.636	0.816	0.671	0.872
Iteration 4	0.623	0.360	0.637	0.817	0.668	0.871
Iteration 5	0.635	0.361	0.650	0.817	0.673	0.863

Table 10. Improvement in predictive accuracy measures for system-wide performance over traditional CF [1].

Framework	Accuracy Increase by %	F-measure Increase by %	MAE Decrease by %	Dataset
Popularity test method				
EM-CF	39.99	0.224	0.094	Serendipity
	59.95	0.632	0.198	MovieLens
EM-Subspace-CF	40.96	0.236	0.047	Serendipity
	60.31	0.636	0.131	MovieLens
Random split test method				
EM-CF	20.87	0.019	0.035	Serendipity
	42.80	0.581	0.243	MovieLens
EM-Subspace-CF	23.91	0.046	0.006	Serendipity
	47.47	0.628	0.195	MovieLens

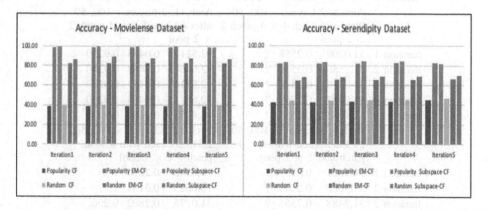

Fig. 3. PUPP framework accuracies on MovieLens and Serendipity datasets [1].

Table 11. Results for Random Split in all architectures against MovieLensExpand dataset.

	Without clustering			With EM clustering		
	Accuracy	MAE	F-measure	Accuracy	MAE	F-measure
	Arch.1: 1 Layer – 100 Filter			Arch.7: 1 Layer – 100 Filter		
Iteration 1	31.808	0.2561	?	98.610	0.0291	0.9860
Iteration 2	31.793	0.2560	?	98.606	0.0292	0.9860
Iteration 3	31.771	0.2562	?	98.626	0.0293	0.9860
Iteration 4	31.720	0.2561	?	98.643	0.0293	0.9860
Iteration 5	31.740	0.2562	?	98.633	0.0290	0.9860
	Arch.2: 2 Layers – 100, 50 filters			Arch.8: 2 Layers – 100, 50 filters		
Iteration 1	31.7011	0.2564	?	98.4412	0.0316	0.9840
Iteration 2	31.4779	0.2564	?	98.3186	0.0317	0.9830
Iteration 3	31.6527	0.2563	?	98.4605	0.0314	0.9840
Iteration 4	31.6280	0.2565	?	98.3600	0.0323	0.9830
Iteration 5	31.5754	0.2564	?	98.5123	0.0312	0.9850
	Arch.3: 3 Layers – 100, 50, 25 filters			Arch.9: 3 Layers – 100, 50, 25 filters		
Iteration 1	31.3238	0.2574	?	98.2671	0.0350	0.9830
Iteration 2	31.2446	0.2574	?	98.2919	0.0350	0.9830
Iteration 3	31.3476	0.2575	?	98.2517	0.0365	0.9820
Iteration 4	31.0654	0.2574	?	98.3252	0.0346	0.9830
Iteration 5	30.9956	0.2574	?	98.1551	0.0368	0.9810
	Arch.4: 1 Layer with 4×4 patch size and 2×2 pool size			Arch.10: 1 Layer with 4×4 patch size and 2×2 pool size		
Iteration 1	31.9727	0.2531	0.2260	93.5398	0.0415	0.9340
Iteration 2	31.9095	0.2533	0.2440	93.5285	0.0416	0.9340
Iteration 3	32.2699	0.2528	0.2360	93.5660	0.0408	0.9340
Iteration 4	32.1882	0.2528	0.2320	93.5153	0.0412	0.9340
Iteration 5	31.9685	0.2525	0.2100	93.5434	0.0411	0.9340
	Arch.5: 2 Layers – 100, 50 filter each with 4×4 patch 2×2 pool			Arch.11: 2 Layers – 100, 50 filter each with 4×4 patch 2×2 pool		
Iteration 1	31.0209	0.2558	?	92.5114	0.0463	0.9230
Iteration 2	31.2586	0.2549	?	92.6466	0.0458	0.9240
Iteration 3	31.0390	0.2548	?	92.5114	0.0457	0.9230
Iteration 4	31.0747	0.2559	?	92.6871	0.0464	0.9250
Iteration 5	31.1985	0.2551	?	92.4755	0.0467	0.9230
	Arch.6: 3 Layers – 100, 50, 25 filters each with 4×4 patch and 2×2 pool			Arch.12: 3 Layers – 100, 50, 25 filters each with 4×4 patch – 2×2 pool		
Iteration 1	31.3621	0.2553	?	19.6546	0.2824	?
Iteration 2	31.3665	0.2549	?	18.6625	0.3134	?
Iteration 3	31.3488	0.2551	?	31.0776	0.2802	0.296
Iteration 4	31.1026	0.2552	?	17.3562	0.3048	?
Iteration 5	31.2530	0.2552	?	27.0162	0.3045	?

Table 12. Results for popularity split in all architectures against MovieLensExpand dataset.

	Without clustering			With EM clustering		
	Accuracy	MAE	F-measure	Accuracy	MAE	F-measure
	Arch.1: 1 Layer – 100 Filter			Arch.7: 1 Layer – 100 Filter		
Iteration 1	32.3328	0.2553	?	98.6855	0.0287	0.9870
Iteration 2	32.3290	0.2554	?	98.6819	0.0283	0.9870
Iteration 3	32.3364	0.2553	?	98.5727	0.0287	0.9860
Iteration 4	32.3878	0.2554	?	98.5865	0.0289	0.9860
Iteration 5	32.3512	0.2553	?	98.5375	0.0286	0.9850
	Arch.2: 2 Layers – 100, 50 filters			Arch.8: 2 Layers – 100, 50 filters		
Iteration 1	32.1711	0.2552	?	98.4277	0.0314	0.9840
Iteration 2	32.3228	0.2554	?	98.4962	0.0313	0.9850
Iteration 3	32.1299	0.2554	?	98.3711	0.0317	0.9840
Iteration 4	32.2562	0.2552	?	98.4459	0.0318	0.9840
Iteration 5	32.1728	0.2553	?	98.3262	0.0321	0.9830
	Arch.3: 3 Layers – 100, 50, 25 filters			Arch.9: 3 Layers – 100, 50, 25 filters		
Iteration 1	31.5767	0.2561	?	98.1899	0.0354	0.9820
Iteration 2	31.6925	0.2566	?	98.2839	0.0351	0.9830
Iteration 3	31.7881	0.2562	?	98.1762	0.0368	0.9820
Iteration 4	31.8678	0.2563	?	98.1674	0.0361	0.9820
Iteration 5	31.5323	0.2563	?	98.1185	0.0398	0.9810
	Arch.4: 1 Layer with 4×4 patch size and 2×2 pool size			Arch.10: 1 Layer with 4×4 patch size and 2×2 pool size		
Iteration 1	32.5612	0.2524	?	93.6614	0.0403	0.9350
Iteration 2	32.5191	0.2522	?	93.6364	0.0408	0.9350
Iteration 3	32.2581	0.2529	?	93.6247	0.0401	0.9350
Iteration 4	32.4751	0.2528	?	93.6772	0.0410	0.9350
Iteration 5	32.3503	0.2528	?	93.6772	0.0410	0.9350
	Arch.5: 2 Layers – 100, 50 filter each with 4×4 patch 2×2 pool			Arch.11: 2 Layers – 100, 50 filter each with 4×4 patch 2×2 pool		
Iteration 1	32.0910	0.2543	?	92.7691	0.0452	0.9260
Iteration 2	31.8594	0.2548	?	92.7830	0.0448	0.9260
Iteration 3	32.0143	0.2549	?	92.6474	0.0450	0.9240
Iteration 4	31.8669	0.2543	?	92.7255	0.0454	0.9250
Iteration 5	31.8077	0.2546	?	92.7314	0.0453	0.9250
	Arch.6: 3 Layers – 100, 50, 25 filters each with 4×4 patch and 2×2 pool			Arch.12: 3 Layers – 100, 50, 25 filters each with 4×4 patch – 2×2 pool		
Iteration 1	32.0923	0.2540	?	37.9286	0.2848	0.2850
Iteration 2	32.0544	0.2544	?	33.4406	0.2839	0.2750
Iteration 3	31.9484	0.2543	?	23.1218	0.3089	?
Iteration 4	32.0119	0.2537	?	30.3928	0.2809	0.2900
Iteration 5	31.8699	0.2543	?	24.4119	0.2692	0.3350

Deep Active Learning Evaluation. In this section, we present and discuss our results with a deep CNN setting. Recall that we use 12 different CNN architectures, as depicted in Table 2. When analyzing Table 11 and Table 12, we found that performing user segmentation with EM clustering results in better models for both random and popularity splits. That is, both techniques resulted in very comparable model performance, therefore not providing much additional insight into the cold-start problem. For this reason, we further evaluated these models by looking at the individual users' prediction as reported above. In terms of system performance, the highest accuracy achieved in the original PUPP framework is 98.81% using the subspace method with the popularity split. In the deep learning setting, both the popularity split and random split methods resulted in comparable performance, indicating that the deep learning method was successful in capturing relationships in between users.

5.2 User Prediction Rates

To further validate our approach, we considered the user prediction rate. In this section, the prediction rates for 10 users from the MovieLens data set are presented. One may conclude based on Table 13 that EM-kNN has the best prediction rates when employing machine learning algorithms, rather than deep learning. However, we noticed that after the third iteration, when a random split is employed, the prediction rate begins to decrease, at least for some users. Also, by taking into consideration the overall performance of the system, it may be concluded that EM-subspace presents the best performance against these data sets when compared to the other two models.

Table 13. New user Prediction accuracy in percentage [1].

Popular user										
User ID	182	274	288	414	448	474	477	599	603	68
CF	80	100	100	100	100	86	100	100	85	80
EM-CF	100	100	100	100	100	100	100	100	100	100
EM-subspace-CF	91	90	91	92	91	92	91	91	91	90
Random split										
User ID	1	225	282	304	34	374	412	450	510	602
CF	71	52	48	61	41	56	71	50	55	76
EM-CF	100	100	100	100	100	100	100	100	100	100
EM-subspace-CF	63	61	61	62	58	62	59	63	61	63

Deep Active Learning. In what follows, we compare the new users' prediction rates for the first two iterations, between the random split and popularity split, while using different deep active learning architectures. We report the total average for users' prediction rates in iterations 1 and 2. For each type of split, as noted earlier, we tested 10 different users, as shown in Table 3. For more details about the individual predictions, the reader is referred to Table 20 in appendix 1.

As reported in Table 14, the prediction rates remain below 50% for almost all users when architectures 1 to 6 are employed. However, with architectures 7 to 11, the models predict the correct product for recommendation with a 100% certainty for at least two items per user. For instance, let us consider architecture 7 where each convolutional layer consists of 100 kernels. In this setting, the prediction rates vary between 76.8% and 100%. Active learning selects the two items with a 100% prediction rate (the two highest prediction rates), labels them, and appends them to the training set. Remember that only the two items with the highest prediction rates are added to the training set during the active learning phase. Therefore, the results for a user are the average of the two movies with the highest prediction rates.

When the popularity split was employed with architectures 7 to 11, accuracies between 92% and 98% were obtained. As depicted in Table 14, during the active learning phase, at least two items had a prediction rate of 100%. Active learning in general did improve the deep learning results for the initial predictions. These initial predictions play a pivotal role in the cold-start setting. While analyzing these results, we further noticed that the prediction rates for some individual users were improving only in the third, fourth, or even fifth iteration. As a result, their profiles were more difficult to learn, which means that more iterations were required for a satisfactory conclusion of the active learning process.

Table 14. Average prediction rates for the 10 test users – results in percentage.

	Random split		Popularity split	
	Iteration 1	Iteration 2	Iteration 1	Iteration 2
Architecture 1	42.30%	41.30%	39.50%	38.30%
Architecture 2	41.00%	39.80%	39.00%	37.80%
Architecture 3	39.10%	35.20%	37.10%	36.20%
Architecture 4	45.50%	45.70%	41.90%	45.80%
Architecture 5	35.50%	36.00%	37.10%	38.90%
Architecture 6	38.10%	38.70%	38.40%	36.80%
Architecture 7	100.00%	99.81%	100.00%	100.00%
Architecture 8	100.00%	99.85%	100.00%	100.00%
Architecture 9	99.99%	99.90%	100.00%	100.00%
Architecture 10	100.00%	100.00%	100.00%	100.00%
Architecture 11	100.00%	100.00%	100.00%	100.00%
Architecture 12	31.10%	30.90%	29.70%	29.30%

5.3 Statistical Validation

This section discusses the results of our statistical significance testing using the Friedman test: the confidence level was set to $a = 0.05$. That is, we wish to determine whether there is any statistical significance between the performance of the baseline CF method using k-NN, the two variants of our PUPP system (EM and EM-subspace).

In this validation, the Friedman yields a p-value of 0.000171 for the Serendipity data set, and a p-value of 0.000139 for the MovieLens data set. Therefore, the null hypothesis is rejected for both data sets, which means there is a significant difference among the three frameworks. We report the results of the pairwise comparisons in Fig. 4 and Fig. 5.

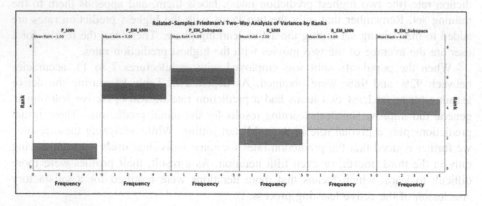

Fig. 4. Friedman test mean ranks for the MovieLens dataset [1].

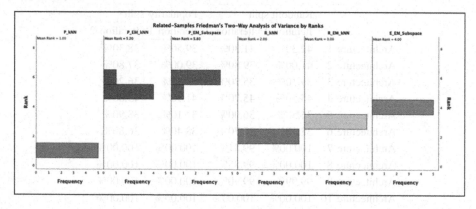

Fig. 5. Friedman test mean ranks for the Serendipity dataset [1].

Furthermore, to determine if there is a significant difference between each pair, we perform the Nemenyi post-hoc test. As shown in Table 15, there is a significant difference among three pairs: EM-kNN versus kNN, EM-subspace versus kNN, and kNN versus EM-kNN. These results confirm that the system benefits from soft clustering and active learning. There is no statistical difference between the versions that use a baseline learning (k-NN) when compared to an ensemble, which indicates that a single classifier may be employed against these data sets. These results confirm our earlier discussion in which EM-k-NN and EM-subspace, when used with the popularity split method, have a significantly better performance when compared with the random split method.

Table 15. Nemenyi p-values for the PUPP framework [1].

Serendipity dataset					
	P-kNN	P-EM-kNN	P-EM-Subspace	R-kNN	R-EM-kNN
P-EM-kNN	**0.005178**				
P-EM-Subspace	**0.000708**	0.995925			
R-kNN	0.958997	0.074302	**0.016639**		
R-EM-kNN	0.538193	0.427525	0.168134	0.958997	
R-EM-Subspace	0.113891	0.91341	0.65049	0.538193	0.958997
MovieLens dataset					
	P-kNN	P-EM-kNN	P-EM-Subspace	R-kNN	R-EM-kNN
P-EM-kNN	**0.009435**				
P-EM-Subspace	**0.000343**	0.958997			
R-kNN	0.958997	0.113891	**0.009435**		
R-EM-kNN	0.538193	0.538193	0.113891	0.958997	
R-EM-Subspace	0.113891	0.958997	0.538193	0.538193	0.958997

5.4   PUPPA-DA Statistical Validation

Friedman Test for All Architectures. In this section, we first validate all architectures we used in the PUPP-DA framework. We perform a Friedman test with a significance level of 0.05, which when considering all architectures resulted in significance level of $2.48E - 013 \cong 0.00$. Therefore, we reject the null hypothesis and determine that there is a significant difference between the 24 architectures we tested. The question, however, is which one is better than the others. To answer this question, we consider the Friedman Two-Way Analysis of Variance by Rank. Figure 6 shows the mean rank for all architectures. In Table 16, which contains the mean rank of all architectures, we set our threshold at mean rank = 15, based on the mean rank results and the model accuracies. Considering Table 16, we notice that architectures 7 to 11 achieved higher ranks using both splits. This also validates our results in Table 11 and Table 12 where the models achieved accuracy higher than 90% for these architectures. Next, we explore these 10 architectures to determine whether there is a superior configuration.

Table 16. Friedman's mean rank for all architectures.

Arch. #	Mean rank	Arch. #	Mean rank
R-Arch. 7	**23.60**	P-Arch. 1	13.00
P-Arch. 7	**23.40**	P-Arch. 4	13.00
R-Arch. 8	**21.60**	P-Arch. 2	11.40
P-Arch. 8	**21.40**	R-Arch. 4	10.40
R-Arch. 9	**20.00**	P-Arch. 6	9.80
P-Arch. 9	**19.00**	P-Arch. 5	8.80
P-Arch. 10	**18.00**	R-Arch. 1	7.20
R-Arch. 10	**17.00**	P-Arch. 3	6.80
P-Arch. 11	**16.00**	P-Arch. 12	6.40
R-Arch. 11	**15.00**	R-Arch. 2	6.00
		R-Arch. 6	4.00
		R-Arch. 3	3.00
		R-Arch. 5	3.00
		R-Arch. 12	1.60

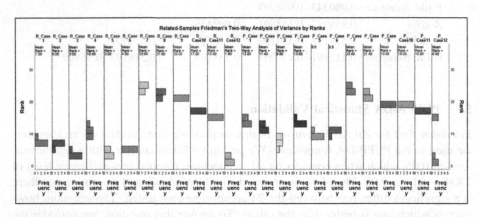

Fig. 6. Test mean ranks for the MovieLensExpand dataset considering all architectures.

Wilcoxon Signed Ranks Test. Recall that we noticed that architectures 7 to 11 achieve higher performance in terms of accuracy and mean rank. However, in this framework, we use two splits to evaluate our model performance: popularity and random splits. Therefore, we proceed to test each architecture for both popularity split (P) and random split (R) to determine whether there a statistical significance in the results. From the following table, we conclude that the results obtained by architectures 9, 10, and 11 are below the significance level of 0.05. Hence, the null hypothesis (that all architectures are equal) is rejected for these three architectures. This implies that, for these architectures, using different splits has an impact on building the learning model. On the other hand, the type of split has no influence on the results for architectures 7 and 8 (Table 17).

Table 17. Wilcoxon test statistics.

	R_Arch. 7 - P_Arch. 7	R_Arch. 8 - P_Arch. 8	R_Arch. 9 - P_Arch. 9	R_Arch. 10 - P_Arch. 10	R_Arch. 11 - P_Arch. 11
Z	−.135b	−.405b	−2.023b	−2.023c	−2.023c
Asymp. Sig. (2-tailed)	0.893	0.686	**0.043**	**0.043**	**0.043**

Friedman Test for Architectures 7 to 11. In this section, we evaluate all results for architectures 7 to 11, considering both splits. The Friedman test resulted in a significance of 0.000001, which is lower than the tested level of 0.05. Therefore, the hypothesis that all architectures perform the same on the given data set is rejected. This means that there is a significant difference between the five tested architectures (7 to 11) for both splits. As mentioned earlier, architectures 7 to 11 resulted in better performance in terms of accuracy and was validated by considering the Friedman's mean rank.

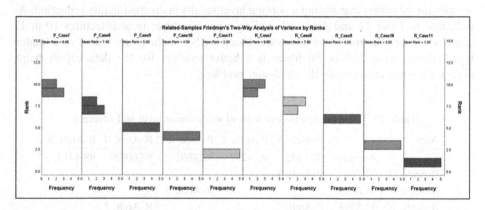

Fig. 7. Friedman test mean ranks for the MovieLensExpand dataset.

We report the results of the pairwise comparisons in Fig. 7, which illustrates the frequency count for each architecture we tested in the PUPP-DA framework. Furthermore, to determine if there is a significant difference between each pair, we perform the Nemenyi post-hoc test. As shown in Table 18, there is a significant difference among the eight pairs highlighted in bold.

Table 18. Nemenyi p-values for Arch. 7 to 11.

	P-Arch. 7	P-Arch. 8	P-Arch. 9	P-Arch. 10	P-Arch. 11	R-Arch. 7	R-Arch. 8	R-Arch. 9	R-Arch. 10
P-Arch. 8	0.989497								
P-Arch. 9	0.390244	0.96351							
P-Arch. 10	0.129563	0.750853	0.999959						
P-Arch. 11	**0.004386**	0.129563	0.864285	0.989497					
R-Arch. 7	1	0.979527	0.324212	0.098774	**0.002898**				
R-Arch. 8	0.995153	1	0.939756	0.682781	0.098774	0.989497			
R-Arch. 9	0.750853	0.999319	0.999959	0.989497	0.535342	0.682781	0.998033		
R-Arch. 10	**0.028557**	0.390244	0.989497	0.999959	0.999959	**0.020181**	0.324212	0.864285	
R-Arch. 11	**0.000487**	**0.028557**	0.535342	0.864285	0.999959	**0.000303**	**0.020181**	0.212132	0.989497

To further the summaries in Table 18, we consider the tests in bold that show that there is a significant difference among the results. To this end, in Table 19 we compare these results in terms of accuracy for the first iteration. Recall that our main purpose for the experiment is to alleviate the cold-start problem in recommendation systems. Also, we mentioned earlier that adding a pooling layer results in dimensionality reduction. As indicated in Table 11 and Table 12, adding a pooling layer in architectures 10 to 12 actually reduced the model performance. Using a CNN architecture with 1 or 2 hidden layers that contain 100 or 50 filters is a better solution for the data set on hand, especially when considering the cold-start problem.

Table 19. Final comparison in term of significance level and accuracy.

Arch. #		P-Arch. 7	P-Arch. 8	P-Arch. 11	R-Arch. 7	R-Arch. 8
	Accuracy	98.6855	98.4277	92.7691	98.6095	98.4412
P-Arch. 11	92.7691	P-Arch. 7				
R-Arch. 7	98.6095				R-Arch. 7	
R-Arch. 10	93.5398	P-Arch. 7			R-Arch. 7	
R-Arch. 11	92.5114	P-Arch. 7	P-Arch. 7		R-Arch. 7	R-Arch. 8

6 Conclusion and Future Work

In this paper, we presented the PUPP-DA framework designed to address the cold-start problem in CF recommendation systems. Our results show the benefits of user segmentation based on soft clustering and the use of active learning to improve predictions for new users. The results also demonstrate the advantages of focusing on frequent or popular users to improve classification accuracy. In addition, our experiments illustrate the value of deep learning algorithms, and notably CNN architectures, when addressing the cold-start problem. In general, our results show that deep learning outperformed the traditional machine learning techniques we tested. Another important conclusion is that deep learning resulted in accurate predictions for each user we randomly tested compared to the regular machine learning in the PUPP-DA framework.

For future work, we want to further evaluate the PUPP-DA framework by labelling more records per iteration. We believe that deep active learning might need the larger sample size of an informative sample to improve its performance. Moreover, in the active learning process, we added informative records regardless of how high the rating was for that movie. Therefore, in future work, we want to focus on adding only records with very high ratings to determine whether this influences the model training process. Additional work will also include the use of social media analysis to further address the cold-start problem.

Appendix 1

See Table 20.

Table 20. Prediction Rates in details for the PUPP-DA framework–results in percentage.

Random split			Popularity split		
User ID	Iteration 1	Iteration 2	User ID	Iteration 1	Iteration 2
Architecture 1					
1	44%	44%	68	36%	34%
225	45%	43%	182	34%	39%
282	31%	41%	274	47%	34%
304	50%	44%	288	49%	42%
34	31%	32%	414	44%	42%
374	49%	43%	448	46%	41%
412	44%	45%	474	34%	42%
450	44%	43%	477	18%	33%
510	32%	32%	599	36%	32%
602	53%	46%	603	51%	44%
Architecture 2					
1	44%	44%	68	33%	32%
225	44%	43%	182	38%	37%
282	31%	30%	274	32%	32%
304	45%	44%	288	45%	43%
34	32%	30%	414	45%	43%
374	46%	43%	448	43%	41%
412	45%	44%	474	45%	43%
450	44%	44%	477	32%	32%
510	32%	31%	599	32%	32%
602	47%	45%	603	45%	43%

(continued)

Table 20. (*continued*)

Random split			Popularity split		
User ID	Iteration 1	Iteration 2	User ID	Iteration 1	Iteration 2
Architecture 1					
Architecture 3					
1	45%	43%	68	30%	30%
225	44%	42%	182	34%	32%
282	29%	28%	274	30%	30%
304	44%	42%	288	44%	42%
34	29%	28%	414	44%	42%
374	41%	39%	448	42%	41%
412	45%	21%	474	44%	42%
450	44%	42%	477	30%	30%
510	29%	28%	599	30%	30%
602	41%	39%	603	43%	43%
Architecture 4					
1	53%	48%	68	33%	32%
225	52%	47%	182	49%	47%
282	30%	31%	274	33%	31%
304	57%	57%	288	54%	58%
34	29%	29%	414	53%	57%
374	54%	54%	448	54%	57%
412	48%	46%	474	53%	54%
450	46%	48%	477	32%	32%
510	30%	30%	599	34%	34%
602	56%	67%	603	24%	56%
Architecture 5					
1	40%	41%	68	27%	30%
225	38%	39%	182	42%	44%
282	27%	26%	274	27%	30%
304	39%	40%	288	46%	45%
34	27%	26%	414	46%	45%
374	40%	42%	448	42%	45%
412	38%	39%	474	44%	45%
450	38%	39%	477	27%	30%
510	27%	26%	599	27%	30%
602	41%	42%	603	43%	45%
Architecture 6					
1	43%	42%	68	27%	30%
225	43%	41%	182	41%	23%
282	29%	27%	274	27%	30%
304	43%	45%	288	47%	44%
34	29%	27%	414	48%	46%
374	40%	46%	448	46%	45%

(*continued*)

Table 20. (*continued*)

Random split			Popularity split		
User ID	Iteration 1	Iteration 2	User ID	Iteration 1	Iteration 2
Architecture 1					
412	42%	42%	474	47%	46%
450	43%	42%	477	27%	30%
510	29%	27%	599	27%	30%
602	40%	48%	603	47%	44%
Architecture 7					
1	100%	100%	68	100%	100%
225	100%	99.50%	182	100%	100%
282	100%	100%	274	100%	100%
304	100%	100%	288	100%	100%
34	100%	99.50%	414	100%	100%
374	100%	99.50%	448	100%	100%
412	100%	99.90%	474	100%	100%
450	100%	99.90%	477	100%	100%
510	100%	99.85%	599	100%	100%
602	100%	99.90%	603	100%	100%
Architecture 8					
1	100%	100%	68	100%	100%
225	100%	99.25%	182	100%	100%
282	100%	100%	274	100%	100%
304	100%	100%	288	100%	100%
34	100%	99.75%	414	100%	100%
374	100%	99.60%	448	100%	100%
412	100%	100%	474	100%	100%
450	100%	99.95%	477	100%	100%
510	100%	99.95%	599	100%	100%
602	100%	100%	603	100%	100%
Architecture 9					
1	100%	100%	68	100%	100%
225	100%	99.65%	182	100%	100%
282	100%	100%	274	100%	100%
304	100%	100%	288	100%	100%
34	99.90%	99.70%	414	100%	100%
374	100%	99.80%	448	100%	100%
412	100%	99.90%	474	100%	100%
450	99.95%	100%	477	100%	100%
510	100%	99.95%	599	100%	100%
602	100%	100%	603	100%	100%

(*continued*)

Table 20. (*continued*)

Random split			Popularity split		
User ID	Iteration 1	Iteration 2	User ID	Iteration 1	Iteration 2
Architecture 1					
Architecture 10					
1	100%	100%	68	100%	100%
225	100%	100%	182	100%	100%
282	100%	100%	274	100%	100%
304	100%	100%	288	100%	100%
34	100%	100%	414	100%	100%
374	100%	100%	448	100%	100%
412	100%	100%	474	100%	100%
450	100%	100%	477	100%	100%
510	100%	100%	599	100%	100%
602	100%	100%	603	100%	100%
Architecture 11					
1	100%	100%	68	100%	100%
225	100%	100%	182	100%	100%
282	100%	100%	274	100%	100%
304	100%	100%	288	100%	100%
34	100%	100%	414	100%	100%
374	100%	100%	448	100%	100%
412	100%	100%	474	100%	100%
450	100%	100%	477	100%	100%
510	100%	100%	599	100%	100%
602	100%	100%	603	100%	100%
Architecture 12					
1	31.10%	30.90%	68	29.70%	29.30%
225	31.10%	30.90%	182	29.70%	29.30%
282	31.10%	30.90%	274	29.70%	29.30%
304	31.10%	30.90%	288	29.70%	29.30%
34	31.10%	30.90%	414	29.70%	29.30%
374	31.10%	30.90%	448	29.70%	29.30%
412	31.10%	30.90%	474	29.70%	29.30%
450	31.10%	30.90%	477	29.70%	29.30%
510	31.10%	30.90%	599	29.70%	29.30%
602	31.10%	30.90%	603	29.70%	29.30%

References

1. Alabdulrahman, R., Viktor, H., Paquet, E.: Active learning and user segmentation for the cold-start problem in recommendation systems. In: Proceedings of the 11th International Joint Conference on Knowledge Discovery, Knowledge Engineering and Knowledge Management (IC3K 2019). Vienna, Austria: KDIR (2019)
2. Lu, J., et al.: Recommender system application developments: A survey. Dec. Support Syst. **74**, 12–32 (2015)
3. Kim, H.M., et al.: Online serendipity: the case for curated recommender systems. Bus. Horizons **60**(5), 613–620 (2017)
4. Bhagat, S., et al.: Recommending with an agenda: Active learning of private attributes using matrix factorization. In: Proceedings of the 8th ACM Conference on Recommender systems. ACM (2014)
5. Minkov, E., et al.: Collaborative future event recommendation. In: Proceedings of the 19th ACM International Conference on Information and Knowledge Management. ACM (2010)
6. Karimi, R., et al.: Comparing prediction models for active learning in recommender systems. In: Comparing Prediction Models for Active Learning in Recommender Systems. (2015)
7. Tsai, C.-H.: A fuzzy-based personalized recommender system for local businesses. In: Proceedings of the 27th ACM Conference on Hypertext and Social Media. ACM (2016)
8. Liao, C.-L., Lee, S.-J.: A clustering based approach to improving the efficiency of collaborative filtering recommendation. Electronic Commerce Res. Appl. **18**, 1–9 (2016)
9. Ntoutsi, E., et al.: Strength lies in differences: Diversifying friends for recommendations through subspace clustering. In: Proceedings of the 23rd ACM International Conference on Conference on Information and Knowledge Management. ACM (2014)
10. Bakshi, S., et al.: Enhancing scalability and accuracy of recommendation systems using unsupervised learning and particle swarm optimization. Appl. Soft Comput. **15**, 21–29 (2014)
11. Acosta, O.C., Behar, P.A., Reategui, E.B.: Content recommendation in an inquiry-based learning environment. In: Frontiers in Education Conference (FIE). IEEE (2014)
12. Saha, T., Rangwala, H., Domeniconi, C.: Predicting preference tags to improve item recommendation. In: Proceedings of the 2015 SIAM International Conference on Data Mining. SIAM (2015)
13. Bajpai, V., Yadav, Y.: Survey paper on dynamic recommendation system for e-commerce. In: International Journal of Advanced Research in Computer Science, vol. 9(1) (2018)
14. Mu, R.: A survey of recommender systems based on deep learning. IEEE Access **6**, 69009–69022 (2018)
15. Zheng, Y., Xu, X., Qi, L.: Deep CNN-assisted personalized recommendation over big data for mobile wireless networks. Wireless Communications and Mobile Computing, (2019)
16. Yu, B., et al.: Multi-source news recommender system based on convolutional neural networks. In: Proceedings of the 3rd International Conference on Intelligent Information Processing. ACM (2018)
17. Karimi, R., et al.: Towards optimal active learning for matrix factorization in recommender systems. In: 2011 23rd IEEE International Conference on Tools with Artificial Intelligence (ICTAI). IEEE. pp. 1069–1076 (2011)
18. Wang, X., et al.: Interactive social recommendation. In: Information and Knowledge Management. ACM (2017)
19. Gope, J., Jain, S.K.: A survey on solving cold start problem in recommender systems. In: 2017 IEEE International Conference on Computing, Communication and Automation, ed. P. N. Astya, et al. pp. 133–138 (2017)

20. Fernandez-Tobias, I., et al.: Alleviating the new user problem in collaborative filtering by exploiting personality information. User Model. User-Adapted Int. **26**(2–3), 221-255 (2016)
21. Pereira, A.L.V., Hruschka, E.R.: Simultaneous co-clustering and learning to address the cold start problem in recommender systems. Knowl.-Based Syst. **82**, 11–19 (2015)
22. Lucas, J.P., Segrera, S., Moreno, M.N.: Making use of associative classifiers in order to alleviate typical drawbacks in recommender systems. Expert Syst. Appl. **39**(1), 1273–1283 (2012)
23. Soundarya, V., Kanimozhi, U., Manjula, D.: Recommendation system for criminal behavioral analysis on social network using genetic weighted k-means clustering. JCP **12** (3), 212–220 (2017)
24. Davoudi, A., Chatterjee, M.: Detection of profile injection attacks in social recommender systems using outlier analysis. In: 2017 IEEE International Conference on Big Data (Big Data). IEEE (2017)
25. Zhou, W., et al.: Deep learning modeling for top-n recommendation with interests exploring. IEEE Access **6**, 51440–51455 (2018)
26. Sun, G.-L., Cheng, Z.-Q., Wu, X., Peng, Q.: Personalized clothing recommendation combining user social circle and fashion style consistency. Multimed. Tools Appl. **77**(14), 17731–17754 (2017). https://doi.org/10.1007/s11042-017-5245-1
27. Xiong, M.T., et al.: TDCTFIC: a novel recommendation framework fusing temporal dynamics, CNN-Based text features and item correlation. IEICE Trans. Inf. an Syst. **102**(8), 1517–1525 (2019)
28. Elahi, M., Ricci, F., Rubens, N.: A survey of active learning in collaborative filtering recommender systems. Comput. Sci. Rev. **20**, 29–50 (2016)
29. Elahi, M., Ricci, F., Rubens, N.: Active learning in collaborative filtering recommender systems. In: E-Commerce and Webtechnologies, M. Hepp and Y. Hoffner, Editors. p. 113–124 (2014)
30. Mishra, R., Kumar, P., Bhasker, B.: A web recommendation system considering sequential information. Deci. Support Syst. **75**, 1–10 (2015)
31. Sridevi, M., Rao, R.R., Rao, M.V.: A survey on recommender system. Int. J. Comput. Sci. Inf. Secur. **14**(5), 265 (2016)
32. Katarya, R., Verma, O.P.: A collaborative recommender system enhanced with particle swarm optimization technique. Multimed. Tools Appl. **75**(15), 9225–9239 (2016). https://doi.org/10.1007/s11042-016-3481-4
33. Flach, P.: Machine learning: the art and science of algorithms that make sense of data. 2012: Cambridge University Press (2012)
34. Pujari, A.K., Rajesh, K., Reddy, D.S.: Clustering techniques in data mining—A survey. IETE J. Res. **47**(1–2), 19–28 (2001)
35. Cho, Y., Jeong, S.P.: A Recommender system in u-commerce based on a segmentation method. in In: Proceedings of the 2015 International Conference on Big Data Applications and Services. ACM (2015)
36. Isinkaye, F.O., Folajimi, Y.O., Ojokoh, B.A.: Recommendation systems: Principles, methods and evaluation. Egyptian Inf. J. **16**(3), 261–273 (2015)
37. Alabdulrahman, R., Viktor, H., Paquet, E.: Beyond k-NN: combining cluster analysis and classification for recommender systems. In: The 10th International Joint Conference on Knowledge Discovery, Knowledge Engineering and Knowledge Management (IC3K 2018). Seville, Spain: KDIR (2018)
38. Bifet, A., Kirkby, R.: Data Stream Mining a Practical Approach. Citeseer: The University of Waikato. pp. 68–69 (2009)
39. Witten, I.H., et al.: Data Mining: Practical machine learning tools and techniques. 2016: Morgan Kaufmann (2016)

40. Sun, S.: An improved random subspace method and its application to EEG signal classification. In: Haindl, M., Kittler, J., Roli, F. (eds.) MCS 2007. LNCS, vol. 4472, pp. 103–112. Springer, Heidelberg (2007). https://doi.org/10.1007/978-3-540-72523-7_11

41. Zhang, S., et al.: Deep learning based recommender system: A survey and new perspectives. ACM Comput. Survey (CSUR) 52(1), 5 (2019)

42. Frank, E., Hall, M.A., Witten, I.H.: The WEKA workbench, p. 4. Practical Mach. Learn. Tools Techn., Data mining (2016)

43. Kotkov, D., et al.: Investigating serendipity in recommender systems based on real user feedback. In: Proceedings of the 33rd Annual ACM Symposium on Applied Computing. ACM (2018)

44. Harper, F.M., Konstan, J.A.: The movielens datasets: History and context. Acm Trans. Int. Intell. Syst. (tiis) 5(4), 19 (2016)

45. Chaaya, G., et al.: Evaluating non-personalized single-heuristic active learning strategies for collaborative filtering recommender systems. In: 2017 16th IEEE International Conference on Machine Learning and Applications, ed. X. Chen, et al. pp. 593–600 (2017)

The Effect of In-Domain Word Embeddings for Chemical Named Entity Recognition

Zainab Awan[1]([✉]) [iD], Tim Kahlke[2] [iD], Peter J. Ralph[2] [iD],
and Paul J. Kennedy[1] [iD]

[1] School of Computer Science, University of Technology Sydney, Sydney, Australia
{zainab.awan,paul.kennedy}@uts.edu.au
[2] Climate Change Cluster, University of Technology Sydney, Sydney, Australia
{tim.kahlke,peter.ralph}@uts.edu.au

Abstract. Research articles and patents contain information in the form of text. Chemical named entity recognition (ChemNER) refers to the process of extracting chemical named entities from research articles or patents. Chemical information extraction pipelines have ChemNER as its first step. Existing ChemNER methods rely on rule-based, dictionary-based, or feature-engineered based approaches. More recently, deep learning-based approaches have been used to approach ChemNER. Deep-learning based methods utilize pre-trained word embeddings such as word2vec and Glove. Previously, we have used embedded language models (ELMo) with Bi-LSTM-CRF to learn the effect of contextual information for ChemNER. In this paper, we further experiment to learn the impact of using in-domain (large unlabelled corpora of chemical patents) pre-trained ELMo for ChemNER and compare it with ELMo pre-trained on biomedical corpora. We report the results on three benchmark corpora and conclude that in-domain embeddings statistically significantly improve F1-score on patent corpus but do not lead to any performance gains for chemical articles corpora.

Keywords: ChemNER · Bi-LSTM-CRF · Word embeddings

1 Introduction

Currently, PubMed indexes over 30 million citations and this number continues to grow [20]. The volume of biomedical literature is increasing at an exponential rate [30]. Availability of such a large amounts of unstructured information makes it difficult for researchers to extract knowledge from articles. Automated biomedical information extraction methods aid researchers to identify biomedical relationships and events from articles. Biomedical named-entity recognition is the process of identifying biomedical named entities from text, such as genes, diseases, chemicals, proteins and cell lines. In this paper, we study chemical named entity recognition only.

© Springer Nature Switzerland AG 2020
A. Fred et al. (Eds.): IC3K 2019, CCIS 1297, pp. 54–68, 2020.
https://doi.org/10.1007/978-3-030-66196-0_3

Chemical named entity recognition (ChemNER) is a preliminary step in chemical informatics pipelines. Errors generated in ChemNER may be propagated to relation extraction or event extraction steps [38]. ChemNER is challenging due to reasons [29], including the facts that a chemical entity may be referred to with its *generic* name or *systematic* name or chemical entities may possibly be represented with acronyms.

Traditionally ChemNER is performed by dictionary-based methods [21, 27, 36] and feature engineering-based methods. Traditional methods have drawbacks such as dictionaries may not be updated and feature engineering is time-consuming. Such methods potentially result in high performing and less generalizable systems. Word embeddings learn representations with minimal to no feature engineering. In the recent past, end-to-end deep learning-based methods have been proposed for ChemNER [8, 14, 16, 22]. In most of the existing methods, the embeddings used are pre-trained on biomedical corpora from PubMed. Dai et al. [31] reported that the NER task can benefit from large vocabulary intersection between source corpora on which word embeddings are pre-trained and target NER data.

In this paper we use three models based on bi-directional long short term memory-conditional random fields (Bi-LSTM-CRF) with different word representations. The first model combines word2vec vectors, LSTM based character representations and a casing feature [1] as an input representation for Bi-LSTM-CRF. The second and third approach employ contextual information in input representation of the baseline model through embedded language models (ELMo) pre-trained on Pubmed corpora and patents. These models are evaluated on three benchmark corpora.

Transfer learning could improve the performance named entity recognition [39]. Word embeddings are an application of transfer learning. In this paper, we explore whether using in-domain embeddings (pre-trained on patents of chemicals) lead to any performance gains as compared to using embeddings pre-trained on Pubmed open access corpora for ChemNER.

The rest of the paper is organised as follows. Section 2 discusses related work, research gaps and our contribution. Section 3 explains the methodology of this paper. In Sect. 4 we descibe the corpora statistics. Section 5 outlines the experimental setup. Section 6 presents results and discussion. In Sect. 7 we conclude our findings.

2   Related Work

We consider six existing state-of-the-art methods for comparison with our approach. All of the below methods are Bi-LSTM based except tmChem which is a feature engineering based method.

2.1   Bi-LSTM-CRF with Word Vectors (word2vec)

One of the earliest deep learning-based biomedical NER methods was proposed by Habibi et al. [8], which was based on a generic NER tagger introduced by Lample et al. [1]. The tagger did not rely on any feature engineering or language-specific resources. Rather it used Google's word2vec [9] for converting into text to word vectors. The vectors are fed into a bi-directional- long short term memory (Bi-LSTM) - conditional random fields network - a forward LSTM and a backward LSTM with conditional random fields (CRF) as a final layer for classification. The input word vectors also included LSTM based character representations to represent out-of-vocabulary terms. Habibi et al. [8] presented an extensive set of experiments of biomedical NER with Bi-LSTM-CRF for five entity classes, namely genes/proteins, species, chemicals, cell lines and diseases on 33 biomedical corpora. The pre-trained word vectors (trained on open access corpora from PubMed) were made available by Moen et al. [15]. The reported performance was comparable to the best performing feature engineered based methods without relying on any language-specific lexicons, features or post-processing.

2.2   Transfer Learning Effect on Bi-LSTM-CRF

Transfer learning is the way of transferring knowledge learned on one problem to another but related problem [40]. In case of biomedical NER, a network could be pre-trained on large source corpus and then be further trained on a target corpora which is smaller than source corpus. To learn transfer learning effect, Giorgi et al. [14] employ a generic Bi-LSTM-CRF tagger, NeuroNER [12] for biomedical NER. They pre-train NeuroNER on a large silver standard corpora [32] (i.e., a corpora tagged by automatic methods) and then initialize training on the gold standard corpora on the pre-trained model. The proposed model was evaluated on benchmark biomedical corpora, and it statistically significantly outperformed the method by Habibi et al. [8].

2.3   tmChem

Generic features based ChemNER system tmChem [21] employs several linguistic features and tags sequences with CRF classifier. The tmChem (Model 2) has been adapted from tmVar [35], which is a sequence variants information extraction tool. In tmChem characters, semantic, syntactic and contextual features have been used with a CRF classifier. Some post-processing rules such as abbreviation resolution have also been employed to tag the mentions that are missed during classification.

2.4 Bi-LSTM-CRF with Attention

Bi-LSTM-CRF model with an additional attention layer was proposed by Luo et al. [13] for ChemNER. Words are represented by word vectors and character embeddings. Also traditional features such as parts-of-speech (POS), chunking and dictionary based features are used. The model has been reported to outperform tmChem [21] in ChemNER on two benchmark corpora.

2.5 LSTMVoter

LSTMVoter is a two-stage method that uses five existing NER taggers including Stanford named entity recognizer [33], MarMot [34], CRF++, MITIE and Glample [1] in an initial stage to label the sequences [22]. The outputs from the initial stage are then transformed into one-hot vectors with an attention layer. One-hot vectors are concatenated with word2vec and attention-based character representation.

2.6 Chemlistem

Chemlistem is a combination of two approaches called traditional and a minimalist approach. The traditional approach uses a token-based feature set with Glove word vectors [37]. Glove word vectors are trained on in-house patents corpus. The minimalist approach relies solely on character representations that are fed into the LSTM layers. This approach does not use a tokenizer. The reason that the minimalist approach does not use a tokenizer is that word segmentation in chemical texts is challenging and character representations will allow a system to avoid tokenization. The results from the two systems are combined to get a final prediction based on a scoring mechanism given in Corbett et al. [23].

2.7 Summary of Research Gaps and Contributions

Existing ChemNER methods rely on static word vectors such as word2vec or contextualized language models such as ELMo which are trained on biomedical domain corpora, such as corpora from PubMed. Existing methods do not rely on embeddings that are specifically trained on an in-domain corpus.

This work is an extension to our previously submitted paper [19]. The contribution of this paper is that we quantify and compare the transfer learning effect by using ELMo embeddings pre-trained on PubMed and chemical patents [11], which was not reported in previous work. We also repeat experiments on chemical entity mentions in patents (CEMP) corpus with different pre-processing techniques and report improved performance. In addition, we employ LSTM based character representation, wherein the previous study we used CNN based character representation. To the best of our knowledge, we are the first to report these results on BC5CDR, CEMP and BC4CHEMDNER corpora.

3   Method

In this section we discuss Bi-LSTM-CRF network in detail. We then explain word representation, word2vec, ELMo, LSTM-based character representation and casing feature.

3.1   Bidirectional Long-Short-Term Memory - Conditional Random Fields (Bi-LSTM-CRF)

Recurrent neural networks (RNNs) are a class of neural network that take a sequence of vectors $(\mathbf{x}_1, \mathbf{x}_2, \ldots, \mathbf{x}_t)$ as input and return a new sequence of vectors $(\mathbf{h}_1, \mathbf{h}_2, \ldots, \mathbf{h}_t)$. Theoretically, RNNs can capture long-range dependencies in sequential data, but in practice, they fail to do so due to the vanishing gradient problem [25,41]. LSTMs have been introduced to address the issue with a memory-cell to retain long-range dependencies. Memory cells, in turn, use several gates to control the proportion of input to keep in memory and the proportion of input to forget [24]. The following equations govern the LSTMs working.

$$\mathbf{i}_t = \sigma(\mathbf{W}_{xi}\mathbf{x}_t + \mathbf{W}_{hi}\mathbf{h}_{t-1} + \mathbf{W}_{ci}\mathbf{c}_{t-1} + \mathbf{b}_i) \tag{1}$$
$$\mathbf{c}_t = (1 - \mathbf{i}_t) \odot \mathbf{c}_{t-1}$$
$$+ \mathbf{i}_t \odot \tanh(\mathbf{W}_{xc}\mathbf{x}_t + \mathbf{W}_{hc}\mathbf{h}_{t-1} + \mathbf{b}_c) \tag{2}$$
$$\mathbf{o}_t = \sigma(\mathbf{W}_{xo}\mathbf{x}_t + \mathbf{W}_{ho}\mathbf{h}_{t-1} + \mathbf{W}_{co}\mathbf{c}_t + \mathbf{b}_o) \tag{3}$$
$$\mathbf{h}_t = \mathbf{o}_t \odot \tanh(\mathbf{c}_t), \tag{4}$$

For a given sentence $(\mathbf{x}_1, \mathbf{x}_2, \ldots, \mathbf{x}_t)$ containing t words, each represented as a d-dimensional vector, an LSTM computes a representation $\overrightarrow{\mathbf{h}_t}$ of the left context of the sentence at every word t. A right context $\overleftarrow{\mathbf{h}_t}$ can also be added, which computes the representation in the reverse direction. The left context network is called a forward layer and the right context network is called a backward layer. Both networks can be combined to form a bidirectional LSTM represented as $\mathbf{h}_t = [\overrightarrow{\mathbf{h}_t}; \overleftarrow{\mathbf{h}_t}]$ [26]. The final representation is computed by concatenating the forward and backward context vectors. A Bi-LSTM runs over each sentence in a forward and backward direction. The final outputs are concatenated together and serve as the input to a CRF classifier.

A linear chain CRF (log-linear model) is used to predict the probability distribution of tags of each word in a complete sentence. Linear chain CRF can also be referred to as a CRF. We have used a CRF classifier instead of a softmax classifier because we do not want to lose the sequential information [28]. Our final architecture is shown in Fig. 1.

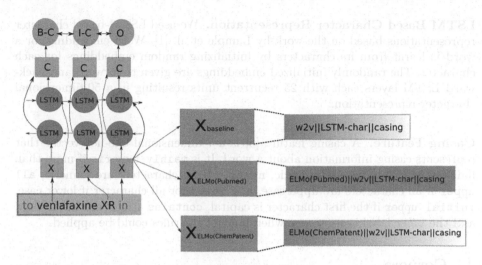

Fig. 1. Bi-LSTM-CRF network in which the sequence "venlafaxine XR in" is an input to the network which is being tagged as "B-C, I-C and O" where B-C is the beginning of chemical entity, I-C is the inside of chemical entity and O is outside the entity. "X" represents word embeddings which are a concatenation of ELMo, word2vec, LSTM-based character embeddings and casing feature. "C" is the concatenation of left and right context.

3.2 Word Representations

We used a combination of word2vec, ELMo, LSTM-based character representations and a casing feature.

Word2vec. Word2vec[9] is a neural network-based model that captures word semantics based on its surrounding words. We evaluated word2vec model pre-trained on four million Wikipedia articles of English language, nearly 23 million PubMed abstracts and nearly 700, 000 full text PMC articles [15].

Embedded Language Models (ELMo). ELMo is a three-layered Bi-LSTM network which is trained on a huge corpus in an unsupervised manner and is completely agnostic to the downstream classification task [10]. ELMo also incorporates character convolutions to learn character representations. Each downstream task learns its linear combination from pre-trained ELMo weights. Unlike word2vec embeddings, ELMo embeddings take into account the context of a word it appears in. We evaluate two pre-trained ELMo embeddings: PubMed version[1] and ChemPatent [11].

ChemPatent embeddings are trained on nearly 84,000 full patent documents (1B tokens) taken from 7 patent offices AU, CA, EP, GB, IN, US and WO.

---

[1] https://allennlp.org/elmo.

LSTM Based Character Representation. We used LSTM-based character representations based on the work by Lample et al. [1]. Word embedding for a word is learnt from its characters by initializing random embeddings for each character. The randomly initialized embeddings are given to forward and backward LSTM layers each with 25 recurrent units resulting in a 50-dimensional character representation.

Casing Feature. A casing feature [6] is a 7-dimensional one-hot vector that represents casing information about a word. It is mainly numeric if more than half of the characters are numeric, numeric if all characters are numeric, all upper if all characters are uppercase, all lower for all character if lower case, initial upper if the first character is capital, contains digit if it has a digit, and the *other* label is set to one when none of the rules could be applied.

4   Corpora

We use three publicly available datasets for benchmarking our results. Statistics of corpora are in Table 1, where the columns Train, Test and Dev indicate the number of sentences in each subset of the data.

Table 1. Gold standard corpora - number of sentences in Train, Test and Development sets.

Data	Train	Test	Dev
CEMP	29,632	14,881	4,869
BC4CHEMDNER	30,682	26,364	30,639
BC5CDR	9,578	4,686	1,774

4.1   Chemical Entity Mentions in Patents (CEMP) Biocreative V.5

CEMP V.5 is based on ChemNER from patents. Twenty-one thousand patents from medicinal chemistry were curated by experts for annotation of chemical entities [4]. Patents are different from regular research articles in that they use a complex language instead and could contain up to 100 pages. For that reason, this task focuses on the detection of chemical entities from patents only.

Training, development and test sets each contained seven thousand patents. Gold labels of the test set that was used for evaluation are not made publicly available. We therefore first combine all fourteen thousand patents and then split into the train, development and test sets in the ratio of 60:10:30. This setting has been chosen to be consistent with [8]. We downloaded the CEMP dataset from the official website[2] and converted into the BIO tagging scheme by using the pre-processing method explained in [17].

4.2   BC4CHEMDNER

This dataset has been provided by BioCreative community challenge IV for the development and evaluation of tools for ChemNER [5]. BC4CHEMDNER was is for the recognition of chemical compounds and drugs from PubMed abstracts. The inter-annotator agreement between human annotators is 91%. Ten thousand abstracts were annotated by expert literature curators. We have downloaded training, development and test sets in the BIO tagging scheme from Github[3].

4.3   BC5CDR

The Biocreative community challenge for chemical-disease relation extraction task (BC5CDR) corpus was made available in a Biocreative workshop [3]. The two subtasks of BC5CDR are identifying chemical and disease entities from Medline abstracts. The corpus has 1500 abstracts from PubMed, and chemical entities are annotated by a team of indexers from Medical Subject Headings (MeSH).

Annotations were done by two groups, and the inter-annotator agreement was 96.05% for chemical entities. The corpus has been split into training, test and development sets, where each set has 500 abstracts. We have used this corpus in BIO (Beginning, Inside, Outside) tagging scheme for ChemNER only.

5   Experimental Setup

In this paper, we used the Bi-LSTM-CRF architecture as explained by Reimers et al. [1]. We run experiments five times for each dataset with a random seed. We use an *early stopping* value of 10 to prevent overfitting. The network stops training if the performance does not increase for ten epochs or else 50 epochs have reached. In addition, we employ *variational dropout* of value (0.5, 0.5) for regularization [18]. The network has a *bi-directional LSTM layer* with *100 recurrent units* in forward and backward layers each. We use the *Nadam optimizer* with the default learning rate. Hyperparameter values were chosen as recommended by Reimers et al. [6].

All the experiments have been repeated five times with random seed value, and their F1-score for test and development sets is reported along with their standard deviation. All four corpora have been used in beginning-inside-outside (BIO) tagging scheme.

---

[2] https://biocreative.bioinformatics.udel.edu/resources/publications/.
[3] https://github.com/cambridgeltl/MTL-Bioinformatics-2016/tree/master/data/
   BC4CHEMD.

6   Results and Discussion

We present and discuss our findings on three benchmark corpora with three different settings. We performed three sets of experiments: a baseline Bi-LSTM-CRF, ELMo (Pubmed) Bi-LSTM-CRF, and ELMo (ChemPatent) Bi-LSTM-CRF. We perform each experiment for five runs with random seeds. We report an average of F1-score ± standard deviation. We also compare our results with the best performing ChemNER methods. Also, we perform a two-tailed t-test with α values of 0.01 and 0.05. We consider a model significantly worse than our best performing model when $p \leq 0.01$ (represented by **) and if $p \leq 0.05$ (represented by *).

Table 2. F1 score on BC5CDR, best F1-score in bold. First three rows show our results which are averaged F1 ± SD over five runs (random seeds). The rest of the results are reported directly from the respective papers.

Method	Dev F1 score	Test F1 score
Bi-LSTM-CRF(baseline)	91.792 ± 0.202	91.768 ± 0.22**
Bi-LSTM-CRF (ELMo-PubMed)	**93.28 ± 0.23**	**93.31 ± 0.12**
Bi-LSTM-CRF (ELMo-ChemPatent)	92.69 ± 15	92.84 ± 0.17**
Maryam Habibi [8]	–	90.63**
Transfer Learning [14]	–	91.64**
Att-Bi-LSTM-CRF [13]	–	92.57**
tmChem [21]	–	87.39**

For the BC5CDR corpus our method Bi-LSTM-CRF (ELMo-PubMed) results in highest F1-score, 93.31, which is statistically significant than our baseline Bi-LSTM-CRF, Bi-LSTM-CRF (ELMo-ChemPatent) and other four existing methods (shown in Table 2). Habibi et al. [8] use Bi-LSTM-CRF without ELMo, and Giorgi et al. [14] also use Bi-LSTM-CRF with pre-training on large silver standard corpora. Likewise, Luo et al. [13] use Bi-LSTM-CRF with attention mechanism and tmChem [21] is a feature-based method. None of these baselines uses contextual information in their representation, and hence our method performs better.

For BC4CHEMDNER corpus our method Bi-LSTM-CRF (ELMo-PubMed) performs with highest F1-score 90.24 which is statistically significant with our baseline, Bi-LSTM-CRF (ELMo-ChemPatent) and three other state-of-the-art methods (shown in Table 3). This high performance of our method can be attributed to the use of ELMo embeddings in word representations. The rest of the methods do not use this information which leads to lower performance.

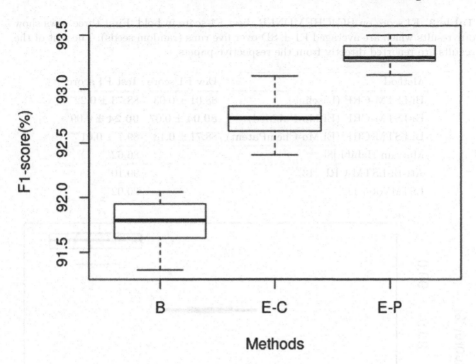

Fig. 2. F1 score on BC5CDR for baseline (B), ELMo-ChemPatent (E-C) and ELMo-Pubmed (E-P).

For BCV.5 CEMP corpus our method is not the best performing method in the list (shown in Table 4). Our initial hypotheses that in-domain ELMo embeddings could lead to performance gains is turned out to be true as Bi-LSTM-CRF (ELMo-ChemPatent) results in higher F1 score than Bi-LSTM-CRF (ELMo-PubMed) and baseline Bi-LSTM-CRF. Chemlistem [23] outperforms six methods. The reason for its higher performance is that it is a combination of two approaches and it uses word embeddings that are pre-trained on their in-house chemical patent corpus. The overlap between their embeddings and target data could be higher than our Bi-LSTM-CRF (ELMo-ChemPatent).

The use of chemical patents embeddings did not improve NER performance for research articles abstract. It only leads to better performance when chemical patent embeddings are used for ChemNER in patent corpora. This reason could be that the patents used for pre-training have different types of chemical compounds which were not present in articles and chemical entities appearing in abstracts were covered well in biomedical domain corpora from PubMed.

Table 3. F1 score on BC4CHEMDNER, best F1-score in bold. First three rows show our results which are averaged F1 ± SD over five runs (random seeds). The rest of the results are reported directly from the respective papers.

Method	Dev F1 score	Test F1 score
Bi-LSTM-CRF (baseline)	88.01 ± 0.03	88.73 ± 0.22**
Bi-LSTM-CRF (ELMo-PubMed)	**89.04 ± 0.07**	**90.24 ± 0.09**
Bi-LSTM-CRF (ELMo-ChemPatent)	88.71 ± 0.13	89.7 ± 0.01**
Maryam Habibi [8]	–	86.62**
Att-Bi-LSTM-CRF [13]	–	90.10*
LSTMVoter [22]	–	90.02**

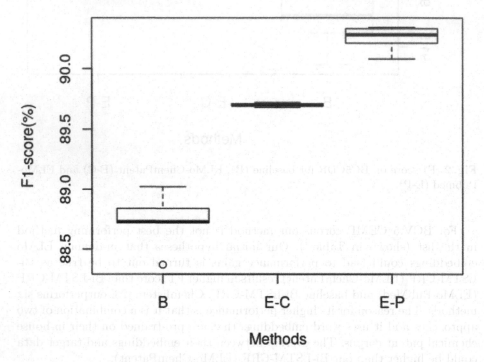

Fig. 3. F1 score on BC4CHEMDNER for baseline (B), ELMo-ChemPatent (E-C) and ELMo-Pubmed (E-P).

We also show the results of three methods over three corpora in Fig. 3, 2 and 4. We report averaged F1 score over five runs of the test set from the epoch with the best development score.

Table 4. F1 score on CEMP, best F1-score in bold. First three rows show our results which are averaged F1 ± SD over five runs (random seeds). The rest of the results are reported directly from the respective papers.

Method	Dev F1 score	Test F1 score
Bi-LSTM-CRF (baseline)	86.67 ± 0.04	86.864 ± 0.069**
Bi-LSTM-CRF (ELMo-PubMed)	86.81 ± 0.05	86.74 ± 0.18**
Bi-LSTM-CRF (ELMo-ChemPatent)	86.79 ± 0.06	87.41 ± 0.08
Maryam Habibi [8]	–	85.38**
Transfer Learning [14]	–	86.05**
LSTMVoter [22]	–	89.01
Chemlistem [23]	–	**90.33**

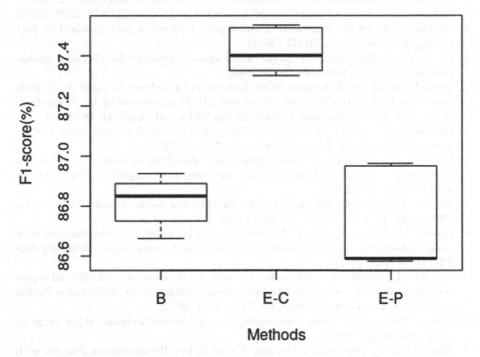

Fig. 4. F1 score on CEMP for baseline (B), ELMo-ChemPatent (E-C) and ELMo-Pubmed (E-P).

7 Conclusion

In this study, we investigated the effect of incorporation of ELMo embeddings (pre-trained on chemical patents) to Bi-LSTM-CRF for ChemNER of research articles abstracts and patents. We present comparisons of ELMo embeddings pre-trained on Pubmed and pre-trained on chemical patents. We conclude that pre-training on biomedical corpora from Pubmed results in highest F1 score on BC5CDR and BC4CHEMDNER corpora when compared to the best performing state-of-the-art methods. For patent corpus, CEMP, our experiments verify that when ELMo pre-trained on patents leads to statisticalally significant performance gains in terms of the F1-score.

For future work, named entity normalization of chemical entities could be experimented with this network in a multi-task setting as ChemNER only assigns a label to an entity, whether it is a chemical or not. Named entity normalization assigns an identifier to a chemical entity from a database such as Pubchem.

References

1. Lample, G., Ballesteros, M., Subramanian, S., Kawakami, K. and Dyer, C. : Neural architectures for named entity recognition. arXiv preprint arXiv:1603.01360 (2016)
2. Akhondi, S.A., et al.: Annotated chemical patent corpus: a gold standard for text mining. PloS one **9**(9), e107477 (2014)
3. Li, J., et al.: BioCreative V CDR task corpus: a resource for chemical disease relation extraction. Database, 1–10 (2016)
4. Pérez-Pérez, M., et al.: Evaluation of chemical and gene/protein entity recognition systems at BioCreative V. 5: the CEMP and GPRO patents tracks. In: Proceedings of the BioCreative Challenge Evaluation Workshop, vol. 5, pp. 11–18 (2017)
5. Krallinger, M., et al.: The CHEMDNER corpus of chemicals and drugs and its annotation principles. J. Cheminformatics **7**(1), S2 (2015)
6. Reimers, N., Gurevych, I: Reporting score distributions makes a difference: Performance study of lstm-networks for sequence tagging. arXiv preprint arXiv:1707.09861 (2017)
7. Ma, X., Hovy, E.: End-to-end sequence labeling via bi-directional LSTM-CNNs-CRF. arXiv preprint arXiv:1603.01354 (2016)
8. Habibi, M., Weber, L., Neves, M., Wiegandt, D.L., Leser, U.: Deep learning with word embeddings improves biomedical named entity recognition. Bioinformatics **33**(14), i37–i48 (2017)
9. Mikolov, T., Sutskever, I., Chen, K., Corrado, G. S., Dean, J. : Distributed representations of words and phrases and their compositionality. In: Advances in Neural Information Processing Systems, pp. 3111–3119 (2013)
10. Peters, M.E., et al.: Deep contextualized word representations. arXiv preprint arXiv:1802.05365 (2018)
11. Zhai, Z., et al.: Improving Chemical Named Entity Recognition in Patents with Contextualized Word Embeddings. arXiv preprint arXiv:1907.02679 (2019)
12. Dernoncourt, F., Lee, J.Y., Szolovits, P.: NeuroNER: an easy-to-use program for named-entity recognition based on neural networks. arXiv preprint arXiv:1705.05487 (2017)
13. Luo, L., et al.: An attention-based BiLSTM-CRF approach to document-level chemical named entity recognition. Bioinformatics **34**(8), 1381–1388 (2017)
14. Giorgi, J.M., Bader, G.D.: Transfer learning for biomedical named entity recognition with neural networks. Bioinformatics **34**(23), 4087–4094 (2018)
15. Moen, S.P.F.G.H., Ananiadou, T.S.S.: Distributional semantics resources for biomedical text processing. Proc. Lang. Biol. Med. 39–44 (2013)

16. Crichton, G., Pyysalo, S., Chiu, B., Korhonen, A.: A neural network multi-task learning approach to biomedical named entity recognition. BMC Bioinf. **18**(1), 368 (2017)
17. Weber, L., Münchmeyer, J., Rocktäschel, T., Habibi, M., Leser, U.: HUNER: improving biomedical NER with pretraining. Bioinformatics **36**(1), 295–302 (2020)
18. Gal, Y., Ghahramani, Z.: A theoretically grounded application of dropout in recurrent neural networks. In: Advances in Neural Information Processing Systems, pp. 1019–1027 (2016)
19. Awan, Z., Kahlke, T., Ralph, P.J., Kennedy, P.J.: Chemical named entity recognition with deep contextualized neural embeddings. In: 11th International Conference of Knowledge Discovery and Information Retrieval (2019)
20. Giorgi, J.M., Bader, G.D.: Towards reliable named entity recognition in the biomedical domain. Bioinformatics **36**(1), 280–286 (2020)
21. Leaman, R., Wei, C.H., Lu, Z.: tmChem: a high performance approach for chemical named entity recognition and normalization. J. Cheminformatics **7**(S1), S3 (2015)
22. Hemati, W., and Mehler, A.: LSTMVoter: chemical named entity recognition using a conglomerate of sequence labeling tools. J. Cheminformatics **11**(1), 1–7 (2019). https://doi.org/10.1186/s13321-018-0327-2
23. Corbett, P., Boyle, J.: Chemlistem: chemical named entity recognition using recurrent neural networks. J. Cheminformatics **10**(1), 59 (2018)
24. Hochreiter, S., Schmidhuber, J.: Long short-term memory. Neural Comput. **9**(8), 1735–1780 (1997)
25. Bengio, Y., Simard, P., Frasconi, P.: Learning long-term dependencies with gradient descent is difficult. IEEE Trans. Neural Netw. **5**(2), 157–166 (1994)
26. Graves, A., Schmidhuber, J.: Framewise phoneme classification with bidirectional LSTM and other neural network architectures. Neural Netw. **18**(5-6), 602–610 (2005)
27. Rocktäschel, T., Weidlich, M., Leser, U.: ChemSpot: a hybrid system for chemical named entity recognition. Bioinformatics **28**(12), 1633–1640 (2012)
28. Lafferty, J., McCallum, A., Pereira, F.C.: Conditional random fields: Probabilistic models for segmenting and labeling sequence data (2001)
29. Liu, S., Tang, B., Chen, Q., Wang, X.: Drug name recognition: approaches and resources. Information **6**(4), 790–810 (2015)
30. Khare, R., Leaman, R., Lu, Z.: Accessing biomedical literature in the current information landscape. In: Kumar, V.D., Tipney, Hannah Jane (eds.) Biomedical Literature Mining. MMB, vol. 1159, pp. 11–31. Springer, New York (2014). https://doi.org/10.1007/978-1-4939-0709-0_2
31. Dai, X., Karimi, S., Hachey, B., Paris, C.: Using Similarity Measures to Select Pretraining Data for NER. arXiv preprint arXiv:1904.00585 (2019)
32. Rebholz-Schuhmann, D., et al.: CALBC silver standard corpus. J. Bioinform. Comput. Biol. **8**(01), 163–179 (2010)
33. Finkel, J.R., Grenager, T., Manning, C.: Incorporating non-local information into information extraction systems by Gibbs sampling. In: Proceedings of the 43rd Annual Meeting on Association for Computational Linguistics, pp. 363–370. Association for Computational Linguistics, June 2005
34. Müller, T., Schmid, H., Schütze, H.: Efficient higher-order CRFs for morphological tagging. In: Proceedings of the 2013 Conference on Empirical Methods in Natural Language Processing, pp. 322–332, October 2013
35. Wei, C.H., Harris, B.R., Kao, H.Y., Lu, Z.: tmVar: a text mining approach for extracting sequence variants in biomedical literature. Bioinformatics **29**(11), 1433–1439 (2013)

36. Usié, A., Alves, R., Solsona, F., Vázquez, M., Valencia, A.: CheNER: chemical named entity recognizer. Bioinformatics **30**(7), 1039–1040 (2014)
37. Pennington, J., Socher, R., Manning, C.D.: Glove: global vectors for word representation. In: Proceedings of the 2014 Conference on Empirical Methods in Natural Language Processing (EMNLP), pp. 1532–1543, October 2014
38. Li, F., Zhang, M., Fu, G., Ji, D.: A neural joint model for entity and relation extraction from biomedical text. BMC Bioinform. **18**(1), 198 (2017)
39. Yang, Z., Salakhutdinov, R., Cohen, W.W.: Transfer learning for sequence tagging with hierarchical recurrent networks. arXiv preprint arXiv:1703.06345 (2017)
40. Zhuang, F., et al.: A Comprehensive Survey on Transfer Learning. arXiv preprint arXiv:1911.02685 (2019)
41. Hochreiter, S.: The vanishing gradient problem during learning recurrent neural nets and problem solutions. Int. J. Uncertainty Fuzziness Knowl.-Based Syst. **6**(02), 107–116 (1998)

An Upper Level for What-If Analysis

Mariana Carvalho and Orlando Belo[(✉)]

Department of Informatics, School of Engineering, ALGORITMI R&D Centre,
University of Minho, Campus de Gualtar, 4710-057 Braga, Portugal
obelo@di.uminho.pt

Abstract. Living in a knowledge-based society, one of the most important tasks of decision makers is to know how to deal with information and knowledge that add value to their activities. Decision makers need to retrieve high-quality sets of information in order to gain competitive advantages in their business world. Otherwise, companies may struggle with several difficulties when it comes to market competition and business reputation. What-If analysis tools can help decision-makers in this matter. This technique allows for simulating hypothetical scenarios without harming the business and helping anticipate future events, by testing hypothesis. Therefore, in this paper, we propose a hybridization approach and develop a hybrid methodology, which aims at discovering the best recommendations for What-If analysis scenarios' parameters using OLAP usage preferences. We also develop a software platform to illustrate the hybrid methodology with a specific case study. This hybridization process will help the user during the design and implementation of a What-If analysis process, overcoming the pitfalls of the conventional What-If analysis process.

Keywords: Business intelligence · Decision support systems · What-If analysis hybridization · OLAP usage preferences · OLAP mining

1 Introduction

Nowadays, the exponential growth of electronic data as well as the increasing competitiveness between companies are quite relevant for business enterprise managers. Improving performance and optimizing decisions often require a better use of analytical information systems, techniques and models for multidimensional data exploration and analysis. Moreover, it is important to retrieve the right and high-quality set of information and make the best of knowledge, in order to gain competitive advantages in relation to other companies. More and more companies use analytical tools and business data for acquiring high quality information, which consequently helps for reducing redundant information, decreasing waste, saving time, and increasing profits.

On-line analytical processing (OLAP) is one of the most important tools used by companies in decision-support systems. Navigating in a multidimensional data structure using OLAP operators is one of many ways of exploring business data. OLAP tools provide a high flexible interactive exploration of multidimensional databases performed in an *ad-hoc* manner, allowing users to see data from different perspectives of analysis. Offering several features useful for business analytics, OLAP also permits

A. Fred et al. (Eds.): IC3K 2019, CCIS 1297, pp. 69–93, 2020.
https://doi.org/10.1007/978-3-030-66196-0_4

multidimensional views of data, data analysis, reporting and complex analytical operations. Turning out to be a very efficient logical way for analyzing businesses activities. OLAP supports the decision process, but it lacks the capability of anticipating or predicting future trends.

What-If analysis [1] is a technology that allows to create hypothetical scenarios and could help filling the lack of capability of OLAP. A data cube [2] is one of the most suitable structures for supporting a simulation of a What-If analysis process due to its characteristics [1]: supporting information analysis and being capable for representing historical trends, supporting information at different abstraction levels.

The process of What-If analysis allows for exploring and analyzing the consequences of changing the considered normal behavior of the business. An ordinary manual analysis of historical data does not allow to discover these effects. What-If analysis allows decision makers to manipulate parameters, create hypothetical scenarios and simulate specific conditions of the business, analyze them and get better decisions about some doubts that could arise during the business management. Therefore, decision makers can use What-If analysis scenarios for testing and validating their business hypothesis to support their decisions, without endangering the real business, and ensuring, if possible, that the consequent decisions will have some success.

During the implementation of the What-If analysis process, the lack of user's expertise may be one of the drawbacks of the process. A user, who is not aware of the What-If process or even the business data, possibly will not choose the most adequate parameters in an application scenario, and consequently may lead to poor results and outcomes. One solution to overcome this pitfall is to integrate OLAP usage preferences [3, 4] in the conventional What-If analysis process. Usually, in OLAP platforms, when complex queries are performed, the outcome could be a huge volume of data and quite difficult to analyze. OLAP preferences allows to filter the volume of data: the returned data is filtered to the users' needs and to the business requirements, consequently significantly reduced and without losing data quality. The integration of OLAP preferences according to each analytic session could come as an advantage, since it provides a way to personalize the outcome of queries of analytical sessions.

The proposed and developed hybridization process [5] consists in the integration of OLAP usage preferences in the conventional What-If scenarios. This hybridization process can recommend OLAP preferences, providing the user the most suitable scenario parameters according to the user needs and turning What-If scenarios more valuable. Therefore, in this paper, we propose a recommendation methodology for assisting the user during the decision-support analysis process. We present and discuss the integration of both technologies and a case example that illustrates the proposed hybridization methodology.

The remaining part of this paper presents an overview about the importance of What-If analysis and its application. As our main goal is to enrich the What-If analysis methodology by overcoming its pitfalls. In Sect. 2, we also do a review about some specific papers that present methodologies that resort to the conventional What-If analysis and others that follows methodologies that aim at improving the What-If analysis process. Next, in Sect. 3, we describe the methodology we propose and expose how What-If scenarios are created and enhanced using OLAP preferences. In Sect. 4, a case example using the proposed methodology is presented and analyzed, and we show

how the process works in a software platform we developed, showing all the steps between the extraction of the rules until the definition of the What-If scenario. Finally, in Sect. 5 we conclude the paper and discuss some possible future research directions. This paper is an extended version of [6]. There are a few differences between the two papers: Sect. 2 was enhanced, Sect. 3 and 4 were significantly increased with more and detailed information about the hybridization process and the case study example.

2 Related Work

2.1 What-If Analysis Applications

Since [1] was published, What-If analysis has been proved to be a valuable resource to use in several areas, as evinced by several papers that were published during the last decade. Next, we reference some papers that shown how What-If analysis can be used in, for example, data warehouse, relational databases, OLAP cubes and other areas of application. In [1], the authors present a solution methodology for resolve problems that need the use What-If analysis for its resolution. They analyzed and discussed some of the lessons learned and the experience obtained, where they found immature technology, complexity of design and lack of design methodology. They also suggest several tools that present What-If features that help to ease users' problems. Following, [7] focused on aided and unaided decision support systems with What-If analysis. These authors presented a formal simulation approach, comparing unaided and aided decision-making performance. The authors conclude that the differences of performance between the both approaches are meaningful, and the effectiveness of the decision-making strategies is dependent on the environmental factors and on the supporting tools. Later, [8] addressed What-If analysis in Multidimensional OLAP environments. The authors mainly focused on storage and organization of hypothetical modified data, when dealing with What-If analysis. The solution proposed by these authors consists in storing the new hypothetical modified data into a HU-Tree data structure (variant of r*-tree). This allows for storing and managing hypothetical modified cells using a hypothetical cube, instead of modifying the original cube directly. When a What-If analysis is processed, the original cube and the What-If cube are manipulated simultaneously. In the next year, [9] focuses on the resolution of a particular problem of a real case study using the What-If methodology and following their previous work, the authors focused on derive a formalism for expressing conceptually the simulation model. They achieve a simulation model that satisfies several issues; for instance, with their methodology, they can model static, functional and dynamic aspects in an integrated fashion, combining use cases, class and activity diagrams, build specific What-If constructs using the UML stereotyping mechanism, and get multiple levels of abstraction using YAM2. Later, [10] aims at improving the traditional What-If analysis. Using a "generate and test" paradigm and integrating a combinatorial optimization and decision-making component. This approach helps identifying the most interesting scenarios. The authors tested this solution approach in a social policy making. Following, [11] focused on improving the performance of What-Ig query processing strategies for Big Data in an OLAP system. They aimed to improve the classical delta-table merge algorithm in the process of What-If, taking advantage from the MapReduce framework. Also, the authors explain a What-If algorithm of BloomFilterDM (Bloom filter-based delta table merging algorithm) and What-If algorithm of DistributedCacheDM (distributed cache-based delta table merging algorithm). Later, [12] addressed how to use What-If analysis process when dealing with conflicting goals. Conflicting goals consists of multiple goals that are contradictory between each other. The authors use data ranges for the input scenario parameters in the simulation, in order to limit the number of scenarios explored. Also, they present ways for optimizing input parameters to get a What-If analysis outcome and balance the defined conflicting goals. In [13], the authors presented the Caravan system. This system was developed for performing What-If analysis and allowing for users to create a personalized session, according to their needs. The main innovation is the use of Provisioned Autonomous Representations (PARs) to store the What-If analysis scenarios information instead of maintaining the all data of the source database. [14] presented an in-memory What-If analysis approach to introduce new dimension values. They presented a system of operators that can introduce new dimension values and store them as scenarios, maintaining the real data cube intact, without changing it. Finally, and more recently, [15] mainly focused on extract temporal models from current and past historical facts to create predictions. The main goal of this paper was essentially to solve problems inherent of predictive analytics. Use novel data models to support large-scale What-If analysis on time-evolving graphs.

2.2 Methodologies Using What-If Analysis

There are several methodologies that use What-If analysis. Most of them use What-If analysis to improve a specific process or other methodologies. In this section, we review some of them. But as far as we know, there are not many papers, only [10], that describes a methodology that aims at improving the conventional What-If analysis. But first, we start analyzing the paper that we consider the landmark of the What-If analysis methodology [1]:

The authors presented a methodology that describes how to use What-If analysis in OLAP environments. The methodology is suggested to be followed when dealing with problems that need the creation of hypothetical scenarios for answering questions during decision-making processes. This methodology considers six phases:

- Definition of the main goal analysis and which are the scenarios to perform in the simulation;
- Business analysis and identification of business variables involved in the defined scenario and the relation between them.
- Analysis of the data source and data content.
- Definition of the multidimensional data structure, considering the variables involved in the simulation and the relation between them.
- Creation of the What-If analysis simulation using the pre-defined multidimensional data structure as the basis for prediction.
- Implementation and validation of the simulation model.

In [16], the authors propose a methodology that uses a What-If engine to predict the performance values of a MapReduce system. The authors use What-If analysis for estimating the performance of a MapReduce job according to several variables: program, input data, cluster resources and job configuration settings. This methodology is composed by four phases:

- Definition of the What-If questions, which need to be translated as changes in the MapReduce jobs executions, like increasing the size of input data, add nodes to the cluster resources.
- Definition of the MapReduce job and other configurations settings of the hypothetical job to perform in the What-If simulation.
- What-If Engine, which consists in estimating the virtual job profile and simulating the MapReduce job execution using the pre-defined parameters.
- Evaluation and Validation, which is the prediction of the MapReduce workflow performance.

In [17], the authors presented a methodology to perform sustainability performance analysis using Sustainable Process Analytics Formalism (SPAF), that aims at helping companies guarantee their sustainable manufacturing goals in their processes. The authors include the What-If analysis in the methodology to help asking What-If questions, make optimization requests and analyze the outcome in order to suggest recommendations to the users. The proposed methodology consists of 5 phases:

- Identification of sustainable manufacturing process scenarios and sustainability performance measures that need to be assessed, analyzed and optimized.
- Collection of knowledge and data: collecting domain knowledge for the relevant indicators and their metrics of the scenario and collecting and processing relevant data that required for the modeling and study.
- Definition of the formal problem representation, when the data and the scenario are modelled using SPAF.
- Execution of the What-If analysis process and make decision optimization.
- Generation of actions to improve the sustainability manufacturing processes.
  [10] is, to our knowledge, the only paper that presents a methodology that aims at improving the What-If analysis process. This paper exposed a methodology that aims to integrate What-If analysis with an optimization-simulation hybridization approach. Firstly, the authors create a Decision Optimization Support System (DOSS and then integrate machine learning in the process. Machine learning helps to synthetize constraints for the decision-making support system using the created simulations results of the What-If analysis simulator. With this, it is possible to avoid the "generate and test" approach of the conventional What-If analysis process. This methodology is composed by several elements, each one has its own function:

- Definition of the hypothetical scenarios for policy making and possible solutions.
- What-If simulator. The simulator takes the scenarios as input and performs What-If analysis. As output the simulator generates a set of tuples, which are composed by decisions and observables.

- Machine learning. The set of tuples is stored as a training set for the learning component.
- Decision Optimization Support System. This system receives as input the set of possible decisions and the output of the machine learning and returns the optimal scenarios.

These methodologies are different in several ways. First, only one of them describes the What-If analysis methodology [1]. [16] and [17] uses What-If analysis in their process. These two papers are examples of methodologies that use What-If analysis to ease the usage of an already developed tool or improve companies' processes. [16] suggests a methodology that uses What-If analysis to predict performance values of MapReduce jobs. [17] developed a methodology to be followed when users pretend to achieve the desired sustainability manufacturing goals in their manufacturing processes. And finally, [10] is the only one that presents a methodology that aims at enhancing the conventional What-If analysis process. But there are some issues related to the methodology presented in [10]. Machine learning requires a large number of simulations before achieving a mature and effective level. Also, in this methodology is necessary to develop an optimization model, specially personalized to the specific problem, to embed in the process.

3   The Methodology

3.1   Conventional What-If Analysis Overview

What-If analysis [1] allows for helping decision makers, influencing the decision-making process. A What-If analysis translates the intention of decision makers to get some doubts or questions answered in order to take future steps in the business. So, decision makers are responsible for creating hypothetical scenarios about the specific business situation to explore and help them to take business decisions. Running the simulation model enables the user to get a better understanding of the business and to explore different outcomes that are likely to occur under different scenarios.

In the What-If analysis process, the data is altered in order to assess the effects of the changes. The user is responsible to change the value of one or more business variables, set the scenario parameters in a specific scenario, taking into consideration the analysis goals. The What-If process calculates the effect of the impact of the change of the business variables, presenting the user a new changed scenario, called the prediction scenario (Fig. 1). It is also the responsibility of the user to accept the prediction scenario or to perform the What-If analysis process again.

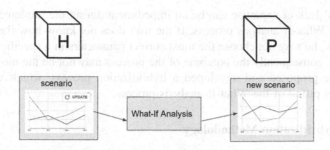

Fig. 1. Historical and prediction scenarios [5].

The What-If analysis process offers several advantages. This technology allows to analyze the system behavior through simulation without building the system or creating the environment to make it functional, undoubtedly reducing time and costs. Also, it is possible through What-If analysis to be aware of circumstances that may lead to an unpredictable or irregular behavior in the system and preventing it.

Users resort to What-If analysis to clarify some doubts, so, typically this technology starts with the definition of a what-if question, for example, "What if...?". This question represents the doubt of the user that symbolizes the intent on exploring the effects of changing the variables and after analyzing the consequences, obtaining the information to answer the previous doubt.

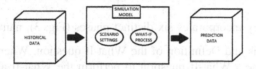

Fig. 2. A general overview of a what-if analysis process [5].

The main element of a What-If analysis application is the simulation model (Fig. 2). This model represents the real business model and usually is composed by several application scenarios. Each application scenario is composed by a set of scenario settings. Each set of scenarios settings, in its turn, is composed by a set of business variables (the source variables) and a set of setting parameters (scenario parameters). As said, the user is responsible to choose the axis of analysis of the simulation, the set of values for analyzing and the set of values to change according to the goal defined previously and in the what-if question.

The What-If process receives as input a data cube with historical data, the simulation model is performed with a proper tool and the outcome would be a prediction scenario. This prediction scenario is a data cube with the new calculated data. The user can explore and analyze the impact of the changes and accept the new data cube, or to return to change the application scenario settings and do the changes required over to the target data.

The users' lack of expertise can be an impediment during the implementation and design of the What-If analysis process. If the user does not know how the process or business work, he may not choose the most correct parameters in a specific application scenario, and, consequently the outcome of the process may not be the most adequate. Therefore, we proposed and developed a hybridization process, which will help to overcome this pitfall of the What-If analysis process.

3.2 The Hybridization Methodology

Integrating OLAP preferences in What-If Analysis defined a general methodology that can be implemented using various methods and different technologies and tools, such as the tool to perform the simulation, or the way preferences are extracted. Clearly, other choices of tools and techniques could be also used. After the overview of the hybridization process we proposed, we define a methodology that scan be followed when dealing with What-If-based problems.

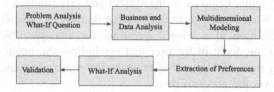

Fig. 3. The schema of the methodology for the hybridization process [5].

Our methodology incorporates six distinct phases (Fig. 3), namely:

1. Problem Analysis and Definition of the What-If question. When doubt arises, it is essential to define a What-If question to perform the What-If analysis. A What-If question translates in a question about what can happen in a specific hypothetical scenario and the consequences of changing the normal behavior of a complex system. So, it is important to know the context of the problem to define the What-If question and the simulation purpose or goal analysis.
2. Business and Data analysis. In this phase, and according to the previous defined What-If question, the set of business variables to add in the simulation must be defined. One should know the set of business variables to be included in the simulation model, and their associations, as well as identifying the dependent and independent ones. The user also needs to perform an analysis of the business and the data and consider the data quality. If the data used in the simulation has some kind of noise, the outcome of the simulation could not be the most adequate.
3. Multidimensional Modelling. To perform the multidimensional modelling, a data structure is created and prepared for discovering user preferences. The multidimensional structure is constructed based on the information collected in the previous phase and the goal analysis defined in the first phase.

4. Extraction of Preferences. A mining technique is applied to the created multidimensional structure. This process is called OLAP mining [18]. The outcome is stored in a mining structure. Then, a filter process, which is explained in detail in Carvalho and Belo (2016), is applied to the outcome of the association rules technique. This filter process consists in filtering the data that is interesting to the user and should be included in the simulation. To do this, it is necessary to filter the set of association rules and return only the set of strong association rules that contain the goal analysis business variable. At the end, this process suggests to the user a set of variables, which frequently occur with the goal analysis in the data set, to introduce in the simulation model.

5. What-If analysis simulation. To perform the simulation process, the user needs to set some scenario settings, namely the source or business variables and the scenario parameters. The set of business variables includes the goal analysis variables, which is the focus of the analysis defined in the first phase, and a set of suggested preferences. The set of scenario parameters, like algorithm to perform the What-If analysis and additional parameters, are defined according to the chosen tool.

6. Validation and Implementation of the decisions. In this last phase, the user evaluates how credible and practicable is the outcome of the simulation. The user needs to compare the conclusions of the simulation model with the real business model outcome and to evaluate if the behavior of the simulation model is adequate. If the behavior is irregular or unacceptable, the user needs to go back and to redefine the whole simulation model.

In the third phase, we used Microsoft Visual Studio 2017 [19] to create the multidimensional structure within an Analysis Services Multidimensional and Data Mining project. Next, and using the same tool, we used a data mining technique for extracting preferences, opting for an Apriori-based algorithm [20] for extracting preferences from the multidimensional structure in the fourth phase. We claim that this algorithm is the most adequate mining technique for extracting preferences from a multidimensional structure. The extracted preferences recommend to the user axis of analysis that are strongly related to the previously defined goal in the What-If question. Preferences consist on information (patterns or knowledge) from previous sessions of analysis derived from the application of a data mining algorithm. They provide access to relevant information as well as eliminate the irrelevant one.

Therefore, preferences help to introduce valuable information to the scenario analysis, which otherwise may not happen. To perform the What-If simulation in the hybridization methodology we chose Microsoft Office Excel functions.

4 Software Platform and Case Study

In this section we present a software platform, called "OPWIF" – OLAP Preferences What-IF analysis integration, that was developed to implement the hybridization methodology described before, and an example of the application methodology on a specific case study. To test our methodology, we used the Wide World Importers (WWI) database [21]. It contains information about a wholesale novelty goods importer and distributer called WWI. As a wholesale, WWI buys goods from suppliers, which can be novelty or toys manufacturers and sells to WWI customers, which are the ones that resell to individuals.

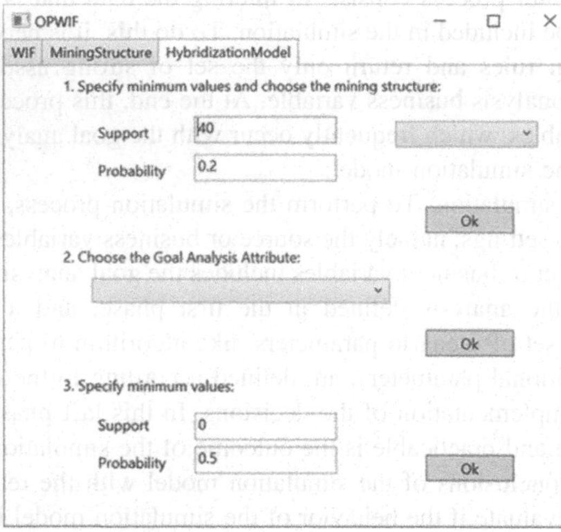

Fig. 4. The hybridization model tab [5].

4.1 The Hybridization Methodology

Let us see now an example of the software platform "OPWIF" (meaning, OLAP Preferences What-IF analysis integration) we developed for implementing the methodology. It allows for the user to:

- create What-If scenarios, choosing the available attributes of his choice (conventional What-If analysis);
- consult the mining models' itemsets and association rules;
- use the hybridization process described in the previous chapter.

Each one of these functionalities is associated to a tab. Figure 4 represents the User Interface (UI) of the "HybridizationModel" tab, which allows for the user to perform the hybridization process.

To illustrate the several functionalities of the software platform we start by describing a case study involving an analysis of the products' mining structure. A mining structure is a data structure that stores the extracted frequent itemsets and association rules. For example, the products' mining structure contains the itemsets and extracted association rules with products' information.

4.2   A Case Study

To illustrate the application of the hybridization methodology we developed, we selected a simple case study, from the WWI data warehouse. The creation and analysis of the small data cube can clearly be generalized to larger complex cases. The WWI database contains information about a fictitious company, which is a wholesale novelty goods importer and distributor.

To proceed in our methodology, in the second phase, we analyze the database content and select the set of interesting data necessary to create the multidimensional structure and by presenting the software platform. Then, we present an example of the application of the proposed hybridization process. We will present and discuss this in the next section.

Data and Goal Analysis. A data warehouse [22] is a subject-oriented, integrated, time-variant and non-volatile collection of data in support of the management decision-making-process. Data warehouses are specially centered on companies' specific concepts, in other words, they are business subject oriented. They intend to store detailed information about the several entities: customers, products, stores, for example; and detailed facts of sales, as, for instance, data, the products bought, the name of the employee who made the sale and the name of the customer.

A data warehouse allows for gathering data from several data sources, integrating all the information in only one place. This eases to access to specific information, turning the process of decision making simpler and faster. Data warehouses are time-variant, which means that all the data warehouse data is dated, allowing for to analyze data from a specific period, like, for example, analyzing product sales of 2017. The use of data warehouses also provides a structured and organized way of analyzing data. And finally, data warehouses are non-volatile, which means that data is consistent and stable. New data can be added to the data warehouse, but it can be never removed. All these data warehouses' properties help companies to get a more consistent view of the business.

A data warehouse data can be represented as a multidimensional view of data, which can be materialized as multidimensional views (data cubes) and used in further inquiry. A data cube structure, also called multidimensional database, is composed by a set of data cells. Each data cell in the data cube stores information about the corresponding entity values in a multidimensional space. A typical multidimensional schema of a data warehouse (Fig. 5) is usually composed by a central table, called fact table, and a set of tables linked to the main table, called dimensions.

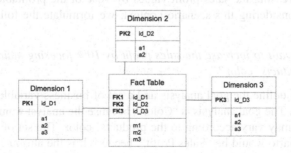

Fig. 5. A typical multidimensional schema of a data warehouse.

Following the formal specifications in [4], we can define a multidimensional schema and its components. Essentially, a fact table can have two types of columns: keys and measures. Fact Tables contain foreign keys from the dimension tables. Measures are numeric values that can be operands in mathematical operations and are used to express business metrics. Foreign keys are responsible for linking fact table's rows to the correspondent dimension table data. Dimensions have primary keys and attributes.

To illustrate the analysis example, we chose a multidimensional view with a fact Table called "Sales" and related dimension tables: "Customer", "Employee", "Stock Item", "City" and "Date", which contains information about customers, employees, stock items, about cities of 49 states of EUA and date details between 'January 1, 2013' and 'December 31, 2016', respectively. These tables are the most adequate to support our goal analysis because this fact table contains the information about sales' details, which is the most adequate taking into consideration the pre-defined What-If question. The database schema of the case study "Sales" is presented in Fig. 6.

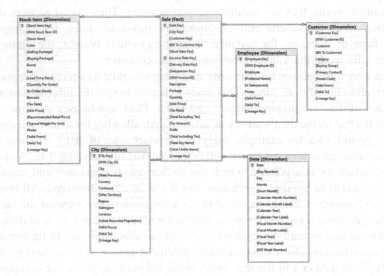

Fig. 6. Selected data warehouse's view "Sales" schema.

The analysis example selected was one want to use What-If analysis for exploring the effects of increasing the sales profit values by 10% of the profitable products of a specific store. Considering this scenario context, we formulate the following What-If question:

– *"What if we want to increase the sales profit by 10% focusing mainly on the most profitable products' color?"*.

Next, we need to define the goal analysis and a set of business variables to add to the analysis scenario. The goal analysis is "Color", because the analyst wants to know how the profit values may vary according to the products' color. The set of variables to be added to the scenario would be "Sales Profit", because it is the attribute that we aim at altering (increasing 10%), and also it would be useful and interesting to analyze the scenario data by year or month.

Applying Conventional What-If Analysis. The developed software platform allows for performing conventional What-If analysis. Let's consider that we are the enterprise managers of WWI and we want to know how the sales profit is going to vary in the next years according to the products characteristics and define the following What-If question: "What if we want to increase the sales profit by 10% focusing mainly on the most profitable products' color?". Figure 7 shows the application UI of this tab, the WIF tab.

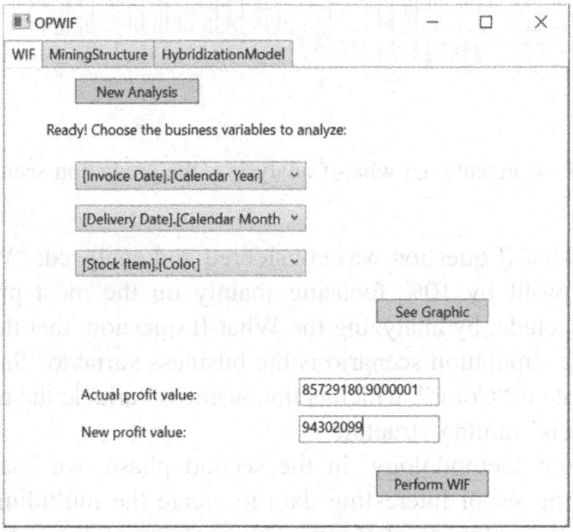

Fig. 7. The WIF tab [5].

Using this tab, the user can create a typical What-If scenario using a conventional What-If analysis. The user chooses the parameters that he wants to introduce in the scenario (according to the pre-defined What-If question) and creates the graphic to analyze the profit values. The set of parameters to be chosen are: "Calendar Year" and "Calendar Month" from the dimension table "Invoice Date" and "Color" from the dimension table "Stock Item", as we want to know which is the most profitable products' color. We opt to choose "Calendar Year" and "Calendar Month to analyze the scenario data by month. Then, after 'See Graphic', the application shows the historical scenario. As we want to analyze the effects of changing the profit value by 10%, we set the new value in the "New profit value". After performing the What-If analysis, the application returns to the prediction scenario (Fig. 8).

The Hybridization Process. In this section, we illustrate the hybridization methodology with an analysis example. In the first phase of the methodology, we need to define the What-If analysis and analyze the problem. Let's consider the same problem described in the conventional What-If analysis example: we want to know how the sales profit is going to vary in the next years according to the products characteristics.

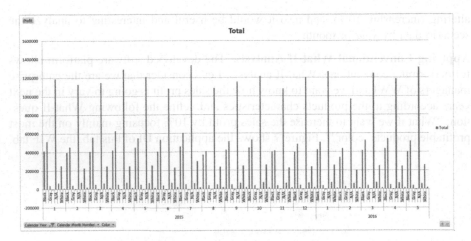

Fig. 8. Conventional what-if analysis – the prediction scenario.

The following What-If question was considered and analyzed: "What if we want to increase the sales profit by 10% focusing mainly on the most profitable products' color?". We can conclude, by analyzing the What-If question, that the attribute that we intend to alter in the simulation scenario is the business variable "Sales Profit" and the goal analysis attribute is "Color", which is the business variable the user wants to focus on, from the products' mining structure.

To proceed in our methodology, in the second phase, we analyze the database content and select the set of interesting data to create the multidimensional structure and by presenting the software platform. The analysis of the database content was already explained previously. Then, we proceed to the construction of the OLAP cube, in the third phase. OLAP consists of a set of techniques developed for analyzing data in data warehouses. The use of a multidimensional database (an OLAP cube) is more advantageous comparatively to using traditional relational data bases in this analysis. It is possible to analyze data in different levels of abstraction, to see queries' output in different formats, to perform operations like navigation of data, and operations like roll up, drill down, slice, dice, etc. To construct the data cube, we used the Microsoft Visual Studio tool, where it is possible to define all the dimensions and the related fact table of the data warehouse and construct the data cube using the defined data. Next, we can use the application UI to extract preferences. Figure 9 represents the application UI of the HybridizationModel tab. The extraction of preferences phase is possible to be done using this tab.

Step 1 is responsible to filter the frequent itemsets of a chosen mining structure. The user can choose the mining structure using the combo box in the right in the application UI: the user selects the mining structure most adequate to answer the What-If question. In this case, the mining structure of "Products" was selected, as shown in Fig. 10.

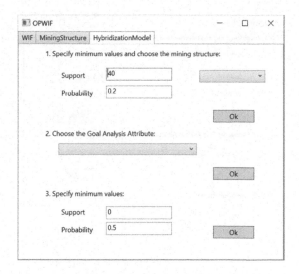

Fig. 9. The UI – Hybridizationmodel tab [5].

Regarding the support and confidence values used to filter the frequent itemsets, the user has the possibility of accepting the default minimum support and probability values or altering them according to the needs. This step filters the set of itemsets of the mining structure and returns the frequent itemsets, in other words, returns the set of frequent itemset that are above the support and probability values. In step 2 the user chooses the frequent itemset of its choice (according to the What-If question), in this case, the "Color" goal analysis attribute. Finally, in step 3, and similarly to step 1, the user specifies the mining values of support and probability to filter the important set of association rules. These association rules are an association rules' subset that contain the chosen goal analysis attribute in step 2. All these steps are resumed in Fig. 10.

After filtering the association rules with default minimum support and probability values in step 3, the application UI shows a new window (Fig. 11), containing the final association rules' list, ordered by probability of happening in the left. The three chosen rules are the association rules in the right:

1. ["Brand" = 'Northwind', "Color" = 'Black' -> "Barcode" = 'N/A'];
2. ["Brand" = 'Northwind', "Color" = 'Black' -> "Buying Package" = 'Each'];
3. ["Brand" = 'Northwind', "Color" = 'Black' -> "Is Chiller Stock" = 'Missing'].

These three top rules are chosen to form OLAP preferences

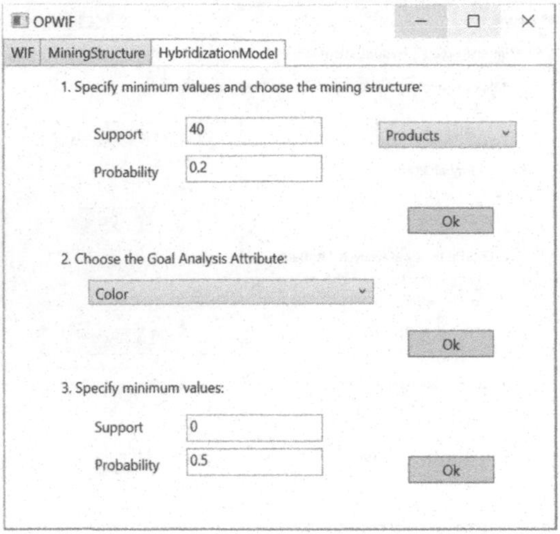

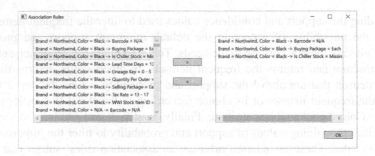

Fig. 10. The hybridizationmodel tab – steps 1, 2 and 3 [5].

Fig. 11. Selection of top association rules [5].

Next, the itemsets contained in the filtered association rules will be suggested to the user as preferences (Fig. 12). The user choses the scenario parameters to be part of the What-If scenario. The preferences are represented by the itemsets of the chosen association rules: "Brand", "Barcode", "Buying Package" and "Is Chiller Stock" in the left. "Calendar Year" and Month Number of Year" are suggested too to be part of the scenario.

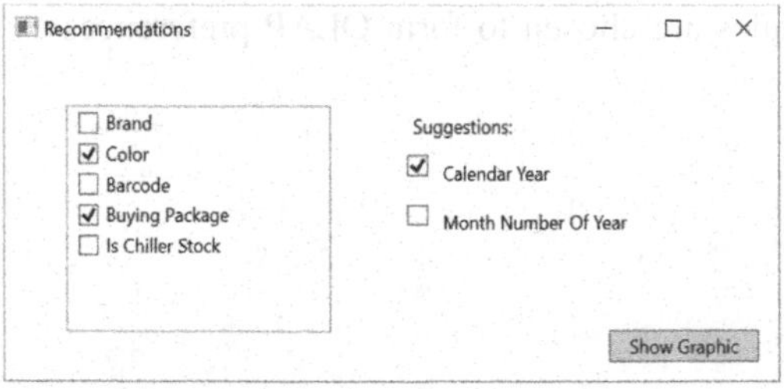

Fig. 12. Recommendations to the user [5].

Then, the application UI creates a historical scenario with the chosen parameters and shows it to the user (Fig. 13).

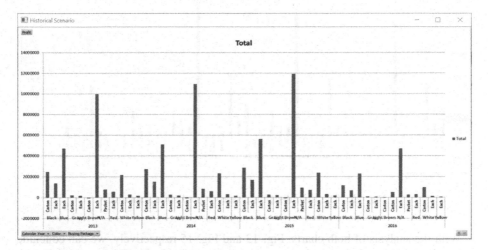

Fig. 13. The hybridization process - historical scenario.

The application UI shows a new window (Fig. 14), in which the user can enter the desired final value. This step is similar to the one in the conventional What-If analysis, in which the user changes the value of the goal analysis variable to the wanted one. In order words, if the user wants to increase the profit value by 10%, we want to alter the profit final value by 10%.

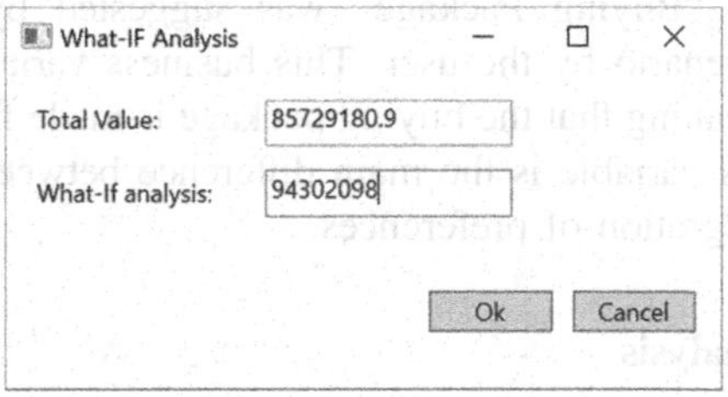

Fig. 14. Changing the variables' values [5].

Next, Microsoft Office Excel [23] performs What-If analysis. Excel takes the historical scenario data, performs the What-If analysis and alters the new final profit value and returns the new prediction scenario (Fig. 15).

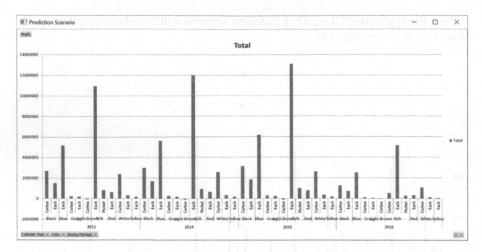

Fig. 15. The hybridization process - prediction scenario.

With the analysis of both charts, Fig. 13 and Fig. 15 respectively, we can conclude that products with unknown color or not available ('N/A') with 'Each type' value for buying package are the most profitable products in '2015', followed by '2014', which resulting in a high profit in both years (over '12,000,000'). Followed by the products' color 'Blue' sold with the 'Each type' buying package in '2015' with total profit value over '6,000,000' and finally the products' color 'Black' sold with 'Carton' buying package with total profit value over '3,000,000' in '2014' and in '2015'. 'White' or 'Black' products with buying package made from 'Carton' are also profitable. Apart from these cases, products that are sold in 'Carton' and 'Packet' (regardless of "Color") generally have low profit values (less than '1,500,000' for year).

The new parameter "Buying Package" was suggested by the application and selected to be in the scenario by the user. This business variable could be 'Carton', 'Packet' and 'Each', meaning that the buying package is made from carton and packet. The introduction of this variable is the main difference between the two approaches, with or without the integration of preferences.

4.3   Comparative Analysis

In this section we compare the outcome of both approaches presented: the outcome of the application of a conventional What-If analysis and the outcome of the application of our approach, the hybridization process. To compare the outcome of both approaches, we use the same What-If question: "What if we want to increase the sales profit by 10% focusing mainly on the most profitable products' color in 2016?".

Conventional What-If Analysis. Here, we consider the outcome of the application of a conventional What-If analysis. In the definition of the scenario, the user chose the business variables "Color" of products, "Sales Profit" in 2016 and then perform the What-If analysis.

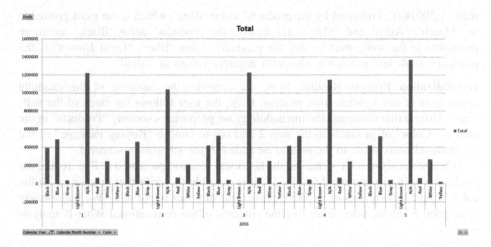

Fig. 16. Conventional what-if analysis - historical scenario.

In the Fig. 16 is possible to analyze the attributes "Profit" represented in the Y axis, with a range from '−200 000' to '1 600 000'; and represented by the X axis: "Calendar Year" '2016', "Month Number of Year" with a range of '1' to '5', which represents the months of a year, from 'January' to 'May'; and "Color" which can be 'Black', 'Red', 'Gray', 'Yellow', 'Blue', 'White', 'Light Brown' and 'N/A' (not available).

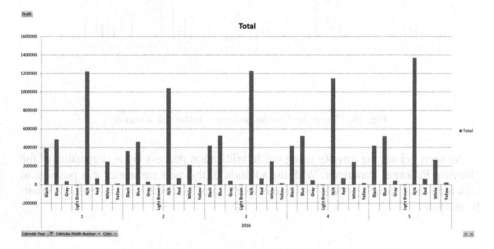

Fig. 17. Conventional what-if analysis – prediction scenario.

The Fig. 17 shows the prediction scenario, revealing that in '2016', products with 'N/A' color are the most profitable and it is the product color that earn more money, especially in 'May', 'March' and 'January', respectively; showing profit vales over than '1,200,000'. Followed by the products' color 'Blue', which is the most profitable in 'March', 'April' and 'May'; and finally, the products' color 'Black' are more profitable in the same months that the products' color 'Blue'. 'Light Brown' is the products' color less profitable, also with negative values in '2016'.

Hybridization Process Results. Now, we consider the outcome of the example application of our hybridization process. Here, the user follows the steps of the software platform that illustrates the methodology we proposed: choosing "Products" in the step 1, "Color" of products in the step 2 and opt to choose "Buying Package" of the recommendations made to the user to be added in the simulation scenario.

When we analyze both scenarios, the historical scenario presented in Fig. 16 and the prediction scenario presented in Fig. 17, it is possible to verify that products with the color 'Light Brown' shows negative profit. But this fact is not new. We had already concluded it before, when analyzing the outcome of the conventional What-If analysis process.

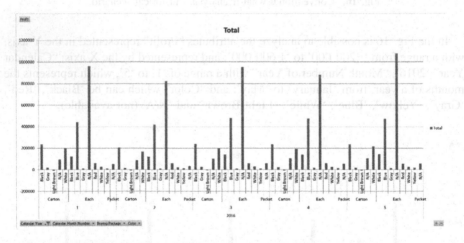

Fig. 18. The hybridization process – historical scenario.

As seen before, the novelty using our hybridization process is the suggestion of the "Buying Package" parameter. With the addition of this new parameter it is possible to conclude more facts beyond what we previously conclude with the conventional What-If analysis.

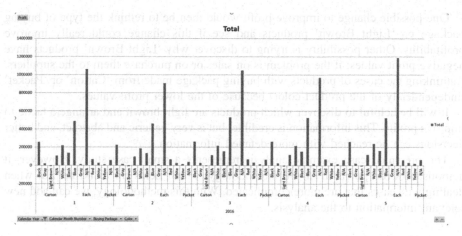

Fig. 19. The hybridization process – prediction scenario.

With the analysis of Fig. 18 and Fig. 19, and similar to the conventional What-If outcome analysis, we can conclude that products with unknown color or not available information about color 'N/A' are the most profitable in 'May', 'March' and 'January'. The information that was hidden from the user in the conventional What-If analysis and now it is possible to conclude that the most profitable products with 'N/A' color were sold with "Each type" buying packages: Products with unknown color or 'N/A' with 'Each type' buying packages are the most profitable products (with profit values over '1,000,000' in 'January', 'March' and 'May'), comparing to 'N/A' color products with 'Carton' and 'Packet' (less than '120,000'), which are less profitable.

Following the 'N/A' color products, the products' color 'Blue' are the second most profitable, especially in 'May', 'April' and 'March' (over '500,000'). This fact is already stated in the last analysis, in the conventional What-If analysis outcome. The novelty here is the fact that the most profitable 'Blue' products were sold with "Each type" buying packages. Another fact that we can analyze is that 'Blue' products sold in 'Carton' and 'Packet' buying packages do not show any profit values.

The products' color 'Black', similar to the previous analysis, are the third most profitable products in 'May', 'April' and 'March' (over '250,000'). The novelty here is that the most profitable 'Black' products were sold with 'Carton' buying packages. This information is hidden in the conventional What-If outcome analysis. Also, 'White' products with buying package made from 'Carton' are also profitable (over '200,000' in 'May', 'April' and 'March'). Apart from these cases, products that are sold in 'Carton' and 'Packet' (regardless of "Color") generally have low profit values (less than '150,000').

Thus, we can conclude that regardless the color, the buying package ('Carton' or 'Packet') influence the negatively the profit. Finally, and already known fact is that 'Light Brown' products have negative profit values. The new information that we can include in this last fact is that 'Light Brown' products have buying package made from 'Carton'.

One possible change to improve profit would then be to rethink the type of buying package on 'Light Brown' products and see if this change could really improve profitability. Other possibility is trying to discover why 'Light Brown' products have negative profit values: if the problem is on sales or on purchase them to the suppliers. Rethinking the cases of products with buying package made from 'Carton' or 'Packet' (independently of the product color) because of the lower profit values.

It will be helpful to discover which products are light brown and arrange a tactic to improve profits. This information is credible, but is very generic and abstract, and better decisions can be reached with more detailed information.

The presented case example analysis represents a small case study. However, it demonstrates the potential of the methodology, which helps up to be helpful when dealing with cases that are more complicated. With this methodology, we can add new relevant information to the analysis.

5   Conclusions

This paper presented a hybrid methodology that can be used for discovering the best recommendations for What-If analysis scenarios' parameters using OLAP usage preferences. This methodology introduces a recommendation engine for assisting users during decision-support analysis processes. The main difference between the approach we propose and a conventional What-If analysis method is to become possible to simulate a system behavior based on past data extracted from OLAP sessions. In other words, our approach integrates the process of extraction of usage preferences in the conventional What-If analysis, forming a hybridization approach. The recommendation engine mainly aims at improving the conventional What-If Analysis process.

The hybridization process suggests OLAP preferences to users, providing more suitable parameters to be included in the scenario in a What-If analysis process. In more detail, this methodology process helps the user by suggesting new axes of analysis, which are obtained using the association rules algorithm and consequently are variables that often appear with the goal analysis in the data set. Therefore, the process suggest these axes of analysis to the user as parameters to be added to the What-If scenario. These axes cannot otherwise be discovered using a manual analysis. At the end, this integration helps analysts by adding new relevant information to What-If scenarios. This contributes significantly to enrich a What-If scenario for a particular business domain.

The choice of the scenario parameters is one of the phases of the conventional What-If analysis that may be quite difficult to a user. A user that is not familiar with the data, may choose wrong or inadequate parameters to add to the scenario. Following the hybridization methodology, the experience of this phase is facilitated. Instead of making the wrong choices or choosing only the scenario parameters included in the What-If question, the hybridization process finds and recommends a set of axes of analysis to the user. Thus, it is possible to the user to add relevant and important information to the scenario, which in a default or usual situation would not be done.

Using usage preferences as recommendations in the hybridization process, the user does not need to know in detail the business domain. Preferences can be defined based on historical data provided from a data mining system. Preferences have the ability to suggest to the user the axes of analysis that are related to the goal analysis, helping him to introduce valuable information in the application scenario he is building. Another advantage that comes with using preferences is that usage preferences can also help to control the returned information, providing access to relevant information, eliminating the irrelevant one. Knowing beforehand usage preferences can have a significant impact on the outcome results of the analytical system. It is possible to provide exactly the most relevant and useful information to each specific user in a specific analysis scenario.

Due to this, query runtime can be enhanced against cases without preferences. There is a significant reduction of the cube implementation costs, processing time and memory usage. The cube will include in its structure only the data that match user preferences and so it will return only the data that interest to user. Moreover, the entire analysis process can be improved. As already noticed, a cube is a very complex data structure and it can be difficult for an analyst to acquire the information he wants. With a simple interface having the ability to recommend the right queries based on the history of past analytical sessions, makes much simpler the process of extracting information. Consequently, using this process, the user can get more focused and refined results, which helps both a user who is not familiar with the business analysis and an analyst who is familiar with the business modelling data.

Nevertheless, we also recognized some limitations that need to be overcome, in order to make the system more efficient, especially at the level of the usage of Microsoft Office Excel functions and within the What-If process itself. Additionally, we need to free the system from some limitations imposed by user's choices and decisions, which are needed in the most parts of the What-If process. This must be avoided, because a user that has limited knowledge about the business domain or even about the simulation process to be implemented influences the entire process negatively, leading consequently to poor results.

This methodology is still dependent on the user. It is the user's responsibility to choose the goal attribute for the analysis. So, if the goal analysis is not done correctly, What-If questions and consequently scenarios will not be correctly defined, and the preferences outcome will not be reliable. What-If Analysis results depend strongly from the data we want to analyze. If it contains some errors, which is a very common situation, the result will not be very useful; to set support and confidence measures and the choice of the set of strong association rules that will form the preferences. These situations influence the filtered set of association rules and consequently the set of preferences. If these steps are done in a wrong manner, the outcome might be inadequate. To overcome these problems, preventive measures were taken. In the filter process, the application suggests default measures for the support and confidence measures. With this, we can guarantee that the outcome is not null and there is at least one rule in the outcome. A solution relatively to the user's choice of strong rules is to automatically choose the set of top 5 strong association rules to form the set of preferences. Finally, as a future work, we intend to overcome the described drawbacks and mainly aim at restructuring automatically the What-If scenarios, in order to discard user dependency.

Acknowledgments. This work has been supported by FCT–Fundação para a Ciência e Tecnologia within the R&D Units Project Scope: UIDB/00319/2020.

References

1. Golfarelli, M., Rizzi, S. Proli, A.: Designing what-if analysis: towards a methodology. In: DOLAP 2006, Arlington, Virginia, USA, pp. 51–58 (2006)
2. Harinarayan, V., Rajaraman, A., Ullman, J.: Implementing data cubes efficiently. ACM SIGMOD Rec. **25**(2), 205–216 (1996)
3. Golfarelli, M., Rizzi, S.: Expressing OLAP preferences. In: Winslett, Marianne (ed.) SSDBM 2009. LNCS, vol. 5566, pp. 83–91. Springer, Heidelberg (2009). https://doi.org/10.1007/978-3-642-02279-1_7
4. Jerbi, H., Ravat, F., Teste, O., Zurfluh, G.: Preference-based recommendations for OLAP analysis. In: Pedersen, T.B., Mohania, M.K., Tjoa, A.M. (eds.) DaWaK 2009. LNCS, vol. 5691, pp. 467–478. Springer, Heidelberg (2009). https://doi.org/10.1007/978-3-642-03730-6_37
5. Carvalho, M., Belo, O.: Enriching what-if scenarios with OLAP usage preferences. In: Proceedings of The 8th International Conference on Knowledge Discovery and Information Retrieval (KDIR 2016), Porto, Portugal, 9–11 November (2016)
6. Carvalho, M., Belo, O.: The added value of OLAP preferences in what-if applications. In: Proceedings of The 11th International Conference on Knowledge Discovery and Information Retrieval (KDIR 2019), Vienna, Austria, 17–19 September (2019)
7. Kottemann, J.E., Boyer-Wright, K.M., Kincaid, J.F., Davis, F.D.: Understanding decision-support effectiveness: a computer simulation approach. IEEE Trans. Syst. Man Cybern.-Part: Syst. Hum. **39**(1), 57–65 (2009)
8. Zhou, G., Chen, H.: What-if analysis in MOLAP environments. In: Sixth International Conference on Fuzzy Systems and Knowledge Discovery, 2009. FSKD 2009, vol. 2, pp. 405–409. IEEE (2009)
9. Golfarelli, M., Rizzi, S.: What-if simulation modeling in business intelligence. In: Business Information Systems: Concepts, Methodologies, Tools and Applications, pp. 2229–2247. IGI Global (2010)
10. Gavanelli, M., Milano, M., Holland, A., O'Sullivan, B.: What-if analysis through simulation-optimization hybrids. In: ECMS, pp. 624–630 (2012)
11. Xu, H., Luo, H., He, J.: What-if query processing policy for big data in OLAP system. In: Advanced Cloud and Big Data (CBD), 2013 International Conference, pp. 110–116. IEEE (2013)
12. Hung, N.Q.V., Tam, N.T., Weidlich, M., Thang, D.C., Zhou, X.: What-if analysis with conflicting goals: recommending data ranges for exploration. In: Proceedings of the VLDB Endowment, vol. 10, no. 5 (2017)
13. Deutch, D., Ives, Z.G., Milo, T., Tannen, V.: Caravan: provisioning for what-if analysis. In: CIDR. ISO 690 (2013)
14. Saxena, G., Narula, R., Mishra, M.: New Dimension Value Introduction for In-Memory What-If Analysis. arXiv preprint arXiv:1302.0351 (2013)
15. Hartmann, T., Fouquet, F., Moawad, A., Rouvoy, R., Traon, Y.L. GreyCat: Efficient What-If Analytics for Data in Motion at Scale. arXiv preprint arXiv:1803.09627 (2018)
16. Herodotou, H., Babu, S.: A what-if engine for cost-based mapreduce optimization. IEEE Data Eng. Bull. **36**(1), 5–14 (2013)

17. Shao, G., Brodsky, A., Shin, S.J., Kim, D.B.: Decision guidance methodology for sustainable manufacturing using process analytics formalism. J. Intell. Manufact. **28**(2), 455–472 (2014). https://doi.org/10.1007/s10845-014-0995-3
18. Han, J.: OLAP mining: An integration of OLAP with data mining. In: Proceedings of the 7th IFIP, pp. 1–9 (1997)
19. Microsoft Visual Studio, Visual Studio - Best-in-class tools for any developer. https://visualstudio.microsoft.com/. Accessed 28 Jan 2020
20. Agrawal, R., Srikant, R. Fast algorithms for mining association rules. In: Proceedings of 20th International Conference Very Large Data Bases, VLDB, vol. 1215, pp. 487–499 (1994)
21. SQL Server Blog. https://cloudblogs.microsoft.com/sqlserver/2016/06/09/wideworldimporters-the-new-sql-server-sample-database/. Accessed 5 Mar 2017
22. Kimball, R.: The Data Warehouse Toolkit: The Definitive Guide to Dimensional Modeling. John Wiley & Sons, Hoboken (2013)
23. Microsoft Office Excel. https://products.office.com/en/excel. Accessed 28 Jan 2020

A Hybrid Sliding Window Based Method for Stream Classification

Engin Maden[✉] and Pinar Karagoz

Department of Computer Engineering, Middle East Technical University (METU),
Ankara, Turkey
{engin.maden,karagoz}@ceng.metu.edu.tr

Abstract. The resources of time and memory space are limited in data stream classification process. Hence, one should read the data only once and it is not possible to store the history as a whole. Therefore, when dealing with data streams, classification approaches in traditional data mining fall short and several enhancements are needed. In the literature, there are stream classifications methods such as stream based versions of nearest neighbor, decision tree based or neural network based methods. In our previous work, we proposed m-kNN (Mean Extended k-Nearest Neighbors) and CSWB (Combined Sliding Window Based) classifiers and presented the accuracy performances in comparison to other data stream classification methods from the literature. In this work, we present two new versions of CSWB, *CSWB-e* and *CSWB-e2*, such that our m-kNN classifier is combined with K* (K-Star) and C4.5, and with K* (K-Star) and Naive Bayes, respectively. In the experiments, accuracy of m-kNN, CSWB-e and CSWB-e2 are analyzed with new data sets in order to observe the relationship between window size and the accuracy. Additionally, the classification performance results for m-kNN are further analyzed and reported in precision, recall and f-score metrics in addition to accuracy.

Keywords: Data stream mining · Classification · Sliding window · Hybrid classifier · Ensemble · CSWB-e · CSWB-e2 · m-kNN · C4.5 · K*

1 Introduction

Due to improvements in hardware technology in recent years, it is possible to collect continuous data from different resources. Daily life activities such as using mobile phone or payment with credit card lead to production of large volumes of continuous data. Such data can be mined to extract interesting and valuable information for various applications. However, processing large volume of continuous data can cause several challenges as [1]:

- It is not possible to pass the data more than once. This is a constraint for the implementation of data stream algorithms.

© Springer Nature Switzerland AG 2020
A. Fred et al. (Eds.): IC3K 2019, CCIS 1297, pp. 94–107, 2020.
https://doi.org/10.1007/978-3-030-66196-0_5

- The data may evolve over time and the stream mining algorithms should be designed to deal with this evolution of data.

In order to work with infinite and continuous data, *sliding window* mechanism is a commonly used approach. We can define a *window* as a set of stream elements within a certain time frame. Sliding windowing has two basic types: *time-based* and *count-based*. In count-based sliding windows, the borders of windows are specified with the counts of instances lying inside the windows. On the other hand, in time-based sliding window mechanisms, the borders are determined by using a time interval [3]. In our previous work [10], we proposed a sliding window based method called *m-kNN*. In m-kNN, we used the conventional kNN within a sliding window, and as an enhancement, one of the k-nearest neighbors is obtained among the centroids of the classes. These centroids indicate the mean values of the features for the classes. In m-kNN, the class having the nearest centroid for the incoming instance is determined and its centroid is utilized as the kth nearest neighbor. Another novelty proposed was a hybrid method, *Combined Sliding Window based Classifier (CSWB)*, combining m-kNN, conventional kNN, and Naive Bayes.

In this work, we propose two new version of CSWB, namely *CSWB-e* and *CSWB-e2*. We conducted experiments on these two hybrid methods for accuracy performance analysis. Additionally, we extended the analysis of m-kNN method on new data sets and under additional classification performance metrics. We can list the contributions of this work as follows:

- The first new version of Combined Sliding Window based Classifier, *CSWB-e*, combines m-kNN with two other methods from the literature, K* and C4.5 algorithms, in a sliding window. The other new version, *CSWB-e2*, is composed of m-kNN, K* and Naive Bayes.
- The performance of *CSWB-e* and *CSWB-e2* are analyzed in comparison to the individual stream classifiers and the previous version, *CSWB*.
- We analyzed the correctness of *m-kNN* further on three data sets: Avila, Poker Hand and LandSat Satillite data sets.
- We extended the analysis for *m-kNN* with additional metrics of precision, recall and f-score.
- Literature survey is extended with additional recent related work.

The rest of the chapter is organized as follows: In Sect. 2, related studies in the literature are summarized. In Sect. 3, an overview of our previous methods, m-kNN and CSWB, which form the basis for this work, is given. In Sect. 4, the new hybrid stream classifiers, CSWB-e and CSWB-e2, are described. In Sect. 5, the experiments and results are presented. The chapter is concluded with an overview of the work and the results in Sect. 6.

2   Related Work

In literature, there is a variety of studies and algorithms developed to deal with data streams in classification, ranging from distance based nearest neighbor approaches, decision tree based solutions to assembler methods that aim to improve the classification performance by combining several methods. One of such assembler method is gEBoost (graph Ensemble Boosting), which classifies imbalanced graph streams with noise. This method partitions the graph stream into chunks where each chunk contains noisy graphs having imbalanced class distributions. A boosting algorithm for each chunk is proposed to combine the selection of discriminative sub-graph pattern. Combination of the chunks forms a unified framework as a learning model for graph classification [11].

As an example to nearest neighbor based methods, MC-NN utilizes statistical summaries of the data stream. In this method, statistical summaries are processed incrementally and it aims to handle concept drifts as well. Additionally, MC-NN has a parallel version, in order to improve efficiency [16].

In [9], VHT method applies vertical parallelism on the features of streaming data. In this method, vertical parallelism divides the instances into partitions with respect to the attributes in order to process the stream more efficiently.

Fuzzy methods can be also utilized in data stream classification. In [14], Silva et al. propose an extension for On-Demand classification algorithm developed by Aggarwal et al. [2]. They include the concepts of fuzzy sets theory and they aim to improve the adaptability of the classification process to changes in data stream.

Yang et al. present an ensemble Extreme Learning Machine (ELPM) that includes a concept drift detection method. The authors utilize online sequence learning strategy in order to handle gradual concept drift. In thier work, it is reported that their ELM algorithm improves the accuracy results for classification and also can adapt to new concepts in a shorter time [18].

In [17], Wozniak et al. propose a data stream classifier based on sliding windows. Their method contains a novel classifier training algorithm and it includes a *forgetting mechanism*. The authors choose *interesting* objects to be labeled by using active learning.

ADWIN (ADaptive WINdowing) also maintains a window for processing data streams but the window has a variable size. ADWIN2 is the improved version for memory usage and time efficiency. In [4], it is proposed to make a combination of ADWIN2 and the Naive Bayes classifiers.

PAW (Probabilistic Adaptive Window) is another windowing based stream learning approach [6]. It contains older samples from dataset as well as the most recent ones. This leads a quick adaptation to new concept drifts and also it enables to maintain information about past concept drifts.

In [7], Bifet et al. propose STREAM DM-C++, which is a framework where decision trees for data streams area implemented in C++. This framework is easy to extend and it includes powerful ensemble methods.

Data stream classification methods can be applied to several domains. Among them, finance includes several interesting sub-problems. Credit card fraud detection or risk assessment for credit are well-known examples of financial application areas for data stream classification. Sousa et al. propose a new dynamic modeling framework which can be used in credit risk assessment. Their framework extend the credit scoring models and they apply it to a real-world data set of credit cards from a financial institution in Brazil [15].

In [13], Shi et al. consider identification of human factors in aviation incidents as another application area for the data stream classification methods. They use four data stream algorithms, Naive Bayes, Very Fast Decision Tree (VFDT), OzaBagADWIN (OBA) and Cost Sensitive Classifier (CSC), which are implemented in MOA (Massive Online Analysis) framework [5].

Our methods for data stream classification, m-kNN and $CSWB$, are sliding window based methods and they are similar to PAW or ADWIN in this aspect. The main difference of our m-kNN method is that we select a nearest neighbor from the historical data and thus, we can associate the past and current behaviour of stream. On the other hand, CSWB an assembler for data stream classification. It differs from other ensemble method in the way singleton classifiers are combined. In CSWB, m-kNN is combined with other classifiers in the literature in a sliding window.

3   Background Information

In our previous work [10], we presented two enhancements for data stream classification approaches. Our first method, m-kNN, is a distance based nearest neighbor classifier. It is based on conventional kNN in a sliding window mechanism. In kNN the prediction for the next incoming sample is made by searching the training samples that are previously classified. After that the first k most similar instances, which are the nearest neighbors for our incoming sample to be classified, are obtained, the sample is classified according to majority voting among these k nearest neighbors. The main difference between m-knn and the conventional kNN is at the selection of the last nearest neighbor for the incoming instance. In m-kNN, we select the k-1 nearest neighbors from the current window. We keep the centroids of the classes as instances and select the kth nearest neighbor from these centroids.

This last nearest neighbor belongs to the class that has the nearest centroid to the incoming sample. We use Euclidean distance for similarity calculation. While sliding the window, it is assumed that the actual class label is available. Hence we update the representative of the class according to this information. To slide the current window, we remove the oldest instance and push this instance into the head of the window. The sliding window mechanism in m-kNN helps us to deal with the concept drift and evolution of data stream [10].

CSWB classifier is our second enhancement, which combines m-kNN, Naive Bayes and conventional kNN classifiers in a sliding window. We use two versions of voting mechanism to obtain the final result of the classification. One of them is majority voting with equal weights. In this voting schema, if two of the classifiers produce the same result, the sample is assigned to their decision. If there is a tie between the decisions of these classifiers, then Naive Bayes makes the final decision since it has higher accuracy results in our experiments. Our second voting mechanism is voting with current accuracy. In this voting procedure, we keep the accuracy values for classifiers and sum up the accuracy of classifiers having the same decision for the incoming sample. Then we assign the incoming sample to the class having the highest accuracy value [10].

4   Extended Hybrid Stream Classifiers: CSWB-e and CSWB-e2

In this paper, we propose two new versions of CSWB where we use new classifiers together with m-kNN. In CSWB-e, m-kNN is combined with K* (K-Star) and C4.5. In CSWB-e2, in addition to m-kNN, K* and Naive Bayes classifier are used. The motivation for including Naive Bayes in CSWB-e2 is based on our previous observation [10] that it contributed well to the performance of CSWB.

The first newly added classifier is K*, which is a nearest neighbor based classifier [8]. In K*, entropy is used as the distance measure. The approach to calculate the distance between two instances is inspired from information theory, and the main idea is that this distance can be viewed as the complexity of transforming one instance into another.

The second classifier that we included in our hybrid model is C4.5 [12], which is a decision tree based classifier, and is the successor of the ID3 algorithm. The algorithm uses the concept of information entropy for node selection. For each node of the decision tree, C4.5 selects the attribute that most effectively splits list of the training data samples. To this aim, C4.5 selects the attribute with the highest information gain. This process is applied recursively on the partitioned data.

As in CSWB, in CSWB-e and in CSWB-e2, we may consider two different voting schemata in the assembler. In [10], it was already shown that the voting under *current accuracy* model performed well. Hence in our experiments, we use voting with current accuracy schema among the participating classifiers.

5   Experiments

In our previous work [10], we compared the classification accuracy performance of m-kNN against MC-NN [16] and VHT [9]. We analyzed CSWB classifier on several real-world and synthetic data sets. We compared the accuracy performance of CSWB in comparison to kNN and Naive Bayes when applied as individual classifiers.

In this work, we conducted two new sets of experiments. In the first one, we analyzed the effect of window size parameter on three new data sets for m-kNN. Additionally, we detailed the analysis on one of the data sets in terms of precision, recall and f-Score metrics. In the second experiment, we analyzed the accuracy performance of CSWB-e and CSWB-e2 under different parameter settings against m-kNN, K*, C4.5, Naive Bayes classifier and CSWB.

5.1 Analysis on the Effect of Window Size for M-KNN

In our first experiment, we analyzed the accuracy of m-kNN on three new data sets:

- **Avila:** This is data set includes 800 images of the "Avila Bible" which is a giant Latin copy of the whole Bible and produced during the XII century between Italy and Spain. The pages are written by 12 copyist and each pattern has 10 features. The data have been normalized by using Z-normalization method. There are 10430 samples in training data set and 10437 samples in testing data set[1].
- **Poker Hand:** In this data set, there are records representing a hand of five playing cards drawn from a standard deck of 52. Each of the cards has two attributes as suit and rank. Therefore there are 10 predictive attributes in the data set. The last attribute for an instance is the class describing the *Poker Hand*[2].
- **Landsat Satellite:** This data set contains multi-spectral values of pixels by 3×3 neighborhood in a satellite image. There are 6435 instances in this data set and each line contains the pixel values in the four spectral bands of each of the 9 pixels in 3×3 neighborhood. The label of each instance shows the classification of the central pixel[3].

In order to analyze the effect of window size on the classification accuracy, m-kNN is run under several window size values for $k = 5$ and $k = 10$ parameters. The window size values we have used in this experiment are $\{10, 20, 30, 40, 50, 75, 100, 200, 300, 500\}$.

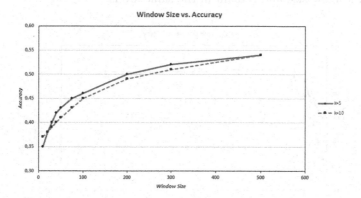

Fig. 1. Accuracy performance for m-kNN on Avila data set under varying window size values with k = 5 and k = 10.

---

[1] https://archive.ics.uci.edu/ml/datasets/Avila.

[2] https://archive.ics.uci.edu/ml/datasets/Poker+Hand.

[3] https://archive.ics.uci.edu/ml/datasets/Statlog+%28Landsat+Satellite%29.

The accuracy values of m-kNN for Avila data set under increasing window sizes can be seen in Fig. 1. In the figure it is seen that the accuracy values are increasing smoothly with the increase in window size and reach the top value for *window size = 500*. The behaviour of the results are similar for *k = 5* and *k = 10* values but the slopes are slightly different.

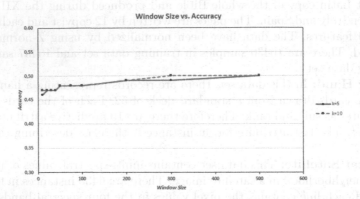

Fig. 2. Accuracy performance for m-kNN on Poker Hand data set under varying window size values with k = 5 and k = 10.

In Fig. 2, the accuracy values of m-kNN for Poker Hand data set under varying window size values are presented. According to the results, the accuracy values for Poker Hand data set is increasing with window size values for both *k = 10* and *k = 10* values but in some steps the accuracy is not affected by the change in window size and remain in the same levels.

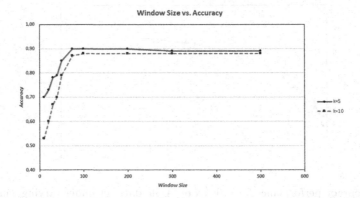

Fig. 3. Accuracy performance for m-kNN on Landsat Satellite data set under varying window size values with k = 5 and k = 10.

In Fig. 3, we can see the accuracy values for Landsat Satellite data set. The results reveal that the accuracy values are increasing in proportional to the window size values up to 100 and this is the maximum value for Landsat Satellite data set. After that the accuracy values remains the same and the trend is similar for both of the $k = 10$ and $k = 10$ values. We can conclude that, for this data set, the classification accuracy is less sensitive to the change in the window size.

The accuracy performance of m-kNN for these data sets is compared against two other methods, MC-NN and VHT, which were used for comparison also in [10]. The comparison of the results for m-kNN, MC-NN and VHT are given Fig. 4. In this analysis, we consider the best window size settings, which were determined in the above mentioned experiments. The results show that m-kNN gives the highest accuracy results for Avila and Landsat Satellite data sets, while the VHT has the highest accuracy value for Poker Hand data set, yet the accuracy value for m-kNN is close to VHT for this data set.

We further analyzed the classification performance for Landset Satellite data set in terms of precision, recall and f-Score metrics. We focused on *Cotton Crop*, *Grey Soil* and *Red Soil* classes, which have higher occurance in the data set.

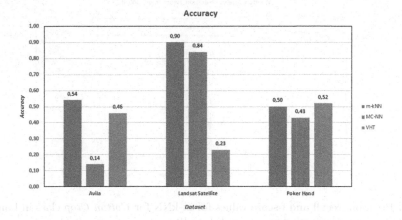

Fig. 4. Comparison of accuracy performance of the methods for Avila, Landsat Satellite and Poker Hand data sets.

The precision, recall and f-Score values for *Cotton Crop* class in Landsat Satellite data set under varying window size is given in Fig. 5 and Fig. 6. According to the results, with $k = 5$, the recall and f-Score values are increasing up to *window size = 100*. On the other hand, precision has a different behavior such that an increase is followed by a decrease and then stable value. F-score value remains around the same level where recall continues to increase up to *window size = 300*. For $k = 10$, we see a similar yet smoother increase and stability in all three metrics.

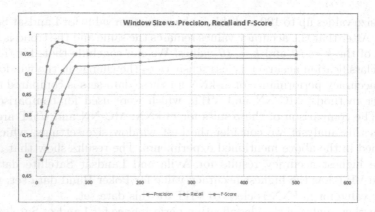

Fig. 5. Precison, recall and f-score values for m-kNN for *Cotton Crop* class in Landsat Satellite under varying window size with k = 5.

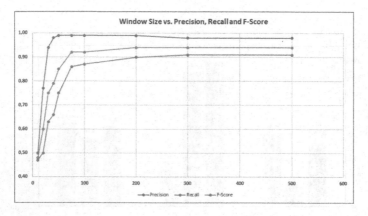

Fig. 6. Precison, recall and f-score values for m-kNN for *Cotton Crop* class in Landsat Satellite under varying window size with k = 10.

The precision, recall and f-score results for *Grey Soil* class under $k = 5$ and $k = 10$ are presented in Fig. 7 and Fig. 8. According to the results, with $k = 5$, the values are increasing up to *window size* $= 75$. Then for all the metrics, the values remain stable followed by a decrease as the window size gets larger. The amount of decrease is observed to be higher for precision. The results reveal that the gap between the precision, recall and f-Score values is smaller under $k = 10$.

The precision, recall and F-Score values of m-kNN for "Red Soil" class in Landsat Satellite data set changing with the window size can be seen in Fig. 9 and Fig. 10. For the first graph for "Red Soil" class in Landsat Satellite data set, the values are increasing up to *window size* $= 75$ and then goes on a straight line where recall continues to increase up to *window size* $= 100$ and then meets the same line with precision and F-score. For the second graph recall and F-Score increases up to *window size* $= 100$ and precision has a decrease after *window size* $= 100$. Then these three values get closer up to *window size* $= 500$.

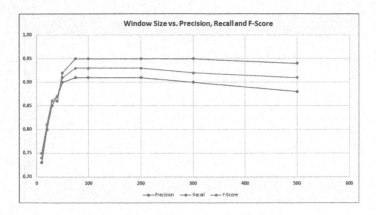

Fig. 7. Precison, recall and f-score values for m-kNN for *Grey Soil* class in Landsat Satellite under varying window size with k = 5.

As a summary, it is observed that the accuracy and other three metric of precision, recall and f-score values increase in parallel to the increase in the window size up to certain values. The stability points change for each data set.

5.2   Analysis on Accuracy Performance of CSWB-e and CSWB-e2

In our next set of experiments, we investigate the accuracy performance of the proposed hybrid methods, *CSWB-e* and *CSWB-e2*, under parameters of k {5, 10} and varying window sizes in comparison to individual classifiers and *CSWB*. We have used the data sets from [10], which are Air Quality[4], Appliances Energy

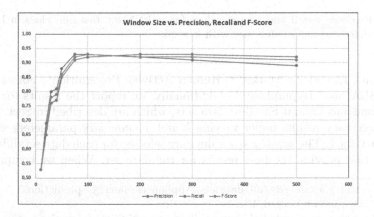

Fig. 8. Precison, recall and f-score values for m-kNN for *Grey Soil* class in Landsat Satellite under varying window size with k = 10.

---

[4] https://archive.ics.uci.edu/ml/datasets/Air+quality.

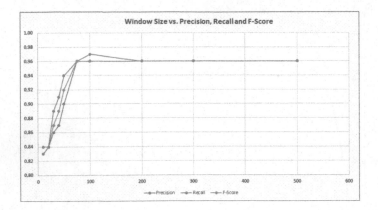

Fig. 9. Precison, recall and f-score values for m-kNN for *Red Soil* class in Landsat Satellite under varying window size with k = 5.

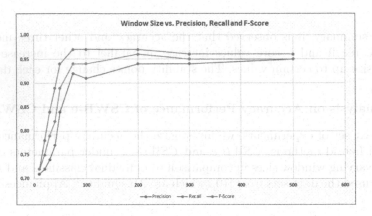

Fig. 10. Precison, recall and f-score values for m-kNN for *Red Soil* class in Landsat Satellite under varying window size with k = 10.

Prediction[5], Electricity Market [6], Human Activity Recognition[7], Forest Cover Type[8], SEA[9] and Hyperplane[10]. Additionally, we report the results for Avila, Poker Hand and Landat Satellite data sets, which are described in Sect. 5.1.

The accuracy results under varying *k* and *window size* parameters are presented in Table 1. The *window size* values are selected for each data set differently as those that provide the best results for the data set. When we compare the

---

[5] https://archive.ics.uci.edu/ml/datasets/Appliances+energy+prediction.

[6] https://www.openml.org/d/151.

[7] https://archive.ics.uci.edu/ml/datasets/human+activity+recognition+using+smart phones.

[8] https://archive.ics.uci.edu/ml/datasets/Covertype.

[9] http://www.liaad.up.pt/kdus/downloads/sea-concepts-dataset.

[10] https://www.win.tue.nl/~mpechen/data/DriftSets/hyperplane1.arff.

Table 1. Accuracy performance comparison for CSWB, CSWB-e and CSWB-e2.

Dataset	k	Win.size	m-kNN	K*	C4.5	CSWB	CSWB-e	CSWB-e2
AirQual	5	250	0.77	**0.79**	0.75	0.74	**0.79**	**0.79**
AirQual.	10	250	0.77	**0.79**	0.75	0.76	**0.79**	**0.79**
AirQual.	5	500	0.77	**0.79**	0.76	0.77	**0.79**	**0.79**
AirQual.	10	500	0.77	**0.79**	0.76	0.78	**0.79**	**0.79**
App.En.Pre.	5	25	0.64	**0.69**	0.65	0.64	0.67	0.67
App.En.Pre.	10	25	0.62	**0.69**	0.65	0.63	0.68	0.67
App.En.Pre.	5	50	0.64	**0.69**	0.65	0.63	0.67	0.66
App.En.Pre.	10	50	0.62	**0.69**	0.65	0.63	0.68	0.66
Elec.Mar.	5	25	0.77	0.90	**0.92**	0.76	0.81	0.79
Elec.Mar.	10	25	0.70	0.90	**0.92**	0.77	0.81	0.79
Elec.Mar.	5	50	0.78	**0.91**	**0.91**	0.77	0.81	0.80
Elec.Mar.	10	50	0.73	**0.91**	**0.91**	0.78	0.81	0.79
Hum.Act.Rec.	5	250	0.91	0.38	0.93	0.76	**0.94**	0.91
Hum.Act.Rec.	10	250	0.88	0.38	0.93	0.75	**0.94**	0.89
Hum.Act.Rec.	5	500	0.92	0.37	0.93	0.89	**0.94**	0.92
Hum.Act.Rec.	10	500	0.91	0.37	0.93	0.91	**0.94**	0.91
For.Cov.Type	5	250	0.86	**0.93**	0.87	0.84	0.91	0.90
For.Cov.Type	10	250	0.81	**0.93**	0.87	0.83	0.91	0.87
For.Cov.Type	5	500	0.90	**0.94**	0.91	0.82	**0.94**	0.92
For.Cov.Type	10	500	0.87	**0.94**	0.91	0.87	0.93	0.91
SEA	5	250	0.81	0.82	0.82	0.79	**0.84**	**0.84**
SEA	10	250	0.83	0.82	0.82	**0.85**	0.84	**0.85**
SEA	5	500	0.82	0.84	0.84	0.84	0.85	**0.86**
SEA	10	500	0.85	0.84	0.84	0.82	**0.86**	**0.86**
Hyperplane	5	250	0.76	0.71	0.70	0.69	0.76	**0.81**
Hyperplane	10	250	0.80	0.71	0.70	0.78	0.81	**0.83**
Hyperplane	5	500	0.78	0.74	0.73	0.81	0.78	**0.83**
Hyperplane	10	500	0.82	0.74	0.73	0.83	0.78	**0.85**
Avila	5	300	0.52	0.56	0.57	0.52	**0.60**	0.56
Avila	10	300	0.51	0.56	0.57	0.51	**0.60**	0.56
Avila	5	500	0.54	0.61	0.62	0.55	**0.64**	0.60
Avila	10	500	0.54	0.61	0.62	0.54	**0.64**	0.60
PokerHand	5	300	**0.49**	0.46	0.45	**0.49**	0.48	**0.49**
PokerHand	10	300	**0.50**	0.46	0.45	0.49	0.49	0.49
PokerHand	5	500	**0.50**	0.46	0.45	0.49	0.49	0.49
PokerHand	10	500	**0.50**	0.46	0.45	0.49	0.49	050
Landsat Satellite	5	100	0.90	**0.92**	0.85	0.90	**0.92**	**0.92**
Landsat Satellite	10	100	0.88	**0.92**	0.85	0.88	0.91	0.91
Landsat Satellite	5	200	0.90	**0.91**	0.86	0.90	**0.91**	**0.91**
Landsat Satellite	10	200	0.88	**0.91**	0.86	0.88	**0.91**	**0.91**

results under the same the parameter values we can see that the proposed hybrid methods, CSWB-e and CSWB-e2, perform better in 6 of the 10 data sets, and in 26 of the 40 cases. In several of the data sets, individual classifiers perform better, but the accuracy performance of the proposed hybrid classifiers are very close. Hence, on the overall, we observe a preferable performance for the hybrid methods, providing good accuracy for any kind of data. Depending on the nature of the data set, the classification accuracy of *CSWB-e* and *CSWB-e2* may vary. In general, among *CSWB-e* and *CSWB-e2* there is almost a tie situation.

6   Conclusions

In this work, we focus on sliding window based stream classification problem and propose two hybrid methods. The hybrid methods, *CSWB-e* and *CSWB-e2*, are improvements over *m-kNN* and *CSWB-e* presented in [10]. For the hybrid methods, our motivation comes from our previous observation for improvement potential via new classifiers. To this aim, we included K^*, *C4.5*, as the new individual classifiers into the assemblers. The results show that the proposed hybrid methods, especially *CSWB-e2*, outperforms the other models.

As another contribution, we analyzed the performance of *m-kNN* algorithm further on additional three data sets. These data sets have different nature from those studied in [10]. Two of them are image data sets, whereas one of them is a streaming set of tuples that represent hands in a poker game. The results show that *m-kNN* provides good performance in comparison to two previous solutions in the literature. Our experiments investigate further details such as the effect of window size on classification performance, and precision, recall and f-score results per class.

For the future work, developing parallel versions of classifiers may be studied to reach a higher performance. Additionally, the proposed methods can be improved to deal with concept drift better. Mixed type data sets can be considered as an open research area for data streams, and working on enhancements for classification in mixed data environments can be another direction for research.

References

1. Aggarwal, C.C.: Data Streams: Models and Algorithms. Springer Science & Business Media, New York (2007)
2. Aggarwal, C.C., Han, J., Wang, J., Yu, P.S.: On demand classification of data streams. In: Proceedings of the tenth ACM SIGKDD international conference on Knowledge discovery and data mining, pp. 503–508 (2004)
3. Badiozamany, S.: Real-time data stream clustering over sliding windows. Ph.D. thesis, Acta Universitatis Upsaliensis (2016)
4. Bifet, A., Gavalda, R.: Learning from time-changing data with adaptive windowing. In: Proceedings of the 2007 SIAM international conference on data mining, pp. 443–448. SIAM (2007)
5. Bifet, A., Holmes, G., Kirkby, R., Pfahringer, B.: Moa: massive online analysis. J. Mach. Learn. Res. **11**, May 2010

6. Bifet, A., Pfahringer, B., Read, J., Holmes, G.: Efficient data stream classification via probabilistic adaptive windows. In: Proceedings of the 28th annual ACM symposium on applied computing, pp. 801–806. ACM (2013)

7. Bifet, A., et al.: Extremely fast decision tree mining for evolving data streams. In: Proceedings of the 23rd ACM SIGKDD International Conference on Knowledge Discovery and Data Mining, pp. 1733–1742 (2017)

8. Cleary, J.G., Trigg, L.E.: K*: an instance-based learner using an entropic distance measure. In: Machine Learning Proceedings, pp. 108–114. Elsevier (1995)

9. Kourtellis, N., Morales, G.D.F., Bifet, A., Murdopo, A.: Vht: vertical hoeffding tree. In: 2016 IEEE International Conference on Big Data (Big Data), pp. 915–922. IEEE (2016)

10. Maden., E., Karagoz., P.: Enhancements for sliding window based stream classification. In: Proceedings of the 11th International Joint Conference on Knowledge Discovery, Knowledge Engineering and Knowledge Management: KDIR, vol. 1, pp. 181–189. INSTICC, SciTePress (2019). https://doi.org/10.5220/0008356501810189

11. Pan, S., Wu, J., Zhu, X., Zhang, C.: Graph ensemble boosting for imbalanced noisy graph stream classification. IEEE Trans. Cybern. **45**(5), 954–968 (2014)

12. Quinlan, J.R.: C4.5: Programs for Machine Learning, 1st edn. Morgan Kaufmann, San Mateo, CA (1992)

13. Shi, D., Zurada, J., Guan, J.: Identification of human factors in aviation incidents using a data stream approach. In: Proceedings of the 50th Hawaii International Conference on System Sciences (2017)

14. da Silva, T.P., Urban, G.A., de Abreu Lopes, P., de Arruda Camargo, H.: A fuzzy variant for on-demand data stream classification. In: 2017 Brazilian Conference on Intelligent Systems (BRACIS), pp. 67–72. IEEE (2017)

15. Sousa, M.R., Gama, J., Brandão, E.: A new dynamic modeling framework for credit risk assessment. Expert Syst. Appl. **45**, 341–351 (2016)

16. Tennant, M., Stahl, F., Rana, O., Gomes, J.B.: Scalable real-time classification of data streams with concept drift. Future Gener. Comput. Syst. **75**, 187–199 (2017)

17. Woźniak, M., Ksieniewicz, P., Cyganek, B., Kasprzak, A., Walkowiak, K.: Active learning classification of drifted streaming data. Procedia Comput. Sci. **80**, 1724–1733 (2016)

18. Yang, R., Xu, S., Feng, L.: An ensemble extreme learning machine for data stream classification. Algorithms **11**(7), 107 (2018)

Beat the Streak: Prediction of MLB Base Hits Using Machine Learning

Pedro Alceo[✉] and Roberto Henriques[✉]

Nova Information Management School, Campus de Campolide, Lisbon, Portugal
{m20170412, roberto}@novaims.unl.pt

Abstract. As the world of sports expands to never seen levels, so does the necessity for tools that provided material advantages for organizations and stakeholders. The objective of this project is to develop a predictive model capable of predicting the odds a baseball player has to achieve a base hit on a given day. After that, using this information to both have a fair shot at winning the game *Beat the Streak* and providing valuable insights to the coaching staff. This project builds upon the work developed previously in Alceo and Henriques (2019), adding a full season of data, emphasizing new strategies, and displaying more data visualization content. The results achieved on the new season are aligned with the previous work where the best model, a Multi-layer Perceptron, developed in Python achieved an 81% correct pick ratio.

Keywords: Machine learning · Data mining · Predictive analysis · Classification model · Baseball · MLB

1 Introduction

In the past few years, the professional sports market has been growing impressively. Events such as the Super Bowl, the Summer Olympics and the UEFA Champions League are excellent examples of the dimension and global interest that can be generated by this industry currently. As the stakes grow and further money and other benefits are involved in the market, new technologies and methods surge to improve stakeholder success (Mordor Intelligence 2018).

The advancement most relevant for this field was the explosion of data creation and data storage systems, during the XXI century, which led to volumes of information that have never been so readily at our disposal before (Cavanillas, Curry and Wahlster 2016). Consequently, sports as many other industries could now use data to their advantage in their search for victory, and, thus the sports analytics began its ascension to the mainstream (Gera et al. 2016).

With the growth of sports popularity and, consequently, the information at our disposable for these events (Principe et al. 2017), so did the development of parallel industries such as gambling or betting. As a consequence, this growth in information was also useful for people outside the sports organizations that could make use of information technologies to develop models to both run betting companies or to gain money in sporting events by betting themselves (Mann 2018).

© Springer Nature Switzerland AG 2020
A. Fred et al. (Eds.): IC3K 2019, CCIS 1297, pp. 108–133, 2020.
https://doi.org/10.1007/978-3-030-66196-0_6

According to Mordor Intelligence (2018), the sport which currently takes the most advantage of sports analytics is baseball. This advantage is a consequence of historical events such as Moneyball, where the use of analytics proved to have significant effects on the outcome of the Oakland Athletics season, a baseball team that had the least budget to spend on players in the League. For most, Moneyball was the turning point in analytics and baseball, which opened the way for the use of analytics in both baseball and other sports (Lewis 2004).

In baseball, a player who can reliably achieve base hits is a valuable asset to help a team win games by both getting into scoring position and to help his other team-mates to score. Base hits are often the best result a player can achieve on an at-bat and thus the importance of knowing which can reliably achieve them.

Keeping this in mind, the objective of this project is to build a database and a data mining model capable of predicting which MLB batters are most likely to get a base hit on a given day. In the end, the output of the work can have two primary uses:

1. To give a methodical approach for coach's decision making and on what players should have an advantage on a given game and therefore make the starting line-up;
2. To improve one's probability of winning the game MLB Beat the Streak.

The dataset was built initially using data from the seasons 2015–2018 of the MLP, from open sources. For the project at hand, we added data from the 2019 season, used mainly as a test run of the previously built models. As for the granularity of the dataset, the samples are from the offensive perspective by game, i.e., a sample is a game from the batter's perspective. Finally, the main categories of the variables used in the models are:

- Batter Performance;
- Batter's Team Performance
- Opponent's Starting Pitcher;
- Opponent's Bullpen Performance;
- Weather Forecast;
- Ballpark Factors.

All in all, the output of the project will be a predictive model capable of fitting the data using one or more types of data mining tools, with the primary objective of maximizing precision on a day-by-day basis. Additionally, the results will be fine-tuned by strategies developed posterior of the models. The results will be analyzed with a variety of tools and compared with other similar work.

Some of the work done in this paper comes from our previous work done in Pedro Alceo and Roberto Henriques (2019). This paper improves the previous work by presenting further developments done in data visualization and a deeper understanding of the features used. Also, we performed tests of the previous models in newly extracted data from the 2019 season as well as proposed new betting strategies tests and a future outlook using a Monte Carlo simulation on the results achieved.

For this, we begin by presenting relevant work and essential concepts in Sect. 2. Section 3, 4 and 5 explain the Data Mining methodology implemented, from the creation of the dataset to the final models achieved. In Sect. 6, it is possible to analyze the most relevant results and insights from the best models. Finally, a brief conclusion is presented, summarizing the project and the most important discoveries found along with this paper and limitations on what points could still be further improved.

2   Background and Related Work

2.1   Sports Analytics

Sports and analytics have always had a close relationship as in most sports, both players and teams are measured by some form of statistics, which provides rankings for both players and teams.

Nowadays, most baseball studies using data mining tools focus on the financial aspects and profitability of the game. The understanding of baseball in-game events is often associated to sabermetrics: "the science of learning about baseball through objective evidence" (Wolf 2015). Most sabermetrics studies concentrate on understanding the value of an individual and, once again, are mainly used for commercial and organizational purposes. The reason behind the emphasis on the commercial side of the sport is that "it is a general agreement that predicting game outcome is one of the most difficult problems on this field" (Valero, C 2016) and operating data mining projects with excellent results often requires investments that demand financial return.

Apart from the financial aspects of the game, predictive modeling is used to try and predict the outcome of matches (which team wins a game or the number of wins a team achieves in a season) and predicting player's performance. The popularity of this practice grew due to the expansion of sports betting all around the world (Stekler, Sendor and Verlander 2010). The results of these models are often compared with the Las Vegas betting predictions, which are used as benchmarks for performance. Projects like these are used to increase earnings in betting but could additionally bring insights regarding various aspects of the game (Jia, Wong and Zeng 2013; Valero, C 2016).

2.2   Evolution of Sports Analytics

This chapter serves as a bridge that will connect the surge of sports statistics in the mid-20th century to the present. The main driver of this portion will be the identification and understanding of the central studies and events that led to the present concept of sports analytics.

In 1968, Charles Reep was the first data analyst connected to football and developed the base for football notation, which helps categorize each play in a match. Together with the statistician Bernard Benjamin, he looked for insights in 15 years' worth of matches using his notation. The study helped the development of football tactics, suggesting that a more direct style of football would be desirable (Reep and Benjamin 1968).

In 1977, Bill James was one of the pioneers in the application of statistics to several aspects of baseball. He defied traditional perceptions on how to evaluate players and highlighted the importance of creating runs versus basic statistics like hitting average and earned run average. His ideas captivated much interest, and he wrote numerous editions of The Baseball Abstract[1], where he presents advanced statistics and methods that are now considered the foundations for modern sabermetrics[2] (James 2001).

During the 1980s, Dean Oliver, inspired by Bill James sabermetrics, began developing analysis on basketball players' performance and their contribution to the team. His research and commitment originated what is now known as APBRmetrics[3]. Due to his significant developments and achievements, in 2004, he was hired as the first full-time statistical analyst in the NBA (Oliver 2004).

Even with the success of Reep, Benjamin, Oliver, and James sports analytics never settled inside sports organizations until the recent event commonly known as Moneyball. Billy Beane and Peter Brand used sabermetrics and other analytics tools to create a roster of players, which were considerate not very good for most teams and reached the playoffs in one of the most exciting seasons in MLB history (Lewis 2004). This event was for most the turning point for the use of analytics in sports.

A recent example of sports analytics, taking a team to the next level, is the history of the Houston Astros road to win over the Los Angeles Dodgers in the 2017 World Series[4]. The Houston Astros had consecutive losing records from 2011 to 2014, where they traded away their star players and veterans for future benefits, also known as tanking[5], which with the use of a data-driven mentally led them to the top of Major League Baseball (Sheinin 2017).

2.3 Statcast

Statcast is a relatively new data source implemented in 2015 across all MLB parks. According to MLB.com Glossary (MLB 2018), "Statcast is a state-of-the-art tracking technology that allows for the collection and analysis of a massive amount of baseball data, in ways that were never possible in the past. (…) Statcast is a combination of two different tracking systems – a Trackman Doppler radar and high definition Chyron Hego cameras. The radar, installed in each ballpark in an elevated position behind home plate, is responsible for tracking everything related to the baseball at 20,000 frames per second. This radar captures pitch speed, spin rate, pitch movement, exit velocity, launch angle, batted ball distance, arm strength, and more."

Before Statcast, the public had access to data through PITCHf/x, which measured several parameters, including pitch speed, trajectory speed and release point. PITCHf/x was created by Sportvision and implemented since 2008 in every MLB stadium (Fast 2010). The video monitoring, provided by Statcast, provides the public access to a broader range of variables, player and ball tracking, which is a significant breakthrough for both baseball analysts and baseball in general.

---

[1] http://baseballanalysts.com/archives/2004/07/abstracts_from_12.php.

[2] http://sabr.org/sabermetrics.

[3] http://www.apbr.org.

[4] The World Series is the annual championship series of Major League Baseball (MLB) in North America.

[5] In sports, tanking is the mentality of selling/losing present assets to achieve greater benefits in the future.

Albert et al. (2018) developed an independent report using Statcast data to analyze possible causes for the recent surge in Home Runs in the MLB. They used variables such as the launch angle, exit velocity, and many others and concluded that this increase was primarily related to a reduction in drag of the baseballs. This is an excellent showing of the potential of Statcast and that it is rapidly surpassing the previous methods, like PITCHf/x, and could consequently lead to more precise measurements of player's abilities (Sievert, Mills 2016).

2.4   Beat the Streak

The MLB Beat the Streak is a betting game based on the commonly used term hot streak, which in baseball is applied for players that have been performing well in recent games or that have achieved base hits on multiple consecutive games. The game's objective is to pick 57 times correctly in a row, a batter that achieves a base hit on the day it was picked. The game is called Beat the Streak since the longest hit streak achieved was 56 by the hall of fame Joe DiMaggio during the 1941 season. The winner of the contest wins US$ 5.600.000, with other prizes being distributed every time a better reaches a multiple of 5 in a streak, for example, picking ten or twenty-five times in a row correctly (Beat the Streak 2018).

Some relevant rules essential for the strategy of reaching higher streaks are: the better can select 1 or 2 batters per day but the streak does not end if no batter is picked for a given day. If the player selected does not start the game for any reason the player is not accounted for an actual pick. Nevertheless, if the player is switched mid-game without achieving a base hit, the streak is reset. Finally, there is a Mulligan which works as a second change for when the streak of a better lies between 10 and 15. If the better incorrectly picks during this state of his streak, his streak will remain (Beat the Streak 2018).

To better visualize the different rules, Table 1 illustrates some examples of how the streak works in different scenarios:

Table 1. Beat the Streak scenario outcomes.

Pick 1	Pick 2	Result
Hit	Hit	Streak increases by two (2)
Not Hit	Not Hit	Streak ends and resets to zero unless a Mulligan applies in which case the streak is preserved at the current level
Hit	Not Hit	Streak ends and resets to zero unless a Mulligan applies in which case the streak is preserved at the current level
Pass	Not Hit	Streak ends and resets to zero unless a Mulligan applies in which case the streak is preserved at the current level
Hit	Pass	Streak is increased by one (1)
Pass	Pass	Streak is preserved at the current level

2.5   Predicting Batting Performance

Baseball is played by two teams who take turns batting (offense) and fielding (defense). The objective of the offense is to bat the ball in play and score runs by running the bases, while the defense tries to prevent the offense from scoring runs. The game proceeds with a player on the fielding team as the pitcher, throwing a ball which the player on the batting team tries to hit with a bat. When a player completes his turn batting, he gets credited with a plate appearance, which can have one of the following outcomes, as seen below:

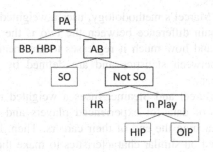

Fig. 1. Breakdown of a plate appearance (Alceo and Henriques 2019).

Denotated in green are the events that result in a base hit and in red the events which are not. This paper tries to predict if a batter will achieve a Home Run (HR) or a Ball hit in play (HIP) among all his plate appearances (PA) during a game. In contrast, it seeks to avoid Base on Balls (BB), Hit by Pitch (HBP), Strikeouts (SO) and Outs in Play (OIP). The most common approach which mostly resembles the model built in this project is forecasting the batting average (AVG). The main difference from both approaches is that the batting average does not account for Base on Balls (BB) and Hit by Pitches (HBP) scenarios.

$$Batting\,Average(AVG) = \frac{HR + HIP}{AB} \qquad (1)$$

$$Hitting\,Percentage(H\%) = \frac{HR + HIP}{PA} \qquad (2)$$

Many systems predict offensive player performance, including batting averages. These models range from simple to complex. Henry Druschel from Beyond the Boxscore identifies that the central systems in place are: Marcel, PECOTA, Steamer, and ZiPS (Druschel 2016):

- **Marcel,** encompasses data from the last three seasons and gives extra weight to the most recent seasons. Then it shrinks a player's prediction to the league average adjusted to the age using a regression towards the mean. The values used for this are usually arbitrary;

- **PECOTA,** uses data for each player using their past performances, with more recent years weighted more heavily. PECOTA then uses this baseline along with the player's body type, position, and age to identify various comparison players. Using an algorithm resembling k-nearest neighbors, it identifies the closest player to the projected player and the closer this comparison is the more weight that comparison player's career carries.;
- **Steamer,** much like Marcel's methodology, uses a weighted average based on past performance. The main difference between the two is the weight given for each year's performance and how much it regresses to the mean is less arbitrary, i.e., these values vary between statistics and are defined by performing regression analysis of past players;
- **ZiPS,** similarly to Marcel and Steamer, uses a weighted regression analysis but precisely four years of data for experienced players and three years for newer players or players reaching the end of their careers. Then, like PECOTA, it pools players together based on similar characteristics to make the final predictions.

Goodman and Frey (2013), developed a machine learning model to predict the batter most likely to get a hit each day. Their objective was to win the MLB Beat the Streak game; to do this, they built a generalized linear model (GLM) based on every game since 1981. The variables used in the dataset were mainly focused on the starting pitcher and batter performance, but also including some ballpark related features. The authors normalize the selected features, but no further preprocessing was carried. The results on testing were 70% precision on correct picks and in a real-life test, achieved a 14-game streak with a peak precision of 67,78%.

Clavelli and Gottsegen (2013), created a data mining model to maximize the precision of hit predictions in baseball. The dataset built was scraped using python achieving over 35.000 samples. The features used in their paper regard batter and opposing pitcher's recent performance and ballpark characteristics, much like the work the previous work analyzed. The compiled game from previous seasons was then inputted in a logistic regression, which achieved a 79,3% precision on its testing set. In the paper, it is also mentioned the use of a support vector machine, which ended up heavily overfitting resulting in a 63% precision in its testing set.

3   Dataset

For the project, there was a need to create a suitable dataset to achieve the goal of predicting base hits in the MLB. With this objective in mind, Microsoft Excel and Python were the tools selected to carry the many processes. Firstly, the collected data was processed in Excel, where some data integration and variable transformation tasks were carried out. Afterward the data was exported to Python in which the remaining data preparation, modeling and evaluation procedures were performed. In Python, the most basic packages used were Pandas (dataset structure and data preparation), Seaborn (data visualization) and Sklearn (for modeling and model evaluation). Below is depicted the dataflow of the project.

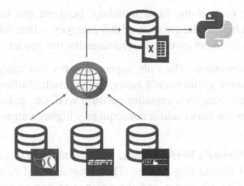

Fig. 2. Data sources and data management diagram (Alceo and Henriques 2019).

The data considered for this project is the games played in Major League Baseball for the seasons 2015, 2016, 2017, 2018 and 2019. All the variables for these games were collected from open sources:

1. **Baseball Reference** is a subsection of the Sports Reference website; the latter includes several other sport-related websites. They attempt to give a comprehensive approach to sports data. In their baseball section, it is possible to find extensive information about baseball teams, baseball players, baseball statistics, and other baseball-related themes dating back to 1871. The data collected from this source is game-by-game player statistics and weather conditions, which could be sub-divided into batting statistics, pitching statistics and team statistics. Data were displayed in a box-score like manner, has seen in Table 2 (Baseball Reference 2018).

2. **ESPN** is a famous North American sports broadcaster with numerous television and radio channels. ESPN mainly focuses on covering North American professional and college sports such as basketball, American football or baseball. Their website contains live scores, news, statistics and other sports-related information up to date. The resource retrieved from the ESPN website was the ballpark factor (ESPN, 2018).

3. **Baseball Savant** provides player matchups, Statcast metrics, and advanced statistics in an easy-to-view and straightforward way. These include several data visualization applications that help users explore Statcast data. The data retrieved from this data source includes Statcast yearly player statistics, such as average launch angle, average exit velocity, and others (Baseball Savant 2018).

3.1   Variable Category Description

Throughout the review of several projects and papers, we could hypothesize the best categories of variables for this paper. Considering that we arrived at six categories of variables:

Batter's Performance. These variables look to describe characteristics, conditions or the performance of the batter. These variables translate into data features like the short/long term performance of the batter, tendencies that might prove beneficial to achieve base hits, or even if the hand matchup, between the batter and pitcher, is favorable. The reason behind the creation of this category is that selecting good players based on their raw skills is an essential advantage for the model.

Batter's Team Performance. The only aspect that fits this category is the on-base percentage (OBP) relative to the team's batter. Since baseball offense is constituted by a 9-player rotation if the batter's teammates perform well, i.e., get on base, this leads to more opportunities for the batter and a consequently higher number of at-bats to get a base hit.

Opponent Starting Pitcher's Performance. The variables in this category refer to the recent performance of the starting pitcher. These variables relate to the pitcher's performance in the last 3 to 10 games and the number of games played by the starting pitcher. The logic behind the category is that the starting pitcher has a significant impact on preventing base hits and the best pitchers tend to allow fewer base hits than weaker ones.

Opponent Bullpen's Performance. This category is quite similar to the previous one. Whereas the former category looks to understand the performance of the starting pitchers, the latter focus on the performance of the bullpen, i.e., the remaining pitchers that might enter the game when starting pitchers get injured, get tired or enter to create tactical advantages. The reasoning for this category is the same as the previous one; a weaker bullpen tends to provide a more significant change of base hits than a good one.

Weather Conditions. In terms of weather conditions, the features taken into account are wind speed and temperature. Firstly, the temperature affects a baseball game in 3 main aspects: the baseball physical composition, the player's reactions and movements, and the baseball's flight distance (Koch and Panorska 2013). If all other aspects remain constant higher temperatures lead to a higher chance of offensive production and thus base hits. Secondly, wind speed affects the trajectory of the baseball, which can lead to lower predictability of the ball's movement and even the amount of time a baseball spends in the air (Chambers, Page and Zaidinis 2003).

Ballpark Factors. Finally, ballpark englobes the ESPN ballpark hit factor, the roof type, and the altitude. The "Park factor compares the rate of stats at home vs. the rate of stats on the road. A rate higher than 1.000 favors the hitters. Below favors the pitcher" meaning that this factor will take into consideration several aspects from this or other categories, indirectly (ESPN 2018). Altitude is another aspect that is crucial to the ballpark. The higher the altitude the ballpark is situated the farther the baseball tends to travel. The previous statement is essential to Denver's Coors Field, widely known for its unusually high offensive production (Kraft and Skeeter 1995). Finally, the roof type of the ballpark affects some meteorological metrics since a closed roof leads to no wind and a more stable temperature, humidity, etc. when compared to ballparks with an open roof.

3.2   Data Visualization

In the context of the paper, the best approach was to use both univariate and bivariate visualization techniques. Several types of plots are presented not only to understand the data but to provide a good perception of the facts hidden in the dataset without needing much knowledge on the topic of baseball.

To give a good understanding of what were the variables experimented and their relationship to the target variable (base hit on a given game) below is depicted both the Pearson's and Spearman's correlation.

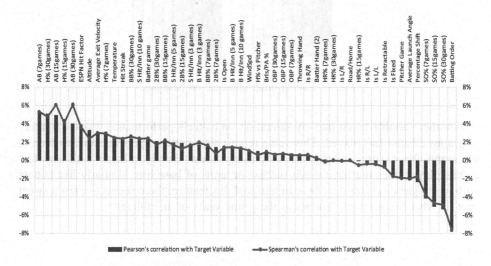

Fig. 3. Pearson's and Spearman's correlation for target variable.

There is no variable with a robust correlation to the target variable but batting order, number of at-bats in previous games and most other batter performance variables present a substantial impact on the target variable at first sight.

In short, most of the relationships of the variables and the target are linear, i.e., if a batter has been performing well, then he is likely to perform well in the future or if a pitcher is performing well, then he is less likely to allow base hits in the future. Nevertheless, we will be showing some examples of this relationship, show some cases where the relation is non-linear and explain details of relations between variables than can influence one another.

Batter's Performance. As mentioned beforehand, most variables in this category are linear. Figure 4 depicts the relation between the batting order and if the batter got a base hit in the game. The graph shown matches the negative correlation value of this pair of variables, where the batters in the first positions of the lineup are considerably more likely to get base hit than the bottom of the lineup. This result is a consequence of the fact that the top of lineup bats more often than the bottom of the lineup. Thus, coaches use these spots for the most talented batters of the team, which usually have the best results. Note that the gap seen in the 9th position is mostly the consequence of removing pitchers batting from the dataset since very often they bat last in the lineup.

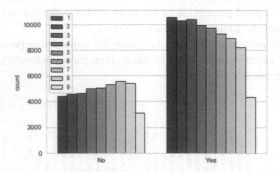

Fig. 4. Batting order influence on base hits.

Another variable taken into consideration on batter's performance was the number of games a batter has played. This value represents a batter experience and, as seen in the graph above, some insights are not entirely linear. Briefly, a batter with very few games played does not have much success in terms of base hits, similarly like batters with many games under their belt. In terms of this feature, there seems to exist a sweet spot or what is commonly known as the prime years of an athlete.

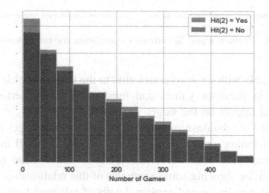

Fig. 5. The number of games played by the batter and base hits.

Finally, the most complicated relationship in this category is the average launch angle. There is no perfect average launch angle in baseball since a launch angle between 15–20° is usually right to make the travel farther where from 5–15° is better to induce ground balls that more often than not end in base hits. The short answer that in the context of our problem (maximizing base hits and not baseball performance) we are looking for players that often induce ground balls to get more base hits. This effect can be seen in Fig. 6 where the launch angle produces more base hits than not.

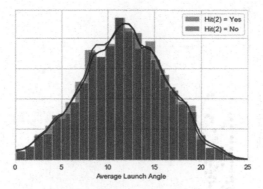

Fig. 6. Average Launch Angle influence on base hits.

Ballpark Factors and Weather Conditions

Finally, Fig. 8 depicts the relationship between the ESPN Hit Factor and the target variableon in every MLB Ballpark. This analysis shows some critical outliers, i.e. ballparks where base hits are more likely or likely to occur, which will be further inspected,in order to gain some valuable insights.

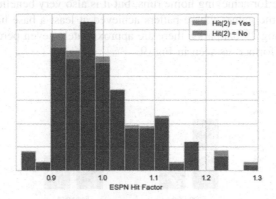

Fig. 7. ESPN Hit Factor influence on base hits.

The graph below represents every MLB ballpark from every year in the dataset. The ESPN Hit Factor values that lie above the 1.2 refer to the Coors Field, which is a very well-known ballpark for its altitude and, it is the only ballpark which is consistently above the rest in terms of batting performance. This ballpark is the home for the Colorado Rockies in Denver, where year after year above-average batting results and Home Runs numbers are achieved. This phenomenon is explained by the low air density, resulting from a high elevation – 5.200 ft of altitude. In Fig. 8, it is quite visible the uniqueness of Coors Field in terms of altitude and ESPN hit factor.

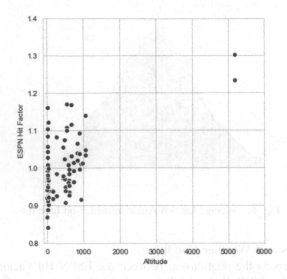

Fig. 8. Ballparks displayed by ESPN Hit Factor and Altitude.

Additionally, the numbers from the count plot below really show that not only the ballpark is suitable for achieving home runs, but it is also very beneficial for base hits. When comparing the games where batters achieved at least a base hit in Coors Field versus the remaining 29 ballparks, there are approximately seven percentage points of advantage for the former, as seen in Fig. 9.

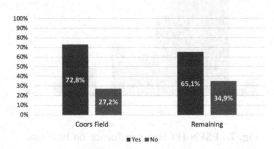

Fig. 9. Coors Field versus remaining ballparks, by base hit percentage.

Finally, to conclude the analysis of the influence of ESPN Hit Factor on other variables, Fig. 11 presents the wind speed associated with each ballpark. Using the average of the wind speed, we can verify that open ballparks are the most influenced by the wind and other weather conditions which promote a higher ESPN Hit Factor. This in conjunction with the altitude and the field dimensions, is the central aspect that influences the ESPN Hit Factor.

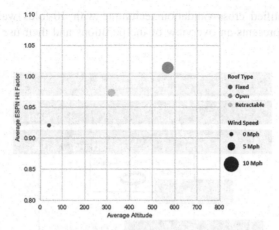

Fig. 10. Average wind speed, ESPN Hit Factor and Altitude on ballparks, by type of roof.

4 Pre-processing

The dataset built for this project consists of 155.521 samples, where around 65,3% are batters that achieved at least a base hit, and the remaining 34,7% are at batters whose game ended without achieving a base hit. Although not very accentuated, it possible to determine that the dataset is imbalanced. These 155.521 records were used to train the model and to run some initial tests on the performance of the models. In the second phase, it further 40.496 samples related to the 2019 season were collected. This last dataset was exclusively used for testing and simulate a real experiment. Note that both the datasets were subject to the same preprocessing methods.

Firstly, to solve the imbalance problem of the initial dataset, both the under-sample and oversample approaches were taken into consideration. However, oversampling was not a feasible solution in the specific context of this problem since the objective of the paper is to predict which are the best players for a given day and, therefore, the creation of random games with random dates would somewhat disturb the analysis. The problem in this approach was the situation of players having to play multiple fictitious games on the same days which would not make sense in the context of the regular season of baseball.

Thus, the method tested for balancing the dataset is under-sampling. It consists of removing random observations from the majority class until the classes are balanced.

We implemented both holdout and cross-validation methods since there was sufficient data. The initial dataset was divided into training set (80%) and test set (20%) using a simple holdout method. For a better simulation, the division was done chronologically, i.e., the first 80% of the games correspond to the training set and the remainder to the test set.

Finally, for the training aspect of the project, the training set was recursively divided into a smaller training set (60% of the total) and a validation set (20% of the total). This division implies that for feature selection, hyperparameter tuning and data evaluation, a stratified cross-validation technique with 10-folds was used. As seen below, Fig. 11 represents an overview of the partitions and their use for the project.

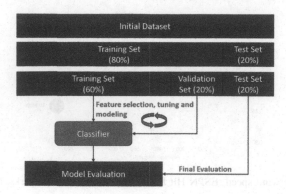

Fig. 11. Data partitioning diagram (Alceo and Henriques 2019).

Regarding normalization, the most common method to obtain normalization of the variables is through normalization, standardization and scaling. The min-max normalization rescales variables in a range between 0 and 1, i.e., the highest value per variable will assume the form of 1 and the lowest 0. It is an appropriate method for normalizing datasets where its variables assume different ranges and, at the same time, solves the mentioned problem of biased results for some specific algorithms that cannot manage variables with different ranges (Larose 2005). This was the solution applied to normalize the numeric variables in the dataset:

$$X^* = \frac{X - \min(X)}{range(X)} = \frac{X - \min(X)}{\max(X) - \min(X)} \tag{3}$$

In contrast, as some algorithms cannot cope with categorical variables, if it is intended the use of these types of variables in all models, there is a need to transform these into a numerical form. Binary encoding was the solution implemented to solve this issue, whereby creating new columns with binary values, it is possible to translate categorical information into 1's and 0's (Larose 2005).

Regarding missing values, only the Statcast variables (Average Launch Angle, Average Exit Velocity, Brls/PA%, and Percentage Shift) had missing values, which comprised around 1% of all the features. These originated from the difference from the two data sources, i.e., some players were not in the Statcast database and therefore did not have a match when building the final database. To solve this issue, the observations with missing values relative to Statcast features were deleted due to their immaterial size.

Additionally, some missing values were created after the variable transformation process. These missing values are the calculated performance statistics for the first game of every player in the dataset (pitcher or batter) and the same for every matchup pitcher vs. batter. In short, every observation which comprises the first game of a player its statistics from the previous "X games" will be NaN since it's their first game in the dataset. These occurrences represented around 4% of the dataset for every batter and pitcher.

Finally, there were two main methods used to detect outliers in this project. In the first phase, we calculated the z-score for the most extreme values for every feature. This enabled us to detect which variables had extremes valuables farther from the mean in a clear way, pointing us in the right direction for what were the most critical variables. In this analysis values that were more than-3 standard deviations or greater than three standard deviations from the mean were analyzed. In the context of our problem, we cannot remove all observations with features that exceed these values but are a good start on understanding which variables have more outliers and their overall dimension in the context of the whole dataset (Larose, D and Larose, C 2014).

The other method used for outlier detection was boxplots, to visualize feature values in the context of their interquartile ranges. In this method, any values under the 1st quartile by more than 1, 5 times the size of the interquartile range or over the 3rd quartile by more than 1, 5 times the size of the interquartile range is considered an extreme value in the context of the respective feature (Larose, D and Larose, C 2014).

In the end, the outlier detection of this project consisted of removing the most extreme values from features using both the information from the z-score analysis and the visualization power of the box-plots. Note that due to the unknown influence of the outliers on the project, every model was tested with outliers and without the identified extreme values. With this, it will be possible to have a good comparison of the performance of the models for both scenarios.

5 Modeling

This chapter focus on presenting the methods used for modeling, feature selection and their respective hyperparameter tuning. Figure 12 depicts an end-to-end view of the paper, where it is possible to perceive the logic behind the processes performed to transform the initial dataset into insight on the problem in question.

Several experiments were created to optimize the set of pre-processing and dimensionality reduction methods. It resulted in the creation of 48 models, which are evaluated and therefore provide an insight on what is the best final model for this problem.

After that, the selected variables already pre-processed are used as inputs to the algorithms, which output a probability estimate i.e. how likely it is a batter to get a base hit in that game. After that, some evaluation metrics are applied to the models and the conclusions are outlined.

Throughout this section, a more in-depth analysis will be presented for feature selection (PCA, no PCA, RFE and RFE without inter-correlated variables), the algorithms and the method used for hyper-parameter tuning and finally what evaluation metrics were applied to compare the final models created.

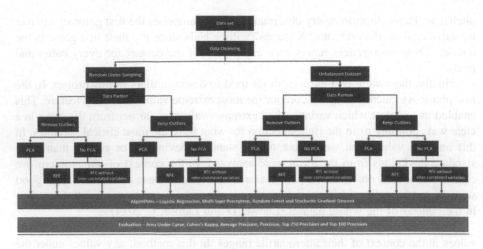

Fig. 12. Top-down project diagram (Alceo and Henriques 2019).

5.1   Algorithms

David Cox developed the logistic regression in 1958. This algorithm is an extension of the linear regression, mainly used for the modeling of regression problems. The former differs from the latter since it looks to solve classification problems by using a sigmoid function or similar to transform the problem into a binary constraint (Cox 1958). The SAGA algorithm was chosen during the hyperparameter tuning for the logistic regression. SAGA follows the path of other algorithms like SAG, also present in the SKlearn library, as an incremental gradient algorithm with a fast linear convergence rate. The additional value that SAGA provides is that it supports non-strongly convex problems directly, i.e., without many alterations, it better adapts to these types of problems in comparison with other similar algorithms (Defazio, Bach and Lascoste-Julien 2014).

A multi-layer perceptron is a type of neural network, inspired by the structure of the human brain. These algorithms make use of nodes or neurons which connect in different levels with weights attributed to each connection. Additionally, some nodes receive extra information through bias values that are also connected with a specific weight (Zhang, Patuwo and Hu 1997).

The optimization algorithm used for training purposes was Adam, a stochastic gradient-based optimization method that works very well with large quantities of data and provides at the same time low computational drawbacks (Kingma and Ba 2015). Regarding the activation functions, during the hyperparameter tuning the ones selected were 'identity'- a no-op activation, which returns f(x) = x and 'relu'- the rectified linear unit functions, which returns f(x) = max (0, x).

The concept of random forest is drawn from a collection of decision trees. Decision trees are a simple algorithm with data mining applications, where a tree-shaped model progressively grows, splitting into branches based on the information held by the variables. Random forests are an ensemble of many of these decision trees, i.e., bootstrapping many decision trees achieves a better overall result, because decision trees are quite prone to overfitting the training data.

The stochastic gradient descent is a standard method for optimizing the training of several machine learning algorithms. As mentioned, it is used in both the multi-layer perceptron and logistic regression approach available in the SKlearn library. This way, it is possible to use gradient descent as the method of learning, where the loss, i.e., the way the error is calculator during training, is associated with another machine learning algorithm. This enables more control over the optimization and less computational drawbacks for the cost of a higher number of parameters (Mei, Montanari and Nguyen 2018).

During parameter tuning, the loss function that was deemed most efficient was 'log' associated with the logistic regression. Therefore, for this algorithm, the error used for training will resemble a standard logistic regression, already described previously.

5.2   Feature Selection

In data mining projects with a high number of variables, it is a good practice to reduce the dimensionality of the dataset. Some of the reasons that make this process worthwhile are a reduction in computational processing time and, for some algorithms, overall better results. The later results from the elimination of the curse of dimensionality – the problem caused by the exponential growth in volume related to adding several dimensions to the Euclidean space (Bellman 1957). In conclusion, feature selection looks to eliminate variables with reductant information and keeping the ones who are most relevant to the model (Guyon and Elisseeff 2003).

The first method used for selecting the optimal set of variables was to use the recursive feature elimination (RFE) functionality in SKlearn. In the first instance, all variables are trained, and a coefficient is calculated for each variable, giving the function a value on which features are the best contributors for the model. After that, the worst variable is removed from the set, and the process is repeated iteratively until there are no variables left.

Another method implemented for dimensionality reduction was the principal component analysis (PCA). This technique looks to explain the correlation structure of the features by using a smaller set of linear combinations of components. By combining correlated variables, it is possible to use the predictive power of several variables in a reduced number of components.

Finally, the correlation between the independent features and the dependent variable was visualized to get the most relevant variables. This had the objective of doing a correlation-based feature selection, meaning that it is desirable to pick variables highly correlated with the dependent variable and the same time with low intercorrelation with the other independent features (Witten, Frank and Hall 2011).

5.3   Hyperparameter Tuning

The method chosen for hyperparameter tuning was Gridsearch with stratified 10-fold cross-validation implemented using the SKlearn library. The process is similar to a brute force approach, where Python runs every possible combination of hyperparameters assigned and returns as the output the best combination for the predefined metrics. This process was performed for every algorithm twice, once for the PCA and once for the no PCA formatted dataset. For unbalanced and balanced datasets comparison, the chosen metric was the area under the ROC curve.

5.4   Evaluation

The final step of the model process was to choose the evaluation metrics that better fit the problem. The main constraints of the problem were to find metrics that enabled the comparison between balanced and imbalanced datasets. The most appropriate metric to fulfill these requirements was precision to define a tight threshold to secure a very high rate of correct predictions on players that would get a base hit. Nevertheless, other metrics that adapt to this type of problem were also applied to get a better overall view of the final models, such as:

- Area Under ROC Curve;
- Cohen Kappa;
- Precision and Average Precision.

Finally, for each model, we calculated the precision for the Top 250 and Top 100 instances, i.e., the instances with the highest probability of being base hits as predicted by the models. This analysis resembles the strategy that will be applied in the real world, for which only the top predictions will be chosen for the game. Note that this analysis will also give an excellent idea of what threshold should be used for this point onward.

6   Results

A total number of 48 different models were created from data collected from the 2015–2018 seasons. Additionally, data from the 2019 season was collected and was used to test the potential of the final model.

6.1   Results on the Models Created with the 2015–2018 Data

All in all, the models showed some differences in performance when considering the different methods used. Firstly, the use of PCA did not provide better results on average, as seen in Fig. 13, these models performed equally or worse than models that were not transformed with this method:

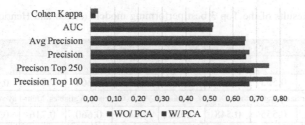

Fig. 13. Average model performance on the test set, by use of PCA (Alceo & Henriques,2019).

Besides PCA, RFE and correction-based feature selection were also game-changers on the final models. As seen already, PCA did not perform better than RFE or the RFE with the removal of correlated variables methods. When comparing the latter two methods, we achieved similar results. However, more often than not, the removal of inter-correlated variables in the RFE selection provided slightly better or equal results than its counterpart. Additionally, removing intercorrelated variables allows a smaller subset of variables that it is faster to compute and might remove unwanted noise in future runs of the model. Note that the most predominant variables cut using the correlation method was related to the batter and pitching performance, which were the variable categories most predominant in the dataset and the overall models.

Additionally on variable usage, and has said previously, the most used variables fall under the batter performance statistics category, it is also important to mention that the models often use at least one variable from each of the remaining categories, where the most prevalent are hits per innings for the starting pitcher (last ten games), ESPN hit factor, temperature and hits per innings for the bullpen (last 3 games). The category with the least representation is the team batting statistics, as on-base-percentage (OBP) does not seem to add much prediction value on the outcome.

With a good understanding of the variables used on the models, Table 2 presents the various metrics of the Top 3 models based on the 10-Fold Cross-Validation, as well as on the Test set. Remember that these results are all extracted from the dataset composed of the 2015–2018 seasons.

All in all, balanced datasets worked well, and the three best models were achieved when using this methodology and without the use of PCA. The Top 3 datasets were selected based mostly on their precision 100 and 250, and in case of similar results, the other metrics were used as tie-breakers. It is also essential to add that when analyzing the Validation set for the imbalanced dataset, the models often tended to choose the most effective outcome (base hit) and therefore these results, although not shown, were ambiguous.

Table 2. Results of the Top 3 best performing models (Alceo and Henriques 2019).

Validation Set (Stratified 10-Fold CV)				Test Set					
AUC	Cohen Kappa	Avg Precision	Precision	AUC	Cohen Kappa	Avg Precision	Precision	Precision Top 250	Precision Top 100
0,566	0,095	0,555	0,550	0,536	0,057	0,664	0,718	0,760	0,850
Random Under Sampling, Without Outliers, Without PCA, No Correlated Variables, Multi-Layered Perceptron									
0,567	0,095	0,555	0,548	0,528	0,043	0,660	0,716	0,768	0,820
Random Under Sampling, Without Outliers, Without PCA, All Variables, Logistic Regression									
0,562	0,078	0,551	0,539	0,545	0,080	0,668	0,690	0,760	0,800
Random Under Sampling, With Outliers, Without PCA, No Correlated Variables, Stochastic Gradient Descent									

Theoretically, the upper model in Table 2 would give us the highest probability of Beating the Streak, due to its capacity of being correct on the model's most confident predictions, shown by both a high precision 250 and 100. Using the probabilities estimates of each model can now define a threshold for future seasons and define an approximation on what are the odds of betting correctly 57 in a row.

Table 3. Threshold analysis on top 3 models (Alceo and Henriques 2019).

Probability Estimates	MLP	LG1	SGD
Maximum probability	0,658	0,671	0,679
Minimun probabilty	0,242	0,218	0,238
Threshold top 100	0,608	0,616	0,643
Z-score threshold	0,880	0,878	0,918
Expected correct ratio	85%	82%	80%

Table 3 shows that the models provided different ranges of probabilities, but all thresholds fall under approximately 80%–90% of the overall distributions, according to the z-score. In short, our strategy, when using the MLP for example, should be to bet only when the model provides a probability of at least 0.608, giving us an approximate probability of 85% of being correct. Additionally, some ensembles techniques were implemented to improve the expected results, such as majority voting and boosting techniques but none of these techniques provided any improvement in the results.

6.2   Results and Betting Strategies Using the 2019 Season

Data from the 2019 season was used to test the best models achieved in the last section. To achieve the best streak possible, under the constraints of the game, there was a need for developing strategies to optimize our picks. Below, we describe, the several possible strategies for betting:

- Betting every day on the two most likely batters, according to the model;
- Betting only when there are batters that are over the pre-defined threshold;
- Betting only when a set of good batters are over the pre-defined threshold.

The three approaches appear naturally as a consequence of the output of the model and common betting strategies. The later approach resembles casual betting and will be an excellent way to understand if this is in fact, as biased as it seems. The other two are much more tied to the core output of the model developed and comparing these to the casual approach will be a good exercise.

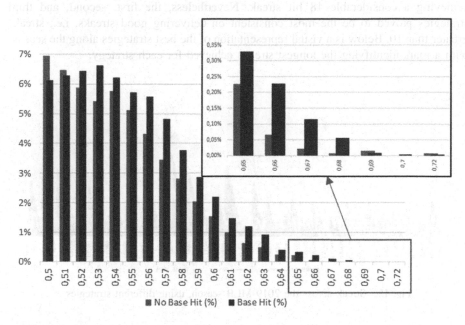

Fig. 14. Probability estimate of MLP vs. target variable, on the 2019 season dataset.

Figure 14 shows that the model is working, and samples with higher probabilities were correct more often than their counterpart. Note that the graph is normalized for the respective outcomes and therefore, the results are not being biased by the number of samples for each class of the target variable and that the samples with low probability estimates are not shown since they are not interesting for the outcome of the strategy.

Table 4. Results for test run of the MLP on the 2019 season.

	Betting everyday most	> 60%	> 55%	Top 15, > 60%	Top 15, > 55%	Top 10, > 60%	Top 10, > 55%
Streaks Started	57	51	51	23	37	22	60
# of Bets	370	340	367	169	348	122	330
Correct Picks	294	274	292	119	251	80	240
% Correct Picks	79,46%	80,59%	79,56%	70,41%	72,13%	65,57%	72,73%
Average % Estimate	63,8%	64,3%	63,9%	61,8%	60,0%	61,7%	59,3%
Quality Streaks	8	7	8	2	5	1	4
Max Streak	14	15	15	13	18	13	15

Table 4 depicts the results for some of the strategies put in place. To understand the table above, let us use the rightmost column as an example. The column depicts the results for picking only the Top 15 best batters last season regarding base hit prowess and when they have higher than 55% on the probability estimate given by the model. The players considered were from best to worst: Mookie Betts, J.D. Martinez, Christian Yelich, Scooter Gennett, Corey Dickerson, Jose Altuve, Jean Segura, Miguel Andujar, Michael Brantley, Jose Martinez, Anthony Rendon, Javier Bayez, Nicholas Castellanos, Yuli Gurriel and Eddie Rosario.

The strategy that led us the farthest in the 2019 season was "Top 15, >55%", achieving a considerable 18 hit streak. Nevertheless, the first, second, and third strategies proved to be the most consistent on delivering good streaks, i.e., streaks greater than 10. Below is a visual representation of the best strategies along the season, with a mark identifying the longest streaks achieved for each strategy.

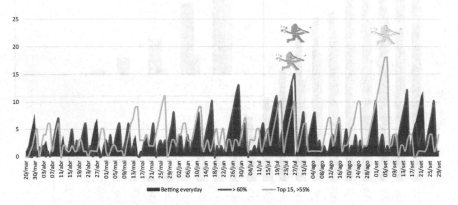

Fig. 15. Streak across the 2019 MLB season, using different strategies.

Finally, to get a better perspective of the probabilities of each of the strategies, we developed a simple Monte Carlo simulation using the % Correct Pick and the number of Bets per season, simulating playing the game over a 10-season period. The results of the simulation are as follows:

Table 5. Monte Carlo simulation on MLP and strategy results.

	Betting everyday most likely	> 60%	> 55%	Top 15, > 60%	Top 15, > 55%	Top 10, > 60%	Top 10, > 55%
Average Streak	3,83	4,32	4,06	2,12	2,55	1,97	2,49
Days in Streak > 10	280	322	336	19	90	18	82
Best streak	34	41	36	15	23	15	19

As mentioned previously, the strategies that both target high probabilities bets, according to the model, and that bet a high number of times will prove to be the best in the long run. Over this 10-year simulation, the best model is the simple betting on players, where the model gives a probability estimate higher than 0, 60.

The main improvements over previous works, mentioned in Fig. 4 and previously discussed at the end of Sect. 2 of this paper, cannot be attributed to a single factor. However, the main differences that, in the end, resulted in a better outcome of this paper, comparatively to the other two, are as follow.

1) A broader scope of variable types. Other authors focused primarily on the use of variables regarding the batter's and pitcher's performance, as well as ballpark characteristics. In this paper, a more comprehensive range of variable types was used, which proved to be essential for a broader understanding of the event being analyzed.

2) The experimentation of several pre-processing methods, and modeling methods. In this paper, no method is deemed to be definitive and by testing a higher number of pre-processing methods and modeling methods, a better fit for the problem was possible. In contrast, other authors tended to experiment with fewer approaches.

3) The overall strategy of evaluation of this paper suits the task presented. In some papers mentioned, the authors focused on standard metrics to evaluate the results of the models, such as precision. However, due to the nature of the game Beat the Streak there was a need to create evaluation criteria that focused on the precision of the top picks, i.e., the picks with the highest probability estimates. This was solved by creating the Top 250 and 100 precision which only highlights the highest probability instances, providing a more effective evaluation of the models. Additionally, this time around it was also analyzed different betting strategies where we tested a variety of approaches using as core the probabilities estimates outputted by the model and therefore arriving at better results in the long run.

7   Conclusion

The main objective of this paper was to build a model able to predict which players were most likely to get a base hit on a given day and, by this, provide a probability estimate for this event. To achieve this objective, the following steps were followed:

1. A dataset was built, using open-source data using a wide variety of variables;
2. Descriptive and visualization techniques were used to explore the features;
3. Built a predictive model capable of providing a good probability estimate for base hits, using a multitude of data mining and machine learning methods;
4. Application of that model on a test set which enabled the extraction of realistic results and consequently identified both the optimal model and strategy.

From the worked carried, 48 models were tested using different constraints such as balancing the dataset, outlier usage, usage of PCA different feature selection techniques. From the final 48 models created, it was possible to retain some insights:

- The use of PCA did not help to generate better results;
- Generally, balancing the datasets using random under-sampling helped to achieve better results than no balancing;
- It was possible to obtain simpler models by removing inter-correlated variables from the RFE selected features and obtain similar or better models.

In an initial stage, after analyzing the performance of the models against the first test set, the top 3 models were chosen as possible candidates for usage in a real-world situation. The best model achieved a correct pick rate of 85% on the top 100 precision metric (precision on top 100 most probable instances). After further testing using the 2019 season, which is a much reasonable size of data than previous tests, we arrived at an 81% correct pick ratio.

The model that arrived at this conclusion was the multi-layered perceptron, not using PCA and with the removal of inter-correlated variables from the original feature selection. When stacked against other projects, our MLP was the best performer, gaining around two percentage points against the best similar work and 15 percentage points for general picking strategies.

The type of event being predicted is very prone to be random since there are many elements that are hard to quantify into features and, thus, cannot be fully translated into a machine learning model. The influence of luck can be diminished but it is hard to obtain a 100% model in predicting these events. The project at hand had some excellent results but it is unlikely that with an 81% expected correct pick ratio, it will predict correctly 57 times in a row.

Using the results of the best model and best strategy to build a simple Monte Carlo simulation, we can expect that in the next ten years to achieve a 40-hit streak or higher, which is very nice considering that for every multiple of 5-hit streak achieved a small prize is delivered. Finally, the main points for improvement for this project would be:

- Collect data from more seasons;
- Experiment with a wider variety of sampling techniques;
- Identify new variables, especially from factors not used in this project, for example, defensive performance from the opposing team;
- Experiment with other algorithms and further tune the hyperparameters used in them;
- Effective use of some form of ensemble techniques.

References

Alamar, B.: Sports Analytics: A Guide for Coaches, Managers, and Other Decision Makers. Columbia University Press, New York (2013)

Alceo, P., Henriques, H.: Sports analytics: maximizing precision in predicting MLB base hits. In: 11th International Joint Conference on Knowledge Discovery, Knowledge Engineering and Knowledge Management (2019)

Baseball Reference (2018). https://www.baseball-reference.com

Baseball Savant (2018). https://baseballsavant.mlb.com

Beat the Streak, Beat the Streak: Official Rules (2018). http://mlb.mlb.com/mlb/fantasy/bts/y2018/?content=rules

Bellman, R.: Dynamic programming. Princeton University Press, Princeton, NJ (1957)

Chambers, F., Page, B., Zaidinjs, C.: Atmosphere, weather and baseball: how much farther do baseballs really fly at Denver's Coors Field. Prof. Geogr. **55**, 491–504 (2003)

Clavelli, J., Gottsegen, J.: Maximizing Precision of Hit Predictions in Baseball (2013)

Collignon, H., Sultan, N.: Winning in the Business of Sports. AT Kearney (2014)

Cox, D.: The regression analysis of binary sequences. J. Royal Stat. Soc. Ser. B **20**(2), 215–242 (1958)

Defazio, A., Bach, F., Lacoste-Julien, S.: SAGA: a fast-incremental gradient method with support for non-strongly convex composite objectives. Adv. Neural Inf. Process. Syst. **27**, 1–9 (2014)

Druschel, H.: Guide to the Projection Systems. Retrieved from Beyond the Box Score. (2016). https://www.beyondtheboxscore.com/2016/2/22/11079186/projections-marcel-pecota-zips-steamerexplained-guide-math-is-fun

ESPN.: ESPN Hit Factor (2018). http://www.espn.com/mlb/stats/parkfactor

Goodman, I., Frey, E.: Beating the Streak: Predicting the MLB Players Most Likely to Get a Hit each Day (2013)

Guyon, I., Elisseeff, A.: An introduction to variable and feature selection. J. Mach. Learn. Res. **3**, 1157–1182 (2003)

Jia, R., Wong, C., Zeng, D.: Predicting the Major League Baseball Season (2013)

Kingma, D., Ba, J.: Adam: a method for stochastic optimization. In: 3rd International Conference for Learning Representations, pp. 1–15 (2015)

Koch, B., Panorska, A.: The impact of temperature on major league baseball. Weather, Clim. Soc. J. **5**(4), 359–366 (2013)

Kraft, M., Skeeter, B.: The effect of meteorological conditions on fly ball distances in north American Major League Baseball games. Geogr. Bull. **37**, 40–48 (1995)

Larose, D., Larose, C.: Discovering Knowledge in Data: An Introduction to Data Mining, 2nd edn. John Wiley & Sons Inc., Hoboken (2014)

Larose, D.: Discovering Knowledge in Data: An Introduction to Data Mining. John Wiley & Sons Inc., Hoboken (2005)

Mann, R.: The Marriage of Sports Betting, Analytics and Novice Bettors (2018)

Mei, S., Montanari, A., Nguyen, P.: A Mean View of the Landscape of Two-Layers Neural Networks, pp. 1–103 (2018)

MLB.: Glossary/Statcast. Retrieved from MLB (2018). http://m.mlb.com/glossary/statcast

Mordor Intelligence, 2018 Sports Analytics Market-Segmented by End User (Team, Individual), Solution (Social Media Analysis, Business Analysis, Player Fitness Analysis), and Region-Growth, Trends and Forecast (2018–2023) (2018)

Principe, V., Gavião, L.O., Henriques, R., Lobo, V., Lima, G.B.A., Sant'anna, A.P.: Multicriteria analysis of football match performances: composition of probabilistic preferences applied to the English premier league 2015/2016. Pesquisa Operacional (2017). https://doi.org/10.1590/0101-7438.2017.037.02.0333

Stekler, H., Sendor, D., Verlander, R.: Issues in sports forecasting. Int. J. Forecast. **26**(3), 606–621 (2010)

Valero, C.: Predicting Win-Loss outcomes in MLB regular season games – A comparative study using data mining methods. Int. J. Comput. Sci. Sport **15**(2), 91–112 (2016)

Witten, I., Frank, E., Hall, M.: Data Mining: Practical Machine Learning Tools and Techniques, 2nd edn. Morgan Kaufmanne Inc., Burlington (2011)

Wolf, G.: The sabermetric revolution: assessing the growth of analytics in baseball by Benjamin Baumer and Andrew Zimbalist (review). J. Sport Hist. **42**(2), 239–241 (2015)

Zhang, G., Patuwo, B., Hu, M.: Forecasting with artificial neural networks: the state of state of the art. Int. J. Forecast. **14**, 35–62 (1997)

A Two-Step Feature Space Transforming Method to Improve Credit Scoring Performance

Salvatore Carta, Gianni Fenu, Anselmo Ferreira, Diego Reforgiato Recupero, and Roberto Saia$^{(\boxtimes)}$

Department of Mathematics and Computer Science,
University of Cagliari, Cagliari, Italy
{salvatore,fenu,anselmo.ferreira,diego.reforgiato,
roberto.saia}@unica.it

Abstract. The increasing amount of credit offered by financial institutions has required intelligent and efficient methodologies of credit scoring. Therefore, the use of different machine learning solutions to that task has been growing during the past recent years. Such procedures have been used in order to identify customers who are reliable or unreliable, with the intention to counterbalance financial losses due to loans offered to wrong customer profiles. Notwithstanding, such an application of machine learning suffers with several limitations when put into practice, such as unbalanced datasets and, specially, the absence of sufficient information from the features that can be useful to discriminate reliable and unreliable loans. To overcome such drawbacks, we propose in this work a Two-Step Feature Space Transforming approach, which operates by evolving feature information in a twofold operation: (i) data enhancement; and (ii) data discretization. In the first step, additional meta-features are used in order to improve data discrimination. In the second step, the goal is to reduce the diversity of features. Experiments results performed in real-world datasets with different levels of unbalancing show that such a step can improve, in a consistent way, the performance of the best machine learning algorithm for such a task. With such results we aim to open new perspectives for novel efficient credit scoring systems.

Keywords: Business intelligence · Credit scoring · Machine learning algorithms · Transforming

1 Introduction

A report from *Trading Economics* [21,22], which is based on the information provided by the *European Central Bank*[1] data, has shown that credit for consumers has been regularly increasing over the last years. Such behavior in the Euro zone, which can be seen in Fig. 1, is also noticed in other markets such as Russia and USA. This increasing phenomenon has forced *Credit Rating Agencies* (CRAs), also known as *ratings services*, to define and establish intelligent

---

[1] https://www.ecb.europa.eu.

© Springer Nature Switzerland AG 2020
A. Fred et al. (Eds.): IC3K 2019, CCIS 1297, pp. 134–157, 2020.
https://doi.org/10.1007/978-3-030-66196-0_7

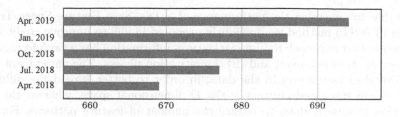

Fig. 1. Euro zone consumer credit in billions of Euros.

strategies to offer credit for the right customers, minimizing financial losses due to bad debts.

Nowadays, CRAs have been using credit scoring systems coupled with machine learning solutions in order to perform credit scoring. Such approaches take into account the big data nature of credit datasets, which can enable machine learning models that can understand credit information from clients and, consequently, discriminate them into *reliable* or *non-reliable* users. Credit scoring systems have been vital in many financial areas [69], as they avoid human interference and eliminate biased analyzes of people information who request financial services, such as a loan. Basically, most of these approaches can be considered probabilistic approaches [52], performing credit scoring by calculating in real time the probability of the loan being repaid, partially repaid and even not repaid based on the given information (*e.g.*, age, job, salary, previous loans status, marital status, among others) in credit scoring datasets, helping the financial operator in the decision of grating or not a financial service [32].

Notwithstanding, credit scoring systems are still limited as a solution for defining loans for three main reasons. The fist one lies in the dataset nature of the problem itself. Similar to other problems, namely fraud or intrusion detection [18, 58,67], the source of data typically contains different distributions of classes [57, 65], which, in the specific case of credit scoring, is more favorable to the reliable instances rather than to the unreliable ones [40]. Such a behavior can seriously affect the performance of classification algorithms, once they can be often biased to classify the most frequent class [30,40]. The second problem comes from the fact that some datasets face the *cold start* issue, on which the unreliable cases do not even exist. Such an issue has motivated several *proactive methods* in the literature to deal with such a problem [60–62]. The last problem, which motivates our solution presented in this work, arises from the heterogeneity of the data. Such limitation highlights the fact that the data, the way they are disposed in datasets, are not enough to describe the different instances. Such information is characterized by features that are very different from each other, even thought they belong to the same class of information. Therefore, further feature transformations are still needed to provide insightful credit scoring.

Based on our previous experience [59–64] to deal with credit scoring, we present in this work a solution for data heterogeneity in credit scoring datasets.

We do that by assessing the performance of a Two-Step Feature Space Transforming (TSFST) method we previously proposed in [66] to improve credit scoring systems. Our approach to improve features information has a twofold process, composed of (i) enrichment; and (ii) discretization phases. The enrichment step adds several meta-features in the data, in order to better spread the different instances into separated clusters in the D dimensional space, whereas the discretization process is done to reduce the number of feature patterns. For the sake of avoiding the risk of overfitting [33] associated to our method and also highlight its real advantages, we adopted an experimental setup that aims at assessing the real performance of financial systems [35]. Such a methodology considers our TSFST method evaluated on data never seen before, which we name *out-of-sample*, and trained on known and different data, which we name *in-sample* data. Experiments considering different classifiers dealing with such feature improvement method spot the effectiveness of such approach, which can mitigate even the data unbalance nature of such datasets.

In summary, the main contributions provided through this work are:

1. The establishment of the Two-Step Feature Space Transforming approach, which enriches and discretizes the original features from credit scoring datasets in order to boost machine learning classifiers performance when using these features.
2. The assessment of the best classifier to be used with the proposed method, done after a series of experiments considering the *in-sample* part of the datasets.
3. The analysis of the method performance considering the *out-of-sample* part of each dataset, adding a comparison with the same canonical approach but without considering our proposed method.

The work presented in this paper is based on our previously published one [66]. Notwithstanding, it has been extended in such a way to add the following new discussions and contributions:

1. Extension of the *Background and Related Work* section by discussing more relevant and recent state-of-the-art approaches, extending the information related to this research field with the aim to provide the readers a quite exhaustive overview on the credit scoring scenario.
2. We changed the order of operations reported in our previous work [66], as we realized that it achieves better results.
3. Inclusion of a new real-world dataset, which allows us to evaluate the performance using a dataset characterized by a low number of instances (690, which is lower than 1000 and 30000 from the other datasets) and features (14, which is also a low number if compared to 21 and 23 from the other datasets).
4. We better discuss the composition of the *in-sample* and *out-of-sample* datasets in terms of number of involved instances and classes. Our choice is based on better providing details about the data imbalance that is present during both the definition of the model (done with the *in-sample* dataset) and the evaluation of its performance (done with the *out-of-sample* dataset).

5. We perform an analysis of the asymptotic time complexity related to the proposed algorithm, which adds valuable information in the context of considering *real-time* credit scoring systems.

The rest of this paper has been structured as follows: Sect. 2 provides information about the background and the related work of the credit scoring domain. Section 3 introduces the formal notation used and provides the formalization of our proposed method. Section 4 describes the experimental environment considered. Section 5 reports and discusses the experimental results in the credit scoring environment and, finally, Sect. 6 makes some concluding remarks and points out some directions for future works.

2 Related Work

In the past few years, it has been witnessed an increasing investment and research over the credit scoring applications with the aim of performing efficient credit scoring. The literature [17] describes several kinds of credit risk models in respect to the *unreliable* cases, which are commonly known as *default* cases. Such models are divided into: (i) *Probability of Default* (PD) models, which investigate the probability of a default in a period; (ii) *Exposure at Default* (EAD) models, which analyse the value the financial operator is exposed to if a default happens; and (iii) *Loss Given Default* (LGD) models, which evaluate the amount of money the operator loses after a default happens. In this section, we discuss the related work of the first kind of models (PD) only, as they are related to our proposed method. Further details of EAD and LGD models can be found in several surveys in the literature [13, 42, 75].

The related work in PD models can be strictly divided into six main branches. The first branch of research is based on statistical methods. For instance, the work in [23] applies Kolmogorov-Smirnov statistics in credit scoring features to discriminate default and non-default users. Other methods, such as the *Logistic Regression* (LR) [70] and *Linear Discriminant Analysis* [39] are also explored in the literature to predict the probability of a default. In [41], the authors propose to use Self Organized Maps and fuzzy k-Nearest Neighbors for credit scoring.

The second branch of research aims to explore data features transformed into other feature domains. The work in [64] processes data in the wavelet domain with three metrics used to rate customers. Similarly, the approach in [63] uses differences of magnitudes in the frequency domain. Finally, the approach in [61] performs comparison of non-square matrix determinants to allow or deny loans.

The third branch of approaches, which is among the most popular ones in credit scoring management, is based on machine learning models. In this topic, the work in [85] considers a Random Forest on preprocessed data. A three-way decision methodology with probability sets is considered in [50]. In [87], a deep learning Convolutional Neural Network approach is applied to pre-selected features that are converted to images. A specific Support Vector Machines with kernel-free fuzzy quadratic surface is proposed in [76]. The work in [10] reports the beneficial use of bagging, boosting and Random Forest techniques to plan and evaluate a housing finance program. An extensive work with machine learning is done in [42], where forty-one methods are compared when applied to eight Credit Scoring datasets.

In the fourth branch of research, approaches based on general artificial intelligence such as neural networks have been explored. For example, authors in [44] present the application of artificial intelligence in the credit scoring area. In [6], the authors use a novel kind of artificial neural network called extreme learning machines. The work in [54] reports credit score prediction using the Takagi-Sugeno neuro-fuzzy network. Finally, the work in [53] performs a benchmark of different neural networks for credit scoring.

The fifth branch of research considers hybrid approaches, where more than one model is used to perform a final decision of credit scoring. The work in [3] used Gabriel Neighbourhood Graph and Multivariate Adaptive Regression Splines together with a new consensus approach. Authors in [77] used seven base different classifiers in dimensionality reduced data with Neighborhood Rough Set. The authors propose a novel ranking technique used to decide the top-5 best classifiers to be part of a layered ensemble. The work in [47] uses several classifiers to validate a feature selection approach called *group penalty function*. In [29], a similar procedure is done, but including normalization and dimensionality reduction preprocessing steps and an ensemble of five classifiers optimized by a Bayesian algorithm. The same number of classifiers is used in [84], but with genetic algorithm and fuzzy assignment. In [24], ensembles are done according to classifier soft probabilities and, in [78], an ensemble with feature clustering-based feature is done in a weighted voting approach.

The last set of models consider specific features of the problem, such as *user profiling* in social networks [7,68,72,79], news from media [86], data entropy [59] , linear-dependence [60,61], among others. One interesting research in this topic is considering *proactive methods* [60–62], which previously assume that the credit scoring datasets are biased and alleviate such a problem before they happen.

Although several approaches have been proposed in literature, there are still many challenges in credit scoring research. All these issues reduce in a significant way the performance of Credit Scoring systems, specially when applied to real-world credit risk management. Such challenges can be enumerated as follows:

1. *Lack of Datasets*, caused mainly by privacy, competition, or legal issues [46].
2. *Non-adaptability*, commonly known as *overfitting*, where Credit Scoring models are unable to correctly classify new instances.
3. *Cold-start*, when the datasets used to train a model do not contain enough information about default and non default cases [4,25,43,71,74].
4. *Data Unbalance*, where an imbalanced class distribution of data [34,37] is found, being typically beneficial to the non-default class.
5. *Data Heterogeneity*, where the same information is represented differently in different data samples [12].

Our approach differs from the previous ones in the literature as it deals with the *Data Heterogeneity* problem in a two step process. To do that, we perform a series of transforming steps in order to make the original heterogeneous data better discernible and separable, which can boost the performance of any classifier. More details of our approach are discussed in the next section.

3 The Two-Step Feature Space Transforming Approach

Before discussing our approach in details, let us define the formal notation used from this section to the rest of this work. Given a set $S = \{s_1, s_2, \ldots, s_X\}$ of samples (or instances) already classified in another set $C = \{reliable, unreliable\}$, we then split S into subsets $S^+ \subseteq S$ of *reliable* or *non default* cases, and another subset $S^- \subseteq S$ of *unreliable* cases, where $S^+ \cap S^- = \emptyset$. Lets also consider another set $P = \{p_1, p_2, \ldots, p_X\}$ as the labels (or predictions) given by a credit scoring system for each sample that will split S as discussed before, and $Y = \{y_1, y_2, \ldots, y_X\}$ their true labels where $P \in C, Y \in C$ and $|S| = |P| = |Y|$. By considering that each sample has a set of features $F = \{f_1, f_2, \ldots, f_N\}$ and that each sample belongs to only one class in the set C, we can formalize our objective as shown in Eq. 1 as follows:

$$\max_{0 \leq \alpha \leq |S|} \alpha = \sum_{z=1}^{|S|} \beta_{(p_z == y_z)}, \tag{1}$$

where β_b is a logical function that converts any proposition b into 1 if the proposition is true, and 0 otherwise. In other words, our goal is to maximize the total number of correct predictions, or $\beta_{(p_z == y_z)} = 1$. To increase α of this objective function, several approaches can be chosen, as discussed previously in the related work in Sect. 2. These can be: (i) select and/or transform features [61,63,64]; (ii) select the best classifier [76,85,87]; or (iii) select the best ensemble of classifiers [3,29,77].

In this work, we choose a solution that includes the first and second approaches simultaneously, proposing a twofold transforming technique that boosts features $f \in F$ and applying them to the best classifier. This boosting is done in such a way to better distribute the features to the classes of interest in the N dimensional space. With such a procedure, we expect to maximize α when applying such boosted features to the best classifier for this task.

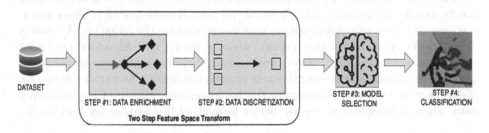

Fig. 2. Full pipeline of credit scoring systems including our proposed Two-Step Feature Space Transforming approach.

As can be seen in proposed model pipeline in Fig. 2, our approach is composed of four main steps, described as follows:

1. **Data Enrichment:** a series of additional features $\hat{F}$ are added to the original ones in F, in order to include useful information for better credit scoring.
2. **Data Discretization:** once enriched, the features are now discretized to lie in a given range, which is defined in the context of experiments done in the *in-sample* part of the dataset.
3. **Model Selection:** chooses the model to use in the context of the credit score machine learning applications.
4. **Classification:** implements the classification algorithm to classify new instances $\hat{S}$ into reliable or unreliable.

We discuss each of the above-mentioned steps of our proposed method in the following subsections.

3.1   Data Enrichment

As discussed previously, several works in the literature have pointed out that transforming features can improve the data domain, thus benefiting any machine learning technique able to discriminate them into disjoint classes. One specific kind of features transformation is adding meta-features [28]. Such transformation is commonly used in a machine learning research branch called *meta-learning* [80]. Such additional features are composed of summarizing or reusing the existing ones, by calculating values such as the minimum, maximum, mean value, among others. Such values can be calculated at each vector domain, or considering all vectors in a matrix of features.

In our proposed method, we use these meta-features in order to balance the loss of information caused by the data heterogeneity issue present in credit scoring datasets, adding further data created to boost the characterization of features F into the *reliable* or *unreliable* classes of interest. Formally, given the set of features $F = \{f_1, f_2, \ldots, f_N\}$, we add $MF = \{mf_{N+1}, mf_{N+2}, \ldots, mf_{N+Z}\}$ new meta-features, obtaining the new set of features shown in Eq. 2.

$$\hat{F} = \{f_1, f_2, \ldots, f_N, mf_{N+1}, mf_{N+2}, \ldots, mf_{N+Z}\}. \tag{2}$$

Therefore, we chose for our proposed method $Z = |MF| = 4$ or, in other words, we add to the original features four additional meta-features. These meta-features have been calculated feature vector-wise and are the following: *Minimum value (min)*, *Maximum value (max)*, *Mean (mean)*, and *Standard Deviation (std)*, then we have $MF = \{min, max, mean, std\}$. By adding more insightful data to the original feature set, this new process minimizes the pattern reduction effects that are normally present in the heterogeneous nature of credit scoring data. Such additional features are better formalized in a parameter u in Eq. 3

$$\mu = \begin{cases} min = min(f_1, f_2, \ldots, f_N) \\ max = max(f_1, f_2, \ldots, f_N) \\ mean = \dfrac{1}{N} \sum_{n=1}^{N}(f_n) \\ std = \sqrt{\dfrac{1}{N-1} \sum_{n=1}^{N}(f_n - \bar{f})^2} \end{cases} \tag{3}$$

3.2 Data Discretization

The data discretization process is commonly used in machine learning algorithms as a way of data transform [45]. It focuses on transforming the features by dividing each of them into a discrete number that falls in independent intervals. It means that numerical features, being discrete or continuous, will be mapped to lie in one of these intervals, standardizing the whole set of original features. Such a procedure was proven to boost the performance of many machine learning models [26,82].

Although the fact that, in one hand, the process of discretization comes with the drawback of filtering some sort of additional information gathered from the meta-features in the previous step of our method, it comes with the advantage of *understandability*, which comes from the conversion of the continuous space to a more limited (discrete) space [45], which guides a faster and precise learning [26]. Figure 3 shows one example of discretizing six feature values in the continuous range $\{0, \ldots, 150\}$ into discrete values in the discrete range $\{0, 1, \ldots, 15\}$.

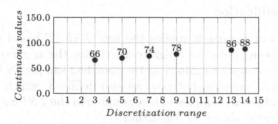

Fig. 3. Discretization process example of continuous features.

In our approach, each of the features $f \in F$ in the enriched $\hat{S}$ from the previous step are transformed through discretization. This is done to move the original continuous range to a defined discrete range $[0, 1, \ldots, r] \in \mathbb{Z}$, where r is found experimentally as will be described later in this work. By defining the discretization procedure $f \xrightarrow{r} d$, we operate in order transform each $f \in F$ into one of the values in the discrete range of integers $d = [1, 2, \ldots, r]$. Such a process reduces significantly the number of possible different patterns in each $f \in F$, as shown in Eq. 4.

$$\{f_1, f_2, \ldots, f_N\} \xrightarrow{r} \{d_1, d_2, \ldots, d_N\}, \ \forall \ \hat{s} \in \hat{S} \tag{4}$$

3.3   Model Selection

The following step of the credit scoring pipeline chooses the model to be applied in preprocessed features by our TSFST approach. According to the u and r parameters from the enrichment and and discretization phases of our approach respectively, a new set of features $TSFST(S)$ is formalized as shown in Eq. 5.

$$
TSFST(S) = \begin{pmatrix}
d_{1,1} & d_{1,2} & \cdots & d_{1,N} & mf_{u(1,1)} & mf_{u(1,2)} & mf_{u(1,3)} & mf_{u(1,4)} \\
d_{2,1} & d_{2,2} & \cdots & d_{2,N} & mf_{u(2,1)} & mf_{u(2,2)} & mf_{u(2,3)} & mf_{u(2,4)} \\
\vdots & \vdots & \ddots & \vdots & \vdots & \vdots & \ddots & \vdots \\
d_{X,1} & d_{X,2} & \cdots & d_{X,N} & mf_{u(X,1)} & mf_{u(X,2)} & mf_{u(X,3)} & mf_{u(X,4)}
\end{pmatrix}
$$
(5)

Such features are used both in the training and evaluation steps of the model. The model chosen in our TSFST model is the Gradient Boosting (GB) algorithm [9]. We chose this algorithm mainly because it follows the idea of *boosting*. In other words, the classifier is composed initially of weak learning models that keep only observations these models successfully classified. Then, a new learner is created and trained on the set of data that was poorly classified before. Decision trees are usually used in GB. Performance experiments done in the *in-sample* part of each dataset assess the choice of such a model, as will be discussed with further details later in this work.

3.4   Data Classification

The last step of our approach applies the new $TSFST$-based classifier in the evaluation (unknown) data, in order to maximize the α metric discussed in Eq. 1. For that, we consider again S as the classified samples, which will be the training (or known) samples, but now we also define $\bar{S}$, which is a new set of unclassified (or unknown) samples to be evaluated in the $TSFST$ classifier. Such a procedure is done as shown in Algorithm 1.

Algorithm 1. TSFST classification pipeline.

Input: cla=classifier, S=classified (training) instances, $\bar{S}$=unclassified instances, u=meta-features to calculate, r=upper bound of the discretization process.

Output: out=Classification of instances in $\bar{S}$

1: **procedure** INSTANCECLASSIFICATION($cla, S, \bar{S}, u, r$)
2:     $MF \leftarrow getMetaFeatures(S, u)$ ▷ Step #1 (enrichment) of TSFST model in the training data
3:     $S \leftarrow concat(S, MF)$ ▷ Concat original data with meta features found
4:     $\hat{S} = getDiscretizedFeatures(S, r)$ ▷ Step #2 (discretization) of TSFP model in the training data
5:     $model \leftarrow ClassifierTraining(alg, \hat{S})$ ▷ Classifier training using the TSFST transformed training data
6:     $MF' \leftarrow getMetaFeatures(\bar{S}, u)$ ▷ Repeat TSFST procedure in the testing samples
7:     $\bar{S} \leftarrow concat(\bar{S}, MF')$
8:     $\hat{\bar{S}} = getDiscretizedFeatures(\bar{S}, r)$
9:     **for each** $\hat{\bar{s}} \in \hat{\bar{S}}$ **do**   ▷ Classifier evaluation in each TSFST transformed testing sample
10:         $c \leftarrow classify(model, \hat{\bar{s}})$
11:         $out.add(c)$
12:     **end for**
13:     **return** out
14: **end procedure**

In the *step 1* of this algorithm, the following parameters are used as input: (i) the classification algorithm *cla* to be trained and tested using the $TSFST$ feature set; (ii) the training classified data S in its original format; (iii) the new instances to be classified $\bar{S}$ also in their original format; and (iv) $TSFST$ parameters, such as the meta-features u to be used in the enhancement step and the upper bound r to be used in the discretization step. The data transformation related to our $TSFST$ approach is performed for sets of training data S and testing data $\bar{S}$ at *steps 2–4* and *6–8* respectively, and the transformed data $\hat{S}$ of the training set trains the model *cla* at *step 5*. The classification process is performed at *steps 9–12* for each instance $\hat{\bar{s}}$ in the transformed testing samples set $\hat{\bar{S}}$, with final classifications stored in the *out* vector. At the end of the process, classification labels generated by our proposed boosted classifier are returned by the algorithm at *step 13*.

In order to evaluate the impact in terms of *response-time* of the proposed approach in a *real-time scoring system*, we evaluated the asymptotic time complexity of the proposed Algorithm 1 in terms of *big-O notation*. According to the formal notation provided in Sect. 3, we can do the following observations:

(i) the complexity of the steps *2–4* and *6–8* is $O(N)$, since our $TSFST$ data transformation performs a discretization of the original feature values F at $N \cdot |F|$ times, after several meta-features are added to them;

(ii) the complexity of the step *5* depends on the adopted algorithms, which in our case is the *Gradient Boosting*, an algorithm characterized by a training complexity of $O(N \cdot |F| \cdot \pi)$, where π denotes the number of used trees;

(iii) the complexity of the cycle in the *steps 9–12* is $O(N^2)$, since it involves the prediction complexity of Gradient Boosting (*i.e.*, $O(N \cdot \pi)$) for each instance in the set $\hat{\bar{S}}$.

On the basis of the aforementioned observations, we can express the asymptotic time complexity of the algorithm as $O(N^2)$, an asymptotic time complexity that can be reduced by distributing the process over different machines, by employing large scale distributed computing models (*e.g.* *MapReduce* [20,31]).

4   Experimental Setup

In this section, we discuss all the experimental environment we considered to perform credit scoring experiments. In the following subsections we discuss: (i) the datasets considered; (ii) the metrics used to assess performances; (iii) methodology used to evaluate the methods; and (iv) models considered and implementation aspects of the proposed TSFST method.

4.1   Datasets

We consider three datasets to evaluate our approach: (i) the *Australian Credit Approval* (AC); (ii) the *German Credit* (GC); and (iii) the *Default of Credit Card Clients* (DC). These datasets represent three real-world data, characterized by a different number of instances and features, and also a different level of data unbalance. Such datasets are publicly available[2], and previous works the literature have used them to benchmark their approaches. Such data distribution is described in Table 1.

Table 1. Datasets information.

Dataset name	Total instances $|S|$	Reliable instances $|S^+|$	Unreliable instances $|S^-|$	Number of features $|F|$	Number of classes $|C|$	Reliable/unreliable instances (%)
AC	690	307	383	14	2	44.50/55.50
GC	1,000	700	300	21	2	70.00/30.00
DC	30,000	23,364	6,636	23	2	77.88/22.12

The *AC* dataset is composed of *690* instances, of which *307* classified as *reliable* (44.50%) and *387* classified as *unreliable* (55.50%), and each instance is composed of *14* features, as detailed in Table 2. For data confidentiality reasons, feature names and values have been changed to meaningless symbols.

Table 2. Features of AC Dataset.

Field	Type	Field	Type
01	Categorical field	08	Categorical field
02	Continuous field	09	Categorical field
03	Continuous field	10	Continuous field
04	Categorical field	11	Categorical field
05	Categorical field	12	Categorical field
06	Categorical field	13	Continuous field
07	Continuous field	14	Continuous field

The *GC* dataset is composed of *1,000* instances, of which *700* classified as *reliable* (70.00%) and *300* classified as *unreliable* (30.00%), and each instance is composed of *20* features, as detailed in Table 3 below.

---

[2] ftp://ftp.ics.uci.edu/pub/machine-learning-databases/statlog/.

Table 3. Features of GC Dataset [66].

Field	Feature	Field	Feature
01	Status of checking account	11	Present residence since
02	Duration	12	Property
03	Credit history	13	Age
04	Purpose	14	Other installment plans
05	Credit amount	15	Housing
06	Savings account/bonds	16	Existing credits
07	Present employment since	17	Job
08	Installment rate	18	Maintained people
09	Personal status and sex	19	Telephone
10	Other debtors/guarantors	20	Foreign worker

Finally, the *DC* dataset is composed of *30,000* instances, of which *23,364* classified as *reliable* (77.88%) and *6,636* classified as *unreliable* (22.12%), and each instance is composed of *23* features, as detailed in Table 4.

Table 4. Features of DC Dataset [66].

Field	Feature	Field	Feature
01	Credit amount	13	Bill statement in August 2005
02	Gender	14	Bill statement in July 2005
03	Education	15	Bill statement in June 2005
04	Marital status	16	Bill statement in May 2005
05	Age	17	Bill statement in April 2005
06	Repayments in September 2005	18	Amount paid in September 2005
07	Repayments in August 2005	19	Amount paid in August 2005
08	Repayments in July 2005	20	Amount paid in July 2005
09	Repayments in June 2005	21	Amount paid in June 2005
10	Repayments in May 2005	22	Amount paid in May 2005
11	Repayments in April 2005	23	Amount paid in April 2005
12	Bill statement in September 2005		

4.2   Metrics

The literature in machine learning has been investigating several different metrics through the last decades, in order to find criteria suitable for a correct performance evaluation of credit scoring models [14]. In [55], several metrics based on confusion matrix were considered, such as *Accuracy*, *True Positive Rate (TPR)*, *Specificity*, or the *Matthews Correlation Coefficient* (MCC). Authors in [11] choose metrics based on the error analysis, such as the *Mean Square Error* (MSE), the *Root Mean Square Error* (RMSE) or the *Mean Absolute Error* (MAE). Finally there are also some works like in [36] that evaluate metrics based on the *Receiver Operating Characteristic* (ROC) curve, such as the *Area Under the ROC Curve* (AUC). Considering that some of these metrics do not work well with unbalanced datasets, like, for example, the metrics based on on the confusion matrix, many works in literature have been addressing the problem of unbalanced datasets by adopting more than one metric to correctly evaluate their results [38].

In our work, we choose to follow that direction, adopting a hybrid strategy to measure the performance of the tested approaches. Our chosen metrics are based on confusion matrix results and ROC curve calculation and are described in the following:

True Positive Rate. Given TP the number of instances correctly classified as *unreliable*, and FN the number of *unreliable* instances wrongly classified as *reliable*, the True Positive Rate (TPR) measures the rate of correct classification of *unreliable* users in a credit scoring model m in any test set S, as can be shown in Eq. 6:

$$TPR_m(S) = \frac{TP}{(TP + FN)}. \tag{6}$$

Such a metric, also known as *Sensitivity*, indicates the proportion of instances from the positive class that are correctly classified by an evaluation model, according to the different classes of a given problem [6].

Matthews Correlation Coefficient. The *Matthews Correlation Coefficient* (MCC) is suitable for unbalanced problems [8,49] as it does a balanced evaluation of performance. Its formalization, shown in Eq. 7, results in a value in the range $[-1, +1]$, with $+1$ when all the classifications are correct and -1 otherwise, whereas 0 indicates the performance related to a random predictor. The MCC of a model m that classifies any new set S is calculated as:

$$MCC_m(S) = \frac{(TP \cdot TN) - (FP \cdot FN)}{\sqrt{(TP + FP) \cdot (TP + FN) \cdot (TN + FP) \cdot (TN + FN)}}. \tag{7}$$

It should be observed that MCC can be seen as a discretization of the *Pearson correlation* [5] for binary variables.

AUC. The *Area Under the Receiver Operating Characteristic* curve (AUC) represents a reliable metric for the evaluation of the performance related to a *credit scoring* model [1,55]. To calculate such a metric, the Receiver Operating Characteristic (ROC) curve is firstly built by plotting the Sensitivity and the False Positive Rate at different classification thresholds and, finally, the area under that curve is calculated.

The AUC metric returns a value in the range [0, 1], where 1 denotes the best performance. AUC is a metric able to assess the predictive capability of an evaluation model, even in the presence of unbalanced data [1].

Performance. This metric is used in the context of our work in order to compare the several classifiers performance. It is calculated by summarizing all metrics presented before in all datasets in just one final metric. Considering ζ the number of datasets in the experiments, the final performance P of a method m in any set S is calculated as:

$$P_m(S) = \frac{\sum_{z=1}^{\zeta} \frac{TPR(S)_z + AUC(S)_z + MCC(S)_z}{3}}{\zeta} \tag{8}$$

We also calculate the performance for a model m in a single dataset z as follows:

$$P_{m,z}(S) = \frac{TPR(S)_z + AUC(S)_z + MCC(S)_z}{3}. \tag{9}$$

Such a metric also returns a value in the range [0, 1], as it comes from three metrics in the same values range.

4.3   Experimental Methodology

We choose an evaluation criterion that divides each dataset into two pieces: (i) the (*in-sample*), used to identify the best model to use to compare with and without our *TSFST* method and the best parameters of our method; and (ii) the (*out-of-sample*), which we use for final evaluation. Such a strategy allows the correct evaluation of the results by preventing the algorithm from yielding results biased by over-fitting [33]. Such an evaluation procedure has also been followed by other works in the literature [56].

For this reason, each of the adopted datasets has been divided into an *in-sample* part, containing 80% of the dataset, and an *out-of-sample* part, containing the remaining 20%. We opt for such a data split to follow some works in literature [2,16,73]. In addition, with the aim to further reduce the impact of the data dependency, we have adopted a *k-fold cross-validation* criterion (k = 5) inside each *in-sample* subset. Information about these subsets are reported in Table 5.

Table 5. In-sample and out-of-sample datasets information.

Dataset name	In-sample				Out-of-sample			
	Reliable	%	Unreliable	%	Reliable	%	Unreliable	%
AC	124	45.0	152	55.0	125	45.5	150	54.5
GC	292	73.0	108	27.0	268	67.2	131	32.8
DC	9307	77.5	2693	22.5	9404	78.4	2595	21.6

4.4 Considered Models and Implementation Details

In order to evaluate the qualities of the proposed transforming approach, we consider several models, represented by machine learning classifiers, in order to select the best one to be used in our approach and to compare its performance before and after our $TSFST$ approach is considered in that model. For this task, we have taken into account the following machine learning algorithms widely used in the credit scoring literature: (i) *Gradient Boosting* (GB) [15]; (ii) *Adaptive Boosting* (AD) [83]; (iii) *Random Forests* (RF) [51]; (iv) *Multilayer Perceptron* (MLP) [48]; and (v) *Decision Tree* (DT) [19].

The code related to the experiments was created with *Python* using the *scikit-learn*[3] library. For the discretization process, we used the *np.digitize()* function, which converts the features to a discrete space according to where each feature value is located in an interval of bins. Such bins are defined as $bins = \{0, 1, \ldots, r-2, r-1\}$, where r is calculated experimentally (we show how we find r later in this section). In order to keep the experiments reproducible, we have fixed the seed of the *pseudo-random number generator* to *1*. In our proposed method, we fixed $|u| = 4$, calculating the four meta-features described in Sect. 3.

5   Experimental Results

To validate our proposed approach, we performed an extensive series of experiments. We classified the experiments as follows:

1. Experiments performed in the *in-sample* part of each dataset: used to assess the benefits of our approach according to several configurations of parameters in credit scoring. For that, we average results of a five-fold cross validation.
2. Experiments performed in the *out-of-sample* part of each dataset: used to compare our approach with some baselines in real credit scoring. For this experiment, we used the *in-sample* part to train and unknown *out-of-sample* data to test.

---

[3] http://scikit-learn.org.

5.1 In-Sample Experiments

In this set of experiments which uses cross validation in the *in-sample* part of each dataset, we choose the following evaluation scenarios:

1. We evaluate the advantages, in terms of performance, of the adoption of some canonical data preprocessing techniques as input to our data transform approach;
2. We report results in order to find the best parameter r of the discretization step of our proposed approach.

We discuss the results of these experiments as follows.

Preprocessing Benchmarking. The literature has been strongly suggesting the use of several preprocessing techniques [27,81] to organize better the data distribution as to training better and boosting machine learning algorithms performance. One straightforward way of doing this is to put feature values in the same range of values, therefore, we decided to verify the performance improvement related to the adoption of two largely used preprocessing methods: *normalization* and *standardization*. In the normalization process, each feature $f \in F$ is scaled into the range $[0, 1]$, whereas the standardization (also known as *Z-score normalization*) re-scales the feature values in such a way that they assume the properties of a *Gaussian distribution*, with mean equals to zero and standard deviation equals to one.

Performance results are shown in Table 6, which reports the mean performance of the five fold cross validation (*i.e.*, related to the *Accuracy*, *MCC*, and *AUC* metrics) measured in all datasets and all algorithms after the application of the aforementioned methods of data preprocessing, along to that measured without any data preprocessing. Premising that the best performances are highlighted in bold, and all the experiments involve only the *in-sample* part of each dataset, on the basis of the obtained results, we can do the following observations:

- the data *normalization* and *standardization* processes do not lead toward significant improvements, since *7* times out of *15* (against *4* out of *15* and *4* out of *15*) we obtain a better performance without using any canonical data preprocessing.
- in the context of the experiments performed without a data preprocessing, *Gradient Boosting* (GB) shows to be the best algorithm between those taken into account, since it gets the best mean performance on all datasets (*i.e.*, *0.6574* against *0.6431* of *ADA*, *0.6388* of *RFA*, *0.5317* of *MLP*, and *0.6147* of *DTC*);
- for the aforementioned reasons we decided to not apply any method of data preprocessing, using *Gradient Boosting* as reference algorithm to evaluate our approach performance.

Table 6. Average performance with preprocessing.

Algorithm	Dataset	Non-preprocessed	Normalized	Standardized
GBC	AC	**0.8018**	0.8005	0.8000
ADA	AC	**0.7495**	0.6735	0.7179
RFA	AC	0.8011	0.7505	**0.8120**
MLP	AC	0.5225	**0.8079**	0.8073
DTC	AC	0.7662	0.7093	**0.7690**
GBC	GC	0.5614	0.5942	**0.6007**
ADA	GC	0.5766	**0.6246**	0.5861
RFA	GC	0.5540	**0.5614**	0.5579
MLP	GC	**0.6114**	0.5649	0.5589
DTC	GC	**0.5796**	0.5456	0.5521
GBC	DC	**0.6087**	0.5442	0.6076
ADA	DC	**0.6031**	0.5361	0.5980
RFA	DC	**0.5613**	0.4909	0.5586
MLP	DC	0.4613	**0.6177**	0.5985
DTC	DC	0.4982	0.4572	**0.5185**
Best cases		7	4	4

Discretization Range Experiments. The goal related to this set of experiments is the definition of the optimal range of discretization r to use in the context of the selected classification algorithm. Figure 4 reports the obtained results in terms of the performance metric for each dataset. Such results indicate *106*, *25*, and *187* as optimal r values for the *AC*, *GC*, and *DC* datasets respectively.

5.2   Out-of-Sample Experiments

Now that we found the discretization parameter of our proposed approach, we focus our attention on discussing the more realistic scenario of credit scoring. For that we perform testing on unseen *out-of-sample* part of the dataset, comparing the effectiveness of such approach with other competitors. We apply the algorithm and the r value detected through the previous experiments in order to evaluate the capability of the proposed *TSFST* model with regard to a canonical data model (*GB*), based on the original feature space. The analysis of the experimental results shown in Fig. 5 leads us toward the following considerations:

1. as shown in Fig. 5, the proposed *TSFST* model outperforms its competitor in terms of *TPR*, *MCC*, and *AUC*, in all the datasets, except for a single case (*i.e.*, *TPR* in the *DC* dataset);
2. although it does not outperform its competitor in terms of *TPR* in the *DC* dataset, its better performance in terms of *MCC*, and *AUC* indicates that

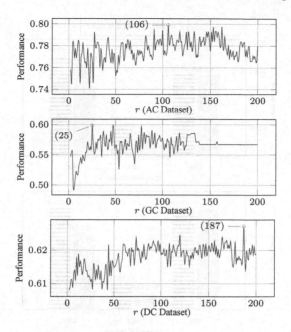

Fig. 4. In-sample r value definition.

the best competitor value has produced a greater number of false positives and/or negatives;

3. for the same reason above, the better performance of our approach in terms of *TPR* can not be considered a side effect related to the increase in terms of *false positive rate* and/or *false negative rate*, since we also outperform the competitor in terms of *MCC* and *AUC*;

4. considering that the *AC*, *GC*, and *DC* datasets are different in terms of data size, level of balancing, and number of features, the obtained results prove the effectiveness of the proposed approach in heterogeneous credit scoring contexts;

5. the adopted validation method, based on the *in-sample/out-of-sample* strategy, combined with a *k-fold cross-validation* criterion, proves the real effectiveness of the proposed approach, since the performance has been evaluated on data never used before, avoiding over-fitting;

In summary, the experimental results have proved that the proposed approach improves the performance of a machine learning algorithm in the credit scoring context, allowing us its exploitation in several state-of-the-art approaches.

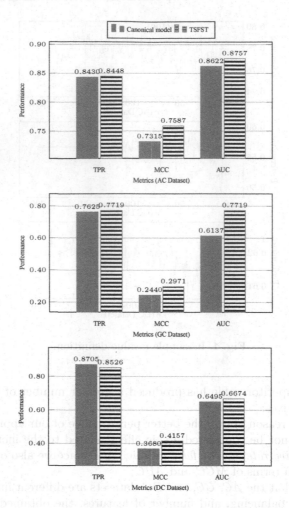

Fig. 5. Out-of-sample classification results, comparing GB with and without our proposed $TSFST$

6   Conclusion

The growth of credit in economy nowadays has required scoring tools in order to allow reliable loans in complex scenarios. Such an opportunity has led an increasing number of research focusing on proposing new methods and strategies. Notwithstanding, similarly to other applications such as fraud detection or intrusion detection, a natural imbalanced distribution of data among classes of interest is commonly found in credit scoring datasets. Such a limitation raises issues in models that could be biased in always classifying samples as the class they have more access in their training. In a such scenario, a slight performance improvement of a classification model produces enormous advantages, which in our case are related to the reduction of financial losses.

In this work, we report a new research inspired by our previous findings [66]. We propose a method composed of a twofold transforming process in credit scoring data, which acts by transforming the features through adding meta-features and also discretizing the resulting new feature space. From our experiments, we could raise the following conclusions; (i) our approach boosts classifiers that use original features; (ii) it is able to improve the performance of the machine learning algorithms; (iii) our approach fits better in boosted-based classifiers such as gradient boosting. Such findings open new perspectives for the definition of more effective credit scoring solutions, considering that many state-of-the-art approaches are based on machine learning algorithms.

As future work, we envision to validate the performance of the proposed data model in the context of credit scoring solutions that implement more than a single machine learning algorithm, such as, for example, homogeneous and heterogeneous ensemble approaches. By achieving good results in this new modelling scenario, we believe we can achieve a more real world solution for credit scoring.

References

1. Abellán, J., Castellano, J.G.: A comparative study on base classifiers in ensemble methods for credit scoring. Expert Syst. Appl. **73**, 1–10 (2017)
2. Adhikari, R.: A neural network based linear ensemble framework for time series forecasting. Neurocomputing **157**, 231–242 (2015)
3. Ala'raj, M., Abbod, M.F.: A new hybrid ensemble credit scoring model based on classifiers consensus system approach. Expert Syst. Appl. **64**, 36–55 (2016)
4. Attenberg, J., Provost, F.J.: Inactive learning?: difficulties employing active learning in practice. SIGKDD Explor. **12**(2), 36–41 (2010). https://doi.org/10.1145/1964897.1964906
5. Benesty, J., Chen, J., Huang, Y., Cohen, I.: Pearson correlation coefficient. Noise Reduction in Speech Processing, pp. 1–4. Springer, Berlin (2009)
6. Bequé, A., Lessmann, S.: Extreme learning machines for credit scoring: an empirical evaluation. Expert Syst. Appl. **86**, 42–53 (2017)
7. Boratto, L., Carta, S., Fenu, G., Saia, R.: Using neural word embeddings to model user behavior and detect user segments. Knowledge-Based Syst. **108**, 5–14 (2016)
8. Boughorbel, S., Jarray, F., El-Anbari, M.: Optimal classifier for imbalanced data using Matthews correlation coefficient metric. PLoS ONE **12**(6), e0177678 (2017)
9. Breiman, L.: Random forests. Mach. Learn. **45**(1), 5–32 (2001)
10. de Castro Vieira, J.R., Barboza, F., Sobreiro, V.A., Kimura, H.: Machine learning models for credit analysis improvements: predicting low-income families' default. Appl. Soft Comput. **83**, 105640 (2019). https://doi.org/10.1016/j.asoc.2019.105640. http://www.sciencedirect.com/science/article/pii/S156849461930420X
11. Chai, T., Draxler, R.R.: Root mean square error (RMSE) or mean absolute error (MAE)?-arguments against avoiding RMSE in the literature. Geoscientific Model Dev. **7**(3), 1247–1250 (2014)
12. Chatterjee, A., Segev, A.: Data manipulation in heterogeneous databases. ACM SIGMOD Rec. **20**(4), 64–68 (1991)

13. Chen, B., Zeng, W., Lin, Y.: Applications of artificial intelligence technologies in credit scoring: a survey of literature. In: International Conference on Natural Computation (ICNC), pp. 658–664, August 2014
14. Chen, N., Ribeiro, B., Chen, A.: Financial credit risk assessment: a recent review. Artif. Intell. Rev. **45**(1), 1–23 (2016)
15. Chopra, A., Bhilare, P.: Application of ensemble models in credit scoring models. Bus. Perspect. Res. **6**(2), 129–141 (2018)
16. Cleary, S., Hebb, G.: An efficient and functional model for predicting bank distress: in and out of sample evidence. J. Bank. Finance **64**, 101–111 (2016)
17. Crook, J.N., Edelman, D.B., Thomas, L.C.: Recent developments in consumer credit risk assessment. Eur. J. Oper. Res. **183**(3), 1447–1465 (2007)
18. Dal Pozzolo, A., Caelen, O., Le Borgne, Y.A., Waterschoot, S., Bontempi, G.: Learned lessons in credit card fraud detection from a practitioner perspective. Expert Syst. Appl. **41**(10), 4915–4928 (2014)
19. Damrongsakmethee, T., Neagoe, V.-E.: Principal component analysis and relieff cascaded with decision tree for credit scoring. In: Silhavy, R. (ed.) CSOC 2019. AISC, vol. 985, pp. 85–95. Springer, Cham (2019). https://doi.org/10.1007/978-3-030-19810-7_9
20. Dean, J., Ghemawat, S.: Mapreduce: simplified data processing on large clusters. Commun. ACM **51**(1), 107–113 (2008). https://doi.org/10.1145/1327452.1327492
21. Economics, T.: Euro area consumer credit (2019). https://tradingeconomics.com/euro-area/consumer-credit?continent=europe
22. Economics, T.: Euro area consumer spending (2019). https://tradingeconomics.com/euro-area/consumer-spending?continent=europe
23. Fang, F., Chen, Y.: A new approach for credit scoring by directly maximizing the kolmogorov-smirnov statistic. Comput. Stat. Data Anal. **133**, 180–194 (2019)
24. Feng, X., Xiao, Z., Zhong, B., Qiu, J., Dong, Y.: Dynamic ensemble classification for credit scoring using soft probability. Appl. Soft Comput. **65**, 139–151 (2018). https://doi.org/10.1016/j.asoc.2018.01.021. http://www.sciencedirect.com/science/article/pii/S1568494618300279
25. Fernández-Tobías, I., Tomeo, P., Cantador, I., Noia, T.D., Sciascio, E.D.: Accuracy and diversity in cross-domain recommendations for cold-start users with positive-only feedback. In: Sen, S., Geyer, W., Freyne, J., Castells, P. (eds.) Proceedings of the 10th ACM Conference on Recommender Systems, Boston, MA, USA, 15–19 September 2016, pp. 119–122. ACM (2016). https://doi.org/10.1145/2959100.2959175
26. García, S., Ramírez-Gallego, S., Luengo, J., Benítez, J.M., Herrera, F.: Big data preprocessing: methods and prospects. Big Data Analytics **1**(1), 9 (2016)
27. Ghodselahi, A.: A hybrid support vector machine ensemble model for credit scoring. Int. J. Comput. Appl. **17**(5), 1–5 (2011)
28. Giraud-Carrier, C., Vilalta, R., Brazdil, P.: Introduction to the special issue on meta-learning. Mach. Learn. **54**(3), 187–193 (2004)
29. Guo, S., He, H., Huang, X.: A multi-stage self-adaptive classifier ensemble model with application in credit scoring. IEEE Access **7**, 78549–78559 (2019)
30. Haixiang, G., Yijing, L., Shang, J., Mingyun, G., Yuanyue, H., Bing, G.: Learning from class-imbalanced data: review of methods and applications. Expert Syst. Appl. **73**, 220–239 (2017)
31. Hashem, I.A.T., Anuar, N.B., Gani, A., Yaqoob, I., Xia, F., Khan, S.U.: Mapreduce: review and open challenges. Scientometrics **109**(1), 389–422 (2016)
32. Hassan, M.K., Brodmann, J., Rayfield, B., Huda, M.: Modeling credit risk in credit unions using survival analysis. Int. J. Bank Mark. **36**(3), 482–495 (2018)

33. Hawkins, D.M.: The problem of overfitting. J. Chem. Inf. Comput. Sci. **44**(1), 1–12 (2004)
34. He, H., Garcia, E.A.: Learning from imbalanced data. IEEE Trans. Knowl. Data Eng. **21**(9), 1263–1284 (2009). https://doi.org/10.1109/TKDE.2008.239
35. Henrique, B.M., Sobreiro, V.A., Kimura, H.: Literature review: machine learning techniques applied to financial market prediction. Expert Syst. Appl. **124**, 226–251 (2019)
36. Huang, J., Ling, C.X.: Using AUC and accuracy in evaluating learning algorithms. IEEE Trans. Knowl. Data Eng. **17**(3), 299–310 (2005)
37. Japkowicz, N., Stephen, S.: The class imbalance problem: a systematic study. Intell. Data Anal. **6**(5), 429–449 (2002)
38. Jeni, L.A., Cohn, J.F., De La Torre, F.: Facing imbalanced data-recommendations for the use of performance metrics. In: 2013 Humaine Association Conference on Affective Computing and Intelligent Interaction, pp. 245–251. IEEE (2013)
39. Khemais, Z., Nesrine, D., Mohamed, M., et al.: Credit scoring and default risk prediction: a comparative study between discriminant analysis & logistic regression. Int. J. Econ. Finance **8**(4), 39 (2016)
40. Khemakhem, S., Ben Said, F., Boujelbene, Y.: Credit risk assessment for unbalanced datasets based on data mining, artificial neural network and support vector machines. J. Modell. Manage. **13**(4), 932–951 (2018)
41. Laha, A.: Developing credit scoring models with SOM and fuzzy rule based k-NN classifiers. In: IEEE International Conference on Fuzzy Systems, pp. 692–698, July 2006. https://doi.org/10.1109/FUZZY.2006.1681786
42. Lessmann, S., Baesens, B., Seow, H.V., Thomas, L.C.: Benchmarking state-of-the-art classification algorithms for credit scoring: an update of research. Eur. J. Oper. Res. **247**(1), 124–136 (2015)
43. Lika, B., Kolomvatsos, K., Hadjiefthymiades, S.: Facing the cold start problem in recommender systems. Expert Syst. Appl. **41**(4), 2065–2073 (2014). https://doi.org/10.1016/j.eswa.2013.09.005
44. Liu, C., Huang, H., Lu, S.: Research on personal credit scoring model based on artificial intelligence. In: Sugumaran, V., Xu, Z., P., S., Zhou, H. (eds.) MMIA 2019. AISC, vol. 929, pp. 466–473. Springer, Cham (2019). https://doi.org/10.1007/978-3-030-15740-1_64
45. Liu, H., Hussain, F., Tan, C.L., Dash, M.: Discretization: an enabling technique. Data Min. Knowl. Discov. **6**(4), 393–423 (2002)
46. López, R.F., Ramon-Jeronimo, J.M.: Modelling credit risk with scarce default data: on the suitability of cooperative bootstrapped strategies for small low-default portfolios. JORS **65**(3), 416–434 (2014). https://doi.org/10.1057/jors.2013.119
47. López, J., Maldonado, S.: Profit-based credit scoring based on robust optimization and feature selection. Inf. Sci. **500**, 190–202 (2019)
48. Luo, C., Wu, D., Wu, D.: A deep learning approach for credit scoring using credit default swaps. Eng. Appl. Artif. Intell. **65**, 465–470 (2017)
49. Luque, A., Carrasco, A., Martín, A., de las Heras, A.: The impact of class imbalance in classification performance metrics based on the binary confusion matrix. Pattern Recogn. **91**, 216–231 (2019)
50. Maldonado, S., Peters, G., Weber, R.: Credit scoring using three-way decisions with probabilistic rough sets. Inf. Sci. (2018). https://doi.org/10.1016/j.ins.2018.08.001. http://www.sciencedirect.com/science/article/pii/S0020025518306078
51. Malekipirbazari, M., Aksakalli, V.: Risk assessment in social lending via random forests. Expert Syst. Appl. **42**(10), 4621–4631 (2015)

52. Mester, L.J., et al.: What's the point of credit scoring? Bus. Rev. **3**, 3–16 (1997)
53. Neagoe, V., Ciotec, A., Cucu, G.: Deep convolutional neural networks versus multilayer perceptron for financial prediction. In: International Conference on Communications (COMM), pp. 201–206, June 2018
54. Pasila, F.: Credit scoring modeling of Indonesian micro, small and medium enterprises using neuro-fuzzy algorithm. In: IEEE International Conference on Fuzzy Systems, pp. 1–6, June 2019. https://doi.org/10.1109/FUZZ-IEEE.2019.8858841
55. Powers, D.: Evaluation: from precision, recall and f-factor to roc, informedness, markedness & correlation. Mach. Learn. Technol. **2**, January 2008
56. Rapach, D.E., Wohar, M.E.: In-sample vs. out-of-sample tests of stock return predictability in the context of data mining. J. Empirical Finance **13**(2), 231–247 (2006)
57. Rodda, S., Erothi, U.S.R.: Class imbalance problem in the network intrusion detection systems. In: 2016 International Conference on Electrical, Electronics, and Optimization Techniques (ICEEOT), pp. 2685–2688. IEEE (2016)
58. Saia, R.: A discrete wavelet transform approach to fraud detection. In: Yan, Z., Molva, R., Mazurczyk, W., Kantola, R. (eds.) NSS 2017. LNCS, vol. 10394, pp. 464–474. Springer, Cham (2017). https://doi.org/10.1007/978-3-319-64701-2_34
59. Saia, R., Carta, S.: An entropy based algorithm for credit scoring. In: Tjoa, A.M., Xu, L.D., Raffai, M., Novak, N.M. (eds.) CONFENIS 2016. LNBIP, vol. 268, pp. 263–276. Springer, Cham (2016). https://doi.org/10.1007/978-3-319-49944-4_20
60. Saia, R., Carta, S.: Introducing a vector space model to perform a proactive credit scoring. In: Fred, A., Dietz, J., Aveiro, D., Liu, K., Bernardino, J., Filipe, J. (eds.) IC3K 2016. CCIS, vol. 914, pp. 125–148. Springer, Cham (2019). https://doi.org/10.1007/978-3-319-99701-8_6
61. Saia, R., Carta, S.: A linear-dependence-based approach to design proactive credit scoring models. In: KDIR, pp. 111–120 (2016)
62. Saia, R., Carta, S.: Evaluating credit card transactions in the frequency domain for a proactive fraud detection approach. In: SECRYPT, pp. 335–342. SciTePress (2017)
63. Saia, R., Carta, S.: A fourier spectral pattern analysis to design credit scoring models. In: Proceedings of the 1st International Conference on Internet of Things and Machine Learning, p. 18. ACM (2017)
64. Saia, R., Carta, S., Fenu, G.: A wavelet-based data analysis to credit scoring. In: Proceedings of the 2nd International Conference on Digital Signal Processing, pp. 176–180. ACM (2018)
65. Saia, R., Carta, S., Recupero, D.R.: A probabilistic-driven ensemble approach to perform event classification in intrusion detection system. In: KDIR, pp. 139–146. SciTePress (2018)
66. Saia, R., Carta, S., Recupero, D.R., Fenu, G., Saia, M.: A discretized enriched technique to enhance machine learning performance in credit scoring. In: KDIR, pp. 202–213. ScitePress (2019)
67. Saia, R., et al.: A frequency-domain-based pattern mining for credit card fraud detection. In: IoTBDS, pp. 386–391 (2017)
68. Sewwandi, D., Perera, K., Sandaruwan, S., Lakchani, O., Nugaliyadde, A., Thelijjagoda, S.: Linguistic features based personality recognition using social media data. In: 2017 6th National Conference on Technology and Management (NCTM), pp. 63–68, January 2017. https://doi.org/10.1109/NCTM.2017.7872829
69. Siddiqi, N.: Intelligent Credit Scoring: Building and Implementing Better Credit Risk Scorecards. John Wiley & Sons, Hoboken (2017)

70. Sohn, S.Y., Kim, D.H., Yoon, J.H.: Technology credit scoring model with fuzzy logistic regression. Appl. Soft Comput. **43**, 150–158 (2016)
71. Son, L.H.: Dealing with the new user cold-start problem in recommender systems: a comparative review. Inf. Syst. **58**, 87–104 (2016). https://doi.org/10.1016/j.is.2014.10.001
72. Sun, X., Liu, B., Cao, J., Luo, J., Shen, X.: Who am i? personality detection based on deep learning for texts. In: IEEE International Conference on Communications (ICC), pp. 1–6, May 2018
73. Tamadonejad, A., Abdul-Majid, M., Abdul-Rahman, A., Jusoh, M., Tabandeh, R.: Early warning systems for banking crises? political and economic stability. Jurnal Ekonomi Malaysia **50**(2), 31–38 (2016)
74. Thanuja, V., Venkateswarlu, B., Anjaneyulu, G.: Applications of data mining in customer relationship management. J. Comput. Math. Sci. **2**(3), 399–580 (2011)
75. Thomas, L.C.: A survey of credit and behavioural scoring: forecasting financial risk of lending to consumers. Int. J. Forecast. **16**(2), 149–172 (2000)
76. Tian, Y., Yong, Z., Luo, J.: A new approach for reject inference in credit scoring using kernel-free fuzzy quadratic surface support vector machines. Appl. Soft Comput. **73**, 96–105 (2018)
77. Tripathi, D., Edla, D.R., Cheruku, R.: Hybrid credit scoring model using neighborhood rough set and multi-layer ensemble classification. J. Intell. Fuzzy Syst. **34**(3), 1543–1549 (2018)
78. Tripathi, D., Edla, D.R., Kuppili, V., Bablani, A., Dharavath, R.: Credit scoring model based on weighted voting and cluster based feature selection. Procedia Comput. Sci. **132**, 22–31 (2018)
79. Vedala, R., Kumar, B.R.: An application of naive bayes classification for credit scoring in e-lending platform. In: International Conference on Data Science Engineering (ICDSE), pp. 81–84, July 2012. https://doi.org/10.1109/ICDSE.2012.6282321
80. Vilalta, R., Drissi, Y.: A perspective view and survey of meta-learning. Artif. Intell. Rev. **18**(2), 77–95 (2002)
81. Wang, C.M., Huang, Y.F.: Evolutionary-based feature selection approaches with new criteria for data mining: a case study of credit approval data. Expert Syst. Appl. **36**(3), 5900–5908 (2009)
82. Wu, X., Kumar, V.: The Top Ten Algorithms in Data Mining. CRC Press, United States (2009)
83. Xia, Y., Liu, C., Li, Y., Liu, N.: A boosted decision tree approach using bayesian hyper-parameter optimization for credit scoring. Expert Syst. Appl. **78**, 225–241 (2017)
84. Zhang, H., He, H., Zhang, W.: Classifier selection and clustering with fuzzy assignment in ensemble model for credit scoring. Neurocomputing **316**, 210–221 (2018)
85. Zhang, X., Yang, Y., Zhou, Z.: A novel credit scoring model based on optimized random forest. In: IEEE Annual Computing and Communication Workshop and Conference (CCWC), pp. 60–65, January 2018
86. Zhao, Y., Shen, Y., Huang, Y.: Dmdp: a dynamic multi-source default probability prediction framework. Data Sci. Eng. **4**(1), 3–13 (2019)
87. Zhu, B., Yang, W., Wang, H., Yuan, Y.: A hybrid deep learning model for consumer credit scoring. In: International Conference on Artificial Intelligence and Big Data (ICAIBD), pp. 205–208, May 2018. https://doi.org/10.1109/ICAIBD.2018.8396195

An Approximate High Quality Nearest Neighbor Distance Profile

Paolo Avogadro[✉] and Matteo Alessandro Dominoni

University of Milano-Bicocca, v.le Sarca 336/14, 20126 Milano, Italy
{paolo.avogadro,matteo.dominoni}@unimib.it

Abstract. In the present research we provide an algorithm for a good quality approximate nearest neighbor distance (*nnd*) profile for a time series, faster than a brute force approach. There are three natural forms of topology embedded in a time series due to different processes: the Euclidean, Symbolic Aggregate Approximation (SAX) and time topology. The first one stems from calculating the Euclidean distance among the sequences; SAX is a quick form of clustering by approximating the values of a sequence; time topology simply refers to the fact that consecutive sequences are naturally similar. By interweaving these three topologies one can prune the calls to the distance function in respect to the brute force algorithm and thus speed up the calculation of the *nnd* profile. We evaluated the algorithm in terms of the speedup in respect to other algorithms and we compared its precision by counting the percentage of exact *nnd*s returned.

Keywords: Time series · Motif · Discord · Nearest neighbor distance · Matrix profile · Topology

1 Introduction and Related Works

Time series analysis is an active research topic [1] since many sensors produce data in this format. As the technology improves, the length of the time series is increasing, thus calling for new faster approaches which allow to process the data more efficiently. A problem which has been gaining attention lately refers to data streams [2] where the attention is shifted at processing the data as soon as it arrives instead of analyzing a time series as a whole.

One of the first tools used at the time of approaching a time series involves dimensionality reduction. This process reduces the complexity of the calculation and can remove redundancies. The Symbolic Aggregate Approximation [3] is a very successful algorithm which allows to turn a sequence into a much shorter symbolic sequence (s-sequence or cluster) and it has been used as the basis of many research works. Among its properties we can enumerate the fact that it scales linearly with the length of the time series, while maintaining high clusterization standards [4] (i.e. sequences within a cluster are similar to each other).

© Springer Nature Switzerland AG 2020
A. Fred et al. (Eds.): IC3K 2019, CCIS 1297, pp. 158–182, 2020.
https://doi.org/10.1007/978-3-030-66196-0_8

At the time of comparing sequences within a time series the most natural method is using the Euclidean distance since it provides a very intuitive indication of the relation among two sequences. A lot of attention has been gained by the usage of z-normalized Euclidean distance. In this case, before calculating the Euclidean distance among sequences, one has to z-normalize its points. These two processes can be combined efficiently by noticing that the Euclidean distance of z-normalized sequences can be obtained in terms of their average, standard deviation and by calculating their scalar product. A completely different approach for comparing distances involves the Dynamic Time Warping (DTW) [5], which is a similarity measure applicable to sequences of different length. The drawback of this technique is its computational complexity.

Two main ideas guide time series analysis: anomalies and recurrent patterns [6–8]. One of the most successful anomaly definitions is the *discord* concept introduced by [9]. The very same article proposed an efficient algorithm to find discords, called HOT SAX which proved to be very quick and exact. The research has been proceeding towards approximate discord algorithms in order to speed up the process. For example Rare Rule Anomaly [10,11] is based on the Kolmogorov complexity of the SAX words and can reduce the amount of distance calls. At variance in respect to SAX the length of the sequences to be analyzed is not an input parameter but it is automatically suggested by the grammar rules.

Instead of searching for anomalies one might be interested in finding recurrent or most similar sequences. For example the concept of motifs [6] goes into this direction. Also in this case there are many algorithms devoted to motif search, including approximate, exact searches, serial and parallel algorithms.

Recently, the articles regarding Matrix Profile have proposed a series of techniques [8,12–14] which can return the calculation of the distances among all the sequences of a time series in approximate or exact, serial and parallelized form, allowing for complete characterization of time series.

The present article is devoted at providing a simple approach where one needs to introduce minor modifications to a HOT SAX code in order to obtain the nearest neighbor distance (*nnd*) profile quickly. This is an extended version of [15] where we clarify some of the concepts, introduce new validation examples, we suggest optimal SAX parameters and we use the approximate nearest neighbor distance profile for finding motifs.

2   Terminology

In this section we detail some of the terms used in the rest of the paper.

- A time series is denoted with the capital letter P, while we use the same letter, lowercase, with subscript, for its points: p_j, $j = 1, .., N$. The points are supposed to equispaced in time and consecutive, the subscript denotes their time position.
- A sequence within the time series is denoted with a capital letter and a superscript: S^k, where the superscript indicates the time of the first point of the sequence. We use the lowercase letter s for the length of the sequence

(the number of points therein contained). Since the length of the sequences is fixed, in the case where no ambiguity arises, it is enough to use the time of their first point to describe them ($S^k \leftrightarrow k$). The points of sequence S^k are $\left(s_1^k, s_2^k, ..., s_s^k\right)$, according to the notation used for the whole time series, these points can also be denoted as $(p_k, p_{k+1}, ..., p_{k+s-1})$.

- The Euclidean distance among two sequences is obtained with

$$d(S^k, S^j) = \sqrt{\sum_{n=1}^{s} \left(s_n^k - s_n^j\right)^2} \tag{1}$$

If one is interested in calculating the z-normalized Euclidean distance, an efficient solution is to resort at first at calculating the average values and standard deviations for all of the sequences and then using the scalar product as described in [12]. Applying a growing strictly monotonic function to Eq. 1, does not change the order of the $nnds$ and simplifies the calculations. For example we will also use the squared Euclidean function since it does not change the order of the $nnds$, thus allowing one to find the positions of the discords or the motifs:

$$d_2(S^k, S^j) = \sum_{n=1}^{s} \left(s_n^k - s_n^j\right)^2, \tag{2}$$

- for each sequence one can calculate the nearest neighbor distance:

$$nnd(S^i) = \min_{j:|i-j|\geq s} d(S^i, S^j), \tag{3}$$

the index j runs on all of the sequences of the time series, with the exception of those which overlap with the one under investigation (sequence i). This non-self match condition [9] is necessary to avoid "spurious" small distances between a sequence and the following ones, since these two sequences partially overlap.

- The nnd profile is the vector containing the nearest distances of all the sequences of the time series. In the first article of the Matrix Profile series, the term *matrix profile* is used with a more general meaning (see definition 6 and 7 of [12]), while in the rest of papers of the series, nnd profile and *matrix profile* coincide.

- The nnd density returns information regarding the number of sequences with a nearest neighbor within a certain distance. Once the nnd profile has been calculated, one needs to consider the max and min nnd values, divide this interval in a given amount of bins (for example 1000) and count the total number of sequences with a nnd belonging to each bin. For example the discord, which is the sequence with the highest nnd value would belong to the righter-most bin.

- the time distance between two sequences is simply:

$$d_t(S^k, S^j) = |k - j| \tag{4}$$

it addresses the amount of points which separate the two sequences.

3   Finding Discords

Since this work is devoted at providing a simple modification allowing to turn HOT SAX into an algorithm for obtaining an approximation of the nnd profile, we detail here HOT SAX, beginning with SAX [3].

3.1   SAX

The Symbolic Aggregate Approximation clusterizes efficiently the sequences of a time series. A summary of this procedure includes:

- All the sequences are divided into r sub-sequences of equal length l. For example a $s = 56$ points sequence can be turned into $r = 7$ consecutive sub-sequences of length $l = 8$ ($s = r \cdot l$)
- Each sub-sequence is summarized by taking its algebraic average value. This procedure is called Piecewise Aggregate Approximation [16]. As a result the PAA shortens a sequence (of s points) into a reduced sequence, or r-sequence (of r points, $r << s$). In the example under consideration we pass from a 56 points sequence to a r-sequence composed of only 7 r-points.
- In order to better handle the single r-points it is possible to group them further, by dividing the range of possible r-points in bins and assigning to each bin a letter. As a result one obtains a short symbolic sequence (containing r symbols) starting from a much longer sequence (made of s points). The set of possible letters which characterize the interval of the r-points is called *alphabet*. The size of the *alphabet* is denoted with the letter a. Usually one chooses the intervals determining the association r-point $\rightarrow$ letter, based on the principle according to which each letter should represent approximately the same quantity of r-points.

With a careful choice of the SAX parameters, the amount of sequences of a time series is much larger than the amount of symbolic sequences (aka s-sequences or clusters), for this reason many sequences correspond to a single symbolic sequence. We refer to *own cluster* of sequence S as the cluster which contains it. The choices of the parameters of the PAA and the amount of possible letters of the *alphabet*, determine the size of the clusters and the quality of the approximation. An example can help to better understand SAX, we consider here a fictitious sequence where the values of its 20 points read: 34433013225661872103. SAX is now used in order to turn it into a symbolic sequence of 5 letters. Let's

Table 1. An example of turning a sequence into a symbolic sequence with SAX, [15].

Sequence	3, 4, 4, 3,	3, 0, 1, 3,	2, 2, 5, 6,	6, 1, 8, 7,	2, 1, 0, 3
r-sequence	14/4,	7/4,	15/4,	22/4,	6/4
r-sequence	3.5,	1.75,	3.75,	5.5,	1.5
s-sequence	b	a	b	c	a

suppose that the alphabet contains 3 letters, determining the following vocabulary: $[0, 3) \rightarrow a$, $[3, 5) \rightarrow b$, $[5, 8] \rightarrow c$ (this choice implies that the whole range of r-points spans the interval $[3, 8]$, as detailed in Table 1).

In this case a 20 points sequence has been turned into a 5 letters s-sequence: *babca*, in a whole time series, however, one expects that many sequences might be turned in the same symbolic sequence, since it contains much less information. The original SAX article provided also an efficient technique to quickly pass from the clusters back to the sequences with the help of a trie and an array. The final result of SAX is thus a quick clusterization of all the sequences of a time series into symbolic sequences.

3.2   HOT SAX

As a reminder, we recall that the first discord of a time series is the sequence with the highest *nnd* value, the second discord is the sequence with the highest *nnd* value which does not overlap with the first one, the third discord has the highest *nnd* and it does not overlap with the previous two, etc. Since one needs to know the *nnd* of a sequence, this implies to make a lot of calls to the Euclidean distance function. In the limit, a brute force algorithm would require to calculate all of the distances from all of the sequences. Such an approach has an asymptotic complexity $O(N^2)$. The reason is that the brute force algorithm requires two nested loops:

- The external one running on all of the ($\approx N$) sequences, in order to understand which of them has the highest *nnd* (this is a maximization procedure).
- The inner loop, instead, is a minimization procedure for determining the *nnd* of the sequence selected by the outer loop. It requires to calculate the distances between the selected sequence and all the ($\approx N$) others.

Such a brute force approach leads to calculating the exact *nnd* profile. On the other hand the aim of HOT SAX is to skip most of the calculation in order to quickly find the first discord(s) of a time series. As a result one expects that HOT SAX should not be able to provide good quality *nnd* profiles.

The idea behind HOT SAX is that the SAX clusterization puts together sequences which are also close Euclidean neighbors. In practice there is a link between the notion of closeness (topology) derived by the Euclidean distance and the notion of closeness (topology) derived by being part of the same SAX cluster. Once this link has been established one can re-arrange the two loops of the brute force approach. At the beginning one will consider those sequences belonging to small clusters, in the limit containing only one sequence. If there is only one sequence in a cluster, it means that, for that sequence, there should be no close (Euclidean) neighbor. This implies that it is a good discord candidate. The minimization procedure associated with this sequence is likely to return a high *nnd* value. With this prescription, the outer loop will likely stumble on good discord candidates quite soon. In the remainder of the external loop, other sequences are being processed. For each of them, the inner loop calculates distances with the other sequences and updates the current nnd value of the sequence. If the current nnd drops below the nnd of the current best discord candidate, one is sure that the sequence under observation cannot be the discord: the remainder of the inner loop, which is a minimization process, can only diminish the current nnd of the sequence. As a result the remaining part of the inner loop can be skipped. Also the inner loop can be rearranged. Instead of calculating the distance between the sequence under observation and all the others just following their time order (S^1, S^2,...), HOT SAX suggests to first calculate the distance with those sequences belonging to the own cluster. The rationale is clear: let's check those sequences which are close according to the SAX topology. By starting the minimization process with good neighbor candidates one is pretty sure that the nnd of the sequence under observation should drop quickly, possibly becoming smaller than the best so far value, and thus allowing to skip the rest of the loop. If the sequence is still a possible discord candidate after checking all of the other sequences of the own SAX cluster, the remainder of the inner loop runs on all of the other sequences in random order. A sequence still having the highest nnd at the end of its inner loop is the new good discord candidate which has set a new best so far nnd value.

In summary, by rearranging the outer and inner loop according to the suggestions of the SAX clusters one is expected to be in a position of skipping most of the inner loop distance function calls and thus obtaining a very quick discord search.

The execution speed of HOT SAX is a function of the time series under observation, however this algorithm is still now one of the fastest exact discord algorithms. We see that the key factor determining the new loop rearrangements is the strong link between the topology induced by the Euclidean distance and the topology induced by SAX. Notice that during the discord search one can keep track of the approximate nnd value associated with all of the sequences. This approximate nnd profile (see for example Fig. 5 left), is likely different from the exact one (Fig. 4 left), exactly because the aim of the algorithm is to skip calculations. For this reason it cannot be used for other purposes (like for example finding motifs).

4   Curse of Dimensionality

The topology (closeness) induced by SAX and the one induced by the Euclidean distance are linked but they are not exactly the same. One of the obvious reasons is that the SAX procedure clusters r-points into letters, however the breakpoints defining the letters are sharp: two very close r-points might be at the opposite sides in respect to a breakpoint. This would give rise to two different letters. Such a result would artificially put two r-sequences in different symbolic sequences although they might be close from the Euclidean point of view (see Fig. 1, right). The passage from the r-sequences to the s-sequences can be visualized as slicing an r-dimensional space where a reduced sequence corresponds to a point, while a SAX cluster to an r-dimensional parallelepiped (aka parallelotope) as in Fig. 1

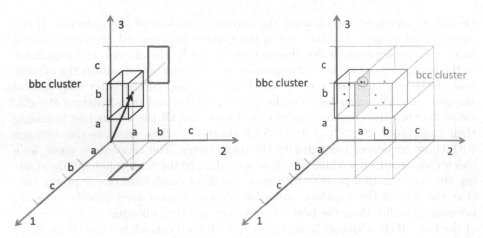

Fig. 1. (Left) We consider an r-point and a 3-dimensional parallelepiped which represents the cluster *bbc*. (Right) Two nearest neighbor r-points that belong to different symbolic sequences (*bbc* and *bcc*). Although these two r-points have likely been obtained by Euclidean close sequences they do not belong to the same SAX cluster [15].

(left). We will limit the rest of the discussion to the case in which the breakpoints defining the letters are equally spaced, thus giving rise to hypercubes. The logic does not change, but the notation and the calculation of the volumes becomes much easier with hypercubes rather than parallelotopes. One might think that the amount of points which are suffering from being close to the border of a hypercube, and thus have a higher chance that their close neighbor belongs to a different cluster, should be a minority. However, with a counter-intuitive logic, as the dimension of the hypercube grows most of its volume becomes close to its surface, thus increasing the probability that an r-point lays close to one of its faces. If one adopts a view where the points are placed at random positions, the fraction of volume over the total available, represents the probability that a point is comprised within the surface surrounding the volume. Let's now divide a hypercube (with edges of length e) in two parts: a inner concentric smaller hypercube with edges of length $e - \epsilon$, and the shell between the full hypercube and the inner one. The inner hypercube represents the volume where the points are far from the surface and thus it is reasonable to expect that the Euclidean neighbor should lay in the same symbolic sequence. At variance the shell is the region of the space where there is a high chance that the closest neighbor of an r-point is outside of the hypercube itself. Let's now consider the ratio between the inner part and the total volume of the hypercube as a function of the dimension of the space r:

$$\frac{\text{inner volume}}{\text{total volume}} = \left(\frac{e - \epsilon}{e}\right)^r = \left(1 - \frac{\epsilon}{e}\right)^r \xrightarrow{r \to \infty} 0. \tag{5}$$

This shows that, as the dimension r increases (ϵ/e being fixed), most of the volume of the hypercube is located close to its borders. According to this view the link between the Euclidean and the SAX topology becomes less and less valid as the length of the symbolic sequences increases.

This reasoning helps to understand why the SAX procedure is known for providing good results for HOT SAX when the number of elements of the PAA is around $3-4$. If these elements were $10-20$ one would obtain symbolic sequences much closer to their sequence of origin, however, the curse of dimensionality would hinder the connection between SAX and Euclidean topology at the basis of the re-ordering of the loop in HOT SAX.

5   Extending the Topological Approach

Up to now we have seen how the link between the Euclidean and SAX topology allowed for a quick calculation of the discords of a time series. In the case in which there is another simple topology one might be tempted to use it for improving the approximate *nnd* profile associated with a HOT SAX calculation.

The idea that time close sequences should share a lot of properties is essentially embedded in the non self-match concept. Two overlapping sequences are similar also from the point of view of the nearest neighbor: we expect that the Euclidean nearest neighbors of two time close sequences should also be time close.

5.1   An Approximate *nnd* Profile

We propose here some simple modifications to HOT SAX which will provide a good quality approximate nearest neighbor profile (we will detail in Sect. 6 the meaning of "good quality approximation"). The approximate *nnd*s returned at the end of a discord search by HOT SAX are obtained by truncating the inner loop. This, in practice, is equivalent to reducing the minimization space of the *nnd*s, by skipping those calculations which are not instrumental for obtaining discords. This reduced search space returns *nnd* values which are equal or higher than the exact ones since the minimization space has been reduced a lot. At this point we want to find indications on two conflicting ideas:

– How to expand the search space for improving the approximate *nnd* of HOT SAX.
– How to limit at most the number of calculations in order to speed up the process of finding the good quality approximate *nnd*.

At the beginning we will list all the procedures to be applied to HOT SAX and later we will explain them in detail.

Before starting the loops one should perform two different SAX clusterizations, one with an alphabet of size a and the second identical but for the size of the alphabet, which should be $a + 1$. At this point each sequence belongs to a cluster obtained with the first SAX procedure and another one with the second SAX procedure. Notice that increasing the number of letters does not augment the dimensionality of the hypercubes, thus it does not go in the direction of disrupting the connection between SAX and Euclidean topologies, although it increases the number of available clusters.

The algorithm proposed in this research has two nested loops which follow the structure of HOT SAX. In particular the outer loop is identical to that of HOT SAX (running on all of the sequences, starting on small clusters). The inner loop, however, is going to be different. For each sequence S of the outer loop one should:

1. Perform a full calculation between S and all of the sequences belonging to its own SAX cluster with alphabet a (but for self matches). The code should keep track of which distance calls have been performed.
2. If the sequence under observation can still be the discord after point 1, perform the same action as point 1, but using the cluster obtained with increased size alphabet $(a + 1)$. Since we expect an overlap between the two clusters, skip those distance calculations which have already been performed at step 1.
3. If the sequence under consideration can still be the discord at this point (i.e. its approximate nnd is higher than the best so far value), call the distance function between S and all the other sequences of the time series in random order. At any point during this procedure, if the approximate $nnd(S)$ becomes smaller than the highest so far nnd, skip the rest of these distance calls.
4. At the end of the outer loop use the properties of the time topology to improve the approximate nnd profile so far obtained

In order to further improve the approximate nnd profile one should search for more than one discord (in our case search for the first 10 discords). During the calculation of a discord following the first one, if a sequence has an approximate nnd value already smaller than the current best one, any further distance call can be skipped. As a general rule, whenever a distance function is called we check if any of the nnds of the two sequences involved can be updated with the results of the distance calculation. We also update the (approximate) nearest neighbor of each sequence.

We will assess the results of this procedure in Sect. 6.

5.2   Double SAX

As detailed in Sect. 4, the neighbor of a sequence close to the surface of a cluster is likely not present in the cluster itself. It is also difficult to pinpoint exactly which is the neighboring cluster which most likely contains that neighbor. In order to overcome these problems with a simple solution we can resort at performing two times the SAX procedure, where the second time we change the amount of letters of the alphabet. There are two main reasons for this:

- By increasing the number of letters of the SAX alphabet we add one breakpoint, among the set of r-points. For this reason those r-points which are close to a breakpoint (when the alphabet contains a letters) should be moved far from it when the alphabet contains $a + 1$ letters. We remind that, in order to create a letters, one needs $a - 1$ inner breakpoints, since the two external ones are fixed.

– A SAX procedure with a bigger alphabet is likely going to produce a more refined clusterization. Many of the clusters of the original SAX procedure should be "covered" by collections of clusters of the SAX procedure with $a+1$. As a result the second own SAX cluster should be smaller and overlapping with the first one, thus not producing an important computational load.

As an example let's consider a 3 letter alphabet (a, b, c) where the r-points range within the interval $[0, 8]$. Let's also suppose that the following breakpoints provide roughly equal amounts of r-values for each letter: $[0, 3) \rightarrow a$, $[3, 5) \rightarrow b$, and $[5, 8] \rightarrow c$. If there are two r-points of the following kind:

$$\begin{pmatrix} 3.95 \\ 2.99 \\ 7.21 \end{pmatrix} \rightarrow \begin{pmatrix} b \\ a \\ c \end{pmatrix} ; \begin{pmatrix} 3.82 \\ 3.01 \\ 7.38 \end{pmatrix} \rightarrow \begin{pmatrix} b \\ b \\ c \end{pmatrix}$$

they become part of two different s-sequences: bac and bbc. The reason is that the second coordinates (2.99 and 3.01), although very close, lay at the two opposite sides of the breakpoint in 3. By adding one letter to the alphabet: $(a, b, c) \rightarrow (a, b, c, d)$, one introduces an additional breakpoint, providing for example the following vocabulary: $[0, 2) \rightarrow a$, $[2, 4) \rightarrow b$, $[4, 6) \rightarrow c$, $[6, 8] \rightarrow d$. As a result the two r-points are prompted in the s-sequence denoted with the letters (b, b, d):

$$\begin{pmatrix} 3.95 \\ 2.99 \\ 7.21 \end{pmatrix} \rightarrow \begin{pmatrix} b \\ b \\ d \end{pmatrix} ; \begin{pmatrix} 3.82 \\ 3.01 \\ 7.38 \end{pmatrix} \rightarrow \begin{pmatrix} b \\ b \\ d \end{pmatrix} .$$

When there are two SAX procedures each sequence is associated to two clusters likely having an important overlap. At this point one can look for neighbors in both of the clusters. Since the number of breakpoints is higher in the second case, the intervals associated will be smaller, leading to finer clusterizations. It should be noted however that, by looking at the neighbors of a sequence in two different clusters increases the search space. This ensures to diminish the nearest neighbor distance at the cost of increasing the computational time. For this reason it is not advisable to do the same procedure many times, otherwise the amount of calculations would increase too much. One could argue that also diminishing the amount of letters might lead to very similar results since the breakpoint would also diminish by one unity thus shifting their positions. The drawback of a smaller alphabet is that the clusters thus obtained would be likely bigger than those obtained with the first SAX procedure, increasing too much the search space.

5.3   Full Search of the Own SAX Clusters

This modification to a HOT SAX code is very easy since it consists in performing the distance calls among the selected sequence and all the other sequences belonging to the own cluster. In practice, in all of the HOT SAX codes there is a *if/then* condition which stops the minimization procedure as soon as the approximate *nnd* of the sequence under investigation drops below the value of the current discord candidate. By removing this condition for the own cluster, one is sure that there is going to be a full search within the original cluster of the sequence. In the case in which the SAX and Euclidean topologies were "identical", this prescription would be enough for finding the nearest neighbor, however as we have seen in Sect. 4, this is not the case and we need to enlarge the search space. As a pre requisite we have already performed SAX with $a + 1$, we can thus extend the full search also to this second own cluster. In order to skip useless calculations we use an integer array of size N initialized to 0. Each time that a distance call between sequence S and one of its SAX neighbors is performed we set the corresponding value of the array to 1. When a new sequence is being investigated it is enough to reset the array. It is also important to remind that the SAX clusters are based on the r-points of the PAA and not on the exact sequences. For this reason, even if the SAX topology had been very close to the Euclidean topology, two close sequences might not belong to the same SAX cluster.

5.4   All the Other Sequences

At the end of the full search of the own SAX clusters, provided that the approximate nnd is still higher than the best candidate, one has to keep on calculating distances with all the remaining sequences. In this case the procedure is aborted as soon as the nnd drops below the current best value.

5.5   Time Topology

The procedures of Sect. 5.3 and Sect. 5.4 exhaust the inner loop of the HOT SAX. Since the search space is bigger than the one of HOT SAX we are sure that the approximated nnds so far obtained are equal or smaller than those of HOT SAX. If one compares this approximated nnd profile and the one obtained from HOT SAX, there is a visible improvement. It is also clear that there are many spikes which appear spurious. One might think of performing another SAX procedure with even further increased alphabets, however this does not produce particularly good results. The amount of calculations increases but there is no obvious improvement of the approximate nnd profile.

In [13] it was described for the first time a form of stability of the nearest neighbor distance profile, called Consecutive Neighborhood Preserving (CNP) Property. This property was also noticed independently in [15] and it is strongly linked with the time topology: sequences close in time have very close nearest neighbors. In particular one can notice that the exact nnd profile shows a degree of regularity, and it can be considered as pseudo-smooth. The discords are the spots of the nnd profile which often show the sharpest peaks, while generally, although there is a considerable noise level, the variations of the nnd profile are not arbitrary. The term pseudo-smooth is to be intended in the following way: once the $nnd(i)$ is known, one can quickly find an upper bound limiting the $nnd(i + 1)$ (its time neighbor). Let's consider a sequence S^i and its closest

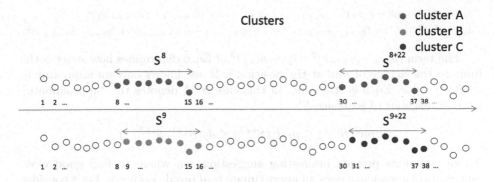

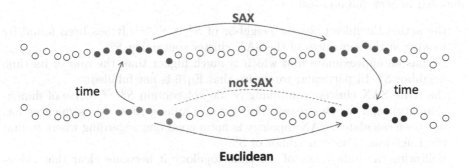

Fig. 2. (Top figure) The two sequences S^8 and S^9 are closest time-neighbors, however they do not fit into the same SAX cluster. S^8 belongs to the red cluster and S^9 to the green one. The red cluster comprises also of sequence $S^{8+22} = S^{30}$, which is the closest Euclidean neighbor of S^8. Unfortunately sequences S^9 and S^{9+22} arc not part of the same symbolic sequence, for this reason the distance among them has not been calculated. (bottom figure) According to the following reasoning: $S^9 \xrightarrow{\text{time}} S^{9-1} \xrightarrow{\text{SAX}} S^{9-1+22} \xrightarrow{\text{time}} S^{9-1+22+1}$ we can guess that S^9 and S^{9+22} are likely Euclidean neighbors [15]. (color figure online)

neighbor S^{i+k} (where $k > s$ in order to avoid self matches). At this point we can provide an inequality limiting the value of $nnd(S^{i+1})$:

$$nnd^2(S^{i+1}) \le d_2(S^{i+1}, S^{i+k+1}) = nnd^2(S^i) + (p_{i+s} - p_{i+s+k})^2 - (p_i - p_{i+k})^2, \quad (6)$$

we used the squared Euclidean distance in order to avoid using the square root and we considered the squared nnds. The first inequality is valid since the definition of nnd implies that it is the minimum among all the distance calls between S^{i+1} and all the other sequences, like for example S^{i+k+1}. The formula $d_2(S^{i+1}, S^{i+k+1})$ can be expressed as a function of $nnd(S^i)$ because there is a strong overlap between these two quantities, and this explains the last part of Eq. 6. This similarity can be seen comparing the two distances:

$$d_2(S^i, S^{i+k}) = (p_i - p_{i+k})^2 + (p_{i+1} - p_{i+k+1})^2 + \cdots + (p_{i+s-1} - p_{i+k+s-1})^2$$
$$d_2(S^{i+1}, S^{i+k+1}) = (p_{i+1} - p_{i+k+1})^2 + \cdots + (p_{i+s-1} - p_{i+k+s-1})^2 + (p_{i+s} - p_{i+k+s})^2.$$

The term $(p_{i+s} - p_{i+s+k})^2 - (p_i - p_{i+k})^2$ of Eq. 6 determines how strict is the limit to the change of nnd at the position i. If one knows only an approximate $nnd(S^i)$ value, Eq. 6 is still valid, in this case S^{i+k} denotes the "approximate" nearest neighbor of sequence S^i:

$$nnd^2(S^{i+1}) \leq nnd_a^2(S^{i+1}) \leq d_2(S^{i+1}, S^{i+k+1})$$

These equations provide interesting suggestions on where to find good close neighbors of a sequence once an approximate nnd profile is known. Let's consider for example the following case, where the sequences under consideration have length 8, and the approximate nnd has been obtained following the procedure detailed in Sect. 5.3 and 5.4:

- the actual Euclidean nearest neighbor of S^8 is S^{8+22}. It has been found by looking at the sequences of the SAX cluster containing S^8.
- S^9 has an approximate nnd which is much higher than the nnd of its time neighbor S^8. In particular we notice that Eq. 6 is not fulfilled.
- the (two) SAX clusters containing S^9 do not contain S^{9+22} (curse of dimensionality), and for this reason the distance among these two sequences has not been calculated. SAX topology is not a good hint regarding where to find the Euclidean nearest neighbor of S^9.
- Following the indications of the time topology it becomes clear that calculating the distance between S^9 and $S^{9-1+22+1}$ is going to improve the actual $nnd(S^9)$, as shown in Fig. 2. Notice that we wrote $S^{9-1+22+1}$ instead of S^{31} in order to decompose the passages: time topology, SAX and time topology again (in the opposite direction).

This procedure can be done from two points of view, e.g. we can check if both of the time neighbors S^8, and S^{10} can suggest good Euclidean neighbors for S^9.

It is also possible to perform longer range sampling, not limited at controlling the closest time-neighbors. In the present work, we check the time-neighbors up to a time distance of 10 steps. In order to avoid useless calculations we invoke the distance function only in the case where there is a violation of Eq. 6.

6   Experimental Results

We provide here examples of nnd profiles obtained with the method exposed in the previous sections. The first data-set under consideration is the ECG 300 which belongs to the MIT-BIH ST change database, part of Physionet [17,18] (Fig. 3).

- Each sequence contains 56 points.
- The PAA is obtained taking sub-sequences of length $l = 8$ points, so each s-sequence comprises 7 letters.
- The basic alphabet size is $a = 3$, and in the case of the extended SAX, $a = 4$.
- We do not z-normalize the sequences.

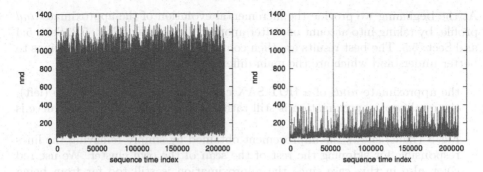

Fig. 3. (Left) The approximate *nnd* profiles returned by a HOT SAX calculation. (Right) With a small modification of HOT SAX, forcing a full calculation of the own cluster, there is a clear improvement the *nnd*s [15].

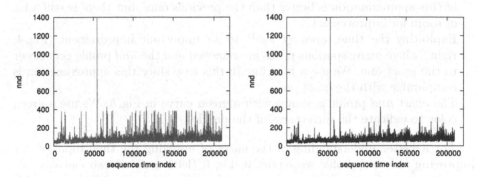

Fig. 4. (Left) By extending the search space also to the SAX cluster with more letters (passing from 3 to 4 letters alphabets) one obtains a further improvement of the *nnd* profile. (Right) With the help of the time topology the quality of the *nnd* profile improves a lot getting very close to the exact one. [15]. (color figure online)

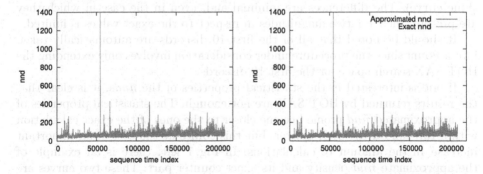

Fig. 5. (Left) Exact *nnd* profile calculated with a brute force approach. (Right) The exact (green curve) and time-topology (blue curve) profiles are superimposed to better understand the differences. The two curves are very similar and require close inspection to detect the differences (provided in Fig. 6), this is a hint of the quality of the approximation [15]. (Color figure online)

At the beginning we provide the incremental evolution of the approximate nnd profile, by taking into account one after another the points of Sect. 5.3, Sect. 5.4 and Sect. 5.5. The best results are then compared with the exact calculations to better understand which are the main differences.

- the approximate nnds of a HOT SAX calculation are shown in Fig. 5 (left), the quality of approximation is still rather low, and the color of the curve is red.
- Fig. 5 (right) shows the improvement obtained by simply removing the lines responsible for skipping the rest of the scan of the own cluster. We use red color also in this case since the approximation is still too far from being acceptable.
- A further extension of the search space which includes controlling the whole SAX cluster with an extended alphabet is shown in Fig. 4 (left). The quality of this approximation is better than the previous ones, but there is still a lot of room for improvement.
- Exploiting the time topology leads to an important improvement (Fig. 4, right) where many spurious peaks are removed and the nnd profile gets closer to the exact one. We use a blue line in this case since this approximation is comparable with the exact one.
- The exact nnd profile is shown with a green curve in Fig. 5. We use a green color to indicate the correctness of the profile.

For a better understanding of the effect of applying the time topology for improving the nnd profile we report in Fig. 6 (left) a detail two calculations, the red curve refers to the approximate nnd profile obtained with the two SAX clusters and the blue one after applying the time topology. The two curves are very similar but for the red spikes of the lower quality approximation. When the time topology is taken into account the curve becomes "smoother". In Fig. 6 (right) we compare the exact nnd profile (green curve) and the approximate one (blue curve). The differences are minimal and, even in the case in which they are present, their relative magnitudes in respect to the exact values is limited.

It should be noted that all of the first 10 discords are automatically taken into account since the procedure under consideration involves only extending the HOT SAX search space for the first 10 discords.

If one is interested in the statistical properties of the nnds, it is clear that the results returned by HOT SAX are not enough. The statistical properties of the approximated nnd profile become closer to the ones of the exact calculation with a full run on the SAX cluster, but this comes at the cost of an important increase in the amount of calculations. In Fig. 7 left, there is an example of the approximate nnd density and its exact counter part. These two curves are very similar and it is safe to study the statistical properties resulting from the approximate nnds. There is an indication that our approximate method becomes more and more convenient in terms of speed in the case of longer time series. For example in Fig. 7 (right) we show the ratio of the times required by a brute force approach and the approximate method. This quantity ranges from 20 to about

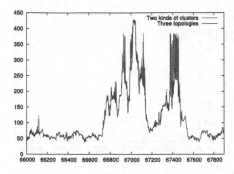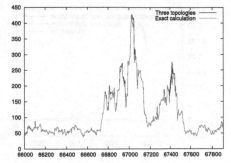

Fig. 6. (Left) An extract of the *nnd* profile obtained by exploiting the time topology (blue) and the one calculated just using two full SAX clusters (red). (Right) The exact calculation (green) and the best approximation with the time topology [15]. (Color figure online)

80. Although the method that we propose is heuristic this graph is a rather strong indication that its speedup grows on on larger data-sets.

6.1   Quantitative Estimate

The main reason for using an approximation, instead of an exact calculation is to shorten the calculation times. In Table 2 we measure this improvement by dividing the number of distance calls of the brute force approach and those of the approximate method, calling this quantity *speedup*.

In order to provide a quantitative estimate of the quality of the approximated *nnd* profile we consider the fractional error (called *Err*) of the approximate *nnd* profile, calculated as:

$$Err = \frac{1}{N_a} \sum_i \frac{nnd_a(S^i) - nnd(S^i)}{nnd(S^i)}, \tag{7}$$

where the quantity N_a indicates the amount sequences for which the procedure returned only an approximate nearest neighbor distance, denoted with $nnd_a(S^i)$. Notice that the exact nearest neighbor distance, *nnd*, is always smaller or equal than nnd_a, since it is obtained from a minimization procedure in a bigger space. In the case of ECG 300: $Err = 3.1 \cdot 10^{-2}$. This implies that the average relative error of the approximated values is in any case small, around 3%. A second indicator of the quality of the approximation is its accuracy, *Acc*, which identifies the percentage of sequences for which the *nnd*s are exact:

$$Acc = \left(1 - \frac{N_a}{N}\right) \times 100, \tag{8}$$

for ECG 300, $Acc = 98.5$. In all of the cases of Table 2 the accuracy is above 98%, while *Err* is usually confined below 10%. The longer time series have a tendency

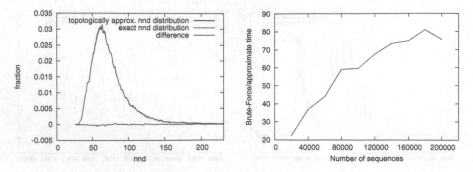

Fig. 7. (Left) The *nnd* densities obtained with our approximate solution and the exact one are very similar, in the limit almost not distinguishable. The *nnd* density have been obtained by dividing the interval of *nnd* values (ranging from about 0 to 1400) in 1000 bins. For a better readability we restrict the picture to values up to 231.5 since the density function includes 99.5% of the nnds. Notice that the differences between the exact and approximate densities diminish as we approach the highest *nnd*s, because by construction we are sure that the first discords are exact [15]. (Right) Speedup in respect to a brute force calculation as a function of the length of the time series under investigation. The present calculation (from the data-set ECG 300) is obtained with alphabet size $a = 3$, number of sub sequences for the PAA equal to $l = 7$, and the number of points in each sub-sequence is $r = 8$ [15].

of showing higher speedups in respect to the shorter ones. The relative error, *Err*, seems more connected with the time series structure than its length since the highest value is obtained for a $bidmc15_2$.

6.2 Tuning the SAX Parameters

The SAX parameters have an important role in determining the speed and accuracy of the calculations. The reason is rather intuitive, if the SAX topology resembles closely the Euclidean one it is possible to expect that the calculation should be faster and more accurate. When selecting the SAX parameters one has to keep in mind the trade-off between having a lot of small clusters (higher speed) or having a few bigger clusters able to really set together close sequences (higher accuracy). It should be noted that most of the time of a calculation is spent within the subroutines performing the full scans of the own cluster of the sequence. The complexity of a full scan of a cluster is quadratic with the size of the cluster itself. The consequences of diminishing the size of the SAX clusters are the following:

– The full scan on the same SAX cluster(s) becomes faster.
– The probability of finding the closest neighbor within the same cluster diminishes.

If one is interested in having more clusters in order to speed up the calculation (a finer resolution in respect to SAX) there are two main parameters which can

Table 2. The quality of the topologically approximated *nnd* profiles as a function of the two indicators *Acc* and *Err*. The data sets of the `sel` series contain 225000 points, while those named `bidmc15` 60000. The subscripts ($_2$, $_3$, $_4$ and $_5$) are the columns: second, third, etc. The *speedup* is calculated by dividing the number of calls to the distance function of the brute force algorithm and those our approximate algorithm.

File name	Acc	Err	speedup	N
$sel0606_2$	99.6	0.05	83	225 000
$sel0606_3$	99.5	0.05	116	225 000
$sel102_2$	98.8	0.05	40	225 000
$sel102_3$	99.7	0.06	26	225 000
$sel123_2$	98.8	0.05	32	225 000
$sel123_3$	99.2	0.04	14	225 000
$bidmc15_2$	99.6	0.15	5	60 000
$bidmc15_3$	99.8	0.09	30	60 000
$bidmc15_4$	98.4	0.05	40	60 000
$bidmc15_5$	98.9	0.06	58	60 000

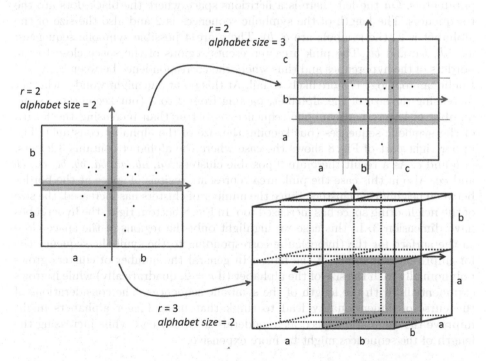

Fig. 8. Representation of the hypercubes associated with symbolic sequences obtained with $r = 2$ and alphabet=2; $r = 2$ and alphabet=3; $r = 3$ and alphabet=2.

be modified: the length of the symbolic sequences, r, and the size of the alphabet, a. There are conceptual differences related with changing these parameters, linked to the geometry of the symbolic sequences and the SAX procedure. The correspondence between the SAX and Euclidean neighborhood depends on two factors:

- The information loss during the PAA approximation (i.e. passing from a 56 points sequence to 8 r-points).
- The spilling of neighbors due to the fact that close r-sequeces might lay on different sides of a face of a hypercube, ending up in two different clusters.

This last problem can be further divided into two parts:

- The curse of dimensionality: when the length of the s-sequences increases the probability that an r-sequence is close to the borders increases, independent on the number of clusters which cover the search space.
- The total bordering surface: many smaller hypercubes (at a fixed dimensionality) lead to a much larger region of space close to the borders.

In Fig. 8 we provide an example of the hypercubes associated with different SAX parameters. On the left there is a fictitious space where the black dots are the r-sequences. The length of the symbolic sequences is 2 and also the size of the alphabet is 2 (the symbols are a, b). There are 4 possible symbolic sequences: aa, ab, ba, and bb. The pink area represents regions of the space close to the borders of the hypercubes and thus where the correspondence between SAX and Euclidean topology is more likely to fail. At this point one might wonder whether increasing the size of the alphabet, passing from 2 to 3 (but keeping the same number of letters per symbolic sequence) is better than increasing the length of the symbolic sequences (but keeping the size of the alphabet constant). The upper right part of Fig. 8 shows the case where the alphabet contains 3 letters: a, b and c. As a result there are 9 possible clusters: aa, ab, ac, ba, bb, bc, ca, cb and cc. Also in this case the pink area represents regions of space at the border between neighboring clusters. Since the number of clusters has increased, the size of the neighboring space has increased too. In Fig. 8 bottom right, the hypercubes have dimension 3. In this case we highlight only the regions of the space close to the surface for the (hyper)cube corresponding to the symbolic sequence bab for improved readability of the figure. In general the number of clusters grows polynomially with the size of the alphabet (if $r = 2$, quadratically) while it grows exponentially with the length of the symbolic sequences. The considerations of the curse of dimensionality lead to think that using bigger alphabets might improve the calculation speed at a moderate accuracy cost while increasing the length of the sequences might be more expensive.

Table 3. Characteristics of the approximate nnd profiles of the time series $sel102_2$, obtained with different SAX parameters. A sequence is divided into r sub-sequences, each containing l points. The r-points are turned into one of the a symbols of the alphabet. In all of the cases the length of the sequences is kept constant $s = r \cdot l = 64$. For example, in the first row the 64 points are grouped into $r = 16$ sub-sequences, each containing $l = 4$ points. These average values are later turned into symbols taken from an alphabet containing $a = 4$ symbols.

Pts per subsequence	Length of the s-sequences	Alphabet			Speedup
l	r	a	Acc	Err	vs Brute
4	16	4	84.5	0.08	91
4	16	8	81.8	0.08	4
4	16	16	97.1	0.06	1
8	8	4	96.5	0.07	133
8	8	8	88.1	0.08	128
8	8	16	86.5	0.07	5
16	4	4	99.4	0.04	42
16	4	8	97.0	0.06	158
16	4	16	87.6	0.09	297

In Table 3 we see the results of the calculations done on the time series $sel102_2$ with different SAX parameters. We are interested in finding a relation between the length of the time series, Acc, Err and the $Speedup$ in respect with the brute force calculation. In the present example the length of the sequences under observation is 64, and can be obtained as the product of l (the amount of points per subsequence) and r (the length of the r-sequences). The last important parameter is the size of the alphabet, which can vary between the following values: 4, 8, 16. A first consideration is that the accuracy can drop to a minimum of $\approx 82\%$ in the worst case scenario but the average error, Err, is always contained within 10%. The more common occurrence is that the accuracy drops as the alphabet size increases. There is an exception: the case of symbolic sequences of length 16, where the alphabet is also equal to 16. The theoretical maximum number of possible clusters is 16^{16} and it greatly exceeds the number of sequences in the time series. For this reason all the clusters contain one single sequence, and the SAX procedure does essentially nothing. When there is a cluster containing only one sequence, the subroutine for the full scan of the own cluster exits immediately: there is no other sequence for which calculating a distance. All of the calculation is left to the subroutine which scans randomly the other clusters in order to find a close neighbor. Notice, however, that this procedure exits as soon as the current value of the nnd drops below the current best candidate. For these reasons a calculation where each cluster contains only one sequence takes essentially the same time of a brute force approach but it is less accurate! As a general indication one should take into account that the total possible amount of clusters is: r^a. When this quantity greatly exceeds the number of sequences of a time series, SAX is likely doomed to fail to clusterize the sequences since the correspondence between the Euclidean and SAX topologies is completely lost.

The best results in terms of speedup (297) are obtained in the case of $l = 16$, $r = 4$, and $a = 16$, however the accuracy, $Acc \approx 88$, is rather low. If one is interested in the density function associated with the nnds this might be a valid choice. At variance with $l = 16$, $r = 4$, and $a = 8$ there is a very high accuracy (97) and a high speedup 158. These data confirm the reported heuristic for the SAX parameters which suggest to use symbolic sequences of length $\sim 3 - 4$ with small alphabets.

6.3   Motifs

The SAX parameters can also affect the precision related to finding motifs. The exact calculations on $sel102_2$ show that there is a tie in regards the first motifs, since there are two couples of sequences which have the same minimum nnd, as shown in Table 4.

Table 4. Index associated to the motifs, their nnd and the position of the nearest neighbor.

Sequence	nnd	Neighbor
204978	$4.74 \cdot 10^{-2}$	157413
157413	$4.74 \cdot 10^{-2}$	204978
204982	$4.74 \cdot 10^{-2}$	157417
157417	$4.74 \cdot 10^{-2}$	204982

In all of the combinations of SAX parameters presented in Table 3, the approximate nnd profiles return the correct motifs. This is a hint of the fact that two very close sequences have a very high chance of being present in the same SAX cluster; since the time approximated nnd profiles include full scans of those clusters one has a high chance of obtaining the right motifs.

6.4   Comparison with Matrix Profile

The algorithm SCAMP [14], of the Matrix Profile series, is the fastest available code able to return the exact distances among all of the sequences. We tested its serial implementation with the time series $sel102_2$. The calculation of the matrix profile required about $138s$. In Table 5 we show the different speedups as a function of the SAX parameters. Our approximate algorithm can be faster than SCAMP in specific occasions, while the worst result happens when the SAX clusterization does not follow the Euclidean topology. In particular we can notice that for $l = 16$, $r = 4$ and $a = 8$ our algorithm retains 97% of exact nnds, including the highest values (the discords) and the lowest values (the motifs) and it is about 6 times faster than SCAMP. At variance the slowest scenario is the one with very long s-sequences ($r = 16$ and $a = 16$) which has a speed comparable with the brute force case, being about 20 times slower than SCAMP.

Table 5. As in Table 3, but in this case the speedup is calculated as the ratio of the execution times between SCAMP and our approximation.

Pts per subsequence	Length of the s-sequences	Alphabet			Speedup
l	r	a	Acc	Err	vs SCAMP
4	16	4	84.5	0.08	3.60
4	16	8	81.8	0.08	0.19
4	16	16	97.1	0.06	0.05
8	8	4	96.5	0.07	4.83
8	8	8	88.1	0.08	4.24
8	8	16	86.5	0.07	0.25
16	4	4	99.4	0.04	1.89
16	4	8	97.0	0.06	6.48
16	4	16	87.6	0.09	10.3

7   Conclusions and Future Work

The nearest neighbor profile of a time series can be particularly useful at the time of finding anomalies, recurrent patterns, ecc. The brute force calculation of this quantity has a complexity which is $O(N^2)$, and for this reason it becomes difficult even for mid range time series. Although the codes of the Matrix Profile series can produce a *nnd* profile very effectively one might be interested in modifying an existing algorithm in order to produce a good quality quick approximate nearest neighbor profile.

In this paper we show that the modifications required by a HOT SAX code for this purpose are easy. The guidelines for these modifications stem from three different kinds of topologies naturally present in time series. The first one is the notion of neighborhood induced by the Euclidean distance, which is at the basis of the nearest neighbor profile. The second notion of closeness is the one induced by the SAX approximation: two sequences belonging to the same cluster are close. This second form of topology partly overlaps with the notion of closeness induced by the Euclidean distance. For this reason, the two were used at the basis of the HOT SAX algorithm in order to quickly have an idea regarding where to find anomalies. The third form of closeness used in this paper regards the time distance between two sequences, i.e. whether they were received one after the other or far in time. This form of topology can be used to significantly improve the quality of an approximated nearest neighbor profile.

During an anomaly search with HOT SAX, it is possible to obtain a low quality nearest neighbor profile since one is interested only in finding the anomalies and to reduce at most the search space. In practice HOT SAX re-arranges the two nested loops of a brute force approach and provides prescriptions regarding when to skip most of the inner loop. If one drops these exit condition and performs a full search on the cluster which includes the sequence under observation, it is possible to notice a clear improvement in respect to the quality of the $nnds$. By applying the same reasoning on a second SAX cluster obtained with an increased alphabet, the quality of the approximation gets even closer to the exact one but for some spurious spikes related with the curse of dimensionality. Resourcing at the time topology helps in removing most of these peaks thus providing a very good approximation of the exact nnd profile. All of these prescriptions increase the search space used by HOT SAX, for this reason one is sure to obtain nnd values which are more accurate. In return this means that those sequences with the highest nnd values are the exact discords of the time series.

In order to quantitatively assess the approximated nnd profiles we resort at calculating the fraction of exact $nnds$ obtained. We find that in many cases more than 98% of the sequences have an exact nnd.

For those sequences with just an approximate nnd value we calculate the average error, called Err, which in most of the cases remains below 10%. This implies that, even when one obtains approximated values they are not very far from the correct ones.

The algorithm proposed in this research is not exact and depends on the parameters of the SAX clusterization. It is thus rather difficult to constrain its complexity, however for the tests that we performed its speed can be almost 2 orders of magnitude faster than a brute force approach.

When compared with the fastest algorithm allowing to calculate the exact nnd profile, SCAMP, our approximate method has shown encouraging results by being up to 6 times faster and with an accuracy of about 97%.

Future works include the possibility to apply the MASS algorithm introduced by [19] in order to further speed up the calculation. It is also important to understand if it is possible to constrain the value of the accuracy as a function of the SAX parameters, or if it is possible to estimate the optimal SAX parameters before a full calculation. A rather simple modification should lead to the possibility to find also the k-th nnd profiles, the accuracy and complexity of this task need to be assessed. A parallel version of this algorithm is expected to be very fast and it is one of our next research directions.

References

1. Chandola, V., Banerjee, A., Kumar, V.: Anomaly detection: a survey. ACM Comput. Surv. (CSUR) **41**(3), 15 (2009)
2. Aggarwal, C.C.: Data streams: models and algorithms. Advances in Database System, vol. 31. Springer, Berlin (2007)

3. Lin, J., Keogh, E., Lonardi, S., Chiu, B.: A Symbolic representation of time series, with implications for streaming algorithms. In: Proceedings of the 8th ACM SIG-MOD Workshop on Research Issues in Data Mining and Knowledge Discovery (2003)
4. Aghabozorgi, S., Shirkhorshidi, A.S., Wah, T.Y.: Time-series clustering - a decade review. Inf. Syst. **53**, 16–38 (2015)
5. Sakoe, H., Chiba, S.: Dynamic programming algorithm for spoken word recognition. IEEE Trans. Acous. Speech Signal Process. **26**(1), 43–49 (1978). https://doi.org/10.1109/tassp.1978.1163055
6. Lin, J., Keogh, E., Lonardi, S., Patel, P.: Finding motifs in time series. In: Proceedings of the Second Workshop on Temporal Data Mining. Edmonton, Alberta, Canada, July 2002
7. Chiu, B., Keogh, E., Lonardi, S.: Probabilistic discovery of time series motifs. In: Proceeding KDD '2003 Proceedings of the Ninth ACM SIGKDD International Conference on Knowledge Discovery and Data Mining, pp. 493-498. (2003). ISBN:1-58113-737-0 https://doi.org/10.1145/956750.956808
8. Zhu, Y., et al.: Matrix profile ii: exploiting a novel algorithm and gpus to break the one hundred million barrier for time series motifs and joins. In: 2016 IEEE 16th International Conference on Data Mining (ICDM), pp. 739–748, December 2016
9. Keogh, E., Lin, J., Fu, A.: HOT SAX: efficiently finding the most unusual time series subsequence. In: Proceedings of the Fifth IEEE International Conference on Data Mining, (ICDM'2005), pp. 226–233 (2005)
10. Senin, P., et al.: GrammarViz 2.0: a tool for grammar-based pattern discovery in time series. In: Proceedings of ECML/PKDD Conference (2014)
11. Senin, P., et al.: Time series anomaly discovery with grammar-based compression. In: Proceedings of The International Conference on Extending Database Technology, EDBT 15 (2015)
12. Yeh, C.C.-M., et al.: Matrix profile I: all pairs similarity joins for time series: a unifying view that includes motifs, discords and shapelets . In: IEEE ICDM (2016)
13. Zhu, Y., Yeh, C.M., Zimmerman, Z., Kamgar, K., Keogh, E.: Matrix profile XI: SCRIMP++: time series motif discovery at interactive speeds. In: 2018 IEEE International Conference on Data Mining (ICDM), Singapore, pp. 837–846 (2018). https://doi.org/10.1109/ICDM.2018.00099
14. Zimmerman, Z., et al.: Matrix profile XIV: scaling time series motif discovery with GPUs to break a quintillion pairwise comparisons a day and beyond. In: Proceedings of the ACM Symposium on Cloud Computing (SoCC '2019), pp. 74–86. Association for Computing Machinery, New York, NY, USA (2019). https://doi.org/10.1145/3357223.3362721
15. Avogadro, P., Dominoni, M.A.: Topological approach for finding nearest neighbor sequence in time series. In: Proceedings of the 11th International Joint Conference on Knowledge Discovery, Knowledge Engineering and Knowledge Management - Volume 1: KDIR, pp. 233–244 (2019). ISBN 978-989-758-382-7. https://doi.org/10.5220/0008493302330244
16. Chakrabarti, K., Keogh, E., Mehrotra, S., Pazzani, M.: Locally adaptive dimensionality reduction for indexing large time series databases. In: ACM Transactions on Database Systems (TODS), January 2002
17. Moody, G.B., Mark, R.G.: The impact of the MIT-BIH arrhythmia database. IEEE Eng. Med. Biol. **20**(3), 45–50 (2001)

18. Goldberger, A.L., et al.: PhysioBank, PhysioToolkit, and PhysioNet: components of a new research resource for complex physiologic signals. Circulation **101**(23), e215–e220, 13 June 2000 [Circulation Electronic Pages; http://circ.ahajournals. org/content/101/23/e215.full];

19. Mueen, A., et al.: The fastest similarity search algorithm for time series subsequences under Euclidean distance, August 2017. http://www.cs.unm.edu/mueen/ FastestSimilaritySearch.html

Knowledge Engineering and Ontology Development

Pitfalls in Networked and Versioned Ontologies

Omar Qawasmeh[1(✉)], Maxime Lefrançois[2], Antoine Zimmermann[2],
and Pierre Maret[1]

[1] Univ. Lyon, CNRS, Lab. Hubert Curien, UMR 5516, 42023 Saint-Étienne, France
{omar.alqawasmeh,pierre.maret}@univ-st-etienne.fr
[2] Univ. Lyon, MINES Saint-Étienne, CNRS, Lab. Hubert Curien, UMR 5516,
42023 Saint-Étienne, France
{maxime.lefrancois,antoine.zimmermann}@emse.fr

Abstract. The listing and automatic detection of ontology pitfalls are crucial in ontology engineering. Existing work mainly focused on detecting pitfalls in stand-alone ontologies. Here, we introduce a new categorization of ontology pitfalls: stand-alone ontology pitfalls, pitfalls in versioned ontologies and, pitfalls in ontology networks. We investigate pitfalls in a situation of ontology co-evolution and we provide a systematic categorization of the different cases that could occur during the co-evolution process over two ontology portals: the Linked Open Vocabulary and BioPortal. We also identify 9 candidate pitfalls that may affect versioned ontologies or ontology networks. We evaluate the importance and potential impact of the candidate pitfalls by means of a web-based survey we conducted in the semantic web community. Participants agreed that listing and investigating ontology pitfalls can effectively enhance the quality of ontologies and affect positively the use of ontologies. Moreover, the participants substantially agreed with the new categorization we proposed. We conclude by providing a set of recommendations to avoid or solve the different pitfalls we identified.

Keywords: Ontology networks · Ontology versions · Ontology pitfalls

1 Introduction

Ontologies provide a common infrastructure for a specific domain, which leads to a better understanding, sharing and analyzing of the knowledge [10]. However, domain description is subject to changes, thus arises the need to evolve ontologies (i.e. versioning) in order to have an up-to-date representation of the targeted domain [33]. Ontology evolution is the process of maintaining an ontology up to date with respect to the changes that might arise in the described domain, and/or in the requirements [41].

Following good practices during the development of ontologies help to increase their quality, which reflects in their usage [3,6]. Reusability is considered

© Springer Nature Switzerland AG 2020
A. Fred et al. (Eds.): IC3K 2019, CCIS 1297, pp. 185–212, 2020.
https://doi.org/10.1007/978-3-030-66196-0_9

as a good practice while designing an ontology [30]. On the one hand, reusability saves time for knowledge engineers while developing ontologies, but on the other hand it raises the problem of adapting one's ontology to the evolution of an imported ontology and thus complicates the maintenance process.

Moreover, reusability leads to the creation of connections between different ontologies. Authors in [28] categorized ontologies based on their connections into: 1. *stand-alone ontologies* that have no connection with other ontologies, or 2. *ontology networks:* sets of ontologies that are connected to each other via relationships, such as imports or uses links.

During the development or the usage of ontologies (stand-alone ontologies or ontology networks), there exist some pitfalls which the knowledge engineers can fall in while developing, evolving or maintaining an ontology. These pitfalls may cause abnormal behavior for the related artifacts (e.g. systems that are using the ontology, or other connected ontologies to it). Several researchers worked on observing (e.g. [8,38]) or listing (e.g. [25]) the set of pitfalls that might affect stand-alone ontologies.

In a previous contribution [27], we investigated the set of pitfalls that are targeted to a specific case of ontology networks, that we name ontology co-evolution (i.e. the evolution of an ontology O that uses terms having the namespace of another ontology O'). We provided an exhaustive categorization of the different cases that could occur for this situation. We observed 74 cases of co-evolution involving 28 different ontologies in the Linked Open Vocabulary (LOV), and 14 cases of co-evolution involving 10 different ontologies in BioPortal. We concluded the paper by listing a set of good practices, bad practices and uncertain practices that could happen within ontologies that use some terms from other ontologies.

In this paper we extend our previous contribution [27] and the current pitfall analysis [8,25,38] by observing and listing the set of pitfalls that can affect versioned ontologies or ontology networks. We propose to distinguish between three types of pitfalls:

1. Stand-alone ontology pitfalls. These pitfalls are addressed by [8,25,38].
2. Versioned ontologies pitfalls (i.e. when an ontology O evolves from v_1 to v_2).
3. Ontology networks pitfalls (i.e. when an ontology O imports a different ontology O').

Moreover, we assess the importance and potential impact of these pitfalls over ontology networks and versioned ontologies.

The rest of the paper is organized as follows: Sect. 2 presents our motivating scenario. Section 3 presents an overview of our research methodology and the related definitions we propose. Section 4 lists our previous contributions at [27], where we presented a theoretical analysis of the need for changes that could stem from the evolution of an imported ontology, in addition to an exhaustive theoretical analysis of how an ontology may be adapted to such evolution. In Sect. 5 we introduce a catalogue of pitfalls that could hamper versioned ontologies and ontology networks. Section 6 presents the survey we distributed to the semantic web community in order to measure the importance and potential impact for the candidate pitfalls. Section 7 discusses and concludes the paper.

2   Motivating Scenario

Let Amal be a knowledge engineer who develops a child care domain ontology called *Childcare*. In the version v1.1 of *Childcare*, created in May 2017, Amal used a specific term `programmOfStudy` from another ontology called *Education* created in January 2017 (Fig. 1). *Childcare* contains at least a link to a term of *Education*. This creates a two ontologies network. In September 2017 the creators of the *Education* ontology released version v1.2. Amal does not notice the evolution. Thus, she thinks that her ontology is still using v1.1 version of the *Education* ontology. Inside this simple ontology network, several issues might arise:

- The term `programmOfStudy` was removed from *Education*, however it is still used in *Childcare*. This has an impact over *Childcare*. As a consequence of this impact, Amal should adapt her ontology.
- New terms were introduced in *Education,v1.2* (e.g. `boarding school`). Amal should be made aware of these new terms in order to possibly make use of them in her ontology.

After noticing the evolution of the *Education* ontology, Amal created v1.2 *Childcare* ontology in November 2017. During this versioning, several issues might arise, such as:

- The v1.1 of *Childcare* ontology is not accessible any more by its IRI. This pitfall is caused by Amal, and she is the responsible of maintaining the *Childcare* ontology.
- Let us assume that the v1.2 of the *Education* ontology is inconsistent, importing this ontology by the *Childcare v1.2* will make it become inconsistent too. This versioned ontology pitfall is caused by the owners of the *Education* ontology, and it is their responsibility to maintain their ontology.

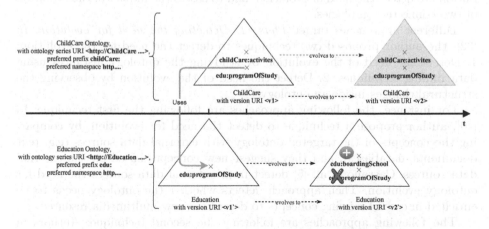

Fig. 1. An illustrative figure for the motivating example.

If Amal publishes a bigger network of ontologies, the connections between these ontologies are expanding, which makes it vulnerable to falling into some pitfalls. For example:

– If Amal presents an inconsistent ontology and she published it. Any other ontology or system (e.g. question answering) that use this ontology might become inconsistent too.

In the next section, we present an overview about ontology evolution, and such approaches that took care of same problem we are targeting in this paper.

3   Research Overview

This section presents the following: Sect. 3.1 presents an overview of ontology evolution. Section 3.2 presents our definition of an ontology network. Section 3.3 presents an overview of ontology pitfalls, and our new categorization for the set of pitfalls.

3.1   An Overview of Ontology Evolution

Ontology evolution is the process of maintaining an ontology up to date with respect to the changes that might arise in the described domain, and/or in the requirements [41]. Zalbith et al. [41] studied the different methodologies and approaches to evolve ontologies, and defined a comprehensive life-cycle of ontology evolution: 1. Detect the need for evolution, 2. Suggest changes to evolve the ontology, 3. Validate the suggested changes, 4. Assess and study the impact of the evolution on external artifacts that rely on the ontology (e.g. other ontologies, systems), 5. Keep track of the implementation of the changes.

We investigated [27] in the first and fourth phases and we introduced two definitions to detect the need of evolution, and to assess the impact of the evolution of two connected ontologies.

Different approaches target *Phase 1. Detecting the need for evolution*. In [32], the author proposed two techniques to detect the need for the evolution: 1. Detect the need of the evolution by studying the ontology instances using data mining techniques. 2. Detect the need of the evolution by observing the structural changes inside an ontology.

For instance, the following approaches are following the first technique: In [40], author propose a technique to detect the need for evolution, by comparing the concepts of the targeted ontology with external data sources (e.g. text documents, databases), and they suggest new concepts based on the external data sources. Castano et al. [5] detect from external data sources the need for ontology evolution. Their approach detects whether the ontology needs to be enriched in case of missing concepts to describe a new multimedia resource.

The following approaches are following the second technique: Authors in [35] and [21] agree that ontology evolution is caused mainly by three reasons:

1. Changes in the described domain. 2. Changes in the conceptualization (e.g. deletion and addition). 3. Changes in the explicit specification. In [23] a change detection algorithm is proposed which relies on a specific language they also proposed. One feature of their algorithm is to detect the need of evolution out of the changes that happen, such as renaming a class (i.e. delete and add).

As for *Phase 4. Assessing the impact of ontology evolution* of [41], different approaches were proposed to study the impact of ontology evolution in different techniques. For instance, Dragoni and Ghidini [7] studied how ontology evolution affects research systems. They observed three operations that could happen during the evolution process of an ontology: 1. rename a concept, 2. delete a concept, and 3. move a concept. They applied 75 queries over a search system for every version of the evolved ontology, they compared the effectiveness of the search system with a baseline.

Abgaz et al. [2] analyzed both structural and semantic impact over ontologies. They predefined a bag of rules to study the impact by detecting undesirable statements and wrong instances. They defined 10 change operations that cover the different change scenarios.

Groß et al. [9] studied how some statistical artifacts are affected by the evolution of the *Gene* ontology[1]. They used CODEX tool [13] to detect the changes (e.g. addition, merging, moving). They created a stability measure by choosing a fixed set of genes to compute the experimental result set at different point of time with freely chosen ontology and annotation versions.

Mihindukulasooriya et al. [20] investigated how *DBpedia* [19], *Schema.org* [11], *PROV-O* [18] and *FOAF* [4] ontologies evolved within time. They observed the changes between the different versions such as, addition and deletion of classes, properties, sub-classes and sub-properties. They show that the process of ontology evolution relies on the size of the ontology, and it becomes more challenging when the ontology size is large. They conclude by showing the need of creating tools that can help during the evolution process.

Abdel-Qader et al. [1] analyzed the impact of the evolution of terms in 18 different ontologies referenced in LOV. Their method consisted of two phases: 1. retrieve all the ontologies that have more than one version, and 2. investigate how terms are changed and adopted in the evolving ontologies. They applied their analysis on three large-scale knowledge graphs: DyLDO[2], BTC[3] and Wikidata.[4] They found that some of the term changes in the 18 ontologies are not mapped into the three knowledge graphs. Also they concluded that there is a need for a service to monitor the ontology changes, which will help to maintain the external artifacts (other ontologies, systems or data sets).

---

[1] http://geneontology.org/.
[2] http://km.aifb.kit.edu/projects/dyldo/data.
[3] https://km.aifb.kit.edu/projects/btc-2012.
[4] https://www.wikidata.org.

3.2   Ontology Networks

This topic has not been widely studied yet. The term "ontology network" (a.k.a. networked ontologies) is informally defined by [12,29,34] as the set of ontologies that are connected to each other via a variety of relationships (e.g. owl:imports, modularization, version). Authors in [26] studied 18,589 terms appearing in 196 ontologies, and they concluded that *Uses* and *Imports* are the main relationships between ontologies. Hence, in this paper we propose a formal definition of an ontology network as:

Definition 1. *An Ontology Network.* *An ontology network is a directed graph $G = (\mathcal{N}, \mathcal{E})$, consisting of a set $\mathcal{N}$ of ontologies and a set $\mathcal{E}$ of relationships, which are ordered pairs of elements of $\mathcal{N}$. Furthermore, every ontology $O \in \mathcal{N}$ has an owner author(O), an IRI iri$(O) \in$ IRI, an ontology series IRI series_iri$(O) \in$ IRI, a namespace ns$(O) \in$ IRI, and a publication date date$(O) \in \mathbb{N}$; Every ontology relationship $e \in \mathcal{E}$ is labeled by a non-empty set of types type$(e) \in \mathcal{T}$.*

We consider only two types of relationships between the different ontologies (regardless of the owner). $\mathcal{T} = \{uses, imports\}$:

uses. uses $\in$ types$\langle O, O' \rangle$ happens when an ontology O uses a term t (that is, an IRI denoting an individual, a class or a property) that has the namespace of a different ontology O'.

imports. imports $\in$ types$\langle O, O' \rangle$ happens when an ontology O imports another ontology O', using the OWL importing mechanism.[5]

3.3   Ontology Pitfalls

In the field of semantic web, several researchers used the term "pitfall" to refer to the set of mistakes/errors that can be made during the development or usage of ontologies. In this research, we propose to distinguish between three types of pitfalls:

1. *Stand-alone ontology pitfalls:* can happen within a single ontology O that is created by *author*(O) (e.g. *Childcare V1.1* from Fig. 1).
2. *Versioned ontologies pitfalls:* can happen when an *author*(O) creates/publishes a new version of the ontology O (e.g. the evolution of *Education* ontology from Fig. 1).
3. *Ontology network pitfalls* can happen within the set of ontologies that are connected to each other, such as when an ontology O is connected to a different ontology O' (e.g. both of the ontologies *Childcare* and *Education* from Fig. 1). The responsible of resolving these pitfalls is either *author*(O) or *author*(O'), depending on if the pitfall occur in O or O'.

---

[5] https://www.w3.org/TR/owl2-syntax/, Sect. 3.4.

Existing work observed and listed the set of pitfalls in different scenarios. Sabou and Fernandez [28] provide methodological guidelines for evaluating both stand-alone ontologies and ontology networks. Their methodology relies on selecting a targeted ontology component to evaluate based on a predefined goal.

Poveda et al. [25] gathered 41 stand-alone ontology pitfalls from different sources in a catalogue[6] and categorized them based on the structural (i.e. syntax and formal semantics), functional (i.e. the usage of a given ontology) and usability (i.e. the communication context of an ontology) dimensions. In addition, they tag each pitfall with it's importance level (i.e. critical, important, or minor).

Gaudt and Dessimoz [8] analyzed annotation pitfalls that exist in the GO-basic ontology.[7] The authors summarized the set of pitfalls (e.g. Annotator Bias and Authorship Bias) and provided good practices to help solving them. They showed how these pitfalls might introduce problems when the data is used in other tasks.

As a conclusion, we see that current research take care of listing or observing pitfalls for stand-alone ontologies, and there is a lack of research papers that observe and list the set of pitfalls that might affect versioned ontologies and ontology networks. In our research we observe and list the set of pitfalls that are related to versioned ontologies and ontology networks.

4 Observing the Impact and Adaptation to the Evolution of an Imported Ontology

In this section we update our findings from [27], where we introduced two situations related to observe the impact and the adaptation to the evolution of an imported ontology. In Sect. 4.1 we target the evolution of an imported ontology (if ontology O uses some terms t from another ontology O', and then O' evolves). In Sect. 4.2 we target the adaptation to the evolution of the imported ontology.

4.1 Observing the Impact of the Evolution of an Imported Ontology

As mentioned in Sect. 3.1, there is a need to detect when to perform changes on ontologies (i.e. Phase 1 from the ontology evolution life-cycle). Two behaviors can be distinguished:

1. There was already a problem: an ontology O uses a term t that has the namespace of another ontology O', however it is not defined in O'.
2. A problem has occurred because of the evolution process: Let's assume that there is an ontology O that uses a term t that has the namespace of another ontology O'. O' evolved which causes the deletion of t. This evolution might cause problems for O. This raises the need to evolve O in order to reflect the changes.

---

[6] Last check January 2020, can be found here: http://oops.linkeddata.es/catalogue.jsp.

[7] http://geneontology.org/docs/download-ontology/.

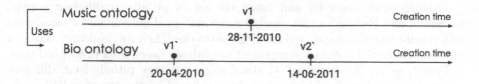

Fig. 2. A time line showing the creation times of the Music ontology and the BIO ontology, where the Music ontology uses terms that are defined by BIO [27].

To represent formally these two situations, in [27] we have defined a situation that can be used to detect the need of the evolution, mainly named "imported ontology evolution":

Definition 2. *Imported Ontology Evolution*
Imported ontology evolution is a situation where: O is an ontology which has at least one version v_1. O' is a different ontology which has at least two versions v_1' and v_2'. O uses terms[8] *that have the namespace of O'. time(v) is the creation time for a version.*
    A case of imported ontology evolution is noted $\langle v_1, v_1', v_2' \rangle$ and holds when the following conditions are satisfied:
$time(v_1') < time(v_2') \wedge time(v_1') < time(v_1)$

To illustrate this definition, Fig. 2 presents a real life example of one case of imported ontology evolution, where *Music* ontology has one version (v_1: mo_2010-11-28) that uses some terms that have the namespace of the *BIO* ontology (v_1': bio_2010-04-20, v_2': bio_2011-06-14). Table 1 lists the different cases that may occur with respect to Definition 2. t is a term that has the namespace of O'. Each circle represents the set of terms terms (t) that exist in the different versions of the two ontologies (i.e. v_1', v_2', and v_1). Four possible cases might happen:

Row 1. No changes over t

Case 1.a There is no change of t to detect, therefore there is no interest in studying this case. This case holds for all the terms t with the namespace of O', that are neither defined in O' nor used in O.

Case 1.b This case holds when O uses a term t with the namespace of O', but that is not defined in O'. Some terms that have the namespace of O' are being used in v_1 without being defined before. This is a mistake, hence there is a need to evolve v_1 to reflect the latest changes.

Row 2. t is deleted in v_2'
The owners of O' decided to stop using a term (e.g. `programmOfStudy`) in v_2':

---

[8] A RDF term is generally defined as: $IRI \cup Blanknodes \cup Literals$. In this research we take into consideration only the IRIs.

Table 1. The set of cases that might happen during the evolution of O' considering a term t that has the namespace of O' [27].

	a	b
uses O / O'	v_1 (circle)	v_1 (circle with t)
1 v_1' ⊕ v_2'	Case 1.a: No changes occurred	Case 1.b: Term is used in v_1 without being defined in O'
2 v_1' (t) v_2'	Case 2.a: No impact occurred	Case 2.b: There is a need for evolution, because the term is no longer in O'
3 v_1' (t) v_2'	Case 3.a: No impact occurred. Suggest to add new terms	Case 3.b: No impact occurred
4 v_1' (t) v_2'	Case 4.a: Suggest to add new terms	Case 4.b: Term used before it is defined

Case 2.a The term is not used in v_1. No problems to be reported, and v_1 was not affected by the evolution of O'.

Case 2.b During the evolution, the term t was deleted. However, it is still being used in v_1. This might introduce a problem of using terms that does not exist anymore. So v_1 should evolve to better reflect the changes of O'.

Row 3. t exist in both v_1' and v_2'
There is no changes on t:

Case 3.a The term is not used in v_1. However, it can be recommended for use in the upcoming versions of v_1.

Case 3.b No changes over the terms during the evolution. This case is not problematic.

Row 4. t is added to v_2'
The owners of O' introduced a new term (e.g. boardingSchool) in v_2':

Case 4.a The term t is not used in v_1. It can be interesting to use, thus this addition can be notified.

Case 4.b The term t is used in v_1, however it was defined later in v_2'.

So far, we have seen the definition and impacts of imported ontology evolution. As a consequence of this evolution, the impacted ontology should be evolved accordingly to better reflect the changes. This creates a situation which we call ontology co-evolution. It will be discussed in the next subsection.

4.2   Observing the Adaptation to the Evolution of an Imported Ontology

The term "ontology co-evolution" has been already used in three research papers. Authors in [15,16] define the co-evolution as the integration between the database schemes and ontologies to design and evolve the targeted ontologies. Also [22] defines the co-evolution as the creation of ontologies by taking advantage of natural language techniques to process some raw text. These definitions are irrelevant to the problem we investigate. In [27] we have defined ontology co-evolution as:

Definition 3. *Ontology Co-evolution*
Ontology co-evolution is a situation where: O is an ontology which has at least two versions v_1 and v_2. O' is a different ontology which has at least two versions v_1' and v_2'. O uses terms that have the namespace of O'. $time(v)$ is the creation time for a version.

In order to have a co-evolution case between O and O' with the ontologies $\langle v_1, v_1', v_2, v_2' \rangle$, the following condition must be satisfied:
$time(v_1) < time(v_2) \wedge time(v_1') < time(v_2') \wedge time(v_1') < time(v_1) \wedge time(v_2') < time(v_2)$

To illustrate this definition, Fig. 3 extends the previous example to show the case of ontology co-evolution: the *Music* ontology has two versions (v_1: mo_2010-11-28, v_2: mo_2013-07-22) that are respectively using the two versions of the *Bio* ontology (v_1': bio_2010-04-20, v_2': bio_2011-06-14).

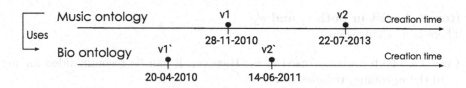

Fig. 3. A time line showing the creation times of the music ontology (mo) and the bio ontology (bio), where mo uses terms that are defined by bio [27].

During the evolution of O', terms may be introduced or deleted. We exhaustively identify the occurrences of adaptation to ontology evolution of O and O' (i.e. co-evolution). We observe the set of terms that have the namespace of O'. Table 2 shows the different cases that may occur. t is a term that has the namespace of O'. Each circle represents the set of terms (t) that exist in the different versions of the two ontologies (i.e. v_1', v_2', v_1, ad v_2).

Table 2. The set of cases that might happen during the ontology co-evolution considering t that has the namespace of O' [27].

	a	b	c	d
1	Case 1.a: No changes occurred	Case 1.b: Term is used in v_1 but doesn't exist in $O`$	Case 1.c: Term is used in both v_1 and v_2 but doesn't exist $O`$	Case 1.d: Term is used in v_2 but doesn't exist $O`$
2	Case 2.a: Term is deleted from $v_2`$ and not used in O	Case 2.b: Term is deleted in $v_2`$ but still used in v_1	Case 2.c: Term is deleted in $v_2`$ but still used in both v_1 and v_2	Case 2.d: Term is deleted in $v_2`$ and still used in v_2
3	Case 3.a: Term exists in both $v_1`$ and $v_2`$ and not used in O	Case 3.b: Term exists in both $v_1`$ and $v_2`$ and used in v_1	Case 3.c: Term exists in both $v_1`$ and $v_2`$ and used in both v_1 and v_2	Case 3.d: Term exists in both $v_1`$ and $v_2`$ and used in v_2
4	Case 4.a: Term introduced in $v_2`$ and not used in O	Case 4.b: Term exists in $v_2`$ and used in v_1	Case 4.c: Term exists in $v_2`$ and used in both v_1 and v_2	Case 4.d: Term exists in $v_2`$ and used in v_2

In our first example of Sect. 2, let us assume that Amal finally noticed the evolution of *Education* ontology and decided to evolve her ontology *Childcare* to V1.2 on November 2017. Based on our definition, the ontology *Childcare* is considered as O which has two versions v_1: *Childcare V1.1*, created in May 2017 and v_2: *Childcare V1.2*, created in November 2017. The ontology *Education* is considered as O' and has two versions v_1': *Education V1.1*, created in January 2017 and v_2': *Education V1.2*, created in September 2017. Amal is using the term `programmOfStudy` from O'. Following each line of Table 2, the following set of cases might occur during the life journey of Amal's ontology:

Row 1. No changes over the terms of v_1' or v_2'

Case 1.a There is no change of t to detect, therefore there is no interest in studying this case.

Case 1.b Amal made a typo by using the term `programOfStudy` (i.e. program is written with one "m" instead of two) in v_1, but then she realizes that this term does not exist in O'. She fixes this mistake by not using it in v_2 anymore.

Case 1.c Amal uses t in both v_1 and v_2. This case might be explained by the fact that t is defined in a previous version (e.g. v_0) of the ontology O' (i.e. $t(v_0') < t(v_1')$).

Case 1.d Amal introduces a mistake by using t in v_2.

Row 2. t is deleted in v_2'

The owners of O' decided to stop using the term `programmOfStudy` in v_2':

Case 2.a Amal does not use t that was recently deleted. Hence v_1 and v_2 were not affected.

Case 2.b Amal realizes that t was deleted, so she stops using it in v_2.

Case 2.c Amal does not realize the deletion of t, and she keeps using it in v_2.

Case 2.d Amal starts to use t in her second version (v_2), which introduces a mistake.

Row 3. t exist in both v_1' and v_2'
None of the cases (3.a, 3.b, 3.c, and 3.d) is problematic.

Row 4. t is added to v_2'
The owners of O' introduced a new term `boardingSchool` in v_2':

Case 4.a Amal has not noticed the addition of t, even if it might be interesting for her to introduce it.
Case 4.b Amal was already using t in (v_1), but she decided to remove it from v_2.
Case 4.c Amal was already using t in v_1, and she continues using it in v_2.
Case 4.d Amal realizes the addition of t, and she starts using it in v_2.

Cases 4.b and 4.c are corner cases that are discussed further Sect. 4.3.

4.3 Identification of the Occurrences of Adaptation to Ontology Evolution

In this section, we update the results of an experiment[9], initially presented in [27], to detect ontology co-evolution using the cases that are defined in Sect. 4.2.

We retrieved and analyzed a set of ontologies from two ontology portals:

- The Linked Open Vocabulary (LOV) [37] which currently references 697 different ontologies.[10] Each ontology is described with different features, such as number of incoming links (i.e. how many ontologies are using ontology O), number of outgoing links (i.e. how many ontologies are used by ontology O), number of different versions, and datasets that are using ontology O.
- BioPortal [39] which currently references 827 different ontologies (see footnote 10) that are related to the biomedical domain. Each ontology is described with different features, such as the number of different versions, along with general metrics (e.g. number of classes, properties and instances).

After examining the different ontologies, we could retrieve from LOV a set of 28 ontologies with 74 co-evolution instances, as for BioPortal we could retrieve a set of 10 ontologies with 14 co-evolution instances.[11] Then, we extracted the set of terms for each version, and the namespaces for the used ontologies (O''s versions), and we used them to compute the number of occurrences of the different co-evolution cases. For interested readers, full details about our retrieval and processing methods are described in [27].

Table 3 shows the number of occurrences for each co-evolution case for LOV (first value in each cell) and BioPortal (second value). We group the results into three categories: 1. good practices, 2. pitfalls, and 3. uncertain cases.

---

[9] The experiments with full results can be found at: https://github.com/OmarAlqawasmeh/coEvolutionTermsExtraction.
[10] Last counted on January 2020.
[11] The co-evolution cases of LOV and BioPortal are inside the *resources* folder at https://github.com/OmarAlqawasmeh/coEvolutionTermsExtraction.

Table 3. The number of occurrences for each co-evolution case for LOV (first value) and BioPortal (second value) with respect to namespace of (O') [27].

	a	b	c	d
1		✓ 0 / 130	✗ 3 / 929	✗ 3 / 115
2	✓ 23 / 27	✓ 0 / 0	✗ 0 / 3	✗ 0 / 0
3	? 16875 / 9135	? 10 / 0	✓ 270 / 2058	? 23 / 0
4	? 2420 / 1560	✗ 0 / 115	✗ 0 / 908	? 0 / 0

✓ Good practices, ✗ Pitfalls, and ? Uncertain cases

Category 1. Good practices

Case 1.b (i.e. a term t is used in v_1, however it does not exist in v'_1 and v'_2): shows a good practice from the owners of O. They noticed that the term t is not defined in both v'_1 and v'_2, so they decided to delete it from v_2. This co-evolution case occurred 130 times in BioPortal but never in LOV. An example is the co-evolution process of the *Schema.org core and all extension vocabularies* (v_1: created in 2014-10-30 and v_2: created in 2017-05-19), with *Schema.org* ontology (v'_1: created in 2012-04-27 and v'_2: created in 2017-03-23). The terms Bacteria, FDAcategoryC and Diagnostic are used in v_1, however they do not exist in v'_1 and v'_2.

Case 2.a (i.e. a term t is deleted in v'_2, and it is not used in any of O's versions): shows a good practice from the owners of O'. They noticed that the term t is not used in both v_1 and v_2 so they decided to delete it from v'_2. This case occurred 23 times in LOV and 27 times in BioPortal. This is a normal case, and no problem occurred during the co-evolution.

Case 2.b (i.e. a term t is deleted in v'_2, and then deleted in v_2): indicates that the set of ontologies stops using the terms after they have been deleted in O' which is a good practice. This case has no occurrence in LOV nor in BioPortal. We are not discussing it further.

Case 2.d (i.e. a term t is deleted in v'_2, however it is added in v_2): indicates that there were no mistake of using the set of deleted terms in the newest version of O. This case has no occurrences in LOV nor in BioPortal. We are not discussing it further.

Category 2. Pitfalls

Cases (1.c and 1.d) demonstrate the problem of using terms that do not exist in v'_1 and v'_2.

Case 1.c (i.e. a term t is used in both v_1 and v_2, however it does not exist in v_1' and v_2'): This case occurred 3 times in LOV and 929 times in BioPortal. An example is the co-evolution process of the *Statistical Core Vocabulary* (v_1: created in 2011-08-05 and v_2: created in 2012-08-09), with *DCMI Metadata Terms* (v_1': created in 2010-10-11 and v_2': created in 2012-06-14). The terms dc:status and dc:partOf are used in v_1 and v_2, however they do not exist in v_1' and v_2'.

Case 1.d (i.e. a term t is used in v_2, however it does not exist in v_1' and v_2'): This case occurred 3 times in LOV and 115 times in BioPortal. An example is the co-evolution process of the *Europeana Data Model vocabulary* (v_1: created in 2012-01-23 and v_2: created in 2013-05-20), with *Dublin Core Metadata Element Set* (v_1': created in 2010-10-11 and v_2': created in 2012-06-14). The terms dc:issued and dc:modified are used in v_2 however they do not exist in v_1' and v_2'.

A possible explanation is that these terms were used from a previous version of O'. Let's assume that this previous version is v_0', then these cases can happen only if the publishing time of $t(v_0')$ is before the publishing time of $t(v_1')$. In these cases, the owners of O, should be notified of the changes, and they should be suggested to delete the terms that do not exist anymore.

Case 2.c (i.e. a term t is deleted in v_2', however it is used in v_1 and still in v_2): shows that some terms are still used in both of O's versions after being deleted from O'. This case occurred 3 times in BioPortal. It shows a problem of using terms that do not exist anymore in O'. For example in the co-evolution process of the *Schema.org core and all extension vocabularies* (v_1: created in 2014-10-30 and v_2: created in 2017-05-19), with *Schema.org* ontology (v_1': created in 2012-04-27 and v_2': created in 2017-03-23). The terms MedicalClinic, Optician and VeterinaryCare are used in both v_1 and v_2, however they do not exist in the latest version of O' (these different terms were deleted from v_2 of *Schema.org*). In order to prevent such kind of problems the owners should be notified about these cases.

Case 4.b (i.e. a term t is added in v_2', and it was already used in v_1): This case occurred 115 times in BioPortal, and it has no occurrence in LOV. An example is the co-evolution process of the *Schema.org core and all extension vocabularies* (v_1: published in 2014-10-30 and v_2: published in 2017-05-19), with *Schema.org* ontology (v_1': created in 2012-04-27 and v_2': created in 2017-03-23). The terms SoundtrackAlbum, Hardcover and SingleRelease are used in v_1, however they were introduced later in v_2'. The v_1 of *Schema.org core and all extension vocabularies* uses terms that were later defined by v_2' of *Schema.org* ontology. The *Schema.org core and all extension vocabularies* is an extension of *Schema.org*, however it has its own namespace. Each reviewed extension for schema.org has its own chunk of schema.org namespace (e.g. if extension name is x, the namespace of this extension is x1.schema.org).[12] We retrieved all terms that have the namespace of *Schema.org*.[13] Other terms with different namespaces

---

[12] More details about the extensions managing of schema.org can be found at: https:// schema.org/docs/extension.html.

[13] Namespace of *Schema.org* is http://schema.org/.

were discarded.[14] This reflects a bad practice in a way of using terms that have not been defined in the second version. These terms could be harbinger to add in the next versions.

Case 4.c (i.e. a term t is added in v_2', and it was already used in both of O's versions): This case occurred 951 times in BioPortal, and it has no occurrence in LOV. An example is the co-evolution process of the *Semanticscience Integrated Ontology (SIO)* (v_1: created in 2015-06-24 and v_2: created in 2015-09-02), with *The Citation Typing Ontology (CITO)* (v_1': created in 2010-03-26 and v_2': created in 2015-07-03). The term `citesAsAuthority` is used in both v_1 and v_2, however it was introduced in v_2'. One explanation for this kind of pitfalls is that the knowledge engineers might have introduced a typos during the development process of the ontology. In these cases, the owners of O, should be notified that the term they use is not a term.

Category 3. Uncertain Cases

In cases (3.a, 3.b, 3.c and 3.d) from LOV and Bioportal, there was no change of terms in the two versions of O'. This indicates that the co-evolution process has no problem to report. Some terms are shared between v_1' and v_2' so there was no addition or deletion over them.

Cases 4.a and 4.d in both LOV and BioPortal show the number of terms that were added during the evolution of O'. These terms were not used in any of O's versions. These cases can be explained in two ways:

1. The owners of O did not notice the addition of these terms, however they might be interested in using some of these new terms. This might reflects a problem, thus further content analysis should be introduced to possibly recommend changes to the owners.
2. The owners of O noticed the addition of these terms and they decided not to add them.

In the next section, we present a catalogue of pitfalls that are related to versioned and networked ontologies.

5 The Set of Pitfalls over Ontology Networks or Versioned Ontologies

Hitherto, we have introduced the different cases (good, pitfalls and uncertain) that could occur inside one particular setting of ontologies combining networked and versioned ontologies (i.e. ontology co-evolution). In this section, we enrich previous work to investigate ontology pitfalls in distinguishing between the two situations: 1. versioned ontologies and, 2. ontology networks. Hence, in Sect. 5.1 we describe 9 candidate pitfalls that are related to versioned ontologies and ontology networks.

---

[14] Some examples of discarded namespaces: https://health-lifesci.schema.org/, https://pending.schema.org/, https://meta.schema.org/.

5.1   Candidate Pitfalls

Pitfall 1. Ontology is not Accessible at Its IRI

This pitfall is related to the ontology relationship $type(e) = \{\,$"uses", "imports"$\}$. It can occur in the following cases:

1. If an ontology was never published on-line, for instance, if an ontology is used internally by a company, and/or if an ontology file becomes private and it is not accessible anymore.
2. If the ontology is not available at its IRI. For example: the IRI of the *pizza* ontology is http://www.co-ode.org/ontologies/pizza/pizza.owl#, but it is not accessible at this IRI.
3. If the IRI of the ontology has been changed. For example: the IRI of the *DOLCE Ultralite upper* ontology was originally http://www.loa-cnr.it/ontologies/DUL.owl#. The website loa-cnr.it closed, and the ontology is now available at http://www.ontologydesignpatterns.org/ont/dul/DUL.owl#.

This pitfall affects ontology networks. Any import of an ontology that has this pitfall will fail. To solve or avoid this pitfall, we suggest to verify the imported IRIs for any changes that could occur or to locally maintain a copy of the ontology and use it offline.

Pitfall 2. Importing an Ontology using a Non Persistent IRI or the IRI of a Representation (the file URL)

This pitfall is related to the ontology relationship $type(e) = \{\,$"imports"$\}$. Persistent IRIs are important, as they ensure that the ontology will be always accessible at the same IRI. This pitfall occurs in two cases:

1. If a knowledge engineer imports a non persistent IRI, for example: the *SEAS* ontology has persistent IRI https://w3id.org/seas/, which no longer redirects to the location https://ci.emse.fr/seas/. Assume an ontology imported the IRI https://ci.emse.fr/seas/. Due to the renaming of the EMSE institution, the IRI now redirects to the location https://ci.mines-stetienne.fr/seas/, thus the import would break.
2. If a knowledge engineer imports the file URL instead of the ontology IRI, for example: the W3C organization ontology has persistent IRI https://www.w3.org/ns/org, with two representations at https://www.w3.org/ns/org.rdf and https://www.w3.org/ns/org.ttl. Assume an ontology imports the ontology representation https://www.w3.org/ns/org.rdf instead of the ontology series https://www.w3.org/ns/org. In case of the deletion of the RDF/XML representation any import would break.

This pitfall affects ontology networks. Any import of an ontology that has this pitfall will fail. To solve or avoid this pitfall, we suggest: 1. to use only persistent IRIs when importing ontologies, and 2. to always use the IRI of the ontology, and not the URL of the file representation.

Pitfall 3. Importing an Inconsistent Ontology
This pitfall is related to the ontology relationship $type(e) = \{\text{"imports"}\}$. It occurs if a knowledge engineer imports an inconsistent ontology, for example: the *SAREF4ENER* ontology (EEbus/Energy@home) https://w3id.org/saref4ee is inconsistent. The importing ontology would become inconsistent too. This pitfall affects both ontology networks and versioned ontologies. To solve or avoid this pitfall, we suggest: 1. to check the consistency of an ontology before importing it, 2. to use only the specific terms that are needed from the ontology (i.e. by their IRIs) instead of importing the whole ontology, and/or 3. to try contacting the ontology owners so that they solve the inconsistency.

Pitfall 4. Only the Latest Version of the Ontology is Available Online
This pitfall is related to the ontology relationship $type(e) = \{\text{"uses"},$ $\text{"imports"}\}$. It occurs when the only available version of the ontology is the latest version. For example, the *S4WATR* ontology is published at https://w3id.org/def/S4WATR, but only the latest version is available online. Let's assume an ontology imports the *S4WATR* ontology at a certain point in time. Later, some terms are deleted or added in S4WATR ontology. Then the importing ontology could break or become inconsistent.

This pitfall affects both ontology networks and versioned ontologies. To solve or avoid this pitfall, the following practices could be followed: 1. to import an ontology with its version URI, and/or 2. to monitor the evolution of the imported ontology to react appropriately.

Pitfall 5. Importing an Ontology Series IRI Instead of an Ontology Version IRI
This pitfall is related to the ontology relationship $type(e) = \{\text{"uses"},$ $\text{"imports"}\}$. It occurs if a knowledge engineer imports an ontology series IRI instead of an ontology version IRI. For example, the *SAREF* ontology series has IRI https://saref.etsi.org/saref#, and version 2.1.1 has IRI https://saref.etsi.org/saref/v2.1.1/saref#. A new version 3.1.1 is under development and will delete terms from version 2.1.1. Let O' be an ontology that imports *SAREF* ontology 2.1.1 using https://saref.etsi.org/saref#. When the new version 3.1.1 is released, the importing ontology O' could break or become inconsistent.

This pitfall affects both ontology networks and versioned ontologies. To solve or avoid this pitfall we recommend to import the ontology version IRI instead of the ontology series IRI.

Pitfall 6. Ontology Series IRI is the Same as the Ontology Version IRI
This pitfall is related to the ontology relationship $type(e) = \{\text{"imports"}\}$. It occurs whenever a IRI refers to a specific version of the ontology. For example, the *Units of Measure (OM)* ontology version 1.8 has IRI http://www.wurvoc.org/vocabularies/om-1.8/, and version 2.0 has IRI http://www.ontology-of-units-of-measure.org/resource/om-2/. Each time a new version is published, the ontology IRI should be updated, this does not conform to the OWL2 specification.[15] This pitfall affects both ontology networks and versioned ontologies. To solve or avoid

---

[15] https://www.w3.org/TR/owl2-syntax/, Sects. 3.1 and 3.3.

this pitfall we recommend to delete the version number from the IRI of the ontology, or to send a notification message with the new IRI when a new version of the ontology is released.

Pitfall 7. A Term is Moved from One Ontology Module to Another

This pitfall is related to the ontology relationship $type(e) = \{\text{"}uses\text{"}\}$. It occurs when a term is moved from one ontology module to another, which causes the change in its IRI. For example, the *SAREF* ontologies [31] consist of 1. *SAREF core*, 2. *SAREF4SYST*, and 3. several ontologies for the verticals, such as SAREF4ENER, SAREF4BLDG, and SAREF4ENVI. In *SAREF-core 1.1.1*, created in 2015, the authors defined the term `saref:BuildingObject`. Later in 2016, SAREF-core 2.1.1 was published without the term `saref:BuildingObject`. However, another ontology SAREF4BLDG was created with the term `s4bldg:BuildingObject`, with the same definition as `saref:BuildingObject`.

In this case, the IRI of the term `BuildingObject` has been changed. This might have a functional impact over the artifacts that are reusing the term (e.g. some queries might be affected by the change of the IRI).

This pitfall affects ontology networks. To solve or avoid this pitfall we recommend to take extra care while moving terms between the different modules, and to notify the users of the ontology in case of changes.

Pitfall 8. Namespace Hijacking [from [24]]

This pitfall is related to the ontology relationship $type(e) = \{\text{"}uses\text{"}\}$. It refers to reusing or referring to terms from another namespace that are not defined in such namespace [24]. For example, the description of classes `qudt-1.1:QuantityValue` and `qudt-1.1:Quantity` are not available at their own IRIs. Instead, they are defined in the ontology http://qudt.org/1.1/schema/quantity#.

This pitfall affects ontology networks as it prevents the retrieval of valid information when looking for the hijacked terms, which violates the Linked Data publishing guidelines [14]. To solve or avoid this pitfall we recommend to define new terms in the namespace that is owned and controlled by the knowledge engineer.

Pitfall 9. The IRI of a Term Contains a File Extension

This pitfall is related to the ontology relationship $type(e) = \{\text{"}uses\text{"}\}$. It occurs if a term's IRI contains a file extension. For example, the terms in the *Dolce ultra lite* ontology have the namespace http://www.ontologydesignpatterns.org/ont/dul/DUL.owl#. Let's assume that some day the publisher of *dolce-very-lite* wants to set up content negotiation to expose an html documentation of their ontology. As the IRI of the terms contains the file extension ".owl", no content negotiation can take place. If a human looks up the term IRI, he/she will access the OWL file, and not the html documentation. To solve or avoid this pitfall we recommend to stop using file extensions inside IRIs, and follow the rules of cool URIs for the Semantic Web.[16]

---

[16] Cool URIs can be found at: https://www.w3.org/TR/cooluris/.

As a summary, Table 4 presents the set of pitfalls based on the following criteria: 1. Affect: whether the pitfall affects ontology networks and/or versioned ontologies, 2. problems that might occur as a consequence of having the pitfall, and 3. recommendations to avoid or solve the pitfall.

6 Evaluating the Importance and Impact of the Candidate Pitfalls

We evaluated the importance and potential impact of the candidate pitfalls using a survey we conducted in the semantic web community. Section 6.1 describes the survey, then Sect. 6.2 quantitatively evaluates the answers. Finally Sect. 6.3 reports on the different opinions and suggestions we gathered from the participants.

6.1 Description of the Survey

The survey[17] first requests some information about the level of expertise of the participant in (1) ontology engineering in general, (2) versioned ontologies, and (3) networked ontologies. We used a Likert scale with values from 1 (beginner) to 10 (expert). Then, each pitfall is described with an illustrative example, and the participant is asked to answer to the following questions:

1. How often have you encountered this pitfall before?
2. How problematic is this pitfall?
3. How would you rate the impact on subsequent versions of the ontology?
4. How problematic is it to import ontologies that have this pitfall?

For the answers, we also use a Likert scale from 1 (Strongly Disagree) to 5 (Strongly Agree). For each pitfall, participants may additionally share known occurrences of the pitfall, and ideas or recommendations to solve or avoid it. Finally, we ask the participant to what extent he/she agrees or not with our pitfalls categorization, and to rate about his/her overall confidence while filling the survey.

6.2 Quantitative Evaluation of Pitfalls

A total of 27 participants answered the survey between November 2019 to January 2020.[18] As shown in Fig. 4, the most of the participants declared expertise in ontology engineering, ontology networks and ontology versioning.

---

[17] The survey can be found at: http://bit.ly/36JQfgO.
[18] Raw results can be found at: http://bit.ly/2RztHKq.

Table 4. A summary for the set of pitfalls.

Code	Description	Affects	Problem caused	Recommendations to solve or to avoid
P1	Ontology is not accessible at its IRI	Ontology networks and versioned ontologies	Import failure	Keep the ontology always available at its IRI by controlling and managing the possible changes during the evolution
P2	Importing an ontology using a non persistent IRI or the IRI of a representation (the file URL)	Ontology networks	Import failure	Try to always use a persistent IRI while importing an ontology
P3	Importing an inconsistent ontology	Ontology networks and versioned ontologies	Inheritance of the inconsistency	Make sure to import consistent ontologies or using specific terms instead of importing the whole ontology
P4	Only the latest version of the ontology is available online	Ontology networks and versioned ontologies	Import failure and/or the ontology become inconsistent	Import an ontology with its version URI, and/or follow the evolution of the imported ontology and change your ontology accordingly
P5	Importing an ontology series IRI instead of an ontology version IRI	Ontology networks and versioned ontologies	Import failure and/or the ontology become inconsistent	Import the ontology version IRI instead of the ontology series IRI
P6	Ontology series IRI is the same as the ontology version IRI	Ontology networks and versioned ontologies	Import failure	Delete the version number from the IRI, and/or to send a notification message with the new IRI when a new version is released
P7	A term is moved from one ontology module to another with different IRI	Ontology network	Functional impact, research queries might break	Take extra care when moving terms, and notify the different users in case of changes
P8	Namespace hijacking	Ontology networks	Retrieve invalid information while looking up for the hijacked terms	Define terms in the namespace that is owned and controlled by the knowledge engineer
P9	The IRI of a term contains a file extension	Stand-alone ontology pitfall, however can affect ontology networks	No content negotiation can take place	Stop using file extensions inside IRIs

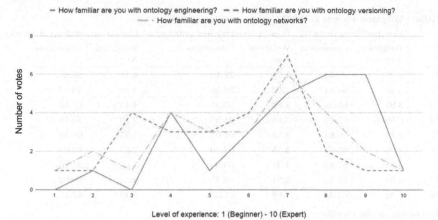

Fig. 4. Level of experience for the participants (weighted average).

We consider that the value of the participants' opinion is increasing with his/her level of experience. Thus, we calculated the weighted average (WA) for the different answers for each pitfall:

$$\text{WA} = \frac{\sum_{i=1}^{N} w_i \cdot x_i}{\sum_{i=1}^{N} w_i}$$

where w_i is the value of expertise of participant i and x_i his response. Then, we assess the agreement level between the different participants using the consensus measure (Cns) proposed by [36]:

$$\text{Cns}(X) = 1 + \sum_{j=1}^{n} p_j \cdot \log_2 \left(1 - \frac{|X_j - \mu_X|}{d_X} \right)$$

where X is the values vector (i.e. values from 1–5), p_j is the relative frequency of answer j, μ_X is the mean of X, and $d_X = X_{max} - X_{min}$ is the width of X.

The value of the consensus measure ranges between 0 (total disagreement) and 1 (total agreement). Authors of [17] proposed the following interpretation for intermediate values: a) Less than 0: poor agreement, b) 0.01–0.20: slight agreement, c) 0.21–0.40: fair agreement, d) 0.41–0.60: moderate agreement, e) 0.61–0.80: substantial agreement, and f) 0.81–1.00: almost perfect agreement.

We adapted the definition of p_j in the consensus (Cns) formula to account for the level of expertise of each participant:

$$p_j = \frac{\sum_{i=1}^{N} w_i \cdot \delta_{vote(i),j}}{\sum_{i=1}^{N} w_i}$$

Table 5. Weighted average and consensus ratio for the survey's answers.

| Pitfall | Weighted average (/5) VS Consensus value (/100) | | | | | |
| | How problematic is it? | | Impact on versioned ontologies | | Impact on ontology networks | |
	Weighted Avg.	Consensus	Weighted Avg.	Consensus	Weighted Avg.	Consensus
P1	4.06	68.61	4.20	77.10	4.18	69.80
P2	3.46	64.81	3.53	58.59	3.59	59.64
P3	3.93	62.52	3.63	55.25	4.10	61.59
P4	3.66	63.96	3.88	61.55	3.60	55.16
P5	3.64	66.61	3.57	54.03	3.57	60.38
P6	2.60	60.63	2.65	68.80	2.59	62.08
P7	3.51	57.89	3.48	60.94	3.60	57.16
P8	3.54	52.86	3.31	62.45	3.32	59.02
P9	3.02	66.40	2.98	61.55	2.49	67.17
Agreement on the classification (/100)			75.59			
Level of confidence (/100)			67.85			

where $\delta_{vote(i),j} = 1$ if participant i voted j, and 0 otherwise. Table 5 presents the weighted average and the consensus value for the different questions of the survey, computed using R.[19]

The overall level of confidence while filling the survey is around 68%, and the participants substantially agreed (Cns = 76%) with the new categorization we proposed for ontology pitfalls (i.e. stand-alone ontology pitfalls, versioned ontologies pitfalls, and pitfalls inside ontology networks). Table 6 categorizes the pitfalls based on their estimated impact into: 1. Major impact (WA > 3.5), 2. Middle impact (3 < WA < 3.5), and 3. Less impact (WA < 3). We rank the pitfalls' impact in descending order (i.e. high to less). As shown in Table 6, there is a substantial agreement that $P1$[20] and $P4$ have a major impact on versioned ontologies, and $P1$ and $P3$ have a major impact on ontology networks. Pitfalls $P1, P2, P3, P4,$ and $P5$ have a major impact on both versioned ontologies and ontology networks. $P7$ has a middle impact on versioned ontology but a major impact on ontology networks. $P8$ has a middle impact on both versioned ontologies and ontology networks. As for $P6$ and $P9$ the participants substantially agree that they have less impact.

---

[19] The source code found in *resources/SurveyExperiments* at https://github.com/OmarAlqawasmeh/coEvolutionTermsExtraction.

[20] P1. Ontology is not accessible at its IRI

P2. Importing an ontology using a non persistent IRI or the IRI of a representation

P3. Importing an inconsistent ontology

P4. Only the latest version of the ontology is available online

P5. Importing an ontology series IRI instead of an ontology version IRI

P6. Ontology series IRI is the same as the ontology version IRI

P7. Term is moved from one ontology module to another with different IRI

P8. Namespace hijacking

P9. The IRI of a term contains a file extension.

Table 6. Pitfalls ranked by their impact over versioned and networked ontologies.

Impact on	Major	Middle	Less
Versioned ontologies	P1$^+$, P4$^+$, P3*, P5*, and P2*	P7*, and P8$^+$	P6$^+$, and P9$^+$
Ontology networks	P1$^+$, P3$^+$, P7*, P4*, P2*, and P5*	P8*	P6$^+$ and P9$^+$

+: substantial agreement

*: moderate agreement

Moreover, Fig. 5 presents how often the participants encountered the different pitfalls. We can see that except for P6, P7, and P8, all participants encountered the different pitfalls before.

How often the participants encountered the set of pitfalls?

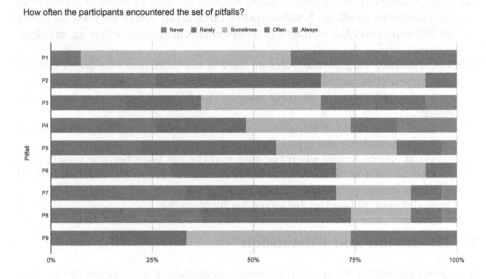

Fig. 5. How often the participants encountered the candidate pitfalls.

6.3   Analyzing the Participants Opinions

For each pitfall, participants could share known occurrences of the pitfall, and ideas or recommendations to solve or avoid it. We summarize the gathered opinions (OPN) below.

OPN 1. *Persistent IRIs are important:* participants agreed about the importance of persistent IRIs when creating or reusing ontologies. Some suggest to use services or catalogues to ensure the usage of persistent IRIs. Using persistent IRIs can effectively help to avoid pitfalls P1 and P2.

OPN 2. *Consistency tests should be made on the imported ontologies:* ontology editors should applying consistency tests on the imported ontologies to avoid pitfall P3.

OPN 3. *When reusing terms, refer only to those that are needed:* Some of the participants suggest to avoid importing the whole ontology and only declare the required terms. Ontology editors should check that these terms are correctly declared (e.g., a term that is originally declared a datatype property should not be declared as an annotation property), and services should be developed to monitor the evolution of the ontologies to prevent pitfall P7.

OPN 4. *Import the ontology using its version IRI.* This point has both advantages and disadvantages, on the one hand, importing an ontology version IRI prevents any issue that may arise if the imported ontology evolves. On the other hand, it may be interesting to update an ontology when a new version of an imported ontology is issued. Again, services could be developed to notify ontology editors about any new version release of the imported ontologies.

OPN 5. *A notification message should be send in case of moving terms from one module to another.* A subscription mechanism could be used to notify the different external artifacts (e.g. systems, ontologies) when an ontology evolves.

OPN 6. *Focusing only on the ontology level is not sufficient enough.* A participant argued that focusing on the quality of ontologies is less important than focusing on the quality of their usage. The following questions have been raised:

- How to improve the integration of heterogeneous data that was designed independently of the ontologies?)
- What can go wrong when the data and the ontology become misaligned?
- How to deal with noisy knowledge situations where the logic embedded in the ontology becomes unusable?

These different points can be topics for future work.

7   Discussion and Conclusion

In a previous contribution, we presented a definition of a situation of ontology evolution which considers the evolution of an ontology O that uses terms that have the namespace of O' (i.e. ontology co-evolution). We systematically listed and described the different cases of the adaptation to ontology co-evolution. We observed occurrences of these cases over two ontology portals: the Linked Open Vocabulary (LOV), and BioPortal. As the outcome of this study, we identified good practices and pitfalls.

Where the state of the art studies addressed stand-alone ontology pitfalls, in this paper we identified 9 candidate pitfalls that may affect versioned ontologies, i.e. when an ontology O_1 evolves to O_2, and/or ontology networks, i.e. when an ontology O uses or imports another ontology O'. In order to measure the importance and potential impact of the candidate pitfalls, we distributed a survey to the semantic web community. Participants agreed that listing and investigating in ontology pitfalls can effectively enhance the quality of ontologies which reflects in a positive way in using these ontologies for the different tasks (e.g. question answering). Moreover, we suggested a set of best practices to be followed in order to prevent or solve the candidate pitfalls.

As for future work, we are interested in targeting the following issues we identified:

1. *Some existing tools leads to the creation of pitfalls.* There exist some tools that could lead to the creation of some pitfalls. For example OnToology tool[21] publishes only the latest version of an ontology, and the documentation of this latest version (even if the ontology includes provenance information and information about the previous versions). It is important to update this tool so that all the versions are published. In case the owners of O' uses OnToology to publish it. Any other ontology that uses O' will be forced to import O' using its ontology series IRI or the latest ontology version IRI. Then using another ontology version IRI will have the risk to break this import in the future.

2. *The inheritance of a pitfall*: Some pitfalls can be inherited either when they evolve or when they are used in other ontologies. For example, if an ontology O' has the pitfall "creating the relationship (is) instead of using rdfs:subClassOf, rdf:type or owl:sameAs"[22], it means that O' has a property called *is*. If another ontology O uses O', then this pitfall will propagate to O automatically.

Moreover, we plan to develop a service that can automatically observe and notify the ontologies' owners during the evolution process. Having such tool can help to keep track of the ontologies in the different setting we proposed (i.e. ontology co-evolution, ontology versioning, and ontology networking). This will reflect positively on the quality of the different ontologies.

Finally, we plan to investigate further on the set of pitfalls that might occur on the data level (suggested by some of the survey's participants), mainly to focus on the set of pitfalls that might occur between the data and the ontologies, such as when the data and the ontology become misaligned due to the evolution of the ontology.

Acknowledgment. The authors would like to thank María Poveda (Universidad Politécnica de Madrid) for her suggestions and comments during the creation of the candidate pitfalls. Additionally, the authors would also like to thank the 27 anonymous participants for their valuable contribution to the experimental evaluation of the candidate pitfalls.

---

[21] http://ontoology.linkeddata.es/.

[22] Pifall number 3 from http://oops.linkeddata.es/catalogue.jsp.

References

1. Abdel-Qader, M., Scherp, A., Vagliano, I.: Analyzing the evolution of vocabulary terms and their impact on the LOD cloud. In: Gangemi, A., et al. (eds.) ESWC 2018. LNCS, vol. 10843, pp. 1–16. Springer, Cham (2018). https://doi.org/10.1007/978-3-319-93417-4_1
2. Abgaz, Y.M., Javed, M., Pahl, C.: Analyzing impacts of change operations in evolving ontologies. In: Proceedings of the 2nd Joint Workshop on Knowledge Evolution and Ontology Dynamics, USA (2012)
3. Bernaras, A., Laresgoiti, I., Corera, J.M.: Building and reusing ontologies for electrical network applications. In: 12th European Conference on Artificial Intelligence, Budapest, Hungary, August 11–16, 1996, Proceedings, pp. 298–302 (1996)
4. Brickley, D., Miller, L.: FOAF vocabulary specification 91 (2010)
5. Castano, S., Ferrara, A., Hess, G.N.: Discovery-driven ontology evolution. In: SWAP 2006 - Semantic Web Applications and Perspectives, Proceedings of the 3rd Italian Semantic Web Workshop, Scuola Normale Superiore, Pisa, Italy (2006)
6. Doran, P., Tamma, V.A.M., Iannone, L.: Ontology module extraction for ontology reuse: an ontology engineering perspective. In: Proceedings of the Sixteenth ACM Conference on Information and Knowledge Management, CIKM 2007, Lisbon, Portugal, 6–10 November 2007, pp. 61–70 (2007)
7. Dragoni, M., Ghidini, C.: Evaluating the impact of ontology evolution patterns on the effectiveness of resources retrieval. In: Proceedings of the 2nd Joint Workshop on Knowledge Evolution and Ontology Dynamics, Boston, MA, USA (2012)
8. Gaudet, P., Dessimoz, C.: Gene ontology: pitfalls, biases, and remedies. In: The Gene Ontology Handbook, pp. 189–205. Humana Press, New York (2017)
9. Groß, A., Hartung, M., Prüfer, K., Kelso, J., Rahm, E.: Impact of ontology evolution on functional analyses. Bioinformatics 28(20), 2671–2677 (2012)
10. Gruber, T.R.: A translation approach to portable ontology specifications. Knowl. Acquisition 5(2), 199–220 (1993)
11. Guha, R.V., Brickley, D., Macbeth, S.: Schema.org: evolution of structured data on the web. Commun. ACM 59(2), 44–51 (2016)
12. Haase, P., Rudolph, S., Wang, Y., Brockmans, S.: D1. 1.1 networked ontology model
13. Hartung, M., Groß, A., Rahm, E.: CODEX: exploration of semantic changes between ontology versions. Bioinformatics (2012)
14. Heath, T., Bizer, C.: Linked data: Evolving the web into a global data space. Synth. Lect. Semant. Web: Theory Technol. 1(1), 1–136 (2011)
15. Kupfer, A., Eckstein, S.: Coevolution of database schemas and associated ontologies in biological context. In: 22nd British National Conference on Databases (2006)
16. Kupfer, A., Eckstein, S., Neumann, K., Mathiak, B.: A coevolution approach for database schemas and related ontologies. In: 19th IEEE International Symposium on Computer-Based Medical Systems (CBMS 2006), Salt Lake City, Utah, USA, pp. 605–610 (2006)
17. Landis, J.R., Koch, G.G.: The measurement of observer agreement for categorical data. Biometrics 159–174 (1977)
18. Lebo, T., Sahoo, S., McGuinness, D.: PROV-O: The PROV ontology. W3C Recommendation 30 (2013)
19. Lehmann, J., Isele, R., Jakob, M., Jentzsch, A., Kontokostas, D., Mendes, P.N., Hellmann, S., Morsey, M., van Kleef, P., Auer, S., Bizer, C.: Dbpedia - a large-scale, multilingual knowledge base extracted from Wikipedia. Semant. Web 6(2), 167–195 (2015)

20. Mihindukulasooriya, N., Poveda-Villalón, M., García-Castro, R., Gómez-Pérez, A.: Collaborative ontology evolution and data quality - an empirical analysis. In: 13th International Workshop, OWLED, and 5th International Workshop, Bologna, Italy, pp. 95–114 (2016)

21. Noy, N.F., Musen, M.A.: PROMPTDIFF: a fixed-point algorithm for comparing ontology versions. In: The Eighteenth National Conference on AI and Fourteenth Conference on Innovative Applications of AI, Canada (2002)

22. Ottens, K., Aussenac-Gilles, N., Gleizes, M.P., Camps, V.: Dynamic ontology co-evolution from texts: principles and case study. In: Proceedings of the First International Workshop on Emergent Semantics and Ontology Evolution, ESOE 2007, Co-located with ISWC 2007 + ASWC 2007, Busan, Korea, pp. 70–83 (2007)

23. Papavassiliou, V., Flouris, G., Fundulaki, I., Kotzinos, D., Christophides, V.: On detecting high-level changes in RDF/S KBs. In: Bernstein, A., et al. (eds.) ISWC 2009. LNCS, vol. 5823, pp. 473–488. Springer, Heidelberg (2009). https://doi.org/10.1007/978-3-642-04930-9_30

24. Poveda Villalón, M.: Ontology Evaluation: a pitfall-based approach to ontology diagnosis. Ph.D. thesis, ETSI_Informatica (2016)

25. Poveda-Villalón, M., Gómez-Pérez, A., Suárez-Figueroa, M.C.: Oops! (ontology pitfall scanner!): An on-line tool for ontology evaluation. Int. J. Semantic Web Inf. Syst. **10**(2), 7–34 (2014)

26. Poveda Villalón, M., Suárez-Figueroa, M.C., Gómez-Pérez, A.: The landscape of ontology reuse in linked data (2012)

27. Qawasmeh, O., Lefrançois, M., Zimmermann, A., Maret, P.: Observing the impact and adaptation to the evolution of an imported ontology. In: Proceedings of the 11th International Joint Conference on Knowledge Discovery, Knowledge Engineering and Knowledge Management, IC3K 2019, Volume 2: KEOD, Vienna, Austria, September 17–19, 2019, pp. 76–86 (2019)

28. Sabou, M., Fernández, M.: Ontology (network) evaluation. In: Ontology Engineering in a Networked World, pp. 193–212 (2012)

29. Complex Networks in Software, Knowledge, and Social Systems. ISRL, vol. 148. Springer, Cham (2019). https://doi.org/10.1007/978-3-319-91196-0

30. Simperl, E.P.B.: Reusing ontologies on the semantic web: a feasibility study. Data Knowl. Eng. **68**(10), 905–925 (2009)

31. SmartM2M, E.: Saref consolidation with new reference ontology patterns, based on the experience from the seas project. 2019 jul. report no.: Ts 103 548 v1. 1.1

32. Stojanovic, L.: Methods and tools for ontology evolution. Ph.D. thesis, Karlsruhe Institute of Technology, Germany (2004)

33. Stojanovic, L., Maedche, A., Stojanovic, N., Studer, R.: Ontology evolution as reconfiguration-design problem solving. In: Proceedings of the 2nd International Conference on Knowledge Capture (K-CAP 2003), Sanibel Island, FL, USA, 23–25 October 2003 (2003)

34. Suárez-Figueroa, M.C., Gómez-Pérez, A., Motta, E., Gangemi, A.: Introduction: Ontology engineering in a networked world. In: Ontology Engineering in a Networked World, pp. 1–6 (2012)

35. Tartir, S., Arpinar, I.B., Sheth, A.P.: Ontological evaluation and validation. In: Poli, R., Healy, M., Kameas, A. (eds.) Theory and Applications of Ontology: Computer Applications. Springer, Dordrecht (2010). https://doi.org/10.1007/978-90-481-8847-5_5

36. Tastle, W.J., Wierman, M.J.: Consensus and dissention: a measure of ordinal dispersion. Int. J. Approx. Reasoning **45**(3), 531–545 (2007)

37. Vandenbussche, P., Atemezing, G., Poveda-Villalón, M., Vatant, B.: Linked open vocabularies (LOV), A gateway to reusable semantic vocabularies on the web. Semantic Web (2017)
38. Vigo, M., Bail, S., Jay, C., Stevens, R.D.: Overcoming the pitfalls of ontology authoring: strategies and implications for tool design. Int. J. Hum.-Comput. Stud. **72**(12), 835–845 (2014)
39. Whetzel, P.L., et al.: Bioportal: ontologies and integrated data resources at the click of a mouse. In: Proceedings of the 2nd International Conference on Biomedical Ontology, Buffalo, NY, USA (2011)
40. Zablith, F.: Ontology evolution: a practical approach. In: Workshop on Matching and Meaning at Artificial Intelligence and Simulation of Behaviour (2009)
41. Zablith, F., et al.: Ontology evolution: a process-centric survey. Knowl. Eng. Rev. **30**(1), 45–75 (2015)

From Semi-automated to Automated Methods of Ontology Learning from Twitter Data

Saad Alajlan[1,2(✉)], Frans Coenen[1], and Angrosh Mandya[1]

[1] Department of Computer Science, The University of Liverpool, Liverpool, UK
{s.alajlan,coenen,angrosh}@Liverpool.ac.uk
[2] College of Computer and Information Sciences, Al Imam Mohammad Ibn Saud Islamic University, Riyadh, Saudi Arabia

Abstract. This paper presents four different mechanisms for ontology learning from Twitter data. The learning process involves the identification of entities and relations from a specified Twitter data set, which is then used to produce an ontology. The initial two methods considered, the Stanford and GATE based ontology learning frameworks, are both semi-automated methods for identifying the relations in the desired ontology. Although the two frameworks effectively create an ontology supported knowledge resource, the frameworks feature a particular disadvantage; the time-consuming and cumbersome task of manually annotating a relation extraction training data sets. As a result two other ontology learning frameworks are proposed, one using regular expressions which reduces the required resource, and one that combines Shortest Path Dependency parsing and Word Mover's Distance to fully automate the process of creating relation extraction training data. All four are analysed and discussed in this paper.

Keywords: Ontology learning · Resource description framework · RDF Relation extraction · Name entity recognition · Twitter · Dependency graphs · Stanford relation extraction · Regular expression

1 Introduction

It is widely acknowledged that social media features a wealth of user-contributed content of all kinds [28,30,32]. The dramatic increase, over recent times, in the usage of social media platforms, such as Facebook and Twitter, has resulted in a rapid increase in the availability of this data. Exploiting this data, by extracting useful information from it, has thus become a research focus in the field of data mining and knowledge discovery. Twitter data has been analysed from many different perspectives to extract information that is both meaningful and useful. For example tweets on Ebola disease have been analysed to examine how users communicate, on social media platforms, regarding disease outbreaks [1]. Another example can be found in [3], where Twitter data was used to investigate

© Springer Nature Switzerland AG 2020
A. Fred et al. (Eds.): IC3K 2019, CCIS 1297, pp. 213–236, 2020.
https://doi.org/10.1007/978-3-030-66196-0_10

whether public sentiment factors can improve the forecasting of social, economic or commercial indicators.

The key challenge in extracting meaningful content from Twitter data arises from its unstructured format, rendering it difficult to query. One possible mechanism whereby some form of structure can be imposed on un-structured data is by preprocessing the data and labelling potential items, for example by identifying entities and relationships between entities. However, it is not enough to simply identify entities and relations to allow the querying of unstructured data. A shared understanding of the entities, and the corresponding relationships between them, is required. In other words what is required is an *ontology*.

In the context of computer science, an ontology is defined as an "explicit formal specification [concerning a given domain of discourse] of terms and the relationships that exist among them" [31]. A general all-encompassing ontology that covers all possible domains of discourse is beyond the means of computer science at present. The research focus has been on specific domains of discourse. Many specific domain ontologies have been proposed, especially to support the notion of the semantic web [15]. Examples include ontologies directed at e-commerce, artificial intelligence and bio-informatics [13]. The challenge of ontology generation is that it is a labour intensive and time consuming activity; the phrase "ontology generation bottleneck" is sometime encountered. The solution is to semi-automate or automate the ontology generation process, so called *ontology learning* [34]. Ontology learning, also known as ontology extraction, ontology generation, or ontology acquisition, is defined as the process of automatically or semi-automatically creating an ontology. The fundamental process is to extract the concepts included in a given domain, and the relationships between these concepts, and encode them using an ontology language so as to facilitate information retrieval [19]. Ontology learning is argued to be the most appropriate solution for providing meaningful structure to unstructured data. Although studies have been conducted to analyse Twitter data from different viewpoints, there are not many studies that have focused on *ontology learning* from Twitter data.

Against this background this paper presents several frameworks for ontology learning from Twitter data, founded on a range of tools and techniques: (a) using the Stanford NLP (Natural Language Processing) tool kit, (b) uisng the GATE (General Architecture for Text Engineering) tool kit, (c) using regular expressions and (d) combining Dependency Parse (DP) with text similarity measures such as Word Mover's Distance (WMD). The first three of these frameworks also present various challenges [2]. For example, the Stanford NLP and GATE frameworks require labelled training data to build a Relation Extraction model. Ontology learning using regular expressions mitigates against the problem of the manual creation of Relation Extraction model training data by defining regular expression patterns to provide a semi-automatic method of creating such data; however, the regular expressions still need to be defined and this remains a difficult, cumbersome and time-consuming task. Given these problems, the last proposed framework, the DPWMD framework, which entirely automates the process of generating Relation Extraction model training data.

The four proposed ontology learning frameworks were evaluated using example Twitter data collections. The entity and relation recognition and extraction models were evaluated using ten-fold cross-validation. The generated ontologies were further evaluated by directing pre-defined SPARQL queries at the populated ontologies. If the retrieved answers matched the expected answers, for a given set of queries, the generated ontology was deemed to be correct.

The rest of this paper is structured as follows. Section 2 gives an overview of previous work on ontology learning and relation extraction systems. Section 3 describes the proposed frameworks for ontology learning from Twitter data. Section 4 then considers the evaluation of the proposed frameworks. Finally, some conclusions are presented in Sect. 5.

2 Previous Work

Ontology learning from structured data such as tabular data, it is argued, is relatively straight forward as such data, by definition, is already structured in that it typically has a data schema associated with it, or at least table column headings; an example of ontology learning from relational databases can be found in [18]. Ontology learning from unstructured data, by definition, presents a greater challenge. There has been significant reported work on ontology learning from document collections. This is typically founded on the idea of relation extraction from text. An early example can be found in [14] where an automated relation labelling for ontology learning was presented. In comparison, there has been very little reported work on ontology learning from Twitter data which presents additional challenges over other forms of ontology learning from unstructured text in that Tweets are short and typically feature many grammatical errors and abbreviations. One example can be found in [2].

A review of relevant previous works on ontology learning from unstructured data is presented in this section. The section is divided into two parts. Work on ontology learning from free text is presented in Subsect. 2.1. Because of its relevance to ontology learning, a review of relation extraction for ontology learning is presented in Subsect. 2.2.

2.1 Ontology Learning

A recent exemplar approach to ontology learning from large collections of text data is presented in [20]. The proposed process starts by building a Word2Vec model [23] and defining some seed entities. The initial seed entities and Word2Vec model are then used to extract all terms representing entities (essentially a list of words) that represent domain concepts founded on those expressed in the seed entities. The list of words, and their Part Of Speech (PoS) tags, is then processed further to identify nouns (entities) and verbs (relations between entities). Finally, a hierarchical ontology is constructed using the Balanced Iterative Reducing and Clustering using Hierarchies (BIRCH) algorithm [33], which is an extended hierarchical clustering algorithm. The problem with this method is the need to manually define the initial seed set, if this is not done appropriately the correct entities and relations will not be identified and hence the ontology will be wrong. From the authors' own experience, a second issue is that using PoS tags is not an effective way to identify the relationship between entities. Further examples of ontology learning from free text can be found in [9,21].

2.2   Entity and Relation Extraction

The identification of the entities and relationships within a domain of discourse is an essential precursor for generating any ontology. There has been much work directed at the automated extraction of entities and relations from free text. This work is typically founded on the use of machine learning, particularly supervised learning, and NLP. A number of tools and techniques are available as a result of this work. Of particular relevance concerning the work presented in this paper is the Stanford CoreNLP which has been extensively used for entity identification and relation extraction, examples can be found in [2,6]. In [6] evaluation was conducted using a corpus of 110 articles relating to the US National Football League. In [2] the evaluation domain used was a Twitter corpus of 300 tweets relating to car pollution; the same evaluation domain as considered in this paper. In [6] a relation extraction system, founded on Stanford CoreNLP, was introduced that could be customised. The Stanford CoreNLP tool kit is also used with respect to the first framework considered in this paper. An alternative NLP tool kit, the GATE (General Architecture for Text Engineering) tool kit [7] is used with respect to the second framework considered in this paper.

A particular challenge of using supervised learning to extract entities and relations is preparing the training data. In many reported cases this is done manually [5,26,29]. In [2] a new method was suggested, founded on Stanford CoreNLP, that reduced the effort required to manually label a training set by using regular expression rules derived from a small number of tweets, a "seed set". This approach is also considered in this paper (the third framework considered). However, regular expressions only offer a partial solution as the expressions themselves have to be defined manually.

The desired solution is to automate the process of identifying entities, and the relations between them, and to then use theses entities and relations to prepare an appropriate training set, which will then help to predict the relations. One potential solutions is to use shortest path dependency parsing to find the most important information (relations) between two entities. There has been some reported work on using dependency parsing to extract relations from free text [4,8,25]. In [4] the authors presented a dependency parsing based approach to extracting relations from the ACE (Automated Content Extraction) newspaper corpus. The corpus consists of 422 documents, with a separate set of 97 documents for testing. The hypothesis was that the information required to captured the relation between two entities in a sentence is contained in the shortest path between the two entities as represented in a dependency graph. In [4] the authors used the Combinatory Categorial Grammar (CCG) and the Context Free Grammar (CFG) parsers to obtain dependencies. In [8] the focus was on biomedical texts. The idea was to identify whether there was any interaction between two protein names featured in a sentence by analysis the paths between the proteins within a given dependency parse tree and a set of pre-labelled parse trees. Two mechanisms for similarity measurement were considered: cosine similarity and modified distance similarity. Support Vector Machines (SVM) and k Nearest Neighbour (kNN) machine learning was used to classify every two proteins within a given dependency parse tree by looking at the label of the most similar pre-labelled parse trees. In [25] relations linking proteins were extracted using constituency syntactic parsing and the shortest dependency path between two proteins using Stanford dependency parsing. Constituent dependency tree nodes associated with the nodes on the shortest dependency path were preserved. The fourth framework presented in this paper considers dependency parsing.

3   Semi-automated and Automated Ontology Learning Frameworks for Twitter Data

The ontology learning frameworks, specifically directed at ontology learning from Twitter data, are presented in this section. As noted earlier, four frameworks are presented: (a) a Stanford NLP tool kit based framework, (b) a GATE based framework, (c) regular expression based framework and (d) a Dependency Parsing and Word Mover's Distance (DPWMD) based framework. The architecture of the Stanford and GATE based ontology learning frameworks are similar to each other, starting with the collecting of tweets and relation extraction. For this purpose, the Stanford NER (Named Entity Recognition) and Stanford Relation Extraction tools were used in the proposed Stanford ontology learning framework. The Gazetteer and GATE relation extraction tools were used with respect to the GATE framework. The regular expression-based ontology learning framework focused on preparing the relation extraction training set in a semi-automated manner by defining regular expression patterns, followed by subsequently using the training set to build a Relation Extraction model. The DPWMD framework is the most sophisticated framework. Further details are presented in the following sub-sections with the greatest emphasis on the fourth framework, the DPWMD framework.

3.1   Stanford NLP Tool Based Ontology Learning Framework

The pipeline architecture for the Stanford NLP tool-based ontology learning framework is given in Fig. 1. From the figure it can be seen that the process starts with a collection of tweets. The Twitter data is cleaned (not shown in the Figure) using various pre-processing steps. For example by deleting the hyperlinks present in a tweet. The next step is the *knowledge extraction* stage, which comprises two tasks, namely: (a) Named Entity Recognition (NER) and (b) Relation Extraction. This is followed by mapping of the identified entities to different classes. For example, entity mentions such as "UK", "USA" and "China" (country names) would be mapped to the class "countries". The mapping entities step is followed by ontology generation. The result is a RDF represented ontology which, once populated, can be queried for information retrieval purposes. More details regarding the NER and Relation Extraction models, and the ontology generation step, are provided below.

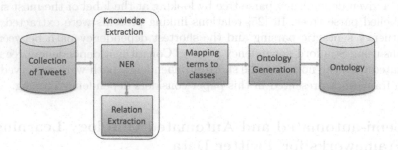

Fig. 1. Stanford ontology learning framework [2].

Named Entity Recognition (NER). The Stanford NER tool was used to create a model to identify entities that featured within a tweet (after which they would be associated with classes). For example, the word "UK" belongs to the class *Location*. Currently, the Stanford NER tool supports the following seven classes: Location, Person, Organization, Money, Percent, Date and Time. Given this limitation, the Stanford NER tools is not able to identify entities belonging to other domains. For instance, in the context of the car pollution data used for the evaluation reported on later in this paper, the Stanford NER tool will not identify entity mentions belonging to classes such as "Fuel vehicles" and "Green vehicles". In order to identify such entities the Stanford NER tool has to be re-trained using an appropriate training set (corpus). The Stanford NER tool provides the facility to do this. Figure 2 shows an example of the training record format that is required to specify a NER training set to create a model to identify the entities belonging to the classes "Location", "Date" and "Fuel vehicles". The tweet shown in the Figure states: "Norway to completely ban petrol powered cars by 2025". The label "Location" indicates that the word "Norway" belongs to the class "Location", "O" indicates a *wild card*, "FuelV" is associated with the class "Fuel vehicles" and "Date" is associated with the class "Date". The re-trained NER model is then used to associate entities with classes, the relation extraction tool (described below) is then used to identify relations between the identified entities.

Relation Extraction. Once a NER model has been created, the Stanford relation extraction tool was used to extract relations from tweets in a specific domain. The Stanford relation extraction tool also provides the ability to train

```
Norway           Location
`                0
to               0
completely       0
ban              0
'                0
petrol           fuelV
powered          fuelV
cars             0
by               0
2025             Date
.                0
```

Fig. 2. Example Stanford NER training record [2].

a relation exaction model using an appropriate training set [27]. The Stanford relation extraction tool has been successfully used for extract relations across different domains. For example, in [6], the tool was used to identify relations in the domain of American football. In [2] it was used to predict relations from Twitter data related to car pollution (the same domain as used with respect to this paper). Figure 3 shows an example of a Stanford relation extraction training record. The example again uses the tweet "Norway to completely ban petrol powered cars by 2025". The entity class is given in column 2, the Part Of Speech (PoS) tag is given in column 5 and the relevant content of the tweet in column 6. The last two lines of the example express the entities and the relations between them: (a) the relation "ban" that exists between word 0 and word 4 (entities "Norway" and "petrol powered"), and (b) the relation "Ban fuelV Date" that exists between words 0 and 6 (entities "Norway" and "2025").

```
0      Location      0     0    NNP     Norway          0    0    0
0      0             1     0    TO      to              0    0    0
0      0             2     0    ``      `               0    0    0
0      0             3     0    RB      completely      0    0    0
0      0             4     0    NN      ban             0    0    0
0      Other         5     0    NN/VBD  petrol/powered  0    0    0
0      0             6     0    NNS     cars            0    0    0
0      0             7     0    IN      by              0    0    0
0      Other         8     0    CD      2025            0    0    0
0      0             9     0    POS     '               0    0    0
0      0            10     0    .       .               0    0    0

0      5      ban
0      8      ban_fuelV_Date
```

Fig. 3. Example of Stanford relation extraction training data record [2].

The Relation Extraction model, once trained, was used to extract relations from tweets (in the specified domain). Results were filtered to include only those relations that were pertinent to the ontology [2]. In other words, only the relations identified in the training set were used to generate the ontology (described further below). All results were saved in the form of triples of the form: ⟨entity1, relation, entity2⟩. For instance, for the example tweet "Norway to completely ban petrol powered cars by 2025", the following triples were saved: $\langle Norway, ban, petrol \rangle$ and $\langle Norway, ban\ fuelv\ Date, 2025 \rangle$. The final step was to re-use the Stanford NER tool to map entities to their respective classes in order to generate the ontology. For example, the entity $Norway$ would be mapped to the class $Location$.

Ontology Generation. The final step in the Stanford ontology learning framework presented in Fig. 1 is ontology generation. To this end, the LODRefine tool, recommended by the the World Wide Web Consortium (W3C), was used to convert entity-relation-entity triples to an RDF represented ontology. The LODRefine tool is a combination of the OpenRefine tool and a RDF extension [12]. The ontology contained four classes "Location", "FuelV", "GreenV" and "Date"; and four relations: "ban", "use", "ban FuelV Date" and "Use GreenV Date".

3.2 GATE-Based Ontology Learning Framework

The GATE-based framework for ontology learning is presented in this section. The architecture for the framework is given in Fig. 4. Comparison of Figs. 4 and Fig. 1 indicate that the distinction between the two is in the *Knowledge Extraction* step. Note that for the purpose of Knowledge Extraction two GATE components were used, the Gazetteer and the GATE relation extraction tool. The gazetteer uses a prescribed lists of words, describing entity classes, and uses this list to identify entities within given texts. The relation extraction component is then used to extract relations that exists between the identified entities. This is followed by the ontology generation step, which is similar to the final step in the Stanford tool based framework described above.

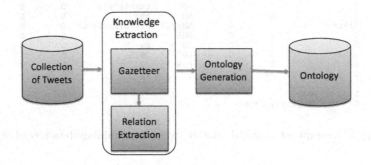

Fig. 4. GATE ontology learning framework [2].

In further detail, the Knowledge Extraction process involves the following steps: (a) data pre-processing, (b) entity extraction using the gazetteer, (c) class pairing, (d) training set generation, (e) Relation Extraction model generation and (f) Relation Extraction model application. The data pre-processing involves word tokenisation and POS tagging. The A Nearly New Information Extraction (ANNIE) tool, available within GATE, was used for the pre-processing step. ANNIE assigns a sequential character ID number, c_i, to each character in a given Tweet T, $T = [c_1, c_2, \ldots c_n]$. Each word is defined by a start (c_s) and end (c_e) id, based on the start and end character location within a tweet; a word id is thus expressed as $\langle c_s, c_e \rangle$; an example annotated tweet is given in Fig. 5. In the next step, the gazetteer was used to annotate words in a tweet so as to identify entities and then assign class labels to those entities. The Gazetteer has predefined lists such as lists of locations, people and organisations. However, in the context of the vehicle pollution scenario used for evaluation purposes an appropriate lists was not available. As a result such a list had to be generated. JAPE [11] was used over the annotated tweets to pair classes. The Gazetteer assigns a unique Entity ID, e, to each entity.

```
<TextWithNodes><Node id="0" />Norway<Node id="6" /> <Node id="7" />to<Node
id="9" /> <Node id="10" />'<Node id="11" />completely<Node id="21" /> <Node
id="22" />ban<Node id="25" /> <Node id="26" />petrol<Node id="32" /> <Node
id="33" />powered<Node id="40" /> <Node id="41" />cars<Node id="45" /> <Node
id="46" />by<Node id="48" /> <Node id="49" />2025<Node id="53" />'<Node
id="54" />.<Node id="55" /></TextWithNodes>

<Annotation Id="1111" Type="RelationClass" StartNode="0" EndNode="45">
<Feature>
   <Name className="java.lang.String">rel-type</Name>
   <Value className="java.lang.String">ban</Value>
</Feature>
<Feature>
   <Name className="java.lang.String">location</Name>
   <Value className="java.lang.String">26</Value>
</Feature>
<Feature>
   <Name className="java.lang.String">fuelV</Name>
   <Value className="java.lang.String">43</Value>
</Feature>
</Annotation>
```

Fig. 5. Example annotated Tweet [2].

Similar to Stanford relation extraction, GATE follows a supervised learning approach. This means that GATE needs a training corpus. The training set was identified by assign relations manually to class pairs identified in the previews step. Once the training set had been identified, the GATE Relation Extraction model was generated. This model was then used to predicate classes and the relations between these classes.

An example of a GATE relation extraction training record is given in Fig. 5. The Figure again shows the example tweet "Norway to completely ban petrol powered cars by 2025" used previously. The relation is "ban", which links entities belonging to the class "Location" and the class "Fuelv". In the example, the character content of the tweet is indexed using a sequential numbering. The specific entities that were identified within the tweet have the IDs 0 to 6 for Norway belonging to the class "Location", and IDs 26 to 45 for petrol powered

```
<AnnotationSet Name="ML">
<Annotation Id="1158" Type="RelationClass" StartNode="0" EndNode="45">
<Feature>
    <Name className="java.lang.String">fuelV</Name>
    <Value className="java.lang.String">43</Value>
</Feature>
<Feature>
    <Name className="java.lang.String">rel-type</Name>
    <Value className="java.lang.String">ban</Value>
</Feature>
<Feature>
    <Name className="java.lang.String">location</Name>
    <Value className="java.lang.String">26</Value>
</Feature>
<Feature>
    <Name className="java.lang.String">prob</Name>
    <Value className="java.lang.Float">0.92415094</Value>
</Feature>
</Annotation>
</AnnotationSet>
```

Fig. 6. Example of a GATE relation extraction result [2].

cars belonging to the class "Fuelv". The GATE Relation Extraction model, once trained, can be used to extract classes and associated relations from Twitter data. The results were of the form $\langle class1, class2, relation \rangle$. The result of the model prediction is shown in the Fig. 6.

3.3 Regular Expression-Based Ontology Learning Framework

While the above described frameworks (using the Stanford coreNLP and GATE) provide useful mechanisms for supporting ontology learning, both involve significant end-user resource, particularly in the preparation of relation extraction training data. The entire process is therefore time consuming and does not generalise over all potential domains. The third mechanism considered in this paper was designed to address the training data preparation overhead by using regular expressions in order to limit the resource required with respect to the previous two frameworks. An overview of the ontology learning using regular expressions framework is given in Fig. 7. Note that the framework interfaces with elements of Stanford CoreNLP, it could equally well be interfaced with GATE, however preliminary evaluation (reported on in Sect. 4 below) indicated that Stanford was a better option.

From Fig. 7 it can be seen that the process starts with a collection of tweets. The first step is to generate a NER model using a "Seed Set"; in the context of the evaluation data set presented later in this paper 100 tweets were selected instead of the 300 used by the Stanford and Gate frameworks. The NER model is generated in a similar manner as described previously in Subsect. 3.1. The seed set was also used to generate a set of regular expression patterns. Three regular expression pattern categories were considered: (a) two entity expressions, (b) three entity expressions and (c) four entity expressions. The form of these patterns was: $\{e_1, ?, r, ?, e_2\}$, $\{e_1, ?, e_2, ?, r, ?, e_3\}$ and $\{e_1, ?, e_2, ?, e_3, ?, r, ?, e_4\}$ respectively, where ? was an arbitrary set of intervening words. In each case there were a number of variations, 6, 24 and 120 respectively. The advantage of

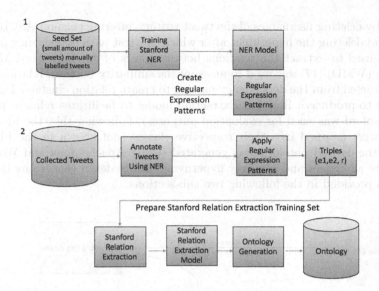

Fig. 7. Regular expressions ontology learning framework [2].

the framework is that it can deal with more than two entities in a tweet, unlike comparable frameworks.

The input set of Tweets were annotated using the NER model. Then, the regular expression were applied to the annotated tweets to extract a set of triples of the form $\langle e_1, e_2, r \rangle$. Note that while, in certain cases, several such triples may be extracted from a single tweet, in some instances no triples were identified. The triples were then used to automatically generate a training set for the generation of the Relation Extraction model as described in Subsect. 3.1 above. The remaining two steps are identical to those included in the previous two frameworks.

3.4 Dependency Parsing and Word Mover's Distance (DPWMD) Based Ontology Learning Framework

The DPWMD ontology learning framework is presented in this section. The framework was designed to avoid the manual labelling of training data so as to reduce the resource required to prepare a training set. The framework is founded on the twin ideas of Dependency Parsing (DP) and Word Mover's Distance (WMD). The architecture of the proposed DPWMD framework is given in Fig. 8. The figure shows a two-stage process: (a) creation of the desired NER model (top of the figure) and (b) creation of the Relation Extraction model (bottom of the figure).

The process starts with the creation of a NER model. With respect to the evaluation presented later in this paper Stanford CoreNLP was again used for this purpose. The input set of tweets were then pre-processed (not shown in the

Figure) by deleting usernames of the tweet writers, filtering the non-ASCII characters and deleting the hyperlinks, after which shortest path dependency parsing [16] was used to extract the relations between pairs of entities. Word Mover's Distance (WMD) [17] was used to measure the similarity between relations that were extracted from the dependency parsing to create relation clusters. The next step was to produce a Relation Extraction model to facilitates relation prediction (Stanford was used for evaluation purposes). Following this, the identified entities were mapped into their respective classes (not shown in the Figure). Finally, the desired ontology was generated (using Apache Jena and WordNet to acquire all classes and property hypernyms). More detail concerning DP and WMD is provided in the following two sub-sections.

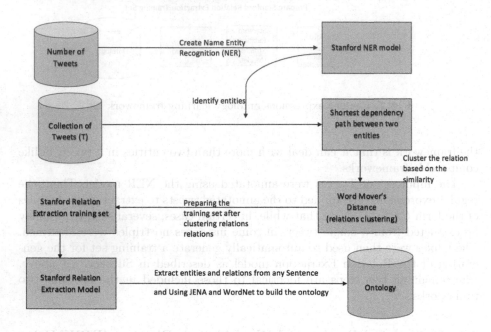

Fig. 8. Dependency Parsing and Word Mover's Distance (DPWMD) ontology learning framework.

Dependency Parsing. Dependency parsing is "the task of automatically analysing the dependency structure of a given input sentence" [16]. In Fig. 8, the goal of the dependency parsing is to find the relationships that link the entities in a given tweet by identifying pairs of entities. The two tools utilized for this purpose were: (i) the Stanford NER tool and (ii) the Stanford Dependency Parsing tool. The Stanford NER tool was used to build a model to identify entities in a tweet by selecting two desired classes; the NER model was then used to capture all entities in the input data to, in turn, help the dependency parsing tool extract relations between the identified entities. The NER model was trained as described previously in Subsect. 3.1.

Once the NER model had been created, DP was used to extract relations between specific classes. For the evaluation presented later in this paper the pretrained Stanford Dependency Parsing model was used. The hypothesis was that the shortest path between two entities described the relation between them [4]. The idea behind using Stanford NER and Stanford Dependency Parsing together is to specify the classes that the user wants to find relations between. The system therefore retrieved all the entities that belonged to the classes of interest and the relations between them. For example, Fig. 9 shows the dependency parse for the tweet: "Norway to completely ban petrol cars by 2025". If the classes "Location" and "FuelV" were specified, the entities *Norway* (e_1) and *petrol* (e_2) would be found, and consequently the relation (r) *ban cars* (according to the short path of the dependency graph shown in Fig. 9). Alternatively, if "Location" and "Date" were selected as the target classes, e_1 would be *Norway* and e_2 would be 2040, and the corresponding relation r would be *ban*. Figure 10 shows the dependency parse for another tweet: "The UK to ban the sale of diesel and petrol cars by 2040 to tackle". In this case e_1 is *UK*, belonging to the class "Location", e_2 is *diesel* belonging to the class "FuelV", and r is *ban sale cars*. Table 9 shows the targeted entities and the relations in these two example tweets. Note that the proposed approach has the advantage, unlike comparable frameworks, of being able to operate with more than two entities.

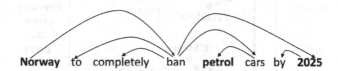

Fig. 9. Example dependency parse 1.

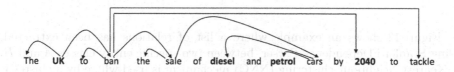

Fig. 10. Example dependency parse 2.

Word Mover's Distance. Most of the relations between entities are sets of words. WMD is used to measure the similarity between relations obtained for

Tweets	Entities and the relations based on the shortest path Dependency parsing		
Norway to completely ban **petrol** cars by **2025**	Norway _____ ban cars_____ **petrol**		
	Norway _____ ban _____ 2025		
The **UK** to ban the sale of **diesel** and **petrol** cars by **2040** to tackle	UK_____ ban sale cars_____**petrol**		
	UK_____ ban sale cars_____**deiseal**		
	UK_____ ban _____2040		

Fig. 11. Entities and relations based on short path dependency parsing.

different entity pairs belonging to similar classes. WMD is based on a word embedding method, which learns semantically meaningful representations for words. WMD "measures the dissimilarity between two text documents as the minimum distance that the embedded words of one document need to "travel" to reach the embedded words of another document" [17]. An example is given in Fig. 12. WMD measures the distance between two text documents by calculating the minimum cumulative distance that all words in the first relation need to travel to match the second relation exactly.

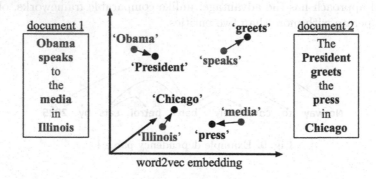

Fig. 12. Example of Word Mover's Distance captured from [17].

Figure 13 shows an example where a list of relations has been extracted, using Stanford Dependency Parser, between two specific entity classes A and B. A Nearest Neighbour clustering (NNC) mechanism is used where by a cluster is created for the first relation. Then, the similarities between the first and second relations are measured using WMD. If the similarities between the two relations are equal to or higher than some threshold the second relation is added to the first cluster. Otherwise, a second cluster is created, and the second relation is added to the second cluster. Next, the third relation is considered and measured against the first cluster, and so on. Several clusters are therefore created, each containing a number of relations. One relation from the biggest cluster is selected to represent all the relations in the clusters. The next step was to automatically generate a training set for Relation Extraction model generation as described earlier in Subsect. 3.1.

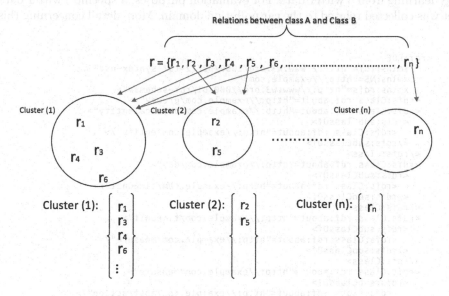

Fig. 13. Relation list and clusters.

DPWMD Ontology Generation. The ontology learning generation step is the final step in the proposed DPWMD ontology learning framework. There are many tools recommended by The World Wide Web Consortium (W3C) to use entity-relation-entity triples to generate an RDF represented ontology. In this paper, Apache Jena was used, which is an open-source Semantic Web framework based on Java. It provides an API to extract data and store a generated ontology in the form of a RDF graph. The resulting RDF data can be queried using SPARQL queries. WordNet was used with respect to the proposed DPWMD framework to enhance the ontology by adding super-classes and super-properties to the classes and relations that were identified. WordNet is an electronic lexical database for English nouns, verbs, adjectives and adverbs [10]. Uisng WordNet "Word forms are grouped into more than 117,000 sets of (roughly) synonymous word forms, so called synsets" and "These are interconnected by bidirectional arcs that stand for lexical (word-word) and semantic (synset-synset) relations, including hyper/hyponymy" [22]. Apache Jena was used with respect to the DPWMD framework instead of OpenRefine as used with respect to the three alternative frameworks described above. During implementation it was found that Apache Jena was easy to use and compatible with lexical databases such as WordNet (use to enrich the ontology in the context of the DPWMD Framework). An example of an RDF schema, generated using the DPWMD Framework, is given in Fig. 14.

4   Evaluation

This section presents the evaluation of the four considered frameworks for ontology learning from Twitter data. For evaluation purposes, a specific Twitter data set was collected related to the car pollution domain. More detail concerning this

```
<rdf:RDF
    xmlns:rdf="http://www.w3.org/1999/02/22-rdf-syntax-ns#"
    xmlns:NS="http://example.com/"
    xmlns:rdfs="http://www.w3.org/2000/01/rdf-schema#">
    <rdfs:Class rdf:about="http://example.com/greenV"/>
    <rdfs:Class rdf:about="http://example.com/physicalentity">
      <rdfs:subClassOf>
        <rdfs:Class rdf:about="http://example.com/entity"/>
      </rdfs:subClassOf>
    </rdfs:Class>
    <rdfs:Class rdf:about="http://example.com/day">
      <rdfs:subClassOf>
        <rdfs:Class rdf:about="http://example.com/timeunit"/>
      </rdfs:subClassOf>
    </rdfs:Class>
    <rdfs:Class rdf:about="http://example.com/timeunit">
      <rdfs:subClassOf>
        <rdfs:Class rdf:about="http://example.com/measure"/>
      </rdfs:subClassOf>
    </rdfs:Class>
    <rdfs:Class rdf:about="http://example.com/measure">
      <rdfs:subClassOf>
        <rdfs:Class rdf:about="http://example.com/abstraction"/>
      </rdfs:subClassOf>
    </rdfs:Class>
    <rdfs:Class rdf:about="http://example.com/Location">
      <rdfs:subClassOf>
        <rdfs:Class rdf:about="http://example.com/object"/>
      </rdfs:subClassOf>
    </rdfs:Class>
    <rdfs:Class rdf:about="http://example.com/Date">
      <rdfs:subClassOf rdf:resource="http://example.com/day"/>
    </rdfs:Class>
    <rdfs:Class rdf:about="http://example.com/abstraction">
      <rdfs:subClassOf rdf:resource="http://example.com/entity"/>
    </rdfs:Class>
    <rdfs:Class rdf:about="http://example.com/object">
      <rdfs:subClassOf rdf:resource="http://example.com/physicalentity"/>
    </rdfs:Class>
    <rdf:Property rdf:about="http://example.com/convert">
      <rdfs:subPropertyOf>
        <rdf:Property rdf:about="http://example.com/change"/>
      </rdfs:subPropertyOf>
    </rdf:Property>
    <rdf:Property rdf:about="http://example.com/transitionvehicles">
      <rdfs:range rdf:resource="http://example.com/greenV"/>
      <rdfs:domain rdf:resource="http://example.com/Location"/>
      <rdfs:subPropertyOf rdf:resource="http://example.com/convert"/>
    </rdf:Property>
    <rdf:Property rdf:about="http://example.com/wantselectric">
      <rdfs:range rdf:resource="http://example.com/Date"/>
      <rdfs:domain rdf:resource="http://example.com/Location"/>
    </rdf:Property>

</rdf:RDF>
```

Fig. 14. Example of RDF File.

data set is presented in Subsect. 4.1 below. The key objectives of the evaluation were as follows:

1. To evaluate the effectiveness, in terms of accuracy, of the Entity and Relation Extraction model generation process.
2. To investigate the effectiveness of the ontology generation process using the identified entities and relations.
3. To evaluate the utility of the generated ontology by querying it using sample queries.

Each objective is discussed in more details in Subsect. 4.2 to 4.3 below.

4.1 Evaluation Data

This section briefly describes the car pollution domain evaluation data set. This dataset was also used in [2]. To create the data set tweets were collected using the Twitter API. The "car pollution" topic was chosen since it is easy to understand and hence any proposed mechanism using this data could be manually analysed, especially the generated ontology. The criteria for the collected tweets were that the tweets should contain content related to the banning of fuel vehicles or promoting the idea of using green vehicles in a certain location. Accordingly, three hundred tweets were collected and labelled manually, which then formed the evaluation data set. The tweets contained four entity classes: (a) *Location*, (a) *FuelV*, (c) *GreenV* and (d) *Date*; and four relation classes: (a) *ban*, (b) *Use*, (c) *ban fuelV Date* and (d) *use greenV Date*. The distribution of the classes and relations across the data set is shown in Figs. 15 and 16; 768, 384, 198 and 1162 for the entity classes; and 241, 125, 166 and 87 for the relations class. Figures 15 and 16 indicate that, as expected, there were many more occurrences of entities than relations which meant that the data set was imbalanced. A typical tweet features eight entities and two relations; not all entities were paired. The DPWMD ontology learning framework featured four different relations to those described above, because an automated method of relation extraction was used: (a) *ban cars*, (b) *transition vehicles*, (c) *ban* and (d) *wants electric*.

4.2 Effectiveness of Ontology Learning Frameworks

Stanford, GATE, Regular Expression and DPWMD relation extraction, and Stanford NER are evaluated in the next two sub-section by providing some statistics that show the accuracy of the models. Further details of this evaluation is presented below.

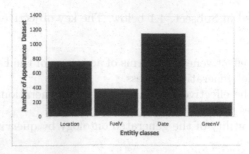

Fig. 15. Distribution of the entities per class across the training data set [2].

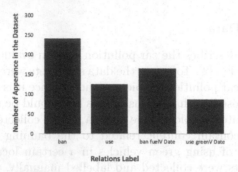

Fig. 16. Distribution of the relations per class across the training data set [2].

Stanford Name Entity Recognition (NER) Evaluation. For the Stanford Name Entity Recognition (NER) evaluation the evaluation data set of 300 tweets was divided into a 270 tweet training set and a 30 tweet test set which were used to generate and evaluate the Stanford NER model generation tool used by the proposed Stanford and DPWMD frameworks. The NER model was trained to identify the four entity classes: *Location, Date, FuelV* and *GreenV*. Table 1 presents the Ten-fold Cross-Validation results of the evaluation of the generated models. Inspection of the table indicates a small Standard Deviation (Stand. Dev.) of 0.71. It can thus be concluded that the generated Stanford NER model was consistent and accurate. Using the regular expression ontology learning framework the Stanford NER model was trained using a seed training set of 100 records, a third of the available evaluation data set. Because of the size of the training set, three-fold Cross-Validation was applied to evaluate the model. The results are presented Table 2. From this table it can be seen that the average F-score was less than that obtained when using 270 records for the training (see Table 1), but within acceptable limits.

Stanford, GATE, Regular Expression, DPWMD Relation Extraction Evaluation. Ten-fold Cross-Validation (TCV) was also used to evaluate all the Relation Extraction models (Stanford, GATE, Regular Expression and DPWMD). Table 3 presents the results obtained. Inspection of the table

Table 1. TCV results for the Stanford NER model evaluation [2].

Fold	F-Score
1	77.3
2	77.7
3	77.2
4	79.3
5	77.2
6	78.0
7	78.0
8	78.9
9	78.4
10	78.3
Average	78.0
Standard Deviation (SD)	0.71

Table 2. Three-fold Cross Validation results for the Regular Expression Stanford NER model evaluation [2].

Fold	F-score
1	49.0
2	53.0
3	55.0
Average	52.3
Standard Deviation (SD)	3.0

indicates a wide spread of results (high standard deviations). The conjectured reason for this was that the training data was imbalanced in nature. Fold 5 is the worst performing fold. Inspection of this fold revealed that nine examples of the *use greenV Date* relationship class were included, but that only two were correctly classified. From Fig. 16 it can be seen that there were only 87 entities within the *use greenV Date* class, which means only nine examples per fold. However, the *ban* relation class appears 241 times. Comparing between the GATE and Stanford Relation Extraction models, the Stanford model produced a better average F-score than the GATE system. This is the reason why it was decided to utilise the Stanford NLP Regular Expression model, as opposed to the GATE model, with respect to the remaining two frameworks. The F-score values ranged from 56.9 to 88.5, again the conjectured reason behind this was the imbalanced nature of the training data. However, what is interesting to note is that the average relation extraction F-score obtained using the Regular Expression approach was better than the GATE approach although not as good at the Stanford approach; whilst using a smaller relation extraction training set.

Table 3. F-Scores using GATE (RE), Stanford (RE) and Regular expression (Stanford CoreNLP) and DPWMD (Stanford CoreNLP) relation extraction.

Fold Num.	GATE (RE)	Stanford (RE)	Regular expression (Stanford CoreNLP)	DPWMD (Stanford CoreNLP)
Fold 1	70.6	76.7.2	78.1	74.5
Fold 2	79.4	85.0	88.5	72.4
Fold 3	71.1	78.4	69.3	89.3
Fold 4	57.6	96.1	75.6	71.8
Fold 5	50.8	56.1	73.7	75.4
Fold 6	82.1	79.3	70.3	65.5
Fold 7	61.4	75.3	73.5	67.6
Fold 8	70.0	72.7	78.5	74.1
Fold 9	72.0	87.9	56.9	76.9
Fold 10	66.8	88.1	81.0	52.9
Average	68.2	79.5	74.5	72.0
Standard Deviation (SD)	9.5	10.9	8.3	9.2

Inspection of the result for the last model, DPWMD, in Table 3 shows that Fold 10 produced the worst performance. Inspection of this fold indicated that there were only 16 examples of *wants electric*, and only four of them were predicted correctly since the number of *wants electric* was so small. The *wants electric* entity featured in the training set only 93 time, unlike other relations such as *ban cars* which was mentioned 493 time. Overall, the average F-scorer seems reasonable, reaching 72.04%. The F-score was less than that obtained using the regular expression framework, however, the relation extraction process using the DPWMD framework was fully automated, unlike in the case of the regular expression framework where the extraction was only semi-automated.

4.3   Evaluation of the Utility of the Generated Ontologies

From a visual inspection of the semantics of the ontologies generated using the Stanford, GATE and Regular expression ontology learning frameworks the ontologies seem correct. Other than visual confirmation, the generated ontologies were automatically evaluated by checking their syntactic integrity using the RDF W3C Validation Tool. It was found that, in this simple Scenario, the generated ontologies were correct semantically and syntactically.

The ontology generated using the DPWMD ontology learning framework, presented in Fig. 14, shows that the class *Location* was linked with three other classes (*Date*, *FuelV* and *GreenV*) and that the connection relations were *bancars*, *transition vehicles*, *ban* and *wantselectric*, since Apache Jena was used to generate the ontology. The *Location* class super-classes were obtained from WordNet as discussed in Subsect. 3.4. Also, the class *Date* had super-classes. Moreover, some properties (relations) had supper properties such as *transitionvehicles* has *convert* and *change*. It is noticeable that some classes did not have a super-classes, such as *FuelV* and *GreenV*; this was because these were not defined in WordNet. Whatever the case, it was concluded that this obtained ontology was also semantically correct.

To evaluate the utility of the generated ontologies, the ontologies were populated using an evaluation data set of 311 tweets, and then SPARQL was used to query the data. In [24] it was noted that "SPARQL could be used to express queries across diverse data sources, whether the data is stored natively as RDF or viewed as RDF via middleware". For the evaluation, Apache Jena was used to support the SPARQL querying of the RDF represented data. Figure 17 shows an example of a SPARQL query. The query asks for all locations that will ban any type of car. From the result of the query it can be concluded that the generated ontology was appropriate. To sum up, the ontology generated using the DPWMD ontology learning framework was considered to be better than that generated using the Stanford, GATE and Regular expression ontology learning frameworks, because it had more classes and properties generated by using WordNet hyponymys.

SELECT   ?Location ?vehicle type
WHERE {

? Location   a:bancars ? vehicle_type

}

Fig. 17. Example of SPARQL query [2].

5   Conclusion

This paper has presented four frameworks for learning ontologies from Twitter data: (a) Stanford, (b) GATE, (c) Regular expression and (d) Dependency Parsing and Word Mover's Distance. The output from these frameworks was an RDF represented ontology generated utilising either LODRefine or Apache Jena. A disadvantage of the Stanford and GATE relation extraction frameworks was that they needed pre-labelling relation extraction training data in a specified format. This was a significant disadvantage since the preparation of this training data required considerable end-user resource. The regular expression ontology learning framework was proposed to solve this problem. However, the regular expression ontology learning framework only provided a partial solution as it was still necessary to manually create the required regular expression patterns. The DPWMD ontology learning framework was therefore proposed which addressed the relation extraction training data problem using dependency parsing and Word Mover's Distance. All four proposed frameworks were evaluated using a car pollution evaluation data set comprised of 300 tweets. The generated ontology was evaluated by populating the generated ontologies with a further set of 311 tweets, and querying the data using SPARQL querying. The results were very encouraging. For future work the authors intend to consider a much larger evaluation data collection. It is anticipated that this will required further modification of the best performing proposed DPWMD ontology learning from Twitter data framework.

References

1. Ahmed, W., Demaerini, G., Bath, P.A.: Topics discussed on twitter at the beginning of the 2014 ebola epidemic in united states. In: iConference 2017 Proceedings (2017)
2. Alajlan., S., Coenen., F., Konev., B., Mandya., A.: Ontology learning from twitter data. In: Proceedings of the 11th International Joint Conference on Knowledge Discovery, Knowledge Engineering and Knowledge Management - Volume 2: KEOD, pp. 94–103. INSTICC, SciTePress (2019)
3. Arias, M., Arratia, A., Xuriguera, R.: Forecasting with twitter data. ACM Trans. Intell. Syst. Technol. (TIST) 5(1), 1–24 (2014)
4. Bunescu, R.C., Mooney, R.J.: A shortest path dependency kernel for relation extraction. In: Proceedings of the Conference on Human Language Technology and Empirical Methods in Natural Language Processing, pp. 724–731. Association for Computational Linguistics (2005)
5. Carlson, A., Betteridge, J., Wang, R.C., Hruschka, E.R., Mitchell, T.M.: Coupled semi-supervised learning for information extraction. In: Proceedings of the 3rd ACM International Conference on Web Search and Data Mining, p. 101. ACM (2010)
6. Chunxiao, W., et al.: Customizing an information extraction system to a new domain. In: Regulatory Peptides, vol. 141, pp. 35–43. Association for Computational Linguistics (2007)
7. Cunningham, H.: Gate, a general architecture for text engineering. Comput. Humanit. 36(2), 223–254 (2002)
8. Erkan, G., Ozgur, A., Radev, D.R.: Semi-supervised classification for extracting protein interaction sentences using dependency parsing. In: Proceedings of the 2007 Joint Conference on Empirical Methods in Natural Language Processing and Computational Natural Language Learning (EMNLP-CoNLL) (2007)
9. Exner, P., Nugues, P.: Entity extraction: from unstructured text to dbpedia RDF triples. In: The Web of Linked Entities Workshop (WoLE 2012), pp. 58–69. CEUR (2012)
10. Fellbaum, C.: Wordnet. In: Theory and Applications of Ontology: Computer Applications, pp. 231–243. Springer, Dordrecht (2010). https://doi.org/10.1007/978-90-481-8847-5_10
11. Cunningham H., Maynard, D., Tablan, V.: JAPE: a Java Annotation Patterns Engine (Second Edition). Department of Computer Science, University of Sheffield (2000)
12. Harlow, C.: Data Munging Tools in Preparation for RDF: catmandu and LODRefine. The Code4Lib Journal 30(30), 1–30 (2015)

13. Iqbal, R., Murad, M.A.A., Mustapha, A., Sharef, N.M.: An analysis of ontology engineering methodologies: a literature review. Res. J. Appl. Sci. Eng. Technol. **6**(16), 2993–3000 (2013)
14. Kavalec, M., Svaték, V.: A study on automated relation labelling in ontology learning. Ontology Learning from Text: Methods, Evaluation and Applications, pp. 44–58 (2005)
15. Klusch, M., Kapahnke, P., Schulte, S., Lecue, F., Bernstein, A.: Semantic web service search: a brief survey. KI - Künstliche Intelligenz **30**(2), 139–147 (2015). https://doi.org/10.1007/s13218-015-0415-7
16. Kübler, S., McDonald, R., Nivre, J.: Dependency parsing. Synthesis Lect. Human Lang. Technol. **1**(1), 1–127 (2009)
17. Kusner, M., Sun, Y., Kolkin, N., Weinberger, K.: From word embeddings to document distances. In: International Conference on Machine Learning, pp. 957–966 (2015)
18. Li, M., Du, X.Y., Wang, S.: Learning ontology from relational database. In: 2005 International Conference on Machine Learning and Cybernetics. vol. 6, pp. 3410–3415. IEEE (2005)
19. Maedche, A., Staab, S.: Ontology learning for the semantic web. IEEE Intell. Syst. **16**(2), 72–79 (2001)
20. Mahmoud, N., Elbeh, H., Abdlkader, H.M.: Ontology learning based on word embeddings for text big data extraction. In: 2018 14th International Computer Engineering Conference (ICENCO), pp. 183–188. IEEE (2018)
21. Mazari, A.C., Aliane, H., Alimazighi, Z.: Automatic construction of ontology from arabic texts. In: ICWIT, pp. 193–202 (2012)
22. McCrae, J., Fellbaum, C., Cimiano, P.: Publishing and linking wordnet using lemon and rdf. In: Proceedings of the 3rd Workshop on Linked Data in Linguistics (2014)
23. Mikolov, T., Chen, K., Corrado, G., Dean, J.: Efficient estimation of word representations in vector space. arXiv preprint arXiv:1301.3781 (2013)
24. Prud'Hommeaux, E., Seaborne, A., Prud, E., Laboratories, H.p.: SPARQL Query Language for RDF. W3C Working Draftd, pp. 1–95 (2008)
25. Qian, L., Zhou, G.: Tree kernel-based protein-protein interaction extraction from biomedical literature. J. Biomed. Inform. **45**(3), 535–543 (2012)
26. Riedel, S., Mccallum, A.: Relation Extraction with Matrix Factorization. In: Proceedings of the 2013 Conference of the North American Chapter of the Association for Computational Linguistics: Human Language Technologies, pp. 74–84 (2013)
27. Roth, D., Yih, W.t.: Global Inference for Entity and Relation Identification via a Linear Programming Formulation. Introduction to Statistical Relational Learning, pp. 553–580 (2019)
28. Stieglitz, S., Dang-Xuan, L.: Social media and political communication: a social media analytics framework. Social Network Anal. Mining **3**(4), 1277–1291 (2012). https://doi.org/10.1007/s13278-012-0079-3
29. Takamatsu, S., Sato, I., Nakagawa, H.: Reducing Wrong Labels in Distant Supervision for Relation Extraction. In: ACL, pp. 721–729. Association for Computational Linguistics (2012)
30. Tanwar, M., Duggal, R., Khatri, S.K.: Unravelling unstructured data: A wealth of information in big data. In: 2015 4th International Conference on Reliability, Infocom Technologies and Optimization (ICRITO)(Trends and Future Directions), pp. 1–6. IEEE (2015)
31. Gruber, T.: A translation approach to portable ontology specifications. Knowl. Acquisition **5**(2), 199–220 (1993)

32. Xiang, Z., Gretzel, U.: Role of social media in online travel information search. Tourism Management **31**(2), 179–188 (2010)
33. Zhang, T., Ramakrishnan, R., Livny, M.: Birch: an efficient data clustering method for very large databases. In: ACM Sigmod Record. vol. 25, pp. 103–114. ACM (1996)
34. Zhou, L.: Ontology learning: state of the art and open issues. Inf. Technol. Manage. **8**(3), 241–252 (2007)

Development and Usability Assessment of a Semantically Validated Guideline-Based Patient-Oriented Gestational Diabetes Mobile App

Garazi Artola[1(✉)], Jordi Torres[1(✉)], Nekane Larburu[1,2(✉)], Roberto Álvarez[1,2(✉)], and Naiara Muro[1,2(✉)]

[1] Vicomtech Research Centre,
Mikeletegi Pasalekua 57, 20009 San Sebastian, Spain
{gartola,jtorres,nlarburu,
ralvarez,nmuro}@vicomtech.org
[2] Biodonostia Health Research Institute,
P. Doctor Begiristain S/N, 20014 San Sebastian, Spain

Abstract. Studies have shown the benefits of following Clinical Practice Guidelines (CPGs) in the daily practice of medicine. Nevertheless, the lack of digitalization of these guidelines makes their update and reliability to be a challenge. With the aim of overcoming these issues, Computer Interpretable Guidelines (CIGs) have been promoted to use in Clinical Decision Support Systems (CDSS). Moreover, the implementation of Semantic Web Technologies (SWTs) to formalize the guideline concepts is a powerful method to promote the standardization and interoperability of these systems. In this paper, the architecture of a CIG-based and semantically validated mobile CDSS is introduced. For that, the development of a patient-oriented mobile application for the management of gestational diabetes is described, and the design and results of its usability assessment are presented. This validation was carried out following the System Usability Scale (SUS) with some additional measurements, and results showed excellent usability scores.

Keywords: Computer interpretable guideline · Semantic web technologies · Ontology · Gestational diabetes · Decision support system · Patient-oriented mobile app · Usability assessment

1 Introduction

Applying Clinical Practice Guidelines (CPGs) in the daily practice of medicine is showing to be beneficial for the medical care quality [1]. They are supposed to promote the latest evidence in medicine and the most reliable and updated clinical practice. However, their implementation in daily practice is still a challenge, as the lack of digitalization of the guidelines makes it difficult to maintain them up-to-date and be interpretable by computers.

A. Fred et al. (Eds.): IC3K 2019, CCIS 1297, pp. 237–259, 2020.
https://doi.org/10.1007/978-3-030-66196-0_11

During the last years, the number of Computer Interpretable Guidelines (CIGs) has increased with the aim of overcoming these issues [2]. Moreover, promoting Clinical Decision Support Systems (CDSS) that use these CIGs have shown to be a powerful method to promote a higher guideline adherence and consequently a better medical practice [2].

In addition, in order to promote interoperability and standardization of the clinical knowledge used in these systems, Semantic Web Technologies (SWTs) can be applied, as they give the opportunity to formalize the guidelines' concepts by means of ontologies.

This work is an extension of the conference paper [3] presented in the 11th International Conference on Knowledge Engineering and Ontology Development, where an architecture that allows the formalization of CPGs into CIGs using SWTs was presented. In our previous work, a use case about the implementation of a gestational diabetes CIG in a patient-oriented mobile application was introduced. In this extension, more details about the development of the final mobile CDSS are given. Moreover, the information about the process of the app's usability assessment and its results are also included.

2   State of the Art

With the aim to support our development, this section presents the current state of the art on the developed technologies.

2.1   Semantic Web Technologies (SWTs)

The healthcare systems' interoperability is being limited by the big number of data produced by the technological breakthrough in biomedical engineering and health informatics [4]. This information is needed to be processed and interpreted by computers in a more effective way. In addition, the creation of frameworks for interoperability between systems and the integration of data from various sources is also necessary. In this context, SWTs provide the tools to manage these needs.

The Semantic Web is defined as an extension of the current Web, in which information is given well-defined meaning (using semantic descriptions of data), better enabling computers and people to work in cooperation [5]. In this context, appropriate technologies must be used to make these data descriptions easy to interpret by computers. To achieve this, data should describe information with terms that have clear meaning to machines [6]. The collections of those terms and their relations form domain vocabularies, and SWTs allow specifying them through formal, shared domain models i.e., ontologies [7].

Many researchers have made use of these technologies to cope with problems related to semantic interoperability of clinical datasets. As an example, the work presented by El-Sappagh et al. [8] introduced the Diabetes Mellitus Treatment Ontology (DMTO) as a basis for shared-semantics, domain-specific, standard, machine-readable, and interoperable knowledge relevant to type 2 diabetes mellitus (T2DM) treatment.

A variety of ontology languages can be found for representing information on the semantic web, such as RDF Schema or Web Ontology Language (OWL). In addition, different programs can be found for editing these ontologies, and one of the widely used ones is Protégé [9], which is fully compatible with the latest OWL and RDF specifications. In Protégé, concepts are represented using classes, slots, and facets [10], and it also allows the use of annotation properties for adding labels to the ontology classes and to link each concept with its definition in validated and available standard terminologies (e.g. SNOMED CT[1], LOINC[2], NCI Thesaurus[3], CIE-10-ES[4]). These permit the representation of the biomedical concepts with stable and unique codes, guaranteeing the interoperability of the implemented knowledge.

2.2 Clinical Practice Guidelines (CPGs)

CPGs are a set of criteria developed in a systematic way to help professionals and patients in the decision-making process, providing the latest evidence-based diagnostic or therapeutic options when dealing with a health problem or a specific clinical condition [11]. Over the past years, these CPGs have been widely used as part of CDSS by formalizing them as CIGs. Such CIG-based CDSS have demonstrated to be able to increase the chance of impacting clinician behavior compared to using only narrative guidelines, as they provide updated patient-specific clinical data and advice at the point of care [2].

Besides the fact that SWTs are demonstrated to be a powerful tool to cope with semantic interoperability problems in ontologies, some other researchers also studied their usage to represent computerized CPGs [12, 13].

It is true that following multiple CPGs in parallel could result in statements that may interact with each other, such as giving conflicting recommendations. Furthermore, it is difficult to find a guideline that offers all the necessary information for attempting a complete care, as each one includes different clinical aspects. Thus, the impetus to deliver customized care based on patient-specific information results in the need to be able to offer guidelines in an integrated manner.

2.3 Computer Interpretable Guidelines (CIGs)

Computer Interpretable Guidelines (CIGs) are formal representations of CPGs that can be executed to provide guideline-based decision support. One of the several well-known approaches for formally representing CIGs are the "Task-Network Models" (TNMs). These models use hierarchical networks to structure the dependencies among actions. When these actions are fulfilled in a satisfactory way, the networks provide a recommendation.

---

[1] http://www.snomed.org/snomed-ct/five-step-briefing

[2] https://loinc.org/

[3] https://ncithesaurus-stage.nci.nih.gov/ncitbrowser/

[4] https://eciemaps.mscbs.gob.es/

There exist several proposals to cope with different clinical modeling challenges [14] such as GLIF [15], PROforma [16], Asbru [17] or EON [18]. All approaches support the main guideline components, but they differ in terminology, as is resumed in Table 1. These types of CIG formalisms have been used in many projects over the past years [19–21].

Table 1. Guideline modelling formalisms.

	PROforma	GLIF	Asbru	EON
Conditions	Decision tasks	Decision steps	Conditions	Decisions
Actions	Action and Enquiry tasks	Action steps	Actions (atomic Plans)	Actions
Entry criteria	Triggers and conditions	Patient state steps	Preferences, intensions and effects	Scenarios
Guideline Modelling	Actions refer to Subplans	Actions refer to Subguidelines	Each plan body contains several Subplans until a nondecomposable plan is encountered	Actions refer to Subguidelines
Functioning	Actions are executed following schedule/temporal constraints and abort/termination conditions	Actions are executed following patient state steps	Actions are executed based on plan's preconditions, intentions or effects	Actions are executed following sequences of structured temporal steps

2.4   Clinical Decision Support Systems (CDSs)

Realizing the potential of using CIGs and ontologies, most of the approaches in this field over the last years focus on guideline development and implementation for decision support. For instance, the work described in [22] proposes an ontological reasoning method to give more flexibility to CDSS and offer the ability to deal with patients suffering from multiple pathologies by including several modeled CPGs. As expected, the system provided more recommendations than the classical approach, as rules of higher level of abstraction were triggered. Another approach was done in [23], where two personalization processes were implemented. First, contents of an ontology were adapted to a concrete patient, providing a personalized care system. Second, the personalized ontology was used as the knowledge base of a CDSS.

It is shown that CDSS aims aiding clinicians in their decision-making process by providing the needed tools to analyze clinical data with the latest evidence in the shortest time [24]. However, they can also support patients in the management of different diseases. For instance, in the approach done by Peleg et al. [25], they presented a personalized and patient-centric CDSS for the monitoring and evaluation of atrial fibrillation and gestational diabetes. In [26] the positive effect of a smartphone-based daily feedback system among women with Gestational Diabetes Mellitus (GDM) for improving patient compliance to treatment and better control of glycemic levels was demonstrated.

2.5   mHealth App Usability Validation

As we have seen, advances in mobile communication for health care (mHealth) allow the design and development of patient-centric models to improve patient's self-management capabilities. These apps are becoming more and more powerful in the last years, and their impact on the patient self-management of health problems is stronger every time [27]. That is why strategies for evaluating these applications are necessary. In this context, researches to identify apps that are effective and provide accurate information, being easy-to-use for the user, have been done recently [28, 29]. The results of these research studies have indicated that well-designed applications can empower patients, improve medication adherence, and reduce the cost of health care [30–33].

In order to assess the usability of mobile applications, a variety of questionnaires have been used for different validations [34, 35]. Although self-written questionnaires are commonly used for this kind of evaluation, the most used standardized questionnaire is the System Usability Scale (SUS) [36]. It is a 10-item questionnaire designed to measure users' perceived usability of a product or system. In addition, the Post-Study System Usability Questionnaire (PSSUQ) [37] is also widely used as an alternative to the previous questionnaire to measure users' perceived satisfaction. This one consists of 16 questions (in its 3rd version) with 7 options to choose from (with an NA additional option).

3   Development of the App for GDM Management

Gestational Diabetes Mellitus (GDM) is the most common metabolic disorder of pregnancy, defined as a glucose intolerance developed in the second or third trimester of pregnancy [38]. It confers an increased risk and complications during pregnancy for both mother and child, and women that develop it have an increased risk to develop type 2 diabetes and cardiovascular diseases after pregnancy [39]. Therefore, strategies to optimize the management of these diseases in its prevention, diagnosis, and treatment are mandatory [40].

In order to develop a semantically validated mobile CDSS for guiding women in the management of GDM, different steps were followed, which are described in the following sections.

3.1   GDM Ontology

The first step of the development of this work was to formalize all concepts and knowledge coming from the different CPGs related to GDM prevention, management and treatment. For that, an ontology was created using the Protégé editor by defining the different gestational diabetes-related clinical concepts and the relationships among them. This ontology was built using NCI Thesaurus terminology to assure a semantic interoperability of the knowledge. The big number of biomedical concepts that NCI Thesaurus contains and the fact that it is open access makes it an appropriate terminology to be used for the GDM ontology. Besides, the Unified Medical Language System (UMLS)[5] code for each of the terminologies was also specified in the ontology. UMLS integrates the most notable vocabularies (e.g. SNOMED CT, ICD-10, etc.) in its repository. The result was validated with a reasoner for ensuring a consistent ontology.

Ontology Formalization. All the conditions and rules expressed in the CIG contain variables and properties that are organized in an ontology. This ontology is composed of a total number of 166 classes, which are separated into two main groups. The first group is under the class named *DMG360Concept* that comprises all the necessary variables' names for creating the CIG. The second group, named *DMG360Value*, compiles the classes that define the possible values of the classes from the first group.

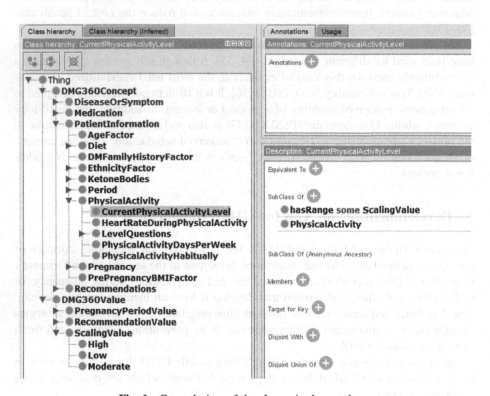

Fig. 1. General view of the classes in the ontology.

5 https://www.nlm.nih.gov/research/umls/

As can be seen in Fig. 1, the group of concepts has four subclasses, and each of them comprises other subclasses. The first concept in the list (i.e. *DiseaseOrSymptom*) is composed of two subclasses: *Disease* class, which contains two diseases definition (*DiabetesMellitus* and *PolycysticOvarianSyndrome*); and *Symptom* class, with a list of 15 different symptoms as subclasses. The second concept (i.e. *Medication*) includes three subclasses corresponding to three different medications: *Antipsychotics*, *Corticosteroids*, and *Insulin*. The third one (i.e. *PatientInformation*) is the concept with the biggest number of subclasses, containing different information about the patient (e.g. information about maternal age, diabetes family history, ethnicity, physical activity, body mass index (BMI), etc.). The last concept (i.e. *Recommendations*) is related to the recommendations that are given to the user, which can vary depending on the stage of pregnancy, as explained in Sect. 3.2. In total, seven different types of recommendations are specified.

Furthermore, two different properties are defined within the ontology to relate the different classes and their values: a data property and an object property. Both are used to specify the range of values that can be taken by these classes; thus, they are both defined using the noun *hasRange*. These ranges can handle either common data types (i.e. integer, Boolean...) when linked by a data property, or other possible values expressed as classes in the *DMG360Value* group when linked by an object property. For example, the *CurrentPhysicalActivityLevel* class is restricted to have a value corresponding to any subclass of the *ScalingValue* class (i.e. *High*, *Low*, or *Moderate*).

In addition, the clinical concepts' names, definitions, and codes were extracted from the NCI Thesaurus repository and defined within the model using annotation properties for its semantic standardization. Five different annotation properties were defined: (i) *NCI_label*, for giving the label of the class as stated in the NCI Thesaurus, (ii) *NCI_definition*, which contains the definition of the concept by the NCI, (iii) *NCI_code*, with the unique code of the term, (iv) *UMLS_CUI*, containing the corresponding UMLS code, and (v) *NCI_version*, specifying the version of the NCI Thesaurus repository used.

For the ontology design in Protégé, OWL language was used, although the model was exported in RDF language for the integration with the CDSS using the Jena API.

Ontology Validation. To validate the defined relationships between the variables and their possible values in the ontology, a tool called Reasoner was used. The reasoners offered by Protégé (i.e. FaCT++, HermiT or Pellet) are programs that evaluate the consistency of an ontology by identifying relationships between classes. In this project, the FaCT++ reasoner was used.

After the triggering of this reasoner without obtaining any unsatisfactory relationship between the classes, the hierarchy of the designed GDM ontology was validated.

Moreover, the SPARQL Query tool in Protégé was used for the validation of the requests that could be done to the ontology in the process of its integration with the CDSS. For that, the SPARQL query language was applied, a language that can be used to express queries across diverse data sources, whether the data is stored natively as RDF or viewed as RDF via middleware. Simple queries, such as requesting data/object properties of a class, finding subclasses of a class, or showing the list of all classes in the ontology, were tested.

3.2   GDM CIG

In this approach, several CPGs for the GDM management were studied. The most known and used guidelines are the ones developed by the National Institute for Health and Care Excellence (NICE) and the World Health Organization (WHO). After analyzing them, the Queensland Clinical Guideline [41] was selected to be used as the backbone guideline, due to its way of representing rules, being the most compatible for the type of formalization used in our system, and also because it is based on data provided by the WHO.

This CPG was then formalized in a computerized way (i.e. as a CIG) containing the concepts defined in the ontology. For this formalization and regarding the needs of this work, a simplified version of Task-Network Models (TNM) was implemented based on inference rules (i.e. IF-THEN type rules). To create the rules, conditions (i.e. clinical statements to be accomplished) and their respective consequences (i.e. the recommendations to be given to the patient) were identified and extracted from the selected CPGs in the GDM domain. Once this knowledge was formalized in our extended CPG, a translation into computer interpretable language was done. For that, statements were translated into IF-THEN kind rules, where the conditional part is preceded by the IF expression and the consequent part by the THEN expression. An example of this kind of formalization is shown in Table 2, where the blood glucose level is used as a variable for detecting hypoglycemia (i.e. low blood sugar).

Table 2. Example of the conversion of glucose level rules from CPG to CIG format.

CPG rule	IF-THEN rule
The glucose level that defines hypoglycemia is variable. In people with diabetes, levels below 3.9 mmol/L (70 mg/dL) is diagnostic. In adults without diabetes, a level below 2.8 mmol/L (50 mg/dL) after not eating or following exercise may be used.	• **IF** (Adult = TRUE) AND (Diabetic = TRUE) AND (BloodGlucoseLevel < 70) **THEN** Hypoglycaemia = TRUE • **IF** (Adult = TRUE) AND (Diabetic = FALSE) AND (BloodGlucoseLevel < 50) **THEN** Hypoglycaemia = TRUE

Each of the statements describing the criteria to be followed for guiding patients in this setup were defined as Rule objects (rules with defined structure), which encompasses (i) a conditional part composed by one or more conditions linked by (ii) a binary operator (i.e. *AND*, or *OR*) and (iii) a consequent part containing the recommendation for the patient, as can be seen in Fig. 2. Each of the conditions is based on a Condition object, which stores (i) the name of the clinical variable to be evaluated (i.e. concept defined in the ontology), (ii) the mathematical operator (i.e. > , $\geq$, = , < , $\leq$) and (iii) the value or the threshold of the clinical variable to be evaluated. When the conditions of the statements are matching a patient's clinical information, a recommendation is provided to the patient.

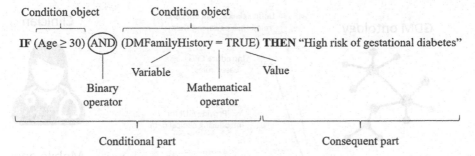

Fig. 2. Components of the Rule object used in our development [3].

Depending on the patient's clinical-stage, different types of interventions for the management of GDM were identified in the rule formalization process. For the stage before pregnancy, information about nutrition, physical activity and GDM risk factors were formalized. For the pregnancy period, guides related to nutrition, weight, physical activity, risk factors, and glucose control were covered. And finally, in the case of the post-pregnancy stage, nutrition, weight control, physical activity, breastfeeding, glucose control, and postpartum depression recommendations were included. The schema describing all this information is represented in Fig. 3.

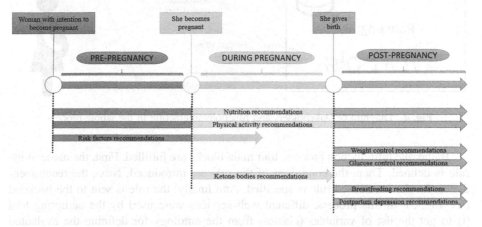

Fig. 3. The pregnancy stages and the different recommendations giving in each of them [3].

3.3 Integration of the Ontology Within the CDSS

Once the CIG was formalized with all computer interpretable rules and the GDM ontology was validated, the next step was to integrate both into the CDSS. For this objective, an authoring tool previously designed [42] was used. This tool enables an intuitive Graphical User Interface (GUI) for including clinical knowledge, such as formalized guidelines, in a computerized way into the CDSS rule base. A general representation of the whole process is shown in Fig. 4.

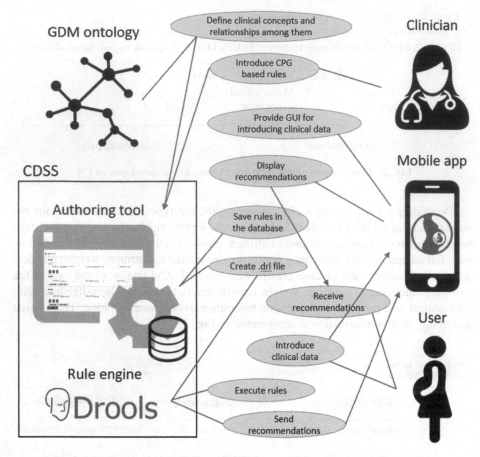

Fig. 4. Diagram of stakeholders and functions interacting in the whole process.

In the rule introduction process, four main blocks are fulfilled. First, the name of the rule is defined. Then, the conditions of the rule are introduced. Next, the recommendation for the introduced rule is specified. And finally, the rule is sent to the backend (see Fig. 5). In this process, different web services were used by the authoring tool (i) to get the list of variables (classes) from the ontology for defining the evaluated variable name within a Condition object, (ii) to get the possible values of the specific variable selected in the Condition object, (iii) to get the list of recommendations for completing the consequent part of the Rule object, and (iv) to post each generated rule to the backend of the system. After a research on different APIs for carrying out the integration of the ontology with the Java-based CDSS (i.e. Protégé-OWL API[6], OWL

Fig. 5. The four-step process for introducing rules in the authoring tool GUI.

API[7], Apache Jena[8], or RDF4J[9]), Jena API was selected because of its ease of use and compatibility advantages with our system.

In the second step, the Condition objects are constructed to introduce rule conditions using the information obtained from querying the integrated ontology (see an example in Fig. 6). The ontology classes used for defining the conditional part of the CIG are subclasses of the *DMG360Concepts* class. These variables are requested and given as options for the first parameter of a Condition object in the authoring tool GUI.

Once the variable name of the Condition object is specified, the respective condition operator is selected. Then, in the third box for specifying the value or threshold of the selected variable, the authoring tool uses the web service for requesting its possible values, and here is where the second type of ontology classes interact. In the case of variables with data properties, the backend of the authoring tool defines the type of data that needs to be used by changing the format of the box in the GUI. For the case of the variables with object properties, a list containing subclasses of the group *DMG360Value* is given (see the first condition example in Fig. 6).

Once the first condition is introduced, the binary operator can be selected from the given options (i.e. AND, or OR) and as many as required conditions can be added to the condition of the rule following the same procedure.

---

[7] https://github.com/owlcs/owlapi/wiki

[8] https://jena.apache.org/documentation/ontology/

[9] http://rdf4j.org/

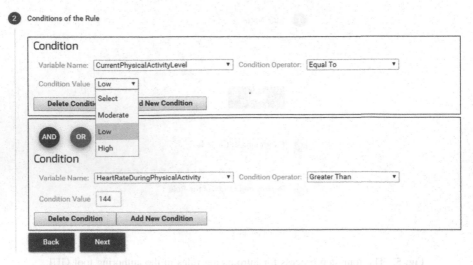

Fig. 6. Examples of the definition of rule conditional statements in the AT.

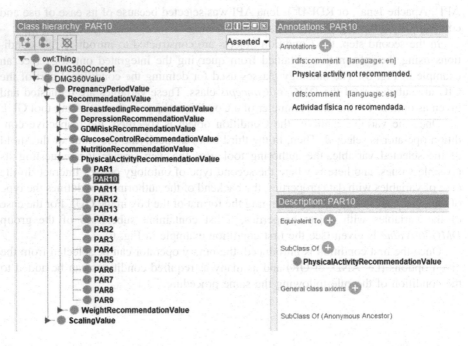

Fig. 7. The different recommendation types and an example of their content in annotation properties.

In the third step of the introduction of the rule, the recommendations are defined by permitting the user to select the recommendation from a drop-down list. This list is the result of the request made by the authoring tool for the subclasses of the class *Recommendation Value* from the *DMG360Value* group in the ontology. When a recommendation is selected by the user using its name or abbreviation, the text corresponding to that recommendation is displayed above the selection box. Each of the texts for the respective recommendation class is specified in the ontology using annotation properties (see example in Fig. 7). The authoring tool uses a web service for obtaining information from those annotations.

The last step of the introduction of rules sends the rules to the backend of the system. This backend is composed of different modules based on Drools[10], (i) a rule engine and (ii) a rule file generator in Drools Rule Language (.drl) extension. For sending the rules, another web service is used, which takes all the values introduced by the clinician in the authoring tool and sends them to the backend, where they are processed and uploaded to the clinical database, and a .drl file is generated. As the structure of the objects generated in the authoring tool is the same as in the Rule object, direct mapping can be done.

3.4   Final Patient-Centered Mobile CDSS

Once the integration of the semantically validated CIG was implemented as a .drl file within the CDSS, a patient-oriented mobile application was developed to interact with it. The user profiles defined for this application are (i) women that want to be pregnant and are monitoring their health status for it, (ii) women already pregnant, or (iii) women that have just given birth, and they all want to receive recommendations for managing gestational diabetes. In the next lines, some examples of the different screens of the designed app and their functionalities are described.

First, a logging page and system was developed for the user to register or sign in (see screen image in Fig. 8). This system will save the basic personal data (i.e. sex, ethnicity…) of the user, which is supposed to be static during the use of the application, to avoid introducing it each time the user logs in.

---

[10] https://www.drools.org/

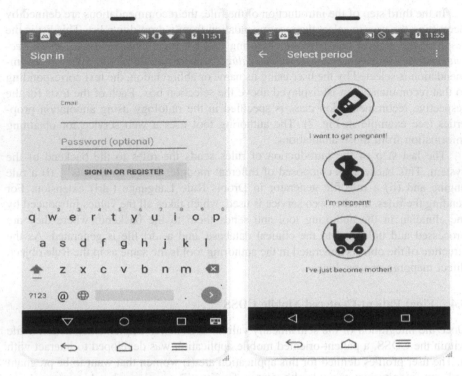

Fig. 8. Left: login page of the application. Right: main menu of the application.

After logging in, a main menu is displayed providing the possible user profiles to start the GDM management depending on their needs. Each of the pregnancy stages will provide specific recommendations, differing ones from the others as each period has a different focus on what to evaluate and how to treat the patient to reach her objective: in pre-pregnancy period, recommendations for nutrition, physical activity and GDM risk factors are given. During pregnancy, nutrition, weight, physical activity, risk factors, and glucose control related guidance is given. For post-pregnancy period, nutrition, weight control, physical activity, breastfeeding, glucose control, and post-partum depression recommendations are given. This information is managed by the app through three different menus, as can be seen in Fig. 9.

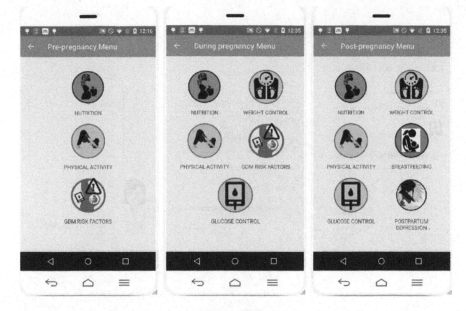

Fig. 9. The three menus for the three different stages of pregnancy in the app.

Each time the user selects an option in the different menus, the Boolean variable corresponding to that specific topic is changed. For example, in the case of the menu for the post-pregnancy stage, when the user touches the image for obtaining recommendation concerning the glucose control, the variable *GlucoseControlRecommendations* is set to true.

If required, the application will retrieve more clinical information by questionnaires (see example in Fig. 10). These questions will have possible answers related to some clinical variables defined in the GDM ontology (mostly Boolean or Object property type variables) to be selected, but sometimes it can require to the user introducing numerical variables' values (e.g. the blood glucose level). Every time the user answers a question, this clinical information will be stored as part of her profile to be evaluated by the CDSS later.

Once all the questions for completing the needed patient profile are answered, they are sent to the CDSS in the backend, getting back the corresponding recommendation (s) to be displayed in the recommendation screen of the mobile application (see Fig. 10).

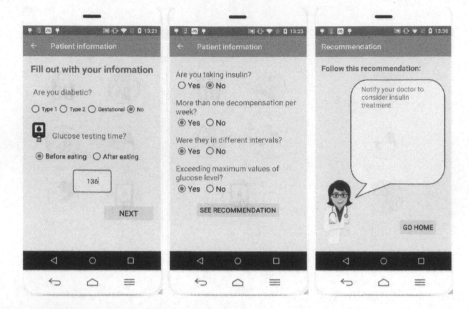

Fig. 10. Questions of the glucose control questionnaire (left and center) and the recommendation screen (right) in the mobile app [3].

4 Usability Assessment of the App

To evaluate our patient-oriented mobile application, a usability test was performed in our research center using the before mentioned System Usability Scale (SUS) questionnaire. In the next sections, the information about the design of the study, the participants, the data analysis, and the results of the test are described.

4.1 Study Design and Participants

The study was conducted following some steps with each of the participants. First, the objectives and aims of the project were explained to the woman. Then, a mobile phone from our research center that had the designed application installed was given to the participant and she was asked to complete three different tasks:

1. To try to obtain recommendations about physical activity by acting as a woman that want to get pregnant after login in the app.
2. To try to obtain advise about glucose control by acting as a woman that is pregnant.
3. To ask the app for information about breastfeeding, weight control, and postpartum depression by acting as a woman that has given birth.

Finally, participants were asked to answer the SUS questionnaire.

Participants. Our study sample consisted of 14 women from all over Spain, aging between 21–33 years. The age range of the participants was selected considering the application of this study, an approximation of the average pregnancy period. Among the 14 participants, one has recently become a mother, while the rest have never been pregnant yet.

4.2 Data Analysis

In order to obtain the most relevant information from the usability study, different data was analyzed during the test. On the one hand, participants were asked twice (first, before starting to do the tasks; and second, just after finishing them) for a score regarding the perception of difficulty for completing the tasks or using the application. For this score, a ten-point scale was used, from Extremely Easy to Extremely Difficult. On the other hand, during the execution of the three tasks, the time spent to complete each one of them was recorded.

For the final SUS questionnaire [36], each question had five response options from Strongly agree to Strongly disagree (Likert scale). Below are the ten items asked (from the original SUS):

- I think that I would like to use this app frequently.
- I found the app unnecessarily complex.
- I thought the app was easy to use.
- I think that I would need the support of a technical person to be able to use this app.
- I found the various functions in this app were well integrated.
- I thought there was too much inconsistency in this app.
- I would imagine that most people would learn to use this app very quickly.
- I found the app very cumbersome to use.
- I felt very confident using the app.
- I needed to learn a lot of things before I could get going with this app.

In addition, two extra variables were also measured using the "Plus" version of the SUS questionnaire. On the one hand, the Adjective Rating Scale was measured, which was added in order to help answer the question: "What is the absolute usability associated with any individual SUS score?". On the other one, the Promoter Rating Scale was considered, which is based on Net Promoter Score (NPS), a management tool that can be used to gauge the loyalty of a firm's customer relationships. For calculating the scores of these variables, participants were asked to answer two additional questions:

- "Overall, I would rate the user friendliness of this product as…" For this question, instead of following the SUS format, a seven-point adjective-anchored Likert scale was used to determine if a word or phrase could be associated with a small range of SUS scores.
- "How likely is it that you would recommend this app to a friend or colleague?" This one has ten possible responses, from Not at all Likely to Extremely likely. Once all the responses from all participants were obtained, data was analyzed using different values:

- **SUS Score.** One of the raw SUS scores, a single number representing a composite measure of the overall usability of the system being studied. It is calculating as follows: first, the score contributions from each item are summed. Each item's score contribution will range from 0 to 4. For items 1, 3, 5, 7, and 9 the score contribution is the scale position minus 1. For items 2, 4, 6, 8 and 10, the contribution is 5 minus the scale position. Then, the sum of the scores is multiplied by 2.5 to obtain the overall SUS score value [36].
- **Learnability and Usability.** Although SUS was originally designed to assess perceived usability as a single attribute, Lewis and Sauro [43] found that there are actually two factors in SUS. Eight of the questions reflect a usability factor and two reflect a learnability factor [44]. So, in order to compute the learnability score, just the fourth and tenth questions' answers need to be considered; while, the usability score is measured considering only the other eight questions.
- **Standard Deviation.** It shows how much variation or dispersion from the average exists. A low standard deviation indicates that the data points tend to be very close to the mean (also called expected value); a high standard deviation indicates that the data points are spread out over a large range of values.
- **Cronbach's Alpha.** It is a measure of internal consistency, that is, how closely related a set of items are as a group. A reliability coefficient of .70 or higher is considered "acceptable" in most social science research situations.
- **Adjective Average.** The absolute usability associated with any individual SUS score, calculated from the answers to the eleventh question of the questionnaire.
- **Net Promoter Score (NPS).** It measures the willingness of customers to recommend a company's products or services to others. It is calculated as the difference between the percentage of Promoters (respondents giving a 9 or 10 score) and Detractors (respondents giving a 0 to 6 score). It is normally presented as an absolute number lying between −100 and +100.

4.3 Results and Discussion

All the participants were able to complete the three of the defined tasks and all of them answered to all the asked questions.

Difficulty Scores. The first-time participants answered this question (before starting to execute the tasks), the results were not consistent for all participants. The scores scaled from 1 (Extremely easy) to 10 (Extremely Difficult) varied, as half of the participants answered with scores between 2–4, both included; and the other half with values between 5–7, both included. However, once the tasks finished, all the participants answered this question with values between 1 and 2.

Task Execution Times. The overall results regarding the times for executing the defined three tasks show that all participants were able to execute them in less than 1:30 min. Moreover, 72% of the tasks were completed in less than a minute.

SUS Questionnaire Results. From the measurements of the final SUS questionnaire, the results of the values described before were obtained, which are represented in the Fig. 11.

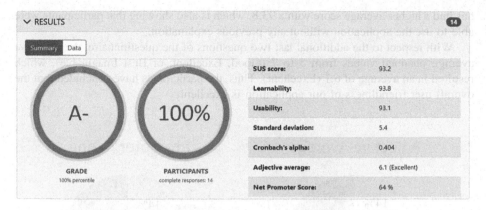

Fig. 11. Results of the SUS questionnaire.

As can be seen in Fig. 11, all the participants completed the entire questionnaire and a final general grade of A- was obtained, which indicates an excellent mark for the app's usability.

In the case of the raw SUS scores, the relationships between them have been studied in the graph below (Fig. 12). As can be seen, the SUS and usability values follow a similar pattern, while the learnability scores track higher in almost all the results. This is a clear indicator of the relationship previously explained between the SUS and the other two values. Regarding the numbers, every SUS and usability scores are showing values above 80/100, with average values of 93.2 and 93.1 respectively. These results indicate an excellent usability perception among all the participants. In addition, the learnability

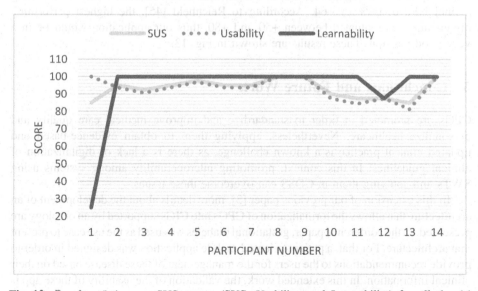

Fig. 12. Results of the raw SUS scores (SUS, Usability, and Learnability) for all the 14 participants.

has had a higher average score with a 93.8, which is also showing that participants were able to use the application without any previous explanation.

With respect to the additional last two questions of the questionnaire, the adjective average obtained values from 5 to 7 (Good, Excellent, or Best Imaginable), which resulted in an average of 6.1 (Excellent). Thus, the participants have concluded that the overall user friendliness of our application is excellent.

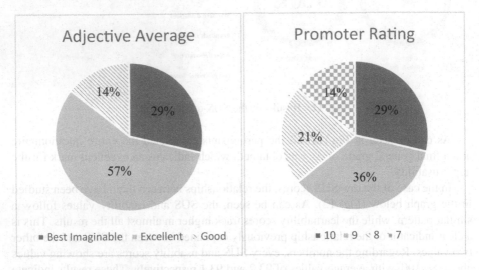

Fig. 13. Results of the additional two questions in the questionnaire.

The promoter rating scores were also high, with values between 7 and 10, obtaining a final NPS of 64% or +64. According to Reichheld [45], the highest performing organizations are situated between +50 and +80, thus our application would be in a very good position. These results are shown in Fig. 13.

5 Conclusions and Future Work

CPGs are promoted in order to standardize and improve medical care quality and personalize healthcare. Nevertheless, applying them to obtain evidence-based and updated clinical practice is a known challenge, as there is a lack of digitalization of clinical guidelines. In this context, promoting interoperability among systems using SWTs and applying them in CDSS can overcome these issues.

In this extension of our previous paper [3], more details about the development of an architecture that allows the formalization of CPGs into CIGs supported by an ontology are presented. In the conference paper, gestational diabetes was used as the use case to present that architecture. For that, a patient-oriented mobile application was designed in order to provide recommendations to the users for the management of these disease based on their clinical information. In this extended work, the validation of the usability of these app is also performed using the System Usability Scale (SUS). The results of the test were excellent, showing a SUS score of 93.2. In addition, all participants agreed that our app is very easy to use, and they would highly recommend it.

As future work, the designed mobile CDSS could be optimized by applying tools for obtaining information from patients' electronic health records. In the same manner, further implementations using wearables are being developed in order to gather users' clinical data in a more flexible way, without needing to introduce them manually. Further work is also needed to facilitate the ontology generation for clinicians. Finally, and considering the usefulness of the presented usability test, a clinical validation of the system will be considered.

Acknowledgments. This work has been developed under the research project DMG360 (2017-2018/Exp. number ZE-2017/00011, in collaboration with INIT Health, SL), which has been funded by the Department of Economic Development and Infrastructure of the Basque Government under the Hazitek program.

References

1. Grimshaw, J.M., Russell, I.T.: Effect of clinical guidelines on medical practice: a systematic review of rigorous evaluations. The Lancet **342**, 1317–1322 (1993). https://doi.org/10.1016/0140-6736(93)92244-N
2. Latoszek-Berendsen, A., Tange, H., van den Herik, H.J., Hasman, A.: From clinical practice guidelines to computer-interpretable guidelines. A literature overview. Meth. Inf. Med. **49**, 550–570 (2010). https://doi.org/10.3414/ME10-01-0056
3. Artola, G., Torres, J., Larburu, N., Álvarez, R., Muro, N.: Development of a gestational diabetes computer interpretable guideline using semantic web technologies. In: Presented at the 11th International Conference on Knowledge Engineering and Ontology Development (2019). https://doi.org/10.5220/0008068001040114
4. Kolias, V.D., Stoitsis, J., Golemati, S., Nikita, K.S.: Utilizing semantic web technologies in healthcare. In: Koutsouris, D.-D., Lazakidou, A.A. (eds.) Concepts and Trends in Healthcare Information Systems. AIS, vol. 16, pp. 9–19. Springer, Cham (2014). https://doi.org/10.1007/978-3-319-06844-2_2
5. Berners-Lee, T., Hendler, J., Lassila, O.: The Semantic Web. Sci. Am. 1–5 (2001)
6. Sabou, M.: An introduction to semantic web technologies. Concepts and Trends in Healthcare Information Systems. AIS, vol. 16, pp. 53–81. Springer, Cham (2016). https://doi.org/10.1007/978-3-319-41490-4_3
7. Gruber, T.: A Translation Approach to Portable Ontology Specifications. Academic Press, New York (1993)
8. El-Sappagh, S., Kwak, D., Ali, F., Kwak, K.-S.: DMTO: a realistic ontology for standard diabetes mellitus treatment. J. Biomed. Semant. **9**, 8 (2018). https://doi.org/10.1186/s13326-018-0176-y
9. Musen, M.A.: The protégé project: a look back and a look forward. AI Matters. **1**, 4–12 (2015). https://doi.org/10.1145/2757001.2757003
10. Noy, N.F., McGuinness, D.L.: Ontology Development: A Guide to Creating Your First Ontology, vol. 25, March 2001
11. Kredo, T., Bernhardsson, S., Machingaidze, S., Young, T., Louw, Q., Ochodo, E., Grimmer, K.: Guide to clinical practice guidelines: the current state of play. Int. J. Qual. Health Care **28**, 122–128 (2016). https://doi.org/10.1093/intqhc/mzv115

12. Hu, S., Kirsner, R.S., Falanga, V., Phillips, T., Eaglstein, W.H.: Evaluation of Apligraf persistence and basement membrane restoration in donor site wounds: a pilot study. Wound Repair Regen. Off. Publ. Wound Heal. Soc. Eur. Tissue Repair Soc. **14**, 427–433 (2006). https://doi.org/10.1111/j.1743-6109.2006.00148.x

13. Huang, Z., ten Teije, A., van Harmelen, F., Aït-Mokhtar, S.: Semantic representation of evidence-based clinical guidelines. In: Miksch, S., Riaño, D., ten Teije, A. (eds.) KR4HC 2014. LNCS (LNAI), vol. 8903, pp. 78–94. Springer, Cham (2014). https://doi.org/10.1007/978-3-319-13281-5_6

14. Peleg, M., et al.: Comparing computer-interpretable guideline models: a case-study approach. J. Am. Med. Inform. Assoc. **10**, 52–68 (2003). https://doi.org/10.1197/jamia.M1135

15. Patel, V.L., Allen, V.G., Arocha, J.F., Shortliffe, E.H.: Representing clinical guidelines in GLIF. J. Am. Med. Inform. Assoc. JAMIA. **5**, 467–483 (1998)

16. Sutton, D.R., Fox, J.: The syntax and semantics of the PROforma guideline modeling language. J. Am. Med. Inform. Assoc. **10**, 433–443 (2003). https://doi.org/10.1197/jamia.M1264

17. Seyfang, A., Miksch, S., Marcos, M.: Combining diagnosis and treatment using asbru. Int. J. Med. Inf. **68**, 49–57 (2002). https://doi.org/10.1016/S1386-5056(02)00064-3

18. Tu, S.W., Musen, M.A.: Modeling data and knowledge in the EON guideline architecture. Stud. Health Technol. Inform. **84**, 280–284 (2001)

19. Isern, D., Sánchez, D., Moreno, A.: Ontology-driven execution of clinical guidelines. Comput. Meth. Prog. Biomed. **107**, 122–139 (2012). https://doi.org/10.1016/j.cmpb.2011.06.006

20. Eccher, C., Seyfang, A., Ferro, A.: Implementation and evaluation of an Asbru-based decision support system for adjuvant treatment in breast cancer. Comput. Meth. Progr. Biomed. **117**, 308–321 (2014). https://doi.org/10.1016/j.cmpb.2014.06.021

21. Peleg, M., et al.: A computer-interpretable version of the AACE, AME, ETA medical guidelines for clinical practice for the diagnosis and management of thyroid nodules. Endocr. Pract. **20**, 352–359 (2013). https://doi.org/10.4158/EP13271.OR

22. Galopin, A., Bouaud, J., Pereira, S., Seroussi, B.: An ontology-based clinical decision support system for the management of patients with multiple chronic disorders. Stud. Health Technol. Inform. **216**, 275–279 (2015)

23. Riaño, D., et al.: An ontology-based personalization of health-care knowledge to support clinical decisions for chronically ill patients. J. Biomed. Inform. **45**, 429–446 (2012). https://doi.org/10.1016/j.jbi.2011.12.008

24. Garg, A.X., et al.: Effects of computerized clinical decision support systems on practitioner performance and patient outcomes: a systematic review. JAMA **293**, 1223–1238 (2005). https://doi.org/10.1001/jama.293.10.1223

25. Peleg, M., et al.: MobiGuide: a personalized and patient-centric decision-support system and its evaluation in the atrial fibrillation and gestational diabetes domains. User Model. User-Adapted Interact. **27**(2), 159–213 (2017). https://doi.org/10.1007/s11257-017-9190-5

26. Miremberg, H., et al.: The impact of a daily smartphone-based feedback system among women with gestational diabetes on compliance, glycemic control, satisfaction, and pregnancy outcome: a randomized controlled trial. Am. J. Obstet. Gynecol. **218**(453), e1–453.e7 (2018). https://doi.org/10.1016/j.ajog.2018.01.044

27. Rehalia, A., Prasad, S.: Global harnessing of advanced mHealth for community mobilization. mHealth **2** (2016). https://doi.org/10.21037/mhealth.2016.03.02

28. McKay, F.H., Cheng, C., Wright, A., Shill, J., Stephens, H., Uccellini, M.: Evaluating mobile phone applications for health behaviour change: A systematic review. J. Telemed. Telecare. **24**, 22–30 (2018). https://doi.org/10.1177/1357633X16673538

29. Boudreaux, E.D., Waring, M.E., Hayes, R.B., Sadasivam, R.S., Mullen, S., Pagoto, S.: Evaluating and selecting mobile health apps: strategies for healthcare providers and healthcare organizations. Transl. Behav. Med. **4**(4), 363–371 (2014). https://doi.org/10.1007/s13142-014-0293-9

30. Parmanto, B., Pramana, G., Yu, D.X., Fairman, A.D., Dicianno, B.E., McCue, M.P.: iMHere: a novel mHealth system for supporting self-care in management of complex and chronic conditions. JMIR MHealth UHealth. **1** (2013). https://doi.org/10.2196/mhealth.2391

31. Seto, E., Leonard, K.J., Cafazzo, J.A., Barnsley, J., Masino, C., Ross, H.J.: Mobile phone-based telemonitoring for heart failure management: a randomized controlled trial. J. Med. Internet Res. **14** (2012). https://doi.org/10.2196/jmir.1909

32. Seto, E., Leonard, K.J., Cafazzo, J.A., Barnsley, J., Masino, C., Ross, H.J.: Perceptions and experiences of heart failure patients and clinicians on the use of mobile phone-based telemonitoring. J. Med. Internet Res. **14** (2012). https://doi.org/10.2196/jmir.1912

33. Fairman, A.D., Dicianno, B.E., Datt, N., Garver, A., Parmanto, B., McCue, M.: Outcomes of clinicians, caregivers, family members and adults with spina bifida regarding receptivity to use of the iMHere mHealth solution to promote wellness. Int. J. Telerehabilitation. **5**, 3–16 (2013). https://doi.org/10.5195/ijt.2013.6116

34. Boceta, J., Samper, D., de la Torre, A., Sánchez-de la Rosa, R., González, G.: Usability, acceptability, and usefulness of an mHealth app for diagnosing and monitoring patients with breakthrough cancer pain. JMIR Cancer **5** (2019). https://doi.org/10.2196/10187

35. Zhou, L., Bao, J., Setiawan, I.M.A., Saptono, A., Parmanto, B.: The mHealth app usability questionnaire (MAUQ): development and validation study. JMIR MHealth UHealth **7** (2019). https://doi.org/10.2196/11500

36. Brooke, J.: SUS: A "Quick and Dirty" Usability Scale. https://www.taylorfrancis.com/. Accessed 22 Jan 2020. https://doi.org/10.1201/9781498710411-35

37. PSSUQ (Post-Study System Usability Questionnaire). https://uiuxtrend.com/pssuq-post-study-system-usability-questionnaire/. Accessed 22 Jan 2020

38. American Diabetes Association: Classification and Diagnosis of Diabetes|Diabetes Care. https://doi.org/10.2337/dc16-S005

39. Bellamy, L., Casas, J.-P., Hingorani, A.D., Williams, D.: Type 2 diabetes mellitus after gestational diabetes: a systematic review and meta-analysis. The Lancet **373**, 1773–1779 (2009). https://doi.org/10.1016/S0140-6736(09)60731-5

40. Chiefari, E., Arcidiacono, B., Foti, D., Brunetti, A.: Gestational diabetes mellitus: an updated overview. J. Endocrinol. Investigat. **40**(9), 899–909 (2017). https://doi.org/10.1007/s40618-016-0607-5

41. Queensland Gobernment: Guideline: Gestational diabetes mellitus, vol. 38, August 2015

42. Muro, N., et al.: Architecture for a multimodal and domain-independent clinical decision support system software development kit. In: 2019 41st Annual International Conference of the IEEE Engineering in Medicine and Biology Society (EMBC), pp. 1399–1404 (2019). https://doi.org/10.1109/EMBC.2019.8856459

43. Lewis, J.R., Sauro, J.: The factor structure of the system usability scale. In: Kurosu, M. (ed.) HCD 2009. LNCS, vol. 5619, pp. 94–103. Springer, Heidelberg (2009). https://doi.org/10.1007/978-3-642-02806-9_12

44. Tullis, T., Albert, B.: Chapter 6 - Self-reported metrics. In: Tullis, T., Albert, B. (eds.) Measuring the User Experience (Second Edition). pp. 121–161. Morgan Kaufmann, Boston (2013). https://doi.org/10.1016/B978-0-12-415781-1.00006-6

45. Reichheld, F.: The Ultimate Question, with Fred Reichheld (2006). https://www.marketingprofs.com/marketing/online-seminars/71

Action Representation for Intelligent Agents Using Memory Nets

Julian Eggert, Jörg Deigmöller$^{(\boxtimes)}$, Lydia Fischer, and Andreas Richter

Honda Research Institute Europe, Carl-Legien Strasse 30, 63073 Offenbach, Germany
{julian.eggert,jorg.deigmoeller,lydia.fischer,
andreas.richter}@honda-ri.de

Abstract. Memory Nets (Eggert et al.: Memory Nets: Knowledge Representation for Intelligent Agent Operations in Real World, 2019) are a knowledge representation schema targeted at autonomous Intelligent Agents (IAs) operating in real world. Memory Nets are targeted at leveraging the large body of openly available semantic information, and incrementally accumulating additional knowledge from situated interaction. Here we extend the Memory Net concepts by action representation. In the first part of this paper, we recap the basic domain independent features of Memory Nets and the relation to measurements and actuator capabilities as available by autonomous entities. In the second part we show how the action representation can be created using the concepts of Memory Nets and relate actions that are executable by an IA with tools, objects and the actor itself. Further, we show how action specific information can be extracted and inferred from the created graph. The combination of the two main parts provide an important step towards a knowledge base framework for researching how to create IAs that continuously expand their knowledge about the world.

Keywords: Memory nets · Semantic net · Common sense · Knowledge graph · Knowledge base · Property graph · Grounding · Situated interaction

1 Introduction

The term **Intelligent Agent (IA)** is commonly used in the artificial intelligence domain for autonomous entities equipped with sensors and actuators which act within an environment in a purposeful way [11,13,35]. Three aspects of this definition point to the very essence of the underlying scientific and technological problems. First, the agent pursues its own goals, limited by some degrees of freedom to decide about its own behavior. Second, since it interacts with the environment, the environment is an integral part in which the IA is embedded. And third, the agent tries to reach its goals by utilizing its own resources and the limiting environment resources (including time) in an efficient way [16].

While an IA interacts with the environment, it uses sensors to collect new information about selected parts of its environment, incorporates it with previously known information about the environment, and derives conclusions on how to achieve goals and deploy actuators. In any case, an internal **Knowledge Base (KB)** system is required that provides two main functions: continuously store and retrieve complex structured

© Springer Nature Switzerland AG 2020
A. Fred et al. (Eds.): IC3K 2019, CCIS 1297, pp. 260–282, 2020.
https://doi.org/10.1007/978-3-030-66196-0_12

and unstructured information about the environment and provide a reasoning engine that allows to infer additional knowledge. That means, the IA expands its knowledge base through exploration, learning and accessing of external knowledge sources that contain related information.

In this paper we introduce the KB system **Memory Nets** which enables IAs to leverage knowledge during their interaction with the real world. We explain how concepts are represented, starting from simple structures up to more complex structures like actions. Our belief is that future IAs need an understanding of who, what and where they are, what the important things are that they have to care about, and how they use all this understanding to pursue their goals in the best way. The important properties of such IAs supported by the KB system are:

1. **Situatedness.** They know about their current context and task.
2. **Operability.** They use this knowledge to operate in the world via actions.
3. **Incrementality.** They expand their knowledge via interaction.

Furthermore, point 1) can be split into three subitems. The most important one is **Grounding** where IAs establish - depending on their task - links to relevant real-world items (objects, subjects). The second subitem is **Common sense** which provides background knowledge about how humans usually process things and general information about world items. **Self-reference** is the third required subitem to give IAs the ability to understand their role(s), capabilities/limitations and own observations.

In the remainder of the paper, we will discuss representational structures that support a KB system with the indicated properties 1)–3). Additionally we consider an inference engine that supports the situatedness, operability and incrementality. With this in mind, we first review the landscape of work in Sect. 2 related to IA knowledge bases. In the following Sect. 3 we explain the main principles of the Memory Nets KB approach. Then we describe an action representation using Memory Nets in Sect. 4 and show reasoning capabilities about actions on an excerpt of an example graph.

2 Related Work

2.1 Knowledge Representation in General Domains

We commonly understand KB systems as a combination of knowledge representation and reasoning capabilities on the knowledge. With the advent of the internet and its huge amount of interlinked documents, it was proposed that it could be beneficial to provide a unified access to the cross-website information stores. Therefore the **Semantic Web** provides an augmentation of the internet by an additional semantic layer which describes the "meaning" of sites in a standardized, human-interpretable way, and which can be used for search and inference in a more effective way than by inspecting the document data [4]. For this purpose, special markup languages based on the XML format have been specified. The Resource Description Framework (RDF) is a specification for a metadata model, as a way to describe formally and conceptually the information that is contained in web resources, with basic capabilities to define classes, subclasses and properties of objects. The Web Ontology Language (OWL) builds on top of the RDF and provides additional levels of semantics to describe ontologies of concepts [1,14]. The underlying triple structure of RDF relates two objects x, y via a predicate P, which can be interpreted as a logical formula $P(x, y)$. On the other hand, it could be seen as a directed graph with x being the subject and y being the object of a statement, which is a **Semantic Net** [7,28] like e.g. the WordNet [20].

Later on, the Linked Data [36] development focused on interfacing as many RDF databases as possible and using them as a huge accessible knowledge source. This organization of knowledge changed the thinking from carefully built databases to **Knowledge Graphs** that collect any kind of machine-readable structured data. In principle, a Knowledge Graph can be seen as any graph-based representation of knowledge [23]. In 2012, Google introduced its "Google Knowledge Graph" that is an accumulated information about the searches, query sessions, and clicks that searchers perform on the Web each day [29]. Other examples of Knowledge Graphs are Freebase [5] or WikiData [33] that are edited by the crowd. DBPedia [17] or Yago [31] extract their knowledge from large-scale, semi-structured web bases such as Wikipedia. The target of all previously mentioned databases is to describe general facts as well as relations of everyday facts, also called **Commonsense Knowledge**, and make them globally accessible.

On the one hand, the Semantic Web facilitates the creation of domain specific databases and shareable ontologies (formal descriptions of knowledge). On the other hand, there are attempts to describe domain independent databases that support a semantic interoperability among the domain specific ones, so-called **Upper Ontologies** [8]. An Upper Ontology usually differentiates between universals and individuals - which are instances of universals located in space and time. Individuals, in turn, cannot have instances. Upper Ontologies are philosophically motivated and try to describe basic categories and relations that are valid among ontologies. Some of the most well-known Upper Ontologies are SUMO [24], Cyc, DOLCE, PROTON and Sowa's ontology [30].

The mentioned standardization and interfacing efforts, together with the growing amount of available knowledge, suggest that a KB system for IAs is increasingly getting into reach. In the ideal case, a large amount of the knowledge that an IA needs would already be available, providing it a jump start when exploiting it to tackle ambitious problems. However, even if the available knowledge is machine readable, its semantics are not yet fully understandable by IAs operating in real world. Nearly all of the available ontologies have been created with a human designer in the loop, requiring human interpretation. This applies especially to the predicates/relationships (such as e.g. "movingTo", "performedBy", but also as complex as "hasLastRegisteredMovementAt") which contain implicit semantics that are not directly accessible to an IA, and difficult to connect to daily operation in real world. In addition, even if inference frameworks are able to operate upon the ontologies, again this is used rather as analyzing tool for humans, and not for an autonomous incremental ontology extension.

2.2 Knowledge Representation for Autonomous Intelligent Agents

On the other side, for real-world operation, the robotics community is trying to make use of the previously mentioned knowledge databases and frameworks to link conceptual information to the physical world. The main focus here is to fill in missing information required by a robot for executing tasks and reaching goals. Unfortunately, most of the knowledge bases in the semantic web were created for understanding and processing text. Hence, even Upper Ontologies like Cyc or SUMO are not very useful from a robotics point of view which has to connect symbols with sensations and actions [10,32].

A promising direction in bringing both worlds together is by describing objects by their affordances [12] or linking capabilities of robots and actions to symbols [15,21]. This resulted in open robot ontologies built for executing special tasks [3,18]. Other branches of research tackle the decomposition of real-world objects into their conceptual components to share situational knowledge on a more fundamental and prototypical level [25,26,37].

Recent developments try to move together actions of IAs and language [6] at an early stage to link observations and experience in the physical world with words. The works show that there is a lack of coupling insights from linguistics like the semantic meaning of words [2,27] with the actual observation from an agents points of view. Other developments concentrate of action representation and learning. For real-world operation, the link of a KB to the world necessarily occurs through sensing and action. The representation and exploitation of action-related knowledge therefore seems to be pivotal in knowledge bases for IA's.

Nevertheless, the gained knowledge representation frameworks are rather domain-specific and constrained in their generalization towards continuous real-world operation. The dynamic extension of an IA's knowledge representation based on situation analysis and a rich existing foundation of available knowledge is still an unsolved problem. The same holds for the ability of an IA to transfer knowledge to different and new situations based on their conceptual description. To tackle these problems, we argue that we likely need KB systems with specific properties. Some of these properties are explained in the following sections, leading to an implementation of an action representation system which can be used to retrieve semantic information about action-related concepts and details like capabilities, affordances, actors and tools.

3   Memory Nets

This section outlines the main guiding principles of Memory Nets representations and the processes operating on it. There are two key principles which strongly differ from standard KB approaches. First, Memory Nets are targeted to be open for intrinsic extension by design. This leads to an open-ended creation of new concepts and problem solving capabilities, and as such to a larger flexibility to react dynamically and adapt to changing situations. Second, as a consequence of the intrinsic extension, the KB can be operated without the knowledge of an external interpreter or designer that needs to make sense of the data.

3.1   General Design Principles

- The elementary representational substrate for Memory Nets are **labeled property graphs**, i.e., graphs with defined link types and with nodes and links which can have key-value attributes. The reason is the expressive power of graphs (e.g., an RDF structure can be easily embedded into a graph), its natural handling in terms of visually discernible structures, and the point that much of the interesting information in KBs lies in the structure of the connectivity.

- Concepts are described in the graph by prototypical **patterns**. A pattern is a reoccurring structure (in terms of graph similarity measures, i.e. arrangement of nodes and links) with an identifiable inner part (nodes and links) and further links which connect to other patterns and which embed the concept within a web of related concepts.
- Compositionality and inheritance are used for **redundancy reduction and minimum description length** principles. The idea is to identify common structures which can be reused as common components in different concepts, and to represent repeated occurrences of structures in a compact way.
- The graph representation should serve as a basis for **different inference paradigms** on the same data or on subsets of the data, e.g. first order logic calculus, graph similarity finding, pattern matching, activity spread algorithms, and probabilistic reasoning.
- Graph elements (especially links) have **no hidden identifier semantics**. Identifier do not provide any item-specific semantic meaning, so that concepts of the KB have meaning without the need of a human-interpretable identifier, and can be used without the knowledge of the data designer. The purpose of different types of links is only to provide operational semantics, i.e., setting constraints on graph structures and specifying how we can operate on them.
- Instead of using natural language identifier to connect from outside (real world) to concepts within the graph, we use **measurement patterns**, which by inference (e.g. pattern matching) have to be matched to the most likely concepts.
- Natural language labels ("utterances") are stored in the same way as all other measurable properties, contributing if desired to pattern matching and pattern finding processes.

3.2 Requirements for Real-World Operation

- The KB is based on **open world** assumptions, i.e., everything we do not know is undefined [19], which is necessary for an open-ended expandability during operation. In addition, the KB should be able to incorporate information from external sources, like semantic web databases and services, which also rely on the open world assumption.
- Within the KB, **new concepts can be created by the system itself** during operation, either by inference or by incorporation of new measurement patterns. The KB should be capable of building new concepts based on existing ones (straightforward examples are hierarchical or chaining compositionality); as well as building specialized or modified concepts from more general ones. This is consistent with the assumption of no item-specific semantic information of graph element identifiers.
- The properties of concepts stored in the KB establish a link to the real world. They should be **measurable**, or derived from measurable properties, and information should be contained in the KB on how the properties are measured (e.g. about sensory devices). As a consequence, there would be no completely isolated parts of the graph with no relation to the real world.

- The KB should be capable of operating in synchronization with a highly dynamic real-world. This implies the support of **grounding** processes that allow the creation of short-lived instances of real-world item representations, their life-time management, keeping them in focus and updating them over time, as well as the generation of short-lived prediction, hypothesis generation and testing. It also implies that time plays a special role both in representational as well as in processing aspects.
- The KB should be able to empower the system to align its knowledge with knowledge from humans during an interaction via the usage of natural language. Therefore not only physical grounding but also language grounding (semantic and communicative grounding) is needed.

3.3   Main Principles of Memory Nets

This section contains a description of the main operational principles of Memory Nets. They are based on the principles of no hidden identifier semantics, measurable properties, compositionality and compact representation. We propose a minimal set of link types which provide operational and inference semantics and on which more complex structures are build upon. Then we explain the notion of concept patterns, specialization and inheritance, transformation chains, and sets.

Link Types. In knowledge graphs, nodes and relationships in form of (source)$\xrightarrow{\text{linktype}}$(target) are often read as semantic subject – predicate – object triples where the link types play a special role, as e. g. in ("robot")$\xrightarrow{\text{"knows"}}$("person x") with the link type "knows" connecting "robot" with "person x". This is also the basis for triplestore databases and the atomic data entity for the RDF data model. The link to the external world is given by the definition of the predicates and the interpretation of their meaning by a human designer. This turns into complex design decisions, as we can see in expressions like "The robot can grasp the plate", where "can – grasp" now works as a predicate between "robot" and "plate".

In Memory Nets, link types do not contain hidden semantics. Therefore, we use a small set of link types which provide operational semantics and which apply to all KB structures regardless of their content. Differently to e.g. RDF triple predicates, Memory Net link types do not encode directly a possible relationship between a subject (the source node) and an object (the target node), but they encode what can be done with the source and target nodes within the graph.

Table 1 shows the basic directed link types of Memory Net and their operational meaning. They provide the framework for the elementary structures that can be built in the Memory Net KB. More complex content semantics are created by exploiting the basic link types. E.g., instead of introducing an "isMadeOf" link ("Robot")$\xrightarrow{\text{isMadeOf}}$("Material"), we would consider a separate concept "Material" which specializes to the concrete material "CMaterial" the object is composed of, and a corresponding relationship ("Robot")$\xrightarrow{\text{hasProp}}$("CMaterial"). In parallel, one could think of separately representing the process of making the robot out of a certain material by using links that indicate transformation. This composition of semantic content that is often hidden in complex, human interpretable predicates forces a representation that is closer to

Table 1. [9] A Memory Net KB is based on a labeled property graph structure with purely operational semantics. Therefore the meaning of concepts is given by the connectivity pattern, and the link types have consequences for the interpretation of the connectivity pattern and for inference processes. The labels of the link types do not convey any semantics related to the concepts stored in the database. E.g. there are no link types with hidden semantics like "knows" or "hasColor", which would require an external interpretation.

Operational link semantics	Forward link type	Abbr. type	Link properties	Source/target roles
Specialization	specializesTo	specTo	Transitive	Parent/child
Transformation	transformsTo	transTo	Transitive	Starting point/result
Properties	hasProperty	hasProp		Property holder/property
Compositationality	hasPart	hasPart	Transitive	Whole/part
Set elements	hasElement	hasEl		Set/element
Binary operator	hasOperator	hasOp		First/second argument
Order/sequentiality	hasNext	hasNext	Transitive	Preceeding/successor

the actual processes and causal chains as they occur in the real world, and this is exactly the target of Memory Nets.

Four link types are transitive (Table 1), i.e. meaning that if (a)$\xrightarrow{\text{link type}}$(b) and (b)$\xrightarrow{\text{link type}}$(c) then it follows (a)$\xrightarrow{\text{link type}}$(c). Transitivity leads to a natural ordering of the involved nodes. In Memory Net, we have at least four dimensions for ordered ontologies: The specialization dimension (which can be used to build class taxonomies), the transformation dimension (for transformation and causality chaining), the compositionality dimension (for building partonomies) and the sequential ordering dimension. All of these provide different semantic views on concepts and coexist within the same KB by crossing at common nodes.

Concepts as Patterns. Concept patterns are knowledge subgraphs with a number of features, represented by characteristic nodes and links, that together describe an aspect of the world, i.e., a concept, relevant for the IA. Single nodes contain describable, derivable resp. measurable components and properties of the concept. Patterns are represented by subgraphs which start from a central node to which all other nodes are directly or indirectly attached. This is the so-called hub node which is often taken as a proxy for the whole concept. The semantic meaning of a concept is given by its own nodes and links and by its contextual embedding within the graph (how is it related with other concepts) and not by a text identifier of its hub node (however in explanatory images of this paper text identifier are included for illustrative purposes).

A property pattern consists of a hub node with "property nodes" attached via "hasProperty" links. Figure 1 displays an example of such a pattern for the concept of a "Robot". A property node has a special value attribute which contributes to a measurable quantity and provides the link to the real world. Property nodes are final, in the sense that they themselves cannot have further properties (e.g., it is not meaningful to speak of a subproperty of "black", however later we will explain the idea of property specialization).

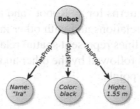

Fig. 1. Property patterns: The simplest Memory Net concept pattern are represented by a hub node (e.g. "Robot") and attached properties ("Name", "Color", "Hight") with values. The node identifier names (e.g. "Robot") are indicated here for illustrative purposes only, since the semantics of the Memory Net are purely given by the structure of the KB graph that contains the concept. Representing properties as separate nodes rather than attributes of a single node enables a better embedding in the graph, e.g. by specializing properties or putting them in relation with each other via links.

From an IA point of view, every pattern that is inserted into the graph has to have properties that make it identifiable or distinguishable from other patterns. As a result, every inserted pattern is stateful, defined by its attached properties. This is an important feature of Memory Nets and will be taken up again in Sect. 4.

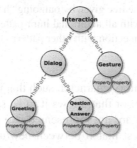

Fig. 2. An example of a non-physical composition of a pattern by subpatterns with "hasPart" links. Subpatterns help in the repeated usage of common modules by different patterns and enable a compact encoding.

Concept patterns are compositional, i.e. they can be composed to form larger patterns. Inversely, a concept pattern can have subpatterns, and subpatterns of subpatterns. The subpatterns' hub nodes are attached to the higher level concept hub node by reverse "hasPart" links, leading to a part-of hierarchy (partonomy). The exact link designation as "hasPart" is somewhat arbitrary and in natural language it suggests mainly physical composition, here however it is used for arbitrary reusable subpatterns that contribute to the identity description of the original pattern. An example of a non-physical partonomy can be seen in Fig. 2.

In detail, a pattern is a tree-formed subgraph that starts from a hub node and which has links of type "hasProperty", "hasPart" and "hasElement". The "hasPart" links form branches. Further, links between pattern nodes can be used to express additional internal (intra-pattern) relations, and inter-pattern relations embed the concept in the KB.

Figure 3 shows two concept patterns for a "Robot" and a "Navigation path" with parts and properties as intra-pattern relations and with other intra- and inter-pattern relations (······▶). In this case, the dotted lines represent spatial relations and ordering, expressing that in the path one waypoint is followed by the other and that the spatial position of the robot is close to one of the waypoints.

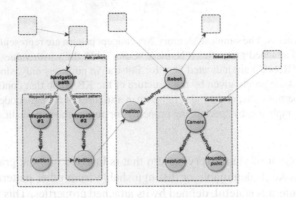

Fig. 3. Patterns with parts and exemplary inter- and intra-pattern relationships. In larger networks, patterns form a dense web of interconnected concepts. The meaning of each concept is given by its internal structure (all nodes of the tree given by outgoing "hasProperty", "hasPart" and "hasElement" links from the hub node with all additional intra-pattern relationships) and its semantic context, which results from the connection with other patterns (indicated by yet unspecified, dotted line relationships). From [9].

A concept pattern has definitory character, such that it should contain the important features that make up a concept or that allows it to be separated from other concepts. All other possible features that are not represented, are assumed to be unknown. One important task is to find the best match between new/unknown and existing concept patterns, e.g. when analyzing sensory measurements.

Specialization and Inheritance. Memory Nets can represent similar concepts in a compact way by specialization. This denotes the operation that starts from a general pattern and then it derives a more specialized pattern from it by addition of further features. Concretely, it is allowed to specialize a concept by incorporation of additional nodes attached by links of "hasProperty", "hasPart" and "hasElement" type compatible with the pattern tree structure described in the previous subsection. This results in a more precise definitory scope of the derived concept. Further, the concept will be applicable in more specific cases only, or, the other way round, if a specialized concept applies to a new pattern, then also does the original concept where it was derived from.

Pattern specialization is indicated by a "specializesTo" link from the general pattern hub node to the specialized pattern hub node. For a compact representation, when specializing a concept we do not repeat all the features of the original concept. Instead, we assume all the parent features (given by further pattern links) to be automatically inherited. The "specializesTo" link therefore indicates that the target node should be read as a proxy, as if it was the equivalent to the source node. This applies to all links from the source node with the exception of the outgoing specialization link to the target node and incoming pattern tree links of the known types "hasProperty", "hasPart" and "hasElement".

In this way, representations with short description lengths can be gained and synergies can be exploited when matching unknown patterns to available concepts. Figure 4 shows a general concept pattern and its specialization. Red nodes and links indicate the inherited features of the specialized pattern.

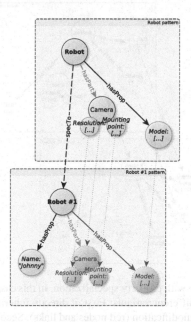

Fig. 4. [9] Pattern extension by specialization and inheritance. Patterns that are extensions of other existing patterns (in the sense that they have additional properties, parts or elements resp. additional intrapattern relations) are represented via "specializesTo" links. Here, we have a general pattern "Robot" that describes a specific robot model, and a concrete robot "Robot #1". By "specializesTo" links, the Memory Net infers that the "Robot #1" concept is a specialization of the concept of "Robot", inheriting all of its pattern features, indicated by the red nodes (these are virtual replicas that do not exist in the network, however during operation the KB treats them as if they would exist). In addition, more specific details can be added to the specialized pattern (e.g. the name property "Johnny"). (Color figure online)

The same principles apply to partial subpattern and property inheritance. Partial subpattern inheritance occurs when the inheritance of features of the specialized pattern applies to only some branches of the original concept pattern. Property inheritance occurs when the property value specializes, i.e., when the property value of the specialized pattern is a subset of the admissible value(s) of the original pattern. A special case is given when the value of the original pattern is undetermined, which we denote by "{}". In this case any value of the specialized property is a valid specialization. Property inheritance lets you create concepts describing features that in principle can/should be measured and which might have a certain value range, and the specialized property then having a concrete property value. If so we speak of specialized pattern nodes, as opposed to inherited ones. Figure 5 shows such a pattern specialization with the different specialization cases. Red nodes and links indicate direct inheritance from the general pattern which are not explicitly represented in the KB but are indicated here for explanation. In addition, there are specialized parts and properties where concrete values of the specialized pattern have been filled, e.g. by sensory measurements.

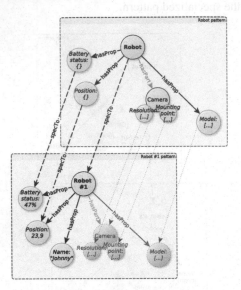

Fig. 5. [9] Pattern inheritance with property specialization. In this case, pattern "Robot #1" is specialized from "Robot" in 3 different variants: First, it directly inherits some of "Robot" features which remain valid without modification (red nodes and links). Second, it specializes its concept further by adding new features, in the case the name property with value "Johnny". And third, it provides concrete values to the measurable properties "Battery status" and "Position", which from the graph are known to be part of the parent concept "Robot". The "specializesTo" links between the parent and child properties indicate here that the values of the properties have been specialized. (Color figure online)

Specialization in Memory Net can be used to construct an ontology in terms of the classical notion of parent and child classes and instances. However, we do not distinguish classes vs. instances, since for purely measurement-based concepts it is impossible to establish a class vs. instance boundary[1]. Just imagine the concepts of "Robot", "My robot" and "My robot yesterday when I talked to him". Whether "My robot" is an instance (of the class "Robot") or "My robot yesterday ..." is an instance (of a class "My robot") depends on the interpretation of the meaning of the concept "My robot". In standard definitions classes refer to abstract, long-lived stable constructs

---

[1] The deeper underlying reason is the contradiction that arises in classical class/instance ontologies when class concepts are interpreted as categorical prototypes and when they are interpreted as the set of instances that together describe a class.

vs. instances, which are supposed to be concrete exemplars and rather short-lived. Since Memory Net concepts ultimately all potentially originate in real-world measurements, this problem is circumvented and the specialization ontologies do not require a class vs. instance decision.

A specialized concept can be derived (inherited) from more than one concept. This allows for parallel ontologies addressing different specialization aspects. For example, consider the two disjunct concepts "robot" and "service agent". A service robot might combine properties of these both concepts. The corresponding multiple inheritance is illustrated in Fig. 6 where it is shown that the pattern which represents the more specialized concept of a service robot inherits from both concepts "robot" and "service agent", directly inheriting or specializing their respective properties.

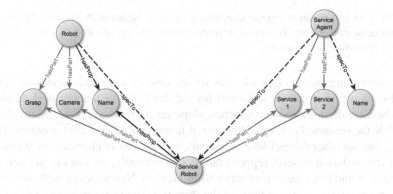

Fig. 6. Multiple inheritance for pattern specialization. Specialized concepts can inherit from several other concepts, which allows for the combination of properties from different specialization ontologies. In this example, a "service robot" concept inherits properties from both the "robot" and the "service agent" concepts, which is represented explicitly using the "specializesTo" links and the introduced inheritance capabilities of Memory Nets. Since the specialization links can always be used to trace properties back to their parents, it can e.g. be inferred that a given service robot has a camera due to its robot function and provides a service because it is also acting as a service agent.

Sets of Patterns. A special structure in Memory Nets is a **Set** structure. A Set is a group of objects with similar characteristics or that belong together. Linguistically, when we speak of certain categories or classes of objects, we implicitly and ambiguously do not refer to the category only, but also to the set of objects that form the category.

Additionally, there are concepts which explicitly mention the set characteristics of a concept. This is the case e.g. for "fleet", which is a group of ships that sail together, engage in the same activity, or are under the same ownership - i.e., they are grouped to one thing, and it does not really matter why.

To be able to represent sets, we use the "hasElement" links. Any node with patterns attached to it with outgoing "hasElement" links, has the characteristics of a set. Hence, one can query set-related information from it, like its number of elements. Figure 7 shows the example of a concept pattern for a concrete "Commercial fleet", with its owner and its single ships as elements that add to the group of ships.

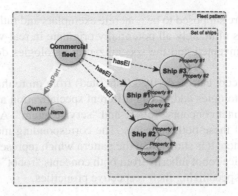

Fig. 7. [9] A set is a group of objects that belong together. Nodes with outgoing "hasElement" links acquire the role of a set. This example represents the concept of a fleet as a set of ships, with additional properties like its owner.

The interesting point is that whereas for the case of a concrete fleet with concrete ships this works, it is not yet sufficient for the definition of a concept of an abstract fleet, where we do not know the concrete ships yet. In this case there are no elements that define the set-based concept. However, it is important that a fleet contains ships or vehicles, but not other things like e.g. animals, so the *types* of elements are a characteristic for the set-based concept representation. Conveniently, we can use the introduced specialization and inheritance properties from Memory Nets together with *element prototypes* for that purpose: If we represent the ships in a compact way by specializing them

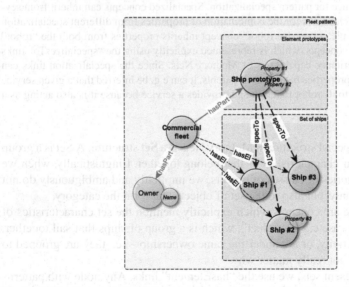

Fig. 8. [9] The fleet concept, this time with a compact representation using ship prototypes. The single ships in the set do not define what a fleet is, but the prototypes do (it is relevant that the elements of the fleet are ships and not, say, animals). In this example we have one prototype but there can be several in a set-based concept, and they can even build specialization hierarchies.

from some common prototypes (there can be several of them, without limitation), then the prototypes are definitory parts of the fleet concept representation. This is shown in Fig. 8, and we can easily see how the "Commercial fleet" concept representation remains valid even if there are no ship elements in the fleet at all.

Transformation Chains. Assume a Memory Net containing items and events registered from the current environment. Over time there are constantly new measurements collected by the system which have to be interpreted in relation to the existing KB structure. Many measurements have a particular property: They are updates of the "same" concept (e.g. describing a real-world object) already registered previously in memory. Processes and structures supporting *concept persistence* are therefore important.

For the purpose of representing concept changes, the link type "transformsTo" is used, which connects two properties or two concept patterns. It expresses that a stored concept undergoes a change to another concept, and it can be used to express concept persistence but also concept transformation. Figure 9 shows an example of the concept for the "Robot #1" measurement before and after charging its battery. The "transformsTo" links indicate that the pattern with some features (in this case the battery status property) are being transformed.

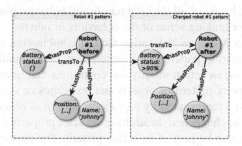

Fig. 9. [9] Transformation from one concept pattern to another using the "transformsTo" type links. In this example, concepts of the robot before and after charging are connected by "transformsTo" links which indicate that the pattern transformation involves the change in its battery status from any ({}) to >90%.

Since the transformation usually only applies to a few features of a pattern, the "transformsTo" link can be used in combination with the previously introduced "specializesTo" link to inherit most of the source pattern features to avoid representation redundancy. In addition, if certain transformations occur repeatedly or should be explicitly represented, a **transformation pattern** can be created. Figure 10 shows such a transformation pattern for the robot example. This can be repeated to gain transformation chains and concatenated transformation patterns, and is an important step towards representing actions and action sequences in an Intelligent Agents' Knowledge Base.

Action Patterns. Since intelligent agents based on an expandable Memory Net knowledge representation are envisaged to always use and update their knowledge by operating in and interacting with the world, the capability to properly represent actions is

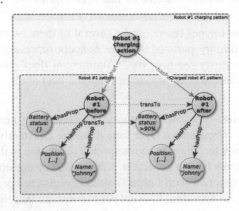

Fig. 10. [9] The two patterns from Fig. 9 linked by "transformsTo" relations combined into a prototypical transformation pattern that represents the overall transformation in a way that is accessible and reusable within the KB.

of crucial importance. Knowledge about actions allow an IA to understand processes, situational contexts and intentions of actors, as well as to infer about what can be done, by whom, on which objects, with which tools and performing which steps. Action representation is also the basis for all the own purposeful behavior planning and execution of an IA, as well as for making sense of the behaviors of others.

Action patterns in Memory Nets arise from a combination of standard property patterns and transformation patterns. In essence, they conceptualize that, similarly to transformation patterns, an action usually has conditions that have to apply at its start, represented by a property pattern of objects and properties or states before the action, and a specific outcome, represented by a property pattern of objects and properties or states after the action has happened. In addition, an actor property pattern and optionally involved tools would also be part of an action pattern. The prototypical action pattern from which specialized action patterns can be derived is shown in Fig. 11. An action pattern is composed of (attached via "hasPart" links) two property patterns representing the state of a part of the world before ("Thing Before") and after ("Thing After") the action, an involved "Actor" pattern specifying who is causing the action and eventually a "Tool" used for the action.

We can see from Fig. 11, that action patterns combine objects, actors, tools and their states in an intertwined way. Furthermore, the different components allow an attachment of dedicated sensing and acting effectors, which is necessary for grounding the respective actions in measured world states, e.g. to infer if an action could be applied or has already been executed.

Using inheritance and specialization, action ontologies can now be build. For example, a general "Locking" action would involve a human as actor, and correspondingly a "Locking Tool", and the "Thing Before" would be an unlocked object and the "Thing After" the same object, but locked. This would specialize further e.g. into a "Locking Door" action, with a key as locking tool and the thing before would be the unlocked door and afterwards, the door would be locked.

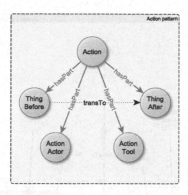

Fig. 11. An Action Pattern, composed of its basic subpatterns. An action pattern serves to represent that something like an object gets transformed from one state (property pattern "Thing Before") into something else (property pattern "Thing After") by involvement of an "Action Actor" that executes the action and eventually an "Action Tool". Action patterns specialize by specialization of any of its subpatterns, e.g. involving specific actors, tools, objects, or object state conditions, forming action hierarchies and sequences.

Furthermore, action patterns can be used in the context of other patterns, e.g. similar to transformation chains concatenating them to describe action sequences, and composing them to build action complexes involving subactions.

All subpatterns that are part of action patterns, i.e., objects, tools and actors, act as proxy nodes. This means that they contribute their specific role, however they are usually derived from other existing patterns that pick up that role by specialization. This is illustrated in Fig. 12, where a robot pattern contributes to the action "Cutting", acquiring the role as "Cutting Actor" (in addition of being a robot). In the same way, the bread pattern undergoes a change and transforms from the uncut state into the cut state in the role of "Thing Before" and "Thing After". The concept that a pattern acquires a certain role through specialization allows it to propagate its specific properties like e.g.. utterances to the corresponding action nodes. In the example of Fig. 12, the node "Uncut Thing" would then have access to its own utterances (e.g. "uncut") but also to the utterances of the robot. In the same way, the cutting tool would have access to additional states and utterances of the "Bread Knife".

Figure 12 shows a concrete action pattern, in this case cutting. It was specialized from the general action pattern (i.e., the "Cutting Action" is an "Action", and its "Cutting Actor" is an "Action Actor", etc.). Connections to external nodes provide details on who is the cutting actor, the manipulated object and the cutting tool. For example, "Cutting Tool" is specialized from "Bread Knife" from an object hierarchy and from "Action Tool" from the action hierarchy, meaning that this specific cutting tool will have all properties of a bread knife as well as of a general action tool.

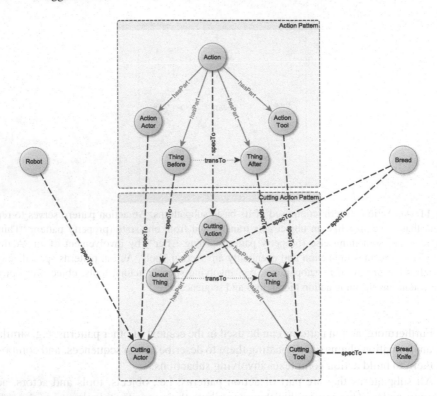

Fig. 12. A concrete action pattern embedded into the Memory Net. The "Cutting Action" is a specialization of the general action pattern, and the concepts "Robot", "Bread" and "Cutting Tool" are attached to it, functioning in the role of the "Action Actor", the object that is acted upon ("Thing Before" and "Thing After") and the "Action Tool".

4   Memory Nets for Action Representation

A major target of Memory Nets is to provide a representation from an acting IA point of view which links abstract database knowledge and natural language to measurements from the physical world. A tight coupling of both worlds through grounding and experiencing is an essential step for IAs to draw intelligent conclusion while interacting in their environment. This view is motivated by well known efforts of philosophers like Plato or Kant [34] to see human thinking as an interplay between opposing concepts like knowledge and experience. Motivated by this idea, we focus on a representation that essentially connects subjects with objects by means of actions.

In the following, we introduce an action representation that combines the principles of Memory Nets which have been explained in the previous chapters. Figure 13 shows the basic structure of the representation, divided into four main categories. The highest pattern, that is the basis for all patterns in the representation is the "Stateful Thing". It supports the idea of Memory Nets that every pattern inserted in the graph is identifiable by its structure of measurable properties or sub-patterns and not by hidden identifiers (cf. Sects. 3.1 and 3.3).

4.1 Main Taxonomic Domains of Action Representation

The main domains in our concept representation are subjects, actions, objects and state determined categories, as depicted in Fig. 13. This separation is driven by drawing a main distinction between the agents capable of performing actions (subjects) and the things that actions are applied on (objects). Within each domain, specialization hierarchies of property patterns form taxonomies of subject and object concepts. The property patterns from the subjects and objects domain are connected via action concepts from the action domain, with the actions describing the transformation of the object in form of its changing properties. As mentioned in Sect. 3.3, subjects and objects specialize to proxy nodes attached to an action pattern. This allows to contribute specific properties to the pattern. By the specialization, subjects and objects then take part in the action in terms of specific roles. A specific object can then be in the role of the object that is manipulated by means of an action as "Thing Before" and "Thing After". Optionally, an object can also be in the role of a tool if it is used for manipulating an object that participates in the same action.

The attribution of roles to everyday objects for the representation of an action resembles the idea of verb semantics as known from linguistics, e.g. discussed in [2]. In verb semantics, words acquire a semantic role in the context of an action.

The remaining concept domain shown in Fig. 13 is that of state determined categories. These are categories of things that are determined by measurable states, like

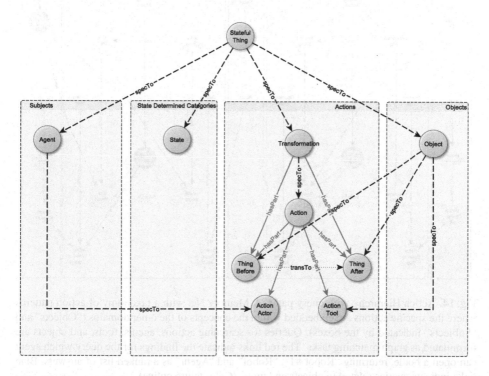

Fig. 13. Memory Nets with their main taxonomic concept domains for action representation.

e.g. the category of all red things, of all locked doors, or of all things that are eatable. These concepts have a close connection to the "Thing Before" and "Thing After" concepts from actions, since actions describe state transformations and therefore, transformations of the state determined categories of the objects involved in an action. For example, a bottle could be in a state "open" or "closed" depending on its properties that have been observed in the physical world, thus belonging to the category of open or closed things. The opening action would be specified as transforming the bottle from the category of open things to the category of closed things, involving these categories by specialization, i.e., the unmanipulated object of the opening bottle action concept would inherit from the concepts "Thing Before" (action domain), "Closed thing" (stateful thing domain), and "Bottle" (object domain), whereas the object after the action would inherit from the concepts "Thing After", "Open thing" and "Bottle". Comparing again state determined categories with linguistics, they reflect the descriptive part just like adjectives in natural language. In this sense important parts of speech like verbs, nouns and adjectives are reflected in segregated taxonomies in the concept domains of action, subjects/objects and state determined categories.

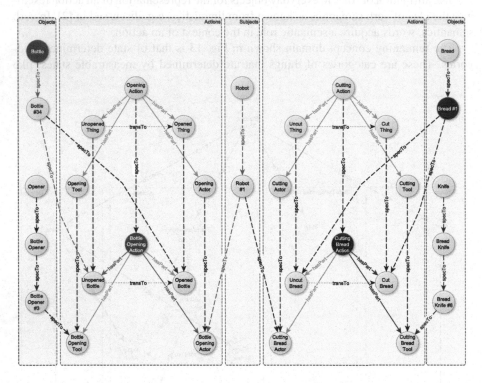

Fig. 14. Action Hierarchy with query paths. A Memory Net with a taxonomy of action patterns where the specific actions are embedded within the concepts of the other domains ("Objects" and "Subjects" indicated by the boxes). Queries for searching actions, agents, tools, and objects are formulated as graph matching tasks. The red links indicate the findings for the query which agent can open a bottle, returning "Robot #1", "Robot" and "Agent" as a ranked list of answers. Blue links indicate queries related to objects and tools. (Color figure online)

4.2   Inference Using Pattern Matching

To demonstrate the reasoning capabilities on the action representation, we use a Memory Net graph snapshot as shown in Fig. 14. The main concept domains that have been explained in the previous chapter are shown as boxes. In the center, a subject hierarchy is shown, starting from a general robot down to a robot instance "Robot #1". The robot participates as actor in two actions, one to the left for opening and one to the right for cutting. The outer boxes show hierarchies of concepts describing objects that participate in actions, like "Bread", "Knife" or "Bottle".

For the exploitation of action knowledge, we are interested in questions related to action properties and roles. For example, we might ask if a specific agent is able to perform a specific operation, which tool can be used, in combination with which object, and so on. For support of behavior planning, we may want to know which actions a certain robot can do (capabilities), or which actions can be applied to transform an object (affordances).

We implemented the node and link representation as well as the Memory Net features from Sect. 3.3 on top of a graph database (Neo4j, [22]), including pattern creation, pattern specialization and pattern query functions. Many reasoning and inference processes, especially those involving transitive link properties, resolve into explicit subgraph matching operations, i.e., specifying characteristic subgraph patterns and querying the database for all matches of these patterns. The query subgraphs can be easiest expressed in a text-type notation as follows. In query subgraphs, known nodes are accessed via round brackets and its properties (e.g. ("Agent")), query/unknown nodes via an additional variable (**a**?"Agent"), links via arrows (e.g. $\xrightarrow{hasProp}$), repeated links via arrows with $*$ (e.g. $\xrightarrow{specTo*}$). Inheritance dependency is expressed in short via "::", so that a (**n**::"Thing Before") is a node **n** that has been specialized from the general "Thing Before" concept from the abstract action pattern.

Now we can explore the relational context of a concept in many different ways. For example, if we want to find which actions involve a bottle as manipulated object, the corresponding query pattern results in ("Bottle"::"Object") $\xrightarrow{specTo*}$ (**tb**?::"Thing Before") $\xleftarrow{hasPart}$ (**a**?::"Action"). In other words, we follow the path of the object "Bottle" playing a role of a "Thing Before" in any action **a** which modifies the state of the bottle.

Expanding the example a bit further, we can also search in the graph for any subject that is involved in opening a bottle. This means that we start with the concepts "Bottle" and "Opening Action" and expand our query pattern from there ("Bottle") $\xrightarrow{specTo*}$ (**tb**?::"Thing Before") $\xleftarrow{hasPart}$ (**a**?::"Opening Action") $\xrightarrow{hasPart}$ (**n**?::"Action Actor") $\xleftarrow{specTo*}$ (**s**?::"Agent"). The returned nodes in the **s** variable are then all possible subjects that are specializations of the general "Agent" which semantically connect to the opening bottle action, e.g. the specialization chain "Agent", "Robot" and "Robot #1". These have a hierarchical order, and introducing path lengths for a ranking, we find "Robot #1" would be the closest and most specific answer, followed by "Robot" and finally "Agent".

Instead of asking for agents involved in actions, we could also query for tools like for example shown by the blue path in Fig. 14. Assuming we have again identified the blue highlighted nodes "Bread #1" and "Cutting Bread Action", the answers for an appropriate tool can be found by ("Bread #1") $\xrightarrow{\text{specTo*}}$ (**tb?**::"Thing Before") $\xleftarrow{\text{hasPart}}$ (**a?**::"Cutting Action") $\xrightarrow{\text{hasPart}}$ (**at?**::"Action Tool") $\xleftarrow{\text{specTo*}}$ (**t?**::"Object"). The query is basically of the same structure as in the previous example, with the only difference that the final node (tool) follows a different path which starts specializing from "Object" and connects to the specific action tool node **at**. With ranking the answers, we then get as result "Bread Knife #8", "Bread Knife" and "Knife".

With the Memory Net structure and the graph-based implementation, the complexity of queries and answers can now be scaled in a straightforward way to different specialization and detail levels of abstract and concrete actions, while retaining a consistent structure.

5   Conclusion

We proposed Memory Nets, a new knowledge representation for IAs that encodes semantics in a graph structure without making use of natural language identifiers that require human interpretation. Memory Nets are defined by a minimal set of link types embedded in patterns with their supporting properties. Such granularity leads to operational semantics and a strong connectedness between nodes - which is the great strength of graphs.

A key component of Memory Nets is the central representation of an IA and its connection through different levels, starting from its own concept, through its capabilities and measurements up to observed patterns and properties. This representation allows for a contextual embedding of a situation an IA is currently in and its operability. An additional important feature is incrementality, that is enabled by possible abstraction from observations or linking of external knowledge sources.

Memory Nets also allow to build action representations where tools, objects and actors play a specific role in the context of an action. We showed how to navigate in a sample graph and retrieve different contextual action related information by pattern matching approaches. We think that the combination of encoding semantics in roles with an operationally driven representation and the ability to enrich the database with measurements and observations is an important step towards an IA that is able to explore its environment and to draw conclusions about the observed.

Future directions of our research are on one hand the enrichment of the knowledge base by accessing common sense information from external databases and using a robot to collect measurements from its environment, as we already outlined in [9]. On the other hand, we focus on using the inference capabilities described in Sect. 4.2 in combination with natural language understanding to retrieve and insert information through speech.

References

1. Antoniou, G., Groth, P., Harmelen, F.V.V., Hoekstra, R.: A Semantic Web Primer. The MIT Press, Cambridge (2012)
2. Baker, C.F., Fillmore, C.J., Lowe, J.B.: The Berkeley FrameNet project. In: In Proceedings of the Coling-ACL (1998)
3. Beetz, M., Beßler, D., Haidu, A., Pomarlan, M., Bozcuoglu, A.K., Bartels, G.: Knowrob 2.0 - a 2nd generation knowledge processing framework for cognition-enabled robotic agents. In: International Conference on Robotics and Automation (ICRA), Brisbane, Australia (2018)
4. Berners-Lee, T., Hendler, J., Lassila, O.: The semantic web. A new form of web content that is meaningful to computers will unleash a revolution of new possibilities. Sci. Am. **284**(5), 34–43 (2001)
5. Bollacker, K., Evans, C., Paritosh, P., Sturge, T., Taylor, J.: Freebase: a collaboratively created graph database for structuring human knowledge. In: Proceedings of the 2008 ACM SIGMOD International Conference on Management of Data, pp. 1247–1250. ACM (2008)
6. Chai, J.Y., Gao, Q., She, L., Yang, S., Saba-Sadiya, S., Xu, G.: Language to action: towards interactive task learning with physical agents. In: AAMAS, p. 6 (2018)
7. Collins, A.M., Quillian, M.R.: Retrieval time from semantic memory. J. Verbal Learn. Verbal Behav. **8**(2), 240–247 (1969)
8. Degen, W., Herre, H.: What is an upper level ontology. In: Workshop on Ontologies. Citeseer (2001)
9. Eggert, J., Deigmöller, J., Fischer, L., Richter, A.: Memory nets: Knowledge representation for intelligent agent operations in real world. In: Proceedings of the 11th International Joint Conference on Knowledge Discovery, Knowledge Engineering and Knowledge Management, IC3K 2019, Volume 2: KEOD, Vienna, Austria, 17–19 September 2019, pp. 115–126 (2019). https://doi.org/10.5220/0008068101150126
10. Fischer, L., et al.: Which tool to use? Grounded reasoning in everyday environments with assistant robots. In: Proceedings of the 11th Cognitive Robotics Workshop 2018, pp. 3–10 (2018). http://ceur-ws.org/Vol-2325/paper-03.pdf
11. Franklin, S., Graesser, A.: Is It an agent, or just a program?: a taxonomy for autonomous agents. In: Müller, J.P., Wooldridge, M.J., Jennings, N.R. (eds.) ATAL 1996. LNCS, vol. 1193, pp. 21–35. Springer, Heidelberg (1997). https://doi.org/10.1007/BFb0013570
12. Horton, T.E., Chakraborty, A., Amant, R.S.: Affordances for robots: a brief survey. AVANT **2**, 70–84 (2012)
13. Kasabov, N., Kozma, R.: Introduction: hybrid intelligent adaptive systems. Int. J. Intell. Syst. **13**(6), 453–454 (1998)
14. Knublauch, H., Oberle, D., Tetlow, P., Wallace, E., Pan, J., Uschold, M.: A semantic web primer for object-oriented software developers. W3c working group note, W3C (2006)
15. Kunze, L., Roehm, T., Beetz, M.: Towards semantic robot description languages. In: 2011 IEEE International Conference on Robotics and Automation, pp. 5589–5595 (2011). https://doi.org/10.1109/ICRA.2011.5980170
16. Kurzweil, R.: The Age of Spiritual Machines: When Computers Exceed Human Intelligence. Viking, New York (1999)
17. Lehmann, J., et al.: DBpedia-a large-scale, multilingual knowledge base extracted from Wikipedia. Semant. Web **6**(2), 167–195 (2015)
18. Lemaignan, S., Ros, R., Mösenlechner, L., Alami, R., Beetz, M.: ORO, a knowledge management platform for cognitive architectures in robotics. In: 2010 IEEE/RSJ International Conference on Intelligent Robots and Systems, pp. 3548–3553. IEEE (2010)
19. Mazzocchi, S.: Closed world vs. open world: the first semantic web battle (2005). http://web.archive.org/web/20090624113015/www.betaversion.org/~stefano/linotype/news/91/. Accessed 23 April 2019

20. Miller, G.A.: WordNet: a lexical database for English. Commun. ACM **38**(11), 39–41 (1995)
21. Mühlig, M., Fischer, L., Hasler, S., Deigmöller, J.: A flexible heterogeneous multi-entity system. In: ICHMS 2020: 1st IEEE International Conference on Human-Machine Systems (2019, submitted)
22. Neo4j: Neo4j graph platform (2019). https://neo4j.com/product/. Accessed 23 April 2019
23. Paulheim, H.: Knowledge graph refinement: a survey of approaches and evaluation methods. Semant. Web **8**(3), 489–508 (2017)
24. Pease, A., Niles, I., Li, J.: The suggested upper merged ontology: a large ontology for the semantic web and its applications. In: Working notes of the AAAI-2002 Workshop on Ontologies and the Semantic Web, vol. 28, pp. 7–10 (2002)
25. Rebhan, S., Richter, A., Eggert, J.: Demand-driven visual information acquisition. In: Fritz, M., Schiele, B., Piater, J.H. (eds.) ICVS 2009. LNCS, vol. 5815, pp. 124–133. Springer, Heidelberg (2009). https://doi.org/10.1007/978-3-642-04667-4_13
26. Röhrbein, F., Eggert, J., Körner, E.: Child-friendly divorcing: incremental hierarchy learning in Bayesian networks. In: Proceedings of the International Joint Conference on Neural Networks, pp. 2711–2716 (2009)
27. Ruggeri, A., Caro, L.D.: Linguistic affordances: Making sense of word senses. In: AIC@AI*IA (2013)
28. Simmons, R.: Semantic networks: their computation and use for understanding English sentences. In: Computer Models of Thought and Language (1973)
29. Singhal, A.: Introducing the knowledge graph: things, not strings (2012). http://googleblog. blogspot.co.uk/2012/05/introducing-knowledge-graph-things-not.html. Accessed 23 April 2019
30. Sowa, J.: Knowledge Representation: Logical, Philosophical, and Computational Foundations. Brooks Cole Publishing Co., Pacific Grove (2000)
31. Suchanek, F.M., Kasneci, G., Weikum, G.: YAGO: a core of semantic knowledge. In: Proceedings of the 16th International Conference on World Wide Web, WWW 2007, pp. 697–706. ACM (2007). https://doi.org/10.1145/1242572.1242667
32. Tenorth, M., Klank, U., Pangercic, D., Beetz, M.: Web-enabled robots. IEEE Robot. Autom. Mag. **18**(2), 58–68 (2011). https://doi.org/10.1109/MRA.2011.940993
33. Vrandecic, D., Krötzsch, M.: Wikidata: a free collaborative knowledge base. Commun. ACM **57**, 78–85 (2014). http://cacm.acm.org/magazines/2014/10/178785-wikidata/fulltext
34. White, D.: Kant on Plato and the metaphysics of purpose. Hist. Philos. Q. **10**(1), 67–82 (1993)
35. Wikipedia: Intelligent agent – Wikipedia, the free encyclopedia (2019). https://en.wikipedia. org/wiki/Intelligent_agent#CITEREFKasabov1998. Accessed 23 Apr 2019
36. Wood, D., Zaidman, M., Ruth, L., Hausenblas, M.: Linked Data: Structured Data on the Web, 1st edn. Manning Publications, New York (2014)
37. Wyatt, J.L., et al.: Self-understanding and self-extension: a systems and representational approach. IEEE Trans. Auton. Ment. Dev. **2**(4), 282–303 (2010)

Ontological Integration of Semantics and Domain Knowledge in Hardware and Software Co-simulation of the Smart Grid

Jan Sören Schwarz[1] , Rami Elshinawy[2], Rebeca P. Ramírez Acosta[1] ,
and Sebastian Lehnhoff[1(✉)]

[1] Department of Computing Science, University of Oldenburg, Oldenburg, Germany
{jan.soeren.schwarz,rebeca.ramirez,
sebastian.lehnhoff}@uni-oldenburg.de
[2] OFFIS – Institute for Information Technology, Oldenburg, Germany
rami.elshinawy@offis.de

Abstract. The transition of the power system to more decentralized power plants and intelligent devices in a smart grid leads to a significant rise in complexity. For holistic and integrated designing and testing of new technologies before their implementation in the field co-simulation is an important approach. It allows to couple diverse software simulation components from different domains for prototyping, but also to couple hardware devices in other testing approaches such as Hardware-in-the-Loop (HIL) and remote laboratory coupling, which enable more complete, realistic, and reproducible validation testing. In the planning and evaluation of co-simulation scenarios, experts from different domains have to collaborate. To assist the stakeholder in this process, we propose to integrate on the one hand semantics of simulation components, their exchanged data and on the other hand domain knowledge in the planning, execution, and evaluation of interdisciplinary co-simulation based on ontologies. This approach aims to allow the high-level planning of simulation and the seamless integration of its information to simulation scenario specification, execution and evaluation. Thus, our approach intents to improve the usability of large-scale interdisciplinary hardware and software co-simulation scenarios.

Keywords: Co-simulation · Energy scenarios · Hardware in the Loop (HIL) · Information model · Ontology · Simulation · Simulation planning · Smart grid

1 Introduction

The intended transition from fossil to renewable energies in the power system poses many new challenges. New technologies have to be developed to deal with fluctuating energy resources and available flexibilities. Additionally, the dependencies between different domains become more and more important and the power system can be considered neither detached from the ICT system nor ecological, economic, or sociotechnical systems. To handle this complexity in the development of new technologies simulation is an important approach. Especially, co-simulation is used to couple diverse simulation

© Springer Nature Switzerland AG 2020
A. Fred et al. (Eds.): IC3K 2019, CCIS 1297, pp. 283–301, 2020.
https://doi.org/10.1007/978-3-030-66196-0_13

components, which is beneficial because in different domains usually specific software, programming languages, and paradigms are used. The coupling allows to reuse existing simulation components without the need for reimplementation and allows to use sophisticated models of the different domains.

While software-based modeling and simulation can be used for testing first prototypes or doing large-scale scenarios, Hardware-in-the-Loop (HIL) and hardware laboratory testing approaches can be used as simulation approaches for more realistic and detailed testing. HIL is an experimental method in which a Hardware under Test (HUT) is coupled with a real-time simulation to be tested under realistic conditions. HIL supports throughout study of dynamic operation of the HUT under realistic conditions [10]. Accordingly, it will entail coupling of different testbed contexts.

Commonly, a simulation expert works together with the experts of the different simulation components in the planning of a co-simulation. This collaboration of simulation and domain experts can be a complex task, because they have to understand at least partly the other domains. For example, in the discussion the used terminology can be unclear, because the same terms may be used for different concepts. Therefore, it would be beneficial for the development of energy scenarios and hardware tests to directly integrate or reference external domain knowledge.

Co-simulation scenarios, which describe an executable co-simulation, are typically developed manually by the simulation expert. Central elements of this process are the parameters, dependencies, and data flows of simulation components. An increasing number of simulation components makes the planning more complex and error-prone, when done manually. Therefore, it is essential for the planning of complex co-simulation scenarios to get assistance in this process, e.g. in getting recommendations of suitable simulation components.

Co-simulation is often not used as standalone tool, but is integrated in, e.g., energy scenarios or hardware experiments adding even more complexity. Energy scenarios are used to describe possible future developments of the energy system [9]. Typically, the future states are defined, tested with simulation and evaluated afterward. For co-simulation with integration of hardware devices the focus is more on the development of new technologies and using HIL or laboratory testing for testing a complex system with reduced time and cost investment compared to field tests. For both, a clear definition of the parametrization, data flows, and results is crucial.

Our approach introduces ontological representations of domain knowledge in hardware and software co-simulation of the smart grid to address the described problems. Additionally, it uses Semantic Web technologies to structure the process of planning, execution, and evaluation of co-simulation. A first version of this approach was already published in the conference proceedings with the focus on software co-simulation [21]. This extended version will also describe the integration of hardware devices in co-simulation.

The first version has been developed in the project NEDS, which consists of an interdisciplinary consortium from the domains of business administration, computer science, economics, electrical engineering, and psychology. In the project a process for the integrated development of energy scenarios, their simulation, and the evaluation of their sustainability has been developed [23] and executed for a future scenario of the German federal state Lower Saxony. The approach was than extended to allow the integration of hardware components in the planning of a co-simulation scenario. In this context, our proposed ontology-based approach offers the following benefits:

Firstly, it enables the integration of knowledge from external ontologies. This allows reuse of existing ontologies from different domains and integrate definitions of used terms. Thus, the terminology used in a co-simulation project can be made clear and transparent.

Secondly, it allows to describe the semantics of data in several steps of co-simulation: The parametrization of simulation models, the exchange of data between simulation models, and the results of simulation. All of these different kinds of data can be semantically annotated to make the interpretation less error-prone.

Thirdly, Semantic Web technologies like RDF, OWL, and SPARQL offer a well-known and widespread structure for knowledge representation and querying. Their usage permits the utilization of manifold available tools and techniques. Especially, the querying based on the ontological description of dependencies and data flows assists the planning of simulation scenarios and enables the simulation expert on the one hand to check high-level scenarios for completeness and missing models or evaluation functions and on the other hand to validate simulation scenarios.

The remainder of this article is structured as follows: Section 2 gives an overview of the foundations and related work. Section 3 describes the proposed approach, gives some examples, and describes the evaluation of the approach in a field study. A conclusion is given in Sect. 4.

2 Foundations and Related Work

In this section, we will give an overview of related work using co-simulation and ontologies in the energy domain (see Sect. 2.1) and introduce our previous work of a process for the planning and evaluation of energy scenarios with an information model and a catalog of components for co-simulation (see Sect. 2.2). Also the aspects of HIL and laboratory testing (see Sect. 2.3) and the Holistic Testing Description (HTD) for the structured development of a experiment (see Sect. 2.4) are described.

2.1 Co-simulation and Ontologies in Energy Domain

As stated in the introduction, the power system is becoming more complex, because multiple domains have to be considered. An approach for handling this issue is software-based co-simulation, which is defined as *"an approach for the joint simulation of models developed with different tools (tool coupling) where each tool treats one part of a modular coupled problem"* [2, p.1].

In energy domain, many different smart grid co-simulation frameworks exist, which are developed for different use cases. For example, the usage of real-time and co-simulators for the development of power system monitoring control and protection applications [18], the coupling with power flow simulators [12], the integration of power system and communication networks [14], or a holistic view on the power system [23]. Schloegl et al. [20] suggest a typification for the available co-simulation frameworks and [33] compare many of them. However, Palensky et al. [17] state that challenges in co-simulation are still massive, which is caused among other things by often missing software interoperability in the modeling.

Although ontologies would offer many benefits for interoperability, the utilization in co-simulation approaches is not common with two exceptions: [28] describe an approach for co-simulation with integration of ontologies for the interoperability between different electricity market multi-agent simulation platforms, which is called TOOCC (Tools Configuration Center). But the focus of this approach seems to be mainly on energy markets and building energy management and the data structure of messages between simulation models. Another approach is CODES (Composable Discrete-Event scalable Simulation), described by [29]. It contains the COSMO ontology, which supports the classification of components to allow component discovery and reuse with a model repository, but it is limited to discrete-event simulation. As our focus is more on the high-level scenario planning, the integration of external domain knowledge, and the usability, our approach aims to be integrated in the established open-source co-simulation framework mosaik[1] [25]. It is focused on providing high usability and flexibility to enable interdisciplinary teams to develop co-simulation scenarios. For the coupling of simulation models mosaik provides an API, which is available in several programming languages and can also be accessed via network packages.

2.2 Process for Assisted Simulation Planning of Co-simulation

In previous work we have introduced the "Process for Integrated Development and Evaluation of Energy Scenarios" (PDES) and an information model for the high-level planning of co-simulation in the context of energy scenarios [3]. The PDES describes an integrated process for the sustainability evaluation of future scenarios based on literature review and co-simulation. The first step of the PDES is the development of qualitative future scenarios, which describe thinkable future states of the power system – the energy scenarios. Afterwards, these qualitative assumptions are quantified and used as input for simulation. The last step is the evaluation of the simulation results based on multi-criteria decision making. The evaluation function for the PDES is sustainability, but also other evaluation functions could be defined in the information model. The information model links future scenarios and simulation scenarios to the sustainability evaluation as shown in Fig. 1. On the left-hand side the domains of interest are modeled and described by attributes, which can be defined based on either future scenarios or simulation. On the right-hand side sustainability is defined as evaluation function and subdivided in facets and criteria. The connection between the two sides is established through transformation functions from attributes to the sustainability criteria. The information model aims to support the information exchange in the PDES. It describes a structure for modeling scenarios and assists the users in the process.

Based on the information model, a process for the planning of co-simulation has been developed and published [22], which is shown in Fig. 2. In this planning of co-simulation, simulation components have to be found, which can provide the results defined in the information model. For this, a catalog of co-simulation components was

---

[1] https://mosaik.offis.de.

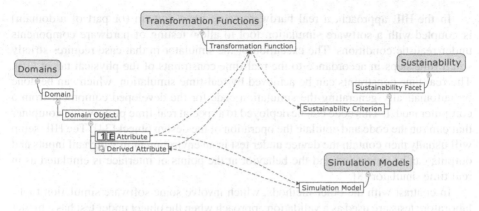

Fig. 1. Structure of the PDES information model [23].

developed to give an overview of the available components. The interfaces of the simulation models are described in the catalog based on the Functional Mockup Interface (FMI) standard, which has been developed to allow the coupling of different simulation models in industrial and scientific projects [4]. A substantial part of FMI is the definition of variables, which define the inputs and outputs of simulation components [15]. Each variable can be described by seven attributes in FMI. For example, the attribute causality can have values like *input*, *output*, *parameter*, or *calculatedParameter* or the attribute variability characterizes time instants when a variable can change its value and can have values like *constant*, *fixed*, *discrete*, or *continuous*.

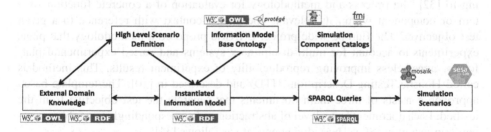

Fig. 2. Overview of the approach for ontological integration of domain knowledge in energy scenario simulation.

2.3   HIL and Laboratory Testing

The design and validation of a new smart grid technologies require the integration of several domains. Co-Simulation, as explained so far, allows to couple different simulation components and environments, taking different depths into account. However, after a software-based co-simulation, for the integration of hardware it is needed to perform more detailed tests. Usually, before a laboratory test or a field test implementation, HIL tests are used to evaluate the integration on a system level, addressing all relevant test domains [26].

In the HIL approach, a real hardware setup for a domain (or part of a domain) is coupled with a software simulation tool to allow testing of hardware components under realistic conditions. The execution of the simulator in that case requires strictly small time steps in accordance to the real-time constraints of the physical target [16]. The real time constraints can be achieved by real-time simulation, which can be done by automatically generating the simulation code for the developed equipment from a computer model. This code can be deployed to a special real-time prototyping computer that can run the code and emulate the operation of the design object [34]. The HIL setup will usually then contain the device under test in an environment in which all inputs and outputs can be controlled and the behavior at the points of interface is emulated as in real time simulator [8].

In contrast with the other methods, which involve some software simulation tools, laboratory tests are used as a validation approach when the object under test has a higher degree of maturity [27]. It requires the proper facility selection (structure or laboratory setup), that allows the tester to evaluate the proper grid configuration.

In OFFIS institute the Smart Energy Simulation and Automation (SESALab) was built to implement pure hardware experiments as well as HIL setups with the integration of software components [5].

2.4   HTD

To manage the complexity of developing a co-simulation, an appropriate testing method is of high importance to reduce the gap between formulating test specification with regard to the different domains (electrical, ICT, and control) and evaluation of the test accordingly. By this, we come to the definition of Holistic Testing which is according to [32] "the process and methodology for evaluation of a concrete function, system or component within its relevant operational context with reference to a given test objective." The Europe-wide project ERIGrid proposed a methodology that plans experiments to account for multi-disciplinary systems and varied experimental platforms, nonetheless improving reproducibility of experiment results. This method is called Holistic Testing Description (HTD) and described in [10]. The template-based approach consists of three main documents that separate the test objective from the testbed. Each document has a level of abstraction and correspondingly resembles a system configuration (SC). These documents are as follows [34]:

Test Case (TC). The starting point of HTD procedure is filling the test case document. The inputs to this document is the Generic System Configuration (GSC), which describes the system boundary in which the Object under Investigation (OuI) lies, a list of use cases that could be realized by this test object, and finally the test objective.

Test Specification (TS). After identifying the GSC and the OuI, the test specification template is of help in identifying the concrete Specific System Configuration (SSC) which is more granular in respect of equipment cardinality and specific connections.

Experiment Specification (ES). The final stage is to map the testing requirement and the system configuration to a testbed or collection of testbeds in an integrated experiment, describing the testbed configuration as Experiment System Configuration (ESC).

The mapping procedure that realizes the test description on a testbed can be semi-automated as suggested by [10]. They Propose two concepts: A web-based open access database that provides information about test labs or co-simulation software plus its component constituents, and a guideline that gives structured advice for the usage of the database for selecting appropriate test environment and test component. The database will give information on the available testbed components and their connection possibilities. The guideline describes a two-stage process for deriving an experiment implementation from a given test specification. During the process the practitioners are asked to assess the degree of precision to which the experimental setup needs to replicate various aspects of the test specification (e.g., grid topology, communication system, static and dynamic parameters), by examining each aspect (component or sub-system) of the test system and assigning one of four different precision levels to it:

Precise. The respective component has to be matched 1:1 (real hardware).
Equivalent. The respective component has to be matched equivalently in a dedicated software simulation tool (e.g., Grid topology modelled in PowerFactory).
Nominal. The respective component can be matched in a software based manner with some deviations.
Irrelevant: The respective system aspect does not influence the test objective and results.

The result of the assessment phase is pairing each system aspect with a precision category. After the assessment table is established, it can be used to communicate the fixed implementation requirements of a test and to prioritize the rest of the system properties. These constraints, together with the prioritization, enable an iterative search of the database. As mentioned above, the method of HTD is a template based documentation of a test and its realization, which in our case not practical enough to produce an automated procedure for testing. Nevertheless, the method and its related concepts such as component assessment is used as guideline for the assisted software and hardware simulation planning.

3 Approach

Our approach for the ontological integration of domain knowledge in co-simulation is based on the information model and component catalog summarized in Sect 2.2. In previous papers, first ideas of this approach were described [3,22,23], which will be detailed in the following regarding the ontological integration and new ideas of integrating hardware simulation and more catalogs.

The information model of the PDES aims to assist the collaboration of a simulation expert and domain experts, which provide components for co-simulation. It can be assumed that the simulation expert is a software expert familiar with the co-simulation framework and several programming languages and simulation tools, but has only limited knowledge about all domains included in simulation. The domain experts may also be software experts, especially, if they provide simulation components. But they could also have no background in computer science or software development. Therefore, an important requirement for our approach is to facilitate the participation of domain experts in the modeling without previous knowledge of Semantic Web technologies. Thus, a semantic diagram in form of a mind map is used for modeling the PDES information model (see *high level scenario definition* in Fig. 2). This allows to start the planning of scenarios with brainstorming in the project team and bringing the information step by step in the correct structure. Objects in the mind map can also be annotated directly with additional information. For example, references to external ontologies (see Sect. 3.1), or the context of the future scenarios can be annotated.

The map has to comply to the structure of the information model shown in Fig. 1 in the end. Other methods for knowledge modeling with the graph-based structure of concept maps also exist, as for example Simon-Cuevas et al. [24] describe it. We argue that a tree-based mind map is sufficient for the described use case and the superior flexibility of a graph-based concept map would distract the users.

For the ontological representation of the modeled information, a base ontology representing the information model structure has been developed (see Sect. 3.2). The mind map tool XMind[2] was used and extended with a plug-in to instantiate the information model ontology. Therefore, the scenario can be modeled inside the mind map and be transformed to RDF (see *instantiated information model* in Fig. 2).

To build an executable co-simulation scenario based on this, information about the available simulation components is needed. In Sect. 2.4 a open access database was described, which is part of the HTD. But as the database tries to cover many different types of labs the complexity is high. Heussen et al. [10] also mention, that many institutions don't want to have all information about their labs publicly available and implement internal solutions. For our approach, the focus is on relevant data for the specific use cases for mosaik and SESALab, which should be aligned with the HTD database to provide the possibility to integrate it in the database. Thus, catalogs for software components [22] and hardware components for co-simulation and a catalog for the experiments have been implemented. The implementation has been done in a Semantic MediaWiki (SMW) [11] based on templates. It was used to facilitate the participation of users without experience in Semantic Web technologies. With the page forms extension[3] based on the defined templates intuitive usable forms have been defined. These forms can be used as a questionnaire to add new components to the catalogs.

The SMW also allows to import vocabularies from external ontologies and to export the content to RDF or to use directly a triplet store as database. Thus, the catalog can directly be integrated in the instantiated ontology of the information model and the user can be assisted in finding the suitable simulation models for his purpose. Some example queries showing this assistance are shown in Sect. 3.3. For the integration of the approach in co-simulation a prototype for the framework mosaik has been developed. It allows to use the information from the information model and the component catalog to assist the simulation expert in the development and validation of executable simulation scenarios. Finally, the integration in data management is shortly described in Sect. 3.4 and the evaluation of the approach in Sect. 3.5.

---

[2] https://www.xmind.net/.

[3] https://www.mediawiki.org/wiki/Extension:Page_Forms.

3.1 Referencing External Ontologies

The ontological modeling allows to reference existing external ontologies in different manners. Exemplary ontologies for the following relevant use cases are described in this section. On the one hand, the objects of interest for the simulation (*domain objects*) and objects of evaluation (*sustainability criteria*) in the information model can be mapped to external ontologies to define their meaning. On the other hand, external ontologies can be used for the definition of units of measurement for different kinds of attributes in the information model.

Definition of Terms. In the energy domain the Common Information Model (CIM) is widespread to facilitate interoperability in the power system. It contains a data model in form of a domain ontology, various interface specifications, and mappings between technologies. Thus, it enables automated communication between components of smart grids. For our approach mainly the first use case for CIM described by [31] is of interest, which is CIM as a large domain ontology providing a vocabulary. This vocabulary can be used to map objects to definitions in the CIM. The CIM is defined as an UML model, but the complete model or subsets (so-called profiles) can be transformed to Web Ontology Language (OWL) with the CIMTool[4].

As in the PDES sustainability is evaluated, it is examined here as example as well. The United Nations defined Sustainable Development Goals (SDGs), which should be fulfilled until the year 2030 [30]. To reference these goals and their indicators the SDG Interface Ontology[5] (SDGIO) based on the Environment Ontology (ENVO) [6] is under development. It contains definitions of indicators for the measurement of the SDGs defined by the United Nations.

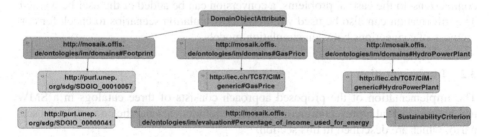

Fig. 3. Mapping of individuals of the instantiated information model from project NEDS to external ontologies [21].

The mapping to external ontologies allows integrating definitions of terms to make clear their meaning in an interdisciplinary simulation or to relate internal evaluation criteria to external criteria. Examples of mapping to the external ontologies CIM and SDGIO are described as follows (see also Fig. 3). The CIM ontology contains

---

[4] http://wiki.cimtool.org.
[5] https://github.com/SDG-InterfaceOntology/sdgio.

definitions for objects of the power system like *CIM-generic#EnergyMarket*, *CIM-generic#HydroPowerPlant*, and *CIM-generic#GasPrice*, which are mapped to domain objects and attributes of the information model in the project NEDS. Additionally, the domain object attribute *footprint* in NEDS is mapped to the class *material footprint (sdg/SDGIO_00010057)* and its definition in the SDGIO. Another example is the sustainability criterion *Percentage of income used for energy* in NEDS, which addresses the SDG 7: *"Ensure access to affordable, reliable, sustainable and modern energy for all"* [30, p. 21], which is represented by the individual *sdg/SDGIO_00000041* in the SDGIO.

Units of Measure. The Ontology of units of Measure (OM) is an OWL ontology of the domain of quantities and units of measure described by [19]. It aims to *"support making quantitative research data more explicit, so that the data can be integrated, verified and reproduced"* [19, p. 1]. In the OM every measure is defined by a unit of measure, which can have a prefix. These units of measure are defined by a quantity and each quantity has a dimension. For example, the measure "3 m" would be defined by the unit "meter", which could be defined by the quantity "length" or "height", which both are in the "length dimension". Additionally, a java library for conversion of units based on the ontology is available[6].

Units play an important role in the attributes, transformation functions, and sustainability criteria in the information model as well as in simulation models and co-simulation. All connections have to be validated in consideration of their unit to ensure the functionality. Therefore, the OM is used to add references to the units of attributes and criteria annotated in the information model. Additionally, the OM is used to assist the user in annotating directly in the mind map, comparable to the assistance with an Excel add-in described by [19]. With this information the OM allows to validate the connections. In the case of problems, a conversion can be added or the user be warned. The information can also be used within the co-simulation scenarios to check for correctness of connections between simulation models.

3.2 Implementation

The implementation of the proposed approach consists of three catalogs in a SMW and the ontological representation of simulation components and the co-simulation scenario, which are described in this section.

Catalogs for Simulation Components and Experiments. As described in [22], a catalog for co-simulation components was already implemented in previous work. The focus was so far on components, which can be coupled in a software-based mosaik co-simulation. To allow the integration in the HTD, additional information is needed in the catalog. Thus, it was extended in regards to the domain information of the components. To align this with the HTD, the type of components was defined based on the documentation from ERIGrid [13, p.32ff.], which contains a list of different domains, areas, levels, components, and attributes.

---

[6] https://github.com/dieudonne-willems/om-java-libs.

In the OFFIS institute the SESALab is used for large-scale, real-time co-simulation of smart grid system under realistic conditions. It contains frameworks and hardware for off-line and real time co-simulation. Additionally, in order to facilitate usage of the lab features, a catalog for the components of the SESALab existed already in the SMW, which is a database to search and explore the hardware and software available in the Lab. The catalog contains information such as component type, functions, its main domain, and its virtual location (IP address) on the lab network. It was extended to be aligned with the HTD.

For the simulation planning another catalog with a questionnaire for the experiments was developed. It was designed based on the HTD templates [10], which also have the goal to lead the development of a test experiment. But with the implementation in the SMW and predefined categorization for answers the goal was to support the user and allow the better automation based on the collected information. To allow this, the questionnaire contains fields to add the types of components, which are needed to run the experiment, and their required precision level, as described in Sect. 2.4. The Questionnaire consists of a section of general questions about the experiment and separated sections for different domains, which have to be filled out only if they are relevant for the experiment.

Ontological Representation. Three base ontologies have been developed and are imported in an additional ontology for integration. This modularity enables the reuse of each of the ontologies.

The first ontology represents the structure of the information model for the high-level scenario planning. For the integration of hardware it has been extended with the possibility to model the in- and outputs of simulation components and to model the grid topology of the components.

The second ontology represents the structure of the SMW catalogs. It contains the description of the co-simulation component catalog and the FMI-based specification of variables for these software components. Additionally, the component catalog of components of the SESALab and a catalog for the experiment definition is part of the second ontology.

The third ontology represents the structure of a simulation scenario modeled in mosaik. Such a scenario consists of multiple simulation component with their parametrization and the connections between simulation components and the exchanged attributes between them. Based on these three ontologies the available data is described and can be used for queries.

3.3 Example Queries

The usage of ontologies provides a structure for querying the data of the planning in the information model, the component catalogs, the experiment catalog, and the mosaik scenario with SPARQL to assist the development of simulation scenarios. In the following, three examples are given, which show the opportunities of the ontological representation in the planning of executable co-simulation scenarios. For all three examples the SPARQL code and a visualization of the query are shown. The following prefixes are used: The prefixes *wiki, fmi, cosicoca,* and *sesalab* are referencing the experiment and component catalogs in the SMW. The prefixes *imDB, imDom,* and *im* are referencing the information model base ontology. The prefix *om* is referencing the OM. In the visualization (see Figs. 4b, 5b, and 6b) the data source is indicated by the background color and label.

```
SELECT DISTINCT ?derAttr ?unit ?omUnit ?dimension ?component ?fmiVar
    ?fmiUnit
WHERE {
    ?derAttr rdf:type imDom:DerivedDomainObjectAttribute; imDB:unit ?unit
    ?omUnit rdf:type om:Unit; om:symbol ?symbol
    FILTER( ?symbol = ?unit )
    ?omUnit om:hasDimension ?dimension
    ?component rdf:type wikiCategory:Component; wiki:fmiVariables ?fmiVar
    ?fmiVar rdf:type wikiCategory:FMIVariable
    ?fmiVar fmi:unit ?fmiUnit; fmi:causality ?fmiCausality
    FILTER( ?fmiCausality = 'output' )
    ?omUnit2 rdf:type om:Unit; om:symbol ?symbol2
    FILTER( ?symbol2 = ?fmiUnit )
    ?omUnit2 om:hasDimension ?dimension }
```
(a) SPARQL code

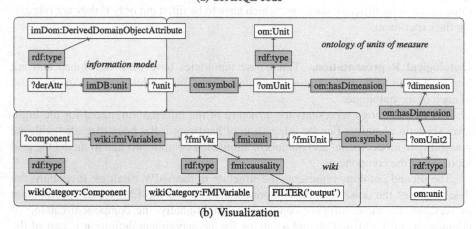

(b) Visualization

Fig. 4. Query 1 – Simulation models from wiki providing output for derived attributes of information model [21]. (Color figure online)

Query 1. This query (see Fig. 4) assist the user in common use cases for the development of a co-simulation scenario. If the simulation models are not predefined, the simulation expert has to find simulation models matching the goal of the simulation. This can be a complex task, because there can be a vast amount of available simulation models, which were usually not developed by the simulation expert. Therefore, the simulation expert does not know all details about the simulation models and is assisted by querying the information model and the specification of the simulation models in the component catalog.

Query 1 shows simulation models, whose output can be used in the information model. These derived attributes in the information model are by definition the output of a simulation. In the query the derived attributes (*?derAttr*) in the information model are mapped to the variables (*?fmiVar*) of simulation models (*?component*) in the component

```
SELECT DISTINCT ?simMod1 ?fmiVar1 ?fmiUnit1 ?derAttr ?fmiVar2 ?fmiUnit2
        ?simMod2
WHERE {
    ?simMod1 im:feedsDerivedAttribute ?derAttr
    ?derAttr im:feedsSimulationModel ?simMod2
    ?component1 rdf:type wikiCategory:MosaikModel
    ?component1 wiki:name ?simMod1; wiki:fmiVariables ?fmiVar1
    ?fmiVar1 rdf:type wikiCategory:FMIVariable
    ?component2 rdf:type wikiCategory:MosaikModel
    ?component2 wiki:name ?simMod2; wiki:fmiVariables ?fmiVar2
    ?fmiVar2 rdf:type wikiCategory:FMIVariable
    ?fmiVar1 fmi:type ?fmiVar1Type; fmi:variability ?fmiVar1Vari
    ?fmiVar2 fmi:type ?fmiVar1Type; fmi:variability ?fmiVar1Vari
    ?component1 wiki:timeDomain ?comp1timeDomain
    ?component2 wiki:timeDomain ?comp1timeDomain
```

(a) SPARQL code

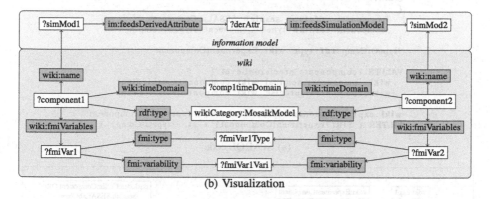

(b) Visualization

Fig. 5. Query 2 – Finding suitable simulation models for coupling with another simulation model [21]. (Color figure online)

catalog. The variables are filtered by their *fmi:causality*, which has to be *output*. To find suitable combinations of derived attributes and variables the units annotated in the mind map are used. In this query the units are not compared directly, but the OM is used to reference the dimension (*?dimension*) of the unit, e.g., the unit "meter" is in the length dimension. Hence, differences in unit prefixes or the system of measurement (imperial or metric system) are of no importance for mapping.

Query 2. This query searches for simulation models that use the output of another simulation model as input (see Fig. 5). In the information model such kind of connection is modeled via a derived attribute, but it is usually realized by a direct coupling of the two simulation models in co-simulation. For these cases, the query checks the technical interfaces and characteristics of the simulation models for compatibility based on the component catalog. In the query, the first simulation model (*?simMod1*) is mapped to the derived attributes (*?derAttr*) and the second simulation model (*?simMod2*). If two simulation models in the information model are modeled this way, the technical characteristics of the simulation models can be checked for compatibility based on the component catalog.

In the example, the characteristics *fmi:variability* and *fmi:type* of the FMI variables (*?fmiVar1* and *?fmiVar2*) are compared. Additionally, the characteristics *wiki:timeDomain* of the simulation models (*?component1* and *?component2*) are compared. This characteristic can have values like "discrete", "continuous", or "stationary" and addresses the common problem of different timing in simulation models. This query can also be adapted to find suitable simulation models based on these characteristics, if one of them is missing in the information model.

```
SELECT DISTINCT ?component ?typeOfComp ?experimentComponent
WHERE {
    {
        ?component rdf:type cosicoca:CoSimComponent .
        ?component cosicoca:typeOfComponent ?typeOfComp .
    }
UNION
    {
        ?component rdf:type sesalab:SESALabComponent .
        ?component sesalab:typeOfComponent ?typeOfComp .
    }
    ?typeOfComp rdf:type wiki:ExperimentComponent .

    VALUES ?components_precisionLevel {
        wiki:components_nominal wiki:components_equivalent
        wiki:components_precise wiki:components_irrelevant
    } .
    wiki:exp1 ?components_precisionLevel ?experimentComponent .
    FILTER ( STR(?experimentComponent) = str(?typeOfComp) ) .
}
```

(a) SPARQL code

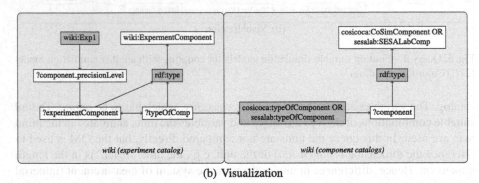

(b) Visualization

Fig. 6. Query 3 – Finding suitable hardware or software simulation components for an experiment. (Color figure online)

Query 3. The third query shows an example in the context of the modeling of a mixed software and hardware co-simulation. It shows available simulation models, which have the type of component modeled in the experiment questionnaire (see Fig. 6).

The starting point is the experiment definition in the SMW (*wiki:exp1*). It contains information about the types of components, which are needed in this experiment and their precision level (*?components_precisionLevel*). For this example, the information about the precision level is not used in detail, but only used to identify the types of components needed for this experiment (*?experimentComponent*). This information could also be used for a more detailed query using the required precision levels to determine if the simulation components have to be a software or hardware component. The types of components are modeled as experiment components (*wiki:ExperimentComponent*) based on HTD documents.

On the other side this query utilizes the component catalogs to find suitable components for the experiment. In the query the components from the software and hardware catalogs are joined (*cosicoca:CoSimComponent OR sesalab:SESALabComp*). The type of component (*typeOfComp*) is used to map them to the experiment, so that suitable simulation components are the result.

3.4 Data Management

In the PDES, values from future scenarios, co-simulation scenario parametrization, and simulation results have to be managed and are directly integrated in the information model. Also for hardware co-simulation the parametrization and simulation results have to be managed. The information model provides one central storage for the semantics of all relevant data in the complete process. Thus, also the data management is integrated with the information model.

As briefly mentioned in [23] the information model was used to generate the schema for a data store, which was implemented in a relational database (RDB) in the NEDS project. To facilitate the collaboration of different domain experts, different views were defined on the schema. To integrate the data from a relational database again Ontology-based Data Access (OBDA) could be used. It is based on a three-level architecture containing an ontology, data sources, and a mapping between them [7]. Thus, OBDA faces the challenge of data heterogeneity by replacing a global scheme in data management with the ontology describing the domains. It allows also to integrate data from other sources like CSV, XML, and XLSX directly in SPARQL queries, which can be helpful in the interdisciplinary environment of co-simulation.

To reduce the complexity the direct usage of a triple store would be preferable compared to a RDB with ODBA, but is not always possible. However, the usage of a triple store or OBDA would allow to access data based on the information model ontology and to integrate the data store directly in SPARQL queries.

3.5 Evaluation

The proposed approach aims to support users in the modeling and management of information in the development of co-simulation scenarios. For its evaluation, the process was used in a field study in the interdisciplinary project team of the project NEDS [3]. Altogether, 28 scientific researchers participated and used the information model to model a simulation scenario, which integrated several simulation models from different domains and to evaluate the results of simulation. The members of the project team came from the domains energy, computer science, business administration, economics, electrical engineering, and psychology. 29 domain objects, 231 attributes, and 19 sustainability criteria where modeled with their dependencies and data flows in the information model and transformed to RDF automatically for further usage. Based on the RDF representation of the information model SPARQL queries were used to check for completeness and correctness of the modeled information. As the project partners were mostly not from computer science, we defined the SPARQL queries to get the needed information. The implementation of a GUI to enable the users to do this themselves would be interesting future work.

The field study showed that the process was helpful to include domain experts in the design of simulation scenarios. The use of the information model allowed easy participation and offered a central model. Also, the semantic diagram was supportive as tool for discussion in the project team. The field study showed that not all participating domains have ontologies which could be referenced for definition of terms. However, the modeling of the information model improved the processes in the interdisciplinary project team during the development of energy scenarios and helped significantly making clear the terminology.

The integration of hardware simulation was implemented in a prototype and tested with a system configuration for automation of the functions on a feeder line in the electrical distribution grid. This system is generic enough to contain a cluster of use cases that could be evaluated separately, additionally an already in-house publication [1] that implemented a test use case in this system's context already existed. This makes the feeder automation system an ideal case for the evaluation of the suggested process. The domains involved in this case are electrical, ICT, and control systems which require collaboration of domain experts. The developed questionnaire helps to define the system under test and give a specific system configuration (SSC), additionally the selected components precision level to determine the experiment setup and the simulation environment suitable to fulfill the test requirements.

4   Conclusion

In this paper, we described an approach for the ontological integration of semantics and domain knowledge in the process of planning, execution, and evaluation of interdisciplinary co-simulation of the smart grid. Our approach incorporates the PDES and its information model representing the process and providing the ontological structures for the modeling of energy scenarios using co-simulation. Additionally, the development of HIL and laboratory testing is integrated based on the HTD. The information model can be instantiated in collaboration of interdisciplinary domain experts and allows to integrate external ontologies for definition of terms and referencing external works. The modeling of the scenarios in the information model allows also the integration in data management of scenario parametrization and results.

Catalogs of software and hardware simulation components and the experiments in a SMW have been integrated, extended, or developed to assist the simulation expert designing suitable environment during the planning of co-simulation. The integration of the approach in the co-simulation framework mosaik has been implemented prototypical. This prototype uses the information model and simulation model specification from the SMW to validate simulation scenarios. Based on this validation, it should also be possible in the future to find wrong connections of simulation components and correct them by automatically added conversions.

In conclusion, the use of ontologies for the development of co-simulation scenarios can assist the user in the process and provides the base for further development in the co-simulation planning in the context of energy scenarios and HIL.

Acknowledgements. The research project'NEDS – Nachhaltige Energieversorgung Niedersachsen' acknowledges the support of the Lower Saxony Ministry of Science and Culture through the'Niedersächsisches Vorab' grant program (grant ZN3043).

References

1. Ansari, S., Castro, F., Weller, D., Babazadeh, D., Lehnhoff, S.: Towards virtualization of operational technology to enable large-scale system testing. In: Proceedings for 2019 Eurocon. IEEE (2019). https://doi.org/10.1109/EUROCON.2019.8861980

2. Bastian, J., Clauß, C., Wolf, S., Schneider, P.: Master for Co-Simulation Using FMI. Proceedings of the 8th International Modelica Conference pp. 115–120 (2011). https://doi.org/10.3384/ecp11063115

3. Blaufuß, C., et al.: Development of a process for integrated development and evaluation of energy scenarios for lower saxony. Final Report of the Research Project NEDS. Cuvillier, Göttingen, band 61 edn. (2019). https://cuvillier.de/de/shop/publications/8139-development-of-a-process-for-integrated-development-and-evaluation-of-energy-scenarios-for-lower-saxony

4. Blochwitz, T., et al.: The Functional Mockup Interface for Tool independent Exchange of Simulation Models. 8th International Modelica Conference 2011, pp. 173–184 (2009)

5. Büscher, M., et al.: dIntegrated Smart Grid simulations for generic automation architectures with RT-LAB and mosaik. In: 5th IEEE International Conference on Smart Grid Communications. pp. 194–199. IEEE (2014). https://doi.org/10.1109/SmartGridComm.2014.7007645

6. Buttigieg, P.L., Pafilis, E., Lewis, S.E., Schildhauer, M.P., Walls, R.L., Mungall, C.J.: The environment ontology in 2016: Bridging domains with increased scope, semantic density, and interoperation. J. Biomed. Semant. **7**(1), 1–12 (2016). https://doi.org/10.1186/s13326-016-0097-6

7. Daraio, C., Lenzerini, M., Leporelli, C., Naggar, P., Bonaccorsi, A., Bartolucci, A.: The advantages of an Ontology-Based Data Management approach: openness, interoperability and data quality. Scientometrics **108**(1), 441–455 (2016). https://doi.org/10.1007/s11192-016-1913-6

8. Ebe, F., Idlbi, B., Stakic, D.E., Chen, S., Kondzialka, C., Casel, M., Heilscher, G., Seitl, C., Bründlinger, R., Strasser, T.I.: Comparison of power hardware-in-the-loop approaches for the testing of smart grid controls. Energies **11**(12), 1–29 (2018). https://doi.org/10.3390/en11123381

9. Grunwald, A., Dieckhoff, C., Fischedick, M., Höffler, F., Mayer, C., Weimer-Jehle, W.: Consulting with energy scenarios: Requirements for scientific policy advice. Series on Science-Based Policy Advice, acatech/Leopoldina/Akademienunion (Eds.) (2016). https://en.acatech.de/publication/consulting-with-energy-scenarios-requirements-for-scientific-policy-advice/

10. Heussen, K., et al.: ERIGrid holistic test description for validating cyber-physical energy systems. Energies **12**(14), 2722 (2019). https://doi.org/10.3390/en12142722

11. Krötzsch, M., Vrandecic, D., Völkel, M., Haller, H., Studer, R.: Semantic wikipedia. Web Semant. Sci. Serv. Agents World Wide Web **5**(4), 251–261 (2007). https://doi.org/10.1016/j.websem.2007.09.001. World Wide Web Conference 2006 Semantic Web Track

12. Lehnhoff, S., et al.: Exchangeability of power flow simulators in smart grid co-simulations with Mosaik. In: 2015 Workshop on Modeling and Simulation of Cyber-Physical Energy Systems (MSCPES), pp. 1–6 (April 2015). https://doi.org/10.1109/MSCPES.2015.7115410

13. Mäki, K., et al.: D-JRA1.1 ERIGrid scenario descriptions. Technical report, ERIGrid Konsortium (2016). https://erigrid.eu/wp-content/uploads/2017/02/DL_D-JRA1.1_ERIGrid_scenario_descriptions_2016-07-02.pdf. Accessed 28 Jan 2020)

14. Mets, K., Ojea, J.A., Develder, C.: Combining power and communication network simulation for cost-effective smart grid analysis. IEEE Commun. Surv. Tutor. 1–25 (2014). https://doi.org/10.1109/SURV.2014.021414.00116
15. Modelica Association Project FMI: Functional Mock-up Interface for Model Exchange and Co-Simulation. Technical report, Modelica Association (2013)
16. Nguyen, V.H., et al.: Real-Time Simulation and Hardware-in-the-Loop Approaches for Integrating Renewable Energy Sources into Smart Grids: Challenges & Actions (2017). https://arxiv.org/abs/1710.02306
17. Palensky, P., Van Der Meer, A.A., Lopez, C.D., Joseph, A., Pan, K.: Co simulation of intelligent power systems: fundamentals, software architecture, numerics, and coupling. IEEE Ind. Electron. Mag. 11(1), 34–50 (2017). https://doi.org/10.1109/MIE.2016.2639825
18. Rehtanz, C., Guillaud, X.: Real-time and co-simulations for the development of power system monitoring, control and protection. In: 2016 Power Systems Computation Conference (PSCC), pp. 1–20, June 2016. https://doi.org/10.1109/PSCC.2016.7541030
19. Rijgersberg, H., Van Assem, M., Top, J.: Ontology of units of measure and related concepts. Semant. Web 4(1), 3–13 (2013). https://doi.org/10.3233/SW-2012-0069
20. Schlögl, F., Rohjans, S., Lehnhoff, S., Velasquez, J., Steinbrink, C., Palensky, P.: Towards a classification scheme for co-simulation approaches in energy systems. In: International Symposium on Smart Electric Distribution Systems and Technologies, pp. 2–7. IEEE/IES (2015). https://doi.org/10.1109/SEDST.2015.7315262
21. Schwarz, J.S., Lehnhoff, S.: Ontological integration of semantics and domain knowledge in energy scenario co-simulation. In: IC3K 2019 - Proceedings of the 11th International Joint Conference on Knowledge Discovery, Knowledge Engineering and Knowledge Management, vol. 2(Ic3k), pp. 127–136 (2019). https://doi.org/10.5220/0008069801270136
22. Schwarz, J.S., Steinbrink, C., Lehnhoff, S.: Towards an assisted simulation planning for co-simulation of cyber-physical energy systems. In: 7th Workshop on Modeling and Simulation of Cyber-Physical Energy Systems (MSCPES), Montreal, pp. 1–6 (2019). https://doi.org/10.1109/MSCPES.2019.8738788
23. Schwarz, J.S., Witt, T., Nieße, A., Geldermann, J., Lehnhoff, S., Sonnenschein, M.: Towards an integrated development and sustainability evaluation of energy scenarios assisted by automated information exchange. In: Donnellan, B., Klein, C., Helfert, M., Gusikhin, O., Pascoal, A. (eds.) SMARTGREENS/VEHITS -2017. CCIS, vol. 921, pp. 3–26. Springer, Cham (2019). https://doi.org/10.1007/978-3-030-02907-4_1
24. Simon-Cuevas, A., Ceccaroni, L., Rosete-Suarez, A., Suarez-Rodriguez, A.: A formal modeling method applied to environmental-knowledge engineering. In: International Conference on Complex, Intelligent and Software Intensive Systems (2009). https://doi.org/10.1109/CISIS.2009.55
25. Steinbrink, C., et al.: CPES testing with mosaik: co-simulation planning, execution and analysis. Appl. Sci. 9(5) (2019). https://doi.org/10.3390/app9050923
26. Strasser, T., et al.: Towards holistic power distribution system validation and testing-an overview and discussion of different possibilities. Elektrotechnik und Informationstechnik 134(1), 71–77 (2017). https://doi.org/10.1007/s00502-016-0453-3
27. Strasser, T.I., Rohjans, S., Burt, G.M.: Methods and concepts for designing and validating smart grid systems. Energies 12(10) (2019). https://doi.org/10.3390/en12101861
28. Teixeira, B., Pinto, T., Silva, F., Santos, G., Praça, I., Vale, Z.: Multi-agent decision support tool to enable interoperability among heterogeneous energy systems. Appl. Sci. 8(3), 328 (2018). https://doi.org/10.3390/app8030328
29. Teo, Y.M., Szabo, C.: CODES: An integrated approach to composable modeling and simulation. In: Proceedings - Simulation Symposium, pp. 103–110 (2008). https://doi.org/10.1109/ANSS-41.2008.24

30. UN General Assembly: Transforming our world: The 2030 agenda for sustainable development (2015). https://doi.org/10.1007/s13398-014-0173-7.2. https://sustainabledevelopment. un.org/content/documents/21252030%20Agenda%20for%20Sustainable%20Development %20web.pdf. Accessed 28 Jan 2020

31. Uslar, M., Specht, M., Rohjans, S., Trefke, J., Gonzalez Vazquez, J.: The IEC Common Information Model. Springer, Berlin (2012). https://doi.org/10.1007/978-3-642-25215-0

32. Van Der Meer, A.A., et al.: Cyber-physical energy systems modeling, test specification, and co-simulation based testing. In: 2017 Workshop on Modeling and Simulation of Cyber-Physical Energy Systems, MSCPES 2017 - Held as part of CPS Week, Proceedings (2017). https://doi.org/10.1109/MSCPES.2017.8064528

33. Vogt, M., Marten, F., Braun, M.: A survey and statistical analysis of smart grid co-simulations. Appl. Energy **222**(March), 67–78 (2018). https://doi.org/10.1016/j.apenergy. 2018.03.123

34. Widl, E., et al.: D-JRA2.1 Simulator coupling and Smart Grid libraries. Technical report, ERIGrid Consortium (2017). https://erigrid.eu/wp-content/uploads/2017/07/DL_D-JRA2.1_ Simulator_coupling_and_Smart_Grid_libraries_2017-05-22.pdf. Accessed 28 Jan 2020

Towards Smart Behavior of Agents in Evacuation Planning Based on Local Cooperative Path Finding

Róbert Selvek and Pavel Surynek[✉][iD]

Faculty of Information Technology, Czech Technical University in Prague,
Thákurova 9, 160 00 Prague, Czech Republic
{selverob,pavel.surynek}@fit.cvut.cz

Abstract. We address engineering of smart behavior of agents in evacuation problems from the perspective of *cooperative path finding* (CPF) in this paper. We introduce an abstract version of evacuation problems we call *multi-agent evacuation* (MAE) that consists of an undirected graph representing the map of the environment and a set of agents moving in this graph. The task is to move agents from the endangered part of the graph into the safe part as quickly as possible. Although the abstract evacuation task can be solved using centralized algorithms based on network flows that are near-optimal with respect to various objectives, such algorithms would hardly be applicable in practice since real agents will not be able to follow the centrally created plan. Therefore we designed a decentralized evacuation planning algorithm called LC-MAE based on local rules derived from local cooperative path finding (CPF) algorithms. We compared LC-MAE with near-optimal centralized algorithm using agent-based simulations in multiple real-life scenarios. Our finding it that LC-MAE produces solutions that are only worse than the optimum by a small factor. Moreover our approach led to important observations about how many agents need to behave rationally to increase the speed of evacuation. A small fraction of rational agents can speed up the evacuation dramatically.

Keywords: Evacuation planning · Cooperative path-finding · Local algorithms · Decentralized algorithms · Agent-based simulations · Real-life scenarios · Network flows

1 Introduction

We address in this paper the evacuation problem from the point of view of engineering of smart behavior of individual evacuated agents. Evacuation planning represents an important real-life problem and is increasingly studied as a topic in artificial intelligence [4,16]. The evacuation task consists of evacuation of people or other agents from the endangered area into the safe zone. The important

© Springer Nature Switzerland AG 2020
A. Fred et al. (Eds.): IC3K 2019, CCIS 1297, pp. 302–321, 2020.
https://doi.org/10.1007/978-3-030-66196-0_14

computational challenge in evacuation represents the fact that centralized planning can hardly be applied as the task involves individual self-interested agents usually not willing to follow a centrally created plan.

Various techniques have been applied to address the evacuation problem both from the *centralized* and *decentralized* point of view including modeling the problem as *network flows* [1] or nature inspired computation such as *bee colony* optimization. The important distinguishing feature of evacuation planning algorithms is whether single evacuation route is being planned [20] or the problem is regarded as multi-agent scenario [19]. In multi-agent evacuation scenarios sometimes multiple types of agents are present such as those assisting the evacuation [15] and those being evacuated.

The environment where the evacuation task takes place is often modeled as a graph where vertices represent locations for agents, and edges model the possibility of moving between pairs of locations [14] (directed case may be used for representing one way path - a case often appearing in practice). Hence the evacuation problem can be interpreted as a variant of *path finding* or *cooperative path finding* [6, 21, 23–25] (CPF).

1.1 Related Work

Specifically in these problems graphs are used as abstractions for the environment. Similarly as in CPF, the evacuation modeling must take into account potential collisions between agents and solving techniques must ensure proper avoidance [7]. The collision avoidance in CPF is usually represented by a constraint of having at most one agent per vertex (in some versions of CPF more than one agent is allowed per vertex).

In contrast to CPF, where agents have unique individual goals (location/vertex), we usually do not distinguish between individual agents in the evacuation task. That is, an agent can evacuate itself to anywhere in the safe zone (not to a specific location in the safe zone). From the theoretical point of view, this feature makes evacuation planning algorithms similar to single commodity network flows [3] while the standard CPF is reducible to the *multi-commodity flow* problem [2].

Another important challenge in evacuation planning is represented by the execution of a plan by real agents. In real-life evacuation scenarios, we cannot simply assume that all agents will want to follow the plan. Centralized control of all agents is not feasible in the setup with self-interested agents. The real agent in evacuation scenario may for example prefer the nearest exit or a path through which it has arrived while a centrally created plan could force the agent go elsewhere, thus not being believable for the agent. This differs from classical planning [8], where the planning authority fully observes the environment, actions are assumed to be deterministic, and plans created in advance are assumed to be perfectly executed.

1.2   Contribution and Organization

Therefore in this work we focus on local evacuation planning relying on local cooperative path finding techniques and agent-based simulations. Our assumption is that evacuation paths planned locally using information available to the agent will be more realistic and could be executed by the real agent. At the same time we do not rule out the central aspect completely, as we also consider some agents to be more informed (about alternative exits, through a communication device) than others.

This paper is an extension of the original conference paper where the idea of evacuation planning using local cooperative path finding algorithms has been presented first time [18]. In this revised version we have extended the set of experiments and added more detailed explanation of network flow based algorithm that was omitted in the conference paper.

The organization of the paper is as follows. We begin with a formal introduction to the concept of evacuation planning, followed by a short summary of local cooperative path finding algorithms. Local CPF algorithms represent a basis of our novel evacuation algorithm called Local Cooperative Multi-agent Evacuation (LC-MAE) described next. Finally we present extensive experimental evaluation of LC-MAE in multiple scenarios using agent-based simulations. As part of the simulations, the algorithm is compared to a network-flow based algorithm which produces near-optimal plans.

2   Background

2.1   Evacuation Planning Formally

We introduce formal definition of evacuation task in this section. The abstract *multi-agent evacuation problem* (MAE) takes place in an undirected graph $G = (V, E)$. The set of vertices is divided into a set of *endangered* (D) vertices and a set of *safe* (S) vertices together modeling the zone to be evacuated and the safe zone. Agents from a set, $A = \{a_1, a_2, ..., a_k\}$, are distributed among the vertices and the task is to evacuate them from endangered to safe vertices.

The crisp variant of the problem requires that all agents are evacuated while in the optimization variant we want to have as many as possible agents in safety.

The MAE problem is similar to *cooperative path finding* (CPF) [21] from which we took the model for agent movement. Each agent is placed in a vertex of G so that there is at most one agent per vertex. The configuration of agents in vertices of the graph at time t will be denoted as $c_t : A \rightarrow V$. Similarly to CPF, an agent can move into a vacant adjacent vertex[1].

Multiple agents can move simultaneously, provided they do not collide with each other (that is, no two agents enter the same target vertex at the same time) and agents only enter vacant vertices.

---

[1] Alternative definitions of possible movements in CPF exist that for example permit train of agents to move simultaneously atc.

Definition 1. Multi-agent evacuation (MAE) *is a 5-tuple* $\mathcal{E} = [G = (V,E), A, c_0, D, S]$, *where G represents the environment, $A = a_1, a_2, ..., a_k$ is a set of agents, $c_0 : A \rightarrow V$ is the initial configuration of agents, D and S such that $D \subseteq V$, $S \subseteq V$, $V = D \cup S$ with $D \cap S \neq \emptyset$, and $|S| \geq k$ represent a set of endangered and a set of safe vertices respectively.*

The task in MAE is to find a plan that moves all agents into the safe vertices (the crisp variant). That is we are searching for a plan $\pi = [c_0, c_1, ..., c_m]$ so that $c_m(a) \in S$ $\forall a \in A$. The total time until the last agent reaches the safe zone is called a *makespan*; the makespan of π is m. An illustration of simple evacuation problem is shown in Fig. 1 and 2.

Fig. 1. Grid map depicting a multi-agent evacuation instance. Green squares represent agents that need to be evacuated from the pink endangered area to the white safe zone. (Color figure online)

The assumption is that everything in the endangered zone will be destroyed at some unknown point in the future. Hence, to increase chances of evacuation, the makespan should be small. An evacuation plan with the near optimal makespan can be found in polynomial time using *network flow* techniques [1, 26, 27]. However, these algorithms require a centralized approach where agents perfectly follow the central plan which is hardly applicable in real-life evacuation scenarios [7, 11].

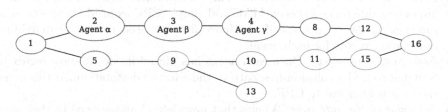

Fig. 2. MAE instance shown using undirected graph with the endangered and safe zone depicted using red and green vertices respectively.

2.2   Cooperative Path Finding Algorithms

We address MAE from a local point of view inspired by CPF algorithms like Local Repair A* (LRA*) and Windowed Hierarchical Cooperative A* (WHCA*) [21]. These algorithms feature a *decentralized* approach to cooperative path finding. Instead of using optimization techniques or network flow, each agent's path is found separately by using local rules, resolving conflicts between agents trying to enter the same vertex as they occur. In other words, each agent's next move is derived from the knowledge of the relative position of the goal vertex and agents in the neighborhood of the agent the move is planned for.

While LRA* only resolves conflicts at the moment agent tries to enter an occupied vertex, a naive strategy which can easily lead to deadlock, WHCA* is more advanced. Instead of only planning agents' paths in space (in graph), agents plan their paths in space-time and share them with other agents using a data structure called *reservation table* which is fact is expanded underlying graph over time. The time expansion is done by making a copy of the graph for each time step. In this data structure, we cab reserve space/time point for an agent once it goes through. When planning, vertices reserved by another agent at a given time are considered to be impassable.

If each agent planned and reserved its whole path to destination, agents planning later would have information about its complete route and their needs and goals would not be taken into account, leading to selfish behavior and deadlocks. The fix to this behavior is *windowing*, in which agents plan their paths only for a certain, small, number of time units and the planning is staggered, so that each agent has an option of reserving a certain vertex. The windowing mechanism supports local behavior of agents which is in line with our assumptions about real-agents in evacuation scenarios.

3   Local Multi-agent Evacuation (LC-MAE)

Our novel *local multi-agent evacuation* (LC-MAE) algorithm divides the evacuation task into three sub-problems:

- *Evacuation destination selection:* This sub-problem arises from the most important difference between MAE and simple CPF as in MAE agents' destinations/goals are not specified. Hence first we need to specify individual destination vertex for each agent.
- *Path-finding to safety:* Once each agent has picked its destination vertex in S, it has to find a collision-free path to the selected destination. At this stage the task is identical to CPF.
- *Behavior in the safe zone:* Agents that have left D and arrived to their destination vertex do not disappear from the map. We need to ensure that their behavior will not block other agents from entering S.

Agent movement in the last two sub-problems is based on modified versions of WHCA* algorithm, described in their respective sections.

3.1   Evacuation Destination Selection

The basic data structure used by LC-MAE when choosing an evacuation destination vertex is the *frontier* denoted F, $F \subseteq S$. The frontier is a set of safe vertices which separates the endangered zone from the safe zone.

In other words, removing F from G will separate D and S into disconnected components. F is created on algorithm initialization. It holds that an agent must enter S by passing a vertex from F. So the frontier can be constructed as a standard *vertex cut* in a graph [17].

Destination selection uses a modified A* algorithm, inspired by the RRA* algorithm [21]. Agent's position is set as the path-finding goal, while all nodes in F are added to the initial *open set*. *Manhattan distance* [12] is used as the heuristic guiding the search of A*.

The result is a vertex in F that is located at the shortest true distance from the agent while, at the same time, being reachable by the agent. With the vertex at hand, the algorithm returns its true distance from the agent. This matches many real-world evacuation scenarios in which people are being evacuated from an area they know and thus have a mental map of the nearest exits [13].

While evacuating, agents keep track of the number of steps they have taken to reach their destination. Since the goal's true distance from the starting position is known, they can compare these two numbers. If the number of steps taken is significantly higher than the distance, it may indicate the agent has veered off the optimal path. This could be, for example, because the path to the chosen destination is congested. In that case, the agent repeats the destination selection process, an action that we call *retargeting*.

3.2   Reservation Table

In LC-MAE we use a variant of the reservation table used in the Cooperative A* algorithm [21]. Every vertex in G is associated with a mapping of time units to reservation structures. Every reservation structure includes a reference to the reserved vertex, the ID of the agent that created the reservation and a priority.

Associating priority with reservations is our primary distinguishing feature. Agents can make a reservation for vertex v and time step t provided they fulfill one of the following conditions:

1. No reservation exists yet for v at time t and the vertex can be reserved at time $t + 1$.
2. A lower-priority reservation exists for v at time t and the vertex can be reserved at time $t + 1$.
3. The agent holds a reservation for vertex v at $t - 1$.

Condition 3 ensures that CPF algorithms used in LC-MAE can always perform at least one action, staying in place, without having to dynamically change the order in which agents' paths are planned or performing invalid actions, like colliding with another agent.

The $t+1$ reservability requirement in conditions 1 and 2 prevents the creation of so-called *trains* - lines or crowds of agents which move in the same direction at the same time and which reduce the simulation realism. A simple example of a train being formed is shown in the right column of Fig. 3.

3.3   Path-Finding to Safety

Once the agent has picked its destination vertex s in S, it plans a path towards s using WHCA* with the RRA* heuristic. An agent plans the next part of its path on-demand when it has to return an action for the next time step and fulfills any of these conditions:

- Is more than halfway through its planned path[2]
- Has to retarget
- Has lost a reservation for a vertex on its planned path
- Is making its first step

Endangered agents are processed before agents located in S, thus being prioritized relative to agents that are in S. This ensures that endangered agents generate their plans first.

As soon as an agent enters S (even if it is not its current destination vertex), it stops following the planned path and switches to the behavior described in the next section.

3.4   Safe Zone Behavior

While some parts of the behavior of an endangered agent, e.g. on-demand planning for a specified number of steps in advance and reserving the vertices for given times do not change once the agents enters a safe zone, the costs for different actions that WHCA* algorithm considers for each step are different and more dynamic.

The major difficulty in the safe zone is that freshly arriving agents must not impede the ongoing evacuation. A simple approach is to move agents as far from D as possible. However, knowing whether an agent is getting away from D is not a trivial problem from the local point of view.

The behavior agents adopt after entering S in LC-MAE (called *surfing*) is based on modified WHCA* algorithm. Costs for the passage from one vertex to another are computed dynamically, depending on the positions of other agents and the type of the agent's target vertex.

The basic idea is that an agent's priorities should vary according to the number of agents following behind, on the same path. When no other agents are following, it will prefer staying in place. With an increasing number of agents behind, the cost of staying in place also increases.

---

[2] Only using half of the planned path before replanning is a simple way of improving agent cooperation described in [22].

Algorithm 1. The algorithm for computing the number of agents following agent a [18].

```
1  previous-reserved (ℰ, π, a, t)
2  │  let π = [c₀, c₁, ..., cₜ]
3  │  Vₐ ← {c_{t−b}(a) | b = 0, ..., ½}
4  │  for v ∈ Vₐ do
5  │  │  if reserved(v, t) then
6  │  │  └  r ← r + 1
7  │  return r
```

The agent determines the number of following agents by checking whether there are reservations created for positions it has passed before. The process is formalized in pseudo-code as Algorithm 1.

Since agents only make this check when they start planning their next few steps, the results have to be adjusted to account for the increasing uncertainty about the steps that other agents will take. This is done by subtracting the number of future time steps from the number of following agents (see line 11 of Algorithm 2).

Algorithm 2. Computing costs of different actions for agents in the safe zone. Actions are considered relative to agent a located at v at time t. t_c specifies the time at which the plan is generated [18].

```
1   neighbors (ℰ, π, a, t, v, t_c)
2   │  let π = [c₀, c₁, ..., cₜ]
3   │  A_p ← previous-reserved(ℰ,π,a,t_c)
4   │  costs ← []
5   │  foreach u ∈ S | {v, u} ∈ E do
6   │  │  if reservable(u, t + 1)∧u ∈ S then
7   │  │  │  if u ∈ {cₜ(a) | t = 0, 1, ..., t} then
8   │  │  │  └  costs ← costs ∪{(u, 3)}
9   │  │  │  else
10  │  │  │  └  costs ← costs ∪{(u, 2)}
11  │  b ← max(1, |A_p| − (t − t_c))
12  │  if reservable(v, t + 1) then
13  │  └  costs ← costs ∪{(u, 1 * b)}
14  │  else
15  │  └  costs ← costs ∪{(u, 4 * b)}
16  │  return costs
```

The complete cost-calculation algorithm can be found in Algorithm 2. With increasing back-pressure, moving into a reservable adjacent vertex becomes the cheapest option. The agent keeps a list of positions it has already visited and assigns them a higher cost. This leads to better diffusion of agents through S as endangered agents can "nudge" safe agents deeper.

4   Centralized Evacuation Based on Network Flows

Near optimal solutions of MAE can be found by modeling an MAE instance as network flow [1, 26] and planning it centrally.

The core concept is to construct a time expanded network having m copies of G in which a flow of size $|A|$ exists if and only if the corresponding *relaxed MAE* has a solution with makespan m. In the relaxed MAE we do not require that agents only enter vacant vertices which is a condition hard to model in the context of network flows.

Only the requirement that there is at most one agent located on a vertex in a single time unit is kept. Hence train-like movements of agents are possible in the relaxed MAE. The illustration of *train like* movement and corresponding movement following the *move to unoccupied* rule is shown in Fig. 3 possible.

The process of construction of flow network G_m based on time expansion of the underlying graph G for m steps is described as follows:

- We add vertices z and s into G_m representing global source and global sink.
- For each vertex v_j from G we add into G_m vertices i_j^0 and o_j^0 and edge (i_j^0, o_j^0). For each j such that v_j contains an agent we add edge (z, i_j^0) into G_m. Intuitively this construction ensures interconnection with the source.
- For each $t \in 1, \ldots, m-1$ and each vertex v_j from G we add into G_m vertices i_j^t and o_j^t connected by an edge. Moreover for each edge $e = \{v_x, v_y\} \in E$ we add into G_m edges $(o_x^{t-1}, i_y^t), (o_y^{t-1}, i_x^t)$.
- For each o_j^{m-1} such that v_j is a safe vertex in G we add edge (o_j^{m-1}, s) into G_m.
- Set the capacity of every edge in G_m to 1.

Finding the minimum makespan for the relaxed MAE can be done for example by the modified binary search algorithm as shown in Algorithm 3. The algorithm uses multiple yes/no queries about the existence of a solution for a specified number of steps to find the optimum.

A solution of a relaxed MAE problem generated by the network flow algorithms can be post-processed into a solution of ordinary MAE by postponing moves that would violate the invariant of not entering a vertex that has just been left by an agent. However, postponing moves may lead to deadlocks, so the post-processing algorithm swaps the paths planned for deadlocked agents when a deadlock is detected. We're calling this planning algorithm based on post-processed network flows *POST-MAE*; the idea of post processing follows the scheme from Fig. 3.

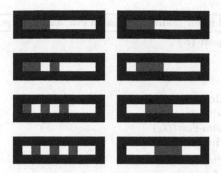

Fig. 3. Movement of agents in ordinary MAE (left) and in relaxed MAE (right) [18].

5   Experimental Evaluation

We implemented LC-MAE in Python and evaluated it in multiple benchmark scenarios. We also implemented the POST-MAE algorithm on top of Push-relabel max-flow algorithm [9] that has been used to find the minimum makespan for the relaxed MAE.

In order to estimate the difference between the makespans of plans generated by LC-MAE and makespans of optimal (if completely unrealistic) plans, we also benchmarked POST-MAE without the post-processing, denoted as *flow* in comparison tables.

Our implementation relies on data structures implemented in the `networkx` library [10]. The visualization is implemented on top of the `arcade` library [5]. In the LC-MAE implementation, the look-ahead window was set to 10 steps.

5.1   Agent Types

To simulate real-life scenarios with higher fidelity we used agents of two types. They differ in their behavior in D, while in S all agents rely on *surfing*. *Retargeting* agents fully implement the destination selection algorithm while *static* agents plan a path to a vertex specified in advance at scenario creation time.

5.2   Setup of Experiments

We used 4 different maps in our evaluations as shown in Fig. 4 - they represent 4-connected grids with obstacles. Free and safe vertices are white (surrounding area), free and endangered vertices are pink. Vertices occupied by agents are green. Black squares signify walls, so no vertices are present in the underlying graph at those positions.

The respective test scenarios try to show evacuation on 3 realistic and 1 synthetic map:

- *Concert* (Fig. 4a) representing a concert hall with an unevenly distributed crowd of 118 agents.

Algorithm 3. Algorithm for finding minimum evacuation time.

```
 1  minimum-makespan (ℰ)
 2      f ← 0
 3      m ← |A|
 4      w_hi ← 0
 5      while f ≠ |A| do
 6          ℰ_e ← expand(ℰ, m)
 7          f ← maximum-flow(G_e)
 8          if f ≠ |A| then
 9              w_hi ← m
10              m ← m * 3/2
11      while true do
12          m_new ← w_hi + ⌊(m − w_hi)/2⌋
13          ℰ_e ← expand(ℰ, m_new)
14          f ← maximum-flow(G_e)
15          if f = |A| then
16              m ← m_new
17              if m = w_hi + 1 then
18                  break
19          else
20              w_hi = m_new
21              if m_new = m − 1 then
22                  break
23      return m
```

- *Office* (Fig. 4c) representing an office building corridor flanked on both sides by small offices. Exits are located on both ends of the corridor. There are 2 agents in each office, the corridor is empty.
- *Shops* (Fig. 4d) representing a shopping center with complicated layout and many exits. 299 agents are present on the map, located both in the shops an on the corridors.
- *Blocker* (Fig. 4b) an unrealistic map of a room with two emergency exits. It's completely filled with 414 agents.

5.3   Experimental Results

We first compared the makespan of evacuation plans generated by LC-MAE with optimal makespans calculated by the flow-based algorithm for relaxed MAE and with makespans of solutions post-processed with POST-MAE - see Table 1. LC-MAE generates plans that are only worse by a small constant factor (ranging from 1.52 to 2.73) than those generated by POST-MAE, which indicates that LC-MAE solutions are close to the true optimal makespan. Moreover, plans generated by LC-MAE are more realistic as they need local communication only.

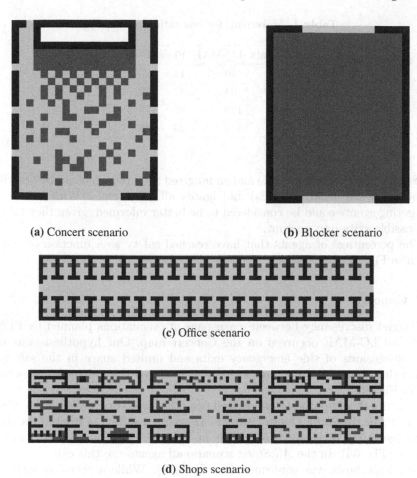

(a) Concert scenario   **(b)** Blocker scenario

(c) Office scenario

(d) Shops scenario

Fig. 4. Maps on which different evacuation scenarios were tested [18].

The performance of LC-MAE is better than the performance of flow algorithm and than that of POST-MAE, as demonstrated in Table 2. An additional advantage is that since LC-MAE is a local algorithm and uses windowing, the plans can be used while they are being generated, since the steps taken by agents do not change.

5.4 Agent-Based Simulations

We also performed a series of experiments to understand the real process of evacuation in scenarios in which various types of agents are mixed together, that is, when some agents are better informed than others.

For each map, we created multiple scenarios with some of the retargeting agents replaced by static agents. These static agents try to exit through the

Table 1. Makespans for evacuation plans [18].

Scenario	Agents	LC-MAE	Flow	POST-MAE
Concert	118	90	17	33
Office	80	94	47	62
Shops	299	129	36	75
Blocker	414	146	23	69

largest opening between the safe and endangered zone (which could be described as the main exit from the area) and ignore all other exits. With this setup, retargeting agents could be considered to be better informed, given they take all the possible exits into account.

The percentage of agents that have reached safety as a function of time is shown in Fig. 5.

5.5   Concert

The largest discrepancy between makespans of evacuations planned by POST-MAE and LC-MAE occurred on the Concert map. Our hypothesis was that small dimensions of side emergency exits and limited space in the safe zone behind them quickly caused congestion and hindered the evacuation, as can be seen in Fig. 6b.

To verify this hypothesis, we created two other scenarios, called *Static Crowd* and *All Static*. In *Static Crowd* there are 42 agents standing in front of the stage. Those agents try to escape through the main exit located on the bottom of the map (see Fig. 6a). In the *All Static* scenario all agents use this exit.

Our hypothesis was confirmed (see Table 3). While a scenario with only retargeting agents has a makespan of 90 time units, when all agents are static, the makespan is only 74 time units. The shortest makespan, 51 time units, occurs in the *Static Crowd* scenario, since informed agents use side exits which don't get congested and free the space in the center of the map for the crowd escaping through the main exit.

5.6   Offices

For the Offices map, we created two modified scenarios, *Half* and *Sixth*. Their names indicate the fraction of agents which was left as retargeting. The rest of the agents is static, using the left exit to evacuate.

In *Sixth*, 14 retargeting agents are located in 7 columns to the right of the map center (see Fig. 7a). We expected the retargeting agents heading right and static agents heading left to collide in the narrow corridor. This expectation was fulfilled. The evacuation of 14 informed agents took 77 time units, only 17 time units less than the evacuation of 80 retargeting agents in the original scenario. Both this collision and the congestion occurring at the left exit impeded the evacuation of static agents, causing their evacuation to take 158 time units. The gap in evacuation flow caused by the collision can be seen in Fig. 7b.

Table 2. Seconds taken by plan generation [18].

Scenario	LC-MAE	Flow	POST-MAE	Speedup
Concert	7	52	62	8.9×
Office	4	57	61	15.3×
Shops	20	379	403	20.2×
Blocker	27	220	243	9.0×

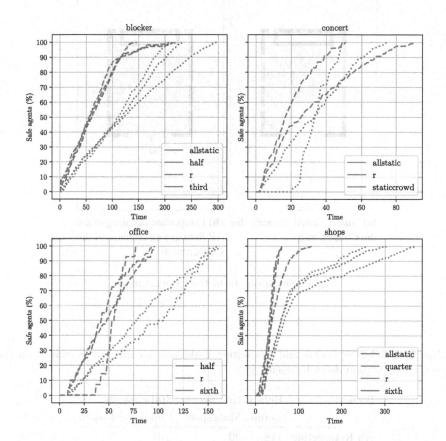

Fig. 5. The percentage of safe agents in time. Line colors differentiate between different scenarios. Dashed lines represent percentage of retargeting agents in S, dotted lines represent the percentage of static agents in S [18].

In *Half*, there was one static and one retargeting agent in each office. In the makespan plot for this scenario, there is a significant slowdown around time unit 60, caused by a crowd forming in front of left exit and making both static and retargeting agents evacuate at the same rate (see Table 4).

5.7 Shopping Center

For the Shopping Center map, we created 3 modified scenarios, called *Quarter*, *Sixth* and *All Static*, named in the same pattern as scenarios for the Offices map. Main exit, used by static agents, is located on the bottom of the map. The different types of agents are distributed randomly throughout the map.

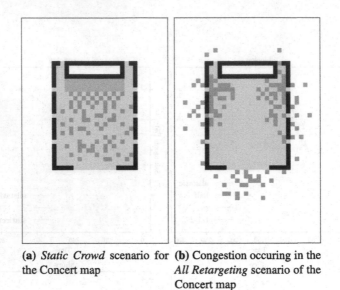

(a) *Static Crowd* scenario for the Concert map

(b) Congestion occuring in the *All Retargeting* scenario of the Concert map

Fig. 6. Situations from the Concert map.

Table 3. Number of agents and evacuation makespan for different scenarios on the Concert map broken down by agent type.

Scenario	Retargeting agents		Static agents	
	Count	Makespan	Count	Makespan
All Retargeting	118	90	0	
Static Crowd	76	51	42	49
All Static	0		118	74

The safe zone around the map is narrow so this scenario tests how the spread of agents between different exits influences the makespan. As can be seen on the plot the evacuation slows down around time unit 90 in all scenarios, because the area in front of the main exit gets filled and agents are not dispersing fast enough. This situation can be seen occurring in *Sixth* scenario in Fig. 8b. Makespan results are summarized in Table 5.

(a) The initial map state

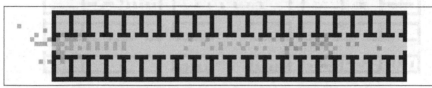

(b) Map state after the collision of retargeting and static agents in the corridor

Fig. 7. The *Sixth* scenario of the Offices map.

Table 4. Number of agents and evacuation makespan for different scenarios on the Offices map broken down by agent type.

Scenario	Retargeting agents		Static agents	
	Count	Makespan	Count	Makespan
All Retargeting	80	94	0	
Half	40	96	40	160
Sixth	14	77	66	158

5.8 Blocking

The Blocking map is specific due to being an unrealistic map used to test agent behavior in a completely filled area. We created 3 modified scenarios, called *Quarter*, *Sixth* and *All Static*, named in the same pattern as scenarios for the Offices map. The exit, used by static agents, is located on the bottom of the map. In each row there is only one type of agents (see Fig. 9a).

Due to map's regularity, the results are unsurprising. The evacuation in *All Static* has a makespan 2.06 times as long as evacuation using both exits (see Table 6). Safe zone saturation effects are similar to the Shopping Center map, being more pronounced for retargeting agents stuck in the crowd in front of the bottom exit.

An interesting situation can be seen in Fig. 9b. Retargeting agents from the upper part of the map choose the upper exit and create reservations for their paths. These reservations block static agents trying to reach the bottom exit. Thus even some of the static agents use the upper exit to get to safety. On the other hand, some of retargeting agents, which get blocked by static agents, use the bottom exit, even though they are closer to the upper one.

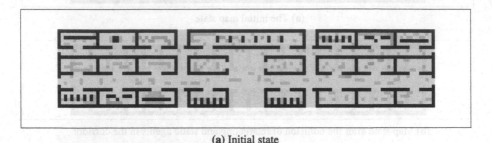

(a) Initial state

(b) Crowding in front of the main exit

Fig. 8. The *Sixth* scenario of the Offices map.

Table 5. Number of agents and evacuation makespan for different scenarios on the Shopping Center map broken down by agent type.

Scenario	Retargeting agents		Static agents	
	Count	Makespan	Count	Makespan
All retargeting	299	129	0	
Quarter	75	61	224	257
Sixth	42	60	257	303
All static	0		299	368

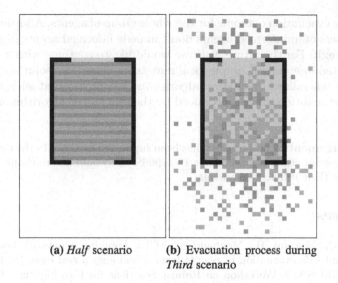

(a) *Half* scenario   (b) Evacuation process during *Third* scenario

Fig. 9. Situations from *Blocking* map.

Table 6. Number of agents and evacuation makespan for different scenarios on the Blocking map broken down by agent type.

Scenario	Retargeting agents		Static agents	
	Count	Makespan	Count	Makespan
All Retargeting	414	146	0	
Half	216	207	198	219
Third	144	214	270	236
All Static	0		414	301

6   Conclusion

We introduced an abstraction for evacuation problems called *multi-agent evacuation* (MAE) based on graph theoretical concepts similar to cooperative path finding. We suggested a new local algorithm called LC-MAE for solving MAE that produces solutions in which individual agents try to behave smartly during the evacuation process. LC-MAE uses a modification of WHCA* as the underlying path-finding process but also introduces several high-level procedures that guide agents' behaviour depending on whether they are in the endangered or the safe zone. We performed experimental evaluation with multiple scenarios including scenarios inspired by real-life evacuation cases as well as synthetic scenarios. The experimental evaluation indicates that LC-MAE generates solutions with makespan that is only a small factor worse than the optimum. We also studied how different ratios of less informed agents affect the process of evacuation. We found that depending on the scenario, the presence of some informed agents can improve the evacuation outcome for the whole group of agents. Additionally, even large numbers of uninformed agents don't impede informed agents from reaching the correct exit. For the future work we would like to continue with a framework for automated inference of simple local movement rules from solutions generated by optimal centralized evacuation algorithms. We expect that such rules could mimic the evacuation process produced by the centralized algorithm at the local level.

Acknowledgements. This research has been supported by GAČR - the Czech Science Foundation, grant registration number 19-17966S. We would like to thank anonymous reviewers for their valuable comments.

References

1. Arbib, C., Muccini, H., Moghaddam, M.T.: Applying a network flow model to quick and safe evacuation of people from a building: a real case. In: Proceedings of the GEOSAFE Workshop on Robust Solutions for Fire Fighting, RSFF 2018, L'Aquila, Italy, 19–20 July 2018, pp. 50–61 (2018)
2. Bompadre, A., Orlin, J.B.: A simple method for improving the primal simplex method for the multicommodity flow problem. Networks **51**(1), 63–77 (2008)
3. Cacchiani, V., Jünger, M., Liers, F., Lodi, A., Schmidt, D.R.: Single-commodity robust network design with finite and hose demand sets. Math. Program. **157**(1), 297–342 (2016)
4. Chalmet, L.G., Francis, R.L., Saunders, P.B.: Network models for building evacuation. Fire Technol. **18**(1), 90–113 (1982)
5. Craven, P.V.: The python arcade library, March 2019. http://arcade.academy
6. Felner, A., et al.: Adding heuristics to conflict-based search for multi-agent path finding. In: Proceedings of the Twenty-Eighth International Conference on Automated Planning and Scheduling, ICAPS 2018, Delft, The Netherlands, 24–29 June 2018, pp. 83–87 (2018)
7. Foudil, C., Djedi, N., Sanza, C., Duthen, Y.: Path finding and collision avoidance in crowd simulation. CIT **17**, 217–228 (2009)
8. Ghallab, M., Nau, D.S., Traverso, P.: Automated Planning and Acting. Cambridge University Press (2016). http://www.cambridge.org/de/academic/subjects/computer-science/artificial-intelligence-and-natural-language-processing/automated-planning-and-acting?format=HB
9. Goldberg, A.V., Tarjan, R.E.: A new approach to the maximum-flow problem. J. ACM **35**(4), 921–940 (1988). https://doi.org/10.1145/48014.61051
10. Hagberg, A.A., Schult, D.A., Swart, P.J.: Exploring network structure, dynamics, and function using networkx. In: Proceedings of the 7th Python in Science Conference, pp. 11–15 (2008)
11. Hudziak, M., Pozniak-Koszalka, I., Koszalka, L., Kasprzak, A.: Comparison of algorithms for multi-agent pathfinding in crowded environment. In: Nguyen, N.T., Trawiński, B., Kosala, R. (eds.) ACIIDS 2015. LNCS (LNAI), vol. 9011, pp. 229–238. Springer, Cham (2015). https://doi.org/10.1007/978-3-319-15702-3_23
12. Korf, R.E., Taylor, L.A.: Finding optimal solutions to the twenty-four puzzle. In: Proceedings of the Thirteenth National Conference on Artificial Intelligence and Eighth Innovative Applications of Artificial Intelligence Conference, AAAI 1996, IAAI 1996, Portland, Oregon, USA, 4–8 August 1996, vol. 2, pp. 1202–1207 (1996)

13. Kurdi, H.A., Al-Megren, S., Althunyan, R., Almulifi, A.: Effect of exit placement on evacuation plans. Eur. J. Oper. Res. **269**(2), 749–759 (2018)
14. Liu, C., li Mao, Z., min Fu, Z.: Emergency evacuation model and algorithm in the building with several exits. Procedia Eng. **135**, 12–18 (2016). 2015 International Conference on Performance-based Fire and Fire Protection Engineering (ICPFFPE 2015)
15. Liu, Z., Wu, B., Lin, H.: Coordinated robot-assisted human crowd evacuation. In: 57th IEEE Conference on Decision and Control, CDC 2018, Miami, FL, USA, 17–19 December 2018, pp. 4481–4486 (2018)
16. Mishra, G., Mazumdar, S., Pal, A.: Improved algorithms for the evacuation route planning problem. In: Lu, Z., Kim, D., Wu, W., Li, W., Du, D.-Z. (eds.) COCOA 2015. LNCS, vol. 9486, pp. 3–19. Springer, Cham (2015). https://doi.org/10.1007/978-3-319-26626-8_1
17. Sánchez-Oro, J., Duarte, A.: An experimental comparison of variable neighborhood search variants for the minimization of the vertex-cut in layout problems. Electron. Not. Discrete Math. **39**, 59–66 (2012)
18. Selvek, R., Surynek, P.: Engineering smart behavior in evacuation planning using local cooperative path finding algorithms and agent-based simulations. In: Proceedings of the 11th International Joint Conference on Knowledge Discovery, Knowledge Engineering and Knowledge Management, IC3K 2019, Volume 2: KEOD, Vienna, Austria, 17–19 September 2019, pp. 137–143 (2019)
19. Sharma, S.: AVATARSIM: a multi-agent system for emergency evacuation simulation. In: 17th International Conference on Software Engineering and Data Engineering (SEDE-2008), 30 June–2 July 2008, Omni Los Angeles Hotel at California Plaza, Los Angeles, California, USA, Proceedings. pp. 163–167 (2008)
20. Shekhar, S., et al.: Experiences with evacuation route planning algorithms. Int. J. Geogr. Inf. Sci. **26**(12), 2253–2265 (2012)
21. Silver, D.: Cooperative pathfinding. In: Young, R.M., Laird, J.E. (eds.) Proceedings of the First Artificial Intelligence and Interactive Digital Entertainment Conference, 1–5 June 2005, Marina del Rey, California, USA, pp. 117–122. AAAI Press (2005)
22. Silver, D.: Cooperative pathfinding. In: AI Game Programming Wisdom, vol. 3 (2006)
23. Surynek, P.: Reduced time-expansion graphs and goal decomposition for solving cooperative path finding sub-optimally. In: IJCAI, pp. 1916–1922 (2015)
24. Surynek, P.: Solving abstract cooperative path-finding in densely populated environments. Comput. Intell. **30**(2), 402–450 (2014)
25. Wang, K., Botea, A.: MAPP: a scalable multi-agent path planning algorithm with tractability and completeness guarantees. JAIR **42**, 55–90 (2011)
26. Yu, J., LaValle, S.M.: Multi-agent path planning and network flow. In: Algorithmic Foundations of Robotics X - Proceedings of the Tenth Workshop on the Algorithmic Foundations of Robotics, WAFR 2012, pp. 157–173 (2012)
27. Yu, J., LaValle, S.M.: Optimal multi-robot path planning on graphs: structure and computational complexity. CoRR abs/1507.03289 (2015). http://arxiv.org/abs/1507.03289

Classification of Tibetan Compounds and Their Modeling in the Formal Grammar and the Computer Ontology

Aleksei Dobrov[1] , Anastasia Dobrova[2] , Maria Smirnova[1]([email]) ,
and Nikolay Soms[2]

[1] Saint-Petersburg State University, Saint-Petersburg, Russia
{a.dobrov,m.o.smirnova}@spbu.ru
[2] LLC "AIIRE", Saint-Petersburg, Russia
{adobrova,nsoms}@aiire.org

Abstract. This article presents the continuation of work on a consistent formal grammatical and ontological description of the model of the Tibetan compounds system, developed and used for automatic syntactic and semantic analysis of Tibetan texts, on the material of a hand-verified corpus. The study of new texts made it possible to develop and correct classes, created for different types of compounds in the formal grammar. New types of compounds were also discovered. In addition, the current research contains the description of the external semantic relations between concepts denoted by compounds components and the overall meaning of a compound.

Keywords: Tibetan language · Compounds · Computer ontology · Tibetan corpus · Natural language processing · Corpus linguistics · Immediate constituents

1 Introduction

The research introduced by this paper is a continuation of several research projects ("The Basic corpus of the Tibetan Classical Language with Russian translation and lexical database", "The Corpus of Indigenous Tibetan Grammar Treatises", "Semantic interpreter of texts in the Tibetan language"), aimed at the development of a full-scale natural language processing (NLP) and understanding (NLU) engine based on a consistent formal model of Tibetan vocabulary, grammar, and semantics, verified by and developed on the basis of a representative and hand-tested corpus of texts.

In Tibetan, there is are no materially expressed boundaries of word forms and, from the point of view of an automatic system, the analysis of compounds is in no way different from the analysis of free combinations of Tibetan morphemes like noun phrases or sentences. Modeling compounds is one of the most important tasks, not only because of the frequency of use of compounds in Tibetan texts is high (at least, as compared with texts in Indo-European languages), but also because without a correct syntactic and semantic model of compounds, a huge ambiguity of Tibetan text segmentation and parsing arises, which leads to a combinatorial explosion [1, p.144].

A. Fred et al. (Eds.): IC3K 2019, CCIS 1297, pp. 322–342, 2020.
https://doi.org/10.1007/978-3-030-66196-0_15

First results achieved in modeling Tibetan compounds were presented in the article "Formal grammatical and ontological modeling of corpus data on Tibetan compounds", prepared for the 11th International Joint Conference on Knowledge Discovery, Knowledge Engineering and Knowledge Management [1]. The article contains the first systematic description of Tibetan compounds, including the description of formal grammar syntactic structure of compounds and methods of their modelling in the computer ontology.

As the study continued, the number of texts in the corpus was increased. For the first time, texts in modern Tibetan language were added. The study of new texts made it possible to develop and correct classes, created for different types of compounds in the formal grammar. New types of compounds were also discovered. In addition, the current research contains the description of the external semantic relations between concepts denoted by compounds components and the overall meaning of a compound.

Thus, the description of Tibetan compounds, presented in this article, was made according to several characteristics taking into account their importance for the tasks of Tibetan NLP: part of speech type, surface syntactic structure, formal grammar syntactic model, internal semantic relations between components of compounds, external semantic relations.

Since the classification was created to meet the needs of Tibetan NLP, the main goal was to create the most complete model of the Tibetan compounds system, which at the same time excludes the ambiguity of morpho-syntactic and semantic analysis.

2 Related Work

Tibetan can reasonably be considered as one of the less-resourced, or even under-resourced languages, in the sense in which this term was introduced in [2] and is widely used now: the presence of Tibetan on the web is limited, it lacks not only electronic resources for language processing, such as corpora, electronic dictionaries, vocabulary lists, etc., but also even such linguistic descriptions as grammars, which could be characterized by at least minimal consistency and validity of linguistic material. The only relatively complete linguistic description of the Tibetan language is the mono-graph by Stephan Beyer [3]. However, this work contains many assumptions that have not been confirmed by any corpus data.

Despite the fact that scholars in different countries are working on the tools for processing Tibetan texts (Germany, Great Britain, China, USA, Japan), still, there is no conventional standard of corpus annotation of Tibetan language material. A number of recent studies were primarily aimed at developing solutions for such stages of Tibetan NLP as word segmentation and part-of-speech tagging. Some researchers use corpus methods within a multidisciplinary approach to solve specific applied problems, as well as tasks in the field of history, literature, linguistics and anthropology (e.g. [4–6]).

Linguistic ontologies in natural language understanding systems are used as ana-logues for the semantic dictionaries that were used before (cf. [7]; [8, 9] etc.); the main difference between an ontology and a conceptual dictionary is that, in a semantic dictionary, semantic valencies are, in fact, postulated, whereas in ontologies, valencies are automatically computed by inference engine subsystems; semantic restrictions are defined not in terms of word lists, but in terms of base classes of ontological concepts (that is the idea behind the mechanism of word-sense disambiguation in [10–13], etc.)

As a formal model, ontology has to predict permissible and exclude impermissible relations between concepts. Despite the clearness and obviousness of these two requirements, there is no generally accepted definition of the term 'ontology' in the scientific literature, which would have reflected them. The most famous and widely cited general definition of the term 'ontology' is 'an explicit specification of a conceptualization' by Gruber [14]. Many different attempts were made to refine it for particular purposes. Without claiming for any changes to this de-facto standard, we have to clarify that, as the majority of researchers in natural language understanding, we mean not just any 'specification of a conceptualization' by this term, but rather a computer ontology, which we define as a database that consists of concepts and relations between them [1, p.145].

Ontological concepts have attributes. Attributes and relations are interconnected: participation of a concept in a relation may be interpreted as its attribute, and vice versa. Relations between concepts are binary and directed.

They can be represented as logical formulae, defined in terms of a calculus, which provides the rules of inference. Relations themselves can be modeled by concepts.

Linguistic ontologies are designed for automatic processing of unstructured natural language texts. Units of linguistic ontologies represent concepts behind meanings of real natural language expressions. Ontologies of this kind actually model linguistic picture of the world that stands for language semantics, as subject domain. Ontologies that are designed for natural language processing are supposed to include relations that allow to perform semantic analysis of texts and to perform lexical and syntactic disambiguation. The ontology, used for this research, was developed according with the above mentioned principles [11]. Its structure is described in detail in the articles [15, 16]. Totally within the framework of this research 4929 concepts were modelled in the ontology.

All Tibetan compounds are created by the juxtaposition of two existing words. Compounds are virtually idiomatized contractions of syntactic groups which have inner syntactic relations frozen and are often characterized by omission of grammatical morphemes [3, p. 102]. E.g., phrase (1) is clipped to (2).

(1) ཕག་པའི་སྣ	(2) ཕག་སྣ
phag-pa 'i sna	*phag-sna*
pig GEN nose	mouth_adornment
'nose of pig'	'snout'

A few attempts were made to classify Tibetan compounds. Depending on part of speech of compound and its components Stephan V. Beyer identifies several models of compound-building in the Tibetan language. The following five models are original Tibetan: noun + noun → noun; noun + adjective → noun; adjective + noun → noun; adjective + adjective → noun; noun + verb → verb [3, p. 103–105]. Stephan V. Beyer also notes that the Tibetan language uses additional devices for compound-building, in part borrowed by Tibetans from Sanskrit within the process of translation: noun + verb → noun; intensifier + verb → verb [3, p. 108–110].

Systematic research of Old Tibetan compounds, based on several approaches, was made by Joanna Bialek. J. Bialek provides a detailed classification of syntactic and semantic structures of compounds based on the Old Tibetan corpus [17].

Both studies are of a descriptive character and therefore can only partially be used for the needs of Tibetan NLP.

3 The Software Tools for Parsing and Formal Grammar Modeling

This study was performed with use of and within the framework of the AIIRE project [10]. AIIRE is a free open-source NLU system, which is developed and distributed in terms of GNU General Public License (http://svn.aiire.org/repos/tproc/trunk/t/). This system implements the full-scale procedure of natural language understanding, from graphematics, through morphological annotation and syntactic parsing, and up to semantic analysis [1, p.146].

The module developed for the Tibetan language is designed taking into account the fact that, since there are no separators between words in Tibetan writing, and morphology and syntax are significantly intermixed, the minimal (atomic) units of modeling (so-called atoms) are morphemes and their allomorphs, not words and their forms; input string segmentation into such units (tokenization) cannot be performed with standard tokenization algorithms, and is therefore performed in AIIRE by means of the Aho-Corasick algorithm (by Alfred V. Aho and Margaret J. Corasick, cf. [18]). This algorithm allows to find all possible substrings of the input string according with a given vocabulary. The algorithm builds a tree, describing a finite state machine with terminal nodes corresponding to completed character strings of elements (in this case, morphemes) from the input dictionary.

The Tibetan language module contains a dictionary of morphemes with their allomorphs, so that this tree can be created in advance at the build stage of the module and just loaded as a shared library in the runtime, which brings its initialization time to minimum. The dictionary of morphemes contains grammatical and morphological attributes (grammemes) for each allomorph; these attributes are mapped into classes of immediate constituents, so that the tree for Aho-Corasick algorithm contains just class and morpheme identifiers for each allomorph and doesn't need to store individual attributes. The module also contains a set of definitions that determines possible types of atoms (atomic units), possible attributes for each type of atom, possible values of each attribute, and restrictions on each attribute value. Both the dictionary of morphemes and the formal grammar are based on these definitions.

Thus, AIIRE first builds all possible hypotheses of recognizing Tibetan atomic units in input strings, including overlapping substrings for separate hypotheses, and then brings them together immediately after they arise into trees of immediate constituents in all possible ways according with the formal grammar, which models the Tibetan morphosyntax. In other words, tokenization and morphosyntactic parsing are carried out simultaneously, so that the ambiguity of tokenization (i.e. the ambiguity of atomic units identification) is partially resolved when building syntactic trees: identification hypotheses are further developed of only those atomic units that can be embedded into syntax trees in accordance with the formal grammar.

This grammar is a combined grammar of immediate constituents and syntactic dependencies, which consists of the so-called classes of immediate constituents (CICs hereinafter). CICs are developed as python-language classes, with the builtin inheritance mechanism enabled, and specify the following attributes: semantic graph template which represents how the meaning of a constituent instance should be calculated from the meanings of its child constituents; lists of possible head and subordinate constituent classes; a dictionary of possible linear orders of the subordinate constituent in relation to the head and the meanings of each order; the possibility of head or subordinate constituent ellipsis; the possibility of non-idiomatic semantic interpretation [1, p.146]. Currently, the formal grammar includes 507 CICs.

The formal grammar is developed in straight accordance with semantics, in a way that the meanings of syntactic and morphosyntactic constituents can be correctly calculated from the meanings of their child constituents in accordance with the Compositionality principle. The procedure of semantic interpretation implies that each constituent is provided with a set of hypotheses of its semantic interpretations; if this set proves to be empty for some hypotheses of constituents, then these hypotheses are discarded; this is how syntactic disambiguation is performed. The hypotheses of semantic interpretations are stored as semantic graphs, i.e. graphs, which have concepts as vertices and relations between them as edges, built by semantic graph templates of CICs in accordance with the underlying ontology.

Thus, AIIRE actually performs simultaneously not only tokenization and morphosyntactic parsing, but also semantic interpretation for each hypothesis of each immediate constituent and, accordingly, of each morphosyntactic tree; impossibility of semantic interpretation of an immediate constituent discards this constituent hypothesis; possibility or impossibility of this semantic interpretation is determined by the semantic graph template of the CIC and the relations involved in this template between the concepts of the ontology, which is also part of the Tibetan language module.

4 The Software Tools for Ontological Modeling

The ontology is implemented within the framework of AIIRE ontology editor software; this software is free and open-source, it is distributed under the terms of GNU General Public License (http://svn.aiire.org/repos/ontology/, http://svn.aiire.org/repos/ontohelper/), and the ontology itself is available as a snapshot at http://svn.aiire.org/repos/tibet/trunk/aiire/lang/ontology/concepts.xml and it is also available for unathorized view or even for edit at http://ontotibet.aiire.org (edit permissions can be obtained by access request).

The ontology, used for this research, is a united consistent classification of concepts behind the meanings of Tibetan linguistic units, including morphemes and idiomatic morphemic complexes. The concepts are interconnected with different semantic relations. These relations allow to perform semantic analysis of texts and lexical and syntactic disambiguation. The basic ontological editor is described with examples from the Tibetan ontology in [15, 16].

Modeling verb (or verbal compound) meanings in the ontology is associated with a number of difficulties. First of all, the classification of concepts denoted by verbs should be made in accordance with several classification attributes in the same time, which arise primarily due to the structure of the corresponding classes of situations that determine the semantic valencies of these verbs. These classification attributes are, in addition to the semantic properties themselves (such as dynamic /static process), the semantic classes of all potential actants and circumstants, each of which represents an independent classification attribute. With the simultaneous operation of several classification attributes, the ontology requires classes for all possible combinations of these attributes and their values in the general class hierarchy. Special tools were created to speed up and partly automate verbal concepts modeling. AIIRE Ontohelper is used together with the main AIIRE ontology editor web interface to build the whole hierarchy of superclasses for any verb meaning in the ontology. The structure and operation of the Ontohelper editor are described in detail in [1, p. 147].

5 Classification of Tibetan Compounds and Their Modeling in the Formal Grammar and the Computer Ontology

Depending on the part of speech classification, nominal and verbal compounds can be distinguished. Initially, the ontology allowed binding concepts to expressions with marking the expression as an idiom and establishing a separate type of token, common for nominal compounds. Since a large number of combinatorial explosions were caused by the incorrect versions of compounds parsing (the same sequence of morphemes can be parsed as compounds of different types) and their interpretation as noun phrases of different types, it was decided to expand the number of token types in the ontology according to identified types of nominal and verbal compounds (see below).

As all Tibetan compounds are idioms, in AIIRE ontology, in addition to the meanings of a compound, meanings of its components are also modeled, so that they could be interpreted in their literal meanings too. This is necessary, because AIIRE natural language processor is designed to perform natural language understanding according with the compositionality principle [19], and idiomaticity is treated not merely as a property of a linguistic unit, but rather as a property of its meaning, namely, as a conventional substitution of a complex (literal) meaning with a single holistic (idiomatic) concept [16, pp. 78–79].

The use of computer ontology allows not only to model correct semantic relations between the components of a compound, but also to model the relations between the components and the overall meaning of a compound. Thus, compounds are characterized simultaneously from two semantic perspectives.

According to basic syntactic relation between the components Tibetan nominal and verbal compounds may be divided into two main classes: compounds with subordinate relations and compounds with coordinate relations (Grokhovskii, Smirnova, 2017, p. 137).

5.1 Nominal Compounds

Nominal Compounds Modeling in the Formal Grammar and the Computer Ontology. Depending on the syntactic model of the compound derivation, the following types were distinguished for nominal compounds with coordinate relations between components: compound noun root group (CompoundNRootGroup); compound attribute group (CompoundAttrGroup); adjunct compound (AdjunctCompound); named entity compound (NamedEntityCompound); and for nominal compounds with subordinate relations between compounds: noun phrase with genitive compound (NPGenCompound); compound class noun phrase (CompoundClassNP).

Coordinate Nominal Compounds. Compound noun root group (3) consists of a nominal component, being the head class, and CompoundNRootGroupArg, attached as a subordinate constituent. The linear order of the subordinate constituent in relation to the head is right. CompoundNRootGroupArg stands for compound argument that consists of a nominal component attached with an intersyllabic delimiter – upper dots (Tib. tshegs). The linear order of the CompoundNRootGroupArg subordinate constituent in relation to the head is left. The syntactic graph for CompoundNRootGroup (3) is presented in Fig. 1.

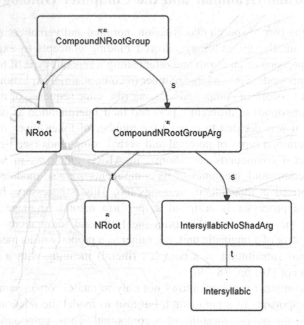

Fig. 1. The syntactic graph for CompoundNRootGroup *pha-ma* 'parents'.

The possible nominal components in both CompoundNRootGroup and CompoundNRootGroupArg include NRoot (nominal root), NForeign (foreign noun and CompoundAtomicVN. CompoundAtomicVN stands for compound atomic nominalized verb within a compound (the nominalizer in compounds is always omitted, thus, the nominalized verb form superficially comprises the verb root only).

CompoundNRootGroup, consisting of two noun roots like in (3) is the most common case. In (4) CompoundAtomicVN is the head class, while in (5) it belongs to the argument class. The example (6) represents CompoundNRootGroup that consists of two foreign nouns.

(3) ཕ་མ་
pha-ma
mother_father
'parents'

(4) འགོག་ལམ་
'gog-lam
cease-path
'cessation and path'

(5) རྩ་འགྲེལ་
rtsa-'grel
root_comment
'root text and commentary'

(6) ཀ་ལི་ཀཱ་ལི་
A-li-kA-li
vowel_consonant
'vowels and consonants'

Heads and arguments of all Tibetan compounds can not be ellipsed. For all compounds the setting 'only_idiom = True' was also made. According to this setting any non-idiomatic interpretations of a compound are excluded.

This type of compounds does not require establishment of any semantic relations in the computer ontology for their components. It is enough that the meaning of the compound and its components are modeled in the ontology, and that the general coordination mechanism is also modeled in the module for syntactic semantics (the meaning of a coordinate phrase is calculated as an instance of 'group' concept which involves 'to include' relations to its elements).

Compound attribute groups also belong to coordinate semantic type. It is a group of superficially homogeneous attributes within a compound. This way of derivation is quite frequent for Tibetan personal names (the name consists of a set of epithets (attributes), without any explicit noun) and for words, denoting size (e.g. (7)). CompoundAttrGroup consists of CompoundAtomicAttributeTopic and CompoundAttrCoord, where the first part is the first attribute or group of attributes and the second part is the last attribute attached as a subordinate constituent. If there are more than two attributes, they are attached in exactly the same way with CompoundAttrGroup self-embedding. The morphosyntactic structure of compounds of this type is described in detail in (Dobrov, Dobrova, Grokhovskiy, Soms, 2017).

Another class of Tibetan nominal compounds is Adjunct compound (e.g. (8)). Compounds of this class are derived from regular noun phrases with adjuncts. Thus, the head class for this CIC is NRoot; and the argument class is CompoundRightNRootArg, consisting of a noun root and the intersyllabic delimiter. It is necessary that the components of the compound belong to the same basic class in the ontology, or that there is no limitation on their equivalence relations (the classes of the concepts should not be disjoint).

(7) རིང་ཐུང
ring-thung
long_short
'length'

(8) རྦ་རླབས
rba-rlabs
wrinkle_swelling
'water wave'

Finally, there is also such class of nominal compounds as NamedEntityCompound that can be considered as a subtype of compound with adjunct. In a broader sense named entity compounds include all compounds where the first component denote an instance from the class, that is specified by the second component like in (9). However to prevent morpho-syntactic ambiguity cases like (9) are considered to be compounds with adjuncts. The NamedEntityCompound CIC was introduced only for combinations of letters or exponents of arbitrary Tibetan morphemes (corresponding classes Letter and Exponent being the head components) with NRoot like in (10).

(9) བོད་ཡུལ
bod-yul
'the country Tibet'

(10) ལ་སྒྲ
la-sgra
la_marker
'grammatical marker *la*'

The NamedEntityCompound CIC is a subclass of named-entity nomination, where the name of the entity is a letter or an exponent of any Tibetan morpheme. Thus, semantic restrictions are imposed on the possible classes of the subordinate constituent concepts, due to the fact that only linguistic units can have such names according with the ontology (there is a corresponding relation between the 'linguistic unit' and 'linguistic unit exponent' concepts).

Subordinate Nominal Compounds. NPGenCompound is a frequent class of Tibetan nominal compounds. These compounds are derived from noun phrases with genitive arguments by omission of the genitive case marker. In accordance with the current grammar version, the head constituents of NPGenCompound can be CompoundAtomicNP, NForeign, PlaceNameForeign, LetterCnt (countable letter), PDefRoot, PIntRoot; the subordinate constituent class can only be NPGenCompoundArg. The linear order of the subordinate constituent in relation to the head is right.

CompoundAtomicNP means atomic nominal phrase within a compound. PlaceNameForeign (foreign place name) was allowed to be the head in NPGenCompound for such cases as e.g. (11). PDefRoot (definitive pronoun) and PIntRoot (indefinite pronoun) were included into possible head classes for such combinations as e.g. (13).

There are cases when one of the components of a compound is itself a compound like in (11) (*mi-rigs* 'nationality' is a genitive compound clipped from a regular genitive nominal phrase (12)). Such cases of compounds with complex structure are discussed in the paragraph 5.3.

(11) ষི་ঁ্ব་ঁ་ঁ་ঁ   (12) ঁ্ঁ་ঁ   (13) གঁর་ঁঁ

si-khron-mi-rigs   *mi 'i rigs*   *gzhan-dbang*

Sichuan-nationality   human GEN class   other-power

'Sichuan people'   'class of people'   'dependent connector'

The CIC NPGenCompoundArg stands for a genitive compound argument that consists of the head immediate constituent, attached with the intersyllabic delimiter (argument immediate constituent) on the left. Head classes of NPGenCompoundArg include: CompoundAtomicVNNoTenseNoMood, IndepNRoot, OnlyCompoundNRoot, NForeign, PersNameForeign (personal name foreign), CompoundAtomicVN. CompoundAtomicVNoTenseNoMood is a CompoundAtomicVN which does not have neither mood, nor tense. As in this case, Tibetan verb roots often do not have different allomorphs for different moods and tenses.

IndepNRoot (independent noun root) is a noun root (allomorph of a noun root), which can be used both within a compound and in free combinations.

OnlyCompoundNRoot stands for a noun root (allomorph of a noun root), which can be used only within a compound. The necessity to create such a class was connected with morphological changes of different kind within compounds. For example, this class includes noun roots that are single-syllabic clips of multisyllabic roots (e.g. *yi-ge* > *yig* 'grapheme').

The relation between NPGenCompound components is subordinate genitive relation. When modeling compounds of this type in the computer ontology, it is necessary to establish specific subclasses of the general genitive relation 'to have any object or process (about any object or process)' between basic classes of compound components. For example, NPGenCompound (14) was formed from the genitive nominal group (15). Thus, the concept 'geographical object' (the basic class for the first component of the compound (14) – *yul* 'area') had to be connected with the concept *skad* 'language', which is a basic class itself, with a relation 'to have a language (about any geographical object)', which is a subclass of the general genitive relation.

(14) ঁঁར་ঁ   (15) ঁঁར་ঁ་ঁ

yul-skad   yul gyi skad

area_language   area GEN language

'dialect'   'local language'

By the moment the class for the general genitive relation 'to have any object or process (about any object or process)' includes the following subclasses: 'to have any object (about anyone)' (17 hyponyms), 'to have any object (about any object)' (72 hyponyms), 'to have any object (about any object or process)' (26 hyponyms). Thus, 115 subclasses of the general genitive relation were created in the ontology.

Another frequent class of Tibetan nominal compounds is CompoundClassNP (16). Compounds of this type are derived from regular noun phrases with adjectival or, more often, quasi-participial (there are no participles in the Tibetan language, but rather nominalized verbs that can act both as participles and as processual nouns) attributes. Possible head classes for the CIC CompoundClassNP are IndepNRoot, OnlyCompoundNRoot, NForeign, PersNameForeign (foreign personal name), PlaceNameForeign, LetterCnt. Its modifier class can be CompoundAtomicAttribute, CompoundAtomicAttributeNoTense, CompoundAtomicAttributeNoTenseNoMood. CompoundAtomicAttribute consists of a state verb, denoting an object feature (the head class), attached by the intersyllabic delimiter (argument class) on the left. For example, CompoundClassNP (16) has the head class IndepNRoot *glang* 'ox' and the modifier class CompoundAtomicAttributeNoTenseNoMood, consisting of the intersyllabic delimiter attached on the left to the verb *chen* 'be big' which does not have neither mood, nor tense.

The only requirement for modeling compounds of this type in the ontology is that the basic class of a nominal component in a compound must be a subclass of the specified verb subject (for the verbal component of the compound). I.e., the verb, from which the attribute is derived, must allow this subject by its valencies.

Finally, there are subject compounds (SubjectCompound) that represent combination of subjects and predicates like in (17).

(16) ग्लन्-ཆेन་
glang-chen
ox_be_big
'elephant'

(17) ཀུན་དགའ་
kun-dga'
all-like
'rejoicing'

Possible head classes for the CIC SubjectCompound are NRoot, PDefRoot, CompoundAtomicVN, CompoundAtomicVNNoTense and CompoundAtomicVNNoTenseNoMood. Its modifier class is CompoundPredicate that consists of a verbal root (VRoot), transformative verbal phrase within a compound (CompoundTransformativeVP), attached by the intersyllabic delimiter (argument class) on the left.

CompoundTransformativeVP is a contraction of a regular Tibetan transformative verb phrase, i.e., a verb phrase with terminative object. As the corpus shows, compound transformative verb phrases can themselves be parts of compound transitive verb phrases, i.e., the complete compound can be a contraction of a verb phrase both with terminative and absolutive objects.

To model the semantic structure of SubjectCompounds in the computer ontology, it is necessary that the concept of the nominal component be a subclass of the basic class specified as a subject class for the concept of the verbal component of the compound.

Thus, some coordinate and subordinate nominal compounds have exactly the same surface structures. For example, compounds of three upper-mentioned classes: NRootGroupCompound, NPGenCompound, and AndjuctCompound can be combinations of two bare noun roots, but they have completely different syntactic structures and completely different internal semantic models (relations between their components). As all compounds are modeled as idioms, when binding ontology concepts, that they denote, to Tibetan language units, it is necessary to specify the syntactic class (type of token) for each concept and to make the natural language processing engine exclude all other possible parses thereof.

External Semantic Relations of Nominal Compounds. The classification of compounds from several perspectives proposed in this research is arranged in such a way that the syntactic structure of a compound determines possible semantic relations between compound's components and its overall meaning.

Understanding the specific of external semantic relations is necessary when modelling concepts denoted by compounds in the computer ontology. In order to create a new concept in the ontology, it is compulsory to incorporate this concept into the general classification hierarchy according with the class-superclass relations (hypo/hypernymy), therefore the whole ontology has the one common superclass. Even at initial stages of work the development of the ontology for the Tibetan language showed that Tibetan compounds reflects special features of Tibetan lexical semantics. Thus, the ontology can be considered as a formalized representation of the real-world knowledge as expressed in the Tibetan lexicon and grammar.

Components of CompoundNRootGroup either form a new meaning or provide a copulative meaning. In the second case components inherit the basic class 'group of objects or processes' in the computer ontology. Components of copulative compounds can have the same hypernym (18) or correspond to different basic classes (19). In some cases the same CompoundNRootGroup (20) can denote a group of elements (20.1) or form a new concept (20.2).

(18) ᨠᨠᨠ
ming-tshig
word-phrase
'words and phrases'

(19) ᨠᨠᨠ
tshig-don
word-meaning
'word and its meaning'

(20) ᨠᨠᨠ
gser-dngul
gold-silver
(20.1) 'gold and silver'
(20.2) 'expenses'

It should be noted that despite the fact that components of such copulative compounds as (21) or (22) have opposite meanings they are also co-hypernymic in the ontology as they have common basic classes in the concepts hierarchy – *cha* 'part' (for (21.1)) or *dus* 'time' (for (21.2)) and *kha-mdog* 'color' (for (22)) respectively.

(21) ᨠᨠ
snga-phyi
previous-subsequent
(21.1) 'previous and subsequent part'
(21.2) 'previous and subsequent period'

(22) ᨠᨠᨠ
dkar-nag
white-black
'white and black'

Compound attribute groups usually denote characteristic (quality) of an object like (7), while their components denote attributes (*ring-po* 'long, having a great length', *thung-thung* 'short, having a short length'). The compound (7) and its components are connected with the corresponding relations in the computer ontology – 'to be a size of any object (about length)' and the inverse one 'to have a length (about any object)' (see Fig. 2).

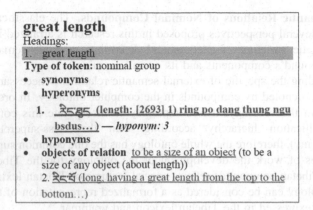

great length
Headings:
1. great length
Type of token: nominal group
*   **synonyms**
*   **hyperonyms**
    1.   རིང་ཚད་ (length: [2693] 1) **ring po dang thung ngu bsdus...**) — *hyponym: 3*
*   **hyponyms**
*   **objects of relation** to be a size of an object (to be a size of any object (about length))
    2. རིང་པོ (long, having a great length from the top to the bottom...)

Fig. 2. The interrelation of the compound *ring-thung* 'length' and its component *ring-po* 'long' in the computer ontology.

In adjunct compounds one or both components can act a generic term to the concept, expressed by a compound. For example both components of (8) – *rba* and *rlabs* have a similar meaning 'wrinkle, swelling'. In named entity compounds the second component always denotes a generic term in relation to the first component and to the compound itself.

Despite a variety of possible semantic relations between components of genitive compounds (possession, participation in an action as an agent or patient, characteristic in relation to another object (material), place or time, the second component of NPGenCompounds most often denotes a generic concept in relation to the overall meaning of a compound like in (9), (11) and (14).

The second component can mean 'type, class' (Tib. rigs, rnam, phyogs, sna) or 'group' (Tib. tshan) of objects. In such cases a compound can also provide either a copulative meaning for e.g. (23), or form a new meaning like (24).

The use of certain nouns as second component of nominal compound words corresponds to the stable word-formation models described by S. Beyer: for example, *sa* 'place' in (25) (Beyer, 1992, p. 129). The status of other words acting in a similar role requires further study.

(23) འབྲུ་སྣ	(24) རྒྱལ་རིགས	(25) ལྷ་ས
'bru-sna	*rgyal-rigs*	*lha-sa*
grain-type	conquer-type	god-place
'grain crops'	'warrior caste'	'Lhasa'

In CompoundClassNP the first component most likely denotes a generic term in relation to compound like in (26); or a compound and its first component are co-hypernymic (16).

(26) གོས་ཧྲུལ   (27) མཁའ་ནོར
gos-hrul   *mkha'-nor*
clothes-tattered   sky-jewel
'ragged clothes'   'sun'

Despite the fact that components of compounds are not always indicated as their direct hypernyms in the computer ontology, nevertheless they often reflect features of the Tibetan naive or proto-scientific picture of the world. The same holds for cases when relation between compound and its components is metaphorical (for e.g. NPGenCompound (28), which literal means 'jewel of the sky').

5.2   Verbal Compounds

Verbal Compounds Modeling in the Formal Grammar and the Computer Ontology. Depending on the syntactic model of the compound derivation, the following types were distinguished for verbal compounds: verb coordinate compound (VerbCoordCompound); compound transitive verb phrase (CompoundTransitiveVP); compound atomic verbal phrase with circumstance (CompoundAtomicVPWithCirc) and compound associative verb phrase (CompoundAssociativeVP). In fact, each of these types is represented by three types in the current grammar version – verbal compound, which varies tense and mood (e.g. CompoundTransitiveVP); verbal compound, which varies only in mood (e.g. CompoundTransitiveVPNoTense); and verbal compound, which doesn't vary in tense and mood (e.g. CompoundTransitiveVPNoTenseNoMood). Verbal compounds like other verbs are processed using the Ontohelper editor.

As it appears from the name only verb coordinate compounds (e.g. 28) belong to the coordinate type. These compounds are contractions of regular coordinate verb phrases with conjunctions omitted. VerbCoordCompound consists of VRoot, being the head of VerbCoordCompound, and VerbCompoundCoord that stands for the second verb (VRoot being the head of VerbCompoundCoord) with the intersyllabic delimiter. Modeling a verb coordinate compound meaning does not require establishing any special semantic relations in the computer ontology, because the upper-mentioned general coordination meaning evaluation is involved.

In compound transitive verb phrase (29), the first nominal component is a direct object of the second verbal component. The head class of CompoundTransitiveVP can be VRoot or CompoundTransformativeVP. The arguments include CompoundInstanceNPArg and CompoundAtomicVNArg. The linear order of the subordinate constituent in relation to the head is left.

Heads of CompoundInstanceNPArg, that is a noun phrase argument within a compound, are IndepNRoot, OnlyCompoundNRoot, PIndRoot and PIntRoot. The argument class is represented by the intersyllabic delimiter.

CompoundAtomicVNArg stands for a compound argument that consists of CompoundAtomicVN, CompoundAtomicVNNoTense, CompoundAtomicVNNoTenseNoMood being head classes, and intersyllabic delimiter argument.

To ensure the correct analysis of compounds of this type, it is necessary that the concept of the nominal component of the compound be a subclass of the basic class specified as a direct object class for the concept of the verbal component of the compound. E.g., the literal meaning of the compound (29) is 'to fasten help'. The class 'any object or process', which includes the concept *phan-pa* 'help', was specified as a direct object for the verb *'dogs* 'to fasten'.

(28) སངས་རྒྱས

sangs-rgyas

be_purified_be_broaden

'awaken and broaden'

(29) ཕན་འདོགས

phan-'dogs

help_fasten

'assist'

The CIC CompoundAtomicVPWithCirc was made for a combination of CompoundAtomicVP (verbal phrase within a compound represented by a single verb root morpheme – the head class) and the modifier – CompoundCircumstance, attached on the left.

Initially CompoundCircumstance stood for a terminative noun phrase within a compound attached with an intersyllabic delimiter. However since circumstances can be expressed by function words of different case meanings (for e.g. terminative in (30), ablative in (31) and ergative in (32)), a common class was created for all of them – CompoundAtomicUnknownCaseNP, where all atomic nominal phrases were embedded.

(30) རྣམ་དབྱེ

rnam-dbye

type_divide

'divide into classes'

(31) མྱང་འདས

myang-'das

suffer-go_beyond

'reach nirvana'

(32) དབང་ཕྱུག

dbang-phyug

power-be_rich

'be rich in power'

The relation 'to have a manner of action or state' was indicated as a hypernym for all case meanings of nominal phrases from which compounds with circumstance are formed. The basic class of the nominal component should be connected by the relation 'to be a relationship object' with this relation 'to have a manner of action or state'. Thus, for the compound (30), this relation was established on the basic class of its nominal component *rnam-pa* 'type' – 'any category'.

The texts, as a rule, use the idiomatized nominalized forms of verbal compounds with the omission of the syllabic formative *–pa* (a nominalizer). Thus, the nominalized form of the verbal compound *rnam-dbye* denotes a grammatical term 'case'. In this regard, in addition to verbal compounds (30), (31), (32), their full nominal forms (33), (34) and (35) respectively are also processed in the computer ontology.

(33) རྣམ་པར་དབྱེ་བ
rnam-pa r dbye-ba
type LOC divide-NMLZ

'case'

(34) མྱ་ངན་ལས་འདས་པ
mya-ngan-las-'das-pa
suffering ABL
go_beyond-NMLZ

'nirvana'

(35) དབང་གིས་ཕྱུག་པ
dbang-gis-phyug-pa
power ERG
be_rich-NMLZ

'lord'

CompoundAssociativeVP is another class of Tibetan verbal compounds which was introduced for contractions of regular associative verb phrases. It consists of the associative verb (the head class) and its indirect object (possible arguments being CompoundInstanceNPArg, CompoundAtomicVNArg).

Thus, the first component of the compound (36) *lhag-ma* 'remainder' should belong to the class of associative objects specified for the verb *bcas* 'to possess' in the Ontohelper editor. Full idiomatized nominal form of this compound (37) is also modeled in the computer ontology.

(36) ལྷག་བཅས
lhag-bcas
remainder_possess
'have a continuation'

(37) ལྷག་མ་དང་བཅས་པ
lhag-ma dang bcas-pa
remainder ASS possess-NMLZ
'continuative'

External Semantic Relations of Verbal Compounds. In most cases, the direct hypernym of verbal compounds is the concept expressed by their verbal component. For example, verbal compounds (38) and (39) have the same hypernym, that is their verbal component *'chad* 'explain'.

(38) གོང་བཤད
gong-bshad
top_explain
'explain above'

(39) རྣམ་བཤད
rnam-bshad
type_explain
'explain completely'

In other cases, there is no class-superclass relation between the meaning of the verbal compound and the verb from which it is derived. However, their type and valency are always the same.

Moreover, it was revealed that such grammatical features of Tibetan verb compounds as transitivity, transformativity, dativity, and associativity are always inherited from the main verb, even when the corresponding syntactic valency seems to be fulfilled within the compound.

5.3 Compounds with Complex Structure

Compound as Component. Typically Tibetan compounds consists of two syllables. However there are cases when one of the components of a compound is itself a compound. For example, in the noun phrase with genitive compound (40) the head class is also a noun phrase with genitive compound (41).

(40) དཔེ་མཛོད་ཁང་
dpe-mdzod-khang
book-repository-house
'library'

(41) དཔེ་མཛོད་
dpe-mdzod
book-store
'book repository'

There are also complex structures with both components being compounds. Most often, such compounds belong to modern vocabulary (42), scientific or religious-philosophical terms (45). For example, the genitive compound (42) consists of two genitive compounds – (43) and (44).

(42) བཙན་དབང་རིང་ལུགས
btsan-dbang-ring-lugs
tyranny-tradition
'imperialism'

(43) བཙན་དབང་
btsan-dbang
violence-power
'tyranny'

(44) རིང་ལུགས
ring-lugs
be_long-tradition
'tradition'

The genitive compound (45) unites named entity compound (46) and genitive compound (47).

(45) ལ་དོན་འཇུག་ཡུལ
la-don-'jug-yul
la_equivalent-place_of_use
'place of use of la-equivalent'

(46) ལ་དོན
la-don
la-meaning
'grammatical marker with the same
meanings that la'

(47) འཇུག་ཡུལ
'jug-yul
place-apply
'place of use'

In poetic texts of the corpus even more complex structures were discovered. In the first Tibetan grammatical treatises Sum-cu-pa (VII c.), we find five verbal roots following each other without any grammatical markers between them (48).

(48) སྡེབ་སྦྱོར་ལེགས་མཛད་མཁས་རྣམས
sdeb sbyor legs mdzad mkhas rnams
poetry be_good do be_skilled-PL

Only the last verb takes the plural marker and thus can be treated as a case of zero nominalization. Relying on the context and several most authoritative commentaries on the grammar this passage can be read in the following way:

(49) སྡེབ་པར་སྦྱོར་བ་ལེགས་པར་མཛད་པའི་མཁས་པ
sdeb [pa r] sbyor-[ba] legs-[pa r] mdzad-[pa 'i] mkhas [pa]
composite-NMLZ TERM join-NMLZ be_good-NMLZ TERM do-NMLZ GEN
be_skilled-NMLZ
'[those who are] skilled in good making joining [of words] for composition'

First four verbs in this passage are obviously in subordinate syntactic relations of different types with the omission of various grammatical markers. Omission of grammatical markers here may be considered acceptable in a poetic text. However, changing the whole formal grammar to ensure correct syntactic parsing of this passage will inevitably cause combinatorial explosions. In this regard, it was decided to model the whole passage as a compound.

According to the created model of Tibetan compounds and reconstructed syntactic relations it is possible to consider *sdeb-sbyor* and *legs-mdzad* as compound atomic verbal phrases with circumstance.

Syntactic relations between *sdeb-sbyor* 'poetry' and *legs-mdzad* 'to do well' are the same as in compound transitive verb phrases, where the first nominal component is a direct object of the second verbal component. Such cases, where both components are compounds, are not common so it was decided not to change immediate constituents of the CICs CompoundTransitiveVP, but to create separate class. Thus for compounds transitive verb phrases with complex structure the CIC CompoundGroupTransitiveVPNoTense was created.

The syntactic relations between *sdeb-sbyor-legs-mdzad* and *mkhas-pa* are the same as those between the components of noun phrase with genitive compounds. Thus, the CompoundGroupTransitiveVPNoTense was added as the head class to the CIC NPGenCompound.

We hope that adding new texts to the corpus and discovering new types of compounds with complex structure will confirm or deny their status and help to determine better way to develop the formal grammar (create separate CIC classes for such compounds or add them as constituents to existing ones) to avoid morpho-syntactic ambiguity.

Personal Names. The vast majority of Tibetan personal names consist of disyllabic terms, including compounds. Such terms usually denote auspicious objects or divine names [3, p. 374]. The corpus, used for this research, contains four-syllable religious and secular names that consist either of two compounds or a compound and disyllabic nominal root.

If between components of a name there is no syntactic relations there are modelled as compound names (CompoundName) in the computer ontology. The components of CompoundName can include compounds, nominal roots and foreign personal names.

For example, the compound name of the Tibetan author of grammatical works *skal-bzang 'gyur-med* consists of two compounds: CompoundClassNP (50) and SubjectCompound (51).

(50) སྐལ་བཟང	(51) འགྱུར་མེད
skal-bzang	*'gyur-med*
fate-be_good	change-not_have
'good fate'	'unchanged'

The literal meanings of both compounds should be modeled in the ontology using the methods described above. In addition, a separate concept must also be created for each of compound; and the class *ming* 'name' should be specified as its hypernym.

Two concepts with different token types are also created for the full name. The first is marked as 'person designation' and the corresponding hypernym is selected. The second is marked as 'compound name' and the concept *ming* 'name' is specified as its hypernym. The concept 'any creature' is connected with this class by establishing a subclass of the general genitive relation 'to have a name (about any creature)'.

Multi-type Compounds. The same Tibetan compound may have different morphosyntactic structures for different meanings. Thus, the compound *sgra-don* is a clip of two different phrases – (52) and (53).

(52) སྒྲའི་དོན་
sgra 'i don
sound GEN meaning
'meaning of sound'

(53) སྒྲ་དང་དོན་
sgra dang don
sound CONJ meaning
'sound and its meaning'

Thus, the correct type of token in the first case is NPGenCompound, and in the second one – CompoundNRootGroup. These cases are represented in the ontology as different concepts of the same expression.

Compounds with Negation. Negation in the Tibetan language is expressed by the negative particle *mI* (the allomorph *mi* is used before the present and future stems of the verb, while the allomorph *ma* is occurred before the past tense and imperative stems), that can precede only verbs. There are two possible contractions of the negative particle and verbs. The equative verb *yin* 'to be' may optionally be contracted to *min* 'is not' in addition to *ma-yin* 'is not'. In addition, the verb *yod* 'to exist' is used in negated form only as *med* 'not exist' [3, p.242].

In the corpus two cases of negation within compounds of different types were discovered. In the first case it is a verb with negation as a head class of the NPGenCompound, which denotes Tibetan grammatical term (54). This compound has the complex structure as its argument includes another NPGenCompound (55). In the second case we see contraction of the equative verb *yin* 'to be' and the negation particle that enters the argument constituent of the SubjectCompound (56).

(54) མི་མཐུན་ཚིག་རྒྱན་
mi-mthun-tshig-rgyan
NEG-correspond-
decoration_of_phrases
'unconformable decoration
of phrases '

(55) ཚིག་རྒྱན་
tshig-rgyan
phrase-decoration
'decoration of phrases'

(56) འོག་མིན་
'og-min
lower_part-not_exist
'Pure land'

According to the current grammar version contractions of the negative particle and verbs are parsed as verbal roots. Thus, as VRoot is already embedded in SubjectCompounds possible constituents the parsing is correct. As for cases like (54) the class VRootImperfNegNoTenseNoMood was embedded in the possible head classes of genitive compounds.

6 Conclusions and Further Work

The current results of the formal grammatical and ontological modeling of Tibetan compounds presented in this article represent the first of its kind consistent systematic formal description of this material that is used to solve tasks of the Tibetan language module of a working automatic text processing system. Thus it is verified by analyzing the results of the automatic syntactic and semantic annotation of the corpus of texts. The work on the development of a full-scale Tibetan NLP and NLU engine will be continued, that help to develop the classification of Tibetan compounds and to create the most complete model of the Tibetan compounds system, which at the same time excludes the ambiguity of morpho-syntactic and semantic analysis.

Acknowledgment. This work was supported by the Russian Foundation for Basic Research, Grant No. 19-012-00616 Semantic interpreter of texts in the Tibetan language.

References

1. Dobrov, A., Dobrova, A., Smirnova, M., Soms, N.: Formal grammatical and ontological modeling of corpus data on Tibetan compounds. In: Proceedings of the 11th International Joint Conference on Knowledge Discovery, Knowledge Engineering and Knowledge Management, vol. 2, pp. 144–153. KEOD (2019). ISBN 978-989-758-382-7. https://doi.org/10.5220/0008162401440153
2. Berment, V.: Méthodes pour informatiser des langues et des groupes de langues peu dotées. Ph.D Thesis, J. Fourier University – Grenoble I (2004)
3. Beyer, S.: The Classical Tibetan Language. State University of New York, New York (1992)
4. Wagner, A., Zeisler, B.A.: syntactically annotated corpus of Tibetan. In: Proceedings of the 4th International Conference on Language Resources and Evaluation, Lisboa, pp. 1141–1144 (2004)
5. Semantic Roles, Case Relations, and Cross-Clausal Reference in Tibetan. http://www.sfb441.unituebingen.de/b11/b11corpora.html#clarkTrees. Accessed 14 Apr 2012
6. Grokhovskii, P., Smirnova, M.: Principles of Tibetan compounds processing in Lexical database. In: Proceedings of the International Conference IMS. Saint Petersburg, pp. 135–142 (2017). ISBN: 978-1-4503-5437-0, https://doi.org/10.1145/3143699.3143718
7. Melcuk, I.: Phrasemes in language and phraseology in linguistics. In: Everaert, M., Van der Linden, E.J., Schenk, A., Schreuder, R. (eds.) Idioms: Structural and Psychological Perspectives, pp. 167–232. Lawrence Erlbaum, New Jersey (1995)
8. Mel'čuk, I.A., Zholkovsky, A.: Explanatory Combinatorial Dictionary of Modern Russian. Ges. zur Förderung Slawistischer Studien (1984)
9. Leont'eva, N.N.: RUSLAN Semantic dictionary as a tool for computer understanding [Semanticheskij slovar RUSLAN kak instrument kompyuternogo ponimaniya]. In: Understanding in communication. Proceedings of the scientific practical conference [Ponimanie v kommunikacii. Materialy nauchnoprakticheskoj konferencii], Moscow, pp. 41–46 (2003)
10. Dobrov, A., Dobrova, A., Grokhovskiy, P., Soms, N., Zakharov, V.: Morphosyntactic analyzer for the Tibetan language: aspects of structural ambiguity. In: Sojka, P., Horák, A., Kopeček, I., Pala, K. (eds.) TSD 2016. LNCS (LNAI), vol. 9924, pp. 215–222. Springer, Cham (2016). https://doi.org/10.1007/978-3-319-45510-5_25

11. Dobrov, A.V.: Semantic and ontological relations in AIIRE natural language processor. Comput. Model. Bus. Eng. Domains. Rzeszow-Sofia: ITHEA, 147–157 (2014)
12. Matuszek, C., Cabral, J., Witbrock, M.J., DeOliveira, J.: An introduction to the syntax and content of cyc. In: AAAI Spring Symposium: Formalizing and Compiling Back-ground Knowledge and Its Applications to Knowledge Representation and Question Answering, pp. 44–49 (2006)
13. Rubashkin, V.Sh., Fadeeva, M.V., Chuprin, B.Y.: The technology of importing fragments from OWL and KIF-ontologies [Tekhnologiya importa fragmentov iz OWL i KIF-ontologij]. In: Proceedings of the conference "Internet and modern society [Materialy nauchnoj konferencii "Internet i sovremennoe obshchestvo"], pp. 217–230 (2012)
14. Gruber, T.R.: A translation approach to portable ontology specifications (PDF). Knowl. Acquis. 5(2), 199–220 (1993). https://doi.org/10.1006/knac.1993.1008
15. Dobrov, A., Dobrova, A., Grokhovskiy, P., Smirnova, M., Soms, N.: Computer ontology of Tibetan for morphosyntactic disambiguation. In: Alexandrov, D.A., Boukhanovsky, A.V., Chugunov, A.V., Kabanov, Y., Koltsova, O. (eds.) DTGS 2018. CCIS, vol. 859, pp. 336–349. Springer, Cham (2018). https://doi.org/10.1007/978-3-030-02846-6_27
16. Dobrov, A., Dobrova, A., Grokhovskiy, P., Smirnova, M., Soms, N.: Idioms modeling in a computer ontology as a morphosyntactic disambiguation strategy. In: Sojka, P., Horák, A., Kopeček, I., Pala, K. (eds.) TSD 2018. LNCS (LNAI), vol. 11107, pp. 76–83. Springer, Cham (2018). https://doi.org/10.1007/978-3-030-00794-2_8
17. Bialek, J.: Compounds and Compounding in Old Tibetan. A Corpus Based Approach, vol. 1. Marburg (2018)
18. Aho, A.V., Corasick, M.J.: Efficient string matching: An aid to bibliographic search. Commun. ACM 18(6), 333–340 (1975)
19. Pelletier, F.J.: The principle of semantic compositionality. Topoi 13, 11 (1994)

Knowledge and Decision Support for Hazard Awareness

Anca Daniela Ionita(✉) , Adriana Olteanu ,
and Radu Nicolae Pietraru

University Politehnica of Bucharest,
Spl. Independentei 313, 060042 Bucharest, Romania
anca.ionita@upb.ro,
{adriana.olteanu,radu.pietraru}@aii.pub.ro

Abstract. In regard to hazards, either produced by natural causes or by human activities, an important issue today is awareness, which is essential not only for the fast response of emergency personnel, but also for people concerned about the risks. The approach described in this chapter is based on making specialists' knowledge accessible to the large public. This was first realized though a selection of fundamental concepts about radiological and nuclear vulnerabilities and their organization in an ontology, used for defining a website. Secondly, the rules followed for making decisions in case of hazardous events were extracted from the public reports elaborated by authorities in atomic energy, were formalized, and were implemented into a software simulator. Thirdly, the processes followed for diverse types of risks were represented graphically, to create awareness about the measurements to be taken, the actions recommended in each situation, and their timing..

Keywords: Knowledge engineering · Hazard management · Process modeling · Decision support

1 Introduction

Hazard awareness is generally approached from the point of view of the authorities who are responsible to make decisions, either for preventive purposes or for diminishing the effects, when a hazardous event happens. From the scientific point of view, Newman et al. analyzed a hundred papers on decision support systems for risk reduction in regard with natural hazards [1], defining a complex analysis framework. They included criteria like end users, external drivers, decision indicators, model integration, software architecture, monitoring and evaluation process etc. Their findings showed that one mostly focuses on risk identification, and less on mitigation measures, with a better coverage of low-level decisions, in the detriment of strategy elaboration and risk-reduction plans. Among the areas indicated to need more attention in the future, there is the interaction with users, both during the development of Decision Support Systems and in the evaluation stages.

From the technical point of view, complementary to prediction methods based on modeling natural phenomena, artificial intelligence has also been applied for managing

A. Fred et al. (Eds.): IC3K 2019, CCIS 1297, pp. 343–364, 2020.
https://doi.org/10.1007/978-3-030-66196-0_16

disaster risks, with supervised and unsupervised machine learning algorithms, applied to data originated from a large variety of sources, like satellites, drones, street cameras etc. A World Bank guidance note presents case studies about two important aspects [2]: i) physical or social vulnerability exposure (e.g. deep learning applied to determine seismic risks of buildings, or conditional random field used for estimating the resistance of roof tops to hurricanes) and ii) damage prediction before the event, in comparison with afterwards assessment (e.g. Bayesian networks and random forest for floods, decision trees for mapping landslide hazard, or deep learning for cyclone damage evaluation). Another method to improve disaster response is to collect messages posted on social media during a hazardous event, and automatically classify them based on artificial intelligence. An example is given in [3], about processing Twitter messages in real-time, with a training algorithm that uses labels characteristic to crisis situations; the tool was validated during an earthquake in Pakistan in 2013. For prevention and preparedness, one also can also apply machine learning over historical information concerning a given type of hazard. Flood events occurred over a period of 24 years were studied in [4] in order to extract behavioral patterns and make classifications to be used in decision trees applicable to future events; among the techniques evaluated, the research proved that the most suitable was the Random Forest collaborative learning, followed by Artificial Neural Networks.

The Sendai Framework for Disaster Risk Reduction 2015–2030 [5] introduced an approach based on risk management, extending the governmental investments in protective measures towards cooperative actions based on a better understanding of risks, and falling into the responsibility of multiple stakeholders. In this new approach, the dissemination and communication of risk information become more important, involving augmented requirements for public awareness [6]. The involvement of local communities also becomes essential, in correlation with larger scale campaigns for creating awareness, and accompanied by teaching notions about vulnerabilities and protection from hazards within formal education programs [7].

Therefore, there are *two important trends* in managing hazards. The former is the investment in developing more sophisticated tools for decision support to learn from historical data, analyzing the situation rapidly and recommending the best actions to be taken in due time. The latter is the involvement of a larger spectrum of stakeholders even in the stage of the simple existence of latent vulnerabilities, like living in the proximity of a volcano or of a nuclear plant. Leaning on these two trends, the work presented in this chapter investigated the use of knowledge engineering to support awareness of the large public and to simulate decisions that are recommended by public documents in case of nuclear or radiological events.

This chapter is an extension of [8], with more insights into the concept of awareness in Sect. 2, were the knowledge available in regard with nuclear hazards is also presented. Section 3 gives further details about the research method from [8], to put forward the important steps involved, and the results concerning the representation of knowledge, the set of rules and the formalization of processes. The proposed ontology organizes nuclear hazards knowledge, targeting the interest of the large public; it is presented in Sect. 4, based on a more technical perspective than in [8], to show how it was used for designing the website to create public awareness. In addition to the conference paper, the chapter also includes a description of scenarios for integration tests, performed in conjunction with a prediction tool for radioactive cloud movement. Section 5 exposes details about the decision support simulator that is part of the website, conceived for general use, but respecting recommendations from public reports of the International Atomic Energy Agency (IAEA); new examples of rule definitions are introduced in respect with [8], along with new graphical representations of operative processes, for protection and response purposes. The chapter ends with an analysis of related work (Sect. 6) and with Conclusion.

2 Background

2.1 Defining Awareness

The Cambridge Dictionary defines *awareness* as: "knowledge that something exists, or understanding of a situation or subject at the present time, based on information or experience". We learn from this that awareness is intrinsically related to knowledge, be it *explicit* (as the one that is found in guidelines, reports, training materials or knowledge basis) or *tacit* (as the one held by domain experts). The conversion between these two types of knowledge is realized, according to the Nonaka model, through: socialization, externalization, combination and internalization. In [9] one proposed a combination between this one and another consecrated model, defined by Endsley, who identified three levels of situational awareness: perception, comprehension, and projection of the future actions [10]. From a technical perspective of data fusion, one also applied another conceptual model, called JDL (Joint Director's of Laboratories), consisting in four levels of assessment - for data, objects, situation and impact - plus a level of process refinement. A framework that integrates JDL with Endsley's model is proposed in [11], with a demonstration based on a war scenario, by integrating tools for processing the routed messages and for parsing free-text, with a system for detecting terrorism evidence and alerts, transmitted to a responsible person for analysis.

According to the same Cambridge Dictionary definition given above, awareness also concerns a given situation. *Situation awareness* is critical in domains like aviation, where it may be the cause of severe incidents (see a review of existing approaches in [12]), and also in emergency management in general. Time is a very important factor in situation awareness and decision support, thus differentiating it from the softer concerns of *public awareness*, where the availability and good organization of the information prevail. Related to them, *context awareness* is also important in pervasive applications that adapt to environmental conditions, characterizing a daily-life situation and not necessarily in relation to hazards. In such a case, the domain knowledge, regarding a smart home environment, for instance, can be formally represented as an ontology, as a basis for further reasoning. The approach given in [13] proposes a hierarchical organization, with a general upper ontology and several other ontologies specific to various sub-domains, for home, vehicle etc., expressed in OWL (Web Ontology Language) and interpreted with context reasoning engines, based on Jena2.

2.2   Knowledge Concerning Nuclear Hazards

All over the world, government agencies, local officials, nuclear plant owners and other stakeholders are directly interested in creating education and awareness about the radiological and nuclear hazards. This concern was also present in the key messages launched in 2013 by the International Federation of Red Cross and Red Crescent Societies (IFRCRCS) to increase public awareness and public education for disaster risk reduction.

The occurrence of severe nuclear accidents in Eastern Europe and Asia, as well as the problems raised by radioactive waste, have increased the general concern on nuclear power plants safety, up to discussing the acceptance by the large public of this form of producing energy [14]. Apart from establishing and maintaining radiation protection measures in nuclear power plants, there are also issues like environment protection, climate change and potential conflicts between technological and social development, leading to the analysis of the people's risk awareness. Thus, the studies show that safety goals and public acceptance have a direct impact on each other [15]. Whereas the geographic proximity to a nuclear facility influences the interest towards the nuclear energy and the awareness of the induced vulnerabilities, it has not been proven to be an important factor in the acceptance of its usage [16]. However, the attitude changes for the population living in the vulnerability area of a former nuclear accident. Kitada [17] analyzed the results of multiple surveys realized in Japan, before and after the Fukushima Daiichi Nuclear Power Plant accident. After the event, the negative opinions about nuclear power increased; people were discussing more about renewable energies and tended to focus on the accident risks. The perception of nuclear energy risks in Taiwan and Hong Kong were also studied in [18]. Similar to Japan, they are seismic countries, densely populated and with nuclear power plants located side by side to urban centers, or in close proximity to numerous underwater volcanoes. The paper presented the implication of the government and media in disseminating crucial information and influencing public opinion and perception of risk. Education on natural disasters in general also has its impact in this respect [19].

For the knowledge of our domain of interest, a major contribution comes from the International Atomic Energy Agency, who also published a "Nuclear Accident Knowledge Taxonomy" [20], along with many other reports, recommendations and guides. A milestone in the European Union was the development of RODOS (Real-time Online Decision Support) – a system for nuclear emergency management [21]. Its main objectives are to provide integrated methodological bases, develop models and databases, and install common hardware and software frameworks for forecasting the consequences of an accident and supporting decisions. The role of multi-criterion analysis to ensure transparency of the decision-making process in the management of emergency situations was described in [22].

There have also been efforts towards an integrated approach of hazards, including Chemical, Biological, Radiological and Nuclear (CBRN), with integrated monitoring, warning and alerting solutions. Sentinel Asia is such an example, functioning since 2005, sharing data from earth observations and in-situ measurements, and creating a link between the space and the disaster reduction communities, at international level [23]. The European Commission also supported multiple projects for an integrated management of crisis situations and for correlated responses in case of disasters [24]. Such efforts are also related to another concern at the international level - the creation of situation awareness tools, to provide a clear perception of a disaster scenario, and to improve decision support and the relations between the involved actors and the environmental factors [25].

3   Research Method

Our work was performed with the purpose to share knowledge on radiological and nuclear hazards with stakeholders concerned of these risks but having medium to zero scientific background on such topics. In the collaboration with professors teaching nuclear technology and with researchers from a physics and nuclear engineering institute, we first played the part of software engineers for developing an educational and awareness platform, but soon discovered that we were also among the potential users of such a platform. It was challenging for them to select which were the basic concepts to be explained and what was important from the point of view of people who may have a technical background but are not accustomed with the specificities of this domain. Our task consisted in organizing the relevant knowledge that was selected by our partners, and of identifying the connections between concepts that would help for an easier understanding and then for a better navigability within the platform. Based on the selection made by specialists in nuclear engineering and physics, we represented a set of concepts that are relevant for understanding the nuclear and radiological vulnerabilities and for creating awareness. The aim was to offer support for education and awareness, necessary for understating and testing the project results, and not to elaborate an exhaustive ontology, because this would have to cover multiple domains that are already characterized by a very detailed terminology.

Furthermore, we wanted to go beyond getting accustomed to a basic terminology and to introduce some insights into the judgement criteria of the relevant authorities, because this might increase the population cooperativeness and trust, and might also offer the possibility to check the validity of some decisions one may be directly affected by. This is particularly important in our country, due to the operation of a nuclear power plant and the proximity of other nuclear facilities that may induce further territorial vulnerabilities [26].

Thus, our method for representing knowledge included the following important steps (see Fig. 1):

- Organization of the concepts
- Identification of connections between concepts
- Establishing references to other ontologies
- Definition of semantic links
- Specification of rules based on the IAEA recommendations
- Representation of processes in a graphical language.

The work was part of a project developing prediction tools about the influence of radioactive clouds on the territory situated in the near and far field of a nuclear facility [27]. Our contribution consisted in:

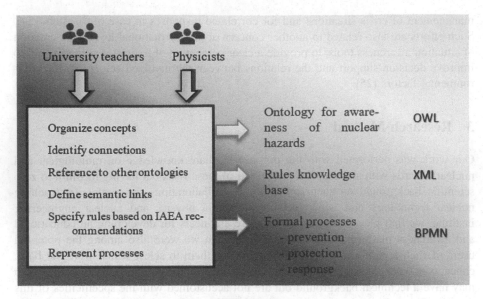

Fig. 1. Research method

- an ontology used to organize the resources for informal education and awareness about the radiological and nuclear hazards;
- the design of a rule-based simulator dedicated to non-specialists, based on criteria, activities and threshold levels conforming to the recommendations of the International Atomic Energy Agency;
- a formal presentation of processes to be followed for prevention, protection and emergency response situations.

The knowledge representation was realized in multiple languages, including UML (Unified Modeling Language), OWL, XML (Extensible Markup Language) and BPMN (Business Process Model and Notation). The representations were then applied for realizing a knowledge integration website, including semantic links, and a tool to simulate the authorities' decisions in a variety of situations related to radiological and nuclear vulnerabilities. The website was also used by students in Power Engineering who chose the Nuclear Power Plant program [28].

4   Knowledge on Nuclear Hazards

4.1   Ontology

Four categories of concepts were considered for realizing the Nuclear-Watch ontology, covering the scope of education and awareness:

- Hazard Management
- Emergency management
- Organizational structure and
- Nuclear and radiological reference terms.

We hereby explain a set of concepts from the first three categories, many of them being relevant for any type of hazard, not just for the nuclear and radiological one. The Nuclear-Watch ontology was represented in OWL, using Protégé (see Fig. 2).

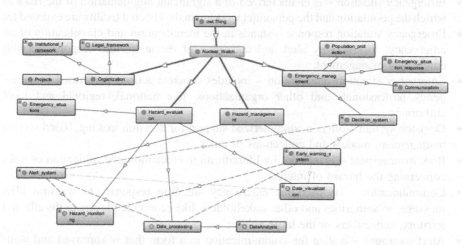

Fig. 2. An OntoGraph representation for the Nuclear-Watch ontology

For the *Hazard* category we selected the following concepts:

- Hazard management system – represents an assembly of physical, software and human components for monitoring, processing and visualization of specific hazards;
- Alert system – supports the decision and communication of alerts in case of disastrous events having happened;
- Early warning system – covers strategic, technical and operational aspects, with the purpose of avoiding or reducing the disastrous effects; its conception and realization considerably depends on the type of hazard, with a clear differentiation between rapid-onset threats, like nuclear plant failures, and slow-onset threats, like climate change [29];
- Hazard monitoring – is specific to the type of hazard and may be realized with diverse measuring instruments, like sensors, satellites, spectrometers, thermometers etc.);
- Data processing – is performed for a variety of goals: estimation of derived physical quantities, prediction, risk assessment, risk mitigation, organizing and storing data for historical purposes, transforming data for communication purposes [30];
- Data visualization – uses data acquired at hazard monitoring and includes maps, graphs, tables, color-coded advisories, video images.

For the *Emergency* category, the concepts considered are:

- Emergency management – represents the overall organization of resources for dealing with emergency situations, possibly realized by existing hazard management systems; a collection of twenty-six definitions of emergency management, along with a comprehensive presentation of the related terminology, are given in [31] and [32];

- Population protection – is performed when a hazard-related event happened, but the effects do not require emergency reactions; in the case of nuclear vulnerabilities, the protection may consist in sheltering, iodine administration, or temporary relocation;
- Emergency situation – is characterized of a significant augmentation of the risks to which the population and the personnel working in the affected facility are exposed to;
- Emergency situation response – stands in the identification and classification of an emergency, followed by alert and activation of the authorities responsible with emergency management;
- Emergency situation intervention – includes concrete actions performed by emergency professionals and other organizations, like national, regional and local authorities;
- Decision system – offers a computerized support for decision making, based on risk management, models and collections of data;
- Risk management – is realized by identification, evaluation and mitigation of risks concerning the hazard of interest;
- Communication – is used for emergency situation response, to transmit alert messages to authorities and other stakeholders, like economic players in the affected territory, subscribers or the large public;
- Alert messages – realize the communication in a form that is approved and well-formatted.

For the *Organization* category, the concepts introduced in the ontology are:

- Legal framework - consists of the main laws and government orders to which the emergency management and a hazard management system must conform to;
- Institutional framework – is an assembly of resources and organizations created for managing emergencies at regional, national or international levels.
- The fourth category, nuclear and radiological reference terms, includes concepts related to radiations, environment radioactivity and nuclear security, accessible to people having a technical background (high school level); a presentation of more advanced terms about nuclear emergencies is given in [33].

The concepts presented above, along with other reference terms necessary for understanding the hazard management fundamentals, were represented in Web Ontology Language, in Protégé. After that, we also added relationships for two reasons: i) to show the connections between them, and ii) to verify whether they have correspondences to concepts from other external ontologies, for validation purposes. Thus, two kinds of relationships were defined:

- relationships between the Nuclear-Watch concepts; see several examples in Table 1;
- correspondences to concepts from other ontologies that represent knowledge from related domains; a selection of correspondent concepts from VuWiki (Vulnerability Ontology 1.0) [34] is given in Table 2.

Table 1. Examples of relationships.

Name	Notation	Description
HasSubclass	———▷—	Nuclear_Watch – HasSubclass –> Hazard_management
HasMonitoring	— — —▷ — — —	Early_warning_system – HasMonitoring (Domain > Range) –> Hazard_monitoring
HasVisualization	- — - —▷ - — -	Alert_system – HasVisualization (Domain > Range) –> Data_visualization
HasResource	· — — —▷— — — -	Early_warning_system – HasResource (Domain > Range) –> Resource
HasDecision	— — —▷— — —	Early_warning_system – HasDecision (Domain > Range) –> Decision_system
HasProcessing	· — — —▷— — — ·	Early_warning_system – HasProcessing (Domain > Range) –> Data_processing

Table 2. Examples of correspondences to VuWiki concepts

Nuclear-Watch Concept	Correspondence	VuWiki concept
Emergency/Population protection	Has definition	Vulnerability assessment/Methodological approach/Theoretical approach/Definition of vulnerability
Emergency/Emergency management	Is based on	Vulnerability assessment/Reference framework of assessment/Target users/Civil protection
Emergency/Risk management	Corresponds to	Vulnerability assessment/Methodological approach/Theoretical approach/Related theoretical concepts/Risk
Hazard/Data processing	Corresponds to	Vulnerability assessment/Methodological approach/Operational approach/Data analysis
Hazard/Hazard monitoring	Corresponds to	Vulnerability assessment/Methodological approach/Operational approach/Data collection
Hazard/Data visualization	Corresponds to	Vulnerability assessment/Methodological approach/Operational approach/Data Analysis//Mapping (spatial or temporal)

4.2 Knowledge Integration Website

The knowledge on nuclear hazards was integrated within an educational and awareness website developed with Tiki Wiki. The wiki pages correspond to the Nuclear-Watch ontology concepts and capitalize the Semantic Links functionality - to define relations between them. Each page contains a brief definition of the concept, followed by a description defined by domain experts, references, a list of connected notions (among the ones presented within the same website) and a category defined within the same ontology.

Apart from this, to improve the navigability and the search capabilities, there are also page relations based on newly introduced link types that are mutually inverted. Thus, we can show, for instance, that a data processing module *is part of* an alert system, or of an early warning system. There is also an invert relation defined in the semantic links, with the label *possible components* and the token *contains*. In this way, the user finds out that an alert system contains components dedicated to: hazard monitoring, data processing, emergency situations, decision support, and data visualization, and can navigate to the correspondent web pages to know further information. The website also incorporates a decision support simulator, whose design is further described in Sect. 5.

Although its main purpose was to create awareness in general, the website was also used in educational settings, for junior students in power engineering, who can visualize fundamental notions about the physical phenomena related to nuclear facilities, understand the alert and early warning systems, study legal aspects, and learn more about the organizational framework responsible of emergency situations. Moreover, the teachers were allowed to define new wiki pages, edit the existing content, and introduce new navigation links based on semantics. Other details on the educational aspects and the tests performed were given in [28].

4.3 Testing Scenarios

The awareness website based on knowledge integration was conceived as a complementary tool to accompany a prediction software concerning radioactive cloud movement and early warning, created by a physics research institute [35]. As a consequence, a set of test cases were defined for scenarios correspondent to different types of risks and decision drivers:

- SC1 Inform population about nuclear vulnerabilities
- SC2 Create population awareness about prevention measures for low-risk nuclear vulnerabilities
- SC3 Protect population from evolving towards a crisis situation
- SC4 Emergency response in case of receiving a high dose of radiations.

For SC2 and SC3, four versions were considered, in respect with four types of events that were simulated numerically by our colleagues from the Power Engineering Faculty:

- an accident at a nuclear plant,
- a fire of a device with radiological dispersions,
- an explosion of a device with radiological dispersion, and
- triggering an improvised nuclear device.

There were two test groups who received access to the above-mentioned prediction tools and to the awareness website presented in this chapter. They were given test forms, as well as teaching and informative materials, and the feedback was interpreted by experts in nuclear power energy.

For example, the list of test cases specified and executed for SC2 is given in Table 3. For a scenario initiated by an accident at a nuclear plant, the suite of tests consisted of: CT.INFO.001 → CT.INFO.002 → CT.INFO.003 → CT.INFO.008 →

CT.SIM.002 → CT.INFO.004 → CT.DEC.001. Four variants of this scenario also included simulations driven by a certain type of event and characterized by a sequence of test cases (CT.SIM.002, CT.SIM.003, CT.SIM.004 and CT.SIM.005). During these integration tests, the awareness website based on the knowledge presented in this chapter was systematically accessed.

Table 3. Test cases included in the low-risk scenario SC2

ID	Test case	Software component
CT.INFO.001	Information about radiation doses	Awareness website
CT.INFO.002	Information about radiation effects on humans	Awareness website
CT.INFO.003	Information about population protection	Awareness website
CT.INFO.008	Data about communities exposed to vulnerabilities	Awareness website
CT.SIM.002	Simulation of an accident at Cernavoda nuclear plant, Romania, with low-risk exposure to radiation	Prediction tool
CT.SIM.003	Simulation of an explosion for a radiological dispersal device	Prediction tool
CT.SIM.004	Simulation of a fire for a radiological dispersal device	Prediction tool
CT.SIM.005	Simulation of an improvised nuclear device	Prediction tool
CT.INFO.004	Weather forecast	Prediction tool
CT.DEC.001	Verification of the prevention decision sequence	Awareness website

5   Decision Support Simulator

5.1   Formalization of Rules

This section describes the knowledge of the rule-based system [36] that simulates the decisions to be taken by responsible authorities, in order to create awareness on the nuclear vulnerabilities. We extracted what can be expressed as a set of rules from the criteria defined for preparedness and response for a nuclear or radiological emergency. They were identified based on reports of the International Atomic Energy Agency [37, 38]. Table 4 presents the structural aspects of the main concepts that characterize the rule-based system (i.e. Rule, Threshold Condition, Time Frame and Action). It includes the concept attributes and their types, whereas the subsequent paragraphs explain their meanings, as they result from domain-specific documentation, but with the purpose of creating awareness to a larger public.

Table 4. Concepts used in the rule-based system

Concept	Attributes	Type
Rule	rule code	String
	category	{A, B, C, D, E, F}
	risk	{R1, R2, R3}
Threshold Condition	threshold code	String
	threshold dose	Real
	unit of measurement	{mSv, Sv, Gy-Eq}
	measured quantity	{E_T, H_AnyOtherOrgan, H_Foetus, H_Skin, H_Thyroid, AD_Torso, AD_Tissue, AD_Foetus, AD_Skin, AD(Δ) RedMarrow}
	operation	Logical Operation
	exposure type	{Internal, External}
	exposure time	{Brief, Unspecified}
	delta days	Integer
Time Frame	time frame code	String
	time frame name	{year, month, week, day, lifetime}
	multiplicity	{1, 2, more than 1}
Action	action code	String
	action name	String
	target	{everybody, pregnant women}
	constraint	{Urgent, Immediately, Temporary, Limited Area, Limited Objects, Discretionary}
	purpose	String

The rules belong to six categories that depend on the dose of radiation, which decreases from A (when "urgent actions are always justified") to F (when there are no "generically justified actions"). They also depend on three types of risks:

- R1 – concerning avertable doses that do not affect population's health, hence it is necessary to take *prevention* measures;
- R2 – when the population *protection* is required due to larger values of projected doses;
- R3 – when the dose has already been received and internal/external exposures are high, so *emergency response* actions are necessary.

A rule behavior depends on a threshold value for the radiation dose, in respect with the generic reference levels adopted by IAEA, and the time frame elapsed from the moment of the nuclear incident. Thus, the premises of the rules are:

- the threshold conditions regarding the radiation doses compared to the specified reference levels,
- the time frames, and
- the risk types.

The conclusion resulted from applying these rules is a set of actions recommended by IAEA, which are supposed to be applied by the organizational structures responsible with emergency management.

The rules are further defined as "if-then" clauses and their codes have the form *Rule_i*, where *i* is the index, as seen in the examples from Table 1. From the analysis of IAEA specifications, we identified 25 rules that were included into the knowledge base.

There are 22 threshold conditions identified from the studied IAEA specifications and we assigned each of them a code, having the form *Threshold_i*, where *i* is the index. A threshold condition represents one of the rule premises and is assigned with a logical operation for checking the condition, and a threshold dose, which is a reference value for a given physical quantity. The physical quantities that are relevant for the purpose of the nuclear and radiological verifications are:

- *E* (Effective dose) – measured for the entire organism or for *T* (the tissue or organ of interest),
- *H* (Equivalent dose) – to express the stochastic health effects on the foetus, thyroid or any other organ, and
- *AD* (Absorbed dose) – due to the external exposure of torso, skin, tissue and foetus, or due to the internal exposure of red marrow, thyroid, lung, colon and foetus.

An action has a name that indicates what are the measures to be taken by the emergency personnel, domain specialists and various responsible authorities, to avoid or reduce the effects of a presumable disaster. See several examples in the last column from Table 5, and other examples were presented in [8]. From the IAEA reports we extracted 25 possible actions, assigned with a code *Action_i*; the conclusion/decision of a rule may reunite several such actions. A constraint for the time or space to apply each action may exist, to specify that it has to be performed urgently or immediately, to certain objects, or to an entire area.

Based on this knowledge base, we defined a decision tree (previously presented in [8]), where the decisions were organized in respect with the types of risks (R1, R2 and R3) correspondent to prevention, protection and emergency response to nuclear and radiological situations.

Table 5. Examples of rule definitions

"If-then" clause	Premises		Conclusion
IF (*Threshold_12*) THEN (*Action_9* AND *Action_5*)	*Threshold_12*: $H_{Thyroid} >= 50$ mSv	L2	*Action_9*: Iodine prophylaxis *Action_5*: Decontamination
IF (*Timeframe_1* AND *Threshold_12*) THEN (*Action_6* AND *Action_16* AND *Action_11*)	*Timeframe_1*: 1 year *Threshold_12*: $H_{Thyroid} >= 50$ mSv	L0 L1	*Action_6*: Limited area/object decontamination *Action_16*: Limited restriction for food, milk, water *Action_11*: Public information
IF (*Threshold_13*) THEN (*Action_20* AND *Action_11* AND *Action_12*)	*Threshold_13*: $AD_{Torso} >= 1$ Gy-Eq	L1	*Action_20*: Protective actions to keep dose below reference *Action_11*: Public information *Action_12*: Public warning
IF (*Threshold_17*) THEN (*Action_21* AND *Action_3* AND *Action_5* AND *Action_22* AND *Action_23* AND *Action_24* AND *Action_25*)	*Threshold_17*: AD $(\Delta)_{Red\ marrow} >= 0.2$ Gy-Eq	L0	*Action_21*: Medical examination, and indicated treatment *Action_3*: Contamination control *Action_5*: Decontamination *Action_22*: Decorporation *Action_23*: Prescription of iodine *Action_24*: Medical follow-up *Action_25*: Psychological counseling

5.2 Rule-Based Engine

The awareness website incorporates a simulator of the rule-based system, processing the following data:

- the date of the presumable nuclear incident,
- a set of values for the relevant physical quantities, i.e. effective, equivalent and/absorbed doses, for various parts of the body, and
- the date when the measurements were taken.

Based on these inputs, an inference engine is run, and the recommended actions are displayed to the user. The engine compares the data introduced by the user to the information stored in the knowledge base. According to the values introduced for the required physical quantities, the user receives appropriate messages, regarding:

- the measures to be taken, like temporary relocation, evacuation, decontamination, and/or contamination control,
- the restrictions related to food, milk or water,
- the medical program to be followed, including, for example, iodine prophylaxis, necessary examinations, medical treatment and/or psychological counseling.

For the purpose of this simulator, the representation of knowledge was done in XML, based on an appropriate schema, for creating a unitary structure and a specific content, in accordance with the rule definitions from Sect. 5.1. The knowledge base has specific files for each concept, necessary for executing the rule behavior, with child elements that correspond to the attributes from Table 4, e.g.:

- the representation of actions, having five child elements: *actionCode, actionName, target, constraint* and *purpose*;
- the representation of timeframes, with three child elements: *timeFrameCode, timeFrameName* and *multiplicity*;
- the representation of threshold conditions, with ten child elements: *thresholdCode, thresholdDose, measuringUnit, measuredQuantity, operation, exposureType, exposureTime, deltaDays, note* and *constraint*.

5.3 Representation of Processes

The IAEA reports studied for obtaining the knowledge base of rules include the representation of several processes, like the situation assessment in the contamination of large or moderate areas [38]. However, for awareness purposes, we needed to show the big picture and not only details for specific procedures to be followed by specialists. For this purpose, we distributed the threshold conditions, rules and activities into three groups, in respect with the type of risk they are recommended for, and we represented three processes, for: prevention (risk type R1), population protection (risk type R2), and emergency response (risk type R3).

Figures 3 and 4 illustrate the protection and response processes, represented in BPMN. The prevention process was previously presented in [8].

The process tasks, notated as rectangles with rounded corners in BPMN, correspond: i) to the measurements of physical quantities necessary in decision making and ii) to the actions recommended by IAEA (previously explained in Sect. 5.1). The decisions, represented as diamonds in BPMN, verify whether the threshold conditions are met, by comparing the measured values with the reference levels from the IAEA safety guides. In respect with the threshold conditions fulfilled or not, the sequence flow advances to the actions recommended in that situation. The timer intermediate events, represented with a clock icon, correspond to the time frames mentioned in Sect. 5.1.

Thus, as resulted from Fig. 3, immediately after an incident, for protection purposes, one has to measure the equivalent radiation dose that shows the effect on the thyroid, and the absorbed doses due to the external exposure of torso, tissues, skin and foetus (if necessary). Public information and warning are generally necessary, but one may also need to impose restrictions on food, milk or water consumption, in respect with the positioning below or above the threshold values; the values from Fig. 3 correspond to those recommended by IAEA, but national authorities may impose different thresholds, generally lower. After a year, the measurements of effective and equivalent doses are repeated, and may determine limited decontamination activities, food restrictions and, as always, public information.

The emergency response process, represented in Fig. 4, includes more specific measures that may be taken immediately, like medical examination, iodine and other treatment prescriptions, contamination control, decontamination, decorporation, registration for medical follow-up, and psychological counseling. The measurements are repeated more often, after one month, after several months and after a year. Note that these processes are conceived according to the IAEA reports, but they are exclusively meant for public awareness; the detailed processes to be followed by emergency professionals and the coordination between them are determined by the authorized committees and organizations, at local, county and national levels.

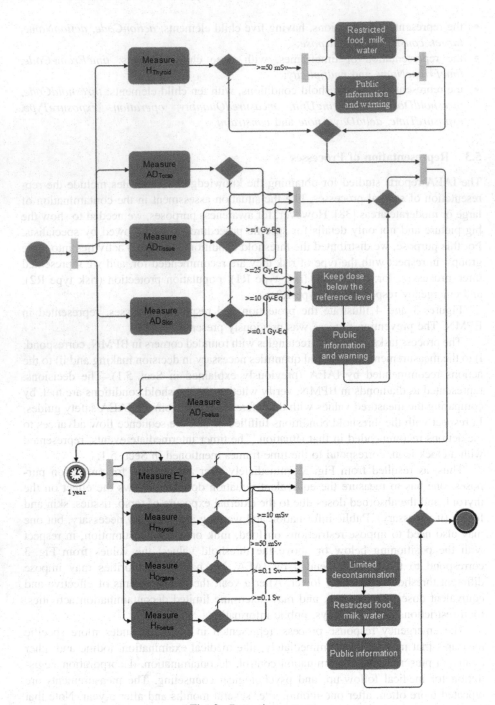

Fig. 3. Protection process.

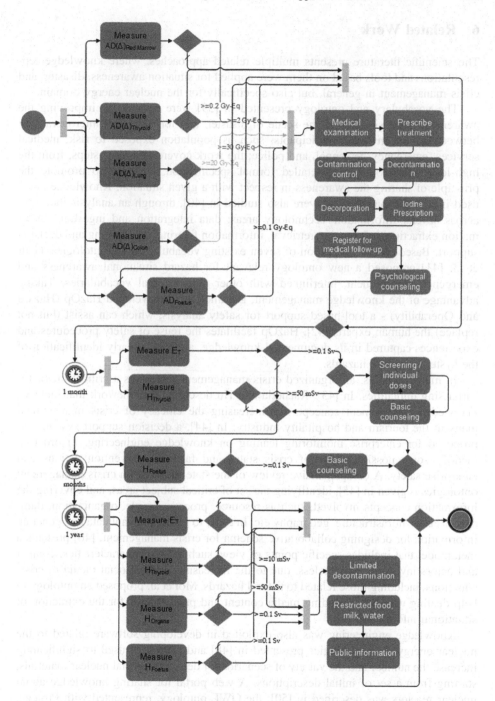

Fig. 4. Emergency response process.

6   Related Work

The scientific literature presents multiple related approaches, where knowledge representations and tools based on them were applied for situation awareness, disaster, and crisis management in general, but also specifically for the nuclear energy domain.

The vocabulary and ontology presented in [39] were defined for improving the awareness of the situation at the scene of disaster, and for providing interoperability between all the involved participants, such as population exposed to risk, medical services, emergency personnel, and police; the work covered multiple steps, from the high-level metamodel to a detailed formal specification, targeting to promote the principle of sharing the awareness in respect with a given situation. Knowledge bases used in disaster management were also studied in [40], through an analysis that goes across several Information Technology areas: data integration and ingestion, information extraction, information retrieval, information filtering, data mining and decision support. Based on the integration of seven existing vocabularies and ontologies, Gaur et al. [41] proposed a new ontology relevant for hazard situational awareness and emergency management, interlinked with other nine external vocabularies. Taking advantage of the knowledge management, Daramola et al. developed HazOp (Hazard and Operability) - a tool-based support for safety analysis, which can assist (but not replace) the human experts [42]. HazOp facilitates the reuse of safety procedures and experiences captured in its documented knowledge, aiming the early identification of the system potential hazards.

In many domains, an organized crisis management represents a critical factor for surpassing difficulties. In [43], Racherla and Hu described a framework that includes knowledge management concepts for increasing the efficacy of crisis management plans in the tourism and hospitality industry. In [44], a decision support system was proposed for enterprise monitoring leaning on knowledge engineering, in order to identify some possible signs of crisis states and facilitate prevention actions and enterprise safety. A comprehensive review of the state of the art in crisis management ontologies is given in [45], identifying the set of critical subject areas, and covering the information concepts involved, such as resource, process, people, organization, damage, disaster, infrastructure, geography etc. In order to gather relevant data and generate information for designing collaborative schema for crisis management, [46] presents a metamodel that includes specific points of view, such as crisis characteristics, context and actors involved. Nonetheless, due to the increasing role of social media in crisis situations, including those related to natural hazards, Moi et al. proposed an ontology to help dealing with the exceeding media content and processing it for the extraction of situational information [47].

Knowledge engineering was also exploited in developing software related to the nuclear energy. The ontologies presented in [48] and [49] were used to significantly increase the number and the variety of scenarios for detecting special nuclear materials, starting from a set of initial descriptions. A web portal for sharing knowledge about nuclear reactors was described in [50]; the OWL ontology, represented with Protégé, includes concepts about neutron energy, steam generator detection and protection, control rod drive mechanisms etc. Furthermore, the design of nuclear power plants is governed by rules that may be expressed in ontological models, using for instance the standard Semantic Web Rule Language (SWRL) [51]. Other research-oriented approaches also exist, like the nuclear or radiological emergency ontology described in [52]. In this context, the work presented in this chapter came with a focus on public awareness, organizing knowledge to create a few insights into the complex expertise and responsibility that stand behind the radiological and nuclear hazards.

7 Conclusion

The awareness of hazards' causes and risks, as well as of the authorized institutions operation framework, has become increasingly important, up to being part of inter-national strategies in regard with disaster management. Overall, many existing appli-cations make use of representations of knowledge and knowledge bases; none of them has been imposed as a standard, but multiple integration attempts are described in the scientific literature. The work presented here was specific for the domain of radio-logical and nuclear vulnerabilities, targeting actors that do not play an active part but are potentially exposed to risks, such as people or industrial players situated in the near-field or in the far-field of nuclear facilities. Thus, the knowledge held by domain experts was organized in an ontology conceived for the awareness and education of non-specialists, accompanied by a set of rules and representations of processes, deduced from public documents on preparedness and response for a nuclear or radi-ological emergency. They were applied for the development of an awareness website that includes a rule-based simulator.

The future involvement of experts from social sciences should get such technical endeavors closer to the end users, based on the study of elements that drive their interest and worries. Nonetheless, we consider that knowledge engineering has been of great help in extracting information and know-how from the experts and it can be further used for a better cooperation between various stakeholders, for facing the risks, understanding them, and acting efficiently in case of hazardous events.

References

1. Newman, J.P., et al.: Review of literature on decision support systems for natural hazard risk reduction: Current status and future research directions. Environ. Model Softw. **96**, 378–409 (2017)
2. GFDRR, 2018: Machine Learning for Disaster Risk Management. Washington, DC: GFDRR. License: Creative Commons Attribution CC BY 3.0. https://www.gfdrr.org/en/publication/machine-learning-disaster-risk-management. Accessed 15 Jan 2020
3. Imran, M., Castillo, C., Lucas, J., Meier, P., Vieweg, S.: AIDR: artificial Intelligence for Disaster response. In: Proceedings of the 23rd International World Wide Web Conference Committee (IW3C2), WWW 2014 Companion, Korea, pp. 159–162 (2014)
4. Saravi, S., Kalawsky, R., Joannou, D., Rivas Casado, M., Fu, G., Men, F.: Use of artificial intelligence to improve resilience and preparedness against adverse flood events. Water **11**, 973 (2019)

5. UNISDR, 2015: Sendai Framework for Disaster Risk Reduction 2015–2030. Geneva, Switzerland. https://www.unisdr.org/filse/43291_sendaiframeworkfordrren.pdf. Accessed 15 Jan 2020
6. Henstra, D., Thistletthwaite, J.: Overcoming barriers to meeting the Sendai framework for disaster risk reduction. Policy Brief 105 (2017)
7. Wilkinson, E., Twigg, J., Weingärtner, L., Peters K.: In Delivering disaster risk reduction by 2030, Overseas Development Institute, UK (2017)
8. Ionita, A., Olteanu, A., Pietraru, R.: Knowledge-based education and awareness about the radiological and nuclear hazards. In: Proceedings of the 11th International Joint Conference on Knowledge Discovery, Knowledge Engineering and Knowledge Management - Volume 2, KEOD, Viena, Austria, pp. 154–163 (2019) ISBN 978-989-758-382-7
9. Yusof, W.S.E.Y.W., Zakaria, O., Zaino, Z.: Establishing of knowledge based framework for situational awareness using Nonaka's and Endsley's models. In: International Conference on Information and Communication Technology (ICICTM), pp. 47–50. IEEE (2016)
10. Endsley, M.R.: Theoretical underpinnings of situation awareness: a critical review. In: Endsley, M.R., Garland, D.J. (eds.) Situation Awareness Analysis and Measurement. Lawrence Erlbaum Associates, Mahwah, NJ (2000)
11. Salerno, J., Hinman, M., Boulware, D.: Building a framework for situation awareness. In: Proceedings of the 7th International Conference on Information Fusion, Sweden (2004)
12. Nguyen, T., Lim, C.P., Nguyen, N.D., Gordon-Brown, L., Nahavand, S.: A review of situation awareness assessment approaches in aviation environments. IEEE Syst. J. 13(3), 3590–3603 (2019)
13. Gu, T., Wang, X.H., Pung, H.K., Zhang, D.Q.: An ontology-based context model in intelligent environments. In: Proceedings of Communication Networks and Distributed Systems Modeling and Simulation Conference, California, USA, pp. 270–275 (2004)
14. Bing, W., Hao, Y., Yi-Ming, W.: Impact factors of public attitudes towards nuclear power development: a questionnaire survey in China. Int. J. Global Energy Issues 36(1), 61–79 (2013)
15. Chao-jun, L., Chun-ming, Z., Yan, C., Jia-xu, Z., Jia-yun, C.: The study on safety goals and public acceptance of nuclear power. Energy Procedia 39, 415–422 (2012)
16. Cale, T., Kromer, M.: Does proximity matter? Plant location, public awareness, and support for nuclear energy. Soc. Sci. J. 52, 148–155 (2015)
17. Kitada., A.: Public opinion changes after the Fukushima Daiichi Nuclear Power Plant accident to nuclear power generation as seen in continuous polls over the past 30 years. J. Nucl. Sci. Technol. 53(11), 1686–1700 (2016)
18. Grano, S.: Perception of risk towards nuclear energy in Taiwan and Hong Kong. Taiwan in Comp. Perspect. 5, pp. 60–78 (2014) ISSN 1752–7732
19. Smawfield, D.: Education as a Humanitarian Response. Education and Natural Disasters, Bloomsbury Academic (2013)
20. IAEA: Nuclear Accident Knowledge Taxonomy. IAEA Nuclear Energy Series No. NG-T-6.8. Vienna, Austria (2016)
21. Bartzis, J., et al.: Rodos: decision support for nuclear emergencies. In: Zanakis S.H., Doukidis G., Zopounidis C. (eds.) Decision Making: Recent Developments and Worldwide Applications. Applied Optimization, vol 45. Springer, Boston, MA (2000) https://doi.org/10.1007/978-1-4757-4919-9_25
22. Geldermann, J., Bertsch, V., Treitz, M., French, S., Papamichail, K., Hamalainen, R.: Multi-criteria decision support and evaluation of strategies for nuclear remediation management. Omega 37(1), 238–251 (2009)
23. Kaku, K., Held, A.: Sentinel Asia: a space-based disaster management support system in the Asia-Pacific region. Int. J. Disaster Risk Reduction 6, 1–17 (2013)

24. European Commission: Security Research and Innovation-Boosting effectiveness of the Security Union, Directorate-General for Research and Innovation (2017)
25. Pavković, B., Berbakov, L., Vraneš, S., Milenković, M.: Situation awareness and decision support tools for response phase of emergency management: a short survey. In: 25th International Workshop on Database and Expert Systems Applications, 1529–4188/14, pp. 154-159. IEEE (2014)
26. Lazaro, P.G., Budu, A.R., Moraru, D.E.: Optimization of energy mix-Nuclear power and Renewable Energy for low emissions energy source a benefit for generations to come. Energy Procedia **112**(2017), 412–417 (2017)
27. N-WATCHDOG: Early Warning and Decision Support Soft System for the Anticipative Assessment of the Fast Dynamics of Territorial Vulnerabilities Induced by Nuclear Facilities, N-WATCHDOG Project, Horia Hulubei National Institute for R&D in Physics and Nuclear Engineering. http://proiecte.nipne.ro/pn2/155-projects.html. Accessed 15 Jan 2020
28. Ionita, A.D., Olteanu, A., Pietraru, R.N., Moraru, D.E., Budu, A., Prisecaru, I.C.: Online learning content for power engineering students, with semantic-based navigability. In: Proceedings of ICERI2016 Conference, Spain, pp. 1152–1157 (2016)
29. UNEP: Early Warning Systems: A State of the Art Analysis and Future Directions. Division of Early Warning and Assessment (DEW/1531/NA), United Nations Environment Programme (UNEP), Nairobi. https://na.unep.net/siouxfalls/publications/Early_Warning.pdf. Accessed 01 May 2019
30. Ionita, A.D., Olteanu, A.: Data acquisition, processing and visualization for early warning information systems. In: IEEE International Symposium on Fundamentals of Electrical Engineering, pp. 1–4 (2014)
31. Wayne Blanchard, B.: Guide to emergency management and related terms, definitions, concepts, acronyms, organizations, programs, guidance, executive orders & legislation: a tutorial on emergency management, broadly defined, past and present. In: CEM (2008)
32. Khorram-Manesh, A.: Handbook of Disaster and Emergency Management. Supported by DGECHO, EU, Sweden (2017)
33. Vamanu, B.I., Acasandrei, V.: Terms of reference for assessing nuclear and chemical emergencies in view of preparedness and response-an outlook. Rom. J. Phys. **59**(9–10), 952–975 (2014)
34. Khazai, B., Kunz-Plapp, T., Büscher, C., Wegner, A.: VuWiki: an ontology-based semantic wiki for vulnerability assessments. Int. J. Disaster Risk Sci. **5**(1), 55–73 (2014). https://doi.org/10.1007/s13753-014-0010-9
35. IFIN-HH: Horia Hulubei National Institute for R&D in Physics and Nuclear Engineering. http://www.nipne.ro/. Accessed 15 Jan 2020
36. Nowak-Brzezińska, A., Wakulicz-Deja, A.: Exploration of rule-based knowledge bases: a knowledge engineer's support. Inf. Sci. **485**, 301–318 (2019)
37. IAEA: Development of an extended framework for emergency response criteria, Interim report for comments jointly sponsored by IAEA and WHO, IAEA-TECDOC-1432, In Vienna: International Atomic Energy Agency (2005)
38. IAEA: Criteria for use in preparedness and response for a nuclear or radiological emergency: general safety guide, jointly sponsored by the Food and Agriculture Organization of the United Nations. In: Vienna: International Atomic Energy Agency (2011)
39. Mescherin, S., Kirillov, I., Klimenko, S.: Ontology of emergency shared situation awareness and crisis interoperability. In: International Conference on Cyberworlds, pp. 159–162 IEEE (2013)
40. Hristidis, V., Chen, S.-C., Li, T., Luis, S., Deng, Y.: Survey of data management and analysis in disaster situations. J. Syst. Softw. **83**(10), 1701–1714 (2010)

41. Gaur, M., Shekarpour, S., Gyrard, A. Sheth, A.: empathi: an ontology for emergency managing and planning about hazard crisis. In: 13th IEEE International Conference on Semantic Computing. California, USA, pp. 396–403. IEEE (2019)
42. Daramola O., Stålhane T., Omoronyia I., Sindre G.: Using ontologies and machine learning for hazard identification and safety analysis. In: Maalej W., Thurimella A. (eds.) Managing Requirements Knowledge. Springer, Berlin, Heidelberg (2013). https://doi.org/10.1007/978-3-642-34419-0_6
43. Racherla, P., Hu, C.: A framework for knowledge-based crisis management in the hospitality and tourism industry. Cornell Hospitality Q. 50(4), 561–577 (2009)
44. Yusupova, N.I., Shakhmametova, G.R., Dusalina, E.K.: Enterprises monitoring for crisis preventing based on knowledge engineering. In: Kovács, G.L., Kochan, D. (eds.) NEW PROLAMAT 2013. IAICT, vol. 411, pp. 343–353. Springer, Heidelberg (2013). https://doi.org/10.1007/978-3-642-41329-2_33
45. Liu, S., Brewster, C., Shaw, D.: Ontologies for crisis management: a review of state of the art in ontology design and usability. In: Proceedings of the 10th International ISCRAM Conference, Germany, pp. 349–359 (2013)
46. Benaben, F., Lauras, M., Truptil, S., Salatge, N.: A metamodel for knowledge management in crisis management. In: 49th Hawaii International Conference on System Sciences, pp. 126–135. IEEE (2016)
47. Moi, M., Rodehutskors, N., Koch, R.: An ontology for the use of quality evaluated social media data in emergencies. IADIS Int. J. WWW/Internet 14(2), 38–57 (2016)
48. Ward, R., Sorokine, A., Schlicher, B., Wright, M., Kruse, K.: Ontology-based software for generating scenarios for characterizing searches for nuclear materials. In: Proceedings of the Sixth International Conference on Semantic Technologies for Intelligence, Defense, and Security, Fairfax, USA, pp. 89–92 (2011)
49. Sorokine, A., Schlicher, B.G., Ward, R.C., Wright, M.C., Kruse, K.L., Bhaduri, B., Slepoy, A.: An interactive ontology-driven information system for simulating background radiation and generating scenarios for testing special nuclear materials detection algorithms. Eng. Appl. Artif. Intell. 43(2015), 157–165 (2015)
50. Madurai, Meenachi N., Sai, Baba M.: Development of semantic web-based knowledge management for nuclear reactor (KMNuR) portal. DESIDOC J. Libr. Inf. Technol. 34(5), 426–434 (2014)
51. Fortineau, V., Paviot, T., Louis-Sidney, L., Lamouri. S.: SWRL as a rule language for ontology-based models in power plant design. In: The 9th International Conference on Product Lifecycle Management (PLM), Canada, pp. 588–597 (2012)
52. Konstantopoulos, S., Ikonomopoulos, A.: A conceptualization of a nuclear or radiological emergency. Nucl. Eng. Des. 284(2015), 192–206 (2015)

Design of a Biochemistry Procedure-Oriented Ontology

Mohammed Alliheedi[1]([✉])[iD], Yetian Wang[2][iD], and Robert E. Mercer[2,3][iD]

[1] Al Baha University, Al Bahah 65527, Saudi Arabia
`malliheedi@bu.edu.sa`
[2] University of Waterloo, Waterloo, Canada
`yetian.wang@uwaterloo.ca`
[3] The University of Western Ontario, London, Canada
`mercer@csd.uwo.ca`

Abstract. Ontologies must provide the entities, concepts, and relations required by the domain being represented. The domain of interest in this paper is the biochemistry experimental procedure. These procedures are composed of procedure steps which can be represented as sequences. Sequences are composed of totally ordered, partially ordered, and alternative subsequences. The ontology language being used is OWL-DL. OWL-DL was adopted due to its well-balanced flexibility among expressiveness (e.g., class description, cardinality restriction, etc.), completeness, and decidability. In the biochemistry procedure-oriented ontology presented here, subsequences are represented with two relations, *directlyFollows* and *directlyPrecedes* that are used to represent sequences. Alternative subsequences can be generated by composing a *oneOf* function in OWL-DL. Each alternative subsequence is referred to as *optionalStepOf* in this work. Two biochemistry procedures, Alkaline Agarose Gel Electrophoresis and Southern Blotting, are used to demonstrate the generality of this procedural ontology. Portions of these procedures are described in detail. SPARQL queries show the versatility of the ontology.

Keywords: Experimental procedure · Procedural steps · Sequence of steps · Biomedical ontology · Formal ontology · Knowledge representation

1 Introduction

Ontologies provide three features to represent a domain: 1) entities (known as individuals in some ontological languages), 2) concepts, and 3) relations among those entities and concepts. Adequacy of an ontology is obtained when the entities, concepts, and relations required to model any situation that can occur in the domain being represented have been provided by the ontology. Our focus is the biochemistry domain, the experimental methodology aspect, in particular. We have attempted to design an ontology that is adequate for this domain. To demonstrate this generality, we show two examples of biochemistry experimental procedures, Alkaline Agarose Gel Electrophoresis and Southern Blotting.

A number of biologically oriented ontologies have been created, one of the best known is the Gene Ontology (GO) [6]. Others have been developed for a variety of other

© Springer Nature Switzerland AG 2020
A. Fred et al. (Eds.): IC3K 2019, CCIS 1297, pp. 365–387, 2020.
https://doi.org/10.1007/978-3-030-66196-0_17

purposes. They are discussed in detail in the Sect. 2. Most of these ontologies describe a set of concepts and categories in the biological domain that shows their properties and the relations between them.

The type of domain that we are attempting to represent consists of *procedures*, experimental procedures, in particular. Procedures are *sequences* of *procedure steps* (simply, *steps*, henceforth). Some ontologies provide descriptions of steps [33]. To the best of our knowledge no current biologically oriented ontology represents sequences of steps. An important aspect of the steps in a procedure is that they immediately follow one another. 'Directly follows' (and 'directly precedes') is an intransitive relation (i.e., if B directly follows A, and if C directly follows B, then C does not directly follow A). Transitive relations are the norm in the current biologically oriented ontologies (e.g., the omnipresent 'subclass' relation; 'proper part of', 'precedes' and 'is causally related to' ([16], Figures 6 and 9)).

Procedures can contain sequences of steps that are totally ordered (i.e., the steps must be done one after the other in the sequence specified), steps that can be partially ordered (i.e., subsequences of steps that can be done in any order), and alternative subsequences of steps (i.e., only one of the alternatives is done). In addition to the intransitive relations 'directly follows' and 'directly precedes' our contribution also includes these three types of sequence orderings.

Descriptions of experimental procedures exist in scientific writing. The scientific domain of interest to us is biochemistry. An important type of information contained in the Method section of biochemistry articles are references to standard biochemistry experiment procedures. These protocols, which typically involve several steps, are described in detail in manuals of standard biochemistry experiment procedures [11,29]. In this paper, which is an extended version of [4], we propose a biochemistry procedure-oriented ontology that explicitly identifies all of the steps of an experimental procedure and provides the relations between the steps of an experimental procedure. Two examples investigate two experimental procedures that exist in the manual of standard biochemistry experimental procedures [29]: Alkaline Agarose Gel Electrophoresis which was first introduced in Alliheedi et al. [4] and an additional procedure, Southern Blotting, which adds to this examination.

The sections that follow include an review of related work in Sect. 2 with special emphasis on ontologies that have been proposed for scientific experimental protocols. This is followed by a description of our ontological framework in Sect. 3. Then, a detailed discussion of two well-known biochemistry protocols is presented in Sect. 4 to demonstrate the capabilities of our developed ontology. These protocols are given textually. Ontological instances of these protocols have been implemented in OWL-DL. Parts of these implementations are described in detail. Six SPARQL queries highlight how information from the protocols can be extracted. Section 5 concludes this paper with a short discussion of further investigations.

2   Related Work

With the increased sophistication of computation in the biomedical domain, ontology development has become more and more important for providing the knowledge needed for these computer applications [28]. Several ontologies have been developed in recent years such as the Gene Ontology [6], the Ontology for Chemical Entities of Biological Interest (ChEBI) [14], the Foundational Model of Anatomy (FMA) [27,28], and the Ontology for Biomedical Investigations (OBI) [9]. The goal of these ontologies is mainlyfm to provide definitive controlled terminologies that describe entities in the biomedical genre.

The main aspect of Gene Ontology (GO) is to provide information that describes gene products using precisely defined vocabulary [6]. GO intially used three model organism databases including FlyBase [18], Mouse Genome Informatics [10,26], and the saccharomyces Genome Database [8]. Recently, the number of model organism databases has increased dramatically [19].

The Chemical Entities of Biological Interest ontology (ChEBI) is a lexicon of molecular entities concerned with small molecules [14]. Information from several resources (e.g., IntEnz [17], KEGG COMPOUND [20], and the Chemical Ontology) was used to create ChEBI. ChEBI used various relations to describe the relationships between ontology entities. These relations include relations required by ChEBI (e.g., 'is conjugate acid of', and 'is tautomer of') as well as relations which are defined by the Relations Ontology[1] (e.g., 'is a' and 'is part of').

The Foundational Model of Anatomy Ontology (FMA) [27,28], a knowledge source for biomedical informatics, is concerned with classes and relationships needed to represent the phenotypic structure of the human body in terms of human anatomy.

The Ontology for Biomedical Investigations (OBI), http://purl.obolibrary.org/obo/obi, [9], a resource for annotating biomedical investigations, provides standard tools to represent study design, protocols and instrumentation used, the data generated and the types of analysis performed on the data.

Several ontologies are based on the OBI ontology. Since these ontologies are closest to our interest in biochemistry procedures, we will describe them in more detail.

- A work predating the above list, [34], proposes EXPO, an ontology of scientific experiments, in general. It remains a descriptive ontology, providing a detailed description of various aspects of scientific experiments and how they are related.
- Descriptions of experimental processes are provided by OBI, and three real-world applications are discussed in [12]. Some of the relations in these applications (e.g., inputs, outputs, etc.) come very close to our purpose here. The beta cell genomics application ontology (BCGO) [35] also uses OBI, but it tends to be a more descriptive ontology than some of the others that use OBI, but some of the relations in RO, the relation ontology [32], that are used (e.g., produces, translate_to) do have an ordering sense.
- The two ontologies that are most similar to the work described below are EXACT [33] and the Semanticscience Integrated Ontology [16]. Both are motivated by a need to describe scientific protocols and experiments. Where they differ from what we are proposing is that they describe *sets* of actions in scientific protocols and experiments, whereas we are proposing to represent *sequences* of actions, or steps in a procedure, if you like. Relations that describe orderings of actions (e.g., 'precedes' [16]) are not applicable to sequences since these relations are transitive.

---

[1] http://www.obofoundry.org/ontology/ro.html.

- The Molecular Methods Database (MolMeth) is a database which contains scientific protocol ontologies that conform to a set of laboratory protocol standards [21].
- Other ontologies describe general concepts that are useful to a biochemistry procedure-oriented ontology include: Ontologies consist of process such as [22] and [30], ontology for units of measure [25], classification of scenarios and plans (CLASP) [15], and materials ontology [7]. Foundational theories such as process calculus and regular grammar are essential for the formalization of procedure-oriented ontologies.

3   Procedure-Oriented Ontology

We propose a framework for procedure-oriented ontologies that explicitly identifies all steps of an experimental procedure and provides a set of relations to describe the relationships between the steps of an experimental procedure. The novelty of this approach is to allow creating a sequence of events (or steps in a procedure) using the ontological concept of "something occurs before". To accomplish this we need to have an ontological concept of "sequence". This is very important concept because one cannot simply call a sequence of events "a sequence" unless these events happen step by step in some sort of ordering.

This approach will be used to provide the necessary information about the experimental procedures for Knowledge Base systems with the required knowledge about experimental processes. There are manuals of standard procedures in biochemistry [11, 29] which in turn will help in building extensions of our ontology.

3.1   Relations

In this section, we describe various properties to satisfy the definition of an experimental procedure. An experimental procedure consists of a series of events (steps). These steps occur in order, either partially or totally. Partial ordering enables steps (more than one step) to precede or follow another step. On the contrary, total ordering allows a step to precede or follow another step intransitively. Both relations have been defined for OWL [24] and are available from http://www.ontologydesignpatterns.org/cp/owl/sequence.owl.

We also aim to represent the choices of a subsequence of steps from more than one possible subsequence. Since the choices among subsequences would be "either" or "or", the relation 'optionalStepOf' needs to be designed based on the different choices of available subsequences in that particular step. To illustrate, the 'optionalStepOf' relation is simply an 'exclusive or' if there are two choices available, or else it would be a generalization of the exclusive or. In this paper, We have implemented the aforementioned relations to satisfy the definition of "procedure".

3.2   Classes and Properties

The proposed ontology framework consists of three core classes: Step, State, and Action. Each of the classes are described in the following sections. We indicate class names with capitalized words, e.g., Step. A property is indicated with single quotes, e.g., 'sub-StepOf'. An instance name is indicated using typewriter font, e.g., step1. When referring to the actual steps from the protocol, we simply use normal font, e.g., step 1.1.

Step. Each step in a procedure is represented by instances of the Step class (see Fig. 1). We defined object properties such as 'precedes', 'follows', and 'parallel' to represent the ordering relations of each step. Note that the aforementioned object properties are transitive. The properties 'precedes' and 'follows', inverses of each other, indicate the chronological order between two steps. The property 'parallel' is symmetrical which indicates steps may occur simultaneously. Intransitive properties 'directlyPrecedes' and 'directlyFollows' are subproperties of 'precedes' and 'follows' respectively. These properties describe the order between steps in which a step immediately precedes or follows another step. Similar to 'precedes' and 'follows', they are also inverses of each other. Therefore, by stating step1.1 'directlyPrecedes' step1.2, and step1.2 'directlyPrecedes' step1.3, a reasoner will automatically infer that step1.1 'precedes' step1.2 as well as step1.3. Also, step1.3 'directlyFollows' step1.2 but only 'follows' step1.1, both being inferable by a reasoner. We indicate only the 'precedes' relation in the figures presented in this paper for cleanliness.

Procedures are often formed by a hierarchical structure among steps. A step may consist of a number of sub-steps required to complete. Suppose we have an arbitrary step called step1 which consists of step1.1 and step1.2. Then both step1.1 and step1.2 must be completed in order to claim that step1 is complete. Thus we introduce the properties 'subStepOf' and 'optionalStepOf'. The property 'subStepOf' indicates that some step(s) must be completed for the completion of the parent step, e.g., the triples (step1.1, 'subStepOf', step1) and (step1.2, 'subStepOf', step1). In the case where one and only one of step1.1 and step1.2 needs to be completed in order to complete step1, the property 'optionalStepOf' can be used to indicate that one of the steps (not both) must be completed in order to complete the parent step, e.g., (step1.1a, 'optionalStepOf', step1.1) and (step1.1b, 'optionalStepOf', step1.1). Both domain and range of the properties are the class Step.

Figure 1 illustrates a scenario with parallel steps step1 and step2. The instance step1 has sub-steps in which step1.1 must complete before step1.2 and thus before step1.3. step1.1 has two optional steps in which at least one must be completed. Ordering relations between step1.1.1 and step1.1.2 since they are optional steps.

Note that all steps mentioned are instances of the class Step. These steps do not necessarily have to strictly follow the organization of steps in a written document. In the previous example, step1 could simply be an abstraction of step1.1 and step1.2 that is not explicitly mentioned in a written procedure. What's important is that the completion of step1 is an indication of the completion of both step1.1 and step1.2, in that order.

State. The relations between instances of the class Step outline the structure of a procedure. Each instance of Step is represented as a set of states and are associated to a set of actions. A step involves a transition from state to state via a single or a series of actions, represented by the classes State and Action (see Fig. 2).

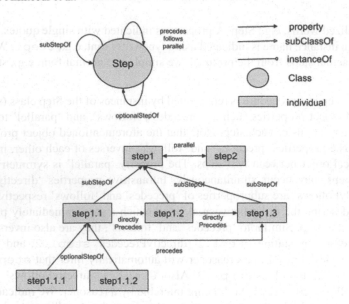

Fig. 1. Step class and example instances. (This figure originally appeared in [4]).

State is connected to Step via the property 'hasState' and has three subclasses, InitialState, MidState, and FinalState. The subclasses are connected via properties such as 'precedes' or 'follows'. InitialState can only precede a MidState or a FinalState. FinalState can only follow an InitialState or MidState. MidState can 'follow' an InitialState and 'precede' a FinalState, as well as 'precede' or 'follow' another MidState. The triple (stateX, 'precedes', stateY) implies (stateY, 'follows', stateX) since 'follows' is an inverse property of 'precedes'. Figures 1 and 2 omit 'follows' to keep the figures clean. Note that a step has at most one instance of InitialState or FinalState but may have multiple instances of MidState. For example, an instance of Step, step1, may involve two instances of State, i.e., step1_state1 and step1_state2, represented by the following triples: (step1, hasState, state1), (step1, 'hasState', state2), (state1, 'precedes', state2), in which state1 and state2 are instances of InitialState and FinalState respectively.

Action. States are connected to the Action class via 'beforeState' and 'afterState', representing the states before and after an action, respectively. In other words, an instance of Action would transition an instance of State to another. For example, when an action action1 is performed in state1, state1 will be modified and thus transitioned into a new state state2. This can be represented by triples (action1, 'beforeState', state1) and (action1, 'afterState', state2).

Restriction. A Restriction class was created to represent certain limitations applied to a state in a step. It is linked to the class State via 'hasRestriction'. For example, (state1, 'hasRestriction', restriction1) means that restriction1 will be

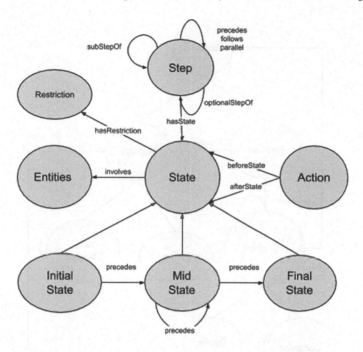

Fig. 2. State and Action classes. (This figure is a modification of the version that originally appeared in [4]).

checked against `state1`. It may be sufficient to apply a restriction to a FinalState but it is also possible to apply restrictions to all states in a step.

Biochemistry Domain Knowledge. The State class is connected to the Entities class (see Fig. 3) via the property 'involves'. Domain knowledge of biochemistry can be described by extending the Entities class with subclasses such as Instruments, Materials, and Devices involved in a specific state. For demonstration purposes, we have included only selected general concepts related to experimental procedures described in Sect. 4. The class Instrument includes Container and Device where Container 'contains' Material which is a class for Chemical and Non-Chemical materials used in biochemistry experiment procedures. Compound materials and assembled instruments are represented using the property 'consistsOf'. Instrument and Material can be connected to the class Measure which is a combination of numerical values and Unit_of_Measure, e.g., $10\,m$ is a measure where the value is 10 with a unit of measure of `meter` [25]. The Measure class was extended with subclasses to represent absolute measures (e.g., $10\,m$), range values (e.g., $5\,m-10\,m$), and ratio (e.g., $1/2$).

4 Two Biochemistry Examples Demonstrating Ontology Instances

In this section, we describe two different experimental procedures namely, Alkaline Agarose Gel Electrophoresis [29] (see Fig. 4) and Southern Blotting [29] (see Fig. 7) using the set of relations described in Sect. 3.

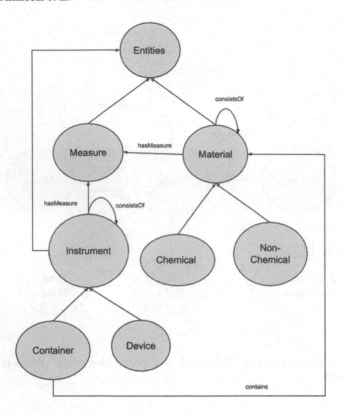

Fig. 3. Demonstration of Entities class. (This figure originally appeared in [4]).

Our primary goal is to analyze experimental procedure sentences found in the Method section of biochemistry articles. Method sections tend to omit some obvious or common steps in experimental procedures that domain experts would interpret from the texts. However, these omitted or hidden steps are crucial to fully understand and interpret the steps and their relations, which in turn will aid in building the ontology for that particular procedure.

For example, in order to understand fully the sentence fragment, "the resulting ca. 900 bp piece was gel purified and ligated using T4 ligase into pUC19" [13], we need to know all the steps and their relations involved in gel purification and ligation. So, with this in mind, we started to design our ontology which meets this essential aspect.

The preparation of both the agarose solution and the DNA samples are the first two main steps of Alkaline Agarose Gel Electrophoresis (see Fig. 4). The preparation of the agarose solution (step1.1) is described in Fig. 5. Essentially, step 1.1 stated that "adding the appropriate amount of powdered agarose to a measured quantity of H2O" consists of two choices either: step 1.1.1 "an Erlenmeyer flask" 'exclusiveOR' step 1.1.2 "a glass bottle". This requires a relation 'optionalStepOf' that demonstrate the option of using one container or another.

Since we have two instruments that we could choose from, two sequences of steps are available: *If* step1.1.1 "an Erlenmeyer flask" *is selected then* proceed to sub-step step1.1.1.1 "loosely plug the neck of the Erlenmeyer flask with Kimwipes"

Alkaline Agarose Gel Electrophoresis

1. Prepare the agarose solution
   1.1. Adding the appropriate amount of powdered agarose to a measured quantity of H2O in either:
       1.1.1. An Erlenmeyer flask (Container 1)
           1.1.1.1. Loosely plug the neck of the Erlenmeyer flask with Kimwipes
       1.1.2. OR a glass bottle (Container 1)
           1.1.2.1. Make sure that the cap is loose
   1.2. Heat the slurry (Item1) in (Container1) for the minimum time required to allow all of the grains of agarose to dissolve using either:
       1.2.1. A boiling-water bath
           1.2.1.1. Check that the volume of the solution (Item 1) has not been decreased by evaporation during boiling in (Container 1):
               1.2.1.1.1. if yes: replenish with H2O in (Container 1)
               1.2.1.1.2. If no: do not add H2O in (Container 1)
       1.2.2. OR a microwave oven
           1.2.2.1. Check that the volume of the solution (Item 1) has not been decreased by evaporation during boiling in (Container 1):
               1.2.2.1.1. if yes: replenish with H2O in (Container 1)
               1.2.2.1.2. If no: do not add H2O in (Container 1)
   1.3. Cool the clear solution (Item 1) to 55 C.
       1.3.1. Add 0.1 volume of 10x alkaline agarose gel electrophoresis buffer in (Container 1)
       1.3.2. And immediately pour the gel (Item 1) into mold (Container 2)
   1.4. After the gel (Item 1) is completely set
       1.4.1. Mount it (Item 1) in the electrophoresis tank (Container 3)
       1.4.2. Add freshly made 1x alkaline electrophoresis buffer until the gel (Item 1) is just covered.
2. Prepare DNA samples
   2.1. Collect the DNA samples (Item 2) by standard precipitation with ethanol2
   2.2. Dissolve the damp precipitates of DNA (Item 2) in 10-20 µl of 1x gel buffer. (Item 3)
   2.3. Add 0.2 volume of 6x alkaline gel-loading buffer
       2.3.1. It is important to chelate all Mg2+ with EDTA before adjusting the electrophoresis samples to alkaline conditions
3. Initiate the electrophoresis
   3.1. Load the DNA samples dissolved in 6x alkaline gel-loading buffer into the wells of the gel (Container 3)
   3.2. Start the electrophoresis at < 3.5 V/cm when the bromocresol green has migrated into the gel approx. 0.5-1 cm; Turn off the power supply, and place a glass plate on top of the gel in (Container 3) and then continue electrophoresis until the bromocresol green has migrated approximately two thirds of the length of the gel in (Container 3).
4. Finalize the experiment
   4.1. Process the gel according to one of the procedures either Southern hybridization by:
       4.1.1. Transfer the DNA either:
           4.1.1.1. Directly (without soaking the gel) from the alkaline agarose gel to a charged nylon membrane. Please see Southern Blotting: Capillary Transfer of DNA to Membranes
           4.1.1.2. OR after soaking the gel in neutralizing solution for 45 minutes at room temperature to either:
               4.1.1.2.1. An uncharged nitrocellulose as described in Southern Blotting: Capillary Transfer of DNA to Membranes
               4.1.1.2.2. OR nylon membrane as described in Southern Blotting: Capillary Transfer of DNA to Membranes
       4.1.2. Detect the target sequences in the immobilized DNA by hybridization to an appropriate labeled probe. Please see Southern Hybridization of Radiolabeled Probes to Nucleic Acids Immobilized on Membranes
   4.2. OR Staining
       4.2.1. Soak the gel in neutralizing solutions for 45 minutes at room temperature
           4.2.1.1. Stain the neutralized gel with 0.5 µg/ml ethidium bromide in 1x TAE or with SYBR Gold
               4.2.1.1.1. A band of interest can be sliced from the gel and subsequently eluted by one of the procedures described Recovery of DNA from Agarose Gels

Fig. 4. The steps of Alkaline Agarose Gel Electrophoresis.

which involves both initial and final states, action and container as seen in Fig. 5; *else if* step1.1.2 "a glass bottle" is selected *then* proceed to sub-step step1.1.2.1 "make sure that the cap is loose". In subsequent steps, the instance container1 refers to the instances of either Erlenmeyer flask (i.e., flask1) or the glass bottle (i.e., glassBottle1). The material of Erlenmeyer flask refers to the instances of kimwipes (i.e., kimwipe1). Figure 1 showed the two main steps (step1, and step2) that are partially ordered, in other words, both steps can be performed in any order (i.e., step1 then step2 or vice versa). Furthermore, each one of the four main steps in Fig. 4 consist of several sub-steps. Figures 5 and 6 include descriptions of step1.1 and step3 because these steps are representative of all other steps in the procedure.

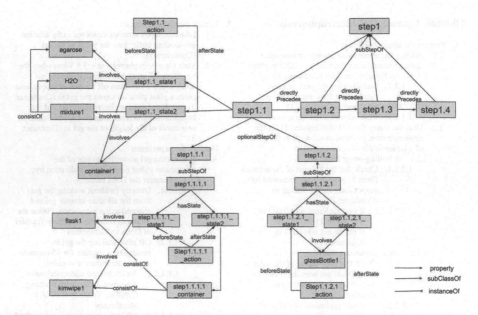

Fig. 5. An example of alternative sub-sequences in steps for preparing the Agarose solution. (This figure is a modification of the version that originally appeared in [4]).

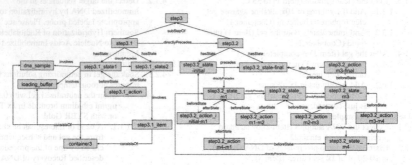

Fig. 6. Instances related to step3 which involves initiating the electrophoresis. (This figure is a modification of the version that originally appeared in [4]).

A total ordered sequence from step1.1 to step1.4 is shown in Fig. 5. Another example, the description of the instances of both sub-steps step3.1 and step3.2, which are parts of step3, that are concerned with initiating the electrophoresis is shown in Fig. 6. Step 3.1 is straightforward (see Fig. 4). Step 3.2 involves a condition to ensure the gel reaches a certain length, so this step needs several MidStates in addition to both the initial and finial states as is shown in Table 1. Table 1 shows a detailed description of all of the entities for step3.2. Note that step3.2 consists of a number of MidStates which represent waiting until the desired amount of migration has been reached (i.e., 2/3 of gel length). The instance step3.2_state_initial and step3.2_state_final are instances of InitialState and FinalState, respectively.

The instances of MidStates are `step3.2_state_m1` to `step3.2_state_m4`, each representing a middle state described below:

- `step3.2_state_m1`: Electrophoresis power is on
- `step3.2_state_m2`: The state where bromocresol green is migrating into gel
- `step3.2_state_m3`: Bromocresol green has migrated into gel approximately 0.5–1 cm, the power of the electrophoresis has been turned off.
- `step3.2_state_m4`: A glass plate has been placed on top of the gel, bromocresol green has migrated less than 2/3 of the gel length.

Table 1. Description of the entities involved in step3.1 and step3.2.

Subject	Property	Object	Description
step3	rdf:type	Step	
step3.1	rdf:type	Step	
	subStepOf	step3	
	directlyPrecedes	step3.2	
	hasState	step3.1_state1	
	hasState	step3.1_state2	
step3.1_state1	rdf:type	InitialState	
	involves	container3	
	involves	dnaSamples	
	involves	gel-loadingbuffer	
	directlyPrecedes	step3.1_state2	
step3.1_action	rdf:type	Action	
	beforeState	step3.1_state1	
	afterState	step3.1_state2	
step3.1_state2	rdf:type	FinalState	
	involves	step3.1_item	
step3.1_item	rdf:type	Material	
	consistOf	container3	
	consistOf	dnaSamples	
	consistOf	gel-loadingbuffer	
container3	rdf:type	Container	
step3.2	rdf:type	Step	
	subStepOf	step3	
	hasState	step3.2_state_initial	
	hasState	step3.2_state_m1	
	hasState	step3.2_state_m2	
	hasState	step3.2_state_m3	
	hasState	step3.2_state_m4	
	hasState	step3.2_state_final	

(continued)

Table 1. (*continued*)

Subject	Property	Object	Description
step3.2_state_initial	rdf:type	InitialState	
	involves	electrophoresis	
	involves	electrophoresis_measure	
	precedes	step3.2_state_m1	
step3.2_action_initial_m1	rdf:type	TurnOn	TurnOn is a subclass of Action
	beforeState	step3.2_state_initial	
	afterState	step3.2_state_m1	
step3.2_state_m1	rdf:type	MidState	
	involves	electrophoresis	
	involves	electrophoresis_measure	
	involves	bg_migrate_measure	A measure for the migration of bromocresol green
	involves	bromocresol_green	
	involves	gel	
	directlyPrecedes	step3.2_state_m2	
step3.2_action_m1_m2	rdf:type	DoNothing	DoNothing is a subclass of Action
	beforeState	step3.2_state_m1	
	afterState	step3.2_state_m2	
step3.2_state_m2	rdf:type	MidState	A measure for the migration of bromocresol green
	involves	bg_migrate_measure	
	involves	bromocresol_green	
	involves	gel	A measure of current length of gel that the bromocresol green has migrated to
	involves	gel_length_portion	
	directlyPrecedes	step3.2_state_m3	
step3.2_action_m2_m3	rdf:type	TurnOff	
	beforeState	step3.2_state_m2	
	afterState	step3.2_state_m3	
step3.2_state_m3	rdf:type	MidState	A measure of current length of gel that the bromocresol green has migrated to, less than 2/3
	involves	electrophoresis	
	involves	electrophoresis_measure	
	involves	gel_length_portion	
	directlyPrecedes	step3.2_state_m4	
	directlyPrecedes	step3.2_state_final	

(*continued*)

Table 1. (*continued*)

Subject	Property	Object	Description
step3.2_action_m3_m4	rdf:type	Action	Put glass plate on gel
	beforeState	step3.2_state_m3	
	afterState	step3.2_state_m4	
step3.2_state_m4	rdf:type	MidState	
	directlyPrecedes	step3.2_state_m1	
	involves	gel	
	involves	gel_length_portion	
	involves	glass_plate	
step3.2_action_m4_m1	rdf:type	TurnOn	
	beforeState	step3.2_state_m4	
	afterState	step3.2_state_m1	
step3.2_action_m3_final	rdf:type	Action	Put glass plate on gel
	beforeState	step3.2_state_m3	
	afterState	step3.2_state_final	
step3.2_state_final	rdf:type	FinalState	
	involves	electrophoresis	A measure of current length of gel that the bromocresol green has migrated to, equal to or more than 2/3
	involves	electrophoresis_measure	
	involves	gel_length_portion2	
	involves	bromocresol_green	
	involves	gel	

The process is a loop since step3.2_state_m4 precedes step3.2_state_m1. step3.2_state_m4 differs with step3.2_state_final in that the bromocresol green has migrated to the targeted amount in the latter. step3.2_state_m3 precedes both step3.2_state_m4 and step3.2_state_final. An instance of Measure could be used to track the amount that bromocresol green has migrated.

Another example demonstrates the step of depurification of agarose gel (step 6) as part of the Southern Blotting procedure. The steps of Southern Blotting are listed in Fig. 7. An ontology diagram for step 6 is presented in Fig. 8. An instance of the class Step was created, i.e., step6. step6 has two sub-steps, represented using instances step6.1 and step6.2. The former is simply placing the gel into a glass baking dish. This process can be explained in terms of our ontology as follows:

1. step6.1 has an initial state step6.1_state1
2. step6.1_state1 involves the instance of the gel (item1) and an instance of glass baking dish (container1)
3. an action step6.1_action (i.e., place) transitions step6.1_state1 to the next state, step6.1_state2
4. step6.1_state2 involves step6.1_item in which the assembled object consists of the gel and the tray

Southern Blotting
(first steps)

1. Prepare the gel
   1.1. Prepare a 1% agarose gel (Item 1). (See Alkaline Agarose Gel Electrophoresis for details.)
2. Prepare DNA samples
   2.1. Digest an appropriate amount of DNA with one or more restriction enzymes to produce the restriction fragments (Item 2)
   2.2. Add the appropriate amount of gel-loading buffer to the digested DNA (Item 2) (giving Item 3)
3. Load the gel (Item 1)
   3.1. Load the DNA fragment mixture (Item 3) on the gel (Item 1)
4. Run the gel (Item 1)
   4.1. OPTION: small gel, follow the standard procedure
   4.2. OPTION: With large gels, 15 cm, it is best to run overnight at about 15-20 volts to ensure sharp band separation
5. Visualization of the gel (Item 1)
   5.1. Stain the gel (Item 1) with ethidium bromide (Solution 1) (giving Item 6)
       5.1.1. Quantity of ethidium bromide: (10 mg/ml)
   5.2. Mark the bottom left-hand corner of the gel (Item 6) by cutting off the corner with a spatula (Item 7)
   5.3. Photograph the gel (Item 6) with a transparent ruler (Item 8) placed alongside to indicate distances in the photograph

6. OPTION: Depurination of the gel (Item 1) (giving Item 4)
   6.1. Place the gel (Item 1) into a glass baking dish (Container 1)
   6.2. Depurination
       6.2.1. Choose volume of 0.25N HCl (Solution 2)
           6.2.1.1. Quantity of Solution 2: 250 ml
           6.2.1.2. OR enough to cover gel completely
       6.2.2. Incubate the gel for 10 min with 0.25N HCl (Solution 2)
           Note: AVOID LONG INCUBATIONS. This process cleaves DNA that allows large fragments to transfer to the nylon membrane
       6.2.3. Agitate gently
7. Denature the gel (Item 1 or Item 4) for transfer of the DNA restriction fragments to uncharged membranes (nitrocellulose or nylon) (giving Item 9)
   7.1. Soak the gel (Item 1 or Item 4) with denaturation solution (Solution 3) with constant gentle agitation
       7.1.1. Composition of Solution 3: 1.5 M NaCl, 0.5 M NaOH
       7.1.2. Quantity of Solution 3: 10 gel volumes
       7.1.3. Time of denaturing: 45 min
       7.1.4. Temperature of denaturing: 15-25°C
8. Wash and Neutralize the gel (Item 9) (giving Item 10)
   8.1. Wash the gel (Item 9) briefly with diH2O (Solution 4)
       8.1.1. Quantity of Solution 4: 250 ml
   8.2. Neutralize the gel (Item 9)with Solution 5 with constant gentle agitation
       8.2.1. Composition of Solution 5: 1 M Tris, pH 4.0, 1.5 mM NaCl
       8.2.2. Quantity of Solution 5: 10 gel volumes
       8.2.3. Time of neutralizing: 30 min
       8.2.4. Temperature of denaturing: 15-25°C
   8.3. Repeat the previous steps.

Fig. 7. The first steps of Southern Blotting.

The instance step6.2 describes the depurification process which involves incubation and agitation of step6.1_item along with the solution 0.266N HCl (solution2). It has three sub-steps, i.e., step6.2.1: choose a volume for solution2, step6.2.2: incubation, and step6.2.3: agitate gently. step6.2.2 and step6.2.3 are parallel steps thus are performed at the same time. In fact, both steps involve the same mixture, i.e., the mixture of solution2 and step6.1_item which is represented by the instance step6.2_item. That is, the instance step6.2_item 'consistOf' solution2 and step6.1_item and is connected to the initial states of step6.2.2 and step6.2.3 via the property 'involves'. Both step6.2.2 and step6.2.3 have three states:

1. step6.2.{1,2}_state1: the initial state which involves step6.2_item created from step6.1.
2. step6.2.{1,2}_state_mid: the middle state in which action incubate or agitate were performed. Note that both actions are continuous, meaning that the actions are constantly being performed while in this state.

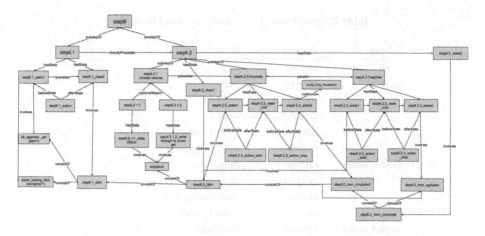

Fig. 8. Instances related to Step6 of Southern Blotting.

3. `step6.2.{1,2}_state2`: the final state which indicates that the duration of incubation has reached 10 min and both incubation and agitation has stopped.

The instances `step6.2.2_state2` and `step6.2.3_state2` involve the instances `step6.2_item_incubated` and `step6.2_item_agitated`, respectively. Since our model sees incubation and agitation as two separate steps, the outcome is also represented using separate instances. However, an instance `step6.2_item_complete` was created to combine the aforementioned instances via the property consistOf. This instance is linked to the final state of the parent step, `step6.2_state` via the property 'involves'. That is, according our definition of sub-steps, in order to complete `step6.2`, both `step6.2.2` and `step6.2.3` must be completed. Therefore the final product, i.e., `step6.2_item_complete`, can be produced only when both `step6.2_item_incubated` and `step6.2_item_agitated` were produced. Note that all three instances `step6.2_item_{incubated,agitated,complete}` may refer to the same real world object. To illustrate, `step6.2_item_incubated` and `step6.2_item_agitated` could be seen as two sides of a coin and the coin itself refers to `step6.2_item_complete`. A restriction `avoid_long_incubation` is connected to the final state of `step6.2.2`, i.e., `step6.2.2_state2` to reflect the restriction applied to step 6.2.2 from the original document. Details of instances of `step6` are listed below in Table 2.

Table 2. Description of the entities involved in step6.

Subject	Property	Object	Description
step6	rdf:type	Step	
step6.1	rdf:type	Step	
	subStepOf	step6	
	directlyPrecedes	step6.2	
	hasState	step6.1_state1	
	hasState	step6.1_state2	
step6.1_state1	rdf:type	InitialState	
	involves	sb_agarose_gel	
	involves	glass_baking_dish	
	precedes	step6.1_state2	
step6.1_state2	rdf:type	FinalState	
	involves	step6.1_item	
	precedes	step6.1_state2	
step6.1_action	rdf:type	Action	
	beforeState	step6.1_state1	
	afterState	step6.1_state_mid	
sb_agarose_gel	rdf:type	AgaroseGel	
	hasMeasure	sb_agarose_gel_m	
	alias	item1	
sb_agarose_gel_m	rdf:type	Measure	
	hasUnit	cm	
glass_baking_dish	rdf:type	Container	
	alias	container1	
step6.1_item	rdf:type	AgaroseGel	
	consistsOf	item1	
	consistsOf	container1	
step6.2	rdf:type	Step	
	subStepOf	step6	
	hasState	step6.2_state1	
	hasState	step6.2_state2	
step6.2_state1	rdf:type	InitialState	
	involves	step6.2_item	
	precedes	step6.2_state2	
step6.2_state2	rdf:type	FinalState	
	involves	step6.2_item_complete	
	precedes	step6.2_state2	
step6.2_item	rdf:type	Item	
	consistsOf	step6.1_item	
	consistsOf	solution2	
solution2	rdf:type	Chemical	
	hasMeasure	sol2_measure	

(continued)

Table 2. (*continued*)

Subject	Property	Object	Description
sol2_measure	rdf:type	Measure	
	hasUnit	mL	
mL	rdf:type	Unit_of_measure	
step6.2.1	rdf:type	Step	Choose volume
	subStepOf	step6.2	
	precedes	step6.2.2	
	precedes	step6.2.3	
step6.2.1.1	rdf:type	Step	
	subStepOf	step6.2.1	
	hasState	step6.2.1.1_state	
step6.2.1.2	rdf:type	Step	
	subStepOf	step6.2.1	
	hasState	step6.2.1.2_state	
step6.2.1.1_state	rdf:type	State	
	involves	solution2	
step6.2.1.2_state	rdf:type	State	
	involves	solution2	
sb_sol2_250ml	rdf:type	Chemical	250mL of solution2
	hasMeasure	sb_sol2_250ml_m	
	alias	solution2	
sb_sol2_250ml_m	rdf:type	Measure	
	hasNumericValue	250	
	hasUnit	mL	
sb_sol2_enough	rdf:type	Chemical	⎰ Enough solution2 to ⎱ cover the gel
	hasMeasure	sb_sol2_enough_m	
	alias	solution2	
sb_sol2_enough_m	rdf:type	Measure	
	hasUnit	mL	
step6.2.2	rdf:type	Step	Incubate
	subStepOf	step6.2	
	parallel	step6.2.3	
	hasState	step6.2.2_state1	
	hasState	step6.2.2_state_mid	
	hasState	step6.2.2_state2	
step6.2.2_state1	rdf:type	InitialState	
	directlyPrecedes	step6.2.2_state_mid	
	involves	step6.2_item	
step6.2.2_state_mid	rdf:type	MidState	
	directlyPrecedes	step6.2.2_state2	
	involves	step6.2_item	

(*continued*)

Table 2. (*continued*)

Subject	Property	Object	Description
step6.2.2_state2	rdf:type	FinalState	
	hasRestriction	avoid_long_incubation	
	involves	step6.2_item_incubated	
step6.2.2_action_start	rdf:type	Action	
	beforeState	step6.2.2_state1	
	afterState	step6.2.2_state_mid	
step6.2.2_action_stop	rdf:type	Action	
	beforeState	step6.2.2_state_mid	
	afterState	step6.2.2_state2	
step6.2_item_incubated	rdf:type	Item	
	consistOf	step6.2_item	
step6.2.3	rdf:type	Step	Agitate
	subStepOf	step6.2	
	parallel	step6.2.2	
	hasState	step6.2.3_state1	
	hasState	step6.2.3_state_mid	
	hasState	step6.2.3_state2	
step6.2.3_state1	rdf:type	InitialState	
	directlyPrecedes	step6.2.3_state_mid	
	involves	step6.2_item	
step6.2.3_state_mid	rdf:type	MidState	
	directlyPrecedes	step6.2.3_state2	
	involves	step6.2_item	
step6.2.3_state2	rdf:type	FinalState	
	involves	step6.2_item_agitated	
step6.2.3_action_start	rdf:type	Action	
	beforeState	step6.2.3_state1	
	afterState	step6.2.3_state_mid	
step6.2.3_action_stop	rdf:type	Action	
	beforeState	step6.2.3_state_mid	
	afterState	step6.2.3_state2	
step6.2_item_agitated	rdf:type	Item	
	consistOf	step6.2_item	
step6.2_item_complete	rdf:type	Item	
	consistOf	step6.2_item_incubated	
	consistOf	step6.2_item_agitated	

4.1   Ontology Queries Using SPARQL

We have used SPARQL to extract some domain knowledge about the experimental procedure of Alkaline Agarose Gel Electrophoresis from our framework. The following shows five queries and their corresponding results.

Query1. Return all devices involved in a state of all steps (1.1, 1.2, 3)

```
SELECT ?step ?state ?
      device
WHERE { ?step rdf:
      type : Step.
?step :hasState ?
      state.
?state :involves ?
      device.
?device rdf:type :
      Device}
```

Query

step	state	device
step1.2	step1.2_state1	device1
step1.2	step1.2_state2	device1
step1.2.1.1	step1.2.1.1_state1	boiling-waterBath
step1.2.1.1	step1.2.1.1_state2	boiling-waterBath
step1.2.2.1	step1.2.2.1_state1	microwaveOven
step1.2.2.1	step1.2.2.1_state2	microwaveOven
step3.2	step3.2_state1	electrophoresis
step3.2	step3.2_state_m3	electrophoresis
step3.2	step3.2_state_m1	electrophoresis
step3.2	step3.2_state2	electrophoresis
step3.2	step3.2_state_m4	electrophoresis
step3.2	step3.2_state_m4	glass_plate

Result

Query2. Which states of step 3 and its sub-steps measure the gel length, and what is the target value?

```
SELECT ?step ?state ?x
WHERE {
: step3 ^: subStep ?step.
?step :hasState ?state.
?state :involves :gel.
: gel :hasMeasure /: hasNumValue ?x}
```

Query

step	state	x
step3.2	step3.2_state_m4	"2/3"^^<http://www.w3.org/2000/01/rdf-schema#Literal>
step3.2	step3.2_state_m2	"2/3"^^<http://www.w3.org/2000/01/rdf-schema#Literal>
step3.2	step3.2_state2	"2/3"^^<http://www.w3.org/2000/01/rdf-schema#Literal>

Result

Query3. Return all steps and states with electrophoresis involved.

```
SELECT ?step ?state ?material
WHERE { ?step rdf:type : Step.
?step :hasState ?state.
?state :involves ?material.
FILTER(?material = :electrophoresis)}
```

Query

step	state	item
step1.2.2.1.2	step1.2.2.1.2_state1	container1
step1.2.1.1.1	step1.2.1.1.1_state1	container1
step1.2.1.1.1	step1.2.1.1.1_state2	container1
step3.1	step3.1_state1	container3
step3.1	step3.1_state2	container3
step1.2.1.1.2	step1.2.1.1.2_state1	container1
step1.2.1.1	step1.2.1.1_state1	container1
step1.2.1.1	step1.2.1.1_state2	container1
step1.2	step1.2_state1	container1
step1.2	step1.2_state2	container1
step1.2.2.1	step1.2.2.1_state1	container1
step1.2.2.1	step1.2.2.1_state2	container1
step1.1	step1.1_state1	container1
step1.2.2.1.1	step1.2.2.1.1_state1	container1
step1.1	step1.1_state2	container1
step1.2.2.1.1	step1.2.2.1.1_state2	container1
step3.2	step3.2_state_m3	electrophoresis
step3.2	step3.2_state_m4	glass_plate
step3.2	step3.2_state_m4	electrophoresis
step3.2	step3.2_state2	electrophoresis
step3.2	step3.2_state_m1	electrophoresis
step1.2.1.1	step1.2.1.1_state1	boiling-waterBath
step1.2.1.1	step1.2.1.1_state2	boiling-waterBath
step1.2	step1.2_state1	device1
step1.2	step1.2_state2	device1
step1.2.2.1	step1.2.2.1_state1	microwaveOven
step1.2.2.1	step1.2.2.1_state2	microwaveOven
step3.2	step3.2_state1	electrophoresis

Result

Query4. Return all materials involved in all steps.

```
SELECT ?step ?state ?material
WHERE { ?step rdf:type :Step.
?step :hasState ?state.
?state :involves ?material.
?material rdf:type/rdfs:subClassOf :
    Material}
```

step	state	x
step3.2	step3.2_state_m4	"2/3"^^<http://www.w3.org/2000/01/rdf-schema#Literal>
step3.2	step3.2_state_m2	"2/3"^^<http://www.w3.org/2000/01/rdf-schema#Literal>
step3.2	step3.2_state2	"2/3"^^<http://www.w3.org/2000/01/rdf-schema#Literal>

Query   Result

Query5. Return all steps and states with the instance agarose1 involved, including any mixtures involving it.

```
SELECT ?step ?state ?material
WHERE { ?step rdf:type :Step.
?step :hasState ?state.
{?state :involves ?material} UNION {?
    state :involves/:consistsOf ?
    material}
FILTER(?material = :agarose1)}
```

step	state	material
step1.1	step1.1_state1	agarose1
step1.1	step1.1_state2	agarose1

Query   Result

Query6. What is the unit used to measure the agarose gel involved in the final product (step6.2_item_complete)?

```
SELECT ?material ?unit
WHERE { :step6.2_item_complete :
    consistsOf+/^:alias ?material.
?material rdf:type :AgaroseGel.
?material :hasMeasure/:hasUnit ?unit }
```

material	unit
sb_agarose_gel	cm

Query   Result

These query and result examples show the true power of knowledge representation by automatically extracting the essential information that a biochemist would use to perform experimental procedures in a lab. These figures show in a few examples how much information can be mined from such a framework with only one experimental procedure. What if all standard experimental procedures in biochemistry [11,29], for example, are modeled and built, one simply cannot imagine how much time and effort will be saved, knowing all essential information is just a few clicks away. Query 1 shows all of the instruments involved in any state for all steps of the Alkaline Agarose Gel Electrophoresis procedure whereas Query 4 shows a query that returned all materials involved in the procedure. Query 2 shows a query that returned the states of step3 and its sub-steps which are concerned with measuring the gel length and returned their target values. The ontology was verified to be consistent using the HermiT 1.3.8.3 reasoner [31].

5 Conclusions and Future Work

Ontologies provide entities, concepts, and relations among those entities and concepts to represent a domain. We have proposed a framework that describes the relations and steps of experimental procedures. Procedures are sequences of steps. We have provided a novel application of the intransitive relations 'directly follows' and 'directly precedes' to model these sequences. Additionally, the ability to model totally ordered, partially ordered and alternative subsequences of steps is enabled. (i.e., only one of the alternatives is done). We have designed an ontology that has been shown to be adequate for this domain using two examples of biochemistry experimental procedures, Alkaline Agarose Gel Electrophoresis and Southern Blotting.

The nature of future work comes in two types. Short term goals include the following: This work will be publicly available for the research community to enhance and expand upon. Such a work could be beneficial for various genres that have similar procedure-oriented characteristics. We also aim to expand our work by incorporating existing ontologies that are essential to this domain such as the ontology for units of measure [25] and the materials ontology [7]. Certain theoretical ontological modelling of states and empirical observations in science can be fruitfully incorporated into our ontology in the future [23].

One of our long term goals is to enrich knowledge based systems with the necessary information about experimental procedures that a scientist would automatically access such as instruments (e.g., laboratory centrifuge) and materials (e.g., buffers). Most importantly, this approach is an important step toward our ultimate goal to analyze biomedical articles. Due to the writing style of biochemistry article authors, not all of the steps of a protocol are explicitly identified, since the authors assume that the knowledgeable reader is able to furnish the missing steps. Natural Language Processing systems need the knowledge that an informed reader would have. We also have started conducting an annotation study for both semantic roles and rhetorical moves, respectively in [1,2]. We have also developed a set of frames for frequent procedural verbs (e.g., "digest") in another work [3]. One of our goals is also to extend the VerbNet project by providing syntactic and semantic information for procedural verbs. Further details can be found in [5].

References

1. Alliheedi, M., Mercer, R.E.: Semantic roles: towards rhetorical moves in writing about experimental procedures. In: Proceedings of the 32nd Canadian Conference on Artificial Intelligence, pp. 518–524 (2019)
2. Alliheedi, M., Mercer, R.E., Cohen, R.: Annotation of rhetorical moves in biochemistry articles. In: Proceedings of the 6th Workshop on Argument Mining, pp. 113–123 (2019). https://www.aclweb.org/anthology/W19-4514
3. Alliheedi, M., Mercer, R.E., Haas-Neil, S.: Ontological knowledge for rhetorical move analysis. Computación y Sistemas 23(3), 633–647 (2019)

4. Alliheedi, M., Wang, Y., Mercer, R.E.: Biochemistry procedure-oriented ontology: a case study. In: Proceedings of the 11th International Conference on Knowledge Engineering and Ontology Development (KEOD 2019) - Volume 2 of Proceedings of the 11th International Conference on Knowledge Discovery, Knowledge Engineering and Knowledge Management (IC3K 2019), pp. 164–173 (2019)

5. Alliheedi, M.: Procedurally rhetorical verb-centric frame semantics as a knowledge representation for argumentation analysis of biochemistry articles. Ph.D. thesis, University of Waterloo (2019). http://hdl.handle.net/10012/15021

6. Ashburner, M., et al.: Gene ontology: tool for the unification of biology. Nat. Genet. **25**(1), 25–29 (2000)

7. Ashino, T.: Materials ontology: an infrastructure for exchanging materials information and knowledge. Data Sci. J. **9**, 54–61 (2010)

8. Ball, C.A., et al.: Integrating functional genomic information into the Saccharomyces genome database. Nucleic Acids Res. **28**(1), 77–80 (2000)

9. Bandrowski, A., et al.: The ontology for biomedical investigations. PLoS ONE **11**(4), e0154556 (2016)

10. Blake, J.A., Eppig, J.T., Richardson, J.E., Davisson, M.T., Group, M.G.D., et al.: The Mouse Genome Database (MGD): expanding genetic and genomic resources for the laboratory mouse. Nucleic Acids Res. **28**(1), 108–111 (2000)

11. Boyer, R.F.: Biochemistry Laboratory: Modern Theory and Techniques. Prentice Hall, Boston (2012)

12. Brinkman, R.R., et al.: The OBI consortium: modeling biomedical experimental processes with OBI. J. Biomed. Semant. **1**(Suppl 1), S7 (2010)

13. Carenbauer, A.L., Garrity, J.D., Periyannan, G., Yates, R.B., Crowder, M.W.: Probing substrate binding to Metallo-β-Lactamase L1 fromStenotrophomonas maltophilia by using site-directed mutagenesis. BMC Biochem. **3**(1) (2002)

14. Degtyarenko, K., et al.: ChEBI: a database and ontology for chemical entities of biological interest. Nucleic Acids Res. **36**(suppl–1), D344–D350 (2007)

15. Devanbu, P.T., Litman, D.J.: Taxonomic plan reasoning. Artif. Intell. **84**(1–2), 1–35 (1996)

16. Dumontier, M., et al.: The semantic science Integrated Ontology (SIO) for biomedical research and knowledge discovery. J. Biomed. Semant. **5**(1), 14 (2014)

17. Fleischmann, A., et al.: IntEnz, the integrated relational enzyme database. Nucleic Acids Res. **32**(suppl–1), D434–D437 (2004)

18. FlyBase Consortium: The FlyBase database of the Drosophila genome projects and community literature. Nucleic Acids Res. **31**(1), 172–175 (2003)

19. Gene Ontology Consortium: The gene ontology: enhancements for 2011. Nucleic Acids Res. **40**(D1), D559–D564 (2011)

20. Kanehisa, M., et al.: From genomics to chemical genomics: New developments in KEGG. Nucleic Acids Res. **34**(suppl-1), D354–D357 (2006)

21. Klingström, T., et al.: Workshop on laboratory protocol standards for the Molecular Methods Data-base. New Biotechnol. **30**(2), 109–113 (2013)

22. Lenat, D.B., Prakash, M., Shepherd, M.: CYC: using common sense knowledge to overcome brittleness and knowledge acquisition bottlenecks. AI Mag. **6**(4), 65 (1985)

23. Masolo, C., Botti Benevides, A., Porello, D.: The interplay between models and observations. Appl. Ontol. **13**(1), 41–71 (2018)

24. McGuinness, D.L., van Harmelen, F.: OWL web ontology language overview. W3C Recommendation, World Wide Web Consortium, February 2004. http://www.w3.org/TR/2004/REC-owl-features-20040210/

25. Rijgersberg, H., Van Assem, M., Top, J.: Ontology of units of measure and related concepts. Semant. Web **4**(1), 3–13 (2013)

26. Ringwald, M., Eppig, J.T., Kadin, J.A., Richardson, J.E.: GXD: a gene expression database for the laboratory mouse: current status and recent enhancements. Nucleic Acids Res. **28**(1), 115–119 (2000)

27. Rosse, C., Mejino, J.L.V.: Anatomy Ontologies for Bioinformatics. In: Burger, A., Davidson, D., Baldock, R. (eds.) The Foundational Model of Anatomy Ontology. Computational Biology, pp. 59–117. Springer, London (2008). https://doi.org/10.1007/978-1-84628-885-2_4

28. Rosse, C., Mejino Jr., J.L.: A reference ontology for biomedical informatics: the Foundational Model of Anatomy. J. Biomed. Inform. **36**(6), 478–500 (2003)

29. Sambrook, J., Russell, D.W.: Molecular Cloning: A Laboratory Manual. ColdSpring Harbor Laboratory Press, Harbor (2001)

30. Schlenoff, C., Schlenoff, C., Tissot, F., Valois, J., Lee, J.: The Process Specification Language (PSL) Overview and Version 1.0 Specification. NISTIR 6459, National Institute of Standards and Technology (2000)

31. Shearer, R., Motik, B., Horrocks, I.: Hermit: a highly-efficient owl reasoner. In: Proceedings of the Fifth OWLED Workshop on OWL: Experiences and Directions. CEUR Workshop Proceedings, vol. 432 (2008)

32. Smith, B., et al.: Relations in biomedical ontologies. Genome Biol. **6**(5), R46 (2005)

33. Soldatova, L., King, R., Basu, P., Haddi, E., Saunders, N.: The representation of biomedical protocols. EMBnet. J. **19**(B) (2013). http://journal.embnet.org/index.php/embnetjournal/article/view/730

34. Soldatova, L.N., King, R.D.: An ontology of scientific experiments. J. Roy. Soc. Interface **3**(11), 795–803 (2006)

35. Zheng, J., Manduchi, E., Jr, C.J.S.: Development of an application ontology for beta cell genomics based on the ontology for biomedical investigations. In: 4th International Conference on Biomedical Ontology, pp. 62–67 (2013)

Formalizing Graphical Modularization Approaches for Ontologies and the Knowledge Loss

Andrew LeClair[✉][iD], Ridha Khedri, and Alicia Marinache

McMaster University, Hamilton, ON, Canada
{leclaial,khedri,marinaam}@mcmaster.ca

Abstract. This paper formalizes the graphical modularization technique view traversal for an ontology component of a Domain Information System (DIS). Our work is motivated by developing the ability to dynamically extract a module (called a view traversal module) based on an initial set of concepts. We show how the ability to quantify the knowledge that is preserved (or lost) in a view traversal module is significant for a multi-agent setting, which is a setting that requires provable privacy. To ensure partial knowledge preservation, we extend the view traversal module to a principal ideal subalgebra module. The cost of this extension is that the obtained knowledge is coarser, as the atoms of the associated lattice are composite yet considered atomic. The presented work constitutes a foundational step towards theories related to reasoning on partial domain knowledge.

Keywords: Ontology · Ontology modularization · View traversal View extraction · Knowledge loss · Provable privacy · Autonomous agents

1 Introduction

Ontology modularization is the process of decomposing an ontology to smaller components for purposes such as reasoning, reusability, and maintenance [60]. In addition to improving a single ontology, the process of modularization can be used to compare and contrast different ontologies [51]. However, despite its wide usage, the process of modularization – and what the precise definition of a module is – is not agreed upon [36]. The lack of a uniform understanding is exemplified when comparing a logical modularization technique [50] to a graphical modularization technique [45]: there are various ways of measuring what a module is, or modules from different techniques may be incomparable to each other. There is a need for having a standard means to assess the quality of an ontology module [2].

Issues such as provable privacy in modules [6,15], co-ordinating multiple autonomous agents [22], data integration [63], and handling the evolution of the domain [9,19] could all be served by a formalized modularization process that precisely defines a module. Problem domains regarding whether agents are able to deduce unintended consequences, or how a new data set is to be interpreted by multiple agents all require a formal definition of a module. By establishing what a module is – and what the process of acquiring one is – in a given ontology-based system, we can begin to define what information a module, and by extension, an agent, can have access to.

© Springer Nature Switzerland AG 2020
A. Fred et al. (Eds.): IC3K 2019, CCIS 1297, pp. 388–412, 2020.
https://doi.org/10.1007/978-3-030-66196-0_18

However, as demonstrated in [42], this is not a trivial set of tasks to solve. It requires a holistic approach to an ontology-based system to discuss how issues such as data integration or autonomous agents can be tackled. This approach is seen with Ontology-based Data Access (OBDA) [47]. OBDA is a system that connects a (possibly heterogeneous) relational dataset to a Description Logic (DL) ontology via mapping. Although OBDA tackles issues such as data integration or evolving concepts, it struggles with multiple agents co-operating [9] or with the evolution of data [59]. Furthermore, OBDA will be limited by the expressivity of the underlying DL fragment [5,40]. This is an issue when considering that for some ontologies, a DL fragment with lower expressiveness is chosen to accommodate the large amount of data or to avoid certain operators or quantifiers [30]. Agents should be empowered with a system that can express complex concepts rather than be limited due to the amount of data.

This work addresses the problems associated with an evolving domain that is rich with data and has many co-operating agents. To reach this goal, rather than using DL, we use Domain Information System (DIS) [39] to formalize an ontology-based system. The use of DIS allows us to create an optimal ontology-based system, as discussed in [31], as well as one that is easily modularizable to avoid monolithic ontologies [38]. The modularization techniques we introduce are formally defined using the theory of the underlying Boolean algebra. Using the established theory, we address the issues of provable privacy, the lack of a precise definition for a module or modularization, and further, we provide a way to relate logical and graphical modularzation techniques.

The remainder of the paper is as follows. In Sect. 2, we evaluate the work of utilizing ontologies in multi-agent systems for customizing views, as well as OBDA. In Sect. 3, we introduce the necessary mathematical background to facilitate discussion on the modularization process and knowledge quantification. In Sect. 4, we provide the findings regarding how a DIS-based ontology can be modularized. In Sect. 5, we discuss how said modularization can be used to characterize the potential knowledge of an agent, followed by a discussion in Sect. 6.

2   Related Work

Ontology modularization is an active research field with the aim of ensuring the ontologies are usable for tractable reasoning tasks, and adhere to established engineering principles that promote maintainability. Examples of recent modularization efforts can be seen in [2,7,17,34,41,61]. These approaches vary by the ontology formalism they modularize on, the ontology component(s) used to modularize (data, concepts, or both), and what types of modules they produce. The utilization of ideals to discuss modularization in the context of DL has been explored in [18], but it requires rigorous computation whereas DIS is able to simply compute ideals using its underlying theory.

In [57], the authors highlight the need for the ontology component of an ontology-based system to be modularizable so as to avoid the issues associated with using a monolithic ontology. These issues include the scalability and tractability of reasoning tasks, reusability of components in another problem domain, or the management of the ontology. In addition to the listed problems that arise from a monolithic ontology, in [31], the authors discuss the need to have the ability for several local ontologies to communicate by using a shared language. DL is the current standard ontology formalism due to its wide usage by research teams and several implementations. However, Wache et al. [57] point to multiple limitations with the formalism such as the static nature of the ontologies created, intractability of reasoning tasks (when using expressive fragments), and tendency to become monolithic. Thus, we investigate DIS (formally introduced in Sect. 3) as an alternative formalism for an ontology-based system.

There exist several recent approaches to multi-agent systems that utilize an ontology at its core (e.g., [33,46,62]). These systems require agents to have their own ontology – or pieces of a shared larger ontology – that they can reason on. As the agents are interacting with a smaller more specialized component of the ontology, the queries are more efficiently conducted. Additionally, it allows for the agents to collaborate, each with their respective expertise as determined by the ontology they contain, to answer more complex queries. However, for collaboration to occur, the agents must have some shared language that is provided by an additional ontology that every agent can communicate through.

By using techniques from the ontology modularization field, a module can be extracted from an ontology that will be assigned to an agent. As all modules come from the same ontology, this mitigates the issue of needing another ontology to facilitate communication between agents. However, this requires an ontology that can be broken into the modules that each agent requires. In other words, this method requires an ontology that conceptualizes the entire domain (rather than a specific view for an agent). Examples of such an implementation can be found in [3,8]. The modularization techniques that are proposed in these papers are heuristic in nature, not able to guarantee properties such as knowledge preservation or correctness. Concerns regarding the modularization process and lack of formal method arise when considering the use of ontologies that consist of hundreds or thousands of concepts, such as in [4,12,13,48,49,53,56]. In addition to this, the lack of an agreed definition of a module results in agents that get possibly inconsistent results to queries [36].

Currently, an ontology-based system will require a full update (recheck for completeness, etc..) whenever an agent's ontology changes due to the domain's evolution [9]. This can be a consuming process depending on how often the agents domain knowledge is expected to change, and can result in a system where the agents are static and seldom react to change.

In addition to the complications associated with ontology evolution, we investigate how the agents can interact with the data. OBDA is the approach used by the Semantic Web for linking data to an ontology [47]. The OBDA paradigm aims to connect an ontology layer to a data layer so that rich queries can be made using the ontology, and answered using the data. Although existing ontologies can be used, in the case study of [36], it is pointed out that several ontologies are not developed with the intent of being reusable (or easily reused). Thus, often times an ontology engineer will need to create a new ontology for the given data. However, it is not a trivial task to create an ontology from a dataset. The task is described as the bootstrapping problem [32], and OBDA is mostly considered as read-only as it puts restrictions on the ability to modify the datasets and handle updates [59]. Additionally, the query transformation process is not simple; it depends on multiple aspects of the ontology, queries, and the data consistency [11].

Our research provides a means for agents to automatically and systematically extract views from an ontology on-the-fly to achieve the tasks they are required to do (such as reasoning). Additionally, we characterize the modules by the knowledge they do or do not preserve, thus providing a means to communicate provable privacy. We seek to have a single ontology that can be dynamically and easily modularized to avoid a monolithic ontology existing at the higher-level. By extracting the modules from a single ontology, we ensure that the agents are able to communicate using the same language. We also seek to have a system that is adaptable to change and evolution, allowing for the data that the agents have to be malleable with minimal changes to the ontology.

3   Mathematical Background

In this Section, we present the necessary mathematical background for the purpose of making this paper self-contained.

3.1   Lattice Theory and Boolean Algebras

A *lattice* is an abstract structure that can be defined as either a relational or algebraic structure [16]. In our work we use both the algebraic and the relational definitions, there we provide them and we present the connection between them.

Let $(L, \leq)$ be a partially ordered set, we define an upper bound and lower bound as follows. For an arbitrary subset $S \subseteq L$, an element $u \in L$ is called an upper bound of S if $s \leq u$ for each $s \in S$. Dually, we define an element $l \in L$ as a lower bound of S if $l \leq s$ for each $s \in S$. An upper bound u is defined as a least upper bound (dually, a lower bound l is defined as a greatest lower bound) if $u \leq x$ for each upper bound $x \in S$ ($x \leq l$ for each lower bound $x \in S$). A least upper bound is typically referred to as a *join*, and a greatest lower bound as a *meet*. If every two elements $a, b \in L$ have a join, then the partially ordered set is called a join-semilattice. Similarly, if every two elements $a, b \in L$ have a meet, then the partially ordered set is called a meet-semilattice. As a relational structure, a lattice is a partially ordered set that is both a join- and meet-semilattice.

A lattice can also be defined as the algebraic structure $(L, \oplus, \otimes)$, which consists of a set L and the two binary operators $\oplus$ and $\otimes$ that are commutative, associative, idempotent, and satisfy the absorption law (i.e., $a \oplus (a \otimes b) = a \otimes (a \oplus b) = a$, for $a, b, c \in L$).

The relational and algebraic structures can be connected by the equivalences $a \leq b \Longleftrightarrow (a = a \otimes b) \Longleftrightarrow (b = a \oplus b)$. The connection between the relational and algebraic definition of a lattice allows us to freely interchange the relational and algebraic aspects in discussion; some concepts are easier to express or explain in one structure over the other.

We also require the notion of a *sublattice*, which is simply defined as a nonempty subset M of a lattice L that satisfies $x \oplus y \in M$ and $x \otimes y \in M$ for all $x, y \in M$. In other words, a sublattice has a carrier set (or supporting set) that is a subset of the carrier set of the lattice in which all joins and meets are preserved in the subset.

A Boolean lattice [52] is defined as a *complemented distributive* lattice. A complemented lattice is bounded (i.e., includes a *top* concept ($\top$) and a *bottom* concept ($\bot$)), and where every element a has a *complement* (i.e., an element b satisfying $a \oplus b = \top$ and $a \otimes b = \bot$). A distributive lattice is one where the join and meet operators distribute over each other, i.e., a lattice L is distributive if for all $x, y, z \in L$, $x \otimes (y \oplus z) = (x \otimes y) \oplus (x \otimes z)$ and $x \oplus (y \otimes z) = (x \oplus y) \otimes (x \oplus z)$.

The algebraic structure for the Boolean lattice is defined as $\mathcal{B} = (B, \otimes, \oplus, 0, 1, ')$. The unique elements 0 and 1 are the top and bottom concepts that bound the lattice, that we denoted above as $\bot$ and $\top$ respectively, and the complement operator $'$ is defined as above for a complemented lattice. In a finite Boolean algebra, an *atom* is defined as an element $a \in B$ where for any $b \in B$, either $a \otimes b = a$ or $a \otimes b = 0$ [26]. In this work, we only consider finite Boolean algebras. The Boolean lattice and its corresponding Boolean algebra is thus generated from the power set of the atoms [29]. As a result, all Boolean algebras with the same number of atoms are isomorphic to each other.

Two distinguished types of substructures are an *ideal* and *filter*. For a Boolean algebra $\mathcal{B}$ with the carrier set B, $I \subseteq B$ is called an ideal in $\mathcal{B}$ if I is nonempty and if for all $i, j \in I$ and $b \in B$ we have $i \otimes b \in I$ and $i \oplus j \in I$. A filter is the dual of an ideal. For a Boolean algebra $\mathcal{B}$ with set of elements B, $F \subseteq B$ is called a filter in $\mathcal{B}$ if F is nonempty and if for all $i, j \in F$ and $b \in B$ we have $i \oplus b \in F$ and $i \otimes j \in F$

An ideal is called *proper* if $I \neq \{0\}$ or B. It is possible to generate an ideal using an element, referred to as the *principal* ideal. Let $\mathcal{B}$ be a Boolean algebra, and $b \in B$, then the principal ideal generated by b is $I(b) = \{a \in B \mid a \leq b\}$. In this paper, we use the symbol $L_{\downarrow b}$ to denote the set of elements in the principal ideal generated by an element b. A filter is defined as the dual to the ideal. For the principal filter generated by an element, we use a symbol with a similar definition to the one used for a principal ideal, but for a principal filter instead: $L_{\uparrow c_{st}}$.

An ideal is *maximal* (or a *prime* ideal) if $I \neq B$ and the only proper ideal containing I is B itself. The dual of of a maximal ideal is the *ultrafilter*. It is also established that for any maximal ideal (or ultrafilter) $I \subseteq B$ and any element $x \in B$, I contains exactly one of $\{x, x'\}$.

3.2 Domain Information System

A Domain Information System (DIS) [39] consists of three components: a domain ontology, a domain data view, and a function that maps the two. This separation of data from the ontology grants us the ability to manipulate the data by adding or removing records without the need for rechecking consistency or reconstructing the ontology. Figure 1 shows these three components. Let C be a set of concepts, e_c an element of C such that $\forall (c \mid c \in C : c \oplus e_c = e_c \oplus c = c)$. Moreover, $\oplus$ is associative, idempotent, and commutative. Hence, $(C, \oplus, e_c)$ is a commutative, idempotent monoid[1].

Let $C_i \subseteq C, R_i \subseteq C_i \times C_i$, and $t \in C_i$. A rooted graph at t, $G_i^t = (C_i, R_i, t)$, is a connected directed graph of concepts with a unique sink $t \in C_i$. We call t the *root* of G_i^t, and define it as follows: $t \in C_i$ is *root* of $G_i^t \iff \forall (k \mid k \in C_i : k = t \lor (k, t) \in R_i^+)$.

---

[1] A monoid is an algebraic structure with a single associative operator, and an identity element.

With this, we present the definition of the ontology.

Definition 1 (Domain Ontology). *Let $\mathcal{C} = (C, \oplus, e_C)$ be a commutative idempotent monoid. Let $\mathcal{L} = (L, \sqsubseteq_C)$ be a Boolean lattice, with $L \subseteq C$, such that $e_C \in L$. Let I be a finite set of indices, and $\mathcal{G} = \{G_i^t\}_{i \in I, \, t \in L}$ a set of rooted graphs at t.*

A domain ontology is the mathematical structure $\mathcal{O} \stackrel{\text{def}}{=} (\mathcal{C}, \mathcal{L}, \mathcal{G})$.

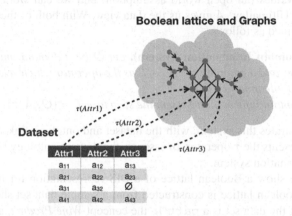

Fig. 1. High-level representation of a Domain Information System. (Color figure online)

We recognize the relation on the set of concepts L as the partOf relation, denoted by $\sqsubseteq_C$. The corresponding Boolean algebra for the Boolean lattice of a domain ontology is defined as $\mathcal{B} = (L, \otimes, \oplus, e_C, \top, ')$. The binary operators $\otimes$ and $\oplus$ are analogous to the meet and join, but are related to $\sqsubseteq_C$ by $a \oplus b = b \iff a \sqsubseteq_C b \iff a \otimes b = a$. The unique elements e_C and $\top$ are the bottom and top concepts of the lattice, and are respectively analogous to 0 and 1.

A concept $k \in C$ is called *atomic* if it has no sub-parts, i.e.,: k is atomic $\stackrel{\text{def}}{\iff}$ $\forall(k' \mid k' \in L : k' \sqsubseteq_C k \implies k' = k \vee k' = e_C)$.

In Fig. 1, the ontology is represented as the components within the cloud. The circles represent concepts, and are differentiated by colour to signify whether they are in the Boolean lattice (i.e., pink) or a rooted graph (i.e., blue).

The second component is the domain data view associated with an ontology $(\mathcal{C}, \mathcal{L}, \mathcal{G})$, which is formalized using a diagonal-free cylindric algebra. Diagonal-free cylindric algebra has been introduced in [28]. Its cylindrification operators are indexed over the elements of the carrier set L of the Boolean lattice. In Fig. 1, it is represented as the dataset.

Definition 2 (Domain Data View Associated to an Ontology). *Let $\mathcal{O} = (\mathcal{C}, \mathcal{L}, \mathcal{G})$ be a domain ontology as defined in Definition 1, where L is the carrier set of $\mathcal{L}$. A domain data view associated to $\mathcal{O}$ is the structure $\mathcal{A} = (A, +, *, -, 0_A, 1_A, \{c_\kappa\})_{\kappa \in L}$ that is a diagonal-free cylindric algebra such that $(A, +, \cdot, -, 0, 1)$ is a Boolean algebra and c_k is an unary operator on A called cylindrification, and the following postulates are satisfied for any $x, y \in A$, and any $k, \lambda \in L$:*

1. $c_\kappa 0 = 0$
2. $x \leq c_\kappa x$
3. $c_\kappa(x * c_\kappa y) = c_\kappa x * c_\kappa y$
4. $c_\kappa c_\lambda x = c_\lambda c_\kappa x$

We adopt cylindric algebra to reason on data as it gives us a data view that goes beyond the relational view of Codd [14]. Cylindrification operations allow us to handle tuples with undefined values (an open world assumption) and we can work on tuples with different length. Ultimatley, $\mathcal{A}$ gives us the data view. With both of these components, a DIS can be defined as follows.

Definition 3 (Domain Information System). *Let $\mathcal{O}$ be a domain ontology, $\mathcal{A}$ be its domain data view, and a mapping $\tau : A \to L$ as the operator which relates the set A to elements of the Boolean lattice in $\mathcal{O}$.*
We call a Domain Information System the structure $\mathcal{I} = (\mathcal{O}, \mathcal{A}, \tau)$.

Figure 1 illustrates this system, with the dataset and ontology linked by the dashed arrows that represents the τ operator. In essence, the domain ontology is the conceptual level of the information system.

In Fig. 2, we show a Boolean lattice of a DIS representation for the *Wine Ontology* [44]. The Boolean lattice is constructed from a sample data set shown in Table 1. Each attribute of the data set is a `partOf` the concept *Wine Product*, and they are the atoms of the Boolean lattice. The remaining concepts are the combinations of these atoms, formed from the power set of the Boolean lattice atoms. Some combinations hold more domain relevance (determined by domain experts), and are signified by larger hollow nodes. These concepts can be named, such as *Estate* being the combination of *Region* and *Winery*, while others may not have explicit names in the domain and instead be referred to by the combination of its parts (e.g., *Grape* $\oplus$ *Colour*).

Table 1. Wine dataset.

Grape	Colour	Sugar	Body	Region	Winery
Merlot	Red	Dry	Full	Niagara	Jackson Triggs
Merlot	Red	Dry	Medium	Okanagan	Jackson Triggs
Pinot Grigio	White	Dry	Medium	Niagara	Konzelmann
Pinot Grigio	White	Semi-sweet	Medium	Niagara	Jackson Triggs
Pinot Blanc	White	Dry	Light	Okanagan	Sperling
Riesling	White	Semi-sweet	Light	Niagara	Jackson Triggs
...	...	...	...	...	...

3.3 Conservative Extension, Local Correctness, and Local Completeness

A prevalent form of modularization (referred to as 'logical modularization techniques') defines a module as a set of concepts and relations such that the knowledge that can be deduced from these concepts is preserved in the module. This presevation of the knowledge is determined by extracting a module such that the ontology conservatively extends it.

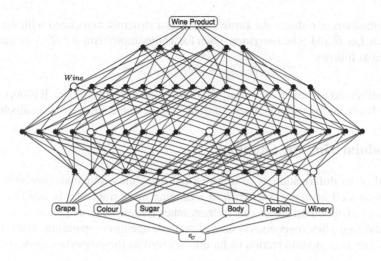

Fig. 2. The Boolean lattice for the Wine Ontology [35].

Conservative extension is a notion from mathematical logic, often used in fields such as proof theory. In [37], we find the (proof theoretic) conservative extension is presented as follows:

Definition 4 ([37])**.** *Let L and L' be logics. We call L' a (proof theoretic) conservative extension of L provided that all formulas of L are formulas of L' and that, for all formulas A of L, A is a theorem of L iff A is a theorem of L'.*

In addition to the definition provided, there exists a stronger notion of conservative extension called *model theoretic* conservative extension. It is presented as follows:

Definition 5 ([37])**.** *Let T and T' be theories. We call T' a (model theoretic) conservative extension of T if every model of T can be extended to a model of T'.*

As seen in [37], both types of conservative extension are used to define an ontological module. In the context of DL, the formulas are the Terminological Box (T-Box) sentences. When demonstrating the conservative extension of the ontology to the module, it is common that it is shown in two parts, such as in [24]. The first part, referred to as *local correctness*, shows that all formulas of L are formulas of L'. The second part, referred to as *local completeness*, shows that for all formulas A of L, A is a theorem of L iff A is a theorem of L'.

3.4 First Isomorphism Theorem

The first isomorphism theorem [58] is used in this work to quantify knowledge loss from modularization.

Theorem 1 (First Isomorphism Theorem [58])**.** *Let R and S be rings, and let ϕ : $R \rightarrow S$ be a ring homomorphism. Then the kernel of ϕ is an ideal of R. In particular, if ϕ is surjective, then S is isomorphic to $R/ker(\phi)$.*

This theorem introduces the *kernel*, which is a structure associated with the homomorphism. Let R and S be two rings. Then for a homomorphism $\phi : R \to S$, the kernel is defined as follows:

$$ker(\phi) = \{r \in R \mid \phi(r) = 0_S\} \tag{1}$$

The kernel is used to measure the non-injectivity of the homomorphism. It is important to note any Boolean ring with the 0-ary constant 1 can be made into a Boolean algebra [54].

4   Modularizing the Ontology

The goal of modularization is to improve the reusability and maintainability of the ontology, as well as make tasks such as reasoning more tractable. In addition to this, the process of modularization can address other issues, such as provable privacy or conceptualizing a heterogeneous system of multiple agents co-operating. In this section, we introduce two modularization techniques as well as the properties of the produced modules.

Figure 2 shows a domain ontology that has been conceptualized for a Wine dataset. Although seemingly large, this is before any processing has been done to improve the maintainability or reusability. For instance, it can be argued that the concept *Wine Product* is composed of two concepts from closely related domains: the *Wine* and *Estate*. The former is composed of *Grape*, *Colour*, *Sugar*, and *Body* whereas the latter is *Region* and *Winery*. In a multi-agent system, it might be more suitable for this ontology to be modularized such that one agent has the module (and the knowledge associated to the concepts therein) for *Wine*, and a different agent has the module for *Estate*. It could also be the case that the agent that has the knowledge about *Wine* must not have knowledge of the *Estate* (and vice versa). For the remainder of this section, we will introduce two modularization techniques: one based on view traversal, and another based on the principal ideal subalgebra. We will then show how the modularization challenges described above are addressed with these modules.

4.1   The Determination of a Graphical Modularization Technique

In the field of ontology modularization, there are several implementations of graphical modularization techniques. This includes Prompt [45], Magpie [21], SWOOP [23], ModOnto [10], PATO [55], and SeeCOnt [1]. We consider these techniques in order to draw parallels between our DIS-based graphical modularization techniques and those that already exist.

Rather than extract a single module, both PATO and SeeCOnt implement techniques that instead partition the ontology. These methods seek to partition an ontology into a (possibly disjoint) set of modules such that every concept belongs to a module. In this paper, we are concerned with extracting a module that meets a specific requirement for an agent. For this reason, we do not consider these two techniques further.

From the remaining techniques, we observe a prominent usage of the view traversal technique or a derivative of it. Prompt is the tool developed as the implementation of view traversal, therefore it is natural that it is the most true to the developed algorithm. Magpie implements a technique that operates similar to view traversal, however, rather than indiscriminately including all traversed concepts, it only retains the ones necessary for the preservation of axioms or consequences of the input. SWOOP is discussed as being able to faciliate a modularization process that factors an ontology into 'subsidiary domains', which are analogous to a view from view traversal. Finally, ModOnto operates similar to Magpie in that it includes concepts necessary for the preservation of axioms and consequences.

All of the presented modularization techniques can be traced to operate similar to view traversal: given an input query, a set of concepts and relationships are produced to answer that query. The techniques vary in how they deem a concept to be eligible for the module or not, but all share this same goal of answering a query with a 'view'. For this reason, our presented graphical modularization technique operates the same. By doing this, the presented technique can be considered an implementation of these techniques.

4.2 Modularization of DIS

To modularize a DIS, a formalized understanding of what a module – and its properties – must be introduced. Thus, we first write a formal definition of a module, and in the context of a DIS, it is defined as follows:

Definition 6 (Module). *Given a domain ontology* $\mathcal{O} = (\mathcal{C}, \mathcal{L}, \mathcal{G})$, *a module M of* $\mathcal{O}$ *is defined as a domain ontology* $M = (\mathcal{C}_M, \mathcal{L}_M, \mathcal{G}_M)$ *satisfying the following conditions:*

- $C_M \subseteq C$
- $\mathcal{L}_M = (L_M, \sqsubseteq_c)$ *such that* $L_M \subseteq C_M$, $\mathcal{L}_M$ *is a Boolean sublattice of* $\mathcal{L}$, *and* $e_c \in L_M$
- $\mathcal{G}_M = \{G_n \mid G_n \in \mathcal{G} \wedge t_n \in L_M\}$

where C_M *and* C *are the carrier sets of* $\mathcal{C}_M$ *and* $\mathcal{C}$, *respectively.*

In short, a module is a sub-ontology. This ensures that the tasks that can be performed on an ontology – such as reasoning or modularization – can also be performed on a module. As the concepts of the module are a subset of the ontology's concepts, we achieve the first goal.

Let $\mathbb{O}$ be a set of ontologies. The *modularization* is a function

$$M : \mathbb{O} \to \mathbb{O}$$

such that $M(O) = O_M$ where O_M is a module of O.

The central piece of a module (and thus, modularization) is the Boolean lattice. More specifically, the process of modularization is the process of determining a Boolean sublattice that will construct the module. With this, we understand the modularization techniques as transformations to the underlying Boolean algebra.

4.3   Generating a Module with View Traversal

A key component of view traversal is the declaration of a concept (or set of concepts), referred to as the starting concept c_{st}, that the module should be focused on. From these starting concepts, the ontology is traversed to acquire the concepts (and the relations) that will be used to populate the module. In a DIS, we define a view traversal using a principal ideal generated by c_{st}, written as $L_{\downarrow c_{st}}$. The principal ideal is a Boolean sublattice defined with a set of concepts such that it contains every concept that is partOf c_{st}. Figure 3 shows a module that has been generated using the starting concept *Wine*.

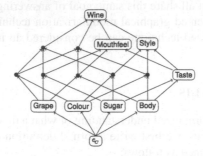

Fig. 3. The Boolean lattice of the module extracted from the Wine Ontology with $c_{st} = Wine$ [35].

As the principal ideal is generated by the input c_{st}, it is critical that c_{st} is well-defined. We envision three cases related to the concept c_{st} under consideration:

1. The starting concept is in the Boolean lattice
2. The starting concept is in a rooted graph
3. There are several starting concepts

The first case is the business-as-usual case, and operates as defined above. In the second case, the starting concept is determined using a *projected concept*, c_p. This projected concept is the root of the rooted graph that contains the desired concept. For example, referring to Fig. 4, if $c_{st} = Location$, then the projected concept would be the root of the graph, *Mouthfeel*. Thus, the principal ideal would be generated using *Mouthfeel*. Finally, in the third scenario where there are multiple desired starting concepts, we denote by C_V the set $C_V \subseteq L$. It is the set of all desired starting concepts or their projected concepts. The starting concept is then defined as[2]

$$c_{st} = \oplus(c \mid c \in C_V : c)^2 \tag{2}$$

For example, referring to Figs. 3 and 4, consider that we wish to modularize based on the starting concepts *Opulent*, *Mouthfeel*, and *Taste*; we first determine all projected

---

[2] Throughout this paper, we adopt the uniform linear notation provided by Gries and Schneider in [25], as well as Dijkstra and Scholten in [20]. The general form of the notation is $\star(x \mid R : P)$ where $\star$ is the quantifier, x is the dummy or quantified variable, R is predicate representing the range, and P is an expression representing the body of the quantification. An empty range is taken to mean **true** and we write $\star(x \mid: P)$; in this case the range is over all values of variable x.

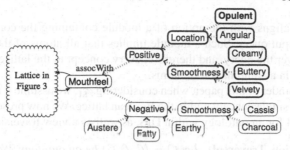

Fig. 4. The Wine Ontology enriched with rooted graphs (i.e., $\mathcal{G}$) with root *Mouthfeel* [35].

concepts. In this case, there is only one concept that belongs to a rooted graph: *Opulent*. The root for this graph is *Mouthfeel*, and so this is taken as the projected concept. Following this, we determine the composition of the three concepts together: $c_{st} = Mouthfeel \oplus Mouthfeel \oplus Taste$. The result is *Mouthfeel*, thus it is the starting concept for view traversal.

In Fig. 5 we present a module that is formed from a starting concept that is the composition of two elements, and the composition is not one of the two concepts. Using starting concepts *Colour* $\oplus$ *Sugar* and *Taste*, we would extract the two modules shown with the respective tops, denoted by bold lines. Simply taking these two modules, would be missing information that could be made from concepts that belong to the two modules: the combination of *Colour* with *Body*, as well as the combination of all three atoms. Therefore, taking a module with the concept that results from Eq. (2), we instead get the module that contains those concepts connected via bold lines, and also via dashed lines. This module includes the two stated concepts, as well as those from the two original modules.

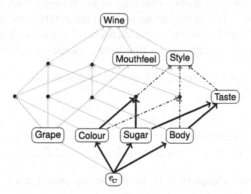

Fig. 5. Modularization with $c_1 = Colour \oplus Sugar$ and $Taste = Sugar \oplus Body$ [35]. (Color figure online)

With this approach, there exist two trivial cases: the first is for $c_i, c_j \in C_V$ we have $c_i \sqsubseteq_c c_j$ for any $c_i, c_j \in C_V$, and the second is the composition of concepts in C_V produce $c_{st} = \top$. In the former, c_i can be disregarded as $c_i \sqsubseteq_c c_j$ implies $c_i \oplus c_j = c_j$. In the latter, the Boolean lattice of the module will be the original ontology. Although counterintuitive to modularization – as the module will not be any smaller than the ontology – this aligns with the notion of a module containing the concepts necessary to answer the input query. Such a module implies that all atoms of the ontology were required to answer the query, and therefore, every concept in the lattice of the ontology can be formed via a combination of atoms.

For the remainder of this paper, when considering c_{st}, we assume it to be normalized such that c_{st} is a single concept within the Boolean lattice. We now present the definition of view traversal for an ontology within DIS, as well as a view traversal module.

Definition 7 (View Traversal). *Let* $\mathcal{O} = (\mathcal{C}, \mathcal{L}, \mathcal{G})$ *be an ontology. We also let* $\mathbb{M}_D$ *be the set of all possible view traversal modules obtainable from* $\mathcal{O}$. *view traversal* vt_D *is a function that is declared as follows*

$$vt_D : \mathbb{M}_D \times C \to \mathbb{M}_D \tag{3}$$

Where $vt_D(\mathcal{O}, c_{st}) = (\mathcal{C}_v, \mathcal{L}_v, \mathcal{G}_v)$ *and is defined as:*

1. $\mathcal{L}_v = (L_{\downarrow c_{st}}, \sqsubseteq_c)$ *is a Boolean lattice*
2. $\mathcal{G}_v = \{G_i \mid G_i \in \mathcal{G} \wedge t_i \in L_v\}$
3. $C_v = \{c \mid c \in L_{\downarrow c_{st}} \vee \exists(G_i \mid G_i \in \mathcal{G}_v : c \in C_i)\}$.

Given a view traversal module and a starting concept, the process of applying view traversal will produce a new view traversal module. It is important to note that the original domain ontology belongs to the set of all possible view traversal modules, i.e., $\mathcal{O} \in \mathbb{M}_D$, as by setting c_{st} to be $\top$, a view traversal module is produced that is equal to $\mathcal{O}$. This, and other trivial scenarios for view traversal, are expressed in the following Lemma. First we introduce the empty ontology and atomic ontology, denoted as $\mathcal{O}_0$ and $\mathcal{O}_a$, respectively. The empty ontology is an ontology with the carrier set being only the empty concept. The atomic ontology is an ontology with the carrier set of the Boolean lattice being two elements: an atom a and the empty concept. Unlike $\mathcal{O}_0$ which characterizes both C and L to be the single element e_c, $\mathcal{O}_a$ only characterizes L as there may still be rooted graphs (with root a) that have concepts populating C.

Lemma 1. *Given a domain ontology* $\mathcal{O}$, *then the following is true:*

1. $vt_D(\mathcal{O}, \top) = \mathcal{O}$
2. $vt_D(\mathcal{O}, \bot) = \mathcal{O}_0$
3. $vt_D(\mathcal{O}, a) = \mathcal{O}_a$ *for any atom* a *in* L
4. $\forall(c_1, c_2 \mid c_1, c_2 \in C : (c_1 \not\sqsubseteq_c c_2 \wedge vt_D(\mathcal{O}, c_2) = (\mathcal{C}_v, \mathcal{L}_v, \mathcal{G}_v)) \implies c_1 \notin C_v)$

Similar to Noy and Musen in [43], we define the analogue to the *composition* and *chaining* view traversals.

Claim (View Traversal Composition). Let $\mathcal{O} = (\mathcal{C}, \mathcal{L}, \mathcal{G})$ be an ontology. Let c_1, c_2 be two concepts in the carrier set of $\mathcal{L}$ such that $c_2 \sqsubseteq_c c_1$.

$$vt_D(vt_D(\mathcal{O}, c_1), c_2) = vt_D(\mathcal{O}, c_2)$$

Proof. A proof by contradiction. Let $\mathcal{O}_1$ be the result of $vt_D(M_v, c_1)$. Assume that there exists a concept c that belongs to the carrier set of $vt_D(M_v, c_2)$ but does not belong to the carrier set of $vt_D(\mathcal{O}_1, c_2)$. As the carrier set of $\mathcal{O}_1$ includes all parts of c_1 as per the definition of a view traversal module, this implies that c is a part of c_2 but is not a part of c_1. Due to the transitivity of the relation, this results in a contradiction that $c \sqsubseteq_c c_2$ and $c_2 \sqsubseteq_c c_1$ but not $c \sqsubseteq_c c_1$.

In essence, view traversal composition is the act of 'modularizing a modularization'. In the situation that c_2 is not a part of c_1, the result is $\mathcal{O}_0$. This is because $vt_D(\mathcal{O}, c_1)$ will not contain c_2. Therefore, to take a module on a concept that does not exist (to the ontology being modularized) should result in 'nothing', which for us is the empty ontology.

The second function introduced is the chaining of two view traversal modules. The chaining of two view traversal modules is the act of combining two modules into a single module, and is defined as follows.

Claim (View Traversal Combination). Let M_1 and M_2 be any view traversal modules from $\mathbb{M}_D$ for a given DIS, $\mathcal{D} = (\mathcal{O}, \mathcal{A}, \tau)$. Let $*$ be an operator with the signature

$$* : \mathbb{M}_D \times \mathbb{M}_D \to \mathbb{M}_D$$

We have $vt(M_1, c_1) * vt(M_2, c_2) = vt(\mathcal{O}, c_1 \oplus c_2)$.

The view traversal combination function inherits the commutativity and associativity from $\oplus$. It is also trivial to show the view traversal combination on view traversals with tops c_1 and c_2 where $c_1 \sqsubseteq_c c_2$ is equal to the view traversal of c_2 as $c_1 \sqsubseteq_c c_2 \Rightarrow c_1 \oplus c_2 = c_2$.

4.4 Properties of DIS View Traversal

We now provide the following proposition which lists a series of claims for a module adhering to Definition 7. We assume $c_{st} \neq \top$ to avoid the trivial case of the module being equal to the original ontology.

Proposition 1. *Let $O = (\mathcal{C}, \mathcal{L}, \mathcal{G})$ be an ontology and $O_v = (\mathcal{C}_v, \mathcal{L}_v, \mathcal{G}_v)$ be a module obtained from O using view traversal. Then:*

1. *The algebra associated to $\mathcal{L}_v$ is not a subalgebra of that associated to $\mathcal{L}$.*
2. *The Boolean algebra associated with the ontology that is produced from view traversal does not preserve the complement operator of the Boolean algebra associated with the original ontology.*
3. *The view traversal module is locally complete but not locally correct with respect to the original ontology.*

The proof for the above results can be found in [35]. Proposition 1.1 indicates that although the Boolean lattice of the view traversal module is a sublattice of the Boolean lattice of the original ontology, the Boolean algebra associated with the view traversal module is not a subalgebra of the Boolean algebra associated with the original ontology. Proposition 1.2 states that specifically, the complement operator is not preserved from the Boolean algebra associated with the original ontology. Proposition 1.3 indicates that due to the inability to preserve the complement operator of the Boolean algebra associated with the original ontology, the module is not locally correct, as defined in [37].

4.5 The Principal Ideal Subalgebra Module

The Boolean lattice of the module produced from view traversal is a Boolean sublattice of $\mathcal{L}$ but the Boolean algebra associated to the module is not a Boolean subalgebra of the algebra associated to $\mathcal{L}$. This may be satisfactory from a pragmatic approach as the resulting module can be utilized in the same ways as an ontology (e.g., reasoning, modularization). However, from a more rigorous perspective, we require an ability to produce a module that preserves the knowledge from the ontology. Thus, we require a module that in addition to preserving the join and meet opertors, also preserves the complement operator, i.e., is a Boolean subalgebra.

The view traversal module is ultimately formed using the principal ideal on a starting concept c_{st}. It is easy to show that the principal ideal generated by c_{st} unioned with the principal filter generated by c'_{st} – the complement of c_{st} – is a Boolean subalgebra of the Boolean algebra associated with the original ontology [27]. Let $c_{st} \in L$ and c'_{st} be its complement. Let $M_v = vt_D(O, c_{st}) = (\mathcal{C}_v, \mathcal{L}_v, \mathcal{G}_v)$ and let $\mathcal{B}$ be the Boolean algebra associated to the lattice of O. We indicated that $\mathcal{L}_{\sqsubseteq}$ is a principal ideal in $B1$, with the carrier set $L_{\downarrow c_{st}}$. We denote by $L_{\uparrow c'_{st}}$ the carrier set of the principal filter generated by c'_{st}. Then the set $L_{\uparrow c'_{st}} \cup L_{\downarrow c_{st}}$ gives us the carrier set for a Boolean subalgebra of $\mathcal{B}$. We call the module that is formed using this set as the *principal ideal subalgebra module* and is formally defined below.

Definition 8 (Principal Ideal Subalgebra Module). *For a given domain ontology* $O \overset{def}{=} (\mathcal{C}, \mathcal{L}, \mathcal{G})$ *and starting concept* c_{st} *in the carrier set L of $\mathcal{L}$, we define the set* $L_P = L_{\downarrow c_{st}} \cup L_{\uparrow c'_{st}}$. *The module* $M_P = (\mathcal{C}_P, \mathcal{L}_P, \mathcal{G}_P)$ *is defined as:*

1. $\mathcal{L}_P = (L_P, \sqsubseteq_c)$ *is a Boolean lattice*
2. $\mathcal{G}_P = \{G_i \mid G_i \in \mathcal{G} \land t_i \in L_P\}$
3. $\mathcal{C}_P = \{c \mid c \in L_P \lor \exists(G_i \mid G_i \in \mathcal{G}_P : c \in C_i)\}$

where C_P is the carrier set for $\mathcal{C}_P$.

We present an example of the principal ideal subalgebra module in Figs. 6 and 7. Figure 6 shows the Boolean lattice for the Wine ontology with the concepts that would populate the carrier set of the principal ideal subalgebra if $c_{st} = Grape \oplus Sugar \oplus Body$. The concept c_{st} corresponds to the concept named *Mouthfeel* in the Boolean lattice of the original ontology. Two disjoint sublattices can be seen. The first one is the magenta principal ideal that is formed by *Mouthfeel*, which contains the empty concept. The second one is the cyan principal filter that is formed by the complement of *Mouthfeel* and which contains the top concept. By extracting these concepts and constructing a new Boolean lattice, we result with the structure shown in Fig. 7. The Boolean lattice in Fig. 7 has a carrier set formed from the union of the principal ideal generated by c_{st} and the principal filter generated by c'_{st}. We note that an atom in this module, the concept $Colour \oplus Region \oplus Winery$, was not an atom in the original ontology. This is because by producing a module in this manner, we effectively change our understanding of what the atomic blocks of the domain are. In the module, the concept $Colour \oplus Region \oplus Winery$ relates to data that is non-decomposable and atomic

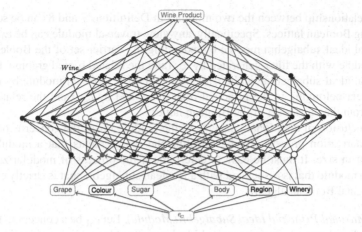

Fig. 6. The Boolean lattice for the Wine Ontology with the principal ideal subalgebra module highlighted for $c_{st} = Mouthfeel$ [35]. (Color figure online)

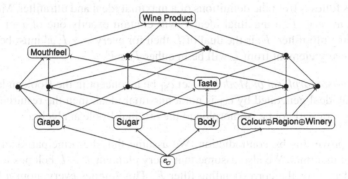

Fig. 7. The Boolean lattice of the principal ideal subalgebra module extracted from the Wine Ontology with $c_{st} = Mouthfeel$ [35]. (Color figure online)

in Fig. 7, whereas in the original ontology, we know that this same concept is composed of the concepts *Colour*, *Region*, and *Winery*. We refer to this as the *coarsening* of the domain, and therefore the knowledge that would be derived from this module would be *coarser* than the knowledge that would be derived from the original ontology.

By extending the view traversal module with the principal filter generated by c'_{st}, we remedy the inability to preserve the complement. Thus, we have the following claim.

Claim. A module obtained by extending view traversal with the principal filter generated with c'_{st} is locally correct and locally complete.

The above claim holds by construction. The module is formed using a Boolean subalgebra, which is conservatively extended by the ontology's Boolean algebra.

According to this result, every satisfiable formula in the module is satisfiable in the ontology, and every satisfiable formula in the ontology written in the language of the module is satisfiable in the module.

The relationship between the two modules in Definitions 7 and 8 can be seen in the underlying Boolean lattices. Specifically, any view traversal module can be *extended* to a principal ideal subalgebra module by extending the carrier set of the Boolean lattice of the module with the filter generated by c'_{st} (and the related rooted graphs). Likewise, a principal ideal subalgebra can be *truncated* to a view traversal module by removing any element belonging to the principal filter generated by c'_{st} (and the related rooted graphs) from the carrier set of the Boolean lattice.

The inclusion of additional concepts to the module raises the concerns of whether the modularization process will be fulfilling the requirements that a module should be smaller in size. It must be easy to determine if the process of modularization will produce a module that is associated with a Boolean subalgebra that is strictly embedded in the original Boolean algebra.

Claim (Maximal Principal Ideal Subalgebra Module). Let c_{st} be a concept in the ontology's Boolean lattice L. If the principal ideal generated by c_{st} is a maximal ideal, then the resulting principal ideal subalgebra module will be equal to the original ontology.

Proof. This follows from the definitions of a maximal ideal and ultrafilter. More specifically, for any $x \in L$, a maximal ideal I will contain exactly one of x or x'. As the corresponding ultrafilter, F, is the dual of I, then for every $x \in I$, x' must belong to F. Therefore, every element from L will be in either I or F.

Claim (Non-isomorphism of Module). Let c_{st} be a concept in the Boolean lattice L. If the principal ideal generated by c_{st} is not a maximal ideal, then the resulting principal ideal subalgebra will not be isomorphic to the original Boolean algebra.

Proof. We prove this by contradiction. We assume that the principal ideal generated by c_{st} is not maximal. We also assume that every element $x \in L$ belongs to either the principal ideal I, or the corresponding filter F. This implies every atom a belongs to either I or F. For the principal ideal to be proper, it cannot include every atom in its set. Similarly, for the filter to be proper, it can at most contain one atom. Therefore, I must contain every atom save for one which must belong to F. An ideal that contains all atoms save one is a maximal ideal (and a filter generated using an atom is an ultrafilter), contradicting the assumption they are not maximal.

As a result of the final claim, a principal ideal subalgebra module generated using any concept that is directly related to the top concept with the partOf relation (i.e., a concept that is the combination of all but one atoms) is guaranteed to be smaller in size than the original ontology.

A result of the module being formed using the principal ideal and a principal filter is that the bottom concept of the principal filter (i.e., c'_{st}) will be an atom of the module's lattice. However, there is no restriction that the principal filter be generated using an atom. In fact, expressed in the proof of the final claim, if the module is non-maximal (i.e., it is not isomorphic to the original ontology) then c'_{st} is not an atom of the ontology. Therefore, an atom of the module *may not be an atom of the ontology.*

4.6 DIS Modularization

Up to this point we have introduced two modules: the view traversal module, and the principal ideal subalgebra module. Both of these modules are defined in terms of a domain ontology $\mathcal{O}$. However, we now introduce how a DIS can be produced from the module's ontology.

Definition 9 (DIS Module). *Given a DIS $\mathcal{I} = (\mathcal{O}, \mathcal{A}, \tau)$, a DIS-module of $\mathcal{I}$ is the DIS $\mathcal{I}_M = (\mathcal{O}_M, \mathcal{A}_M, \tau_M)$ such that:*

1. $\mathcal{O}_M = (\mathcal{C}_M, \mathcal{L}_M, \mathcal{G}_M)$ is a module of $\mathcal{O}$
2. $\mathcal{A}_M = (A_M, +, \cdot, -, 0, 1, c_k)_{k \in L_M}$
3. τ_M is the restriction of τ to only the elements of A_M.

where L_M is the carrier set of the Boolean lattice $\mathcal{L}_M$, A is the carrier set of $\mathcal{A}$, and $A_M = \{a \mid a \in A \wedge \tau(a) \in L_M\}$.

When determining a DIS module, either a view traversal module or a principal ideal subalgebra module can be used as the $\mathcal{O}_M$. The remaining components – the cylindric algebra and the τ function – are redefined from the original DIS for the DIS-module by using the new domain ontology's (i.e., the module's) Boolean lattice. With this definition of a DIS-module, a modularized DIS will result in a new DIS that can be further modularized or reasoned on.

5 Quantifying Knowledge Loss

The process of modularizing implies the loss of a part of the original ontology. The knowledge that could be obtained from the lost part becomes unattainable. By leveraging that the view traversal module is constructed using the principal ideal generated by c_{st}, we are able to both determine the scope of the domain knowledge that is lost, and quantify it.

A Boolean lattice is the underlying structure of both the original ontology that is modularized, as well as the view traversal module. More specifically, the Boolean lattice of the view traversal module is a principal ideal of the Boolean lattice of the original ontology. Using this fact and the first theorem of isomorphism [58], there must be a homomorphism from the Boolean algebra associated to the original ontology to some other Boolean algebra to which the Boolean algebra associated to the view traversal module is its kernel. In other words, the existence of the view traversal module implies the existence of another Boolean algebra, and thus, a module that can be built around it. We denote the homomorphism which maps one Boolean algebra to another as $f : \mathcal{B}_1 \rightarrow \mathcal{B}_2$, where $\mathcal{B}_1$ is the Boolean algebra associated with the original ontology, and $\mathcal{B}_2$ is some other Boolean algebra. Let B_1 be the carrier set of $\mathcal{B}_1$, the kernel of f is the set of all elements from B_1 that are mapped to the identity element e_c of $\mathcal{B}_2$. The kernel of f contains only one element if and only if f is injective.

In the following, we construct an example of the function f. Let p_0 be any element from B_1. We define an instance of f as the f_{p_0} for a given $p_0 \in B_1$ and every $p \in B_1$:

$$f_{p_0}(p) = p \otimes p_0 \tag{4}$$

The kernel of f_{p_0} is defined as the set of all elements which map by f_{p_0} to the identity element:

$$ker(f_{p_0}) = \{p \in B_1 \mid f_{p_0}(p) = e_C\} \tag{5}$$

To illustrate the significance of the relationship between the view traversal module, the homomorphism, the kernel, and the knowledge lost, we return to the original Boolean lattice illustrated in Fig. 2. We set $p_0 = Taste$, where $Taste = Sugar \oplus Body$. The use of Eq. 4 signals the intent to map every concept from the Boolean lattice of the original ontology to a new Boolean lattice which is focused on the concept $Taste$. In this case, the function f_{p_0} in Eq. 4 maps every concept from the original Boolean lattice to $Taste$ or one of its parts. As the original Boolean lattice consists of 2^6 concepts, and the Boolean lattice with $Taste$ as the top consists of 2^2 concepts, the mapping will not be injective. The elements that map to e_C will populate the kernel of f_{p_0}, as given in Eq. 5.

For example, consider the following four evaluations where $p_0 = Taste$,

$$f_{p_0}(Sugar) = Sugar \otimes Taste = Sugar,$$
$$f_{p_0}(Wine) = Wine \otimes Taste = Taste$$
$$f_{p_0}(Grape) = Grape \otimes Taste = e_C$$
$$f_{p_0}(Region \oplus Winery) = (Region \oplus Winery) \otimes Taste = e_C$$

The function f_{p_0} maps any value that is a part of $Taste$, such as $Sugar$, to itself, such that $f_{p_0}(Sugar) = Sugar$. Any value that an element of $Taste$ is a part of, such as $Wine$, is also mapped to itself. Finally, any other element is mapped to the empty concept. Thus, with the starting concept $p_0 = Taste$, the kernel of the homomorphism f_{p_0} is composed of the concept $p_0' = Grape \oplus Colour \oplus Region \oplus Winery$ and all of its parts:

$$ker(f_{p_0}) = \{c \in L \mid c \sqsubseteq_C p_0'\} \tag{6}$$

Equations 4 and 5 together state that any concept $p \in B_1$ where $p \otimes p_0 = e_C$ is a part of $ker(f_{p_0})$. Using the definition of the concept complement and Boolean lattice meet, we get $p_0' \otimes p = e_C$. Therefore, $p_0' \in ker(f_{p_0})$. For any $c \sqsubseteq_C p_0'$, according to the definition of partOf, $c \sqsubseteq_C p_0' \iff c \otimes p_0' = c$. With this definition of partOf and Eq. 4, we get $f_{p_0}(c) = (c \otimes p_0') \otimes p_0$. Using the associativity of $\otimes$ operator, we get $f_{p_0}(c) = c \otimes (p_0' \otimes p_0) = c \otimes e_C = e_C$. Therefore, any element $c \sqsubseteq_C p_0'$ also belongs to the kernel of f_{p_0}, which explains Eq. 6.

Figure 8 displays both Boolean lattices: the one mapped to by f_{p_0} and the one constructed using $ker(f_{p_0})$.

The kernel of f_{p_0} for the example is populated by the concepts p_0' and all its parts. This is the same set as the one obtained by determining the principal ideal generated by p_0' on the original ontology. This aligns with the first isomorphism theorem which states the kernel is the carrier set for a principal ideal of the original Boolean algebra. In our example, p_0' is the complement of $Taste$ since it is the concept that is created from combining all atoms that are *not* part of $Taste$. Therefore we observe the following relationship between the three Boolean algebra structures. Let B_1, B_2, B_3 be three Boolean algebras, and p_0 be a concept from the carrier set B_1 of $\mathcal{B}_1$. Applying the function in

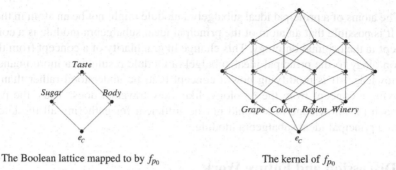

The Boolean lattice mapped to by f_{p_0} The kernel of f_{p_0}

Fig. 8. $f_{p_0}(p) = p \otimes Taste$, where $p_0 = Taste$.

Eq. 4 with p_0 will result in a homomorphism that maps $\mathcal{B}_1$ to $\mathcal{B}_2$. This homomorphism has a kernel, which is itself associated with a Boolean algebra, $\mathcal{B}_3$. $\mathcal{B}_3$ corresponds to a module that is equivalent to, using the view traversal function defined in Definition 7, $vt_D(p'_0)$.

With this relationship between the Boolean lattices of the original ontology, the one determined by the homomorphism f_{p_0}, and its kernel, we revisit measuring the loss of knowledge. As introduced, the process of modularizing implies the possible loss of knowledge that can be derived from the omitted part of the ontology. The kernel of f_{p_0} represents a quantifiable measure of the lost part of the ontology. It is quantifiable because, as the kernel is a measure of how non-injective the homomorphism is: the larger a kernel is, the more concepts that were 'lost' in the mapping. This use of measuring the kernel to determine how much knowledge is lost aligns with our example in Fig. 8. The chosen p_0 was one made of only two constituent concepts, *Sugar* and *Body*. It is to be expected that, given the original ontology has six atoms and we are only using two, a significant amount of knowledge is lost. The kernel of f_{p_0} is a Boolean lattice formed from the four missing atoms, and represents all the concepts that are lost. Thus, from an ontologist's perspective, the manipulation of the homomorphism and the kernel allow for the control of what domain knowledge will be present in the module, or, what domain knowledge will *not* be there by ensuring it is in the kernel. In [35], an equation giving a measure of the knowledge loss is provided. It is based on comparing the number of atoms in the kernel to the total number of atoms in the original ontology. This can be made into a percentage which represents how many total concepts are lost. For our example, as we are using two of the six atoms, we are losing roughly 67% of the domain knowledge.

A view traversal modularization certainly results in the loss of knowledge which can be measured as described in the previous paragraph, but this does not capture all knowledge that is lost. For instance, the view traversal module does not preserve the complement operator, and the knowledge that is lost due to this is not captured using this approach. However, since the principal ideal subalgebra module preserves the complement operator, it does not lose this knowledge.

The atoms of a principal ideal subalgebra module might not be an atom in the ontology. It is possible that an atom of the principal ideal subalgebra module is a composite concept in the original ontology. This change in granularity of a concept from the original ontology to the principal ideal subalgebra module results in a more nuanced loss of knowledge. It is modifying how a concept is to be understood rather than simply removing a concept from the ontology, like view traversal does. Thus, the proposed approach for knowledge loss would not be sufficient for gathering all the knowledge lost in a principal ideal subalgebra module.

6   Discussion and Future Work

A major consequence of the view traversal module not being locally correct is that the complement operator is not preserved. As the lattice operations of join and meet are preserved, the knowledge that is deduced using these operators will be preserved, but anything deduced with the complement operator will not be. Contextually, this has its own significance: the view traversal module is a focused snapshot of the domain. It removes concepts from the context that is being evaluated by entirely removing the concepts and its parts. Given that a query for the complement of a concept is to ask for the concept that is built from the atoms of those that do not build the queried concept, it does not make sense for the answer to be a concept that is not a part of the context. Instead, the answer should be one which is a part of the context. However, there is still a significant need for being able to utilize the complement on a module, and be able to use the result without it being incorrect in the original context. For this, the principal ideal subalgebra module is useful. The cost of preserving the complement operator is the size of the principal ideal subalgebra module being greater than that of a view traversal module, as well as modifying the granularity of some concepts in the principal ideal subalgebra module. The application of either type of modularization approach can be seen dependent on priority of the engineer: view traversal produces lightweight and easily usable modules, but do not preserve the complement operator, whereas the principal ideal subalgebra module is one that preserves all knowledge from the Boolean algebra operators, but are larger and contain composite concepts as atoms.

The use of the algebraic notion of a homomorphism associated to an ideal allows for the measurement of the knowledge that is lost due to modularization. This is a significant step towards being able to not only modularize based on preserving certain pieces of knowledge, but also by ensuring certain knowledge is not able to be determined via reasoning on the module. For fields related to privacy or determining the knowledge an autonomous agent can know via the module it has, this is a significant result. With the result of knowledge being quantified using the size of the kernel, we are able to determine the amount of domain knowledge that is being lost (or retained). However, as there are many different types, or facets of knowledge beyond simply the concepts themselves, there is work to be done in exploring how modularization on a DIS ontology can be characterized to capture these properties.

Lastly, the result of composite concepts being an atom in a principal ideal subalgebra module demonstrates insight to the different ways a single domain can be understood. A single non-decomposable concept to one agent might be a concept made of many smaller parts to another. In this case, the second agent has a *finer* understanding of that concept, whereas the first agent has a *coarser* understanding. A modularization technique that, instead of focusing on the omission or retention of concepts, but rather the coarsening or refinement of a concept could prove significant. By coarsening a concept, you produce a light-weight module at the cost of not being able to recognize or use the parts of the coarsened concept. In contrast, the refinement of a concept would result in a *larger* ontology, but distinguish the composing atoms of the refined concept.

7 Conclusion

In this paper, modularizing a DIS ontology with view traversal was introduced. The ability to leverage both the underlying Boolean lattice and the Boolean algebra associated with the ontology allows for a simple deterministic way to modularize the ontology. It is shown that the view traversal module is equal to a principal ideal, which is itself a Boolean sublattice. The Wine Ontology was utilized to demonstrate an example of extracting a view traversal module from a DIS ontology. Additional to the view traversal module, the principal ideal subalgebra module is introduced as a way of extending the view traversal module so that the complement operator is preserved.

Finally, the topic of measuring the knowledge that is lost due to modularization is introduced using the view traversal module. Using the first isomorphism theorem, we show the view traversal module is associated to the kernel of a homomorphism f that maps the Boolean algebra associated to the original ontology to another separate Boolean algebra. Since the kernel is a measure of the non-injectivity of a homomorphism, the size of the kernel is used to quantify the domain knowledge that is lost by the modularization process. It is also shown how the modularization process can be guided by ensuring the retention (or exclusion) of knowledge by their existence within the kernel. Other types of knowledge, such as the knowledge associated with the coarsening or refinement of a concept is introduced as a rich area for future work.

References

1. Algergawy, A., Babalou, S., Kargar, M.J., Davarpanah, S.H.: SeeCOnt: a new seeding-based clustering approach for ontology matching. In: Morzy, T., Valduriez, P., Bellatreche, L. (eds.) ADBIS 2015. LNCS, vol. 9282, pp. 245–258. Springer, Cham (2015). https://doi.org/10.1007/978-3-319-23135-8_17
2. Algergawy, A., Babalou, S., König-Ries, B.: A new metric to evaluate ontology modularization. In: SumPre@ ESWC (2016)
3. Anand, N., van Duin, R., Tavasszy, L.: Ontology-based multi-agent system for urban freight transportation. Int. J. Urban Sci. **18**(2), 133–153 (2014)
4. Ashburner, M., et al.: Gene ontology: tool for the unification of biology. Nat. Genet. **25**(1), 25 (2000)
5. Baader, F.: The Description Logic Handbook: Theory, Implementation and Applications. Cambridge University Press, Cambridge (2003)
6. Baader, F., Borchmann, D., Nuradiansyah, A.: The identity problem in description logic ontologies and its application to view-based information hiding. In: Joint International Semantic Technology Conference, pp. 102–117. Springer (2017)

7. Babalou, S., Kargar, M.J., Davarpanah, S.H.: Large-scale ontology matching: a review of the literature. In: 2016 Second International Conference on Web Research (ICWR), pp. 158–165. IEEE (2016)
8. Belmonte, M.V., Pérez-de-la Cruz, J.L., Triguero, F.: Ontologies and agents for a bus fleet management system. Expert Syst. Appl. **34**(2), 1351–1365 (2008)
9. Benomrane, S., Sellami, Z., Ayed, M.B.: An ontologist feedback driven ontology evolution with an adaptive multi-agent system. Adv. Eng. Inform. **30**(3), 337–353 (2016)
10. Bezerra, C., Freitas, F., Euzenat, J., Zimmermann, A.: Modonto: a tool for modularizing ontologies. In: Proceedings 3rd Workshop on Ontologies and Their Applications (Wonto), pp. No-pagination (2008)
11. Bienvenu, M., Kikot, S., Kontchakov, R., Podolskii, V.V., Zakharyaschev, M.: Ontology-mediated queries: combined complexity and succinctness of rewritings via circuit complexity. J. ACM (JACM) **65**(5), 28 (2018)
12. Bodenreider, O.: The unified medical language system (UMLS): integrating biomedical terminology. Nucleic Acids Res. **32**(suppl-1), D267–D270 (2004)
13. Brickley, D., Miller, L.: FOAF vocabulary specification 0.91 (2010)
14. Codd, E.F.: A relational model of data for large shared data banks. Commun. ACM **26**, 64–69 (1983)
15. Cuenca Grau, B.: Privacy in ontology-based information systems: a pending matter. Semant. Web **1**(1, 2), 137–141 (2010)
16. Davey, B.A., Priestley, H.A.: Introduction to Lattices and Order. Cambridge University Press, Cambridge (2002)
17. De Giacomo, G., Lembo, D., Lenzerini, M., Poggi, A., Rosati, R.: Using ontologies for semantic data integration. In: Flesca, S., Greco, S., Masciari, E., Saccà, D. (eds.) A Comprehensive Guide Through the Italian Database Research Over the Last 25 Years. SBD, vol. 31, pp. 187–202. Springer, Cham (2018). https://doi.org/10.1007/978-3-319-61893-7_11
18. Del Vescovo, C., Parsia, B., Sattler, U., Schneider, T.: The modular structure of an ontology: atomic decomposition and module count. In: WoMO, pp. 25–39 (2011)
19. Dietz, J.L.: What is Enterprise Ontology? Springer, Heidelberg (2006). https://doi.org/10.1007/3-540-33149-2_2
20. Dijkstra, E., Scholten, C.: Predicate Calculus and Program Semantics. Springer, New York (1990). https://doi.org/10.1007/978-1-4612-3228-5
21. Domingue, J., Dzbor, M.: Magpie: supporting browsing and navigation on the semantic web. In: Proceedings of the 9th International Conference on Intelligent User Interfaces, pp. 191–197. ACM (2004)
22. Freitas, A., Panisson, A.R., Hilgert, L., Meneguzzi, F., Vieira, R., Bordini, R.H.: Applying ontologies to the development and execution of multi-agent systems. In: Web Intelligence, vol. 15, pp. 291–302. IOS Press (2017)
23. Grau, B.C., Parsia, B., Sirin, E.: Combining owl ontologies using e-connections. Web Semant. Sci. Serv. Agents World Wide Web **4**(1), 40–59 (2006)
24. Grau, B.C., Parsia, B., Sirin, E., Kalyanpur, A.: Modularity and web ontologies. In: KR. pp. 198–209 (2006)
25. Gries, D., Schenider, F.: A Logical Approach to Discrete Math. Springer Texts and Monographs in Computer Science. Springer, New York (1993)
26. Halmos, P.R.: Lectures on Boolean Algebras. Courier Dover Publications, Mineola (2018)
27. Harding, J., Heunen, C., Lindenhovius, B., Navara, M.: Boolean subalgebras of orthoalgebras. Order pp. 1–47 (2017)
28. Henkin, L., Monk, J., Tarski, A.: Cylindric algebras. II. Studies in logic and the foundations of mathematics **115** (1985)
29. Hirsch, R., Hodkinson, I.: Relation Algebras by Games. Elsevier, Amsterdam (2002)

30. Hustadt, U., Motik, B., Sattler, U.: Data complexity of reasoning in very expressive description logics. IJCAI **5**, 466–471 (2005)
31. Jaskolka, J., MacCaull, W., Khedri, R.: Towards an ontology design architecture. In: Proceedings of the 2015 International Conference on Computational Science and Computational Intelligence, pp. 132–135. CSCI 2015 (2015)
32. Jiménez-Ruiz, E., et al.: BOOTOX: practical mapping of RDBs to OWL 2. In: Arenas, M., et al. (eds.) ISWC 2015. LNCS, vol. 9367, pp. 113–132. Springer, Cham (2015). https://doi.org/10.1007/978-3-319-25010-6_7
33. Kantamneni, A., Brown, L.E., Parker, G., Weaver, W.W.: Survey of multi-agent systems for microgrid control. Eng. Appl. Artif. Intell. **45**, 192–203 (2015)
34. Khan, Z.C., Keet, C.M.: Toward a framework for ontology modularity. In: Proceedings of the 2015 Annual Research Conference on South African Institute of Computer Scientists and Information Technologists, p. 24. ACM (2015)
35. LeClair, A., Khedri, R., Marinache, A.: Toward measuring knowledge loss due to ontology modularization. In: Proceedings of the 11th International Joint Conference on Knowledge Discovery, Knowledge Engineering and Knowledge Management - Volume 2: KEOD. INSTICC, SciTePress (2019)
36. Legat, C., Seitz, C., Lamparter, S., Feldmann, S.: Semantics to the shop floor: towards ontology modularization and reuse in the automation domain. IFAC Proc. Vol. **47**(3), 3444–3449 (2014)
37. Lutz, C., Walther, D., Wolter, F.: Conservative extensions in expressive description logics. IJCAI **7**, 453–458 (2007)
38. Maedche, A., Motik, B., Stojanovic, L., Studer, R., Volz, R.: Ontologies for enterprise knowledge management. IEEE Intell. Syst. **18**(2), 26–33 (2003)
39. Marinache, A.: On the Structural Link Between Ontologies and Organised Data Sets. Master's thesis (2016)
40. Motik, B.: Reasoning in description logics using resolution and deductive databases. Ph.D. thesis, Karlsruhe Institute of Technology, Germany (2006)
41. Movaghati, M.A., Barforoush, A.A.: Modular-based measuring semantic quality of ontology. In: 2016 6th International Conference on Computer and Knowledge Engineering (ICCKE), pp. 13–18. IEEE (2016)
42. Nadal, S., Romero, O., Abelló, A., Vassiliadis, P., Vansummeren, S.: An integration-oriented ontology to govern evolution in big data ecosystems. Inf. Syst. **79**, 3–19 (2019)
43. Noy, N., Musen, M.: Traversing ontologies to extract views. Modular Ontologies pp. 245–260 (2009)
44. Noy, N.F., McGuinness, D.L., et al.: Ontology development 101: a guide to creating your first ontology (2001)
45. Noy, N.F., Musen, M.A.: Specifying ontology views by traversal. In: McIlraith, S.A., Plexousakis, D., van Harmelen, F. (eds.) ISWC 2004. LNCS, vol. 3298, pp. 713–725. Springer, Heidelberg (2004). https://doi.org/10.1007/978-3-540-30475-3_49
46. Pakdeetrakulwong, U., Wongthongtham, P., Siricharoen, W.V., Khan, N.: An ontology-based multi-agent system for active software engineering ontology. Mob. Networks Appl. **21**(1), 65–88 (2016)
47. Poggi, A., Lembo, D., Calvanese, D., De Giacomo, G., Lenzerini, M., Rosati, R.: Linking data to ontologies. In: Spaccapietra, S. (ed.) Journal on Data Semantics X. LNCS, vol. 4900, pp. 133–173. Springer, Heidelberg (2008). https://doi.org/10.1007/978-3-540-77688-8_5
48. Raimond, Y., Abdallah, S.A., Sandler, M.B., Giasson, F.: The music ontology. In: ISMIR, vol. 2007, p. 8th. Citeseer (2007)
49. Rector, A., Rogers, J., Pole, P.: The galen high level ontology (1996)
50. Romero, A.A., Kaminski, M., Grau, B.C., Horrocks, I.: Module extraction in expressive ontology languages via datalog reasoning. J. Artif. Intell. Res. **55**, 499–564 (2016)

51. Santos, E., Faria, D., Pesquita, C., Couto, F.M.: Ontology alignment repair through modularization and confidence-based heuristics. PLoS ONE **10**(12), e0144807 (2015)
52. Sikorski, R.: Boolean Algebras, vol. 2. Springer, Heidelberg (1969). https://doi.org/10.1007/978-3-642-85820-8
53. Spackman, K.A., Campbell, K.E., Côté, R.A.: Snomed RT: a reference terminology for health care. In: Proceedings of the AMIA Annual Fall Symposium, p. 640. American Medical Informatics Association (1997)
54. Stone, M.H.: The theory of representation for Boolean algebras. Trans. Am. Math. Soc. **40**(1), 37–111 (1936)
55. Stuckenschmidt, H., Klein, M.: Structure-based partitioning of large concept hierarchies. In: McIlraith, S.A., Plexousakis, D., van Harmelen, F. (eds.) ISWC 2004. LNCS, vol. 3298, pp. 289–303. Springer, Heidelberg (2004). https://doi.org/10.1007/978-3-540-30475-3_21
56. Suchanek, F.M., Kasneci, G., Weikum, G.: YAGO: a large ontology from Wikipedia and wordnet. Web Semant. Sci. Serv. Agents World Wide Web **6**(3), 203–217 (2008)
57. Wache, H., et al,.: Ontology-based integration of information-a survey of existing approaches. In: IJCAI-01 Workshop: Ontologies and Information Sharing, Seattle, USA, vol. 2001, pp. 108–117 (2001)
58. Van der Waerden, B.L., Artin, E., Noether, E.: Moderne algebra, vol. 31950. Springer (1950)
59. Xiao, G., et al.: Ontology-based data access: a survey. IJCAI (2018)
60. Xu, D., Karray, M.H., Archimède, B.: A knowledge base with modularized ontologies for eco-labeling: application for laundry detergents. Comput. Ind. **98**, 118–133 (2018)
61. Xue, X., Tang, Z.: An evolutionary algorithm based ontology matching system. J. Inf. Hiding Multimedia Signal Process. **8**(3), 551–556 (2017). high heterogeneity; Matcher combination; Matching system; Ontology matching; Optimal model; Recall and precision; Semantic correspondence; State of the art
62. Zhou, L., et al.: Towards an ontological infrastructure for chemical process simulation and optimization in the context of eco-industrial parks. Appl. Energy **204**, 1284–1298 (2017)
63. Ziegler, P., Dittrich, K.R.: Three decades of data intecration — all problems solved? In: Jacquart, R. (ed.) Building the Information Society. IIFIP, vol. 156, pp. 3–12. Springer, Boston, MA (2004). https://doi.org/10.1007/978-1-4020-8157-6_1

FoodOntoMapV2: Food Concepts Normalization Across Food Ontologies

Gorjan Popovski[1,2]([⊠]) [iD], Barbara Koroušić Seljak[1] [iD], and Tome Eftimov[1] [iD]

[1] Computer Systems Department, Jožef Stefan Institute, Jamova cesta 39,
1000 Ljubljana, Slovenia
{gorjan.popovski,barbara.korousic,tome.eftimov}@ijs.si
[2] Jožef Stefan International Postgraduate School, Jamova cesta 39, 1000 Ljubljana, Slovenia

Abstract. Nowadays, the existence of several available biomedical vocabularies and standards play a crucial role in understanding health information. While there is a large number of available resources in the biomedical domain, only a limited number of resources can be utilized in the food domain. There are only a few annotated corpora with food concepts, as well as a small number of rule-based food named-entity recognition systems for food concept extraction. Additionally, several food ontologies exist, each developed for a specific application scenario. To address the issue of ontology alignment, we have previously created a resource, named FoodOntoMap, that consists of food concepts extracted from recipes. The extracted concepts were annotated by using semantic tags from four different food ontologies. To make the resource more comprehensive, as well as more representative of the domain, in this paper we have extended this resource by creating a second version, appropriately named FoodOntoMapV2. This was done by including an additional four ontologies that contain food concepts. Moreover, this resource can be used for normalizing food concepts across ontologies and developing applications for understanding the relation between food systems, human health, and the environment.

Keywords: Food data normalization · Food data linking · Food ontology · Food semantics

1 Introduction

"End hunger, achieve food security and improved nutrition and promote sustainable agriculture" is one of the sustainable development goals of the United Nations set to the target date of 2030 [19]. To achieve this ambitious goal, big data and AI technologies can significantly contribute in the domain of global food and agricultural systems. A huge amount of work that has been done in biomedical predictive modelling [14, 31] is enabled by the existence of diverse biomedical vocabularies and standards. Such resources play a crucial role in understanding biomedical information, as well as the sheer amount of biomedical data that is collected from numerous sources (e.g., drug, diseases, treatments, etc.).

The number of biomedical resources available to researchers is tremendous. This can pose an additional challenge when different data sets described by these resources

© Springer Nature Switzerland AG 2020
A. Fred et al. (Eds.): IC3K 2019, CCIS 1297, pp. 413–426, 2020.
https://doi.org/10.1007/978-3-030-66196-0_19

are to be fused to provide more accurate and comprehensive information than that provided by any individual data set. For example, the Unified Medical Language System (UMLS) is a system that brings and links together several biomedical vocabularies to enable interoperability between computer systems [3]. It maps these vocabularies and thus allows one to normalize the data among the various terminological systems. It additionally provides tools for natural language processing that are mainly used by systems developers in medical informatics. The UMLS system consists of over one million biomedical concepts and five million concept names, all of which stem from over 100 incorporated controlled vocabularies and classification systems. Some examples of the controlled vocabularies that are part of UMLS are CPT [2], ICD-10 [28], MeSH [9], SNOMED CT [10], and RxNorm [20].

In contrast to the biomedical domain, the food and nutrition domain is relatively low-resourced. For example, there is only one publicly available annotated corpus with food concepts, known as FoodBase [27], and there are few food named-entity recognition systems for the extraction of food and nutrient concepts [13,25]. In addition, the 0available food ontologies are developed for very specific use cases [4].

To address such shortcomings, we have created a resource that consists of food concepts extracted from recipes, named FoodOntoMap. Each food concept was assigned its corresponding semantic tags from from four food vocabularies (i.e. Hansard taxonomy and three food ontologies: FoodOn [15], OntoFood, and SNOMED CT [10]). With this, the resource provides a link between different food ontologies that can be further used to create embedding spaces for food concepts, as well as to develop applications for understanding the relation between food system, human health, and the environment [26].

In this paper, we have extended the FoodOntoMap resource by adding four additional vocabularies (i.e. ontologies: RCD [7], MeSH [9], SNMI [32], and NDDF [8]) that can be used for food data normalization. With the inclusion of these new vocabularies, the resource becomes more comprehensive, which can further assist in easier food data integration. We have appropriately named this extended resource FoodOntoMapV2.

2   Related Work

In this section, we are mainly going to discuss i) different ontologies that can be used for normalization of food concepts, and ii) food named-entity recognition methods, which are used for extracting food concepts from textual data. Additionally, we are going to provide an overview of food data normalization approaches that have already been published.

2.1   Food Semantic Resources

There are several ontologies that can be used for normalizing food concepts. Some of them are developed specifically for the food domain (i.e. FoodWiki [6], AGROVOC [5], Open Food Facts [4], Food Product Ontology [18], FOODS [30], and FoodOn [15]), while others are related to the biomedical domain, but also include links to food and environmental concepts (i.e. SNOMED CT [10], MeSH [9], SNMI [32], and NDDF [8]). A comprehensive review of these publicly available food ontologies was provided by Boulos et al. [4].

BioPortal is an open repository that consists of 816 different biomedical ontologies and services that enable access to and exploration of those ontologies [22]. Notwithstanding its definition as a repository for the biomedical domain, it contains ontologies that consist of food concepts as well.

The Hansard corpus is a collection of text and concepts created as a part of the SAMUELS project (2014–2016). One of its advantages is that it allows semantic searching of its data. More details about the semantic tags that it uses can be found in [1,29]. The concepts are organized in 37 higher level semantic groups, one of which is *Food and Drink* (i.e. AG).

Table 1 provides an overview of the most commonly used ontologies that can be explored for food data normalization, while in Table 2 their availability is presented. In our case, after manually exploring the ontologies available in BioPortal, we have concluded that the aforementioned ontologies are to be included in the final mapping methodology, as their domain is in accordance with the task and they contain a significant number of classes.

2.2   Food Information Extraction

Before the process of food data normalization can be done, we should mention that some food concepts can be presented as parts of unstructured textual data. Thus, the first step would be to perform food information extraction [25]. Information extraction (IE) is the task of automatically extracting structured information from unstructured data. In our case, the information that should be extracted are the food concepts. One way to do this is to use a named-entity recognition method (NER), whose main goal is to locate and classify the entity (concept) mentions in the unstructured data into predefined categories [21].

There is a tremendous amount of work that has been done regarding NERs for biomedical tasks, especially focusing on disease, drug, procedure entities and other similar concepts in the biomedical domain. However, the situation is completely different in the food and nutrition domain. There are only a few rule-based systems that can be used as well as some general tools that work in combination with available ontologies. A supervised machine learning (ML) model that can be used for food information extraction still does not exist, since the first annotated corpus with food entities was just recently published [27].

The UCREL Semantic Analysis System (USAS) is a framework for semantic text analysis. It can be used for named-entity recognition with 21 major classes. The class of interest to our application is "food and farming" [29]. However, one of its significant drawbacks is that it only works on a token level. To illustrate what this means, let us take the text "steamed broccoli" as an example which represents one food entity that should be extracted and annotated. In this case, the USAS tagger would extract and annotate the words "steamed" and "broccoli" as separate entities.

Moreover, there are also only two rule-based systems that can be used for extraction of food entities. One of them, titled drNER, focuses on extracting food and nutri-

Table 1. Overview of the resources that are used for the process of food data normalization.

Ontology	Description
FoodOn [15]	• Semantics for food safety, food security, agriculture and animal husbandry practices linked to food production, culinary, nutritional and chemical ingredients and processes
	• Its usage is related to research and clinical data sets in academia and government
OntoFood (OF)	• An ontology with SWRL rules regarding nutrition for diabetic patients
SNOMED CT [10]	• A standardized, multilingual vocabulary of clinical terminology that is used by physicians and other health care providers for electronic health records
	• Apart from the medical concepts that are the main focus of this ontology, it additionally contains the concept of *Food* that can be further used for food concept normalization
Read Codes, Clinical Terms Version 3 (RCD) [7]	• Available as a part of the UMLS system
MeSH [9]	• Thesaurus that is a controlled and hierarchically-organized vocabulary produced by the National Library of Medicine
	• It is used for indexing, cataloging, and searching the biomedical and health-related information
SNMI [32]	• A previous version of SNOMED CT
NDDF [8]	• Widely-known terminology regarding drugs, which combines a comprehensive set of drug elements, pricing and clinical information
	• Approved by the U.S. Food and Drug Administration (FDA)
	• It additionally consists of concepts related to herbals, nutraceutical and dietary supplements
Hansard corpus [1,29]	• A collection of concepts created as part of the SAMUELS project (2014–2016)
	• It allows semantically-based searches of its data
	• The concepts are organized in 37 higher level semantic groups, one of which is *Food and Drink* (i.e. AG)

ent concepts from evidence-based dietary recommendations [13]. Recently, this work was extended with the creation of FoodIE [25], which is another rule-based system for extracting food entities. FoodIE uses rules based on computational linguistics, which also combine and utilize the knowledge available in the Hansard corpus.

Another tool that can be used for information extraction, in general, is the NCBO Annotator [17]. It utilizes the ontologies that are part of the BioPortal [22]. The methodology leverages these ontologies to create annotations of the raw input text and returns them by adhering to semantic web standards.

Table 2. Availability of the resources that are used for the process of food data normalization.

FoodOn	https://bioportal.bioontology.org/ontologies/FOODON/?p=summary
OntoFood	https://bioportal.bioontology.org/ontologies/OF/?p=summary
SNOMED CT	https://bioportal.bioontology.org/ontologies/SNOMEDCT/?p=summary
RCD	https://bioportal.bioontology.org/ontologies/RCD/?p=summary
MeSH	https://bioportal.bioontology.org/ontologies/MESH/?p=summary
SNMI	https://bioportal.bioontology.org/ontologies/SNMI?p=summary
NDDF	https://bioportal.bioontology.org/ontologies/NDDF/?p=summary
Hansard corpus	https://www.hansard-corpus.org/

2.3 Food Data Normalization

Recently, food concept normalization poses an open research question that is highly researched by the food and nutrition science community. Food concepts that are available in unstructured data can be represented in various unstandardized ways, which simply depend on how people express themselves. It is always good practice to normalize the data in order to ease further analyses. This is a task where the same food concept, represented in different ways, should be mapped to the single corresponding food concept that exists in some food resource (e.g., taxonomy or ontology).

To propose a solution to this issue, StandFood [12] has recently been introduced. It is a semi-automatic system for classifying and describing foods according to a description and classification system. Specifically, it adheres to FoodEx2, which is proposed by the European Food Safety Agency (EFSA) [11]. It uses a combination of machine learning, methods from natural language processing, and probability theory to perform food concept normalization. Additionally, we have created a resource that consists of food concepts extracted from recipes, named FoodOntoMap. Each food concept was assigned its corresponding semantic tags from four food vocabularies (i.e. Hansard taxonomy and three food ontologies: FoodOn [15], OntoFood, and SNOMED CT [10]). With this, the resource provides a link between different food ontologies that can be further used to create embedding spaces for food concepts, as well as to develop applications for understanding the relation between food system, human health, and the environment [26]. To go one step further, we have developed a heuristic model based on lexical similarity and propose two new semantic similarity heuristics based on word embeddings [24]. Moreover, we have explored the LanguaL hierarchy [23], which is a standard used to describe foods, in order to see if different food concepts that are part of this hierarchy are linked together properly. To do this, we have trained a vector representation (i.e. embedding) for each food concept that is a part of the hierarchy and have found the most similar products for a subset of products. The results indicate that further efforts should be made to link all these standards together in order to provide a unified system for describing and standardizing food concepts.

3 Methodology

The methodology is an extension of the methodology used to build *FoodOntoMap*, presented in [26]. It is constructed by including an additional four ontologies taken from the BioPortal. With this extended pipeline the second version is created, appropriately named *FoodOntoMapV2*. The flowchart on Fig. 1 illustrates the extended methodology.

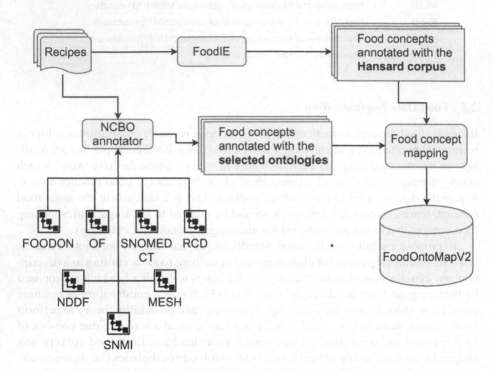

Fig. 1. Flowchart depicting the FoodOntoMapV2 methodology.

3.1 Data Collection

The data of interest is in the form of free-form text, i.e. recipe texts that are composed of i) lists of (raw or already treated) ingredients with amounts and units, and ii) descriptions of the preparation method with the specification of potential treatment methods and timing (i.e. time units and degrees). To provide a substantial amount and diversity of data, the recipes were taken from the most popular recipe sharing social media platform called AllRecipes [16]. More than 23,000 recipes were taken from the site, spanning across five different categories: "Appetizers and snacks", "Breakfast and Lunch", "Desserts", "Drinks", and "Dinners". It is important to mention the difficulties while working with raw textual data. As it is free-form text, i.e simply natural language text, there is no predefined data representation (format) that is followed. This implicates that the sentence structures, vocabulary, and in essence the very way people express themselves vary significantly from text to text. This imposes a challenge in the pre-processing of such textual data.

3.2   Text Pre-processing

In order to provide some consistency in the recipe texts, a text pre-processing step is useful. With this step, some issues that arise due to the nature of free-form text are resolved.

In our case, the pre-processing methodology, originally a constituent of FoodIE, is done prior to running all of the NER methods. It consists of several steps:

1. Removing excess white-space characters.
2. Removing semantically irrelevant punctuation (i.e. quotation marks).
3. Substituting commonly occurring non-ASCII symbols (i.e. degree symbol(°)).
4. ASCII transliteration.
5. Standardizing fractions to decimal notation.

The pre-processing is described in more detail in [25].

3.3   Information Extraction and Annotation

NCBO Annotator with Selected Ontologies. By using the aforementioned NCBO annotator in conjunction with each ontology once, we obtain annotations for all the recipes. With this, we have seven different annotation sets, one per ontology. As each ontology is primarily constructed for various different purposes, each NCBO run provides us with unique semantic information regarding the annotated food concepts. It is important to note that not all ontologies are able to extract every mentioned food concept. Consequently, some recipe annotations are empty, which is also due to the insufficient domain coverage of the ontology in question.

Each concept extraction and annotation produced by the NCBO annotator is defined by its:

- ordinal number within the recipe text;
- *urls* - The semantic type(s) taken from the ontology;
- *text* - The textual representation of the food concept;
- *from* - The start position of the food concept in the recipe, as expressed in terms of characters from the beginning of the text;
- *to* - The end position of the food concept in the recipe, as expressed in terms of characters from the beginning of the text;
- *matchType* - The type of match that is found by the NCBO annotator.

An example of an annotated recipe can be seen in Table 3.

Table 3. An example recipe annotated by the NCBO annotator using the SNOMED CT ontology.

	SNOMED CT ID	Text	From	To	MatchType
1	226890008	MARGARINE	60	68	PREF
2	735030001	GARLIC	77	82	PREF
3	443701000124100	WORCESTERSHIRE SAUCE	90	109	PREF
4	227519005	SAUCE	105	109	PREF
5	227260004	PUMPKIN	115	121	PREF

FoodIE Method. As mentioned in Sect. 2.2, FoodIE is a rule-based system for extracting food entities. Since its rule-engine utilizes the semantic information in the Hansard corpus, each extraction is accompanied by its corresponding semantic tag from the Hansard corpus. With this, an annotation for the food concept is provided.

The FoodIE rule-based system is used to extract and annotate the food concepts in each recipe, in a similar a fashion to the usage of the NCBO annotator. This process produces one more annotation set, bringing the total to eight annotation sets containing semantic annotations for the concepts in each recipe, subject to the domain coverage of the used ontology.

Similarly to the previous method, each food concept annotation is defined by its:

- *annotation id* - The ordinal number within the recipe text;
- *offset* - The start position of the extracted food concept within the recipe, as expressed in terms of words (tokens) from the beginning of the text;
- *length* - The length of the textual representation of the food concept, as measured by its length in characters;
- *text* - The textual representation of the food concept;
- *semantic_tags* - The semantic tag(s) from the Hansard corpus which correspond to the food concept.

It is important to note that the positions of the extracted food concepts by FoodIE are measured differently compared to the NCBO annotator.

An example of an annotated recipe can be seen in Listing 1.1. This is the same convenient format used by FoodBase.

```
<document>
  <id>0recipe43</id>
  <infon key="category">Appetizers and snacks</infon>
  <infon key="full_text">
  Preheat oven to 275 degrees F (135 degrees C). Combine the margarine, salt,
  garlic salt, Worcestershire sauce and pumpkin seeds. Mix thoroughly
  and place in shallow baking dish. Bake for 1 hour, stirring occasionally.
  </infon>
  <annotation id="1">
    <location offset="15" length="9"/>
    <text>margarine</text>
    <infon key="semantic_tags">
      AG.01.f [Fat/oil];
    </infon>
  </annotation>
  <annotation id="2">
    <location offset="17" length="4"/>
```

```
<text>salt</text>
<infon key="semantic_tags">
  AG.01.1.01 [Salt];AG.01.w [Setting table];
</infon>
</annotation>
<annotation id="3">
  <location offset="19" length="11"/>
  <text>garlic salt</text>
  <infon key="semantic_tags">
    AG.01.h.02.e [Onion/leek/garlic];AG.01.1.01 [Salt];AG.01.w [Setting table];
  </infon>
</annotation>
<annotation id="4">
  <location offset="22" length="20"/>
  <text>Worcestershire sauce</text>
  <infon key="semantic_tags">
    AG.01.h [Fruit and vegetables];AG.01.1.04 [Sauce/dressing];
  </infon>
</annotation>
<annotation id="5">
  <location offset="25" length="13"/>
  <text>pumpkin seeds</text>
  <infon key="semantic_tags">
    AG.01.h.02.f [Fruits as vegetables];
  </infon>
</annotation>
</document>
```

Listing 1.1. The same recipe shown in Table 3, but annotated by the FoodIE method instead.

3.4 Datasets with Unique Extracted Food Concepts per Ontology

Before the food concept mapping can be done, it is useful to have a standardized representation for the food concepts found across all the different ontologies, as the semantic tags provided by each resource differ regarding their representation. After the process of extracting and annotating the recipes, all the unique food concepts extracted by each ontology can be condensed into eight simple datasets, i.e. one per ontology. Each code is represented by a single uppercase letter, followed by six digits (e.g. "A000832"). The digits are simply ordinal numbers, while each letter represents a semantic resource, namely:

A. FoodIE + Hansard corpus
B. FoodOn
C. SNOMED CT
D. OntoFood
E. Read Codes, Clinical Terms Version 3 (RCD)
F. Medical Subject Headings (MeSH)
G. Systematized Nomenclature of Medicine, International Version (SNMI)
H. National Drug Data File (NDDF)

With this, each food concept from each semantic resource has its own unique identifier by which it is represented in the final map. The number of unique food concepts per method is presented in Table 4.

Table 4. Total number of unique extracted entities per method.

Method	Number of unique extracted entities
FoodIE + Hansard corpus (A)	13111
FOODON (B)	1069
SNOMED CT (C)	583
OF (D)	111
RCD (E)	485
MESH (F)	105
SNMI (G)	42
NDDF (H)	54

3.5 Food Concept Mapping

After all the annotations have been done by using the different methods and semantic resources, the mapping process can be performed. The first thing that must be done here is to convert the positions of the food concepts into the same unit. In this case, all of the positions are converted as to be expressed in terms of words (tokens) from the beginning of the recipe text.

Now that all the positions are expressed in the same way, the mapping can be done. For each concept that is extracted and annotated by any method, we check if it is extracted and annotated by every other method. From here, three things are possible for each pair of methods:

1. The food concept is extracted and annotated by both methods.
    (a) The positions given by both methods are the same.
        - In this case, the food concepts' texts are double checked for robustness. If they are the same, a link is added in the map between the codes for both concepts. If the texts are different, an error is to be raised and the concepts are to be manually checked. However, as is expected, this did not happen when performing the mapping. Additionally, this step takes the different spelling variants of the words into account, e.g. "colour" is the same as "color".
    (b) The positions from one annotator lie within the positions from the other.
        - In this case, the food concept is only partially recognized by one of the methods. The encompassed food concept is mapped with the encompassing food concept. If several of these partial matches are present, then the semantic tags from each concept are mapped to the food concept that encompasses them. This implicates that a single food concept from one ontology can have multiple corresponding food concept mappings with another ontology. To illustrate this with an example let us consider the food concept "fruit juice". Here, one annotator might extract the concept as "fruit juice", while the other might extract two separate concepts: "fruit" and "juice". As the positions of these two concepts lie within the position of the food concept extracted by the first annotator, the semantic tags from both shorter concepts are mapped to the semantic tag of the single food concept.

2. One or both of the methods do not extract and annotate the food concept.
   - In this case, there exist no links between the food concepts, and therefore no mapping is performed.

The map consists of 1,398 instances, where each instance is a tuple of corresponding food concept codes. There are a total of eight columns, one for each semantic resource. If a food concept is not annotated by a specific semantic resource, then there is no corresponding food concept code from that ontology, and such missing data is filled with "NULL". An example entry, where all of the three possible matches occur, is presented in Table 5.

Table 5. An example of a FoodMapOntomapV2 instance which contains all types of matches.

Hansard	FOODON	SNOMEDCT	OF	RCD	MESH	SNMI	NDDF
A000630	B000066; B000022	C000018	NULL	E000018	F000007	G000002	H000003

In this example the codes represent the following food concepts:

- A000630 - "VEGETABLE OIL SPRAY"
- B000066 - "SPRAY"
- B000022 - "VEGETABLE OIL"
- C000018 - "VEGETABLE OIL"
- E000018 - "VEGETABLE OIL"
- F000007 - "VEGETABLE"
- G000002 - "VEGETABLE"
- H000003 - "VEGETABLE OIL"

Finally, the map was manually checked in order to ensure that no inconsistencies are present. The code used to perform this mapping is available at https://github.com/ GorjanP/FOM_mapper_client, while the final map can be found at https://doi.org/10. 5281/zenodo.3600619.

4 Discussion

Analyzing the data presented in Table 4, we can observe that the first method, which uses FoodIE and the Hansard corpus, provides the largest domain coverage of all the methods presented. This is due to the performance of the NER method FoodIE, which can extract previously unseen combinations of tokens that represent a food concept. Concretely, this means that the entities extracted and annotated by FoodIE do not have to be present as a whole in the semantic resource, as long as each token that is part of the food concept is correspondingly extracted and annotated.

Moreover, there is quite a large variation between the number of extracted food concepts among the other seven methods. As each one is built with a specific purpose in mind, it defines different points of interest that should be captured by the semantic information of the concepts it describes. However, with such a map between these different semantic resources a broader perspective is represented for each food concept that is found in it. This is especially useful regarding achieving interoperability, as well as working towards creating a definitive, universal, and standardized semantic resource for food concepts that could be used for any purpose. Such a target resource is reminiscent of the Unified Medical Language System (UMLS).

5   Conclusions

In this paper we have presented an extension of the FoodOntoMap methodology, which performs food concept normalization across different food ontologies, aptly named *FoodOntoMapV2*.

Each food ontology contains different semantic information regarding its constituent classes and concepts, as they are developed for a specific problem domain. Therefore, the process of food concept normalization across such ontologies presents an important task which aims at providing interoperability between the ontologies in the form of an ontology concept map. With this, each specific concept that is found in several ontologies is linked by this mapping.

Moreover, the same methodology can be applied in order to normalize data of any nature, provided there exist adequate semantic resources (e.g. ontologies) and a corresponding NER method.

Acknowledgements. This work was supported by the Ad Futura grant for postgraduate study; the Slovenian Research Agency Program P2-0098; and the European Union's Horizon 2020 research and innovation programme [grant agreement No 863059].

References

1. Alexander, M., Anderson, J.: The hansard corpus **1803–2003** (2012)
2. Association, A.M., et al.: CPT, 1989: Physician's Current Procedural Terminology. American Medical Association Press (1989)
3. Bodenreider, O.: The unified medical language system (UMLs): integrating biomedical terminology. Nucleic Acids Res. **32**(suppl-1), D267–D270 (2004)
4. Boulos, M.N.K., Yassine, A., Shirmohammadi, S., Namahoot, C.S., Brückner, M.: Towards an "internet of food": food ontologies for the internet of things. Future Internet **7**(4), 372–392 (2015)
5. Caracciolo, C., Stellato, A., Rajbahndari, S., Morshed, A., Johannsen, G., Jaques, Y., Keizer, J.: Thesaurus maintenance, alignment and publication as linked data: the AGROVOC use case. Int. J. Metadata Semant. Ontol. **7**(1), 65–75 (2012)
6. Çelik, D.: Foodwiki: Ontology-driven mobile safe food consumption system. Sci. World Jo. **2015** (2015)
7. Chen, Y., Lasko, T.A., Mei, Q., Denny, J.C., Xu, H.: A study of active learning methods for named entity recognition in clinical text. J. Biomed. Inform. **58**, 11–18 (2015)
8. First DataBank: National drug data file (NDDF) (2008)
9. Díaz-Galiano, M.C., García-Cumbreras, M.Á., Martín-Valdivia, M.T., Montejo-Ráez, A., Ureña-López, L.A.: Integrating MeSH ontology to improve medical information retrieval. In: Peters, C., Jijkoun, V., Mandl, T., Müller, H., Oard, D.W., Peñas, A., Petras, V., Santos, D. (eds.) CLEF 2007. LNCS, vol. 5152, pp. 601–606. Springer, Heidelberg (2008). https://doi.org/10.1007/978-3-540-85760-0_76

10. Donnelly, K.: SNOMED-CT: The advanced terminology and coding system for eHealth. Stud. Health Technol. Inform. **121**, 279 (2006)
11. (EFSA), E.F.S.A.: The food classification and description system foodex 2 (revision 2). EFSA Supporting Publications **12**(5), 804E (2015)
12. Eftimov, T., Korošec, P., Koroušić Seljak, B.: Standfood: Standardization of foods using a semi-automatic system for classifying and describing foods according to FoodEx2. Nutrients **9**(6), 542 (2017)
13. Eftimov, T., Koroušić Seljak, B., Korošec, P.: A rule-based named-entity recognition method for knowledge extraction of evidence-based dietary recommendations. PLoS ONE **12**(6), e0179488 (2017)
14. Gligic, L., Kormilitzin, A., Goldberg, P., Nevado-Holgado, A.: Named entity recognition in electronic health records using transfer learning bootstrapped neural networks. arXiv preprint arXiv:1901.01592 (2019)
15. Griffiths, E.J., Dooley, D.M., Buttigieg, P.L., Hoehndorf, R., Brinkman, F.S., Hsiao, W.W.: Foodon: a global farm-to-fork food ontology. In: ICBO/BioCreative (2016)
16. Groves, S.: How allrecipes. com became the worlds largest food/recipe site. roi of social media (blog) (2013)
17. Jonquet, C., Shah, N., Youn, C., Callendar, C., Storey, M.A., Musen, M.: NCBO annotator: semantic annotation of biomedical data. In: International Semantic Web Conference, Poster and Demo Session, vol. 110 (2009)
18. Kolchin, M., Zamula, D.: Food product ontology: initial implementation of a vocabulary for describing food products. In: Proceeding of the 14th Conference of Open Innovations Association FRUCT, Helsinki, Finland, pp. 11–15 (2013)
19. Lartey, A.: End hunger, achieve food security and improved nutrition and promote sustainable agriculture. UN Chronicle **51**(4), 6–8 (2015)
20. Liu, S., Ma, W., Moore, R., Ganesan, V., Nelson, S.: RXNORM: prescription for electronic drug information exchange. IT Prof. **7**(5), 17–23 (2005)
21. Nadeau, D., Sekine, S.: A survey of named entity recognition and classification. Lingvisticae Investigationes **30**(1), 3–26 (2007)
22. Noy, N.F., et al.: Bioportal: ontologies and integrated data resources at the click of a mouse. Nucleic Acids Res. **37**(suppl-2), W170–W173 (2009)
23. Pennington, J.A., Smith, E.C., Chatfield, M.R., Hendricks, T.C.: Langual: a food-description language. Terminology. Int. J. Theoret. Appl. Issues Special. Commun. **1**(2), 277–289 (1994)
24. Popovski, G., Ispirova, G., Hadzi-Kotarova, N., Valenčič, E., Eftimov, T., Koroušić Seljak, B.: Food data integration by using heuristics based on lexical and semantic similarities. In: Proceedings of the 13th International Conference on Health Informatics (2020, in Press)
25. Popovski, G., Kochev, S., Koroušić Seljak, B., Eftimov, T.: Foodie: a rule-based named-entity recognition method for food information extraction. In: Proceedings of the 8th International Conference on Pattern Recognition Applications and Methods, (ICPRAM 2019), pp. 915–922 (2019)
26. Popovski, G., Koroušić Seljak, B., Eftimov, T.: FoodOntoMap: linking food concepts across different food ontologies. In: Proceedings of the 11th International Joint Conference on Knowledge Discovery, Knowledge Engineering and Knowledge Management - Volume 2: KEOD, pp. 195–202. INSTICC, SciTePress (2019). https://doi.org/10.5220/0008353201950202
27. Popovski, G., Seljak, B.K., Eftimov, T.: FoodBase corpus: a new resource of annotated food entities. Database 2019, November 2019. https://doi.org/10.1093/database/baz121
28. Quan, H., et al.: Coding algorithms for defining comorbidities in icd-9-cm and icd-10 administrative data. Medical care pp. 1130–1139 (2005)
29. Rayson, P., Archer, D., Piao, S., McEnery, A.: The UCREL semantic analysis system (2004)

30. Snae, C., Brückner, M.: Foods: a food-oriented ontology-driven system. In: 2nd IEEE International Conference on Digital Ecosystems and Technologies, DEST 2008 pp. 168–176. IEEE (2008)
31. Wang, Q., Zhou, Y., Ruan, T., Gao, D., Xia, Y., He, P.: Incorporating dictionaries into deep neural networks for the Chinese clinical named entity recognition. J. Biomed. Inform. 103133 (2019)
32. Wang, Y.: An empirical evaluation of semantic similarity measures using the wordnet and UMLS ontologies. Ph.D. thesis, Miami University (2005)

Knowledge Management and Information Systems

Knowledge Life Cycle Management as a Key Aspect of Digitalization

Eduard Babkin[✉] ⓘ, Tanja Poletaeva ⓘ, and Boris Ulitin ⓘ

National Research University, Higher School of Economics,
B. Pechorskaya St, Nizhny Novgorod, Russia
{eababkin, tpoletaeva, bulitin}@hse.ru

Abstract. Digital transformation of organizations became a significant research and engineering challenge worldwide. Implementing such a transformation requires not only a change in the technical equipment of the enterprise, but also developing new methods of knowledge life cycle management which include extraction of individual, interpersonal or organizational knowledge to explicit machine-readable forms and their conscious application during enterprise reengineering. Successful accomplishment of these tasks vitally relies on a rigorous scientific theory and formal methods. This work presents a new approach to knowledge life cycle management of different forms of knowledge based on combination of ontology engineering and evolvable domain-specific languages.

Keywords: Digital transformation · Enterprise engineering · Ontology development · Domain-specific languages

1 Introduction

During last decades we became witnesses of unprecedented advances in various domains of micro-electronics, communications and computer sciences. These advances have great impact on almost every aspect of economic and social structures. Such concepts as Industry 4.0 [6, 57, 65] Logistics 4.0 [6, 43], as well new models of government and public administration services [5, 11, 53] demonstrate new trends in development of organizational theory and business models based on digital technologies. That development assumes the wide-scope conversion process from mainly analog information into the binary machine-understandable languages, accompanied by the notion of digital innovation as "the concerted orchestration of new products, new processes, new services, new platforms, or even new business models in a given context" [28]. A large-scale combination of these digital innovations has a name of digital transformation, emphasizing crucial synergetic effects on an institutional level [28, 30, 32, 33, 35, 53, 65]. Despite intrinsic processes of digital transformation in each application domain, common characteristic features are clearly visible: institutionalized disruptive changes of social and business domains, intensification of networking and cooperation, emergence of complex cyber-physical systems [28, 30, 33, 35, 53, 57].

Radically new conditions of information processing, planning and strategic management of digitalized enterprises call to engineering of various flexible organizational

© Springer Nature Switzerland AG 2020
A. Fred et al. (Eds.): IC3K 2019, CCIS 1297, pp. 429–452, 2020.
https://doi.org/10.1007/978-3-030-66196-0_20

forms on the solid ground of enterprise engineering principles: virtual enterprises [45], agile enterprises [37] and distributed autonomous organizations (DAO) [34].

Recent achievements in enterprise engineering [15, 55, 66] provide a design blue print as well as offer a certain set of methodological implications. During recent years within the enterprise engineering community the notion of Enterprise Architecture (EA) became manifestation of the systemic engineering approach to understanding and redesigning organizations [27, 28, 57]. First of all, EA-based methods of digital transformation should lead to design of cohesive socio-technical systems because, as it is stated in [6], the digital transformation aim is not to replace humans in their works, but to avoid inaccuracies and to have faster processes where the information can be shared effortless and in real time.

Modern researches determine a complicated manner of relations and multiple perspectives on socio-technical systems [6, 57, 65]. According to [65] vertical integration requires the intelligent cross-linking and digitalization of business units in different hierarchal levels within the organization. Such complexity makes practical implementation of digital transformation quite difficult in general and in particular domains as well. Recent analysis of Westerman et al. [68] shows that none of the 50 companies, most of which had a turnover of more than $1 billion, had successfully transformed all elements of EA. At the same time Hafsi et al. conclude that despite the ongoing research in academia, the benefits and the role of EA management in digital context are still a topic of lively discussions, and there is a gap in research on how to leverage EA for digital transformation [27]. It is concluded in [32] that the characteristics of the industry raise barriers for process innovations and effectively constrain application of EA for digital transformation. By a similar manner Oleśków-Szłapka and Stachowiak [43] point out significant problems of digitalization in Logistics 4.0, while Oliva and Kotabe determine significant barriers to knowledge management in startups [44].

Performed analysis shows, that successful implementation of digital transformation strategy vitally depends on further progress in liaison of EA practices and enterprise knowledge management in new contexts of virtual organizations and evolvable cyber-physical systems. Supporting the concept of digital transformation "as the third and ultimate level of digital literacy" [27] we have a strong reason to augment the notion of digital transformation by the concept of knowledge-based digital transformation as a new paradigm of organizational theory. That augmentation revives relevance of the pioneering work on design of inquiring systems by C.W. Churchman [12].

According to [67] during knowledge-based digital transformation enterprise modeling and knowledge management could combine their efforts to develop reference and reusable core enterprise ontologies and behavior representations as required by the smart, sensing and sustainable (S3) digital enterprises of tomorrow. Following the pioneering work of Fox and Gruninger [20] and the Enterprise Ontology of Uschold et al. [63] several ontology-based modeling approaches were proposed, such as: DEMO [14] or MRO [64].

In the enterprise engineering studies of knowledge management within a digital enterprise an important problem arises which is proper extraction of tacit individual, interpersonal or organizational knowledge to explicit machine-readable forms and their conscious application during enterprise reengineering. In that context research multiple researchers show that tacit knowledge greatly influences behavior of enterprise [39, 48].

By our view in most applied engineering methods availability of structured externalized knowledge is usually only a requirement to construct models and necessary for enterprise models [45]. Specific features of tacit knowledge require development of new forms of its machine-based representation, and support mechanisms for knowledge life cycle management. In our studies a following principal research question was specified: which theoretical backgrounds facilitate design or integration of artifacts which comprise a unified solution to knowledge life cycle management fostering knowledge-based digital transformations? Fig. 1 depicts such a research framework.

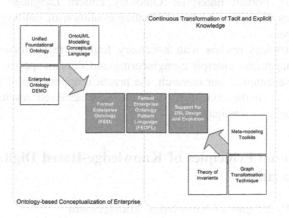

Fig. 1. The research framework of studies [4].

In order to pursue an answer we hypothesize that:

1. Implementation of the knowledge triad model [40], which facilitates mutual transformations of explicit and tacit knowledge, can be a practically achievable form of knowledge-based digital transformation if enterprise engineering methods are designed in accordance with social constructivism paradigm.
2. Combination of three elements becomes critical for developing these new enterprise engineering methods:
   a. methodology for extracting tacit knowledge;
   b. a constructivist view – aligned theory of comprehensive ontology-based knowledge modeling for proper conceptualization of enterprise;
   c. a theory and methodology for continuous transformation of tacit and explicit knowledge according the model of knowledge triad (using phronesis).
3. Following design artifacts may instantiate the elements a), b) and c):

   – mathematical and psychological principles of repertory grids by G. Kelly [21] can be used for the purpose of reconstruction of a personal world view and developing a solid methodology for extracting tacit knowledge by application of factual approach to knowledge construction;

- a constructivist-based theory of knowledge modeling which combines advances of designing top-level ontologies and formal ontology of enterprise proposed by J. Dietz;
- an ontology-grounded theory of domain-specific languages with proper methods of their transformation and evolution, providing an explicit-tacit knowledge combination engine.

In that article we wish overview key results in developing artifacts for the elements b) and c) for comprehensive understanding of socio-technical systems, and providing a reliable decision support for digitalization. These results include Formal Enterprise Ontology (FEO), Formal Enterprise Ontology Pattern Language (FEOPL) and a specific approach to supporting transformative evolution of ontology-based domain-specific languages.

Section 2 provides readers with necessary foundational information concerning knowledge management, enterprise engineering and domain-specific languages. Section 3 offers description of our research, the practical application of which results are shown in Sect. 4. In the conclusion we overview achieved results and determine directions for further investigation.

2 Foundational Principles of Knowledge-Based Digital Transformation

2.1 Generic Paradigms of Knowledge Management

Hafsi et al. in [27] provide a direct connection between digital transformation and knowledge management as a specific organizational discipline that aims to acquire, transform, store, use and discard knowledge that is important in generating value for the organization. Oliva and Kotabe [44] consider the knowledge management as one of the key enterprise processes that supports the dynamic capabilities of emerging digital organizations. In the context of digital transformation Nonaka et al. [40] argue that the company needs to have organizational forms that achieve a dynamic synthesis of knowledge exploration and exploitation. Weichhart, Stary and Vernadat provide even a more radical viewpoint – the rate of new product introduction is a function of a firm's ability to manage, maintain and create knowledge [67].

We may distinguish several aspects of knowledge-based digital transformation. Interoperability becomes the first aspect because dynamic synthesis of knowledge exploration and exploitation during digital transformation raises grand challenges. For example, in [45] authors show unprecedented nature of these challenges for the case of mapping the Industry 4.0 elements to the European Enterprise Interoperability Framework. A detailed set of interoperability includes such elements as interoperability of models and processes, explicit knowledge, knowledge management systems. Undoubtedly, as Weichhart, Stary and Vernadat noted in [67] with respect to semantic interoperability, the key element of that set is mutual ontological commitment on the basis of machine-readable shared ontologies. For instance, the Ontology of Enterprise Interoperability (OoEI) proposed by Naudet et al. [38] can give an example of ontology-based support for enterprise modeling.

We see the second aspect of knowledge-based digital transformation in a more precise stratification of knowledge onto different types. From the time of ancient Greece epistemology determines three subsets of knowledge: *techne* (the practical skill required to be able to create), *episteme* (context-independent knowledge), and *phronesis* (practical wisdom) [67, 69]. Simultaneously in the modern knowledge creation theory, two types of knowledge are distinguished: tacit and explicit [40]. Polanyi [49] defines explicit or codified knowledge as the type of knowledge that can be effectively transferred through a formal language, and tacit knowledge as having a personal quality that makes its formalization and communication difficult. At the same time tacit knowledge can be shared, developed, and extended by physical collaboration [39]. In [48] the authors argue that the distinction between tacit and explicit knowledge is the key to understanding organizational knowledge. Nonaka and Nishihara even emphasize the importance of tacit knowledge over explicit knowledge, through an understanding that tacit knowledge is the foundation of all knowledge [39].

Distinction of two knowledge types supposes presence of a dynamic approach to the knowledge management [41, 42]. In order to achieve deep understanding of such knowledge dynamics, which is very important for digital innovations and digital transformations [44, 48] some conceptualization of knowledge synthesis is required. To pursue that goal Nonaka et al. propose to combine traditional and modern taxonomies of knowledge within a unified conceptual framework of knowledge triad [40]. In that framework dynamic synthesis of knowledge is realized through the knowledge dialectics of tacit knowledge, explicit knowledge and phronesis. According that model of "knowledge triad" phronesis drives the conversion of tacit and explicit knowing. Practical evaluation of that framework in modern conditions of digital enterprises has been provided in [36], which confirms existence of four phases of the process of generating and converting knowledge phases: Socialization, Externalization, Combination, Internalization.

In that framework dynamic synthesis of knowledge is realized through the knowledge dialectics of tacit knowledge, explicit knowledge and phronesis. As it is stated in [40] it is the phronesis of the leaders with their practical wisdom that facilitates and propels new business models of dynamic fractal organizations. Taking such a holistic view point leads to the conclusion that modern foundations of knowledge management need "to synthesize the subjective and the objective, the personal and the organizational perspective" [67].

2.2 Foundations for a Proper Conceptualization of Knowledge About Enterprise

Being paired with generic principles of knowledge management Enterprise Engineering aims at developing a holistic systemic view on the construction and the operation of enterprises [16]. However, there is no agreement about the best shared conceptualization of enterprises even in terms of a foundational organizational paradigm.

We strongly believe that it is the social constructivism paradigm which reflects the key characteristics of digital transformation and is becoming a prevailing approach in construction and evolution of organizational knowledge. According to the constructivist view, individuals actively participate in a construction of their own knowledge through interactions within complex social systems [26]. As a clear example of well-founded conceptualization and a constructivist view on enterprise knowledge evolution and management the enterprise ontology [14] can be distinguished. That approach includes the ontology-based concise, comprehensive, coherent, and consistent enterprise modeling language, and the corresponding modeling methodology (DEMO - Design & Engineering Methodology for Organizations). Providing a consistent set of micro-theories grounded in Language-Action Perspective (PSI – Performance in Social Interaction theory), the enterprise ontology represents a coordination viewpoint underlying other ontological theories of enterprises.

2.3 Definition and Classification of Ontologies

Ontology is a representational artifact, comprising a taxonomy as a proper part, whose representations are intended to designate some combination of universals, defined classes, and certain relations between them [3].

According to this definition, the following considerations can be deduced: (1) the ontology is a representational artifact = def. the scheme of a certain area; (2) the ontology contains concepts of a certain area, its properties and relations between them; (3) a proper part of relations are taxonomy-type relations.

Based on these considerations, the ontology can be represented as a triple (O, R, F), where $O = U \cup C$ is a set of objects, where $U = \{u_1, u_2, \ldots, u_N\}$, $N \in \mathbb{N}$ (where u_i, $i = 1, N$ is a concept (universal) of a certain area an can be represented as a set of its attributes $u_i = \{attr_1, attr_2, \ldots, attr_M\}$, $M \in \mathbb{N}$, , $i = 1, N$), C(class)is a set of c_i, $i = 1, K$, $K \in \mathbb{N}$, where c_i is an exemplar of some u_j, R is a set of relations between elements of O, and F is an interpretation function assigning values to the non-logical constants of the language [23].

From this point of view, the ontology can be naturally perceived as a graph (O, R), with a set of functions of constraints F.

On the other hand, the ontology is some kind of representation, created by the designer [24]. From this point of view, development of the ontology has always some certain goal, which affects the whole design process and its final result, the ontology itself. As a result, the following classification of ontology kinds based on their level of dependence on a particular task (or a viewpoint) can be identified [3, 23]: top-level ontologies, which describe very general concepts, independent of a particular problem or domain; domain (task) ontologies, which describe, respectively, the vocabulary related to a generic domain (task) and application ontologies, which describe concepts that depend both on a particular domain and a task, and often combine specializations of both the corresponding domain and task ontologies.

In the current research, we pay attention mostly to the enterprise ontologies, which refer to the Application ones. But as the Domain ontology contains only the necessary concepts of a subject area, Application ontology operates with a subset of these concepts necessary to achieve a certain goal. That allows us to consider the Application ontology as the reduced Domain ontology and can be used as a basis for development of DSM which in turn is used in the development of domain-specific languages.

2.4 Domain Specific Languages

Static conceptual structures of the enterprise ontology alone are not capable of maintaining mutual transformations of explicit and tacit knowledge during knowledge life cycle management. For that purpose, ontology should be fused with a specific mechanism for dynamic generating and converting knowledge. Evolvable domain-specific languages may be considered for that role.

A number of research results demonstrate suitability of using Domain-Specific Languages (DSL) for defining the context for different knowledge modeling and management tasks of modern companies [17, 18, 23, 24, 47, 52, 54, 58]. For example, Sprinkle [58] describes the implementation of DSL for modelling logistic interactions within the organization. Pereira et al. [47] prove the effectiveness of DSL usage for the definition of the context of the resource allocation problem.

In the context of our studies frontiers of DSL application for extraction and transformation of tacit knowledge attract special interest, because as Colins states – language plays a role of a repository for tacit knowledge [13]. Indeed, domain-specific languages can be considered as a practical implementation of interactional expertise, which may be viewed also as an attempt to introduce the tacit dimension of linguistic knowledge [56]. In [70] ontologies and domain-specific languages were considered as among the primary tools for extraction and representation of explicit and tacit knowledge in the safety domain. Gross demonstrates application of visual domain-specific languages for grasping tacit knowledge in a complex domain of artistic lighting [22].

Formally a domain-specific language is a computer language specialized to a particular application domain. This is in contrast to a general-purpose language, which is broadly applicable across domains, and lacks specialized features for a particular domain [19]. In [46] two parts of the DSL are identified: (1) a syntactic part, which defines the constructions of DSL; (2) a semantic part, which manifests itself in the semantic model. The syntactic part allows us defining the context for working with the second one, which defines meaning of DSL commands in terms of the target domain. The syntactic part itself contains the domain concepts and rules (abstract syntax), as well as the notation used to represent these concepts – let it be textual or graphical (concrete syntax).

A syntactic part of DSL can also be separated into two levels: the level of objects and the level of functions. The object-level is equivalent to the set of objects of the meta-model. The functional level contains operations, which specify the operational context for the objects. That two-level division of the DSL syntactic part provides the maximum correspondence between the ontological model of the target domain and the DSL model, and the most convenient way of organizing conversions between them.

A semantic part of DSL is derived from the conceptual model of the target domain. According to Parr [46] we will call such a model as Domain-Semantic Model (DSM). DSM can be constituted by either just small pieces of domain knowledge (e.g. small taxonomies equipped with few rules) or rich and complex ontologies (obtained, for example, by translating existing ontologies). That gives respectively weak or rich and detailed representation of a domain [7]. In our research DSM becomes the bridge between the enterprise ontologies and DSL.

Static features of DSL are well studied and a lot of automated tools exists to design and exploit DSL in the enterprise practice. However, as a dynamic complex structure, any domain demonstrates the tendency to the evolution over time: new concepts may arise, while others unite into more general ones or become obsolete. In accordance with these changes, DSL should also support the possibility of evolution.

The simplest option in this case is to rebuild DSL whenever the domain model changes. But this process has several disadvantages. First of all, the process of DSL development is really time-consuming, since DSL contains internal and external parts, connected with the domain model and DSL syntax correspondingly. Secondly, DSL development, since DSL is a language, is often associated with the use of grammar tools that require special skills from developers. Finally, while a new version of DSL is being created, the domain can be changed again. Thus, the DSL changes may not be synchronized with the domain changes, making DSL not fully compliant with the needs of the end users.

3   Developing Own Unified Solution

In that section we perform a synthesis of aforementioned foundations and describe own contributions to the theory and practice of knowledge life cycle management and knowledge-based digital transformations. At first, an ontology-based conceptualization of enterprise is described, which facilitates ontology-based description of cornerstone enterprise concepts. Secondly, an ontology-based methodology for continuous transformations and verification of DSL is given, which can play a role of the mechanism for continuous transformation of tacit and explicit knowledge.

3.1   Building an Ontology-Based Conceptualization of Knowledge About Enterprise

In order to play a role of an ontological basis for knowledge-based digital transformation enterprise ontology should be fused with a corresponding foundational ontology because the core enterprise theory provided by DEMO is not fully axiomatized yet. Rephrasing the definitions made by Guizzardi in [23] with regard to enterprise modeling, the domain appropriateness and the comprehensibility appropriateness of an enterprise conceptual modeling language is guaranteed by the meta-model of this language representing a full axiomatization of enterprise ontology. Despite the plurality of existing foundational ontologies, in our work we exploit the Unified Foundational Ontology (UFO) and its compliant conceptual modeling language OntoUML [23] in order to build and to represent an ontological theory of enterprise interactions with the basis on a solid theoretical framework.

Practical implementation of such fusion requires performing two intellectual tasks. At first hand, a consistent ontology-based conceptual modeling language with a strong referential semantics should be designed. Secondly, a set of design-oriented practices should be developed which impose relevant constraints on the modeling language application during solution of recurrent modeling problems of enterprises.

For the solution of the task of developing a conceptual modeling language, the OntoUML conceptual modeling language [23] was taken as a basis. Restating the DEMO enterprise ontology in terms of OntoUML allowed us to combine modeling elements of enterprise ontology and reference ontology (UFO), as well as to reveal some gaps and inconsistencies on the analysis of the DEMO foundations. Moreover, we added some additional ontological categories based on their relevance for the theory of enterprise ontology.

This work resulted in a fully axiomatized Formal Enterprise Ontology (FEO) [50]. This is the domain- and standard-independent ontological theory that provides a referential semantics for metadata. The UFO-C part (a foundational ontology of social entities) [25] guarantees a well-defined ontological foundation of FEO and expressiveness of the essence of an organization in the ontological categories of foundational ontology.

The OntoUML-based FEO language provides modeling primitives that reflect the conceptual categories and axioms defined by the whole ontological theory. For example, FEO includes the axioms in first order logic that supplement the forgoing definitions by relevant constraints and formally specify the notion of an ontological transaction.

The second task aimed at solving recurring conceptual modeling problems of enterprises by adapting a generic notion of ontological patterns to FEO. Ontology patterns [18] were considered as a promising approach to capture standard domain-specific solutions to recurrent problems of conceptual modeling [17]. In general, each pattern has to be dedicated to a particular type of modeling issues, provide a solution, be accompanied with the instructions about its applicability in a right situation, and be associated with the set of related patterns. A set of interrelated patterns comprises a certain pattern language which can be applied systematically depending on requirements of the modeled situation and the goals of the modeler.

Following the method proposed by Guizzardi in [23], we created a set of modeling constructs (ontology patterns) represented in OntoUML, and called it the Formal Enterprise Ontology Pattern Language (FEOPL) [51]. All patterns of that language inherit axiomatization of the FEO ontology, thus making the meta-model of the language isomorphic to this ontology. FEOPL patterns include the following:

- a Transaction pattern, intended (1) to specify the notion of transaction and (2) to tackle problems related to modeling of properties and an evolution of basic units of business processes;
- the pattern of Coordination actions and their resulting commitments, which puts together Actor Role, C-act, C-act Intention, C-act Proposition, Transaction, C-commitment and their interrelations;
- the pattern of Production Actions, which states that propositional contents of production actions are abstract representations of allowable/desired states of the production world of an enterprise;
- the pattern of Production Facts, which explicitly defines semantics of the notion of a production fact.

A more detailed description and analysis of the presented templates is contained in [51]. As patterns description shows, FEOPL facilitates formalization of rules and conditions for social coordination actions based on the information derived from domain ontologies. Moreover, the language meta-model correlated with both the upper level ontology and the FEO preserves real-world semantics in a broad sense. That is reducing the number of semantic conflicts in representation of enterprise domain.

Grounding FEOPL in the DEMO modelling language leverages application of formal methods for knowledge management because the FEOPL patterns define precise semantics for interrelation between lifecycles of social objects (including transactions, commitments and claims) and lifecycles of enterprise products.

The modelling power of FEOPL was investigated in application to modelling problems of test-bed case studies. The results of modelling confirmed relevance and efficiency of FEOPL application for modelling knowledge-based digital transformations.

3.2 Evolution of Domain-Specific Languages for Managing Knowledge

Having reliable tools of conceptualization in terms of formal enterprise ontology, we may consider further advancing of DSL design on that solid ground. Application of the ontology as a model of DSL guarantees that DSL is identical to the corresponding domain, thereby allows the users interacting with it more effectively.

In our approach [60] we apply the formalization of the semantic DSL level in a model-oriented manner as a combination (O, R) of some objects of the target domain and relations between them, where each object is a set of its attributes and operations

$$o_i = (Attr_i, Opp_i) = \left(\begin{array}{c} \{attr_{i_1}, attr_{i_2}, \ldots, attr_{i_M}\}, \\ \{opp_{i_1}, opp_{i_2}, \ldots, opp_{i_K}\} \end{array} \right), M, K \in \mathbb{N}, \ i = 1, N).$$

In these terms, the syntactic part of DSL can be represented as a subset of the semantic level, needed for representation of a certain problem situation. The very one difference is that the syntactic part may not absolutely reflect the semantic constructions but identify its own definitions (pseudonyms) for the semantic constructions, according to the user's needs.

As follows, the structure of the syntactic level can be formalized as a triple $\left(O_{syntax}, R_{syntax}, Alias_{syntax} \right)$, where $O_{syntax} \subseteq O$ and $R_{syntax} \subseteq R$ are the subsets of objects and relations between them of the semantic DSL level respectively, and $Alias_{syntax}$ is a set of pseudonyms for objects' components (attributes and operations).

By a similar object-oriented manner Domain-Semantic Model can be derived from the corresponding FEO and can be represented as a seven-tuple: $DSM = (\mathcal{H}_C, \mathcal{H}_R, O, R, A, M, D)$, where

- $\mathcal{H}_C$ and $\mathcal{H}_R$ are sets of classes and relations schema. Each schema is constituted by a set of attributes, the type of each attribute is a class. In both $\mathcal{H}_C$ and $\mathcal{H}_R$ are defined partial orders for the representation of concepts and relation taxonomies;
- O and R are sets of class and relation instances also called objects and tuples;
- A is a set of axioms represented by special rules expressing constraints about the represented knowledge;

- M is a set of reasoning modules that are logic programs constituted by a set of (disjunctive) rules that enables reasoning about the represented and stored knowledge, so new knowledge not explicitly declared can be inferred;
- D is a set of descriptors (i.e. production rules in a two-dimensional object-oriented attribute grammar) enabling the recognition of class (concept) instances contained in O, so their annotation, extraction and storing is possible.

In our research, we focus only on the sets O and R. Consideration of other parts of DSM is beyond the scope of our study, since it determines more meta-characteristics of DSM itself, rather than the objects and connections between them, which are the most interesting for the further development of the DSL semantic model.

Finally, taking into account previously mentioned formalization of the ontology as a triple (O, R, F) [23], we can argue, that the ontology can be naturally perceived as a set (O, R), with a set of functions of constraints F. Such definition of the ontology guarantee, that an ontology can be completely transformed into DSM, which ensures complete consistency of all three models (ontology, DSM and DSL model) with each other.

Under these circumstances, we can tell about the complete ontology-based and model-oriented representation of the DSL structure. That representation corresponds to principles of model-driven engineering [8]. From this point of view, we can derive DSL semantics as result of transformation of DSM. Similarly, using transformation rules on entities and relationships between them from the DSM, the meta-model of a DSL can also be defined. Finally, reflecting DSL abstract syntax terms on the concrete visual icons or textual constructions DSL concrete syntax can be defined.

Such a hierarchical model-driven approach allows us not only to describe both levels of DSL in structured and unified manner but optimize the process of DSL development and evolution by introducing several syntactic DSL dialects on one fixed semantic level. Furthermore, the versification of DSL can be provided in a similar way on the semantic level as well as on the syntactic level, without need to re-create the whole DSL structure every time, when the changes are required. All these features open practical opportunities for proper reflection of transition between tacit and explicit knowledge of the users in a corresponding evolution of different DSL dialects with varying syntactic or semantic elements. Also, automation of DSL syntactic and semantic transformation using MDE principles forces traceability between different DSL dialects and allow us to use advanced methods of formal verification, as it will show later.

Combining the object-oriented model of the DSL structure with the formal definition of DSM on the basis of a single meta-meta-model, we can specialize a well-known semantic hierarchy of meta-models for our approach to model-oriented development and evolution of DSL (Fig. 2). In our case this hierarchy is separated into four layers, according to the stages of the DSL development. Each lower level is based on the model artefacts of the upper level A single M3 meta-meta-model determines common grounds for all meta- and models of the lower levels. This meta-level defines also notations in which concrete models will be defined and what rules for their transformations will be used.

We propose to create a DSL structure from the Domain-semantic model (DSM) through the so-called semantic projection mechanism. The semantic projection is an operation, which is conducted over DSM. Any semantic projection performs a certain model-to-model transformation (M2M) of DSM to some its fragment. Thus, semantic projection fully determines the semantic model of a particular dialect of DSL.

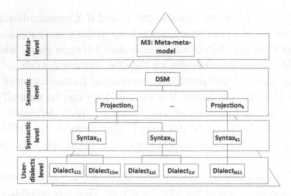

Fig. 2. The semantic hierarchy of projection-based DSL development [4].

We suggest application of a group of model-to-model transformations for practical implementation of semantic projections and producing corresponding DSL artefacts. In this case the semantic model becomes an object-temporal structure, because it should be adopted according changes in DSM over the time, thereby defining a new object filling of the DSM.

After the semantic projection was performed, the syntactic level of DSL can be developed by a M2M transformation of the result of the corresponding projection. What is important, these DSL syntactic models are independent of each other and are determined by end-users in accordance with the adaptation of the semantic projection to their own tasks. Finally, created syntaxes are used by the end-users of DSL, who determine the set of DSL dialects within the single specific syntactic model.

Figure 3 shows differences between traditional approaches and our proposals. Traditional approaches start with the manual definition of the DSL concrete syntax which is followed by the translation of the syntax in terms of grammars. Consequently, every change in the target domain leads to the need to redefine the DSL concrete syntax and re-create the corresponding grammar. A similar process repeats in a case, when changes in DSL are caused by the end-users. As a result, outcomes of traditional approaches contain inconsistent dialects of DSL, which cannot be mapped among themselves due to differences in all levels of the DSL structure.

In order to provide such transformations, it is sufficient to adjust the system of matching rules between the components of the ontological model of the target domain and the components of the DSL model. One of the possible solutions to this problem can be the mechanism of graph transformations between the graph representation of the ontology and the DSL model. If we interpret the entities of our model as vertices of the corresponding graph and relations between them as corresponding edges, we can

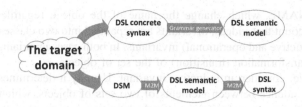

Fig. 3. The scheme of differences between traditional (top) and projection-based (bottom) DSL development approaches [4].

postulate, that any model can be described using graph-oriented manner. This fact logically results in the opportunity to describe model transformations and the corresponding dynamic operational semantics of DSL using graph transformations rules (Fig. 3). It is important to note, that such advanced methods of graph transformation as Graph Grammars (TGGs) [29] enable specification of direct and inverse transformation rules facilitating bi-directional DSL transformation.

Practical implementation of such transformation can be achieved by using one of specialized graph-transformation languages such as ATL Transformation Language, GReAT (Graph REwriting and Transformation) [1], AGG (Attributed Graph Grammar), QVT. In our current research, we propose to use QVT, because this language allows us to describe the transformation rules from any original model into any target model, conducting a transformation at the level of meta-models. Using that instrument we demonstrated evolution of DSL in the railway allocation domain as an example of knowledge-based digital transformation [59]. In that case our method enabled evolutionary changes of syntax and semantics of DSL in response to changing the knowledge model of the users. Such changes frequently occur during modification of the business model of the railway services.

In the scope of automated transformation between different variants of DSL an important issue of transformation verification arises. If the verification succeeds, then we conclude that the model transformation is correct with respect to each pair (p, q) of properties (objects, relations) for the specific pairs of source and target models having semantics defined by a set of graph transformation rules. Otherwise, property p is not preserved by the model transformation and debugging can be initiated based upon the error traces retrieved by the model checker. That debugging phase may fix problems in the model transformation or in the specification of the target language.

In what follows, we offer the unified and highly automated approach, allowing developers to formally verify by model checking that a model transformation (specified by meta-modeling and graph transformation techniques) from an arbitrary well-formed model instance of the source modelling language into its target equivalent preserves (language specific) dynamic consistency properties. In that approach the notion of invariants is specialized for a particular case of DSL verification.

In terms of the most general approach [9], the invariant is a property, held by a class of objects, which remains unchanged when transformations of a certain type are applied to the objects. From this point of view, invariant can be interpreted in two ways: (i) a set of objects, which leave unchanged during the transformation provided, (ii) an operation, which can be applied to several objects at the same time (e.g.

operation RENAME, which change the name of the object, regardless of its type). Taking into account these ideas, invariants are separated into two classes: structural and functional (inductive and operational) invariants. In both cases invariants are defined on top of some transformation (transition) of the set of objects.

For example, consider an inductive invariant. Usually it determines that there is a strong correspondence between elements of two sets of objects, which are connected during some relation (transformation). Such definition is very close to the relational approach for model transformation definition, when the relationship between objects (and links) of the source and the target language are declared. That results in the insight, that the inductive invariant can be an effective mechanism for the definition of such model transformations and for the validation of the feasibility of obtaining one model by transforming another. We may conclude that the process of graph transformation resembles the search for various structural invariants in the source and the target with consequent application of corresponding graph transformation rules to them. Consequently, we can reformulate model transformations using the double-pushout approach (DPO) with injective matching for graph transformations and an invariant technique.

According to these principles, we can conclude, that validation of the model transformation correctness can be fully described through invariant mechanisms. Such definition allows us to automate the process of formal validation of the model transformation, reducing it to verifying the presence of invariants of both types among defined model (graph) transformations.

Since we describe the model transformation using the graph-oriented approach in QVT transformation language, the procedure to derive the OCL invariants need be implemented. With application of OCL invariants both problems can be solved using existing OCL verification and validation tools for the analysis of model transformations. With these inputs, verification tools provide means to automatically check the consistency of the transformation model without user intervention. Checking consistency enables the verification of the executability of the transformation and the use of all validation scenarios.

In our resent work [61] details of our approach to invariant-based transformation are provided together with the overview of an actual implementation of the verification algorithm for a case of transformation between different enterprise models.

4 Demonstration in a Practical Case

In that section we demonstrate practical application of our approach for the case of the railway station resource allocation domain. Partially aspects of this evolution were considered in our previous works [59, 60], therefore, here we will pay more attention directly to demonstrating the evolution of the language than to analyzing the process of its development and content.

4.1   DSM for Railway Allocation Domain

The domain of railways services represents an interesting and significant case of dynamic management of knowledge and enterprise digitalization. In particular the context of the railway allocation problem can change frequently because of arrivals of new trains, or changing the priority of existing services. As a result, we have to have a clear and simple way to adapt new changes in terms of the proposed framework, responsible for finding the optimal resource allocation. In the process of DSL design for the railway allocation process, it's vital to identify all the types of resources in this domain.

There are three general resources for any railway station, each with specific attributes: railways, trains and service brigades. All of them are represented in the DSM for the corresponding domain, which is more complete in comparison with that considered in our previous work [60], since it contains the specification of the requirements (Skills) both for the Services and for the Brigades providing them.

After the DSM created, we can identify the semantic level of DSL, describing the DSL meta-model. For this purpose, M2M transformation rules can be used, as it was described in [59]. This is reasonable since both DSM and DSL meta-model are described in a model-oriented way. In addition, M2M transformations are independent from the notation of model definition, that allows us to describe DSM and DSL meta-model independently, in the most appropriate way. As a result, we will have the complete DSL meta-model, which can be used during the following DSL syntax definition. This definition includes two parts: definition of objects for DSL syntax, which are the equivalents to the objects, described on the semantic level of DSL, and grammar, describing the operations and correct terms for the future DSL syntax. In our case, we used the Backus-Naur form of grammar definition, because this form allows us to identify rules, based on the previously created objects, and automatically convert the resulting rules into an abstract, language-independent form.

As a result, the created DSL semantic and syntactic levels are wholly coherent and can be evolved using transformations in real time. In addition, such changes are provided separately, since the invariants on both levels are identified.

In order to demonstrate how the evolution of users' knowledge reflects into the transformation of DSL terms we analyze to states of the DSL: original one, derived from the DSM, and its further development using evolution tools.

4.2   The Original DSL

As a starting point for our DSL development we consider, that DSL supports only basic constructions and operations on objects defined in the DSM (railways, trains and service brigades) and the relationship between them. As a result, the following structure of DSL terms exists (Fig. 4and Fig. 5). As you can see, these constructions are sufficient to perform the basic operations of the domain: creating objects and establishing links between them (Fig. 6).

On the other hand, these commands do not reflect the time perspective of the domain, distributing only the set of resources available at a given moment in time between arriving trains.

```
Trains
({id type priority length [services] wagonsToService})*
EndTrainsBlock;

Railways
   ({id type totalLength usefulLength [equipment]})*
endRailwayBlock;

Services
   ({name priority [skills] standartDuration[equipment]})*
endServiceBlock;

Brigades ({id [ skills ] capacity})* endBrigadeBlock;
```

Fig. 4. DSL objects.

```
Put idTrain to idRailway with startNick;
```
This command allows to move Train with identifier idTrain to railway idRailway on start nick startNick

```
Relocate idTrain [from idOldRailway] to idNewRailway;
```
This command allows to move Train with identifier idTrain from railway with identifier idOldRailway to railway idNewRailway.

```
Move forward/back idTrain by countShifts;
```
This command allows to move Train within current railway forward or back by the count of shifts equals to countShifts.

Fig. 5. DSL functions.

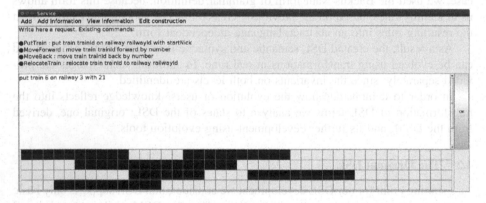

Fig. 6. Example of scenario in terms of the original DSL.

In order to improve the quality of DSL and provide the user with the ability to plan resource allocation over time, it is necessary to make changes to the original DSL. As a result, we need to provide the user with the ability to change the design of the DSL, which creates a more complex version of the subject-oriented interface.

4.3   Subject-Oriented GUI

Developing subject-oriented GUI we should take into account, that it pursues two goals: writing and executing scenarios in the current version of DSL, as well as making changes (evolution) into DSL.

As a result, the interface created contains two parts: the first one, responsible for the DSL scenario definition and processing, and another one, needed for evolution of DSL. The first part, which contains only a visual panel, representing all the DSL components needed for definition of DSL scenarios, was properly described in our previous work [62] and mentioned in previous section. In what follows, the second part of the interface (see Fig. 7 and Fig. 8) responsible for DSL evolution is more interesting for us.

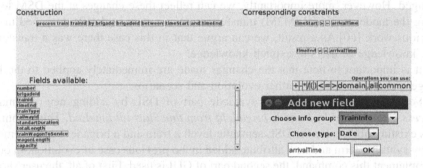

Fig. 7.   Evolution of DSL implementation.

Fig. 8.   Scenario with added command.

This part of interface allows us to adopt DSL automatically whenever the evolution is provided. Such automation allows us to support DSL evolution by end-users without the need to re-compile the whole framework and to have special programming skills.

In order to design such evolution, the second part of the interface is used (Fig. 7). This part contains three main components: the component to define/change a new/existing command of DSL, the component for definition of constraints, connected with the command and the component for definition of syntactic terms, related to the new command. All these components are identified in accordance with the structure of DSL: objects, which contain attributes and operations and relations between them. As a result, the created interface allows us to define the whole DSL structure and change it in real time without need to re-create the DSL manually.

4.4   Evolution of DSL

The first change we want to provide to the user is to add a time perspective to all objects. In fact, this means that each of the objects will have an additional attribute associated with time. For example, arrival time at the trains, the start and end time of servicing at the servicing brigades, etc.

From a formal point of view, this DSL development scenario is an example horizontal evolution. In more details, this classification of evolution was described in [59, 60].

In this case, using the evolution part of the interface, we add a new attribute *arrivalTime* to the *TrainInfo* object. For this purpose, the corresponding interface component can be used (Fig. 7, right). Similarly, we add other time attributes to other objects. After making such changes, we can argue that the structure of DSL objects has changed. However, more importantly, we can reflect these changes at the DSM level, using the model-to-model (M2M) transformations, as it as in details described in our previous work [60].As a result, we can argue that in this case there was a transfer of tacit knowledge of users to explicit knowledge.

It is important to note that the changes made are immediately applied to the language and can be used in further evolution and scenarios.

For example, we can extend syntactic part of DSL by adding new command: *process train trainId by brigade brigadeId from timeStart till timeEnd*. This command uses existing objects for the DSL semantic level: a train and a brigade, but implements a new syntactic term and new attribute added in the previous case of evolution. In order to implement this command, the second part of GUI is used. First of all, the user should define a needed command, using the block of available fields of DSL objects. As a result, the following construction and constraints, related to this, are defined (Fig. 7). Finally, the created term is compiled and added to the DSL, ready to use.

What is the most important, in this case, we only define new commands, without need to re-create the DSL structure and can use them in sceneries in real time. For example, the result of added command is represented in Fig. 8. As follows, the approach proposed allows us to implement all types of DSL evolution in real time, correctly transforming new commands into DSL syntactic and semantic objects and terms.

Currently existing approaches, allowing also to allocate resources of railway station, are targeted to one concrete type of resources (for example, to brigades by Wang et al. [67], or to trains by Chen et al. [10]). Furthermore, such approaches use static models of resource allocation and cannot be adopted according to new types of resources or solving models in real time. In comparison to existing approaches, the approach proposed is independent from the nature of the resources and can be adopted to any other domain.

The only limitation for our approach is the fact, that it can provide the opportunity to define only unidirectional transformation of DSL, according to changes in the domain model. This limitation can be explained by the fact, that languages of model transformations do not support bidirectional transformations, because symmetric transformation means using the opposite to the original operation (delete instead of add, etc.). However, such limitation can be resolved using the idea of closure operations necessary for organizing the DSL evolution [60].

5 Conclusion

Critical aspects of digital transformations, including the cross-institutional level of changes, dynamic nature of emerging business models and increasing importance of knowledge management strategies in the course of designing digital enterprises as inquiring systems, lead us to the conclusion that successful digital transformation requires application of a systemic engineering approach.

That article aimed at observing a complex phenomenon of digital transformation from the systemic viewpoint of enterprise engineering. Our attention was attracted to further progress in combination of enterprise engineering techniques and different knowledge types in order to facilitate knowledge life cycle management in the context of knowledge-based digital transformations because the practice of continuous defining, acquiring, disseminating, storing, applying, and assessing knowledge in organizations prepares people and potentializes internal changes.

Along that way several contributions were proposed in the ontology engineering. A new ontology modelling language of Formal Enterprise Ontology (FEO) was proposed which restates DEMO in precise terms of UFO. FEO gives a modeling language with precisely defined formal semantics provides an input for inference procedures and engines with a minimal information loss. Represented in OntoUML the FEOPL patterns fully inherit the FEO. In addition to a modeling power inherited from OntoUML, the FEOPL patterns enforce a correlated modeling of changes (the behavioral perspective of an organization) and objects undergoing these changes (the structural perspective of an organization).

We believe that proper combination of FEO and FEOPL with evolvable domain-specific languages facilitate continuous transformation of explicit and tacit knowledge. In our research, we explored an opportunity to provide the method of co-evolution of the ontology, used as a model of the subject area, and DSL. We proposed a formal ontology-based DSL structure together with a method of semantic projections. This method combines graph representation of the ontology and DSL with the set of rules, formulated in terms of an automated graph-transformation language. This mechanism has several advantages: the DSL designer does not need to know the semantic domain (s), nor the relationship between the concepts of his/her DSL and the concepts of the semantic domain, and he/she can still be benefited from its analysis tools. We call semantic bridges to those general mappings between different domains from which DSL-specific semantic mappings can be automatically derived. Models can then cross these bridges to benefit from each world without being aware of how they were constructed.

In comparison to traditional approaches, the proposed projection-based method of DSL development is organized in the strong correspondence of the target domain. Such correspondence is provided by the consequent projections among different models in a semi-automatic way through M2M transformations: from DSM into a DSL semantic model and then into a syntactic model of the specific DSL dialect. In comparison with existing approaches to transformation verification like [2] and [31], which also use the ideas of automated model generation with subsequent correctness property checking, our approach doesn't depend on the modelling language and property chosen. Such independency follows from deriving invariants as stable logical structures from the model transformation rules. As a result, the verification procedure reduces to a simple check of two sets of OCL constraints between themselves.

Using our approach, we can define several DSL syntactic dialects over one specific DSL semantic model expressed in the form of FEO, which will be consistent and can be transformed between themselves without the redefinition of the DSL semantic models. Applicability of the proposed approach was demonstrated using a real-life example of co-evolution of the ontology and DSL in the railway transportation domain. Evaluation of the software prototypes has demonstrated that our approach to fusion practically enables continuous transformation of domain-specific languages in response to changes of the underlying enterprise ontology or knowledge of the users.

That example demonstrated an attractive feature of our method regarding the ratio of explicitly formulated knowledge. As Fig. 9 shows, evolution of DSL leads to increasing complexity of the user interface in terms of number of available elements and relations between these elements. As far as the user expresses knowledge about the subject area in terms of DSL more and more implicit knowledge can be reformulated explicitly.

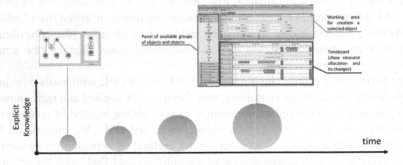

Fig. 9. Growth of explicit knowledge alongside using DSL.

Changing the focus to the second pillar of our approach, namely ontology-based methods of dynamical evolution of domain-specific languages, we also can recognize some important directions of further research. In present kind our software prototypes require manual elaboration of user's insights and transformation of their tacit knowledge to the explicit knowledge via modification of ontology. It will be beneficial to adapt machine learning algorithms for automatic production of recommendations for ontology changes on the basis of intellectual analysis of users' interactions with a DSL. Another improvement includes design of more efficient model transformation algorithms for cases of complex domains.

In our vision achieved results and prospective plans clearly envisage importance and great potential of designing deep interconnections between such elements of enterprise engineering as enterprise ontologies and domain specific languages. We hope that results of such interconnections will facilitate efficient and effective knowledge-based digital transformations.

References

1. Agrawal, A., Karsai, G., Shi, F.: Graph transformations on domain-specific models. In: International Journal on Software and Systems Modeling, pp. 1–43. Nashville: Vanderbilt University Press (2003)
2. Akehurst, D., Kent, S.: A relational approach to defining transformations in a metamodel. In: Jézéquel, J.M., Hussmann, H., Cook, S. (eds.) UML 2002. LNCS, vol. 2460, pp. 243–258. Springer, Heidelberg (2002). https://doi.org/10.1007/3-540-45800-X_20
3. Arp, R., Smith, B., Spear, A.D.: Building Ontologies with Basic Formal Ontology. The MIT Press, Cambridge (2015)
4. Babkin, E., Poletaeva, T., Ulitin, B.: Digitalization: a meeting point of knowledge management and enterprise engineering. In: Proceedings of 11th International Joint Conference on Knowledge Discovery, Knowledge Engineering and Knowledge Management, vol. 3, pp. 22–36. SciTePress (2019)
5. Bani, M., De Paoli, S.: Ideas for a new civic reputation system for the rising of digital civics: digital badges and their role in democratic process. In: ECEG2013–13th European Conference on eGovernment: ECEG (2013)
6. Barreto, L., Amaral, A., Pereira, T.: Industry 4.0 implications in logistics: an overview. Procedia Manuf. **13**, 1245–1252 (2017)
7. Bell, P.: Automated transformation of statements within evolving domain specific languages. In: Computer Science and Information System Reports, pp. 172–177 (2007)
8. Beydeda, S., Book, M.: Model-Driven Software Development. Springer, Heidelberg (2005)
9. Chandy, K.M.: Parallel program design. Opportunities and Constraints of Parallel Computing, pp. 21–24. Springer, New York (1989)
10. Chen, W., Dong, M.: Optimal resource allocation across related channels. Oper. Res. Lett. **46**(4), 397–401 (2018)
11. Chou, J., Hsu, S., Lin, C., Chang, Y.: Classifying influential for project information to discover rule sets for project disputes and possible resolutions. Int. J. Project Manag. **34**, 1706–1716 (2016)
12. Churchman, C.: The Design of Inquiring Systems: Basic Concepts of Systems and Organization. Basic Books Inc., Publishers. NY, London (1971)
13. Collins, H.: Language as a repository of tacit knowledge. The Symbolic Species Evolved, pp. 225–239. Springer, Dordrecht (2012)
14. Dietz, J.L.G.: Enterprise Ontology: Theory and Methodology. Springer, Berlin (2006)
15. Dietz, J.L., et al.: The discipline of enterprise engineering. Int. J. Organ. Des. Eng. **3**(1), 86–114 (2013)
16. Dietz, J.L.G., Hoogervorst, J.A.P.: Enterprise ontology in enterprise engineering. In: Proceedings of the 2008 ACM Symposium on Applied Computing, pp. 572–579 (2008)
17. Falbo, R.A., Barcellos, M.P., Ruy, F.B., Guizzardi, G., Guizzardi, R.S.S.: Ontology pattern languages. Ontology Engineering with Ontology Design Patterns: Foundations and Applications. IOS Press, Amsterdam (2016)
18. Falbo, R.A., Ruy, F.B., Guizzardi, G., Barcellos, M.P., Almeida, J.P.A.: Towards an enterprise ontology pattern language. In: Proceedings of 29th Annual ACM Symposium on Applied Computing (ACM 2014), pp. 323–330 (2014)
19. Fowler, M.: Domain Specific Languages. Addison Wesley, Boston (2010)
20. Fox, M.S., Gruninger, M.: Enterprise modeling. AI Mag. **19**(3), 109–121 (1998)
21. Fransella, F., Bannister, D.: A Manual For Repertory Grid Technique. Academic Press, Cambridge (1977)

22. Gross, J.B.: Programming for artists: a visual language for expressive lighting design. In: 2005 IEEE Symposium on Visual Languages and Human-Centric Computing (VL/HCC 2005), pp. 331–332. IEEE (2005)

23. Guizzardi, G.: Ontological Foundations for Structural Conceptual Models. Telematics Instituut Fundamental Research Series, The Netherlands (2005)

24. Guizzardi, G.: On ontology, ontologies, conceptualizations, modeling languages, and (meta) models. In: Proceedings of the 2007 Conference on Databases and Information Systems IV, pp. 18–39. IOS Press, Amsterdam (2007)

25. Guizzardi, G., Falbo, R.A., Guizzardi, R.S.S.: Grounding software domain ontologies in the Unified Foundational Ontology (UFO): the case of the ODE software process ontology. In: XI Iberoamerican Workshop on Requirements Engineering and Software Environments, pp. 244–251 (2008)

26. Guizzardi, R.S.S.: Agent-Oriented Constructivist Knowledge Management. Centre For Telematics and Information Technology PhD.-thesis series, The Netherlands (2006)

27. Hafsi, M., Assar, S.: What enterprise architecture can bring for digital transformation: an exploratory study. In: 2016 IEEE 18th Conference on Business Informatics (CBI), vol. 2, pp. 83–89. IEEE (2016)

28. Hinings, B., Gegenhuber, T., Greenwood, R.: Digital innovation and transformation: an institutional perspective. Inf. Organ. **28**(1), 52–61 (2018)

29. Königs, A., Schürr, A.: Tool integration with triple graph grammars-a survey. Electron. Notes Theor. Comput. Sci. **148**(1), 113–150 (2006)

30. Krimpmann, D.: IT/IS organisation design in the digital age – a literature review. Int. J. Soc. Behav. Educ. Econ. Bus. Ind. Eng. **9**(4), 1189–1199 (2015)

31. Küster, J.M., Abd-El-Razik, M.: Validation of model transformations – first experiences using a white box approach. In: Kühne, T. (ed.) MODELS 2006. LNCS, vol. 4364, pp. 193–204. Springer, Heidelberg (2007). https://doi.org/10.1007/978-3-540-69489-2_24

32. Linderoth, H.C.J., Jacobsson M., Elbanna A.: Barriers for digital transformation: the role of industry. In: Australasian Conference on Information Systems, vol. 48 (2018)

33. Loebbecke, C., Picot, A.: Reflections on societal and business model transformation arising from digitization and big data analytics: a research agenda. J. Strat. Inf. Syst. **24**(3), 149–157 (2015)

34. MacDonald, T.J., Allen, D., Potts, J.: Blockchains and the boundaries of self-organized economies: predictions for the future of banking. Banking Beyond Banks and Money, pp. 279–296. Springer, Cham (2016)

35. Mangematin, V., Sapsed, J., Schüßler, E.: Disassembly and reassembly: an introduction to the special issue on digital technology and creative industries. Technol. Forecast. Soc. Change **83**, 1–9 (2014)

36. Maravilhas, S., Martins, J.: Strategic knowledge management a digital environment tacit and explicit knowledge in fab labs. J. Bus. Res. **94**, 353–359 (2019)

37. Moreira, M.F.: Agile Enterprise. Apress, New York (2017)

38. Naudet, Y., Latour, T., Guédria, W., Chen, D.: Towards a systemic formalisation of interoperability. Comput. Ind. **61**, 176–185 (2010)

39. Nonaka, I., Hirose Nishihara, A.: Introduction to the concepts and frameworks of knowledge-creating theory. In: Hirose Nishihara, A., Matsunaga, M., Nonaka, I., Yokomichi, K. (eds.) Knowledge Creation in Community Development, pp. 1–15. Springer, Cham (2018). https://doi.org/10.1007/978-3-319-57481-3_1

40. Nonaka, I., Kodama, M., Hirose, A., Kohlbacher, F.: Dynamic fractal organizations for promoting knowledge-based transformation–a new paradigm for organizational theory. Euro. Manage. J. **32**(1), 137–146 (2014)

41. Nonaka, I., Toyama, R., Hirata, T.: Managing Flow: A Process Theory of the Knowledge-Based Firm. Palgrave Macmillan, New York (2008)
42. Nonaka, I., von Krogh, G.: Perspective—tacit knowledge and knowledge conversion: controversy and advancement in organizational knowledge creation theory. Organ. Sci. **20**, 635–652 (2009)
43. Oleśków-Szłapka, J., Stachowiak, A.: The framework of logistics 4.0 maturity model. In: Burduk, A., Chlebus, E., Nowakowski, T., Tubis, A. (eds.) ISPEM 2018. AISC, vol. 835, pp. 771–781. Springer, Cham (2019). https://doi.org/10.1007/978-3-319-97490-3_73
44. Oliva, F.L., Kotabe, M.: Barriers, practices, methods and knowledge management tools in startups. J. Knowl. Manage. (2019)
45. Panetto, H., Iung, B., Ivanov, D., Weichhart, G., Wang, X.: Challenges for the cyber-physical manufacturing enterprises of the future. Ann. Rev. Control (2019)
46. Parr, T.: Language Implementation Patterns: Create Your Own Domain-Specific and General Programming Languages. Pragmatic Bookshelf (2012)
47. Pereira, M., Fonseca, J., Henriques, P.: Ontological approach for DSL development. Comput. Lang. Syst. Struct. **45**, 35–52 (2016)
48. Pérez-Luño, A., Alegre, J., Valle-Cabrera, R.: The role of tacit knowledge in connecting knowledge exchange and combination with innovation. Technol. Anal. Strateg. Manage. **31** (2), 186–198 (2019)
49. Polanyi, M.: The Tacit Dimension. University of Chicago Press, Chicago (1966)
50. Poletaeva, T., Babkin, E., Abdulrab, H.: Ontological framework aimed to facilitate business transformations. In: 1st Joint Workshop ONTO.COM co-located with 8th International Conference on Formal Ontology in Information Systems (FOIS 2014), vol. 1301 (2014)
51. Poletaeva, T., Abdulrab, H., Babkin, E.: From the essence of an enterprise towards enterprise ontology patterns. In: Aveiro, D., Pergl, R., Gouveia, D. (eds.) EEWC 2016. LNBIP, vol. 252, pp. 118–131. Springer, Cham (2016). https://doi.org/10.1007/978-3-319-39567-8_8
52. Quirino, G.K., et al.: Towards a Service Ontology Pattern Language. In: Johannesson, Paul, Lee, M.L., Liddle, S.W., Opdahl, A.L., López, O.P. (eds.) ER 2015. LNCS, vol. 9381, pp. 187–195. Springer, Cham (2015). https://doi.org/10.1007/978-3-319-25264-3_14
53. Reis, J., Santo, P.E., Melão, N.: Artificial intelligence in government services: a systematic literature review. In: Rocha, A., Adeli, H., Reis, L.P., Costanzo, S. (eds.) WorldCIST'19 2019. AISC, vol. 930, pp. 241–252. Springer, Cham (2019). https://doi.org/10.1007/978-3-030-16181-1_23
54. Ruy, F.B., Falbo, R.A., Barcellos, M.P., Guizzardi, G.: Towards an ontology pattern language for harmonizing software process related ISO standards. In: 29th Annual ACM Symposium on Applied Computing, pp. 388–395 (2015)
55. Sandkuhl, K., et al.: From expert discipline to common practice: a vision and research agenda for extending the reach of enterprise modeling. Bus. Inf. Syst. Eng. **60**(1), 69–80 (2018)
56. Schilhab, T.: Derived Embodiment in Abstract Language. Springer, Cham (2017). https://doi.org/10.1007/978-3-319-56056-4
57. Schmidt, R., Zimmermann, A., Möhring, M., Nurcan, S., Keller, B., Bär, F.: Digitization–perspectives for conceptualization. European Conference on Service-Oriented and Cloud Computing, pp. 263–275. Springer, Cham (2015)
58. Sprinkle, J.: A safe autonomous vehicle trajectory domain specific modelling language for non-expert development. In: Proceedings of the International Workshop on Domain-Specific Modeling, pp. 42–48 (2016)
59. Ulitin, B., Babkin, E., Babkina, T.: Ontology-based DSL development using graph transformations methods. J. Syst. Integr. **9**(2), 37–51 (2018)

60. Ulitin, B., Babkin, E.: Ontology and DSL Co-evolution using graph transformations methods. In: Johansson, B., Møller, C., Chaudhuri, A., Sudzina, F. (eds.) BIR 2017. LNBIP, vol. 295, pp. 233–247. Springer, Cham (2017). https://doi.org/10.1007/978-3-319-64930-6_17

61. Ulitin, B., Babkin, E., Babkina, T., Vizgunov, A.: Automated formal verification of model transformations using the invariants mechanism. In: Pańkowska, M., Sandkuhl, K. (eds.) BIR 2019. LNBIP, vol. 365, pp. 59–73. Springer, Cham (2019). https://doi.org/10.1007/978-3-030-31143-8_5

62. Ulitin, B., Babkin, E., Babkina, T.: Combination of DSL and DCSP for decision support in dynamic contexts. In: Řepa, V., Bruckner, T. (eds.) BIR 2016. LNBIP, vol. 261, pp. 159–173. Springer, Cham (2016). https://doi.org/10.1007/978-3-319-45321-7_12

63. Uschold, M., King, M., Moralee, S., Zorgios, Y.: The enterprise ontology. Knowl. Eng. Rev. 13(1), 31–89 (1998)

64. Usman, Z., Young, R.I.M., Chungoora, N., Palmer, C., Case, K., Harding, J.A.: Towards a formal manufacturing reference ontology. Int. J. Product. Res. 51(22), 6553–6572 (2013)

65. Ustundag, A., Cevikcan, E.: Industry 4.0: Managing the Digital Transformation. Springer, Berlin (2017)

66. van Gils, B., Proper, H.A.: Enterprise modelling in the age of digital transformation. IFIP Working Conference on The Practice of Enterprise Modeling, pp. 257–273. Springer, Cham (2018)

67. Wang, H., Wang, X., Zhang, X.: Dynamic resource allocation for intermodal freight transportation with network effects approximations and algorithms. Trans. Res. Part B: Method. 99, 83–112 (2017)

68. Westerman, G., Bonnet, D., McAfee, A.: The nine elements of digital transformation. MIT Sloan Manage. Rev. 55(3), 1–6 (2014)

69. Yoon, K.S.: Measuring the influence of expertise and epistemic engagement to the practice of knowledge management. Int. J. Knowl. Manage. 8(1), 40–70 (2012)

70. Zhang, S., Boukamp, F., Teizer, J.: Ontology-based semantic modeling of construction safety knowledge: towards automated safety planning for job hazard analysis (JHA). Autom. Constr. 52, 29–41 (2015)

Towards Web Browsing Assistance Using Task Modeling Based on Observed Usages

Benoît Encelle[1](✉) ⓘ and Karim Sehaba[2] ⓘ

[1] Université de Lyon, CNRS, Université de Lyon 1. LIRIS, UMR5205,
69622 Lyon, France
benoit.encelle@liris.cnrs.fr
[2] Université de Lyon, CNRS, Université de Lyon 2. LIRIS, UMR5205,
69676 Lyon, France
karim.sehaba@liris.cnrs.fr

Abstract. This article deals with knowledge extracted from observed usages of Web sites/applications for assistance purposes. The extracted knowledge is used to develop assistance systems in order to help a) users in carrying out Web browsing tasks, or b) designers to adapt/redesign Web applications. The suggested approach involves the generation of task models from interaction traces, which are then used to perform assistance. Task metamodel characteristics for assistance purposes are firstly identified and then used to develop a comparative study of some well-known task metamodels, resulting in the selection of the ConcurTaskTrees (CTT) metamodel. In order to generate CTT task models, a set of algorithms that identify CTT operators from interaction traces - represented as deterministic finite state automata - are presented. We also expose an approach for performing assistance, for users and designers, based on task models and finally conducted unit testing and validation based on two real web browsing scenarios.

Keywords: Knowledge extraction · Interaction traces · Task model ·
ConcurTaskTrees (CTT) · Web browsing/redesign assistance

1 Introduction

This article is an extended version of [1] and deals with knowledge extraction from observed usages. This work is situated in the field of Web browsing assistance/Web automation, and Web application redesign assistance. The question we address is how to develop a system able to assist Web users in carrying out Web browsing tasks and Web designers in the adaptation and/or the redesign of Web applications.

In many current assistance systems, the helps typically provided and, on the whole, the assistance knowledge, are predefined during the design phase and correspond to the uses envisaged by the designers. However, it is usually difficult to anticipate the entire spectrum of the real uses for a given system, and for an online application more particularly. Indeed, the Web users can have very diverse profiles, their requirements can be in continuous evolution, they may have various conditions of use, etc. Even if tools and methodologies exist to predict particular uses (including requirements

A. Fred et al. (Eds.): IC3K 2019, CCIS 1297, pp. 453–471, 2020.
https://doi.org/10.1007/978-3-030-66196-0_21

analysis, rapid prototyping and assessments in ecological situation), these will remain intended uses and could sometimes not cover/correspond to all real uses. This may be due to several difficulties related to: the analysis of all the contexts of use, the representativeness of the observed sample of users, the achievement of truly ecological conditions in assessments, etc. Thus, the design of an assistance system with a complete representation of the needs of upcoming users and their evolution is extremely difficult, if not impossible.

To solve these kinds of difficulties, we propose to base the assistance on the real uses, observed right after system deployment. The approach developed in this work aims to produce task models based on these real uses. As an input in the task model generation process, we start from interaction traces (i.e. logs). Here, a trace represents the history of the actions of a given user on a Web application. At the output, a task model represents the different possibilities of performing a given task. Formally, a task model is a graphical or textual representation resulting from an analysis process, making it possible to logically describe the activities to be carried out by one or more users to achieve a given objective, such as booking a flight or hotel room.

The task models obtained by the proposed process will then be used, in an assistance system, to guide the users in the accomplishment of their tasks and the designers in the analysis of their applications, to carry out redesigns of them.

In this article, we studied the characteristics that should be supported by task models to ensure that they can be used for providing assistance. Two main properties have been identified, namely:

1. The intelligibility of the task model for the user; and
2. The expressiveness of the task model and its ability to be manipulated by a software, more specifically an assistance system.

Several metamodels have been suggested to represent task models in the literature. Therefore, we challenge these metamodels with the previously identified characteristics to identify the most suitable ones for our assistance need. This study leads us to choose the ConcurTaskTrees (CTT) metamodel. Then, we establish a process for generating task models, representing real uses, based on interaction traces. Finally, we then suggest an approach for providing Web task assistance based on these task models.

In summary, the work presented in this paper aims at four contributions:

1. The specification of the characteristics of the task metamodels for assistance purposes;
2. The confrontation of existing metamodels regarding the characteristics previously identified (cf. 1). The study we conducted allowed us to choose the CTT metamodel;
3. A process for generating CTT task models from interaction traces;
4. An assistance approach based on these task models.

This article is organized as follows. Section 2 presents a state of the art on web browsing assistance based on traces and task models. Section 3 details the target characteristics of a task metamodel for assistance purposes. Section 4 presents a comparison of existing task metamodels against our target characteristics, leading to the choice of the CTT metamodel that we present next. Section 5 describes our approaches for a) generating task model from interaction traces and b) providing assistance based upon these task models. Section 6 is dedicated to the validation process and results. Finally, we conclude and state some perspectives in Sect. 7.

This article, in comparison with [1] mainly a) gives more details on the process for generating CTT task models from interaction traces (third contribution) and b) provides an approach for task model-based assistance (fourth contribution).

2 Related Works

The design and/or the generation of task models has been the subject of several studies in the literature. In this work, we are interested in generating task models from traces. In this context, the methods proposed in the literature can be classified into two main approaches, namely: the generation of task models from a) one task instance and b) from multiple task instances.

2.1 From an Instance to a Task Model

The first approach is to start from one instance (i.e. a particular way of performing a task) to generate a task model. In this way, let us mention the CoScripter system [2] which makes it possible to automate web tasks via a scripting language, used among other in the Trailblazer Web assistant [3].

```
1. goto "http://www.mycompany.com/timecard/"
2. enter "8" into the "Hours worked" textbox
3. click the "Submit" button
4. click the "Verify" button.
```

Fig. 1. Example of a CoScript (from [3]).

Figure 1 shows an example of a CoScript representing the actions for performing a "book purchase" task on Amazon. As this example shows, a CoScript is very close to a trace and possibly generalizes it to a minimum. Indeed, the scripting language integrates only one element of generalization (with the notion of personal database [2]). Therefore, a CoScript is more an instance than a task model itself. In addition, control structures such as conditional (e.g. if A then B else C) or iterative ones do not exist in CoScripter [2]. Therefore, to generate a task model from a CoScript, the challenges of a generalization process from an instance remain open as pointed out in [4].

To answer these challenges, namely the elicitation of a task model from an instance, the approach used in PLOW (Procedural Learning on the Web) [4] increases the description of a task instance by knowledge provided during its performance. This knowledge makes it possible to represent conditions, iterations, etc. This "expert" knowledge is, within the framework of PLOW, provided by a certain kind of user named demonstrator. The latter teaches the system new task models by providing this expert knowledge orally, while he/she is performing the task. This knowledge is then interpreted using Natural Language Processing technologies. This approach requires 1) that the demonstrator keeps in mind to bring a maximum of knowledge and 2) that the tool is able to correctly interpret this knowledge to modify the model accordingly. Thus, the more a demonstrator brings knowledge and the more a model can be generic. Overall, with respect to this knowledge, the more it is expressed in language similar to that used by the system to model the task, the less likely it is that it will be misinterpreted.

2.2   From Instances to a Task Model

The second approach attempts to eliminate the need of expert knowledge by using multiple instances to generate a task model, as in LiveAction [5]. The latter focuses on the identification and modeling of repetitive tasks, tasks being represented as CoScripts. In LiveAction, a task model is generated using a set of CoScripts and Machine Learning techniques. With this kind of approach, task models are represented as finite state automata (FSAs) [5, 6]. However, to our knowledge, an assistance system based on such automata has not been developed yet.

With this kind of approach, the level of genericity of the models obtained depends on the quantity of instances as well as their quality (variability in particular). It should be noted that, as suggested in [5] and with the aim of quickly reaching satisfactory models, users should be able to add knowledge to generated models by manipulating them directly.

2.3   Synthesis

The research works on generating task models from interaction traces can be classified into two distinct approaches. The *instance to model* approach produces more specific than generic task models. This approach requires a lot of expert knowledge and reaches its limits in a Web context with a large amount of "*open and massive*" applications. The approach *instances to model* requires a large number of different instances to generate sufficiently complete and generic models.

To fulfill our needs, we base our work on the generation of task models from several instances to reduce the expert knowledge that has to be initially provided to obtain sufficiently complete and generic models. In order to minimize the number of instances needed and the necessary variability among them, we will opt for "*user-friendly*" task models. By user-friendly task models, we mean task models that could be quickly and easily understandable and handleable by users (users can easily modify these models).

These modifications that add knowledge to a generated model, will have to be carried out directly by handling the model itself, thus evacuating the risks of misinterpretations which can lead to erroneous models (risks existing in PLOW for example). Therefore, reusing an approach such as the one described in LiveAction seems interesting to us, except that the generated models are represented by finite state automata (FSAs). These FSAs are indeed difficult to understand and manipulated by end users:

- There is no decomposition or hierarchical relationships between the tasks and their subtasks, which does not facilitate model reading and understanding.
- FSAs generally have a large number of states and transitions, even for representing simple tasks, which causes difficulties in reading and understanding models.

To remedy these problems, we argue for the use of task meta-models that are more user-friendly than FSAs. To achieve this objective, we will first identify all the characteristics that have to be supported by a metamodel dedicated to browsing assistance. Then, we will confront some well-known existing task metamodels with the characteristics identified in order to guide our choice. The metamodels studied were designed to be quickly understandable and handleable by "novice" (i.e. user-friendly metamodels).

3 Metamodel Characteristics Study

As mentioned above, task models generated from traces must be user-friendly, easily understandable, and even directly handleable by the user. In addition, these models must also be machine-friendly to be automatically used by an assistance system to guide the user in performing his/her task. This characteristic implies that a machine can a) be able to identify models that do not conform to the metamodels (i.e. models that can lead to misinterpretations) and b) understand and interpret these models at a certain level. This requires a certain level of formality, a precise semantics of the elements constituting these metamodels.

We complement these two main characteristics with other secondary characteristics. The first is related to the set of tasks we want to model and their intrinsic properties. We want to model web browsing tasks, essentially sequential tasks (actions to be carried out one after another) and single-user tasks (collective tasks are not considered). This characteristic therefore corresponds to the expressiveness of the metamodels and more specifically to their ability to represent browsing tasks. In this perspective, elements of a metamodel must make it possible to specify the component of the user interface to be manipulated. Another important thing is that the metamodels must also allow the expression of optionality (to model the fact that a sub-task is optional to carry out a given task), for a sufficiently generic modeling of Web browsing tasks. For example, the modeling of a "ticket reservation" task must be able to represent optional steps, such as the possibility of entering a discount card id.

The second secondary characteristic is related to the adaptability and extension capabilities of metamodels: these are initially designed to be used in a set of software engineering phases [7], but they must be adaptable to meet our assistance goal. However, these adaptations may require complements (e.g. concepts), i.e. new elements added to the metamodels. As a result, metamodels have to be extensible if necessary (extensibility characteristic).

The third is related to the plurality of devices that can be used to browse the Web (smartphone, tablet, computer, etc.) and their respective characteristics (screen sizes, proposed interaction modalities, etc.). Indeed, several variants of user interfaces or process of accomplishing tasks may exist for the same Web application ("responsive" aspect). These variations of the context of use must be able to be supported by the chosen metamodel: the same task has to be described in several ways according to the context of use.

To sum up, a "candidate" metamodel that could integrate the assistance process we wish to develop, must have key characteristics (user-friendly and machine-friendly) and secondary ones (expressivity, adaptability/extensibility, support variations in the context of use). The following section presents a study comparing existing metamodels with the above characteristics.

4 Task Models for Assistance Purposes

4.1 Comparison of Metamodel with Target Characteristics

Comparative studies of the most well-known metamodels have been proposed in the literature [7–9], including:

- HTA: Hierarchical Task Analysis,
- GOMS: Goals, Operators, Methods and Selection rules,
- CTT: Concur Task Trees,
- MAD: "Méthode Analytique de Description".

These studies suggest analysis frameworks to compare metamodels between them in order to guide the choice of one or more specific metamodels according to a given objective. These analyses are based on a set of characteristics, including those we target (see previous section).

Concerning the user-friendly aspect, the authors of [7] refer to it through the "usability axis in communication" and specify in particular that, in relation to textual or formal metamodels, the graphic metamodels are more suitable. The author of [10] also approve this position. For example, the highly textual GOMS metamodel is moderately user-friendly [7]. Being able to break down tasks into sub-tasks (decomposition characteristic [7]), how to break down tasks and thus describe the relationships between tasks and sub-tasks are also important. For example, a tree-like representation of tasks/sub-tasks appears intuitive [11], as in MAD or CTT, and offers several levels of detail, including the ability to unfold/fold branches of the tree. Similarly, the ability of the metamodel to allow the reuse of elements helps to minimize the number of elements present and improve readability.

Concerning the machine-friendly characteristic, the degree of formality of a metamodel is related to what must be generated [7]: a formal metamodel can be used for the automatic generation of code while a semi-formal model can be used to generate user documentation for example. The authors of [8] confirm the need for a certain level of formality of the metamodels to be machine-readable: for example, a plan in HTA described informally (textual descriptions) the logic of execution of the sub-tasks that make up a task, which can lead to interpretation ambiguities. On the contrary, CTT has a set of formal operators, based on the LOTOS language [12], to describe this same logic, which guarantees an unambiguous automatic interpretation.

Regarding the secondary characteristics, concerning the expressivity of the meta-models for Web browsing tasks, in addition to sequentiality and single-user criteria, models such as MAD or GOMS do not allow the expression of the optionality [7], unlike CTT. In addition, some models, such as HTA for example, are not intended to indicate the user interface components that must be manipulated to perform the tasks/subtasks while others, such as CTT, allow it. We also have to mention that the W3C Working Group "*Model-Based User Interfaces*" has chosen CTT to model web tasks.

Concerning adaptability/extensibility, graphical metamodels are more easily extensible to express relationships or concepts that were not initially planned [7]. For example, several extensions have been proposed for models of this type, such as MAD or CTT (e.g. MAD*, CCTT).

Regarding the characteristic "context of use variations support", few metamodels integrate this dimension as underlined by [8]. Nevertheless, CTT integrates this dimension through the platform concept [10].

Table 1. Comparison of metamodels with target characteristics [1].

	User-friendly	Machine friendly	Expressivity	Adaptability/extensibility	Variations to the context of use
CTT	+	+	+	+	+
HTA	+	−	−	−	−
MAD	+	+	−	+	−
GOMS	−	+	−	−	−

Table 1 gives a summary of our confrontation of metamodels with regard to our target characteristics. It thus appears that the CTT metamodel, among the metamodels studied, is the only one that meets all the characteristics previously identified. The following section provides a short introduction to this model.

4.2 CTT Metamodel Overview

A Concur Task Tree (CTT) model exposes a hierarchical structure of tasks as a tree. Each tree node represents a task or a subtask. The node icon identifies the category of the task or subtask:

- cloud: abstract task, decomposable;
- user and keyboard: interaction task;
- computer: task performed by the system.

Logical or temporal relationships between tasks are indicated by operators. For example, the operator "[]" represents the choice and "|=|" represents the order independency operator. In Fig. 2, the room booking task can only be done if the user has specified the type of the room he wants to reserve (single or double). Thus, the "Make reservation" sub-task is only activated if the "Select room type" task has been performed.

These operators are formally defined (mainly from the LOTOS language [12]). CTT allows to add features to tasks as needed: iteration (indefinite or finite) and optionality. Finally, the tasks can be correlated to the application domain objects (the type of room for example) and to their representation(s) on a given user interface (for the selection of a type of room for instance, radio buttons or other).

5   Task Model Generation and Assistance

Remember that our goal is to propose a task model generation approach based on observed usages. These task models will assist users in performing web browsing tasks and the designers in the adaptation and redesign of web applications. To represent the tasks, we propose to use CTT and, for the observed usages, we rely on the traces/logs resulting from the actions of users on Web applications.

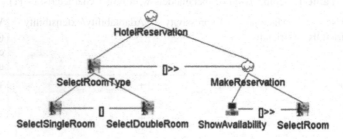

Fig. 2. CTT modeling of a room booking task [10].

Figure 3 presents the process workflow involved in our approach. At first, the logs/traces are transformed (T1) into a finite state automaton (FSA) or, more precisely, a deterministic finite state automaton (DFSA). We already mentioned that a bunch of work related to web browsing assistance generate FSAs from the traces, such as LiveAction. If these automata have the advantage of being relatively simple to process automatically (machine-friendly), they remain difficult to understand for the general public given: a) the large number of states and transitions they can contain, even for represent a simple browsing task, and b) their linear reading as there is no hierarchy of states to represent task/subtask relations. Therefore, the second step of our approach is to transform these automata into CTT models (T2).

In this section, we are interested in 1) the transformation T2 (FSAs -> CTT models), since T1 (Traces -> FSAs) has already been treated by other works - notably [5], and 2) the assistance process based on task models.

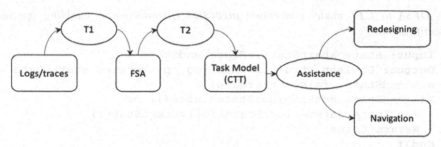

Fig. 3. Task model generation process and assistance [1].

5.1   Task Model Generation from Deterministic Finite State Automata

Formally, a deterministic finite state automaton (DFSA) is a 5-tuple (Q, Σ, R, qi, F) consisting of:

- Q: a finite set of states (Web resources/pages)
- Σ: an input alphabet, which in our case represents all the events applied to web resources (e.g. button click, typed text, etc.)
- R: a part of Q × Σ × Q called the set of transitions
- qi: the initial state. qi ∈ Q
- F: a part of Q called the set of final states

Since the automaton is deterministic, the relationship R is functional in the following sense: If (p, a, q) ∈ R and (p, a, q') ∈ R then q = q'.

In the following subsections we detail the algorithms for converting DFSAs to CTT models, focusing on CTT operator identification on DFSAs.

Enabling Operators ("≫", "[]≫"). The CTT enabling operators (without "≫" or with information passing "[]≫") indicates that a subtask B cannot start until a subtask A is performed. From the DFSA point of view, if there is an *endState* state for which there is only one previous *startState* state, we can deduce that there is an enabling operator (see Table 2 for an example of conversion from DFSA to CTT).

Table 2. Example of an DFSA to CTT conversion, two enabling operators (between states 1, 2 and 2, 3).

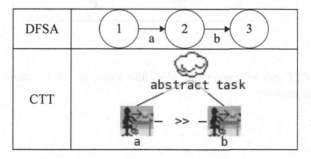

DFSA to CTT model conversion algorithm (pseudocode) - enabling operator identification:

```
Input: State startState, State endState
Output: Boolean (true if enabling op. between startState
and endState, false otherwise)
If((endState.getPreviousStates.size>1) or
  (endState.getPreviousStates[0]!=startState))
  Return false
EndIf
Return true
```

Order Independency Operator ("|=|"). There is an order independency operator between two or more subtasks if they can be performed in any order. From the DFSA point of view, if there are for a couple of states (*startState, endState*) n paths (n > 1) that link them and that each of these paths has the same k transition labels (which then will be in a different order) and n = k!, then we can conclude that these are subtasks that can be performed in any order, expressed in CTT using independence operators (see Table 3 for an example of conversion from DFSA to CTT).

Table 3. Example of an DFSA to CTT conversion, one order independency operator (between states 1 and 4, two equivalent paths (through states 2 and 3)).

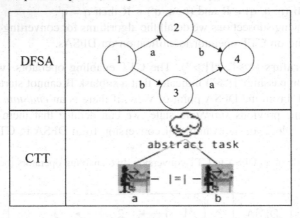

DFSA to CTT model conversion algorithm (pseudocode) - order independency operator identification:

```
Input: State startState, State endState
Output: Boolean (true if order independancy op. exist,
false otherwise)
paths=getAllPossiblePaths(startState, endState)
If(paths.size<=1)
  Return false
EndIf
j=paths[0]
If(factorial(j.transitions.size)!= paths.size)
  Return false
EndIf
For i=1 to paths.size-1
  If(!hasSameTransitionLabels(j,paths[i]))
    Return false
  EndIf
EndFor
Return true
```

Choice operator ("[]"). The CTT choice operator indicates that a task T can be performed either performing subtask A or B. From the DFSA point of view, if - from a *startState* state to an *endState* state - there is two or more paths and at least two of these paths start with a different state, we can conclude that there is a choice operator (see Table 4 for an example of conversion from DFSA to CTT).

Table 4. Example of an DFSA to CTT conversion, choice operator (between states 2 and 5).

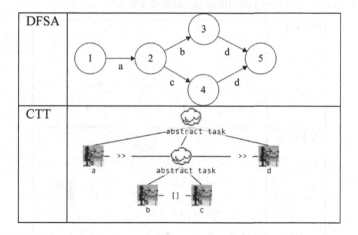

DFSA to CTT model conversion algorithm (pseudocode) - choice operator identification:

```
Output: Boolean(true if choice exist, false otherwise)
paths=getAllPossiblePaths(startState, endState)
If(paths.size<2)
  Return false
EndIf
ts=paths[0].getStates[0]
For i=1 to paths.size-1
  If(paths[i].getStates[0]!=ts)
    Return true
  EndIf
EndFor
Return false
```

Optional Subtask Detection ("[ST]"). Given a task T = A»[B]»C meaning that T is done by performing either subtasks (A, B and C), or (A and C).

B is an optional subtask that can or cannot be performed. To identify an optional task in an DFSA, all paths from a *startState* state to an *endState* state are collected before checking if each path last transition label is the same. After that, if a direct path (one transition) between *startState* and *endState* exists, we can conclude that there is (at least) an optional subtask (see Table 5 for an example of conversion from DFSA to CTT).

Table 5. Example of an DFSA to CTT conversion, one order independency operator (between states 1 and 4, two equivalent paths (through states 2 and 3).

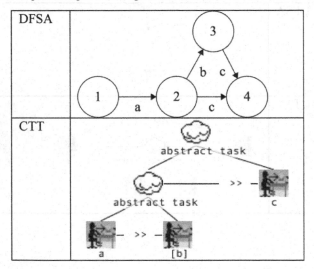

DFSA to CTT model conversion algorithm (pseudocode) - optional subtask detection:

```
Input: State startState, State endState
Output: Boolean (true if optional task exists, false oth-
erwise)
paths=getAllPossiblePaths(startState, endState)
lastTransitionLabel=paths[0].getLastTransition().label
For i=1 to paths.size()-1
  If(paths.get(i).getLastTransition().label<>lastTransi-
tionLabel)
    Return false
  EndIf
EndFor
For i=0 to paths.size()
  If(paths[i].transitions.size=1)
    Return true
  EndIf
EndFor
Return false
```

Iterative Subtask Detection ("ST*"). An iterative subtask ST corresponds from the DFSA point of view to a cycle. i.e. a *startState* state that has a path to an *endState* state, that also has a path to *startState* (see Table 6 for an example of conversion from DFSA to CTT). As a comment, an iterative subtask is usually linked with a disabling operator (not represented in Table 6).

Table 6. Example of an DFSA to CTT conversion, including an iterative subtask (states 2, 3, 4).

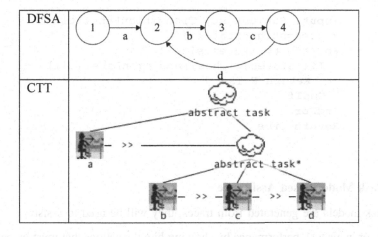

Disabling Operator ("[>"). The CTT disabling operator indicates that a first subtask (usually an iterative one) is completely interrupted by a second subtask. From the DFSA point of view, if there exist, for each state of a subtask *st*, transitions to states that are out of the task with a same label t, we can conclude that there is a disabling operator (see Table 7 for an example of conversion from DFSA to CTT).

Table 7. Example of an DFSA to CTT conversion, disabling operator (for subtask containing states 2, 3, 4).

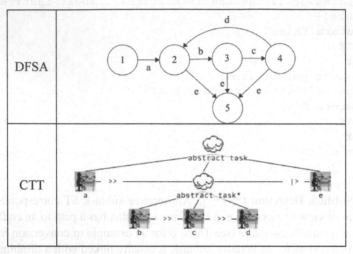

DFSA to CTT model conversion algorithm (pseudocode) - disabling operator identification:

```
Input: SubTask st, TransitionLabel tl
states=st.getStates()
For i=0 to states.size-1
  If(!states[i].hasTransitionLabel(tl))
    Return False
  EndIf
EndFor
Return true
```

5.2   Task Model-Based Assistance

Once task models are generated from traces, they will be used to assist:

- the user in his task performance by showing him the actions that must be performed to achieve his objective, or

- the designer in the adaptation of his Web application by highlighting the observed usages of his application.

In both cases, we assume that tasks are organized by categories and that each task model is associated with metadata specifying the name of the task, its purpose and, possibly, the traces that generate it.

User Assistance. User assistance can be provided in three modes: manual search, search through the declaration of the purpose of the task and automatic search.

Manual Search. In this first mode, as a classic help, the user is supposed to select the task by navigating in a task tree. Tasks are structured hierarchically, thereby representing the different functionalities of the web application. For instance, for a booking site such as booking.com, the first level of the hierarchy will contain main tasks: accommodation, flights, car rental and Airport taxis. The second level will contain the different tasks of each functionality, for example for accommodation, the tasks to "search hotel", to "book hotel", to "pay" can be associated with it.

Search through the Declaration of Purpose. The second mode is a keyword search, entered by the user, specifying his objective. It is a question of searching in the task database those whose objective matches the user's keywords. This search is based on a similarity measure. Several metrics can be used, particularly those used in text mining, like Cosine Similarity between the words in the task database and the words introduced by the user describing its task.

The word-vector cosine metric can consider each set of words as a vector in which each dimension corresponds to a different term, and in which the length is set to the frequency with which each word has been observed. For the calculation, a list of stopwords is removed. The similarity between the task description word vector A and the potential suggestion word vector B is calculated as follows:

$$\cos(\theta) = \frac{\mathbf{A} \cdot \mathbf{B}}{\|\mathbf{A}\|\|\mathbf{B}\|} = \frac{\sum_{i=1}^{n} A_i B_i}{\sqrt{\sum_{i=1}^{n} A_i^2} \sqrt{\sum_{i=1}^{n} B_i^2}}$$

where A_i and B_i are components of vectors A and B respectively. The similarity value ranges from -1 (meaning exactly opposite) to 1 (meaning exactly the same).

Automatic Search. In automatic mode, as the user performs his task, the assistance system displays the tasks that match the actions performed by the user. If several tasks match, the system will order them according to two possible options, namely the popularity of the tasks and the browsing history of the target user. Regarding the popularity of tasks: the tasks most requested by users will be displayed in the first positions followed by the least requested tasks. For browsing history, tasks that have never been requested by the target user will be displayed in the first positions, followed by tasks already performed by the target user.

Designer Assistance. Re-design assistance simply consists of displaying some usage indicators allowing the designer to become aware of the Web application uses and eventually adapt his Web application to these uses through CHI re-design for instance. The following classes of indicators are adapted versions of those defined in [13].

1. Stickiness class of indicators: this class of indicators specifies the ability of a task to attract and retain users' interest. Stickiness is evaluated by using stats (basic indicators) related to the "popularity" of a task, for instance: the count of the task accomplishments, the number of unique users that performed the task, etc.
2. Performance class of indicators: this class of indicators is related to the ease/difficulty encountered by users while performing a task. Performance is based on stats related to the time needed for accomplishing a task, the count of back and forth during the task accomplishment, etc.
3. Navigation class of indicators: this class of indicators analyses the way users performed tasks on an application (the order of tasks performed, task paths). Navigation is based on the analysis of transitions between tasks (tasks that follow/precede a given task).
4. Stop & resume class of indicators: this class of indicators analyses the distribution of interruptions in task accomplishments and seeks to explain how - and ultimately why - users interrupt and resume a task. In general, these interruptions are correlated to a decrease in users' understanding or motivation (too much steps to perform, data to provide). Some interruptions are final (final stops – drops out of ongoing tasks), others are followed by resumes.

6 Tests and Results

In order to validate our approach, we implemented the previously mentioned CTT operator identification from DFSAs algorithms, performed unit testing first and then tested our approach on two real scenarios. The Java language was used for coding the algorithms and the DFSAs were stored in XML files.

6.1 Unit Testing

We checked our algorithms for generating CTT operators on a set of 24 XML files, each containing a DFSA that correspond to a particular CTT operator. The identification of CTT operators was successful for 21 out of 24 files, that leads to an average success rate of 87.5% (see Table 8).

Table 8. Results of unit testing. Each row represents a DFSA (an XML file) that corresponds to a CTT operator [1].

Operator	Nb. of states	Result	Rate
Enabling	5	Success	100%
	7	Success	
	13	Success	
	5	Success	
	3	Success	
Disabling	9	Success	100%
	4	Success	
	3	Success	
Choice	4	Success	100%
	12	Success	
	14	Success	
	48	Success	
Order independency	4	Success	100%
	12	Success	
	14	Success	
	48	Success	
Optionality	6	Failure	50%
	4	Success	
Iteration	5	Failure	33%
	6	Success	
	4	Failure	
Finite iteration	9	Success	100%
	9	Success	
	13	Success	

6.2 Real Scenarios Testing

We have also checked our algorithms on two real scenarios that represent respectively the booking of a flight on "www.airfrance.fr" and the search for an itinerary on "www.google.fr/maps". For testing these scenarios and thus evaluating our algorithms, we studied algorithm capacities to correctly identify CTT operators.

The Air France scenario DFSA is composed of 265 states and mainly contains CTT operators that are often encountered in web browsing tasks (choice, order independency, enabling, disabling, iteration). We obtained an average operator identification accuracy rate of 76.58% (see Table 9). Some identification errors are related to each other, especially in the case of the disabling operator which very often take place in iterations. Therefore, if the identification of an iteration operator that contains a disabling operator fails, then the disabling operator will not be identified either.

Table 9. Results of the Air France scenario CTT operator identification [1].

Operator	Instances	Identified instances	Rate
Enabling	104	80	76,92%
Disabling	1	0	0%
Choice	49	38	77,55%
Order independency	3	3	100%
Iteration	1	0	0%
Total	**158**	**121**	**76,58%**

For the Google Maps scenario, the DFSA is composed of 64 states and the average operator identification accuracy rate is 71.73% (see Table 10). Most operators are correctly identified except the optional one (i.e. optionality of tasks).

Table 10. Results of the Google maps scenario CTT operator identification [1].

Operator	Instances	Identified instances	Rate
Enabling	30	21	70%
Choice	13	10	76,92%
Order independency	2	2	100%
Optionality	1	0	0%
Total	**46**	**33**	**71,73%**

7   Conclusion

This paper deals with the development of assistance systems, based on knowledge extracted from observed usages. With our approach, such assistance systems are based on task models, generated using interaction traces (logs) represented as finite state automata. A task represents all the user's actions performed on a device to achieve a given objective. A trace represents the history of the user's actions on the digital environment. The idea is to consider the traces left by users as sources of knowledge that an assistance system can employ to perform user-specific assistance, and thus overcome the limitations of assistance based on intended uses, sealed during the design phase of a system.

Task models generated from traces could thus be used to guide a user in performing his task or a designer in adapting the digital environment to the observed uses.

Our contributions are the following 1) the specification of the characteristics of task metamodels for user assistance, 2) the comparison of well-known existing task metamodels, that lead us to the selection of the CTT metamodel, 3) the development of a set of algorithms for the generation of CTT task models from traces and 4), the development of an assistance approach, based on task models.

In future work, we plan to deepen the study of existing task metamodels - being aware that not all of them have been covered. To our mind, UML statecharts support of identified characteristics strongly deserve to be studied. A comparative study of the compliant metamodels, assessing their ability to be quickly understood and manipulated by "novice" - "first time users", could also be carried out to strengthen the selection of a given metamodel.

An interesting study about Web task model generation using CTT could be performed in order to compare our approach against another one based on the analysis of web sites code [14], and for investigating to what extend both of them could be employed in a complementary manner. We also plan to continue the development and evaluation of our conversion process and assistance system in using a large corpus of Web browsing data.

References

1. Sehaba, K., Encelle, B.: Generation of task models from observed usage - application to web browsing assistance. In Proceedings of the 11th International Joint Conference on Knowledge Discovery, Knowledge Engineering and Knowledge Management, KMIS, vol. 3, pp. 74–82 (2019). https://doi.org/10.5220/0008068300740082. ISBN 978-989-758-382-7
2. Leshed, G., Haber, E.xM., Matthews, T., Lau, T.: CoScripter: automating & sharing how-to knowledge in the enterprise. In: Proceedings of the SIGCHI Conference on Human Factors in Computing Systems, pp. 1719–1728. ACM, April 2008
3. Bigham, J.P., Lau, T., Nichols, J.: Trailblazer: enabling blind users to blaze trails through the web. In: Proceedings of the 14th International Conference on Intelligent User Interfaces, pp. 177–186. ACM, February 2009
4. Allen, J., et al.: Plow: a collaborative task learning agent. In: AAAI, vol. 7, pp. 1514–1519, July 2007
5. Amershi, S., Mahmud, J., Nichols, J., Lau, T., Ruiz, G.A.: LiveAction: automating web task model generation. ACM Trans. Interact. Intell. Syst. (TiiS) 3(3), 14 (2013)
6. Mahmud, J., Borodin, Y., Ramakrishnan, I.V., Ramakrishnan, C.R.: Automated construction of web accessibility models from transaction click-streams. In: Proceedings of the 18th International Conference on World Wide Web, pp. 871–880. ACM, April 2009
7. Balbo, S., Ozkan, N., Paris, C.: Choosing the right task-modeling notation: a taxonomy. In: The Handbook of Task Analysis for Human-Computer Interaction, pp. 445–465 (2004)
8. Limbourg, Q., Vanderdonckt, J.: Comparing task models for user interface design. The Handbook of Task Analysis for Human-Computer Interaction 6, 135–154 (2004)
9. Jourde, F., Laurillau, Y., Nigay, L.: Description of tasks with multi-user multimodal interactive systems: existing notations. Journal d'Interaction Personne-Système (JIPS) 3(3), 1–33 (2014)
10. Paternò, F.: ConcurTaskTrees: an engineered notation for task models. In: The Handbook of Task Analysis for Human-Computer Interaction, pp. 483–503 (2004)
11. Paternò, F.: Task models in interactive software systems. In Handbook of Software Engineering and Knowledge Engineering: Volume I: Fundamentals, pp. 817–836 (2001)
12. Bolognesi, T., Brinksma, E.: Introduction to the ISO specification language LOTOS. Comput. Netw. ISDN Syst. 14(1), 25–59 (1987)
13. Sadallah, M., Encelle, B., Maredj, A., Prié, Y.: Leveraging learners' activity logs for course reading analytics using session-based indicators. Int. J. Technol. Enhanc. Learn. 12(1), 53–78 (2020). https://doi.org/10.1504/IJTEL.2020.103815
14. Paganelli, L., Paterno, F.: A tool for creating design models from web site code. Int. J. Softw. Eng. Knowl. Eng. 13(02), 169–189 (2003)

Format Matters! And People do, too! Tools and Insights from an Innovation Network

Harriet Kasper[1]([⊠]), Verena Pohl[1]([⊠]), and Monika Kochanowski[2]

[1] Fraunhofer IAO, Fraunhofer Institute for Industrial Engineering IAO,
Nobelstr. 12, 70569 Stuttgart, Germany
{harriet.kasper,verena.pohl}@iao.fraunhofer.de
[2] Baden-Württemberg Cooperative State University,
Rotebühlpl. 41, 70178 Stuttgart, Germany
monika.kochanowski@dhbw-stuttgart.de

Abstract. Communication is one important key to successful innovation culture within companies. We developed three lightweight formats to support innovation communication – future personas, describing the needs of future customers, anchorvideos, for giving technological trends "a face" and anchoring them within a company, and the InnoDeck for efficiently spreading innovative methods and inspiration in practice. In this work, we extend previous work on the three topics by describing how the three artifacts work together and can be combined within a company or in innovation networks. We show this in three case studies. Two describing how companies use the artifacts internally. A third case study from an innovation network shows concrete visualization of the combination of the three concepts. Additionally, we provide new evaluation results for the innovation communication within the network based on a questionnaire. Concluding, we illustrate how we will extend and interleave the concepts for supporting communities of practice in the future.

Keywords: Future persona · Anchorvideo · InnoDeck · Innovation · Innovation facilitation · Knowledge management · Communities of practice · CoP · Applied science

1 Introduction

It has shown in various studies, e.g. in the publication by Linke and Zerfass [1], that innovation is strongly supported by culture and communication can foster a company's ability to innovate. However, each company is different and therefore needs a different set of tools and processes to support innovation. One common challenge across company boarders is the question how to enable a company with lightweight formats to create its own communication structures for innovation communication. We tackle this challenge from three sides: the communication of needs of future customers, the communication of innovative trends from outside the company, and the communication of innovation topics from inside the company. This paper is based on three peer-reviewed papers previously published by the authors: [2–4]. They describe these three different tools from the field of knowledge management developed in a contract

© Springer Nature Switzerland AG 2020
A. Fred et al. (Eds.): IC3K 2019, CCIS 1297, pp. 472–496, 2020.
https://doi.org/10.1007/978-3-030-66196-0_22

research project. The aim of the so-called innovation network digitization for insurance companies is to enable the digital transformation in the participating companies. Therefore, the InnoDeck [2] and Future Personas [3] offer valuable content but also focus on the way this content is presented because we have found that in the context of innovation and digital transformation format matters and we argue that in our dynamic environment it is essential for every context. Anchorvideo [4] is a new format in itself that facilitates the adoption of new trends and topics within an organization. We will show that an individual combination of all three tools is one key ingredient for effective and successful innovation communication within the participating companies (Fig. 1). Additionally, we will provide two case studies, how the members of the network incorporate the three proposed methods within their innovation process for their maximum profit. In a third case study we apply the combination in a hackathon within the innovation network.

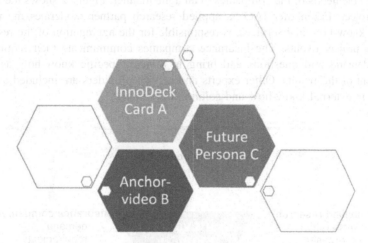

Fig. 1. Interleaving lightweight innovation communication artifacts InnoDeck [2], future personas [3] and anchorvideos [4] for tailored innovation support and individual communication strategies.

In the introduction, we give a quick overview of the innovation network we are working in and look at research regarding the importance of innovation communication, knowledge management and innovation management. In Sects. 2, 3 and 4, we present the three tools we developed. In each case we start with the motivation why the tool was created, we give an overview of the format, its implementation and use and discuss the benefits in the end. Adding to previous work we will show how these tools can be combined together for optimal results. An evaluation of the innovation network is presented in Sect. 5. This is based on a questionnaire and includes new facts and figures. Additionally, we describe three case studies on the combination of the artifacts. We conclude with an outlook to future work in Sect. 6. It handles the innovation network as a community of practice, and shows how the three created tools are connected to it.

1.1　Overview Innovation Network

The innovation network digitization for insurance companies (Innovationsnetzwerk Digitalisierung für Versicherungen) has been founded 2016. The Fraunhofer Institute for Industrial Engineering IAO stands for applied research and is the main contributor in the consortium. It prepares input and projects for 5 to 6 insurance companies represented by 50–80 people in total. The companies' benefits are shared cost for the content that can be base of their future products and activities and networking per se. Aim of the project is to advance the participating insurers innovation ability by providing relevant insights in future trends, especially of digital nature but also training the project participants in new technologies and innovation methodology [5].

One director per insurance company and one director from the applied research institution form the steering committee that regularly jointly agrees upon the next core areas of work as proposed by the researchers' project team. Activities in the project are adapted to the needs of the companies in an agile manner. Figure 2 shows the structure of the project. Fraunhofer IAO as applied research partner moderates the network, provides know-how and services, is responsible for the aggregation of the results and organizes project events. The insurance companies communicate their requirements, general demand and questions and bring in domain specific know-how as well as assessment of the results. Other experts and service providers are included as needed bringing in external know-how and solution elements.

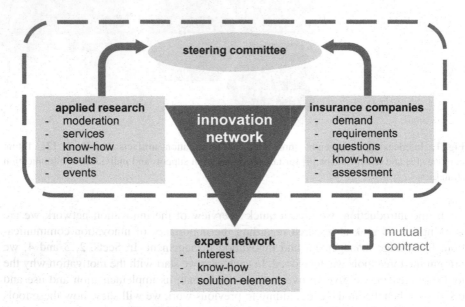

Fig. 2. Structure of the innovation network

The major results of the innovation network are soft skills and knowledge anchored in the people participating in the project. Additionally tangible assets are created within the network and available for the insurance companies, e.g. reports and newly developed methodologies like the ones presented in this paper. Moreover, the innovation network has published a popular scientific study on future trends [6].

1.2 Related Work

The innovation network has more and more developed into a community of practice [7]. The network's common goal lies in learning about innovation in a community. Innovation processes being highly interactive require simultaneous networking across companies, functional groups and business units [8]. Managing the knowledge within the network on the one hand and the bringing in trends from outside the network to spark innovations shape the characteristics of the network.

Innovation Communication. Communication issues are imperative for successful innovation management. Product innovation involves synthesizing and reusing existing knowledge and information. However, skills developed during the design and development process are often lost after the project is finished. Furthermore, many organizations face difficulties in transferring knowledge and information from one organizational unit to another [9].

Another important influencing factor for innovations in our world today is technology. Whether an upcoming technology is used in a company not seldom determines the ability to create future-proof products. Underlying technologies for software development – such as artificial intelligence, internet of things, or blockchain – form the basis of software innovation. It is of paramount importance to foster the acceptance and use of new technologies by the employees. The acceptance of a technology is strongly determined by the way it is introduced to the intended users [10]. An increasingly large part of innovation in an organization is driven by software – introduction of new software or software improvement. As software is not tangible, its "packaging" is especially important. There is a need to focus on communication, on how information is transported to the recipients, in order to counterpart complexity and abstractness [4].

Knowledge Management. Nonaka and Takeuchi [11] state that there are two types of knowledge: explicit knowledge that is written down in textbooks for example and tacit knowledge within individuals e.g. their intuition. Capturing tacit knowledge and transforming it to explicit knowledge and the constant creation of knowledge are major success factors for companies and therefore an important goal of knowledge management.

A variety of information technology (IT) solutions support the process of creation/identification, documentation and distribution of knowledge: from document management tools to content management tools, collaboration solutions or e-learning platforms [12]. But often these systems lack of participation and contributions as Standing and Kiniti [13] point out for company-wikis. Ownership and individualization and the mere length and format of the presented information may be other levers [1]. The lack of time [14] to acquire new knowledge is a current challenge knowledge management needs to address the easing of the access to knowledge. Another lever is reducing the time to acquire new knowledge and making it more memorable e.g. by presenting summaries or new formats like videos [4].

Innovation Management. "The doing of new things or the doing of things that are already done, in a new way" is Schumpeter's definition of innovation [15]. Not only new products, but also new production methods, new markets, new suppliers or other new resources or organizational changes can be innovations and are the drivers for economic growth. Therefore, they need to be managed.

From today's perspective: Innovation is an outcome, a process and a mind-set and companies need to concentrate on all of these qualities to be successful innovators [16]. New products, services, business models etc., but also the methods to generate them and the organizations' culture towards innovation are necessary. In IT organizations knowledge acquisition from the customer base enables innovation [17]. Design thinking is a widely used human-centered process for innovation today and comprises the following steps: inspiration, ideation and implementation [18]. Especially in the ideation phase, personas as archetypes of users or customers [19] help product developers to focus on the needs of the end user. Many use cases for personas prove their benefits [19] and thus they have been widely adopted [20, 21]. Openness, servitization and digitization currently transform the innovation landscape [22] and this requires adaptation of innovation management and the related knowledge management.

Altogether, it can be summarized that various approaches for innovation communication are possible. Each format has its advantages and disadvantages. It is necessary to find tailored lightweight approaches, and to the best of our knowledge, a combination of the three approaches as proposed in this paper has not yet been part in the current research.

2   InnoDeck: Card Based Innovation Support

2.1   Motivation

It has shown that information in a well-designed format can be grasped and remembered better. Some might fall victim to the prejudice that design is a matter of taste and therefore not a serious source of information. But pictures and visual elements are an important means to transport information types like text [23]. A format were we combine well readable texts with an appealing design and suitable visual elements is the InnoDeck.

For innovation projects two types of knowledge is necessary – methodological knowledge on the one hand and inspirational/informative knowledge on the other. We developed the concept of the InnoDeck as a toolbox a facilitator can choose from to prepare a workshop or project. The modular InnoDeck approach is therefore suitable for agile contexts. The InnoDeck offers knowledge as a set of two-sided cards and acts as a toolbox, a source of inspiration and an idea repository. It is intended to meet the needs of innovators. Like the design thinking process itself, it is not constructed sequentially, but allows revisiting certain points and individual deepening as needed. [2]

Design Thinking uses a variety of methods. Which method to use in which stage of the process not only depends on the problem to solve but also on the people involved in the project: which methods are they familiar and comfortable with and which methods do they actually understand and consider suitable for their challenge? The facilitators answer these questions for themselves and the design thinking team and provide the group the corresponding card as quick reference. Due to its shortness a method card can be read and referred to during a workshop, but it is usually not sufficient to master a method from scratch. Design thinking facilitators should have experienced the methods they suggest themselves or at least have further discussed them with an experienced facilitator. However, with an InnoDeck method card workshop participants after having experienced the method will have a starting point to facilitate the method themselves. The InnoDeck therefore is a tool for information sharing and organizational learning. The handy two-sided format is also used for other information necessary in the innovation process (inspiration cards). InnoDeck cards can be combined with other formats and serve as input when it comes to the creation of new products and services with future personas and formats like anchorvideos. At the same time, InnoDeck cards [2] serve as a format to sum up workshop results in order to use them as input for upcoming workshops (Fig. 3).

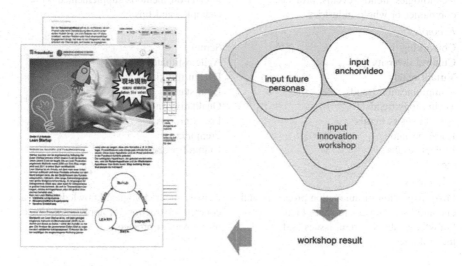

Fig. 3. The InnoDeck cards can either serve as input for anchorvideos or future personas workshops and all sorts of other innovation workshops or as a result format.

2.2 Format Overview

To make the InnoDeck as easy to use as possible, we designed a set of categories. Each card is classified into one category to make it simple for employees to find a suitable bit of knowledge for their specific need. To keep the complexity on a low level, it is important to set up a manageable amount of categories. We defined two categories of cards as they are employed in workshops: (1) method cards and (2) inspiration cards.

Method cards describe empirical, innovation and creativity methods, which come into operation for example in innovation processes in companies, especially in innovation workshops. On the one hand a method card can contain the brief introduction to broad methods like Scrum, Design Thinking or Lean Startup, which is important if these build the foundation of a workshop. On the other hand, practical method guides can be provided e.g. for agile estimation, qualitative interviewing and focus groups. Inspiration cards contain information about trends and technologies and thus serve as inspiration in the ideation phase, for example in product development workshops. For example, we produced cards on trends like coworking or virtual reality. Inspiration cards were also used to present results in a well-arranged way. The InnoDeck overview lists all the cards available with their name and ID number subdivided into the two categories (Table 1). The overview card provides a low-threshold access to the existing cards, making it easy to pick the right card for the particular scenario.

Table 1. Contents and aims of the different card types [2].

Inspiration cards	Method cards
Contents	
Information about technologies, trends, events, projects, companies or whole industries	Information about empirical, creativity and innovation methods supplemented with examples and tips
Examples	
Coworking	Scrum
Cultural diversity	Agile estimation
Virtual reality	Design thinking
Communication trends	Lean startup
Technology trends	Qualitative interviewing
New business trends	Focus groups
Location info	Premortem
Project results	Cultural probes
etc.	etc.
Objectives	
Give inspiration in innovation processes and encourage employees to share their knowledge about certain issues and technologies	Convey methodological knowledge and give concrete instruction for applying the method in innovation projects

Standardization is an important factor in knowledge management. The most important formal feature of an InnoDeck card is that it only comprises two pages, so it can be printed on one sheet of paper. This is in order to make it a quick read, but also for printed versions not to get separated in a workshop environment. Since the Inno-Deck is an expandable treasure of knowledge that is intended to be expanded by many, it is necessary to define formal guidelines that create a uniform appearance and ensure the discoverability of the cards. Each card is equipped with a definite ID, consisting of a consecutive number and the letter "m" for method or "i" for inspiration. To provide transparency concerning the update status of a card, a version number is obligatory. References need to be specified, as well as the creation date and authors of the card. Note that InnoDeck cards are not scientific publications – only one or two references should be stated on a card. Additionally, few other sources may be linked within the text. Both links and references should be an optional read – an InnoDeck card should be self-contained. As explained before, the InnoDeck cards are classified into different categories. Using an icon for the specific category helps to assign the particular card to a certain category. An appealing key visual arises interest, illustrates the topic and makes it more memorable. Subheadings structure the content and give useful information about the particular paragraph. The main headline needs to be as clear and short as possible. The two-column layout ensures readability and clarity [2].

2.3   Implementation and Use

The InnoDeck concept has been developed and refined within the network of insurance companies and has come to use in different application areas. For example, the card deck was handed to selected employees of those companies in order to apply the cards in seminaries and innovation projects as well as to share the information with their colleagues [2].

The first set of cards has come to use in a three-day boot camp where participants used innovation methods to create the next big insurance product. This hands-on experience was essential to demonstrate the usefulness of the InnoDeck and make the boot camp participants ambassadors for the InnoDeck and its contents [2].

In June 2018, one of the insurance companies from the network launched in-house innovation circles. 4 to 7 people of different departments were selected to work together on all kinds of different innovation projects on products, processes, sales and customer structures as well as on specific issues like mobility. Before starting the work on the innovation project, the participants received special training. For the preparation of these training seminaries, the facilitators used method cards of the InnoDeck. In the seminaries, the participants were equipped with printed InnoDeck cards. A digital version of the cards was provided on a project platform for download. Until today, 6–7 seminaries of this kind have kicked off several innovation projects in this insurance company. We do not have exact data on how often InnoDeck cards have been used within the proceeded innovation projects, but it has been confirmed that the InnoDeck has enabled an intra-corporate cultural change towards innovation. In an interview the facilitators stated that the InnoDeck benefitted the seminaries directly, since the participants gained inspirations from the inspiration cards. The method cards served especially the facilitators by giving them necessary tools for the preparation of the seminaries. From the facilitators' point of view, the InnoDeck should be enhanced to serve as an enduring source of methodical and inspirational content in their companies, for example by using short videos clips to explain complex issues. The facilitators also expressed the wish for an easier possibility to share the contents of the InnoDeck with their colleagues – via intranet, blog or wiki [2].

Another interesting scenario for the application of InnoDeck cards are hackathons. In February 2018, the InnoDeck was used for the preparation of a network-internal hackathon dedicated to the development of chatbots in the insurance sector. During the hackathon, the participants in four different teams were equipped with a set of cards compiled in order to contribute to the objective of the hackathon. The InnoDeck served both as a library of methods eligible to evaluate the created concepts and pieces of software and as a stimulus for the creation of ideas.

The third setting, where the InnoDeck came into use, were strategic meetings within an IT department of an insurance company. The meetings in this use case took place in March 2019 and focused on the restructuring of the IT department. The initiators knew the InnoDeck from the innovation network and deployed it in this particular setting to find out about the needs and expectations of the employees regarding the new organizational structure of the department. The example shows: the InnoDeck does not only contribute to innovation processes, but can also be employed in other contexts [2].

2.4   Benefits and Discussion

Golembewski and Selby [24] emphasize the advantages of card-based systems in design processes, especially by providing general support to overall design process. Previous experience with the InnoDeck within the innovation network supports this thesis.

It has shown in our work with companies that the combination of InnoDeck cards with future personas form a very good basis for workshop design. In some companies, it has become "normal" to take both artifacts into innovation workshops on various topics, for example about the future of IT cooperation, the future for innovation process design, process design in general, and others. When an InnoDeck card is especially fruitful and useful for a workshop and the contents are of great value to a broader public, the transition from InnoDeck card to anchorvideo is helpful. This has been done for example for the topics blockchain and hackathon. The videos give a great insight, especially for the vivid innovation processes, and insights on the application from outside trends within a company.

3   Future Personas as a Tool for Designing Products and Services for the Customer of the Future

3.1   Motivation

For the innovation network we condensed the following six future megatrends i.e. long-term trends from different sources [25–29]. KNOWing stands for the knowledge society where knowledge is the most important asset. LIVing includes topics like health, demographic change and ecology. MOVing addresses mobility but also globalization and urbanization. BEing is about the importance of individualization whereas WEing is about networks and new work issues. SECURing like KNOWing builds the brace around the megatrends. Figure 4 shows the representation of our megatrends. We also created a leporello with tag clouds for each megatrend as a brief enough format to be used in an innovation workshop. Nevertheless, it remains abstract and hard to consider at every point of the innovation process.

Future Ways of ...

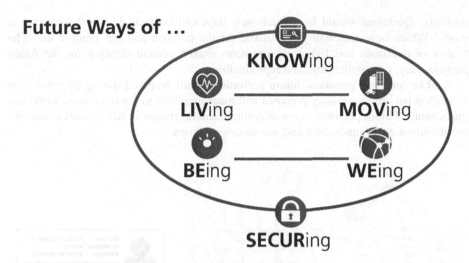

Fig. 4. Megatrends in the innovation network on which our future personas are based on

In human computer interaction and the design of products and services in general personas as first described by Cooper [18] are a widely used tool. They ease the communication about the end-user or customer and therefore this communication happens more often in the developers' team and this results in products and services that fit the customers' needs.

Personas and future trends and technologies are only two aspects that need to be considered during the innovation process. To reduce the mental load, we developed future personas as a concept that combines personas and future trends in a way that makes it easy to consider both in the innovation process.

3.2   Format Overview

The process of creating a future persona is explorative empiric-analytic [28] and besides the megatrends a lot of desktop research and analysis of technology trends is necessary. Additionally, we used a participative-formative approach by sourcing from expert interviews and discussions involving more than 50 people within the innovation network. Besides megatrends for the creation of future personas microtrends, e.g. from the Trendone Trendexplorer [30] are necessary. These can be new technologies, prototypes, products, services, business models, marketing and media innovations from the present. Such microtrends are very concrete and tangible and necessary to make a good future persona story.

Creating a future persona is a creative editorial process (Fig. 5). First, a present persona is created. Individually for each present persona you then must examine if and how a trend, which was also defined before, will influence the present persona in the future. We use a matrix of questions and living environments. E.g. for the megatrend KNOWing one could ask which new data will be available to the persona. And specify the answer in some or all the different living environments which we adapted from the Sinus Milieus [31] as follows: work, family, leisure, money, consumption, media and mobility. Questions would be: Which new data will be available to the persona at work? Which new data will be available for the persona and her family? Etc. The matrix of questions and living environments makes content creation for the future persona easy, comprehensible and reproducible.

Unlike (present) personas, future personas are not prepared during an innovation workshop but are preliminary prepared and made available to the innovation workshop participants. Future personas serve as communication means in (developer) teams and are mainly used in innovation and scenario workshops.

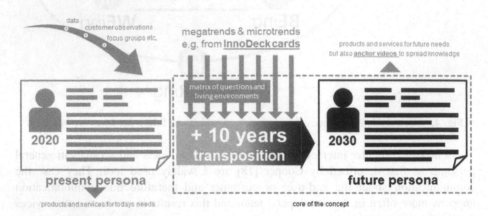

Fig. 5. Concept of transposing a present persona into a future persona by using future trends e.g. from InnoDeck cards – extended by interaction with other formats, original in [3]

3.3   Implementation and Use

Figure 6 shows the (present) persona Erkan Bilgin – a 15 year old student. Basis for this persona was a workshop with 15 year old high school students. Several fictional personas were created and discussed during this workshop. The present persona is represented on two pages which are both clearly marked with the year number – here 2017. The title on the first page consists of name, age and occupation of the persona. A picture and a profile are placed directly underneath. The profile contains hobbies, marital status, source of the persona and target group segment. For target group segmentation we used Sinus Milieus [31], which are widely used in product development and communication. These target groups are not as concrete as personas are, but besides the focus group observation and discussion which we used here, Sinus Milieus provide a good data based foundation for personas.

Core of the persona representation are several paragraphs of text that narrate different aspects of the persona's life in correlation (storytelling). Possible topics are the living environments of the transposition matrix: work, family, leisure, money, consumption, media and mobility. The persona representation is finalized by a typical quotation and a photo collage that depicts life and mood of the persona. These visual elements are especially important, because they offer nonverbal, quick and good to remember further perspectives for the user of the persona. The persona thereby becomes more concrete and dense.

Fig. 6. Example for a present persona from [3]

Instead of a photo collage the future persona in Fig. 7 uses a graphic, that represents the weight of the megatrends in this individual persona. Each megatrend is represented by a symbol and the size of the symbol stands for its importance. Keywords are added to clarify which megatrend-aspects the future persona incorporates. The manifesting trends are described in the written out text. The weight of the megatrends is also added to the quick profile below the hobbies. The future persona also has a portrait, since this is essential for the credibility. Furthermore, the future persona includes three new technologies, products or services, which are sourced from todays' microtrends. These are represented through a short headline, a picture and a shortlink that provides a more detailed description of the microtrend.

Fig. 7. Example for a future persona from [3].

3.4   Benefits and Discussion

Despite the structured way of creation, future personas are not intended to depict representative people of the future or predict the use of technologies or other developments in the future. Future personas are supposed to be a tool and inspiration source for innovation.

Especially when products and services of a faraway future are supposed to be created, future personas reduce the complexity for the developers. They must not think about the end-user, his future *and* future trends at the same time. Future personas are inspirational, comprehensive and save time.

Of course, several aspects need to be considered and offer room for extending and improving the concept of future personas. Future personas could be created from the perspective of certain sectors, although we prefer a universal view. A-B testing must show if the present persona can be omitted from the final result, making future personas 50% briefer and quicker to grasp. The megatrends representation in the future persona could be replaced by microtrends that are more comprehensible. A process to automatically choose from a pool of microtrends would therefore be helpful. Although based on long-term trends, the life period of future personas must be defined. To map people's diversity, a future persona database would be reasonable.

Fergnani [32] recently published an own concept of future personas as an add-on to enrich future scenarios. His future personas derive directly from the scenarios in a much lighter process than the one used by us, but considering the effort to create the scenarios the total invest is probably similar to ours. The two approaches could produce very similar personas that have the same purpose: to make the incorporated knowledge remembered, used and applied.

Since future personas have been published, several consultancies have adopted the method [33, 34]. And most importantly, future personas have become one of the most used assets from the innovation network within the participating companies. This is for sure because of its easy to grasp and appropriate format.

4 Anchorvideos

4.1 Motivation

Identifying, assessing and adopting new software and technologies plays an important role for the innovation capability of an organization. People are probably *the* most important factor when it comes to the diffusion of technological innovations in organizations [1, 35].

The anchorvideo format is aimed at the goal to attract interest and engage the employees in software and other departments and in consequence to foster innovation in the organizations. In the working context videos need to overcome an invisible barrier. Employees might not want to watch a video; they might just not be interested in the specific topic their organization wants to convey. In addition, long-term employees and elder staff members might face new technologies with some fear or aversion. In order to increase acceptance for software and new technology in companies it is essential to engage future users as an active part in the process of transformation. Anchorvideos combine the concept of engaging future users with the idea that, besides explaining a technology using animated graphics, people should stand in the spotlight to attract interest. One of the main characteristics of the novel format is involving staff members as talking heads in the video. Thereby the technology literally gets "a face" that functions as contact point for coworkers. At the same time, the employees will identify with one out of their own lines; reputation of the talking head makes follow their remarks with more attention [36]. Curiosity and some voyeurism might increase chances to watch a video a colleague participated. Anchorvideos anchor the innovative technology they give a stage within an organization. Persons providing statements within the anchorvideo (the so-called talking heads) become anchorwomen and anchormen for the presented technology. They are not necessarily involved in the initiative that further works on investigating the technology but they can refer any interested person to the right contact person within the organization. [4]

4.2 Format Overview

Anchorvideos usually consist of three parts. The videos start with a quick explantion and definition on what technology they are about, e.g. using an animation. This introduction is followed by possible areas of applications and examples for the use of the technology, which can be presented as animations, as real footage of the technology in action or as talking heads, i.e. in person employee statements. Examples of use are not limited to the companies' sector, since innovation often includes transferring an idea from another sector. The last part of the anchorvideo consists of talking heads of employees, which convey their vision of how the organization should apply the technology. Within the video itself or in the context in which the video is embedded, it is possible to include a call to action: What should the spectator do? The length of the video should be just a few minutes and its content despite being correct should not state every detail. It should be acted on the maxim of keeping it short and simple [4].

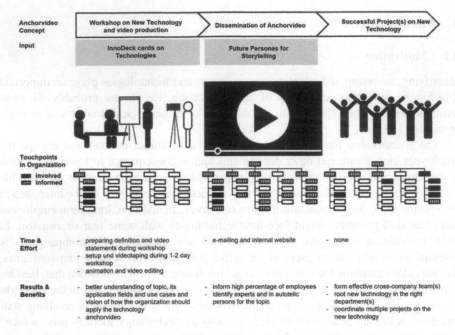

Fig. 8. The anchorvideo concept based on [4] extended by the aspect of useful input from InnoDeck cards and future personas.

It is advisable to produce the talking head material for an anchorvideo as part of a workshop on the same topic, e.g. a new technology like blockchain. Figure 8 shows the general anchorvideo concept. On the organizational level, the participants of such workshops typically come from the same department and if the results are not shared throughout the company similar workshops may occur in other departments. The explanatory part is best produced by somebody experienced in animation software or by using self-service explainer-video-tools. By collaborating with the workshop participants and picking up their thoughts and views, the video contents become more individual and offer specific information. [4].

The produced video is supposed to be widely shared throughout the company by email or other internal communication tools. In the context of open innovation, anchorvideos may be publicly available. Although a clear contact (topic lead) should be given with the distribution of the anchorvideo, the talking heads will instantly become contact points for their direct co-workers. They must refer relevant information to the topic lead [4].

4.3   Implementation and Use

We first applied and refined the anchorvideo concept within a network of insurance companies. Ten participants from four companies attended a two-day seminary "Blockchain and Distributed Ledger" to explore the new technology for their industry. Besides the direct training on the topic, an anchorvideo on blockchain was produced and distributed within the four companies. Preparing the in person statements for the talking heads in the video was incorporated in group work during the seminary. Condensing the group's opinions to statements proved beneficial for everyone's understanding and must not be regarded as extra-work for the video. The questions to be answered in the video (application fields in general and vision for the company) are part of the concept and must not be altered. An external expert who gave a talk at the seminary was also videotaped with his one sentence definition of blockchain [4].

4.4   Benefits and Discussion

In general, we observe that results including videos are clicked more often than e.g. slides or documents. The participants of the seminary requested the blockchain video before it was even finished. We see that moving image is an appropriate format for transferring complex content. Fuchs and Graichen [37] point out that cognitive information processing in audiovisual content is far more effective than purely visual or auditory content. A video has advantages over other formats as it can prevail in the general sensory overload by sending out strong stimuli [38]. In the recent years, videos have become a popular and time efficient resource not only for information but also as a learning tool. As Guo, Kim and Rubin [36] found out, certain video properties and production styles affect the engagement of students in a positive way. When an instructor's talking head is displayed, the video is more engaging than if it contains slides alone.

5   Evaluation

5.1   Interleaving of InnoDeck, Future Personas and Anchorvideos

Inspirational cards from the InnoDeck can fuel and enrich the representation of future personas. To transfer a future persona into a wide use throughout a company an anchorvideo can be used, where e.g. the employees involved in the creation of the future persona present the content to their coworkers.

It has shown that anchorvideos are especially useful for showing results of innovation workshops based on innovation methods like described on InnoDeck cards or technologies likewise to a broader audience. Future personas are often used as basis for storytelling a service or product idea within an anchorvideo, efficiently supporting the video creation process.

5.2   Innovation Network Evaluation

As described above, the formats presented have been developed and used as part of an innovation network. Therefore, the application scenarios often refer to cross-company workshops and the participants of the network have evaluated projects and the benefits of the formats. Nevertheless, the findings can be transferred to an intra-corporate use of the formats. The predominant part of the evaluation took place in 2017, at the end of the first contract phase.

Since innovation capability of an organization is always closely linked to people, we aim to reach as many employees as possible with the methods, topics and materials from the network. An indicator of the benefits of the formats in the innovation process and therefore for the successful spread of innovative content is the extent of its distribution. To measure the extent of the distribution, we questioned the participants about the amount of people they spoke with in their company about the topics from the innovation network. The results show that, with over 70%, the majority of the participants told more than 10 people about topics from the network (Fig. 9).

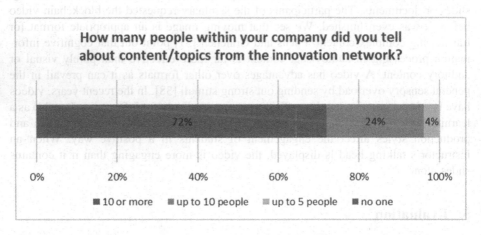

Fig. 9. The distribution of contents by participants of the innovation network (n = 25).

In addition to the reach, the use of methods and results for later innovation projects certainly allows conclusions to be drawn about their benefits. More than half of the respondents state that they have been able to integrate knowledge from the innovation network into their daily work (Fig. 10).

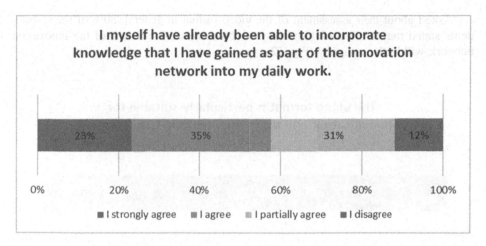

Fig. 10. Usefulness of the knowledge for daily work (n = 26).

5.3   Evaluation of InnoDeck, Anchorvideos and Future Personas

In the evaluation, we see high acceptance of the formats. Figure 11 shows that almost 70% agree on the statement, that the result "Blockchain and Distributed Ledger" represents benefits for their company. The result comprises the seminary as well as the anchorvideo on the topic. Nearly 50% of the respondents called the result "Future Personas" beneficial for their company. Due to the time of the evaluation in late 2017, the result "InnoDeck" could not be evaluated as the first set of cards has come to use in early 2018.

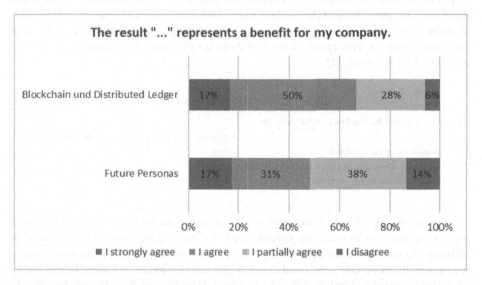

Fig. 11. Evaluation of the results "Blockchain anchorvideo and seminary" (n = 18) [4] and "Future Personas" (n = 29) by the participants of the innovation network.

Asked about their assessment of the video format in general, 80% of the respondents stated that it is a useful and way to communicate the results of the innovation network within the company (Fig. 12).

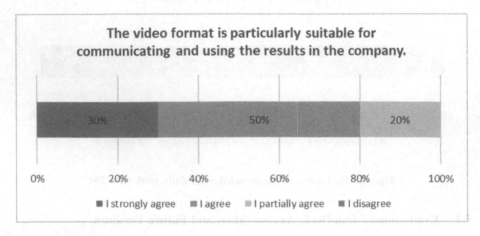

Fig. 12. Assessment of the video format for representing results (n = 30).

To evaluate the benefits of the InnoDeck, we asked the users of the InnoDeck separately about the advantages of the format. The evaluation presented here focuses on the way the InnoDeck is used in the companies participating in the innovation network. The method cards in particular are often used in workshops - either for distribution to the participants or to prepare the facilitators. 70% that means 14 of 20 respondents stated that they had applied the methods of the InnoDeck. This result underlines the usefulness of the method cards. 60% said, they had read InnoDeck cards to inform themselves. Only 35% answered that they downloaded the cards to hand them to colleagues. This result shows that there are still obstacles when it comes to the sharing of information. [2]

Table 2. The InnoDeck in use [2].

How have you used the InnoDeck so far? (n = 20)	
Usage	Approval rate ("I agree" and "I strongly agree")
Applied methods of the InnoDeck	70%
Downloaded InnoDeck cards to hand them to colleagues	35%
Read InnoDeck cards to inform myself	60%

Despite the high level of acceptance, we also see room for improvement. The users ask for mechanisms to select the suitable cards for the specific workshop or project. In addition, the users wish for a possibility for easier distribution [2]. In further evaluation, we need to focus on this aspect and develop alternative formats and identify alternative channels to transfer contents not only to direct members of the network but also to other employees of their organizations. Nevertheless, the results show clearly that the InnoDeck makes an important contribution to the innovation culture within an organization [2].

Table 3. Survey after the use of future personas [3].

Future Personas are a useful tool for the development of future products. (n = 30)	
Statements	*Approval rate*
"I agree" and "I strongly agree"	90%
"I partially agree"	6, 7%
"I don't agree"	3, 3%

The future personas tool was developed to accompany an industry working group and was validated by the participants from five participating companies with regard to the requirements provided in the concept. In addition, future personas were applied in a workshop and discussed with the workshop participants. Finally, the opinion of the workshop participants was collected using a questionnaire. Table 3 shows that almost all workshop participants (90%) see future personas as a useful or rather useful tool for the development of future products. Only one out of thirty participants disagreed with the statement. The first evaluation of future personas briefly outlined here confirms the concept as well as its high relevance for and acceptance by users [3].

5.4   Individual Use of the Three Tools

Communication is unique for every company. However, in the first phase of the network, when there were less artifacts available (fewer InnoDeck cards, no anchorvideos, fewer future personas) the innovation communication posed a challenge for the participants of the network. This was the starting point for the current toolset of these three tools, as the feedback showed room for improvement beforehand.

In three case studies, we show the combination and use cases for the three introduced artifacts InnoDeck, anchorvideos and future personas. We present the use cases of two companies and their individual strategies for incorporating these artifacts within their processes. The third use case describes how we used the three artifacts to support a hackathon within the innovation network. Figure 13 illustrates how several tools can be individually combined to fit a company's specific needs.

First case study is company A that likes future personas and established them as a standard for product development. They refer to the InnoDeck and anchorvideos from time to time, but rather innovate themselves in own workshops. This forms innovation islands, which then spread their results within the company if successful. Company B established an innovation circle, which is spreading the knowledge actively by distributing the videos and cards. This aims more at targeting the complete company instead of innovation islands. Depending on the overall strategy, different approaches and combinations of the concepts may be the fit. Additionally, due to the growing amount of sheer number of InnoDeck cards, videos and personas, a review and selection process is part of the innovation strategy an individual company needs to establish.

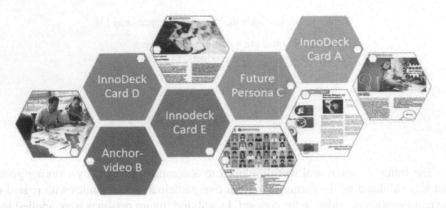

Fig. 13. Several InnoDeck cards, future personas and anchorvideos [2–4] can be individually combined and adapted for the specific purpose for tailored innovation support and communication strategies

A third case study C within the innovation network is the chatbot hackathon [39]. For supporting a hackathon on chatbots as described above, InnoDeck cards were amongst others created for following topics: voice technology, chatbot technology, premortem, storytelling, virtual reality. Future personas were used as key customers for various needs for a chatbot. For communicating the results of the hackathon, a video was created[1]. For details on the results see [39].

6 Conclusions and Outlook

In today's dynamic digital world, it is becoming more and more evident that the survivors in this new age will be those companies who are rigorous in their pursuit of innovation, in order to develop and deploy new products more efficiently, effectively and profitability. It is also increasingly clear that the only way to achieve this goal is to support the employees as enablers of innovation. In order to do this, companies must provide the appropriate formats and methods in the innovation process to support people in the best way possible: people matter!

The presented tools are not limited to the domain of insurances and universally usable in processes towards the digital transformation of organizations and innovation in general. We summarized the tools in this paper, because of their common fundamental that format matters, which we take for granted. However, for the innovation network the created community is the most important asset.

---

[1] See https://www.youtube.com/watch?v=yHRLYJ_olZ8

In 2020 the innovation network is planned for a third phase and like a community of practice it needs to be cultivated to not enter a phase of stewardship and eventually end because the need for the participating companies to be innovative is still high. Wenger et al. [40] propose several principles to keep such a community alive, which may be adapted for the innovation network like presented in Table 4. We will use the three described formats and created tailored bundles of information for supporting especially these communities of practice, by topic and by individual needs.

The platform the innovation network members use to exchange data already changed between phase one and two and will possibly change again in the next phase since collaboration means is such an important handle. Although managing all the involved people is a challenge already, we will involve more outside experts to nurture the community. The commercial nature of the innovation network and the steering committee assure that value stays in focus. We have always added new activity formats to the innovation network and will continue doing this, since it keeps people excited and this momentum is necessary for innovation. Big gatherings 2–3 times a year remain important and in addition to the agile project work in-between, a digital rhythm may keep the spirit high.

The knowledge created in the innovation network and its use must be measured better and more often in the future. We will especially consider community activities, knowledge resources and business processes like proposed by Wenger et al. [40]. In our distributed community, the data must not come from the joint parts, but from the activities, resources and processes triggered through the innovation network within the insurance companies.

Table 4. Principles for designing communities of practice [40] and implications for the next contract phase of the innovation network

Principle of designing CoPs	Plans and implications for innovation network
1. Design for evolution	allow continuous change by providing better technical communication and collaboration means and promote the good of change in the steering board
2. Open dialogue between inside and outside perspective	reinforce the involvement of outside experts
3. Invite different level of participation	see 1 – a better communication collaboration tool could offer new possibilities to get involved
4. Develop both public and private spaces	consider private spaces for the participating insurance companies where they only interact with the Fraunhofer IAO
5. Focus on value	put topics relevant for the insurance companies first
6. Combine familiarity with excitement	preserve some familiar artifacts or activities, but unconditionally add new things
7. Create a rhythm	communicate regular gatherings and agilely plan the in-between activities, maybe a digital rhythm may also help

Acknowledgements. We thank all people involved in the innovation network for their energy and trust that made working together so far big fun. It is great that we have the possibility to publish some of the content and we hope to continue this journey towards more innovative insurance companies and insurance products.

References

1. Linke, A., Zerfass, A.: Internal communication and innovation culture: developing a change framework. JCOM **15**, 332–348 (2011)
2. Kasper, H., Kochanowski, M., Pohl, V.: InnoDeck: card based innovation support - a modular human-centered approach to facilitate innovation workshops. In: Proceedings of the 11th International Joint Conference on Knowledge Discovery, Knowledge Engineering and Knowledge Management, pp. 83–91. SCITEPRESS - Science and Technology Publications (2019)
3. Kasper, H., Kintz, M., Kochanowski, M., Weisbecker, A.: Future Personas als Werkzeug zum Entwurf von Produkten und Dienstleistungen für den Kunden der Zukunft. In: Binz, H., Bertsche, B., Bauer, W., Spath, D., Roth, D. (eds.) Stuttgarter Symposium für Produktentwicklung SSP 2017 - Produktentwicklung im disruptiven Umfeld. Stuttgart, 29. Juni 2017: wissenschaftliche Konferenz. IRB Mediendienstleistungen - Fraunhofer Informationszentrum Raum und Bau, Stuttgart (2017)
4. Pohl, V., Kasper, H., Kochanowski, M., Krause, T.: Anchorvideos as a means to engage with software and technology innovations in large organizations. In: 44th Euromicro Conference on Software Engineering and Advanced Applications (SEAA), pp. 206–209 (2018)
5. Fraunhofer IAO: Innovationsnetzwerk Digitalisierung für Versicherungen. Innovationen anstoßen, Einsatzmöglichkeiten Künstlicher Intelligenz erkennen, https://www.digital.iao.fraunhofer.de/de/leistungen/Digitalisierung/innovationsnetzwerk-digitalisierung-fuer-versicherungen.html. Accessed 30 Jan 2020
6. Pohl, V., Kasper, H., Kochanowski, M., Renner, T.: Zukunftsstudie 2027 - #ichinzehnjahren. Wie aktuelle Technologien und Entwicklungen unsere Lebenswelten verändern. Fraunhofer Verlag, Stuttgart (2017)
7. Lave, J., Wenger, E.: Situated Learning. Legitimate Peripheral Participation. Cambridge Univ. Pr., Cambridge (1991)
8. Swan, J., Newell, S., Scarbrough, H., Hislop, D.: Knowledge management and innovation: networks and networking. J of Knowl. Manage. **3**, 262–275 (1999)
9. Cormican, K., O'Sullivan, D.: Auditing best practice for effective product innovation management. Technovation **24**, 819–829 (2004)
10. Quirke, B.: Making the Connections. Taylor and Francis (2017)
11. Nonaka, I., Takeuchi, H.: The knowledge-creating company: how Japanese companies create the dynamics of innovation. Res. Policy **26**, 598–600 (1997)
12. Janev, V., Vraneš, S.: The role of knowledge management solutions in enterprise business processes. J. Univ. Comput. Sci. **11**, 526–545 (2005)
13. Standing, C., Kiniti, S.: How can organizations use wikis for innovation? Technovation **31**, 287–295 (2011)
14. Riege, A.: Three-dozen knowledge-sharing barriers managers must consider. J. Knowl. Manage. **9**, 18–35 (2005)
15. Schumpeter, J.A.: The creative response in economic history. J. Econ. Hist. **7**, 149–159 (1947)

16. Kahn, K.B.: Understanding innovation. Bus. Horiz. **61**, 453–460 (2018)
17. Badr, N.G.: Empowering capability for innovation in IT organizations - a confluence of knowledge for continual organizational learning. In: 9th International Conference on Knowledge Management and Information Sharing (KMIS), pp. 17–28 (2017)
18. Cooper, A.: The Inmates are running the Asylum. Sams, Indianapolis (Ind.) (1999)
19. Marshall, R., Cook, S., Mitchell, V., Summerskill, S., Haines, V., Maguire, M., Sims, R., Gyi, D., Case, K.: Design and evaluation: end users, user datasets and personas. Appl. Ergon. **46**(Pt B), 311–317 (2015)
20. Rönkkö, K., Hellman, M., Kilander, B., Dittrich, Y.: Personas is not applicable. Local remedies interpreted in a wider context. In: Clement, A. (ed.) Proceedings of the Eighth Conference on Participatory Design Artful Integration Interweaving Media, Materials and Practices, New York, NY, vol. 1, pp. 112–120. ACM (2004)
21. Pruitt, J., Grudin, J.: Personas. In: Arnowitz, J., Chalmers, A., Swack, T., Anderson, R., Zapolski, J. (eds.) Proceedings of the 2003 Conference on Designing for User Experiences – DUX 2003, New York, New York, USA, p. 1. ACM Press (2003)
22. Frishammar, J., Richtnér, A., Brattström, A., Magnusson, M., Björk, J.: Opportunities and challenges in the new innovation landscape: Implications for innovation auditing and innovation management. Eur. Manage. J. **37**, 151–164 (2019)
23. Alexander, K.: Kompendium der visuellen Information und Kommunikation. Springer, Berlin Heidelberg, Berlin, Heidelberg (2007)
24. Golembewski, M., Selby, M.: Ideation decks. In: Halskov, K. (ed.) Poceedings of the 8th ACM Conference on Designing Interactive Systems. DIS 2010, Aarhus, Denmark, August 16 – 20, pp. 89–92. ACM, New York, NY (2010)
25. Huber, T., Gatterer, H.: Megatrend-Dokumentation. die Wegweiser des Wandels. Zukunftsinstitut, Kelkheim (2015)
26. Maas, P., Cachelin, J.L., Bühler, P. (eds.): 2050 Megatrends, Alltagswelten Zukunftsmärktc. Institut für Versicherungswirtschaft der Univ. St. Gallen, St. Gallen (2015)
27. TrendOne: Mega-Trends.   http://www.trendone.com/trenduniversum/mega-trends.html. Accessed 30 Jan 2020
28. Kreiblich, R.: Die Zukunft der Zukunftsforschung. Berlin (2009)
29. Zweck, A., Holtmannspötter, D.: Geschichten aus der Zukunft 2030. Ergebnisbericht 3. VDI Technologiezentrum, Düsseldorf (2015)
30. TrendOne: TrendExplorer - From Trends to Innovations. https://www.trendexplorer.com/en/ . Accessed 30 Jan 2020
31. Sinus Insitut: Sinus-Milieus(R) Deutschland. http://www.sinus-institut.de/sinus-loesungen/sinus-milieus-deutschland/. Accessed 30 Jan 2020
32. Fergnani, A.: The future persona: a futures method to let your scenarios come to life. FS 21, pp. 445–466 (2019)
33. TrendOne: Wie Trends die Zielgruppe verändern – Meet your Future Persona. http://blog.trendone.com/2017/06/28/wie-trends-die-zielgruppe-veraendern-meet-your-future-persona/. Accessed 30 Jan 2020
34. Neef, A. and Schaich, A.: Den Kunden der Zukunft erlebbar machen. https://www.z-punkt.de/de/themen/artikel/den-kunden-der-zukunft-erlebbar-machen/550. Accessed 30 Jan 2020
35. Mumford, M.D., Scott, G.M., Gaddis, B., Strange, J.M.: Leading creative people: Orchestrating expertise and relationships. Leadersh. Q. **13**, 705–750 (2002)
36. Guo, P.J., Kim, J., Rubin, R.: How video production affects student engagement. In: Sahami, M., Fox, A., Hearst, M.A., Chi, M.T.H. (eds.) Proceedings of the First ACM Conference on Learning @ Scale Conference - L@S 2014, New York, New York, USA, pp. 41–50. ACM Press (2014)

37. Fuchs, H., Graichen, W.U.: Bessere Lernmethoden. Effiziente Techniken für Erwachsene. Orbis, München (1994)
38. Lanzenberger, W., Müller, M.: Unternehmensfilme drehen. Business Movies im digitalen Zeitalter. UVK Verlagsgesellschaft, Konstanz und München (2012)
39. Koetter, F., Blohm, M., Drawehn, J., Kochanowski, M., Goetzer, J., Graziotin, D., Wagner, S.: Conversational agents for insurance companies: from theory to practice. In: van den Herik, J., Rocha, A.P., Steels, L. (eds.) ICAART 2019. LNCS (LNAI), vol. 11978, pp. 338–362. Springer, Cham (2019). https://doi.org/10.1007/978-3-030-37494-5_17
40. Wenger, E., McDermott, R.A., Snyder, W.: Cultivating Communities of Practice. A Guide to Managing Knowledge. Harvard Business Review Press, Boston (2002)

Rethinking Hackathons' Strategies: The Findings of a Global Event

Nelson Tenório[1,2](✉) , Gisele Caroline Urbano Lourenço[2] ,
Mariana Oliveira[2] , Steffi Aline Stark Becker[2] ,
Fabrício Tomaz Bernardelli[2] , Hassan Atifi[3] , and Nada Matta[3]

[1] Cesumar Institute of Science, Technology, and Innovation (ICETI),
Av. Gudner 1610, Bl. 7, sl. 9, 87100-00 Maringá, Paraná, Brazil
nelson.tenorio@unicesumar.edu.br
[2] Knowledge Management of the Organizations,
UniCesumar, Maringá, Paraná, Brazil
gisele_urbano@hotmail.com,
mariana_santosoliveira@hotmail.com,
steffi_aline@hotmail.com, bernardelliwolf@gmail.com
[3] Department of Computer Science, University of Technology of Troyes,
Troyes, France
{hassan.atifi,nada.matta}@utt.fr

Abstract. Hackathons are events that have become increasingly common around the world. This kind of event, described as a programming marathon, is based on problem-solving that can go beyond the technological boundary. This paper presents the findings of a global hackathon to aid its organizers to rethink their strategies to leverage the knowledge management of the teams to solve the hackathon challenges. Our research is a mixed research approach followed by ethnography based on a questionnaire, interviews, and observations. The findings point out that the organizers should consider four factors to rethink hackathons strategies to leverage knowledge management for the event: *knowledge processes*, r*esolving conflicts*, *individual learning*, and *experienced emotions*. Moreover, our findings could inspire the tech industry to consider those factors to leverage the innovation and creativity in the team workers.

Keywords: Knowledge process · Solving conflict · Individual learning · Emotions

1 Introduction

Hackathon is a typical event to create innovative solutions for social and industrial challenges. This kind of activity can be described as a programming marathon that aims to solve a challenge that can go beyond the technological world [1]. Flores et al. [2] point out that a hackathon is a competition where participants work in teams for a short time, in which they need to idealize, design, prototype, test, and launch their solutions to a given challenge. Those events encourage both individual and organizational learning through innovative ways [3]. Knowledge, then, is considered one of the most

© Springer Nature Switzerland AG 2020
A. Fred et al. (Eds.): IC3K 2019, CCIS 1297, pp. 497–515, 2020.
https://doi.org/10.1007/978-3-030-66196-0_23

valuable corporate assets. In this way, the organization that manages its knowledge benefits from a hackathon, and other activities have a higher possibility of creating innovative products and services, remaining sustainable in the market in which it operates [4]. Knowledge Management (KM) is indispensable for stimulating innovation in organizations. KM is a collection of processes that govern the creation and dissemination of knowledge to achieve organizational team goals [5].

In this paper, we extend our findings presented in [8], deepening our analysis through data mining techniques, in particular, clusters, and also discussing means to help the organizers of the hackathons to rethink strategies in order to leverage knowledge management during the event. Our findings pointed four factors as follows: knowledge process, solving conflicts, individual learning, and experienced emotions, once those might impact directly in the solutions proposed during the event. Therefore, KM is a trigger to increase innovation and creativity in which could improve problem-solving in the hackathons. Firstly, our findings concerning the knowledge process show that hackathons provide team members to accomplish knowledge creation, acquiring, storage, sharing, and use in which are useful to organizers perform KM of the events. Secondly, the findings concerned solving conflicts, for instance, may help the organizers to gather information about team member's conflicts during the hackathon once it aids the groups to find ways for supporting in the next event. Thirdly, individual learning happens mainly through the interaction with team members or executing different activities to solve the hackathon challenge. Finally, emotions experienced, such as tiredness, lead organizers to rethink about hackathons' duration. Thus, although the participants experienced different positive emotions at the event, tiredness was hard highlighted by them in which might lead.

To show our findings, we organized this article into six sections. Following this introduction, the second section presents the concepts and related works regarding hackathons and knowledge management processes, emotions, conflicts, and individual learning. Section three presents our research method in which we present the empirical settings, data collection, and data analysis. Section four summarizes the results, and Sect. 5 presents our discussion. Finally, section six presents our conclusions, followed by references.

2   Hackathons and Knowledge Management

Hackathons are events in which they use different cultures and expertise concerning each participant to apply their vision to solve a specific challenge [6]. Facing the hackathon challenge, the participants have the opportunity to interact with each other, providing insights into the creation of the content [7]. Thus, hackathons provide means to share and create knowledge by seeking solutions to everyday problems posed as challenges by resorting to the production of innovative tech solutions for the benefit of society [8].

According to Zukin and Papadantonakis [9], hackathons promote the opportunity for participants to develop new skills, e.g., coding, applications, designs, and mockups, as well as do networking. In this way, hackathons stimulate the creativity of participants, who have the opportunity to deal with technology [10]. However, hackathons are applicable in a variety of settings, as they seek innovative solutions for a real challenge [11]. In this context, [3] emphasize that hackathons have accomplished in different areas such as music, fashion, and fitness and even inside of companies by mean of internal hackathons [12]. The authors further underline that hackathons encourage experimentations and creativity to figure out different challenges. Hackathons, therefore, aim to stimulate innovation as individuals share ideas and looking for solutions to the nowadays issues [13].

Organizations have to manage their knowledge to get business sustainability in a competitive market. In this sense, Knowledge Management (KM) can be useful as a resource for (managing) organizational knowledge. According to [5], KM is the deliberate and systemic coordination of people, technologies, processes, and organizational structures to add corporate value through knowledge reuse and innovation. So, the organizations which manage their knowledge to create innovative products and services remain sustainable in the market in which they act [14]. So, KM arises through the process of knowledge creation, in which it requires a physical environment to create new knowledge. Regarding this, it is necessary to highlight two types of knowledge: implicit and explicit. The implicit knowledge is complex, developed, and internalized by people over a while, compounded by lifelong learning [15]. Explicit knowledge is easily communicated, either through product specifications, scientific formulas, or computer programs [4].

Knowledge creation starts with socialization and passes through the four modes of knowledge conversions [4]. Firstly, the socialization, which is presented as the sharing and creation of implicit knowledge through direct experiences. Secondly, the outsourcing that aims to articulate tacit knowledge through dialogue. Thirdly, the combination that suggests both implicit and explicit knowledge application. Finally, the internalization suggests the need to acquire and learn new tacit knowledge in practice. Since the individual has the knowledge internalized, it is necessary to apply this experience so that the organization gains innovation and creativity [8]. Therefore, organizations that use their knowledge properly achieve competitive advantages and notorious place in a competitive market.

Turban et al. (2006) highlight that KM is a cyclical process because the knowledge's environment is continually changing and, consequently, the knowledge needs to be updated to reflect these changes. According to Dalkir (2011), those processes compose the KM cycles, and they have a relationship with each KM stage representing the path taken by the information and becoming a strategic asset for the organization. Providing a knowledge-sharing space can offer significant benefits to organizations as it helps their employees acquire, distribute, store, and retrieve information during work routines (Detlor 2000). As the organizational team members seek out new learning such as knowledge tool resources and sharing practices, it facilitates the creation of an environment in which individuals talk about knowledge requirements and assist in measures for the implementation of a knowledge repository which supports the objectives of the company (Cepeda and Vera 2007).

Thus, KM processes need to be supported by structures or tools based on technology to assure the efficiency and effectiveness of their functions. Those tools have a vital extraction role to transform tacit knowledge from people to explicit knowledge available in the whole company. The cycles of KM are processes formed by some procedures that seek to create/capture, store, share and use knowledge efficiently. The literature presents different KM cycles [5, 16, 17]

From the perspective of the KM, a hackathon group practices for creating, sharing, and use knowledge once it encourages the participants to work together, sharing information for generating experience on the challenges. The creation in a perspective of Nonaka's theory [18], suggests that knowledge is created from socialization (tacit to tacit), externalization (tacit to explicit), internalization (explicit to implicit), and combination (explicit to explicit). So, some organizations formally encourage and support workers' participation in events like hackathons. Moreover, most of them sponsor internal or external hackathons around the world. Therefore, hackathons provide participants an environment that helps to learn new skills as well as interaction with other participants and networking, also stimulating its participants' creativity to solve a real challenge innovatively.

2.1 Emotions

The emotions are our evolution legacy in which gives us individual impulses for immediate actions. Thus, emotions refer to feelings and reasoning – psychological and biological states, and the range of propensities for action. There are hundreds of emotions, including their combinations, variations, mutations, and shadows [18].

Emotions are a mental state of readiness that arises from cognitive evaluations of events or thoughts, and that can be perceived by gestures, postures, and facial features [19]. Therefore, emotion is a natural way of evaluating the environment that surrounds us and reacts adaptively [20, 21].

Human emotions are negative or positive. One of the theories that explain negative and positive emotions, namely the theory of control over behavior, considers the view of the behavior that could show the nature of emotions. The theory suggests how feelings can arise and function in human behavior [22]. Positive emotions allow an individual to know what is being done toward a desirable goal. In this context, there is compelling evidence that positive emotions are not just the result of well-being, but can also drive success and prosperity [23]. Inversely, negative emotions are the way of realizing that no behavior, progress, or action is being taken toward goals [22].

Negative emotions occur when we perceive a negative meaning in personal situation changes or related ones [24–26] in which represents an overall dimension of subjective suffering and unpleasant engagement. Moreover, that includes a variety of aversive mood states including anger, contempt, repulsion, guilt, fear, and nervousness [27] frustrated, angry, depressed, harassed, hostile, worried, and unmotivated [28]; anxious and sad [29]. Positive emotions work as effective antidotes to the persistent effects of negative emotions, correcting or undo the subsequent effects of the negative emotions [21, 26]. In this sense, some positive emotions are joy, interest, contentment, love [29], satisfaction, pleasure, pride, relief, affection, love, hope [19].

Emotions are complex reactions triggered by a stimulus or thought with personal sensations, an answer involving different components, which is an unusual reaction, a physiological excitation, a cognitive interpretation, and subjective experience. Therefore, all human emotions directly influence personal-life as well as work-life.

2.2   Conflicts

Conflicts may occur in a wide range of settings involving people in the individual or work-life. Those conflicts are social and psychological phenomena in which they have different sources, processes, and results. So, various disciplines, such as sociology, economics, philosophy, and management, try to explain the conflicts in different ways [30]. Thomas [31] points out that conflict is a process that begins when one party realizes that the other had frustrated or was about to disappoint some of their concerns. In this way, conflict is a state, in which disharmonious phenomena trigger hostile actions, under a state of confrontation or emotion.

Nowadays, conflicts are widespread due to the competition and the growing expectations of all business stakeholders [32]. Furthermore, conflicts are an indicator of a lack of reliability of some sources which adopt inappropriate conduct for such situations [33]. According to Rao [34], conflicts can occur for a variety of reasons, e.g., personality clashes, ego clashes, differences of opinion or culture, perceptions, lack of communication, lack of information, ambiguity in roles and responsibilities, stress, and lack of resources. In this scenario, conflicts arise when there is a gap between expectations and realities.

However, if the conflicts are not well solved, they have detrimental effects on the organization, team, or project progress [35], impacting the creative process [36]. Since the conflict is a confrontational relationship, it shows up a hard way to achieve the goals of a project, team, or organization, resulting in excessive waste of time and expanse of costs [37]. Deal with conflict means effectively solve a disagreement among individuals, in which it occurs once none of the two equal persons perform and think the same task in the same way [34]. In this sense, the organizations must pay more attention to finding out the critical factors of conflicts and related mechanisms.

The conflicts exist in organizations, teams, or projects (i.e., in all that involves people), and the expertise to deal with such disputes is essential. The lack of conflict's experience could cause knowledge loss impacting directly into team creativity and innovation of products and services.

2.3   Individual Learning

The concept of individual learning as an object of study is still uncommon in the literature since it is relatively new, and, as of that moment, not much is known about its conceptualization and empirical [33]. However, individual learning is a lifelong process that enables us to learn and develop individuals' cognitive skills [38]. Also, learning is the personal experience throughout the life that occurs individually, through the person's interaction with groups of people, or in situations lived in its work environment [39]. In this sense, all the interactions of the individuals are incorporated into the person's lifelong learning. This learning later gets knowledge that might be shared with other individuals [40].

A unique learning project is one that has a specific time, and that seeks to teach some relevant subjects to the individual [41]. One of the reasons for using an individual learning project refers to the fact that individuals need other ones to learn. This context comes from friends, co-workers, or anyone who contributes to the personal learning process by providing models and constructive feedback [42]. Thus, a unique learning project is in a constructivist approach, in that it can adhere to diverse contexts, e.g., personal or work [43]. Collaboration for individual learning is a way out once the help of one's specific knowledge in practice [44].

Therefore, interactions with other people may help to acquire individual learning. So, this learning gets substantial knowledge application when required.

3   Method

To aid the organizers of the hackathons rethink strategies to leverage knowledge management during the event, we accomplished a mixed approach [45]. Furthermore, we collected empirical evidence based upon an ethnographically informed [46]. We collected data between 19 and 22 of October of 2018. Firstly, we conducted a face-to-face questionnaire regarding the emotions of the participants at the beginning of the event. Secondly, we observed all teams – one-by-one, during the first phase of their project definition, and the final solution. Thirdly, on the last day, we conducted face-to-face interviews with the participants through a semi-structured interview protocol. Finally, we repeat the face-to-face emotions questionnaire one day after the event. Our empirical material was recorded, transcribed, analyzed as following.

3.1   Empirical Settings

Hackathons are public marathons that involve participants for hours, days, or weeks to discuss ideas and develop software or hardware projects that can create or disseminate productions and especially digital innovations [47, 48]. Usually, such events are sponsored by entities (public or private), which presents a challenge to the participants, being related to the most diverse areas of knowledge. They are distributed into teams that must propose solutions for the proposed trial. Hackathon event is the scenario behind NASA Space Apps, a NASA-sponsored hackathon. The event was held between October 19, 2018, until October 21 of the same year and involved professionals and students from different fields of knowledge. The Space Apps event took place simultaneously in 75 countries, with more than eighteen thousand participants [49]. The event was taking place by a University in the city of Maringá, Brazil. During the three days of the event, several activities took place. On Saturday morning (the first day of the challenge) mini-courses, workshops and mentoring were held. The participants randomly segregated into teams, had twenty-four hours to develop projects on one of six themes set by NASA: freestyle, better earth, natural impact, big rocks, and space mindfulness. At the end of twenty-four hours, the teams were previously submitted to a short pitch with the event's mentors who assessed each project and selected the 'ten best choices' of them. Those ten best choices presented to all participants and the referees at the beginning of the afternoon of October 21st to vote the three best solutions.

3.2 Data Collection

We collected data through a questionnaire, interviews, and observation. The questionnaire was conducted face-to-face even though the questionnaire was available in the google form. We chose face-to-face questionnaire since it is essential to get data precisely, i.e., avoiding distortions [50]. Moreover, four researchers accomplished 24 h observation across the teams during the event focused on interaction among the team members and the design solutions for the challenging choice. The researchers took notes concerned their impressions of the team interactions. After the presentations – the last day of the event, we conducted eight different team member interviews following a semi-structured interview protocol in order to identify the knowledge management in the hackathon. We recorded all the interviews with the interviewee's permission and conducted the interviews at the same local of the event. One day after the event, we repeated the emotions' questionnaire to identify how were the emotions of the participants after the event.

3.3 Data Analysis

We analyzed our empirical material obeying three steps. Firstly, we analyzed the emotions of the participants from the google form questionnaire using data mining techniques. For that, we prepared the data and designed a workflow into the *Orange* tool. The *Orange* is a free intuitive data science tool based on workflow concept [51]. Even though the data coming from google forms, our most laborious task was to get the data into standards form to be analyzed [52]. Secondly, we transcribed each interview recorded word-by-word. So, we imported all transcribed interviews to *ATLAS.ti* and codified them following coding suggestions of [53]. Finally, we revisited our empirical notes of the observation to get insights regarding team interactions and challenge solutions.

4 Results

In this section, we present our results based on the questionnaire – quantitative results, in which we used data mining techniques to analyze the emotions experimented by the participants of the hackathon. Next, we present the results of the interviews and our empirical observations.

4.1 Results Based on the Questionnaire

We conducted a face-to-face questionnaire with twenty participants of the hackathons for identity positive and negative emotions. The questionnaire data were collected during [pre, post]-event. The emotions are essential to understand how they impact on participants' behavior while the event is running. The questionnaire is comprising of forty-one Likert scale questions concerned following emotions: Alert, Frightened, Loving, Distressed, Cheered up, Anxious, In love, Active, Calm, Tired out, Full of energy, Comfortable, Happy, Determined, Dynamic, Willing, Funny, Enthusiast,

Hopeful, Happy, Strong, Thankful, Humiliated, Troubled, Restless, Inspired, Angry, Motivated, Nervous, Proud, Optimistic, Patient, Disturbed, Worried, Spiteful, Relaxed, Serene, Fearful, Tense, Tranquil, and Vigorous.

We have used data mining techniques to prepare our data for analysis. So, firstly we prepared a '.csv' file in which containing all forty-one emotions with the answers on a Likert scale (i.e., strongly agree, agree, non-agree neither disagree, disagree, strongly disagree) about [pre, post]-hackathon. We have considered the sum of the answers agree and strongly agree as well as disagree and strongly disagree, discarding the neutral answers once they were not coming up any novelty concerned the participant's emotions. Secondly, we loaded the '.csv' files into the Orange data mining tool, splitting the data in four combinations of flows as follows: pre-agree vs. post-agree; pre-agree vs. pre-disagree; pre-disagree vs. post-disagree; post-agree vs. post-disagree. Below, we show four flows executed according to the data set combinations (see Fig. 1).

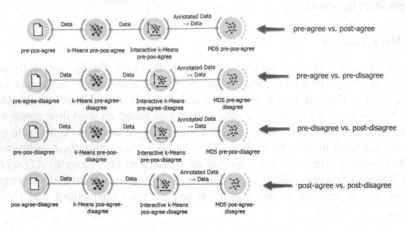

Fig. 1. Clusters implementation to analyze the answers based on pre-agree, post-agree, pre-disagree, and post-disagree.

Thirdly, we execute the four flows using the k-Means algorithm to find out emotion clusters and the Interactive k-Means to remove the outliers. Based on our data set, the k-Means step suggested to us automatically a quantity of four clusters. We have run the k-Means algorithm over four combinations of our data set. Finally, we plotted a multidimensional scaling to discover the clusters based on those combinations. We did not observe any difference between the four combinations, i.e., the clusters of emotions were the same in all of our data sets. The clusters resulted in our four data sets are presented in Fig. 2 (a, b, c, d).

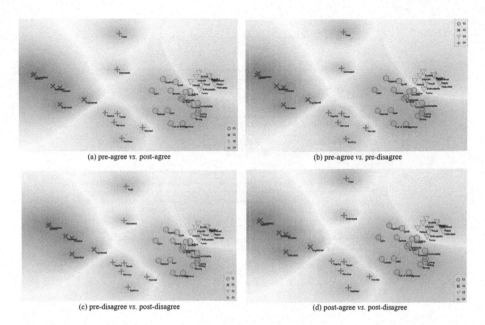

(a) pre-agree vs. post-agree

(b) pre-agree vs. pre-disagree

(c) pre-disagree vs. post-disagree

(d) post-agree vs. post-disagree

Fig. 2. Clusters of emotions based on four data sets of pre-agree, post-agree, pre-disagree, and post-disagree answers.

Thanks to the clusters, we classified the emotions in four categories based on [25, 54] (see Table 1).

Table 1. The categories of the emotions experienced by the participants of the hackathon.

Category	Emotions
Opportunity	Alert, Loving, Anxious, Comfortable, Dynamic, Willing, In love, Active, Calm, Full of energy, Hopeful, Strong, Optimistic, Relaxed, Serene, Quiet, Vigorous
Joy	Excited, Funny, Enthusiastic, Motivated, Inspired, Determined, Happy, Thankful, Patient, Proud, Happy
Fear	Tired, Distressed, Fearful, Tense, Worried, Nervous, Restless
Dominance	Humiliated, Bothered, Irritated, Frightened, Disturbed, Spiteful

Finally, we calculated the percentual of each category of emotion experienced by the participants, in which they reported to us what kind of emotions they were feeling (pre-agree) or not feeling (pre-disagree) at the beginning of the hackathon as well as at the end of the event – post-agree and post-disagree (see Fig. 3).

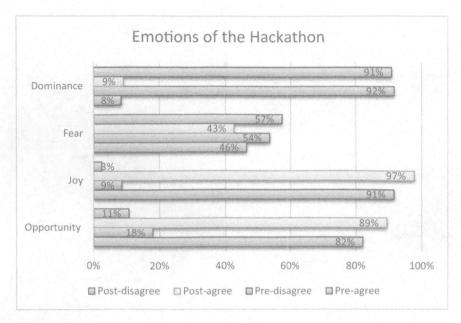

Fig. 3. Categories of emotions experienced by the participants.

We observed that most of the participants were experiencing positive emotions represented by Opportunity and Joy categories. We also observed that, despite a tiny increase in the negative emotions (1% in category Dominance), there was a curiously gain of positive emotions. In this way, the data lead us to reflect that the hackathons bring in most of the participant's positive emotions even at the end in which the teams are tired. Therefore, such emotions leverage the participants' chances of sharing their knowledge, as well as acquiring and using it, enhancing individual learning, engagement, creativity, and innovative solutions before the challenge.

4.2   Results Based on Interviews and Observations

To identify knowledge management in the hackathon, we interviewed post-event eight participants from different teams, i.e., immediately after team presentations. Our results were considerably remarkable once it reinforced our quantitative results presented previously.

During the interviews, when asked regarding previous knowledge and how they handle that in the event, the participants reported us that they brought their individual experience to combine with new knowledge acquired during team discussions. They reinforced that the new knowledge provided to them a sustainable and competitive advantage for the problem solve all long of the hackathon. In this context, the 'Interviewee A' quoted a previous experience, as observed below.

"Even being my first year at the university, I've already applied some of my knowledge that I have brought from my personal experiences to the hackathon." (Interviewee A, 21/10/2018).

"You know, through my previous experience, I contributed to my team in different sort of discussion. It's nice because I improved my knowledge regarding astronomy since we discuss the universe stuff." (Interviewee B, 21/10/2018).

In this way, we observed that interviewee A able to apply the knowledge acquired during the first University year in a proper solution and share the knowledge with the team. On the other hand, group discussions made interviewee B gain considerable knowledge concerning astronomy. The interviewee 'C' reported to us regarding work in the software development area and applied this knowledge to design solutions in the hackathon.

"I already work in IT area, and I applied my design and prototype knowledge for a good solution in my team. I helped them [the team] promptly." (Interviewee C, 21/10/2018).

Those quotes represent how relevant is the hackathons and how these events are linked with the processes od knowledge creation, sharing, and application. It is obvious apparently, but observing the event under the KM processes perspective is possible to get innovative insights and stimulate creative solutions skills for the participants both inside or outside of the event. On the other hand, we have missed the knowledge store process, relevant to the registration of the knowledge and solutions. We observed teams registering the solutions through knowledge products (i.e., software artifacts such as diagrams and code). Although we observed physical registration like post-it and notes, at the end of the event, the teams got rid of that material. This observation saddened us since this kind of knowledge produced during hard 24 h could be used in future projects or hackathons or even could be used by the organizers to improve the next hackathons.

During the interviews, some participants reported several cases of team members' conflict. Those conflicts comprise different proposals to solve hackathon challenges and to decide what proposal was 'the best' one. The interviewee also reported how they solved such conflicts, as shown in the quote below.

"I had several ideas, but each team member suggested different ideas, […] that conflict discouraged me." (Interviewee F, 21/10/2018).

"There was no disagreement in our team, each one of us arrived with three proposals, and we were tapering them considering positive and negative points. We discussed each one of those proposals, and we ranked those that would be most interesting until we reached an agreement of the team members." (Interviewee B, 21/10/2018).

"There were many different opinions to define the project, so we decided to take place a 'vote system' to support our decision." (Interviewee C, 21/10/2018).

"[…] we haven't problems [conflict] with the idea but concerned the technology to use. I know Java and my colleagues would like Python […] However, I saw an opportunity to learn Python" (Interviewee D, 21/10/2018).

Two most observed type of conflicts was regarding different project ideas and technologies to use. Those conflicts referred to divergences of opinion occurred during the solution design, i.e., when the teams are discussing the hackathon challenge and the tech to use. Most important than ideas and the tech was the path that the team members found out to solve those conflicts and further not discourage the team members – as quoted interviewee 'F'. Even though the conflict established in the team of intervie-wees 'B', 'C', and 'D', they had the maturity to figure those conflicts out. While the team of the interviewee 'C' found a democratic path to solve the conflict, the inter-viewee 'D' saw in the conflict the opportunity to knowledge improvement. It is fas-cinating since we have observed various conflicts at the beginning of the hackathon and some 'crisis' among the team members.

Moreover, the solution of the interviewee B team seemed more appropriate once they ranked positive and negative points of each proposal. Our further observations revealed that most of the team formation was not arranged in the event, i.e., the teams came to the hackathon already formed. We also observed just three people who came alone to find a team. So, conflicts may occur due to the degree of friendship between the teams, or because one team member wants to show more knowledge than the others to see the idea implemented satisfying the ego.

We know that each hackathon provides means to individuals learning about the challenge, solution, interpersonal relationship, and tech. Individual learning is the base of the knowledge once it mixes experience and learning. The learning is visible by the participants as well as they may see knowledge application. Learning is visible by the participants as well as they may see knowledge application. The quotes below show how interviewees 'E', 'G', and 'F' learned in terms of interaction.

"In this hackathon, I have learned a lot how to work in the team and interpersonal relationships because my team members had different points of view concerned the challenge. Hackathon is an amazing event" (Interviewee E, 21/10/2018).

"I felt an evolved of my interaction skills in this hackathon because I have negotiated solutions with my team. I'm proud of me for this because I really learned it [negotiation]" (Interviewee G, 21/10/2018).

"I have learned useful things in this hackathon to be practiced out of here and in my life, such as interpersonal relationships, technology skills, and fair play" (Interviewee F, 21/10/2018).

We observed the participants learning new matters in the hackathon. Interpersonal relationships paid our attention since, even the teams having a strong friendship bond, they had conflicts and learned to manage it. So, hackathons bring people to accomplish a challenge pushing the participants out and requiring skills such as interpersonal relationships. It shows us the teams executing the knowledge sharing process and the knowledge acquisition process.

At the beginning of the hackathon, the participant has demonstrated positive emotions and such as joy, motivation, happiness. Although our quantitative data have not demonstrated, after several hours in the event, the participants are before some negative emotions. Nonetheless, our research is a novel in the context of identifying the participant's [post, pre]-emotions in the hackathons. This verification is relevant so that the organizers could outline some strategies regarding the event to reduce the conflicts and keep positive emotions. So, when it comes to emotions, the interviewees 'A', 'C' and 'F' revealed some negative of them, such as tiredness.

"The hackathon was a lot of fun and the motivating environment, but after several hours here, it gets very tiring" (Interviewee A, 21/10/2018).

"There were disagreements in our team, I think because of tiredness [...]" (Interviewee C, 21/10/2018).

"I'm feeling [emotion] pleased to be here [in the hackathon]. However, now I'm tired because I'm in the event since it started [twelve-hours ago]" (Interviewee F, 21/10/2018).

In this sense, 24 h of 'keeping push' the intellectual work cause mental and physical tiredness in which is a trigger to other negative emotions. For instance, we observed two of 20 teams giving up the event after 12 h. Moreover, we observed some team members giving up of the hackathon after 16 h. When we asked why the teams and members gave up, they told us tiredness. So, our data suggested interesting findings, revealing four factors to be thinking for hackathons as follows: knowledge process, solving conflicts, individual learning, and experienced emotions. We discuss those findings deeply in the next section.

5 Discussion

Looking at this global hackathon closely, we empirical insights based on the literature to aid organizers manage future events leveraging KM. It is relevant since KM provides a set of processes capable of improving innovation and creativity, which should improve the solutions to the challenges. Following, we present our four factors in which impacts in KM leverage.

Knowledge Process. Looking at our empirical material closely, we observe the following knowledge management processes: creation, acquiring, sharing, storage, and use [5, 15, 16]. Knowledge use occurs through knowledge acquired and stored is shared among team members obeying a KM cycle [4] SECI model. The team members perform socialization, which provides knowledge creation through their interaction (tacit to tacit), creating knowledge sharing. Externalization is the design and discussion of the solution of the challenge through schemas, graphs, diagrams, or texts (implicit to explicit), creating knowledge storage. Internalization, whereas team members understand the answer (explicit to implicit) creating knowledge acquiring; and, finally, the combination in which team members can use previous experience with new acquire knowledge to propose solutions to hackathon's challenge (explicit to explicit) creating knowledge use. So, in hackathons, the individual's tacit knowledge is the leading way to solve the problems once the essence of problem-solving, innovative suggestions, creativity, design, analysis, and project management is based on more implicit, rather than explicit knowledge. In this sense, the hackathon organizers must rethink the ways to potentialize knowledge application to stimulate creativity and, consequently, knowledge creation, problem-solving, and innovation. They must offer pre-events such as workshops, training, mentoring, and so on. The NASA hackathon suggests a pre-event, namely boot camp. The boot camp intends to 'equalize' team members' knowledge to figure out the challenge with innovative solutions. We have observed different kinds of hackathons in our region; however, the hackathons which do not provide pre-events end up less innovative products than those which do.

Solving Conflicts. Team members' disagreements are frequent mainly over a creative process when a person wants his idea to overlap others. This kind of dispute results in lowered creativity [36]. When we look at the conflicts deeply, we observe that those are relevant to the hackathon's organizers since they improve the solution quality. So, the organizers should collect information regarding conflicts among team members during the event in different moments, such as the beginning and middle, once it involves different emotions of the participants. It concerns to learn more about discussions and organize means to support teams to figure their conflict out in the hackathons' event. A possibility to avoid team conflict is offering lectures to the participants regarding interpersonal relationships within the pre-event. Those lectures should be conducted by inviting psychology professionals and students in which would present techniques of conflict solving.

Individual Learning. We observed that all respondents reported that a hackathon is an event in which it facilitates learning practically and interactively. This solid form refers to the fact that such projects are elaborated and executed during the same period of the event. Furthermore, the interactive way can be related to the socialization that the event provides among the participants. Once hackathons are events of challenges based on basic functionalities due to the short time of the event, [41] highlights that the individual learning project is one that has a specific time, seeking to teach something relevant from the project and interaction with the team. Working on a project, the individuals might learn in practice, internalizing their knowledge [5]. Thus, hackathons bring a constructivist approach in which aligned to different personal or work contexts [43]. So, the hackathon's organizers should stimulate individual learning in hackathons offering online courses, tutorials, and materials before the hackathon begins to afford creative insights for the participants.

Experienced Emotions. The participants experienced different emotions, some of them positive (i.e., joy and opportunity) [21, 26] in contrast with dominance and fear. According to [21, 26], the effects of positive emotions share the capacity to enlarge people's momentary repertoires and create their enduring personal resources, from physical and intellectual resources to social and psychological resources. Positive emotions occur when positive changes are perceived, significantly improving a situation [24]. The positive emotions reflect how much a person feels enthusiastic, active, and alert, being a state of high energy, total concentration, and pleasurable engagement [27]. Also, the other participant highlighted the happiness of attending the event.

However, the hackathons closely, we observed the motivation and engagement of the participants. On the other hand, we found tiredness and discouragement. Despite an environment all prepared and conducive to creativity, we noted some team members are giving up their participation in the hackathon. Unfortunately, we have not interviewed the members who gave up on the event, but we interviewed some of their team members in which reported us some motivations for the withdrawal of its members, namely tiredness, discouraged, and afraid to be ashamed of the proposed solution during the pitches.

Based on this kind of behavior, we should rethink the hackathon's design, trying to avoid those negative emotions (i.e., tiredness, discouraged, and afraid). Hackathons' organizers should reduce twenty-four hours to twelve-hours proposing short challenges in a format of mini-hackathons like mini-marathons. Secondly, take place the hackathons during daylight, e.g., three days of eight-hours-day. Finally, allow some members, particularly those who feel more tiring, might participate virtually.

Therefore, our findings pointed out that the hackathon's organizers should rethink the design of the hackathons considering four factors. The first category, knowledge process, shows that the hackathon takes place a KM cycle, which converts knowledge tacit to explicit and vice-versa, providing the store and use of hackathons knowledge for future events. The second category, solving conflicts, show a fragility of the team members to handle the clash of ideas and how this is detrimental to the team's creativity and coexistence during the event most of the time discourage the team members from continuing the challenges. The third category brought to us how individual learning is essential to and should be stimulated before the event to improve the solutions to afford ideas and creativity to the participants. Finally, the fourth category, namely experienced emotions, show how relevant is the feelings of the individuals during the event and how the tiredness can be unfavorable to solve the challenges given in the hackathon. Moreover, our contribution could be tested within tech (or non-tech) companies through internal hackathons or even new projects. Table 2 summarizes our findings of this research.

Table 2. Summarizing the research findings.

Finding	Strategy
Knowledge process	To potentialize problem-solving, innovation, and the creativity of the participants. A pre-event should offer workshops, training, and mentoring regarding knowledge management tools and practices
Solving conflicts	Gather information regarding conflicts that occurred within team members to try to avoid conflicts. Offer in pre-event courses or lectures concerning the interpersonal relationship
Individual learning	Stimulate individual learning before the event through online courses, mentoring, and knowledge database (i.e., wiki, yammer)
Experienced emotions	Try to avoid tiredness and negative emotions rethinking about the period of the event, maybe reducing from twenty-four hours to twelve-hours offering short challenges (e.g., mini-hackathon). Alternatively, take place the event during daylight (*e.g.*, three days during eight-hours by day). Finally, allow members who feel tiring to continue its participation from home, i.e., virtually

5.1   Study Limitations

Although we investigated a global hackathon, we limited in just one venue. It might create a bias in the analysis of our empirical data. So, we encourage researchers to investigate those four factors in different venues or even hackathons to improve our understanding of the relation between KM and this sort of event. Moreover, we did not analyze the emotions of the participants closely. Finally, for the future works, we intend to improve our understanding of positive and negative emotions and how organizers should stimulate positive to avoid the negative ones.

6 Conclusion

This paper presented the findings of an international hackathon to help its organizers rethink their strategies to leverage KM, aiming to stimulate innovation and creativity to solve the proposed challenge. To this end, we conducted mixed through a questionnaire – regarding participants' emotions and interviews conducted post-event. Moreover, we observed the participants in the event for 24 h visiting different teams and taking notes. The results pointed out that organizers should consider strategies for improving knowledge application, conflict resolution, individual learning, and emotions experienced during the [pre, post]-event. In this way, our findings pointed out four factors in which should be considered to rethink the strategies of the hackathon to leverage KM and, consequently, innovation and creativity in this sort of event as follows: *knowledge process*, *solving conflicts*, *individual learning*, and *experienced emotions*.

References

1. Vivanco-Galván, O.A., Castillo-Malla, D., Jiménez-Gaona, Y.: HACKATHON multidisciplinario: fortalecimiento del aprendizaje basado en proyectos. Rev. Electrónica Calid. en la Educ. Super. **9**, 119–135 (2018)
2. Flores, M., et al.: How can hackathons accelerate corporate innovation? Cambridge Serv. Alliance. **1**, 1–8 (2018)
3. Briscoe, G., Mulligan, C.: Digital innovation: the hackathon phenomenon. Creat. London. 1–13 (2014)
4. Nonaka, I., Toyama, R., Konno, N.: SECI, ba and leadership: a unified model of dynamic knowledge creation. Long Range Plann. **33**, 5–34 (2000). https://doi.org/10.1016/S0024-6301(99)00115-6
5. Dalkir, K.: Knowledge Management in Theory and Practice. Cambridge, MA (2017). https://doi.org/10.1002/asi.21613
6. Seravalli, A., Simeone, L.: Performing hackathons as a way of positioning boundary organizations. J. Organ. Chang. Manag. **29**, 326–343 (2016). https://doi.org/10.1108/JOCM-04-2013-0060
7. Serrano-Laguna, Á., Rotaru, D.-C., Calvo-Morata, A., Torrente, J., Fernández-Manjón, B.: Creating interactive content in android devices: the Mokap Hackaton. In: Díaz, P., Pipek, V., Ardito, C., Jensen, C., Aedo, I., Boden, A. (eds.) IS-EUD 2015. LNCS, vol. 9083, pp. 287–290. Springer, Cham (2015). https://doi.org/10.1007/978-3-319-18425-8_31
8. Tenório, N., et al.: Rethinking strategies of hackathons to increase team's creativity: findings of a qualitative research. In: IC3K 2019 – Proceedings of Joint Conference on Knowledge Discovery, Knowledge Engineering and Knowledge Management, vol. 3, pp. 92–101 (2019). https://doi.org/10.5220/0008164300920101

9. Zukin, S., Papadantonakis, M.: Hackathons as Co-optation Ritual: Socializing Workers and Institutionalizing Innovation in the "New" Economy. In: Precarious Work. pp. 157–181. Emerald Publishing Limited, Bingley (2017)

10. Richterich, A.: Hacking events. Converg. Int. J. Res. into New Media Technol. 135485651770940 (2017). https://doi.org/10.1177/1354856517709405

11. Calco, M., Veeck, A.: The Markathon: adapting the hackathon model for an introductory marketing class project. Mark. Educ. Rev. **25**, 33–38 (2015). https://doi.org/10.1080/10528008.2015.999600

12. Lourenço, G.C.U., Gonçalves, R. de C.B., Miguel, G., Tenório, N.: Aprendizagem Na Indústria De Software: A Investigação De Um Hackathon Interno. In: Anais do Encontro de Ensino, Pesquisa e Extensão da Unoeste - ENEPE 2018. p. 8. Unoeste, Presidente Prudente (2018)

13. Lourenço, G.C.U., Gonçalves, R.deC.B., Oliveira, G.M.de, Tenório, N.: Aprendizagem Na Indústria De Software: A Investigação De Um Hackathon Interno. In: ENEPE - Encontro de Ensino, Pesquisa e Extensão da Unoeste, pp. 1–8. Unoeste, Presidente Prudente (2018)

14. Nonaka, I., Toyama, R., Hirata, T.: Managing Flow: A Process Theory of the Knowledge-Based Firm. Springer (2008)

15. Davenport, T.H., Prusak, L.: Working knowledge: how organizations manage what they know [Book Review]. IEEE Eng. Manag. Rev. **31**, 137–137 (2003). https://doi.org/10.1109/EMR.2003.1267012

16. Tenório, N., Pinto, D., Ferrarezi Vidotti, A., Santos de Oliveira, M., Caroline Urbano, G., Bortolozzi, F.: Tool based on knowledge management process: an interview protocol to gather functional requirements from software industry experts. MATTER Int. J. Sci. Technol. **3**, 45–54 (2017). https://doi.org/10.20319/Mijst.2017.31.4554

17. Santos, M., Lourenço, G.C.U., Gomes, L.R.L., Bortolozzi, F., Tenório, N.: Managing knowledge products: a system architecture addressed to software industry. Perspect. em Gestão Conhecimento. **8**, 151–166 (2018). https://doi.org/10.21714/2236-417x2018v8nep151

18. Nonaka, I.: A dynamic theory of organizational knowledge creation. Organ. Sci. **5**, 14–37 (1994). https://doi.org/10.1287/orsc.5.1.14

19. Goleman, D.: Emotional intelligence (10th anniversary trade pbk. ed.). New York (2005)

20. Bagozzi, R.P., Gopinath, M., Nyer, P.U.: The role of emotions in marketing. J. Acad. Mark. Sci. **27**, 184–206 (1999). https://doi.org/10.1177/0092070399272005

21. Fredrickson, B.L.: What good are positive emotions? Rev. Gen. Psychol. **2**, 300 (1998)

22. Fredrickson, B.L.: Positive Emotions Broaden and Build. Copyright © 2013, Elsevier Inc. All rights reserved. (2013). https://doi.org/10.1016/B978-0-12-407236-7.00001-2

23. Carver, C.S., Scheier, M.F.: Origins and functions of positive and negative affect: a control-process view. Psychol. Rev. **97**, 19 (1990)

24. Hazelton, S.: Positive emotions boost employee engagement. Hum. Resour. Manag. Int. Dig. (2014)

25. Ben-Ze'ev, A.: The Subtlety of Emotions. MIT Press, Cambridge (2001)

26. Shaver, P., et al.: Emotion Knowledge : Further Exploration of a Prototype Approach 52 (1987)

27. Kleef, G.A. Van, Dreu, C.K.W. De, Manstead, A.S.R.: An Interpersonal Approach to Emotion in Social Decision Making: The Emotions as Social Information Model. Elsevier Inc. 2010 (2010). https://doi.org/10.1016/S0065-2601(10)42002-X

28. Watson, D., Clark, L.A., Tellegen, A.: Development and validation of brief measures of positive and negative affect: the PANAS scales. J. Pers. Soc. Psychol. **54**, 1063–1070 (1988). https://doi.org/10.1037/0022-3514.54.6.1063

29. Kahneman, D., Krueger, A.B., Schkade, D.A., Schwarz, N., Stone, A.A.: A survey method for characterizing daily life experience: The day reconstruction method. Science (80). **306**, 1776–1780 (2004)

30. Fredrickson, B.L.: The role of positive emotions in positive psychology. The broaden-and-built theory of positive emotions. Am. Psychol. **56**, 218–226 (2001). https://doi.org/10.1037/0003-066X.56.3.218

31. Wu, G., Zhao, X., Zuo, J.: Effects of inter-organizational conflicts on construction project added value in China. In: Int. J. Confl. Manag. (2017)

32. Thomas, K.W.: Thomas-Kilmann Conflict Mode Instrument. Xicom, New York (1974)

33. Wang, Q., Fink, E.L., Cai, D.A.: The effect of conflict goals on avoidance strategies: what does not communicating communicate? Hum. Commun. Res. **38**, 222–252 (2012). https://doi.org/10.1111/j.1468-2958.2011.01421.x

34. Pichon, F., Jousselme, A.-L., Abdallah, N.: Ben: several shades of conflict. Fuzzy Sets Syst. **366**, 63–84 (2019)

35. Rao, M.S.: Tools and techniques to resolve organizational conflicts amicably. Ind. Commer. Train. **49**, 93–97 (2017). https://doi.org/10.1108/ICT-05-2016-0030

36. Chen, Y.Q., Zhang, Y.B., Zhang, S.J.: Impacts of different types of owner-contractor conflict on cost performance in construction projects. J. Constr. Eng. Manag. **140**, 04014017 (2014). https://doi.org/10.1061/(ASCE)CO.1943-7862.0000852

37. Reiter-Palmon, R., Murugavel, V.: The Effect of problem construction on team process and creativity **9**, 2098 (2018). https://doi.org/10.3389/fpsyg.2018.02098

38. Hwang, B.-G., Zhao, X., Ng, S.Y.: Identifying the critical factors affecting schedule performance of public housing projects. Habitat Int. **38**, 214–221 (2013). https://doi.org/10.1016/j.habitatint.2012.06.008

39. Cornford, I.R.: Imperatives in teaching for lifelong learning: Moving beyond rhetoric to effective educational practice. Asia-Pacific J. Teach. Educ. **27**, 107–117 (1999)

40. Sanchez, R.: Knowledge Management and Organizational Competence. Oxford University Press, New York (2010)

41. de Melo, A.V.C., de Araújo, E.A.: Competência informacional e gestão do conhecimento: uma relação necessária no contexto da sociedade da informação. Perspect. em Ciência da Informação. **12**, 185–201 (2007)

42. Roberson Jr., D.N., Merriam, S.B.: The self-directed learning process of older, rural adults. Adult Educ. Q. **55**, 269–287 (2005)

43. O'Hara, S.: Organizational change through individual learning. Career Dev. Int. (1996)

44. Voinea, M., Purcaru, M.: Individual Learning plan in teaching mathematics for children with SEN–a constructivist approach. Procedia-Soc. Behav. Sci. **187**, 190–195 (2015)

45. Zambrano, J., Kirschner, F., Sweller, J., Kirschner, P.A.: Effects of prior knowledge on collaborative and individual learning. Learn. Instr. **63**, 101214 (2019)

46. Creswell, J.W., Creswell, J.D.: Research Design: Qualitative, Quantitative, and Mixed Methods Approaches. Sage Publications, Thousand Oaks (2017)

47. Randall, D., Harper, R., Rouncefield, M.: Fieldwork for Design. Springer, London (2007). https://doi.org/10.1007/978-1-84628-768-8

48. Topi, H., Tucker, A.: Computing Handbook: Information Systems and Information Technology. CRC Press, Boca Raton (2014)

49. Leckart, S.: The hackathon is on: Pitching and programming the next killer app. Wired, San Fr. 17, (2012)
50. NASA: Space Apps Challenge. https://2018.spaceappschallenge.org/
51. Fowler, F.J.: Survey Research Methods, 5th edn. SAGE Publications, London (2014)
52. Orange: Orange Documentation. https://orange.biolab.si/docs/. Accessed 28 Mar 2020
53. Bramer, M.: Principles of Data Mining. Springer, London (2019). https://doi.org/10.1007/978-1-4471-7307-6
54. Saldaña, J.: The Coding Manual for Qualitative Researchers. SAGE Publications, London (2013)
55. Hart, C.M., Van Vugt, M.: From fault line to group fission: understanding membership changes in small groups. Personal. Soc. Psychol. Bull. 32, 392–404 (2006). https://doi.org/10.1177/0146167205282149

Guide for the Implementation of Sustainable Development Through a Territorial Ontology Within Enterprises

Amer Ezoji[✉], Nada Matta, and Robain Lallier

ICD/TECH-CICO, University of Technology of Troyes,
12 Rue Marie Curie, Troyes, France
{amer.ezoji,nada.matta,robin.lallier}@utt.fr

Abstract. Studying territorial knowledge can increase decision-makers' information when considering sustainable development implementation. Enterprises consider territorial resources in terms of sustainability when selecting a location. This paper proposes a territorial ontology to help the enterprise and organizations to capture the territorial resources when they want to integrate these resources into their activities for sustainable development. This application ontology tested in three organization of sustainable development to validate the usability of it. These tests validate that territorial application ontology enhances strategic decision making for sustainability. Moreover, the ontology of the domain of DOKT, as a guide, provides to capture the territorial knowledge of every geographic territory. Also, this paper suggests ongoing research for visualization of territorial knowledge on the site for the usage of all enterprises and organizations.

Keywords: Territorial knowledge · DOTK · Sustainable development · Enterprises

1 Introduction

Regarding the increasing role of sustainability, implementation of sustainability is often difficult because of poor communication between experts from different academic fields. Moreover, enterprises need to integrate sustainability into their activities for sustainable development goals [21]. In the literature review and in consulting with sustainable development's organization, lack of territorial knowledge is distinguished as the main problem for improving the sustainability within enterprises. So, it needs to capture and represent territorial knowledge. Thus, Ontology can facilitate information sharing and exchange in the various engineering domains by providing concept structures and clarifications that make explicit and precise important notions. Therefore, a descriptive ontology of territorial knowledge (DOTK) modeled to prepare a model for capturing the intangible and tangible resources of each geographic territory [9]. DOTK aims to provide territorial resources for the needs of sustainable development organizations and enterprises.

This research is centered on sustainable development's organization embedded in a territory whining 5 dimensions (5D) of sustainability. Sustainability with 5 dimensions has been adapted with the environmental, social, economic, political sphere, and territorial dimensions [13]. Three-use cases scenario is defined about the usability of DOTK in cooperation with top-managers of organization. These use cases clarify how DOTK ontology can use by these organizations to help the sustainable development of enterprises. To validate of usability of these scenarios, application ontology is defined by DOTK. Thus, application ontology is extracted the intangible and tangible resources of Troyes city in France that these organizations located in this geographic territory. The aim is to demonstrate the usability of DOTK for extracting territorial resources for sustainable development objectives within industries. Territorial resources of Troyes are extracted by the essence and meaning of concepts of DOTK that show the usability of DOTK to explore the resources of each geographic territory.

Extracted territorial resources by application ontology of territorial are validated by Top-manger of sustainable development organizations that provide the resources for them to make a sustainable decision at the strategic level.

This paper proposes the visualization of DOTK on the website to use it by every enterprise or organization in every geographic territory. The different methods of visualization discuss and one method is selected to visualize DOTK. The first phase of visualization is the realization of the visualization that is performed. The second phase is the development of the site that is ongoing work.

2 Implementation of Sustainable Development Within Industries

The growing attention given to sustainable development is encouraging companies to integrate sustainable issues into their activities. To increase the performance of this integration, some literature points out that sustainable aspects should be embedded at all corporate hierarchical levels, from global strategic decisions by top management, through planning and organization by tactical management, to daily engineering and production activities of the operational area [21].

Sustainability issues affect every component from individuals to regional and global organizations: major ecological or social crises are due to natural resource overconsumption and rising inequality at both local and global scales [1]. Sustainability is a system property; therefore products, services, technology or organization cannot be sustainable on their own but may be elements of sustainable systems [14]. Therefore, sustainable strategy cannot be considered an independent issue: it must be integrated into corporate global development strategy. This integration needs to support sustainable goals to be in line with other existing global corporate tendencies and constraints. To do so, the company needs to carefully and reasonably break down "sustainability" into several actions or attributes to help its comprehension [15]. Social, ecological, economic, territorial and governance dimensions of sustainability are explored and a set of sustainability principles are integrated into an industrial organizational governance [1].

It focuses sustainability objectives on human development (social sphere). The environment is considered as the limiting factor for anthropic activity (ecological sphere). The economic sphere is investigated as a mean (not a goal), which enables the realization of social objectives with respect to ecological boundaries. The political sphere has to define development guidelines and must be strong enough to take precedence over economic actors. The political sphere is addressed as the place for public debate and long-term societal orientation and decision-making. In fact, public policies are the only legitimate way to define public interest and the common good; consequently, they must coordinate sustainable industrial strategies and expectations from civil society [7]. The territorial dimension should also be taken into account, adapting global policy to local specificities to develop appropriate solutions. Over and above its administrative boundaries, a territory is an evolving and complex combination of a set of actors and the geographical space that these actors use, landscape and manage [18]. Moreover, 'Territory' is studied as a value creation network where tangible and intangible resources flow [1]. Therefore, it's need to depth understanding of structure of territory for sustainable objective by industrial organization to integrate territorial resources to their activities. So, in the following sub- section, importance of industrial organization for implementation of sustainable development is explained.

2.1 Industrial Organization for Integration of Sustainability

The integration of sustainability can be improved by developing a coherent and systematic approach between strategic, tactical, and operational levels. Sustainable integration could be improved by better cooperative circulation between the different company levels (strategic, tactical, and operational). The strategic level assists "top managers" who define the corporate strategic goals that will create multi-values for all stakeholders. In order to respond to strategic goals, the tactical level analyzes and organizes the corporate material and immaterial resources (for example cost, knowledge, human resource, relationship with stakeholders, or organization.) and develops an efficient and implementable roadmap. This matches the strategic goals with specific technological solutions and identifies related "activity tables/chains" to help meet these goals. Lastly, the operational level supports the deployment of the process in the company in accordance with the tactics (and tools) chosen [21]. So, strategy and tactical level within the industry have the main role to organize and integrate the material and immaterial resources for sustainability. These material and immaterial resources are territorial resources as defined.

The strategies aim at facilitating exchanges of tangible or intangible resources between actors of a local network in order to create value for both the companies and the territory. Organizational innovation has come to be a key factor for a company and its stakeholders in a changing, competitive, and constrained environment [2]. Moreover, governance principles in order to facilitate coordination between political, territorial, and company spheres are needed [1].

The necessary coordination between these three organizational levels supports by the three principles for sustainable governance proposed by [6]: capability, proximity, and participatory democracy. Participatory Democracy aims to build a balance between individual preferences and the common interest in meeting the challenges of sustainable development. This reconciles company and social expectations. Capability/ empowerment aims to maintain and develop the capacity of organizations/individuals to meet their own expectations. Proximity aims to bring together the decision-making level and the level impacted by the decision. So, the organizational level in industries has a significant role to coordinate between political, territorial, and company sphere. In addition, it can help the integration of tangible and intangible resources of territory within the industrial organization for sustainable goals.

2.2   Necessity of Territorial Knowledge for Sustainability

French public policymakers as a promising both economic and social value creation consider territorial competitiveness. Companies consider territorial specificities when selecting a location (e.g. low production costs, highly qualified labor pool) from a utilitarian perspective. Allais (2015) at her research encourage the companies to consider territory as a value creation network and integrate these latent territorial resources into the product development process to create value for both the company and its territory from a sustainable perspective [2]. In fact, he demonstrated from industrial cases that integration of tangibles and intangible territorial resources into the product design process adds value for the customer, the company, and its territory. Moreover, Allais (2015) aids industrial companies to both explore the use of latent resources from their territory and to their responsibility facing their stakeholders in a sustainable perspective [2].

In another research by Zhang et al. (2013), better circulation between the different organizational functions in a company is considered to show the improvement of the integration of sustainable issues [21]. Moreover, studying a product's environmental impact on an interacted territory's environmental statues can increase decision maker's information when considering design for sustainability [19].

There are different sustainable development organizations in Troyes city in France that implement the sustainable development for companies according to territorial resources of this city. Troyes is the capital of the department of Aube in north central of France and Textile companies' production is a popular clothing brand as the economy of this city.

These organizations are: Troyes Champagne Métropole (TCM), Biogaz vallée and Business Sud Champagne (BSC). The organizations are presented in Table 1.

Table 1. Presentation of organizations of sustainable developments.

Organizations	Troyes Champagne Métroploe (TCM)	Business Sud Champagne (BSC)	Boigaz Vallée
Sector	Sustainable development of municipalities and communities	Is the new economic development agency of the Aube	An organization that it is open to all players, national and international, to advance the biogas sector by creating value in the territories, in France
Activity and missions	Economic development in industrial area, Landscaping, Social balance of housing, City policy, Environment and sustainable development	The promotion of the territory, Business prospecting, Support for strategic businesses, ensuring the operational implementation of the strategic action plan, enhance the attractiveness of the territory	Accelerate the connection and networking, Share best practices to promote sustainability, Facilitate access to financing, Develop the creation of skilled industrial jobs, Stimulate innovation

During of interviews with top-mangers of these organizations, they clarified about the needs of territorial resources as territorial knowledge to use them for implementation of sustainable development within companies. For example, there are the enterprises in Troyes that don't have enough knowledge about the territorial resources for implementation sustainable development within their enterprises. Another example is related to the enterprises that are intended to transfer their companies to Troyes. But they don't know about the exiting territorial resources in Troyes. So, they request from these organizations to implement the sustainable development in their company. Therefore, these organizations need to know about the types of existing territorial resources to present them to these enterprises.

In addition, TCM presented an example about the integrating of territorial knowledge in their projects for urban transport in Troyes (TCAT). TCM is pointed the problem for capturing of knowledge about all of existing and non- existing territorial resources in Troyes to implement the sustainable development in TCAT's projects. Because TCM helps the TCAT in different social, economic and environmental projects. While, it is necessary to know which types of these resources can help it in their project. So, TCM need to know about geographical, human, economic and political capital of Troyes in order to integrate these resources in the project of TCAT. So, the general question for the enterprises and organizations is: which types of territorial resources do exist?

There are so many researches about the territory that didn't consider the capturing and representation of territorial resources. Therefore, it can be concluded that it should capture and make explicit the territorial resources because, at first, there are not enough knowledge about all of existing territorial resources for sustainable development and, secondly, identification of territorial resources facilitates to make a decision for sustainability.

So, interviews with these organizations and literature review show that there is not enough knowledge about the territory's features, its environment and their integrity for implementation of sustainable development. They are barriers to search a possible concept and knowledge in order to improve the sustainable objective of local and regional companies. Moreover, it wasn't identified which type of territorial resources affect the sustainable development of industrial companies. So, the following research questions are extracted to answer the research problem and needs of organizations for implementation of sustainable development:

1. Which type of territorial Knowledge affects the sustainability's goal of industrial companies?
2. How represent and share this knowledge for sustainability's objective within industrial companies?
3. Territorial knowledge helps which level of hierarchical corporate level for sustainable development?

So, it is need to find a tool to capture the territorial knowledge. It is assumed to represent this knowledge by ontology. In other words, territorial ontology can facilitate territorial knowledge sharing and justify the resources of territory for implementation of sustainable development within industries. Moreover, territorial ontology can present to these organizations to provide the answer for these research questions and their needs through the usability of this ontology in their activities for sustainable development.

The aim is helping the companies' hierarchical levels in order to increase their knowledge about their territorial resources to integrate this knowledge into their activities for sustainable development goal and especially, the decision making of hierarchical level to create the value for human in regard to existing territorial knowledge. In the following section, the methodology for modeling a territorial ontology introduces.

3 Methodology

Ontology is a suitable method for the representation of dispersed knowledge of tangible and intangible resources of the territory. Ontology is a formal, explicit specification of a shared conceptualization. So, it provides a common understanding of a domain that can be communicated between people and the application system [12]. Moreover, ontology can explicit the assumptions and analyze the domain knowledge [20]. Territorial knowledge's ontology is a tool to manage territorial resources and facilitate the consideration of the complex relationships among different types of territorial knowledge to make the decision toward sustainability.

Therefore, some necessary principles for constructing of territorial ontology are needed. The first principle for modeling ontology is issues of knowledge representation to complete the definitions for the categories of objects by descriptive knowledge. So, Normalizing helps the use of notions and agreement on the meaning of notions by their explicit descriptions. The second principle is normalizing by necessary and sufficient conditions. A usual way of normalizing the descriptive knowledge consists of the stating of necessary relations between notions. So, the normalizing condition makes the explicit distance between the intentional definition of a type and its extension. So, the knowledge normalization must be carried out to assign the complete definitions of types. The last principle is characterizing the essential and taxonomy. The essence of notions should capture by assigning the definitions of notions and their essential properties. Thus, the types are defined by deciding the essential characteristics to build the ontology of the domain. Also, the meaning of properties must be understood through its positions in the ontology [3, 5, 10].

Therefore, the methodology for modeling ontology of territorial knowledge according to the mentioned principles is:

1. The taxonomy of elements of territorial knowledge. This taxonomy is made according to four categories of geographical, human, economic, and political capital. Also, their sub-elements are identified in regard to five dimensions of sustainability [8].
2. The second step is the normalizing of these elements based on the foundational ontology of DOLCE (Descriptive Ontology for Linguistic and Cognitive Engineering) [14] which extracted their basic meaning [9].
3. Finally, the ontology of territorial knowledge is modeled [9].

4 Ontology of Territorial Knowledge

Characterizing the ontological taxonomy of territorial knowledge is made according to the essence of notions and basic meaning of DOLCE ontology [4] that help to understand the meaning of territorial knowledge's concepts through its position in the ontology. So, a Descriptive Ontology for Territorial Knowledge (DOTK) according to the mentioned methodology is modeled [10] as can be seen in Fig. 1. DOTK has three main top entities such as endurant, perdurant, and abstract.

Endurants are wholly present in which they exist and mainly as a physical object. In other words, they are physical and non- physical, according to whether they have entities with spatial qualities or not. Perdurants just extend in time by accumulating different temporal parts, so that, at any time they are present, they are only partially present, in the sense that some of their proper temporal parts (e.g., their previous or future phases) maybe not present such as event and processes. Abstracts are entities that exist neither in time nor in space. In fact, abstracts do not have spatial or temporal qualities such as fact and attribute [14].

DOTK identifies the meaning and why reasoning of the element of territorial knowledge. In other words, the essence of each territorial element can follow in DOTK to understand its meaning. So, DOTK provides more details about the intention of territorial knowledge taxonomy. Moreover, DOTK is a guide for the identification of resources of a specific territory. Entities of DOTK assist to extract the resources of the territory. So, in this way, application ontology is made that the identified resources can help the hierarchical levels of industries for sustainable development goals.

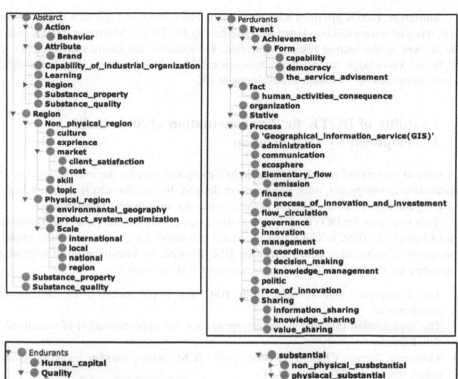

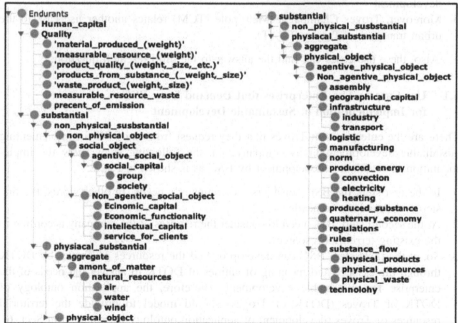

Fig. 1. Hierarchy class of DOTK [10].

Moreover, DOTK provides a response to the first and second research questions. In fact, types of territorial knowledge are identified by DOTK [8]. Moreover, DOTK gives the answer to the second research question. It explicates the essence of concepts of territorial knowledge for actors of hierarchical level of companies and helps their communications for sustainable development [9].

5 Usability of DOTK for Implementation of Sustainable Development by Organization

In order to understand how DOTK can help the organization for the implementation of sustainable development, three use cases are defined. In fact, the aim is to demonstrate how organizations can use DOTK in their works for sustainable development.

Two use cases for DOTK of Troyes is discussed during of interview with Business Sud Champagne (BSC). These two use cases can assist the companies in the implementation of sustainable development by BSC through the identification of territorial resources by DOTK. So, these two use cases of BSC consist:

1. The enterprises that demand from BSC for implementation of sustainable development.
2. The organization that search the enterprises for the implementation of sustainable development
3. Moreover, Troyes Champagne Métropole (TCM) relates another use case to the urban transport in Troyes (TCAT).

Also, these use cases can find the answer to the third research question.

5.1 Use Case 1: The Enterprises that Demand from BSC for Implementation of Sustainable Development

There are the enterprises in Troyes that they request from the BSC for implementing sustainable development in its company. So, the following steps show the implementation of sustainable development by BSC as is shown in Fig. 2:

1. In the first step, the BSC considers the company's needs. In other words, the first step is the analysis of needs.
2. At the second step, BSC need to consider the requires of the company according to the existing territorial resources.
3. So, at the third step, BSC can develop or find the resources of Troyes by DOTK through the essence and meaning of entities of DOTK to answer the needs of the enterprise for sustainable development. Therefore, the application ontology of DOTK of Troyes (DOTK of Troyes) should model to provide the territorial resources of Troyes (development of application ontology is explained in Sect. 6). So, in this way, the BSC can find the resources or one alternative solution to respond to the demand of the enterprise.

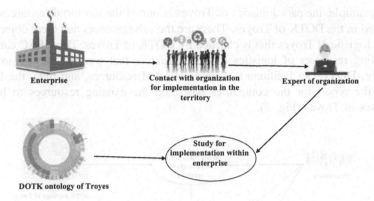

Fig. 2. Scenario of use case 1.

So, it is clarified how the BSC uses the application ontology of DOTK of Troyes for executing sustainable development in different projects of companies. Therefore, BSC by this application could aid the decision making for sustainable development within companies. The sequence model this use case is demonstrated in Fig. 3.

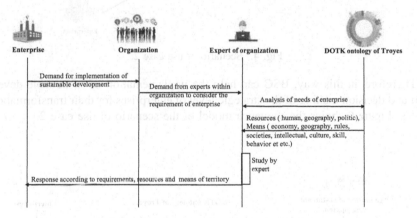

Fig. 3. Sequence model of use case 1 [11].

5.2   Use Case 2: The Organization that Search the Enterprises for Implementation of Sustainable Development

BSC, also, searches the other companies in the other geographical territory to transfer them to Troyes and help them for implementing sustainable development. The scenario of this use case explains below and it is demonstrated in Fig. 4.

1. At first, BSC needs to consider all of the existing territorial resources in DOTK of Troyes.
2. In the second step, the BSC searches the enterprises that can be interested in these territorial resources in a particular domain.

For example, the park logistics of Troyes is one of the territorial resources that are mentioned in the DOTK of Troyes. There are the sub-resources and clear objectives for the park logistic of Troyes that is clarified by DOTK of Troyes. Thus, BSC can present the existing resources of logistics to the companies that want to transfer to Troyes. Therefore, DOTK can facilitate the presentation of resources, and then, the BSC can prepare the report for the companies based on the existing resources to bring the enterprises in Troyes (Fig. 5).

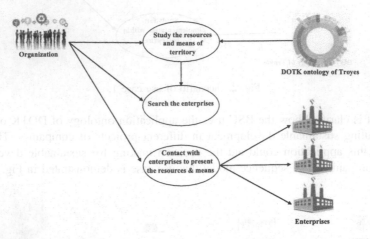

Fig. 4. Scenario of use case 2.

Therefore, in this way, BSC can help the implementation of sustainable development and decision making of the strategic level of enterprises for their transformation to Troyes. Figure 6 shows the sequence model of the scenario of use case 2.

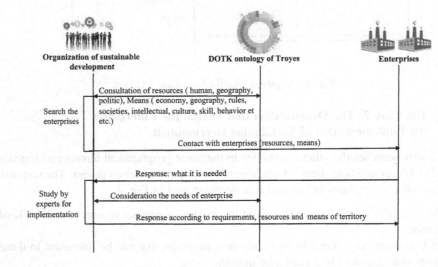

Fig. 5. Sequence model of use case 2.

5.3   Use Case 3: Usage of DOTK of Troyes for TCAT

As mentioned, TCAT cooperates with TCM to apply the global travel policy in Troyes. TCM implements sustainable development for a different project of TCAT in the following steps.

1. In the first step, TCM considers what TCAT needs for its project.
2. In the second step, TCM searches the existing and non-existing territorial resources in DOTK of Troyes about the project of TCAT.

Then, TCM develops the resources for the improvement of the project of TCAT. Therefore, DOTK of Troyes helps the TCM to analyze the real resources, real needs, and develop the resources for its project of sustainable development. These steps are shown in Fig. 6.

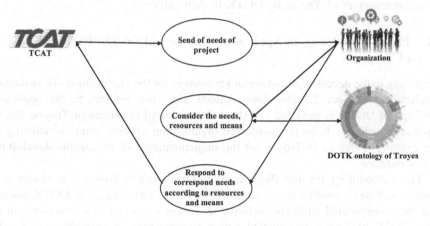

Fig. 6. Scenario of use case 3.

Therefore, resources of DOTK of Troyes in the project of TCAT cover the three dimensions of sustainable development (social, economic and environmental) because there are the resources such as culture, behavior, social object, environmental regulation, rules, the quaternary economy in the DOTK which justify the usability of all dimensions of sustainable development.

It is concluded from three use cases that DOTK of Troyes gives the strategic development viewpoint to top-managers for implementing sustainable development within companies. The existing territorial resources of Troyes help the top-manager during their communication with the strategic and tactical level of the enterprise to decide for sustainability. It is concluded that DOTK of Troyes could help the decision making of the strategic and tactic level of companies through the top-mangers of organizations indirectly.

Besides, providing the DOTK of Troyes for organizations aid them to know the existing resources of Troyes. In the following section, the methodology for modeling DOTK of Troyes presents.

6   DOTK of Troyes for Implementation of Sustainable Development by Organizations

This step aims to make application ontology to show how DOTK provides territorial resources for organizations and companies. In other words, this application ontology can be used by organizations in three use cases mentioned. Two phases consider in this section. The first phase is modeling the application ontology of DOTK to extract the intangible and tangible resources of the geographical territory of Troyes. The second phase is a survey interview with mentioned organizations about the usability of extracted resources of Troyes by DOTK in their activities.

6.1   Phase 1: Modeling an Application Ontology of DOTK (DOTK of Troyes)

According to the necessity of territorial knowledge for the organizations of sustainable development in Sect. 2.2 and three defined use cases in Sect. 5, the application ontology of DOTK is modeled to extract the territorial resources of Troyes. So, this application ontology helps the mentioned organization to know about the existing and non-existing resources in Troyes for the implementation of sustainable development within industries.

The methodology for identifying territorial resources of Troyes is to search in the Internet websites according to concepts of DOTK. So, each concept of DOTK assists to find the corresponded territorial resource in Troyes according to its meaning. In this way, DOTK of Troyes is modeled which is consisting of intangible and tangible resources of Troyes for the sustainable goal of companies as shown in Fig. 7. The entities with the blue bolded frame show the resources of Troyes that are extracted by the concepts of DOTK [9].

So, this ontology provides all resources according to 5 dimensions of sustainability that can be used by organizations to perform sustainable development within companies in Troyes. Thus, in the following section, the usability of extracted resources of Troyes through the survey with top-manager of organization investigates.

6.2   Phase 2: Finding from Survey Interviews with Organizations

In this step, a multiple-choice survey conducted by researchers enabled the evaluation of DOTK of Troyes. The main goal of the survey was the presentation of territorial resources of Troyes to understand whether the extracted resources of Troyes by DOTK are useable for their sustainable development goal or not.

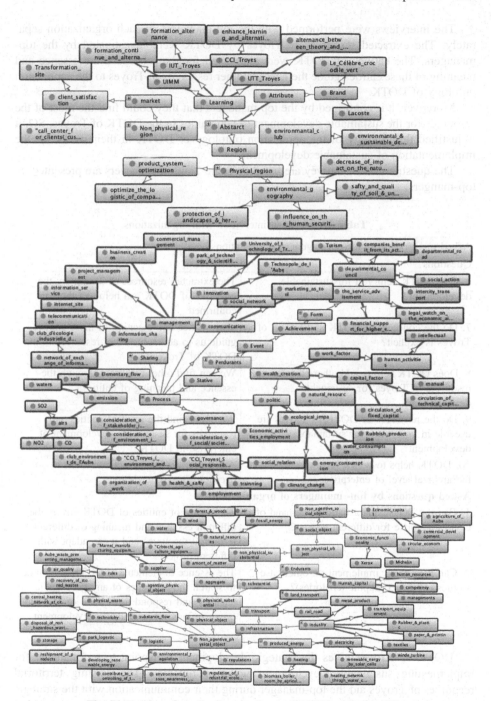

Fig. 7. Entities of application ontology of DOTK of Troyes [9].

The interviews were performed with the top-managers of each organization separately. The extracted resources of Troyes by DOTK were investigated by the top-managers. The entities of DOTK were explicated for them because the essence and meaning of these entities guide them to add other resources of Troyes to the application ontology of DOTK.

Moreover, it is confirmed by the top-managers that they could find the most of the resources for the sustainable development of companies in the DOTK of Troyes. SO, it is justified the usability of the application ontology of DOTK in their works for the implementation of sustainable development.

The questions of this survey are listed in Table 2 and the answers are presented by top-mangers.

Table 2. Survey of interviews with organizations.

Asked questions from top- managers of organizations	
Questions	Answers
1. Can DOTK help you for sustainable development?	The extracted resources of Troyes by the concepts of DOTK can help and they are confirmed
7. Do the concepts of DOTK and DOTK of Troyes is explicit?	The essence and meaning of these entities guide us to add some other resources to the DOTK of Troyes
8. Does DOTK help to add other elements to resources of Troyes for sustainable development?	We can find other resources through the essence and meaning of entities
9. Do the resources of DOTK of Troyes are useable in your work for sustainable development?	We could find the most of entities and resources for sustainable development of enterprise in DOTK
10. DOTK helps to which level of hierarchical level of enterprises?	Aid the strategic and tactic to make a decision for sustainability
Asked questions by top- managers of organizations	
1. Can the DOTK adapt with the demand of every enterprise for different project?	The nature of entities of DOTK covers the different essence and meaning of different territorial resources and it can adapt with different projects
2. Can the DOTK implement on other case studies (other geographic territories)?	The essence of elements of DOTK can guide to search the resources of any geographic territory and respond to demand of organizations for sustainable development

DOTK of T.royes gives the strategic development viewpoint to top-manager for implementing sustainable development within companies. The existing territorial resources of Troyes aid the top-manager during their communication with the strategic and tactical level of the enterprise to decide for sustainability. It is concluded that DOTK of Troyes could assist the decision making of the strategic and tactic level of companies through the top-mangers of organizations indirectly.

Also, one of the questions of the top-managers was about the adaptability of DOTK with the demands of companies according to their project for sustainable development. It was important for them to know whether the concepts of DOTK can be adapted to the demands of companies for the project of sustainable development in every geographic territory or not. This question is answered by the nature of the entities of DOTK. DOTK covers the different essence and meaning of different territorial resources because it has: (i) has a large scope, (ii) can be highly reused in different modeling scenarios, (iii) is conceptually well-founded, and (iv) is semantically transparent.

So, these results of the survey conducted to validate the usability of DOTK of Troyes in activities of sustainable development of these organizations. Moreover, it was concluded that the DOTK ontology of Troyes could assist the tactical and strategic levels of companies. Moreover, DOTK ontology can utilize in the scenario of three use cases, which explained.

7 Visualization of DOTK of Troyes

Visualization of DOTK of Troyes provides the opportunity to put the ontology on the websites to use directly by companies and organizations. In this way, all companies or organizations can find the concepts of DOTK and territorial resources of Troyes on the websites to integrate into their activities for sustainable development. Moreover, it is not possible to put the DOTK of Troyes on the website as Fig. 7. So, it needs to find a method for visualization of concepts of DOTK of Troyes.

Data visualization helps to represent a set of complex data in order to make it understandable graphically. So, several criteria make it possible to separate different data visualization techniques.

There are 2 different types [16]:

- Quantitative data are data that can be measured and represented in quantities.
- Qualitative data is categorized separately.
  - Ordinal qualitative data can be prioritized (for example, the degree of satisfaction of a user is an ordinal).
  - Nominal qualitative data describe a name or category and are not a priori uniquely hierarchical (there is a multitude of ways to represent them hierarchically). Nominal data are often analyzed by linking them to other types of data [17].

So, the concepts of DOTK are nominal qualitative. Moreover, there are different types of representation of vitalization such as comparative, hierarchical, relational, spatial, temporal and textual.

Roughs have been explored in several ways: the nested hierarchical representations, in the form of Treemaps or Sunburst diagram, which allows to visualize trends according to categories, as well as more conventional node tree techniques allow us to highlight the relationships between different classifications and entities. The Sunburst diagram is a representation of Treemap in a circular form. It maximizes the space available for each element of territorial resources.

The implementation has two main stages: the realization of visualizations and the development of the site. So, it is necessary to find tools and solutions to realize the graphical representations and to develop the site.

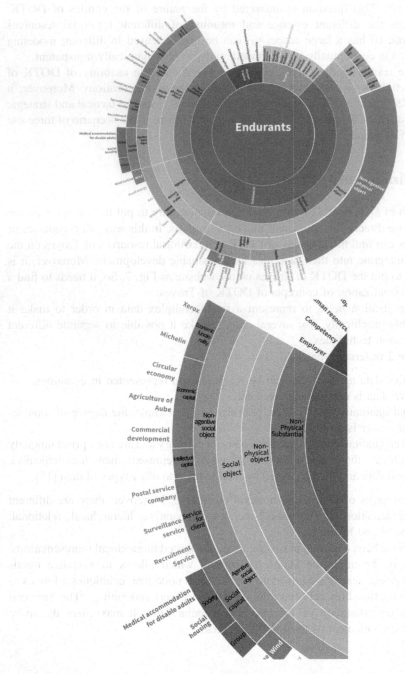

Fig. 8. Circular sunburst diagram of DOTK of Troyes for endurant's territorial resources.

Application of RAWgraphs[1] as open-source application in the university of technology of Troyes allows visualizing the concepts of application ontology of DOTK of Troyes. So, the hierarchical concepts of DOTK of Troyes entered in RAWgraphs. Then, RAWGraphs generates a raw Sunburst diagram in a vector image format. Figure 8 shows the circular sunburst diagram of the DOTK ontology of Troyes, which can be visualized on websites.

RAWgraphs as open-source application in the university of technology of Troyes allows visualizing the concepts of application ontology of DOTK of Troyes. So, the hierarchical concepts of DOTK of Troyes entered in RAWgraphs. Then, RAWGraphs generates a raw Sunburst diagram in a vector image format. Figure 8 shows the circular sunburst diagram of DOTK ontology of Troyes, which can be visualized on websites.

The next step is the development of the site. It is found from the literature review that D3.js library can use for the realization of the site because it is an extremely comprehensive data visualization library and provides the ability to create a table nesting from a simple table. This step is an ongoing step that allows realizing the visualization of DOTK of Troyes on the websites.

8 Conclusion

This article lays the foundation for capturing of territorial knowledge to search the possible concepts for sustainable development of companies. It appears from an organizational case that the integration of tangible and intangible territorial resources into their activities helps the better implementation of sustainable development within companies. Therefore, the strategy for extracting territorial knowledge was adapted with 5 dimensions (environmental, economic, social, politic and territorial) of sustainability. To support this strategy, it assumes that an ontology can explicit this territorial knowledge for actors of the organization to integrate this knowledge in their activities. This proposition aims to support organizations with territorial resources through ontology. Therefore, three scenarios of usability of the ontology of territorial knowledge define to supply the needs of organizations and companies for the implementation of sustainable development. These defined scenarios justify the usability of DOTK by organizations in their activities and project. Application ontology defines to prepare the tangible and intangible resources of the territory. This application ontology provides the territorial resources of Troyes city in France for the organizations of sustainable development in this city.

The main contribution of this research was the usability of identified territorial resources in the activities of organizations. Therefore, the second survey interview with top-mangers of organizations proves the defined scenarios use cases. Also, it is justified the identified territorial resources by DOTK can help the strategic decision of enterprises for sustainability. Also, it is confirmed by the top manager of these organizations that the essence and meaning of DOTK help them to extract other territorial resources. Also, DOTK can be used for every geographic territory to identify their resources.

---

[1] http://app.rawgraphs.io/.

Finally, the different method considers visualizing DOTK on the website. The first step of visualization is made and the second step for the development of the website is ongoing research. As future work, this research will be interested to consider how DOTK can help the operational level of companies.

References

1. Allais, R., Roucoules, L., Reyes, T.: Governance maturity grid: a transition method for integrating sustainability into companies? J. Clean. Prod. **140**, 213–226 (2017)
2. Allais, R., Roucoules, L., Reyes, T.: Inclusion of territorial resources in the product development process. J. Clean. Prod. **94**, 187–197 (2015)
3. Bachimont, B.: Engagement sémantique et engagement ontologique: conception et réalisation d'ontologies en ingénierie des connaissances. Ingénierie des connaissances: évolutions récentes et nouveaux défis, pp. 305–323 (2000)
4. Borgo, S., Masolo, C.: Foundational Choices in DOLCE. In: Staab, S., Studer, R. (eds.) Handbook on Ontologies. IHIS, pp. 361–381. Springer, Heidelberg (2009). https://doi.org/10.1007/978-3-540-92673-3_16
5. Bouaud, J., Bachimont, B., Charlet, J., Zweigenbaum, P.: Methodological principles for structuring an "ontology". In: Proceedings of the IJCAI 1995 Workshop on "Basic Ontological Issues in Knowledge Sharing, pp. 19–25, August 1995
6. Buclet, N.: Territorial and industrial ecology, local strategies for a sustainable development (Ecologie industrielle et territoriale, strate_gies locales pour un developpement durable). Septentrion presses universitaires (2011)
7. Capron, M., Quairel, F.: Evaluating strategies for sustainable development of enterprises: the mobilizing utopia of overall performance (E_valuer les strate_gies de de_veloppement durable des entreprises: l'utopie mobilisatrice de la performance globale). Rev. l'organisation Responsab. **1**, 5e17 (2006)
8. Ezoji, A., Matta, N.: How Territorial Knowledge Effects on the Sustainable Development within Companies. In: Proceeding of the 10th International Joint Conference on Knowledge Discovery, Knowledge Engineering and Knowledge Management (IC3K), vol. 3, p. 8. IC3K (2018)
9. Ezoji, A., Matta, N.: Territorial Knowledge Ontology as a Guide for the Identification of Resource of the Territory Toward Sustainability. In Proceedings of the Design Society: International Conference on Engineering Design, vol. 1, no. 1, pp. 3391–3400. Cambridge University Press, July 2019
10. Ezoji, A., Matta, N.: Identification of territorial resources based on domain ontology (DOTK) for sustainability. IFAC-PapersOnLine **52**(13), 683–688 (2019)
11. Ezoji, A., Matta, N.: Assist the sustainable development within industries through the territorial knowledge ontology. In: Proceedings of the 11th International Joint Conference on Knowledge Discovery, Knowledge Engineering and Knowledge Management, KMIS, vol. 3, pp. 102–112 (2019). ISBN 978-989-758-382-7, ISSN 2184-3228 https://doi.org/10.5220/0008165201020112
12. Fensel, D.: Ontologies. In: Ontologies, pp. 11–18. Springer, Heidelberg (2001). https://doi.org/10.1007/978-3-662-04396-7_2
13. Figuière, C., Rocca, M.: Un développement véritablement durable: quelle compatibilité avec le capitalisme financier?. In Colloque international" La problématique du développement durable vingt ans après: nouvelles lectures théoriques, innovations méthodologiques et domaines d'extension", CLERSE, Lille, 20–22 novembre 2008, November 2008

14. Gangemi, A., Guarino, N., Masolo, C., Oltramari, A.: Sweetening wordnet with dolce. AI Mag., **24**(3), 13 (2003)

15. Hallstedt, S., Ny, H., Robèrt, K.H., Broman, G.: An approach to assessing sustainability integration in strategic decision systems for product development. J. Clean. Prod. **18**(8), 703–712 (2010)

16. Lagnel, J.-M.: Manuel of Data Visualisation. Dunod, s.l. (2017)

17. Meirelles, I.: Design of Information- Represent the information visually s.l.: Parramon (2013)

18. Moine, A.: Le territoire comme un système complexe: un concept opératoire pour l'aménagement ct la géographie. LEspace geographique **35**(2), 115–132 (2006)

19. Vadoudi, K., Bratec, F., Troussier, N.: A GIS-oriented semantic data model to support PLM for DfS. Int. J. Product Lifecycle Manage. **10**(3), 210–230 (2017)

20. Wijesooriya, C., Heales, J., McCoy, S.: Multi-dimensional views for sustainability: ontological approach. In: 21st Americas Conference on Information Systems (AMCIS 2015), pp. 1–14, January 2015

21. Zhang, F., et al.: Toward an systemic navigation framework to integrate sustainable development into the company. J. Clean. Prod. **54**, 199–214 (2013)

What Promotes Intention? Factors Influencing Consumers' Intention to Purchase Animal-Welfare Friendly Beef in Japan

Takuya Washio(✉) , Takumi Ohashi , and Miki Saijo

Tokyo Institute of Technology, 2-12-1 Ookayama,
Meguro, Tokyo 152-8550, Japan
washio.t.aa@m.titech.ac.jp

Abstract. Food industries are required to face both increasing demand from a growing population with social development and enhancement of its sustainability. Farm animal welfare has become an important aspect of sustainable business development, but is still an unfamiliar concept for consumers in Japan, although Japanese society is under pressure to catch up with global trends. Researchers have been working around the world to explore consumer behavior concerning animal welfare in markets, but few such studies have been performed in Japan. In this study, we explored factors influencing consumers' intention to purchase animal welfare friendly beef products (AWFBP) in Japan, by considering them as food products purchased involving ethical decision-making and empathy for beef cattle and farmers. An online questionnaire was used to identify consumer characteristics and perceived attributes of AWFBP among 620 consumers in the three largest cities in Japan. Based on the Theory of Planned Behavior, we found that perception of attributes perceived behavioral controls, and empathy for beef cattle were likely to influence consumers' intention to purchase AWFBP.

Keywords: Animal welfare friendly products · The theory of planned behavior · Consumer intention to purchase · Online questionnaire

1 Introduction

Farm animal welfare (FAW) has been increasing its impacts on stockbreeding and the food business sector. Japan is known as a market that has paid less concern to this world trend, and the relevant business standards are seen as risks for market growth. In summer 2021, Japan will host the Olympic and Paralympic Games in Tokyo and other satellite venues in several other cities. These massive events with global attention have been expected to be opportunities to raise the standard of FAW as one of their "legacies" in this island-country in East Asia; however, changes have not met expectations [1].

However, the increasing global attention on FAW as an environmental, social, and governance indicator for companies in their investment decisions has forced Japanese food companies to respond to FAW concerns. It will be important to understand consumers' behavior in regard to FAW-friendly products for those companies who

© Springer Nature Switzerland AG 2020
A. Fred et al. (Eds.): IC3K 2019, CCIS 1297, pp. 536–549, 2020.
https://doi.org/10.1007/978-3-030-66196-0_25

want to succeed in future business. Thus, we explored factors influencing consumers' intention to purchase animal welfare-friendly beef products (AWFBP).

This paper is an extended version of the paper presented at KMIS2019 [2]. Further analysis and discussion were made since the conference for this extension. We applied linear multi-regression analysis (MRA) to explore factors which influenced consumers' intention to purchase AWFBP, and discussed the possible market implementation to increase consumers' intention for the purchase.

1.1 Farm Animal Welfare

The definition of animal welfare (AW) published by the World Organisation for Animal Health (OIE) is the most accepted worldwide. According to their Terrestrial Animal Health Code, AW refers to "the physical and mental state of an animal in relation to the conditions in which it lives and dies." The OIE's Terrestrial Code set "the Five Freedoms" which consist of the following: (1) freedom from hunger or thirst; (2) freedom from discomfort; (3) freedom from pain, injury or disease; (4) freedom to express normal behavior; and (5) freedom from fear and distress [3]. They are five major aspects of AW under human control, and are accepted internationally as a standard definition of AW.

Animal welfare should be considered as "actual states of animals" or "the quality of life which individual animals experience" in a scientific context, although it tends to be considered as humanitarian demands to take care of animals in general public. Sonoda et al. set an example for better understandings; if a wild animal is suffering from illness or low-nutrition, even if the situation is not caused by human beings and there is no ethical demand on human beings, scientifically the animal's welfare is considered to be low [4]. It is the responsibility of humans today to improve the welfare of animals that are under human control through livestock production and other means.

Balancing productivity in volume and quality, economic efficiency, and FAW in stockbreeding is strongly demanded in today's world. Initiatives toward AW improvement in relation to companies' business have become a concern for investors.

1.2 Effects on Japanese Stockbreeding and Food Business

Environmental, social, and governance (ESG) factors are increasingly recognized as critical determinants in the success or failure of corporations of every type, together with traditional indexes represented by finance statements [5]. Institutional investors, e.g. pension funds, who invest their large-scale and long-term funds now pay attention to ESG as benchmarks to evaluate corporate sustainability and business-creation opportunities. Principles for Responsible Investment (PRI), established by the United Nations in 2005, is the world's leading proponent of responsible investment. It contains a set of six principles that offer a menu of possible actions for incorporating ESG issues [6]. In Japan, the Government Pension Investment Fund signed to PRI in 2015, and this has led to Japanese corporations paying more attention to ESG [7]. Among investors in North America and Europe, it has become popular to take account of FAW in ESG for stockbreeding and food-related enterprises.

Farm Animal Investment Risk and Return (FAIRR) initiatives is an investor network that aims to include factory farming as an ESG agenda, established by the Jeremy Coller Foundation in 2015. The FAIRR issues the Coller FAIRR Protein Producer Index every year, which is a livestock industry-related initiative for institutional investors with 176 organizations worldwide and total assets under management of more than USD 20 trillion. Based on the Sustainable Development Goals announced by the United Nations, this grading system has been applied to nine items – greenhouse gases, deforestation and biodiversity loss, water use and scarcity, waste water and pollution, antibiotics, animal welfare, working conditions, food safety, and sustainable protein – on a trial basis since 2019 using a four-point scale: best practice, low risk, medium risk, and high risk. According to the ratings from the latest announcement in September 2019, 39 out of 60 meat and fish food companies were rated as "high risk", as were all three evaluated Japanese companies: Nippon Suisan Kaisha, Prima Ham, and Nippon Ham [8].

The Business Benchmark on Farm Animal Welfare (BBFAW) is another corporate rating indicator that addresses AW. This has assessed and published the annual results of the world's major retail, wholesale, food production, food manufacturing, and food-related companies' commitments to AW since 2012. As of the end of August 2019, there were 31 credit rating agencies worldwide with total assets under management of GBP 2.4 trillion. Benchmarks evaluate the feeding environment and transportation of livestock animals; methods, targets, and practices of supply chain management and supervision; and customer satisfaction; and also reports on the performance of AW initiatives. The evaluation criteria are ranked from Tier 1, a group of global leadership companies, to Tier 6, a group of companies that are not recognized as a business challenge. The BBFAW 2019 Benchmark, the latest edition at the time of writing, evaluates all five companies from Japan (out of a total of 150 companies) that are ranked in Tier 6: Aeon Group, Maruha Nichiro, Meiji Holdings, Nippon Ham and Seven & i Holdings. However, foreign companies operating in Japan and also transforming their business to AW friendly are included in higher tiers: Nestlé is in Tier 2, Unilever, and McDonald's are in Tier 3, and Kraft Heinz is in Tier 4 [9, 10].

Thus, in order for food companies to gain international competitiveness, it is essential to respond to AW in terms of both corporate financing and corporate value. If the current situation is left unaddressed, this will certainly affect livestock farmers and general consumers of the products of the companies. It is important to investigate the factors influencing consumers' intention to purchase AW-friendly products in order to develop effective communication of relevant information with consumers. In Japan, only a few researches have made to investigate consumer acceptance of AW-friendly products. Sonoda et al. examined the relationship between willingness to pay for the labels indicate AWFBP and consumers' personal values, and it has been the only study was made for beef specifically until today [1]. This present study may bring better understandings of consumers' acceptance and insights for the market implication in Japan.

2   Theories

In this study, our challenge was to explain AW-friendly products, which are not well-recognized in the Japanese market, to Japanese consumers. To overcome this problem, we decided to explain AW-friendly products as a type of organic food that is consumed ethically with empathy for farmers and livestock.

2.1   Ethical Consumption

According to the Ethical Association, ethical consumption in Japan refers to "thinking and acting with consideration for people, society, the global environment, and the local community." [11] Based on the report of the Consumer Affairs Agency in 2015, ethical consumption is a broad class, and under the large umbrella called "ethical consumption" there is a wide range of consumption forms, such as fair trade, organic, local production for local consumption, products that help people with disabilities, traditional craft, AW, endowed products, recycling, and ethical finance [11, 12]. According to Carrigan et al., it is difficult to sum up the full range of activities that can possibly be included under the term "ethical consumption", but it is the conscious and deliberate choice to make confident consumption choices due to personal and moral beliefs [13]. In addition, Ethical Consumer, the world's largest non-profit and multi-stakeholder ethical consumption promotion activity founded in 1989 and based in Manchester, UK, lists three activities to be targeted: environmental issues (e.g. environmental pollution, wildlife conservation, and climate change), human rights issues (worker rights protection, corporate tax avoidance, and excessive lobbying), and AW against animal testing and industrial animal husbandry [14]. In the same way, high AW products are sometimes positioned as a type of organic food [15, 16]. Therefore, in this paper, we consider purchasing behavior of AW-friendly products as a kind of purchasing behavior of organic food, which is a part of ethical consumption, and attempt to discuss this type of consumer behavior in the form of a systematic behavior theory that is often used.

2.2   Theory of Planned Behavior

The Theory of Planned Behavior (TPB) is a major theory applied in consumer behavior research. According to TPB, an individual's intention to take a certain action has a great influence on whether or not the individual takes an action. Furthermore, it is said that the intention to take action is formed by the attitude of an individual toward his/her action, the pressure from society that he/she feels they should/should not take the action, and the consciousness of whether he/she can actually take the action [17]. The main factors that constitute TPB based on Ajzen [17] are described below.

Attitude toward behavior (attitude) is the first factor that shapes an individual's intention toward behavior (intention). An assessment of the consequences of an individual's beliefs and actions shapes an attitude toward action. Subjective norms are those that are influenced by an individual's perception of behavior, particularly by the evaluation of others that are important to the individual. Social trends, reputation, and awareness of others' expectations of the individual shape this factor. Behavioral controllability (behavioral control) is an awareness of the ease/difficulty with which individuals act. With regard to the purchase of food, factors such as price and convenience of access to the place where it is sold may form this factor. According to the TPB, these three factors influence each other to form an intention to perform behavior, and the intention to perform behavior guides an individual's action.

The TPB has been used to explain consumer behavior in relation to the selection of production-sustainability related products, such as organic foods and ethical products. Ma et al. tried to explain the purchasing behavior of young women in the United States in regard to fair trade products using this theory. They concluded that beliefs about the concept of fair trade and the nature of the product, attitudes toward the purchasing behavior of fair trade products, and perceived control over the purchasing behavior of fair trade products were all important factors in shaping the purchasing intent concerning fair trade products [18]. Voon et al. attempted to explain the purchasing behavior of organic food among Malaysian consumers during the early period of organic food proliferation by using TPB. An analysis of 406 questionnaire samples collected in Kuching, the capital of the largest state in the country, identified factors affecting the formation of consumers' purchase intentions and concluded that the influence of behavioral controllability factors was small and that subjective normative factors of consumers played a significant role in the formation of purchase intentions [19]. Because this study is one of the few similar studies conducted in Asia, we refer to this study and extend TPB by adding additional factors.

The TPB is a theoretical model which is "open to the inclusion of additional predictors" [17]. Studies have exploited this property to attempt to explain more complex consumer behaviors by introducing additional factors. Using TPB as a basis, Shaw and Shiu introduced "ethical obliteration" and "self-identity" as additional factors in an attempt to explain the decisions of ethically conscious consumers in the United Kingdom [20, 21]. McEachern et al. attempted to analyze consumers' purchasing behavior for a specific brand of AW-friendly products and concluded that consumer ethical responsibility for food animals and consumer location influence consumer choice [22]. Based on these previous results, we considered it appropriate to introduce new factors and expand the model in this study. In this paper, "empathy" is assumed as a new factor.

2.3 Empathy

Hoffman explained empathy as an individual's affective response more appropriate to someone else's situation than to one's own [23]. Empathy is considered to influence consumers' ethical decision-making or prosocial behavior. Previous studies have shown that empathy affects consumers' ethical decision-making and prosocial behavior, which is voluntary behavior by individuals for society. Mencl and May concluded that the experience of empathy for the subject has a positive effect on ethical decision-making [24]. Davis et al. concluded that individual personality traits and emotional reactions that lead to empathy play an important role in strategic thinking in response to a need for help [25]. Verhofstadt et al. found that empathy by supporters plays a role in social support activities [26].

Debate continues on the structure of empathy as a psychological response that affects human behavior. According to these studies, empathy can be broadly divided into two different cognitive responses. Stern found that the effects of drama advertising were caused by emotional empathy and cognitive sympathy [27]. According to Stern, empathy is a participatory response toward another person with less differentiation from oneself, whereas sympathy is an identificatory response involving more differentiation and detachment. Following this study, Escalas and Stern concluded that cognitive empathy is perceived prior to emotional empathy, and that both cognitive and emotional empathy positively influence attitudes toward drama advertising, with emotional empathy being stronger [28]. Tamaki examined the impact of emotional and cognitive empathy on purchasing intent for ethical products in Japan [29]. A survey was conducted on the purchase of products that contribute to the maintenance of local industries and the environment as well as improvement of the welfare of prefectural residents, targeting the members of a consumer cooperative that engages in local development, the advance maintenance of the environment, and the welfare of prefectural residents. An analysis using a sample of 736 collected questionnaires confirmed that consumers with greater emotional and cognitive empathy were more likely to purchase ethical products.

According to these previous studies, when considering consumers' behavior based on empathy, it is thought that factors affecting the behavior can be examined in a more detailed manner by considering the nature of the psychological distance that consumers feel from the subject of empathy.

2.4 Objectives

The literature review showed that TPB was appropriate for the examination of consumer behavior regarding high AW products, and there was scope to include empathy in the discussion. The present study investigated determinants of willingness to purchase high AWFBP in the three greater urban areas in Japan. We set the objectives as using TPB to (1) explore the factors influencing willingness to purchase high AW products and (2) explain how empathy influences consumer behavior.

3 Methodology

In this study, we explored factors influencing consumers' intention to purchase AWFBP through statistical analysis of data collected through an online questionnaire.

3.1 Data Collection

The data collected through the online questionnaire are summarized in Table 1. In this paper, AWFBP are defined as beef products produced through AW-friendly processes from feed to food processing. All 620 samples were used in the analysis because the online survey was unable to provide incomplete responses. Also, when checking complete individual data, no strange response patterns or outliers were found.

Table 1. Summary of data collection.

Period	25–26 March 2019
Data collection	An online questionnaire through a market research company
Target	Consumers aged 20–69 years residing in Tokyo, Osaka, and Nagoya Prefectures (evenly allocated to gender and age layers)
Screening	Eligibility to eat beef products (e.g. allergy and religion)
Total sample size	N = 620

3.2 Questionnaire Design

The questionnaire was primarily based on the original questionnaires designed and used in Voon et al. [19] and Tamaki [29], and our literature review. We translated their questionnaire into Japanese and also modified some of the questions to adjust for the AW-friendly products and the cultural background of Japan. We made repeated translations and had them reviewed by other Japanese native speakers until we had confirmation that Japanese people would easily understand the translated version. Details of questionnaire design and structure were explained in our previous conference paper [2].

3.3 Analysis Flow

At first, we conducted exploratory factor analysis (EFA) to extract factors from questionnaire items and to calculate factor scores for each factor. Then we applied linear multi-regression analysis (MRA) to explore factors which influenced consumers' intention to purchase AWFBP.

4 Results

4.1 Efa

The EFA was applied to identify and confirm the factors within each component (Table 2). Factors were extracted with the Maximum Likelihood method, and Promax rotation was used based on a prediction of a high correlation between factors. Items with loading smaller than 0.4 were eliminated from further analysis. Likewise, items loaded with more than one factor were assigned to the factors where they achieved the highest factor loadings. The Kaiser–Meyer–Olkin (KMO) measures of sampling adequacy had a value of 0.911 and Bartlett's test of sphericity was significant ($p < 0.01$), indicating that the data were suitable for factor analysis.

Table 2. Components and scale reliability for consumers' perception (N = 620).

Factors and questionnaire items	Alpha
Intention to purchase AWFBP	*.884*
I am willing to buy animal-welfare friendly products even though choices are limited.[a]	.886
I am willing to buy animal-welfare friendly products because the benefits outweigh the cost.[a]	.784
I would still buy animal-welfare friendly products even though conventional alternatives are on sale.[a]	.689
I do not mind spending more time searching for animal welfare friendly products.[a]	.569
Perception of AWFBP attributes	*.848*
Purchasing animal-welfare friendly products improves the quality of farmers' lives.[a]	.846
Purchasing animal-welfare friendly products improves the welfare of livestock.[a]	.788
Consuming animal-welfare friendly products positively affects my health[a]	.675
Purchasing animal-welfare friendly products improves the quality of my life.[a]	.537
Animal-welfare friendly products taste better.[a]	.437
Empathy and sympathy for cattle	*.879*
I feel as if the beef cows' feelings are my own.[a]	.920
I feel as though the beef cows' situation and problems are happening to me.[a]	.812
I try to understand the beef cows' feelings.[a]	.528
Concerns about food production processes	*.820*
I am concerned about the type and amount of nutrition in the food that I consume daily.[a]	.811
I am concerned about food additives.[a]	.792
I care about cholesterol and fat.[a]	.727
I am concerned about how food is processed.[a]	.548
Trust in AWFBP	*.818*
If there is a certification system for animal-welfare friendly products, I can trust the nature of the products.[a]	.769
I trust that those selling (or will be selling) organic food are honest about the animal welfare related to their products.[a]	.698
I trust the information on animal-welfare friendly product labels.[a]	.670
I trust that the producers of animal welfare friendly products are practicing animal welfare concerned production.[a]	.629
Perceived behavioral control	*.726*
The stores where I frequently shop do not sell a variety of animal-welfare friendly products[a]	.691
Animal-welfare friendly products are only available in limited stores/markets.[a]	.663
Animal-welfare friendly products are beyond my budget (or will be beyond my budget shortly).[a]	.631
Buying animal-welfare friendly products is highly inconvenient.[a]	.587
Only consumers with higher income can afford animal-welfare friendly products.[a]	.438
Sympathy for farmers	*.849*
I try to understand the situation and problems of farmers using animal welfare practices.[a]	.937
I try to understand the motivation of farmers using animal welfare practice	.712

[a] Scale used: 1 (strongly disagree) to 5 (strongly agree)
Cronbach's alpha value is shown beside each factor, and factor loadings are shown beside each item
Exploratory factor analysis: Promax rotation with Kaiser normalization; loadings less than 0.4 are not shown
KMO = 0.911

Seven factors were extracted in total. Although several items were dropped due to low factor loadings, most of the remaining items that were expected to measure a similar construct did indeed load the same factor. In order to assess the reliability of the items in measuring the factor, Cronbach's alpha value for each factor was calculated (Table 2). Reliability was assured because the Cronbach's alpha values (0.73–0.88) exceeded the minimum threshold of 0.7.

4.2 Linear MRA

Linear MRA was applied with intention to purchase AWFBP as the dependent variable. Initial explanatory variables were socio-demographics variables (gender, age group, marital status, number in household, resident prefecture, household income, occupation, and education history), perception of AWFBP attributes, empathy and sympathy for cattle, concern about food production processes, trust in AWFBP, perceived behavioral control, and sympathy for farmers. Reliability for factors were confirmed using variance inflation factor (VIF). Outliers were examined using Cook's distance larger than 1 after first analysis. The final model was chosen using stepwise selection including exploratory variables expressing a P-value larger than 0.05 and excluding exploratory variables expressing a P-value smaller than 0.10. The result is shown in Table 3.

Table 3. Coefficients selected from MRA.

Coefficient	b	S.E.	p	β	VIF
Perception of AWFBP attributes	.481	.045	.000	.474	3.016
Empathy and sympathy for cattle	.295	.028	.000	.293	1.236
Perceived behavioral control	-.333	.032	.000	-.305	1.367
Concern on food production process	.257	.032	.000	.254	1.544
Trust in AWFBP	.119	.045	.008	.115	2.895
(Constant)	.012	.025	.625		
R^2	.703				
Adjusted R^2	.699				
df	5				
N	620				

5   Discussion

The results of MRA suggested the factors influencing consumers' intention to purchase AWFBP. Each of these factors is discussed, and actions that may be effective in enhancing purchase intent are also mentioned.

5.1 Attitudes Promote Consumers' Intention to Purchase AWFBP

Consumer attitudes toward AWFBP were found to promote consumers' intention to purchase.

Perception of AWFBP Attributes. It was shown that consumers' attributes perception of AWFBP promoted willingness to purchase. In an experiment on organic beef, the information presentation to consumers on an all organic production system promoted more expectations of consumers than partial information on AW and environmental pollution [30]. In this way, the effects from various aspects obtained by improvement of AW will shape consumer expectations. In addition, the same study points out that the main concerns of consumers, such as product safety, consideration of AW, and environmental pollution, are mutually taken positively by assimilation. Although the increase in willingness to pay for products with organic certification labels is largely explained by consumer ethical considerations, Sirieix and Tagbata point out that the positive impact of such information also depends on intrinsic quality and perception of quality [31]. It was suggested that to increase consumer expectations of AW, it is effective to enhance positive impressions other than AW, such as taste.

Concern about the Food Production Process. It was shown that the interest in the food production process promoted consumers' purchase intention regarding AWFBP. Previous studies indicated that willingness to pay for grass-fed beef is positively influenced by consumers' knowledge of nutrition and is also influenced by the health condition of the consumer or family members within the household [32]. Thus, consumers who are highly interested in the nutrients contained in their regular foods may be promising targets for AWFBP.

Trust in AWFBP. It was suggested that trust in AWFBP would promote consumers' intention to purchase. The importance of product labeling as a source of information used by consumers to obtain information about AW-friendly products was pointed out in past studies, including in Europe [33–35]. A study conducted in Italy, the United Kingdom, and Sweden found that labeling on products and in-store information were important. This study also points to the importance of a product's AW rating to consumers. An attempt to rank livestock products has actually been made in Europe. In some regions, livestock products on the market are ranked in three levels and displayed as labeling. In Japan, measures will be necessary to enhance the credibility of AW-friendly products.

5.2 Perceived Behavioral Control Obstructs Consumers' Intention to Purchase AWFBP

Farm practices that consider AW are expected to result in higher production costs than conventional feeding methods. Some studies suggest that the value of AW is negative from a rigorous economic point of view because unmitigated costs are incurred by both producers and consumers [36]. McInerney, however, states that consumers are not always looking for cheap food; they are looking for the greatest value for money for the amount they intend to pay [37]. In a study of Italian consumers' willingness to purchase organic food, Napolitano et al. cited higher prices due to the greater space required for production, feed costs, and small-scale production systems as major limitations to purchasing organic beef. In addition, they pointed out that it may be effective to provide ethical value to consumers by labeling in conjunction with conventional livestock production methods [38].

Regarding the availability of products, the duality of having the consumers' intention to purchase while not taking any buying action can be explained by the limited number of products that can be distributed to the market in response to the growing consumer concern about AW [39, 40]. Therefore, in actual product sales, it is necessary to reduce the sense of high cost and to make consumers feel that they can buy without much effort.

5.3 Empathy and Sympathy for Cattle Promotes Consumers' Intention to Purchase AWFBP

It was suggested that empathy and sympathy for cattle would promote consumers' intention to purchase. Previous studies suggested that positive information about farm-based practices can influence consumer preferences for meat [41, 42] and that information about farm practices can influence expectations in regard to organic certification and associated high quality [30] for value-added growth-oriented practices such as organic and grass-fed beef. Similarly, it may be possible to promote consumers' empathy toward beef cattle and increase intention to purchase by reminding consumers of the situation in which beef cattle are actually raised.

6 Limitations and Future Research

Our study had several limitations. First, the data are based on a limited number of samples from online surveys. By increasing the sample size and performing the analysis, it would be possible to approach actual market conditions.

We attempted to explore factors that affect consumers' purchase intentions, but the relationship between the extracted factors could not be examined. It would be possible to explore more complex relationships by examining the effects of factors through such methods as structural modeling.

Consumer surveys of purchasing and willingness to pay indicate that the results are affected by part-whole bias and also by warm-glow bias. It should be noted that our results may be distorted by bias [43].

Finally, behavioral research using TPB often shows discrepancies between intention and actual behavior [44, 45]. In other words, there is a problem that although positive opinions are given in answer to a question of whether a certain action is desired, the intention may not necessarily lead to actual behavior. This is the case when an individual wants to take a particular action, but is blocked by the possibility of action control, for instance by money, time, or convenience. In this paper, we focus on the formulation of intention to purchase in TPB, and do not discuss the relationship with actual purchasing behavior. In the future, it will be desirable to conduct additional research such as experiments with more realistic environmental and product preparations, and use test marketing of actual products.

We are planning interviews with actual consumers in the future, and anticipate that results of this qualitative survey will deepen our understanding.

Acknowledgement. This study is partly supported by the Center of Innovation Program under Japan Science and Technology Agency (Grant Number: JPMJCE1309).

References

1. Sonoda, Y., Oishi, K., Chomei, Y., Hirooka, H.: How do human values influence the beef preferences of consumer segments regarding animal welfare and environmentally friendly production? Meat Sci. **146**, 75–86 (2018)
2. Washio, T., Ohashi, T., Saijo, M.: Consumers' willingness to purchase high animal-welfare beef products in Japan: exploratory research based on the theory of planned behavior. In: IC3K 2019–Proceedings of the 11th International Joint Conference on Knowledge Discovery, Knowledge Engineering and Knowledge Management, pp 130–138 (2019)
3. World Organisation for Animal Health Terrestrial Animal Health Code Article 7. 1. 1. https://www.oie.int/index.php?id=169&L=0&htmfile=chapitre_aw_introduction.htm. Accessed 18 Jan 2020
4. Sonoda, Y., Oishi, K., Kumagai, H., Hirooka, H.: A review: the effects of animal welfare on beef productivity and the consumers' demand. Nihon Chikusan Gakkaiho **90**, 1–11 (2019)
5. Allianz Global Investors: ESG is going mainstream because it's business-critical. https://jp.allianzgi.com/ja-jp/jp-insights/investment-themes-and-strategy/esg-is-going-mainstream. Accessed 18 Jan 2020
6. PRI Association. https://www.unpri.org/about-the-pri/about-the-pri/322.article. Accessed 18 Jan 2020
7. Government Pension Investment Fund ESG investment. https://www.gpif.go.jp/investment/esg/ [in Japanese]. Accessed 18 Jan 2020
8. Farm Animal Investment Risk and Return Coller FAIRR Protein Producer Index. https://www.fairr.org/index/. Accessed 18 Jan 2020
9. McLaren, J., Appleyard, T.: Improving accountability for farm animal welfare: the performative role of a benchmark device. Account. Audit Account. J. **33**, 32–58 (2019)
10. Business Benchmark on Farm Animal Welfare. https://bbfaw.com/media/1788/bbfaw_full-report_2019.pdf/. Accessed 06 Jul 2020
11. Ethical Association About ethical consumption. https://ethicaljapan.org/ethical-consumption. [in Japanese]. Accessed 18 Jan 2020
12. Consumer Affair Agency Research group for "Ethical consumption", Your consumption changes the world [in Japanese] (2015)
13. Carrigan, M., Szmigin, I., Wright, J.: Shopping for a better world? An interpretive study of the potential for ethical consumption within the older market. J. Consum. Mark. **21**, 401–417 (2004)
14. Ethical Consumer. Why shop ethically? https://www.ethicalconsumer.org/why-shop-ethically, Accessed 18 Jan 2020
15. Hughner, R.S., McDonagh, P., Prothero, A., Shultz, C.J.I., Stanton, J.: Who are organic food consumers? A compilation and review of why people purchase organic food. J. Consum. Behav. **6**, 94–110 (2007)
16. Makatouni, A.: What motivates consumers to buy organic food in the UK?: results from a qualitative study. Br. Food J. **104**, 345–352 (2002)

17. Ajzen, I.: The theory of planned behavior. Organ. Behav. Hum. Decis. Process. **50**, 179–211 (1991)
18. Ma, Y.J., Littrell, M.A., Niehm, L.: Young female consumers' intentions toward fair trade consumption. Int. J. Retail Distrib. Manag. **40**, 41–63 (2012)
19. Voon, J.P., Ngui, K.S., Agrawal, A.: Determinants of willingness to purchase organic food: an exploratory study using structural equation modeling. Int. Food Agribus. Manag. Rev. **14**, 103–120 (2011)
20. Shaw, D., Shiu, E.: An assessment of ethical obligation and self-identity in ethical consumer decision-making: a structural equation modelling approach. Int. J. Consum. Stud. **26**, 286–293 (2002)
21. Shaw, D., Shiu, E.: Ethics in consumer choice: a multivariate modelling approach. Eur. J. Mark. **37**, 1485–1498 (2003)
22. McEachern, M.G., Schröder, M.J.A., Willock, J., Whitelock, J., Mason, R.: Exploring ethical brand extensions and consumer buying behaviour: the RSPCA and the "Freedom Food" brand. J. Prod. Brand Manag. **16**, 168–177 (2007)
23. Hoffman, M.L.: Empathy and justice motivation. Motiv. Emot. **14**, 151–172 (1990)
24. Mencl, J., May, D.R.: The effects of proximity and empathy on ethical decision-making: an exploratory investigation. J. Bus. Ethics **85**, 201–226 (2009)
25. Davis, M.H., Mitchell, K.V., Hall, J.A., Lothert, J., Snapp, T., Meyer, M.: Empathy, expectations, and situational preferences: personality influences on the decision to participate in volunteer helping behaviors. J. Pers. **67**, 469–503 (1999)
26. Verhofstadt, L., Devoldre, I., Buysse, A., Stevens, M., Hinnekens, C., Ickes, W., Davis, M.: The role of cognitive and affective empathy in spouses' support interactions: an observational study. PLoS ONE **11**, e0149944 (2016)
27. Stern, B.B.: Classical and vignette television advertising dramas: structural models, formal analysis, and consumer effects. J. Consum. Res. **20**, 601–615 (1994)
28. Escalas, J.E., Stern, B.B.: Sympathy and empathy: emotional responses to advertising dramas. J. Consum. Res. **29**, 566–578 (2003)
29. Tamaki, S.: Empathy and ethical consumption. Shokei-gakuso J. Bus. Stud. **61**, pp. 709–722 (2015) [in Japanese]
30. Napolitano, F., Braghieri, A., Piasentier, E., Favotto, S., Naspetti, S., Zanoli, R.: Effect of information about organic production on beef liking and consumer willingness to pay. Food Qual. Prefer. **21**, 207–212 (2010)
31. Tagbata, D., Sirieix, L.: Measuring consumer's willingness to pay for organic and Fair Trade products. Int. J. Consum. Stud. **32** (5), 479–490 (2008)
32. Xue, H., Mainville, D., You, W., Nayga, R.M.: Consumer preferences and willingness to pay for grass-fed beef: empirical evidence from in-store experiments. Food Qual. Prefer. **21**, 857–866 (2010)
33. Clark, B., Stewart, G.B., Panzone, L.A., Kyriazakis, I., Frewer, L.J.: A systematic review of public attitudes, perceptions and behaviours towards production diseases associated with farm animal welfare. J. Agric. Environ. Ethics **29**, 455–478 (2016)
34. Clark, B., Stewart, G.B., Panzone, L.A., Kyriazakis, I., Frewer, L.J.: Citizens, consumers and farm animal welfare: a meta-analysis of willingness-to-pay studies. Food Policy **68**, 112–127 (2017)
35. Lagerkvist, C.J., Hess, S.: A meta-analysis of consumer willingness to pay for farm animal welfare. Eur. Rev. Agric. Econ. **38**, 55–78 (2011)
36. Henneberry, S.R., Tweeten, L.G.: A review of international agricultural supply response. J. Int. Food Agribus. Mark. **2**, 49–95 (1991)
37. McInerney, J.: Animal welfare, economics and policy. Rep. Study Undertaken Farm Anim. Health Econ. Div. Defra **68** (2004)

38. Napolitano, F., Girolami, A., Braghieri, A.: Consumer liking and willingness to pay for high welfare animal-based products. Trends Food Sci. Technol. **21**, 537–543 (2010)
39. Verbeke, W.: Stakeholder, citizen and consumer interests in farm animal welfare. Anim Welf. **18**, 325–333 (2009)
40. Verbeke, W., Pérez-Cueto, F.J.A., de Barcellos, M.D., Krystallis, A., Grunert, K.G.: European citizen and consumer attitudes and preferences regarding beef and pork. Meat Sci. **84**, 284–292 (2010)
41. Napolitano, F., Caporale, G., Carlucci, A., Monteleone, E.: Effect of information about animal welfare and product nutritional properties on acceptability of meat from Podolian cattle. Food Qual. Prefer. **18**, 305–312 (2007)
42. Napolitano, F., Braghieri, A., Caroprese, M., Marino, R., Girolami, A., Sevi, A.: Effect of information about animal welfare, expressed in terms of rearing conditions, on lamb acceptability. Meat Sci. **77**, 431–436 (2007)
43. Nocella, G., Hubbard, L., Scarpa, R.: Farm animal welfare, consumer willingness to pay, and trust: results of a cross-national survey. Appl. Econ. Perspect. Policy **32**, 275–297 (2010)
44. Rezai, G.: Consumers' awareness and consumption intention towards green foods. Afr. J. Bus. Manag. **6**, 4496–4503 (2012)
45. de Graaf, S., et al.: Determinants of consumer intention to purchase animal-friendly milk. J. Dairy Sci. **99**, 8304–8313 (2016)

Author Index

Printed in the United States
By Bookmasters